Instructor's Resou~~rce~~

for

Berk

Child Development

Ninth Edition

prepared by

Sara Harris
Illinois State University

Laura E. Berk
Illinois State University

Leah Shriro

Judy Ashkenaz

PEARSON

Boston • Columbus • Indianapolis • New York • San Francisco • Upper Saddle River
Amsterdam • Cape Town • Dubai • London • Madrid • Milan • Munich • Paris • Montreal • Toronto
Delhi • Mexico City • Sao Paulo • Sydney • Hong Kong • Seoul • Singapore • Taipei • Tokyo

Copyright © 2013, 2009, 2006, 2003, 2000, 1997, 1994, 1991, 1989 by Pearson Education, Inc.
All rights reserved. Printed in the United States of America. This publication is protected by Copyright and permission should be obtained from the publisher prior to any prohibited reproduction, storage in a retrieval system, or transmission in any form or by any means, electronic, mechanical, photocopying, recording, or likewise. To obtain permission(s) to use material from this work, please submit a written request to Pearson Education, Inc., Permissions Department, One Lake Street, Upper Saddle River, New Jersey 07458 or you may fax your request to 201-236-3290.

10 9 8 7 6 5 4 3 2 1

> **This work is protected by United States copyright laws and is provided solely for the use of instructors in teaching their courses and assessing student learning. Dissemination or sale of any part of this work (including on the World Wide Web) will destroy the integrity of the work and is not permitted. The work and materials from it should never be made available to students except by instructors using the accompanying text in their classes. All recipients of this work are expected to abide by these restrictions and to honor the intended pedagogical purposes and the needs of other instructors who rely on these materials.**

ISBN-10: 0-205-25687-2
ISBN-13: 978-0-205-25687-7

PEARSON

CONTENTS

PREFACE *vii*

CHAPTER 1 HISTORY, THEORY, AND APPLIED DIRECTIONS 1
    Chapter-at-a-Glance *1* • Brief Chapter Summary *2*
    Learning Objectives *2* • Lecture Outline *2* • Lecture Enhancements *11*
    Learning Activities *15* • Ask Yourself *17* • Suggested Readings *21*
    Media Materials *21*

CHAPTER 2 RESEARCH STRATEGIES 23
    Chapter-at-a-Glance *23* • Brief Chapter Summary *23*
    Learning Objectives *24* • Lecture Outline *24* • Lecture Enhancements *29*
    Learning Activities *33* • Ask Yourself *36* • Suggested Readings *39*
    Media Materials *40*

CHAPTER 3 BIOLOGICAL FOUNDATIONS, PRENATAL DEVELOPMENT, AND BIRTH 41
    Chapter-at-a-Glance *41* • Brief Chapter Summary *42*
    Learning Objectives *42* • Lecture Outline *43* • Lecture Enhancements *56*
    Learning Activities *59* • Ask Yourself *62* • Suggested Readings *69*
    Media Materials *69*

CHAPTER 4 INFANCY: EARLY LEARNING, MOTOR SKILLS, AND PERCEPTUAL CAPACITIES 71
    Chapter-at-a-Glance *71* • Brief Chapter Summary *71*
    Learning Objectives *72* • Lecture Outline *72* • Lecture Enhancements *81*
    Learning Activities *83* • Ask Yourself *86* • Suggested Readings *90*
    Media Materials *91*

CHAPTER 5 PHYSICAL GROWTH 93
    Chapter-at-a-Glance *93* • Brief Chapter Summary *94*
    Learning Objectives *94* • Lecture Outline *95* • Lecture Enhancements *103*
    Learning Activities *106* • Ask Yourself *109* • Suggested Readings *113*
    Media Materials *114*

CHAPTER 6 COGNITIVE DEVELOPMENT: PIAGETIAN, CORE KNOWLEDGE, AND VYGOTSKIAN PERSPECTIVES 117
    Chapter-at-a-Glance *117* • Brief Chapter Summary *118*
    Learning Objectives *119* • Lecture Outline *119* • Lecture Enhancements *130*
    Learning Activities *133* • Ask Yourself *136* • Suggested Readings *142*
    Media Materials *142*

**CHAPTER 7 COGNITIVE DEVELOPMENT: AN INFORMATION-
            PROCESSING PERSPECTIVE 145**

Chapter-at-a-Glance *145* • Brief Chapter Summary *146*
Learning Objectives *147* • Lecture Outline *147* • Lecture Enhancements *154*
Learning Activities *157* • Ask Yourself *160* • Suggested Readings *165*
Media Materials *165*

CHAPTER 8 INTELLIGENCE 167

Chapter-at-a-Glance *167* • Brief Chapter Summary *168*
Learning Objectives *168* • Lecture Outline *169* • Lecture Enhancements *177*
Learning Activities *179* • Ask Yourself *182* • Suggested Readings *185*
Media Materials *186*

CHAPTER 9 LANGUAGE DEVELOPMENT 187

Chapter-at-a-Glance *187* • Brief Chapter Summary *188*
Learning Objectives *188* • Lecture Outline *189* • Lecture Enhancements *196*
Learning Activities *199* • Ask Yourself *201* • Suggested Readings *207*
Media Materials *207*

CHAPTER 10 EMOTIONAL DEVELOPMENT 209

Chapter-at-a-Glance *209* • Brief Chapter Summary *210*
Learning Objectives *210* • Lecture Outline *211* • Lecture Enhancements *220*
Learning Activities *223* • Ask Yourself *226* • Suggested Readings *231*
Media Materials *232*

CHAPTER 11 SELF AND SOCIAL UNDERSTANDING 235

Chapter-at-a-Glance *235* • Brief Chapter Summary *236*
Learning Objectives *237* • Lecture Outline *237* • Lecture Enhancements *245*
Learning Activities *249* • Ask Yourself *251* • Suggested Readings *255*
Media Materials *255*

CHAPTER 12 MORAL DEVELOPMENT 257

Chapter-at-a-Glance *257* • Brief Chapter Summary *258*
Learning Objectives *259* • Lecture Outline *259* • Lecture Enhancements *270*
Learning Activities *274* • Ask Yourself *276* • Suggested Readings *280*
Media Materials *280*

**CHAPTER 13 DEVELOPMENT OF SEX DIFFERENCES AND GENDER
            ROLES 283**

Chapter-at-a-Glance *283* • Brief Chapter Summary *283*
Learning Objectives *284* • Lecture Outline *285* • Lecture Enhancements *292*
Learning Activities *295* • Ask Yourself *298* • Suggested Readings *303*
Media Materials *304*

CHAPTER 14   THE FAMILY   307
    Chapter-at-a-Glance *307* • Brief Chapter Summary *308*
    Learning Objectives *309* • Lecture Outline *309* • Lecture Enhancements *320*
    Learning Activities *323* • Ask Yourself *326* • Suggested Readings *330*
    Media Materials *331*

CHAPTER 15   PEERS, MEDIA, AND SCHOOLING   333
    Chapter-at-a-Glance *333* • Brief Chapter Summary *333*
    Learning Objectives *334* • Lecture Outline *335* • Lecture Enhancements *346*
    Learning Activities *349* • Ask Yourself *352* • Suggested Readings *358*
    Media Materials *358*

ADDITIONAL INSTRUCTIONAL IDEAS   361

MEDIA DISTRIBUTION INFORMATION   363

PREFACE

This Instructor's Resource Manual, which accompanies *Child Development,* Ninth Edition, is designed to assist both the novice and the experienced teacher in preparing lectures and guiding students' learning. During the months that we wrote the manual, we tried to think of the kind of supports that might help instructors seasoned by years of experience bring freshness, stimulation, and inspiration to the teaching of child development. At the same time, we paid great attention to addressing the needs of beginning teachers—only a breath ahead of the syllabus in class preparation and scrambling to find good sources that amplify text discussion. The resources in this manual are intended to lighten the busy schedules of instructors; bring new insights and lively discussion to the classroom; and, most of all, deepen the understanding of students of child development.

The *Instructor's Resource Manual* consists of the following instructional resources keyed to each chapter of the text:

1. **Chapter-at-a-Glance.** Located at the beginning of each chapter, the Chapter-at-a-Glance tables provide easy reference to available resources in the manual as well as outside supplements. Main topics are page-referenced, and instruction ideas (Learning Objectives, Lecture Enhancements, Learning Activities, and Ask Yourself questions) and the supplement (Test Bank) relevant to each text section are listed.

2. **Brief Chapter Summary.** This feature is designed to provide quick familiarity with the coverage of topics in each chapter. It can serve as the basis for deciding which subjects treated by the text to review and extend in class lecture and which supplementary topics to add that reflect the instructor's unique perspective, interests, and personal experiences.

3. **Learning Objectives.** For each text chapter, a comprehensive set of Learning Objectives is provided. We believe that students learn best when they actively grapple with text material and integrate new information with what they already know. Students can be asked to write a paragraph or two in response to each objective, include important terms in their responses, check their answers against the text's discussion, and revise each response accordingly. This exercise yields a student-generated summary of the content of each chapter. Once completed, it provides a useful review written in the student's own words that can be referred to while preparing for examinations. Further, the objectives are tied to individual items in the accompanying Test Bank.

4. **Lecture Outline.** The purpose of the Lecture Outlines is to provide a detailed synopsis of each chapter. Material is organized by text headings and subheadings and page-referenced to the text. Important terms and concepts appear in boldface and in italics, as in the text narrative. The outlines permit a "quick read" of each chapter and can serve as the basis for lecture notes or PowerPoint® Presentations.

5. **Lecture Enhancements.** Four Lecture Enhancements, page-referenced to relevant text material, accompany each chapter. Each expands on information treated in the text by addressing new theory and research, considering controversial issues that promote student discussion and debate, and extending the text's emphasis on the vital connections among theory, research, and applications. To assist instructors with the time-consuming task of lecture preparation, the Lecture Enhancements go beyond merely suggesting appropriate topics to providing the general direction of each lecture's content. Enough detail is given so that instructors who are pressed for time can integrate information from the manual directly into their lectures. Each Lecture Enhancement is accompanied by one or two current sources that can be used to develop a more extensive lecture presentation. Finally, for Lecture Enhancements calling for student participation, specific instructions have been boldfaced.

6. **Learning Activities.** From seven to eleven Learning Activities per chapter are included. Many of the activities provide students with opportunities to see "live" examples of research findings by observing and interviewing children and adolescents. Also included are written assignments that permit students to extend their knowledge of topics in the text.

7. **Ask Yourself.** The Ask Yourself feature consists of critical-thinking questions, designed to support students' active engagement with the subject matter. Each question can be found at the end of major sections in the text and is page-referenced in this manual. The focus of these questions is divided between theory and application. Many describe problematic situations and ask students to resolve them in light of what they have learned. In this way, the questions inspire high-level thinking and new insights.

8. **Suggested Readings.** Many instructors wish to assign or recommend supplementary readings to their students. A list of three to four additional readings complements each text chapter. The readings have been carefully selected for their interest, value, and readability; the majority are recently published. Each entry is annotated so instructors can discern the topic and general orientation of the reading prior to consulting the original source.

9. **Media Materials.** Each chapter contains a related list of available DVDs, including the date of production, the name of the distributor, the length of the presentation, and a description of content.

Sara Harris
Laura E. Berk
Leah Shriro
Judy Ashkenaz

CHAPTER 1
HISTORY, THEORY, AND APPLIED DIRECTIONS

CHAPTER-AT-A-GLANCE

Chapter Outline	Instruction Ideas	Supplements
The Field of Child Development pp. 4–6 Domains of Development • Periods of Development	Learning Objectives 1.1–1.2 Lecture Enhancement 1.1	Test Bank Items 1–12 Please contact your Pearson publisher's representative for a wide range of video offerings available to adopters.
Basic Issues pp. 6–10, 11 Continuous or Discontinuous Development? • One Course of Development or Many? • Relative Influence of Nature and Nurture? • A Balanced Point of View	Learning Objective 1.3 Lecture Enhancement 1.2 Learning Activities 1.1–1.2 Ask Yourself p. 9	Test Bank Items 13–26, 136–137, 141
Historical Foundations pp. 10–14 Medieval Times • The Reformation • Philosophies of the Enlightenment • Scientific Beginnings	Learning Objective 1.4 Learning Activity 1.3 Ask Yourself p. 14	Test Bank Items 27–46
Mid-Twentieth-Century Theories pp. 14–21 The Psychoanalytic Perspective • Behaviorism and Social Learning Theory • Piaget's Cognitive-Developmental Theory	Learning Objective 1.5 Learning Activities 1.3–1.4 Ask Yourself p. 21	Test Bank Items 47–80
Recent Theoretical Perspectives pp. 21–31 Information Processing • Developmental Cognitive Neuroscience • Ethology and Evolutionary Developmental Psychology • Vygotsky's Sociocultural Theory • Ecological Systems Theory • New Directions: Development as a Dynamic System	Learning Objective 1.6 Lecture Enhancement 1.3 Learning Activities 1.3–1.5 Ask Yourself p. 31	Test Bank Items 81–117, 138–140
Comparing Child Development Theories pp. 31–32	Learning Objective 1.7	Test Bank Items 118–121, 141
Applied Directions: Child Development and Social Policy pp. 32–38 Culture and Public Policies • Contributions of Child Development Research • Looking Toward the Future	Learning Objective 1.8 Lecture Enhancement 1.4 Learning Activities 1.6–1.7 Ask Yourself p. 38	Test Bank Items 122–135, 142

BRIEF CHAPTER SUMMARY

Child development is the study of human constancy and change from conception through adolescence. It is part of the larger, interdisciplinary field of developmental science, which includes the entire lifespan.

Researchers often divide the study of development into three broad domains—physical, cognitive, and emotional and social—and divide development into five age periods from conception through adolescence. In recent decades, researchers have posited a new period, emerging adulthood, which describes the prolonged transition to adulthood typical of contemporary young people in industrialized nations.

Theories of child development provide organizing frameworks that guide and give meaning to the scientific study of children. All major theories of child development take a stand on three basic issues: (1) Is the course of development continuous or discontinuous? (2) Do all children follow one course of development, or are there many possible courses? (3) Are genetic or environmental factors more important in influencing development? Recent theories generally take a balanced view of these issues.

Contemporary theories of child development are rooted in ideas about children that go back many centuries. The theories that have been major forces in child development research vary in their focus on different domains of development, in their view of development, and in their strengths and limitations.

In recent years, the field of child development has become increasingly concerned with applying its vast knowledge base to solving pressing social problems. Public policy—favorable laws and government programs aimed at improving current conditions—is essential for safeguarding children's positive experiences in family, school, and community contexts. Such policies are strongly affected by cultural values like individualism versus collectivism. To be effective in meeting children's needs, public policies must be guided by research. As researchers in child development collaborate with community and government agencies, they can help to create a sense of immediacy about the need to improve the condition of children and families.

LEARNING OBJECTIVES

After reading this chapter, you should be able to answer the following:

1.1 What is the field of child development, and what factors stimulated its expansion? (p. 4)

1.2 How is child development typically divided into domains and periods? (pp. 4–6)

1.3 Identify three basic issues on which child development theories take a stand. (pp. 6–10, 11)

1.4 Describe major historical influences on theories of child development. (pp. 10–14)

1.5 What theories influenced child development research in the mid-twentieth century? (pp. 14–21)

1.6 Describe recent theoretical perspectives on child development. (pp. 21–31)

1.7 Identify the stand taken by each major theory on the basic issues of child development. (pp. 31–32)

1.8 Explain the importance of social policies for safeguarding children's well-being, and cite factors that affect the policy-making process, noting the role of child development research. (pp. 32–38)

LECTURE OUTLINE

I. THE FIELD OF CHILD DEVELOPMENT (pp. 4–6)
   A. **Child development** is an area of study devoted to understanding constancy and change from conception through adolescence.
   B. Child development is part of the field of **developmental science,** which includes all changes that humans experience throughout the lifespan.
   C. Research in child development has both scientific and *applied* (practical) importance.
   D. Our large storehouse of information about child development is *interdisciplinary*.

E. Domains of Development (pp. 4–5)
   1. Development often is divided into three broad domains, which combine in an integrated, holistic fashion to yield the living, growing child.
   2. The three domains are *physical, cognitive,* and *emotional and social.*
F. Periods of Development (pp. 5–6)
   1. Researchers usually segment child development into age periods.
   2. *The prenatal period: from conception to birth:* In this nine-month period, a one-celled organism is transformed into a human baby.
   3. *Infancy and toddlerhood: from birth to 2 years:* This period brings dramatic changes in the body and brain that support the emergence of a wide array of motor, perceptual, and intellectual capacities.
   4. *Early childhood: from 2 to 6 years:* In this period, motor skills are refined, children become more self-sufficient, make-believe play blooms, and thought and language expand rapidly.
   5. *Middle childhood: from 6 to 11 years:* In this period, children learn about the wider world and master responsibilities that increasingly resemble those of adults.
   6. *Adolescence: from 11 to 18 years:* During this period, puberty leads to an adult-sized body and sexual maturity, thought becomes abstract and idealistic, and schooling focuses on preparation for higher education and work.
   7. *Emerging adulthood: from 18 to 25 years:*
      a. Some researchers posit this as a new period of development for contemporary youths in industrialized nations.
      b. During this period, young people intensify their exploration of options in love, career, and personal values before making enduring commitments.

II. BASIC ISSUES (pp. 6–10, 11)
   A. Speculations about child development combined with research have inspired the construction of *theories* of development.
   B. A **theory** is an orderly, integrated set of statements that describes, explains, and predicts behavior.
   C. Most theories of development take a stand on three basic issues: (1) Is the course of development continuous or discontinuous? (2) Does one course of development characterize all children, or are there many possible courses? (3) What are the roles of genetic and environmental factors in development?
   D. Continuous or Discontinuous Development? (pp. 7–8)
      1. **Continuous** development is a process of gradually adding more of the same types of skills that were there to begin with.
      2. **Discontinuous** development is a process in which new ways of understanding and responding to the world emerge at specific times.
      3. Theories that accept the discontinuous perspective see development as taking place in **stages**—*qualitative* changes in thinking, feeling, and behaving that characterize specific periods of development.
   E. One Course of Development or Many? (p. 8)
      1. Stage theorists assume that children everywhere follow the same sequence of development.
      2. The field of child development is becoming increasingly aware that children grow up in distinct **contexts**—unique combinations of personal and environmental circumstances that can result in different paths of change.
      3. Contemporary theorists regard the contexts that shape development as many-layered and complex.
         a. Personal contexts include heredity and biological makeup.
         b. Environmental contexts include both immediate settings (home, school, and neighborhood) and more remote circumstances such as community resources and societal values.
   F. Relative Influence of Nature and Nurture? (pp. 8–9)
      1. The age-old **nature–nurture controversy** asks: Are genetic or environmental factors more important in influencing development?
         a. *Nature* refers to inborn biological givens—hereditary information we receive from our parents.
         b. *Nurture* means the complex forces of the physical and social world that influence our biological makeup and psychological experiences before and after birth.
      2. Investigators disagree on the question of *stability versus plasticity.*
         a. Some theorists emphasize *stability*—that children who are high or low in a characteristic will remain so at later ages. These theorists typically stress the importance of *heredity.*

b. If theorists regard environment as important, they usually point to early experiences as establishing a lifelong pattern of behavior.
c. Other theorists see development as having substantial **plasticity** throughout life—as open to change in response to influential experiences.
G. A Balanced Point of View (pp. 9–10, 11)
1. Today, some theorists believe that both continuous and discontinuous changes occur.
2. Many acknowledge that development can have both universal features and features unique to each individual and his or her contexts.
3. A growing number of investigators regard heredity and environment as inseparably interwoven.
4. The relative impact of early and later experiences varies greatly from one domain of development to another, and even across individuals, who vary in **resilience**—the ability to adapt effectively in the face of threats to development.

III. HISTORICAL FOUNDATIONS (pp. 10–14)
A. Contemporary theories of child development are the result of centuries of change in Western cultural values, philosophical thinking about children, and scientific progress.
B. Medieval Times (pp. 10–11)
1. Childhood was regarded as a separate period of life as early as medieval Europe.
2. Laws recognized that children needed protection from people who might mistreat them.
3. Medieval religious writings sometimes portrayed infants as possessed by the devil, at other times as innocent. Both ideas foreshadowed later views of childhood.
C. The Reformation (pp. 11–12)
1. In the sixteenth century, the Puritan belief in original sin gave rise to the view that children were born evil and stubborn and had to be civilized.
2. Harsh, restrictive child-rearing practices were recommended, but love for their children prevented most Puritan parents from using extremely repressive measures.
3. As the Puritans emigrated from England to the New World, they brought the belief that child rearing was one of their most important obligations.
D. Philosophies of the Enlightenment (p. 12)
1. John Locke (1632–1704)
a. Locke, a British philosopher, viewed the child as a *tabula rasa,* Latin for "blank slate." He saw parents as rational tutors who could mold the child through instruction, example, and rewards.
b. Locke championed *nurture*—the power of the environment to shape the child—a belief that suggested the possibility of *many courses of development* and of *high plasticity at later ages* due to new experiences. He regarded development as *continuous*.
c. Locke's view of children as doing little to influence their own destiny has been discarded.
2. Jean-Jacques Rousseau (1712–1778)
a. The French philosopher Rousseau saw children as *noble savages,* naturally endowed with a sense of right and wrong and with an innate plan for orderly, healthy growth.
b. The role of adults was to be receptive to the child's needs at each of four stages: infancy, childhood, late childhood, and adolescence.
c. Rousseau's philosophy includes the idea of *stage* and the concept of **maturation**—a genetically determined, naturally unfolding course of growth.
d. Rousseau saw development as a *discontinuous, stagewise* process following a *single, unified* course mapped out by *nature*.
E. Scientific Beginnings (pp. 13–14)
1. Darwin: Forefather of Scientific Child Study
a. British naturalist Charles Darwin (1809–1882) constructed his *theory of evolution* after joining an expedition to distant parts of the world, where he observed infinite variation among plant and animal species.
b. Darwin's theory emphasized two related principles:
(1) According to *natural selection,* certain species survive because they have characteristics that are adapted to their surroundings, while others, less well-suited to their environments, die off.

Chapter 1 History, Theory, and Applied Directions

   (2) *Survival of the fittest* refers to Darwin's explanation that individuals within a species who best meet their environment's survival requirements live long enough to reproduce and pass on their beneficial characteristics to future generations.
 c. Darwin observed that the early prenatal growth of many species is strikingly similar.
   (1) Other scientists concluded that human child development follows the same general plan as the evolution of the human species.
   (2) Although this belief proved inaccurate, efforts to chart parallels between child growth and human evolution prompted researchers to document all aspects of children's behavior, giving rise to the field of scientific child study.
 2. The Normative Period
  a. The American psychologist G. Stanley Hall (1844–1924) is generally regarded as the founder of the child-study movement.
  b. Hall and his student Arnold Gesell (1880–1961) developed theories of child development based on evolutionary ideas. They regarded child development as a *maturational process*—a genetically determined series of events that unfolds automatically.
  c. Hall and Gesell are best remembered for their intensive efforts to describe all aspects of child development, which launched the **normative approach,** in which measures of behavior are taken on large numbers of individuals and age-related averages are computed to represent typical development.
  d. Gesell was among the first to make knowledge about child development meaningful to parents by telling them what to expect at each age.
 3. The Mental Testing Movement
  a. French psychologist Alfred Binet (1857–1911) and his colleague Theodore Simon constructed the first successful intelligence test as a way of identifying children in the Paris school system with learning problems who needed to be placed in special classes.
  b. Binet defined intelligence as good judgment, planning, and critical reflection.
  c. The English-language version of Binet's test, the *Stanford-Binet Intelligence Scale,* sparked interest in individual differences in development, and intelligence tests rose quickly to the forefront of the nature–nurture controversy.
 4. James Mark Baldwin: Early Developmental Theorist
  a. American psychologist James Mark Baldwin (1861–1934) granted nature and nurture equal importance in development, and he believed that children actively revise their ways of thinking about the world but that they also learn through habit, or by copying others' behaviors.
  b. Baldwin argued that heredity and environment should not be viewed as distinct, opposing forces.

IV. MID-TWENTIETH-CENTURY THEORIES (pp. 14–21)
 A. In the mid-1900s, the field of child development expanded into a legitimate discipline.
  1. The Society for Research in Child Development (SRCD), established in 1933 to promote interdisciplinary research, now has an international membership of about 5,500.
  2. In the theories that have emerged, the European concern with the child's inner thoughts and feelings contrasts sharply with the North American focus on scientific precision and observable behavior.
 B. The Psychoanalytic Perspective (pp. 15–17)
  1. By the 1930s and 1940s, parents increasingly sought professional help to deal with children's emotional difficulties. Psychiatrists and social workers turned to an emerging approach to personality development that emphasized the unique history of each child.
  2 According to the **psychoanalytic perspective,** children move through a series of stages in which they confront conflicts between biological drives and social expectations. How these conflicts are resolved determines the person's ability to learn, to get along with others, and to cope with anxiety.
  3. Freud's Theory
   a. Viennese physician Sigmund Freud (1856–1939) sought to cure emotionally troubled adults by having them talk freely about painful events of their childhoods.
   b. Examining his patients' unconscious motivations, Freud constructed his **psychosexual theory,** which emphasizes that how parents manage their child's sexual and aggressive drives in the first few years is crucial for healthy personality development.

c. Freud identified three parts of the personality that become integrated during five stages of development.
   (1) The *id,* the largest portion, is the source of basic biological needs and desires.
   (2) The *ego,* the conscious, rational part of the personality, emerges in early infancy to redirect the id's impulses so they are discharged in acceptable ways.
   (3) The *superego,* or conscience, develops between ages 3 and 6 through interactions with parents, who insist that the child conform to the values of society.
d. Freud believed that during childhood, sexual impulses shift their focus from the oral to the anal to the genital regions of the body.
   (1) If parents strike an appropriate balance between permitting too much or too little gratification of the child's basic needs at each stage, the child will grow into a well-adjusted adult.
   (2) Freud's perspective was eventually criticized in part because it overemphasized the influence of sexual feelings in development.
4. Erikson's Theory
   a. Erik Erikson (1902–1994), a neo-Freudian in the field of child development, developed his **psychosocial theory,** which emphasizes that in addition to mediating between id impulses and superego demands, the ego also makes a positive contribution to development, acquiring attitudes and skills that make the individual an active, contributing member of society.
   b. Erikson believed that a basic psychosocial conflict is resolved positively or negatively at each stage, determining healthy or maladaptive outcomes.
   c. Erikson's first five stages of development parallel Freud's stages, but Erikson added three adult stages.
5. Contributions and Limitations of the Psychoanalytic Perspective
   a. A strength of the psychoanalytic perspective is its emphasis on the individual's unique life history as worthy of study and understanding. Reflecting this view, psychoanalytic theorists accept the *clinical,* or *case study, method.*
   b. Despite its extensive contributions, the psychoanalytic perspective is no longer in the mainstream of child development research.
   c. Erikson's broad outline of psychosocial change remains relevant because it captures the essence of psychosocial attainments at each age period.

C. Behaviorism and Social Learning Theory (pp. 17–19)
1. Child study was also influenced by the perspective of **behaviorism,** which views directly observable events—stimuli and responses—as the appropriate focus of study.
2. North American behaviorism began in the early twentieth century with the efforts of psychologist John Watson (1878–1958) to create an objective science of psychology.
3. Traditional Behaviorism
   a. Inspired by Russian physiologist Ivan Pavlov's studies of animal learning, Watson wanted to find out if *classical conditioning* could be applied to children's behavior.
   b. Watson concluded that adults can mold children's behavior by carefully controlling stimulus–response associations.
   c. B. F. Skinner (1904–1990) developed another form of behaviorism, *operant conditioning theory,* which holds that the frequency of a child's behavior can be increased by following it with a variety of *reinforcers* or decreased through *punishment.*
4. Social Learning Theory
   a. The rise of behaviorism sparked the emergence of several kinds of **social learning theory** based on the principles of conditioning.
   b. The most influential form of this theory, devised by psychologist Albert Bandura, emphasized *modeling,* also known as *imitation* or *observational learning,* as a powerful source of development.
   c. Bandura's work is still influential, but he now calls his theory a *social-cognitive* rather than a social learning approach because it stresses the importance of *cognition.*
   d. In Bandura's revised view, through watching others and feedback about their own actions, children develop *personal standards* for behavior and a *sense of self-efficacy*—the belief that their own abilities and characteristics will help them succeed.

Chapter 1 History, Theory, and Applied Directions

5. Contributions and Limitations of Behaviorism and Social Learning Theory
   a. **Behavior modification,** consisting of procedures that combine conditioning and modeling to eliminate undesirable behaviors and increase desirable responses, has been used to relieve serious developmental problems and also to deal with everyday difficulties, such as thumb sucking.
   b. Many theorists believe that behaviorism and social learning theory offer too narrow a view of important environmental influences.
   c. Behaviorism and social learning theory have been criticized for underestimating children's role in their own development.
D. Piaget's Cognitive-Developmental Theory (pp. 19–21)
   1. Swiss cognitive theorist Jean Piaget (1896–1980) has influenced the contemporary field of child development more than any other individual.
   2. In Piaget's **cognitive-developmental theory,** children actively construct knowledge as they manipulate and explore their world.
   3. Piaget's Stages
      a. Central to Piaget's theory is the biological concept of *adaptation,* whereby structures of the mind develop to better fit with, or represent, the external world.
      b. Piaget believed that young children's understanding differs from adults' and that children eventually revise these incorrect ideas in their ongoing efforts to achieve *equilibrium,* or balance, between internal structures and information they encounter in their everyday life.
      c. According to Piaget's theory, as children's brains develop and their experiences expand, they move through four broad stages characterized by qualitatively distinct ways of thinking:
         (1) *Sensorimotor stage (birth–2 years):* Cognitive development begins as the baby uses the senses and movements to explore the world.
         (2) *Preoperational stage (2–7 years):* The baby's action patterns evolve into the symbolic but illogical thinking of the preschooler.
         (3) *Concrete operational stage (7–11 years):* Cognition is transformed into the more organized, logical reasoning of the school-age child.
         (4) *Formal operational stage (11 years on):* Thought becomes the abstract, systematic reasoning system of the adolescent and adult.
      d. To investigate how children think, Piaget first observed his three infant children's responses when he presented them with everyday problems. Later, to study childhood and adolescent thought, he conducted open-ended *clinical interviews.*
   4. Contributions and Limitations of Piaget's Theory
      a. Contributions
         (1) Piaget convinced the field of child development that children are active learners whose minds consist of rich structures of knowledge.
         (2) Piaget investigated both children's understanding of the physical world and their reasoning about the social world.
         (3) Piaget's stages sparked research on children's conceptions of themselves, others, and human relationships.
         (4) Piaget's theory encouraged the development of educational philosophies and programs that emphasize discovery learning and direct contact with the environment.
      b. Limitations
         (1) Research indicates that Piaget underestimated the competencies of infants and preschoolers.
         (2) Studies show that children's performance on Piagetian problems can be improved with training, calling into question Piaget's assumption that discovery learning, not adult teaching, is the best way to foster development.
         (3) Also, adolescents generally reach their full intellectual potential only in areas of endeavor in which they have had extensive education and experience.
V. RECENT THEORETICAL PERSPECTIVES (pp. 21–31)
   A. Information Processing (pp. 21–23)
      1. The **information-processing** perspective views the human mind as a symbol-manipulating system through which information flows.

2. In this view, from the time information is presented to the senses at *input* until it emerges as a behavioral response at *output,* the information is actively coded, transformed, and organized.
3. Information-processing researchers seek to clarify how both task characteristics and cognitive limitations (for example, memory capacity) influence performance.
4. Some information-processing models track children's mastery of one or a few tasks; others describe the human cognitive system as a whole.
5. The information-processing approach is being used to clarify the processing of social information.
6. The information-processing approach, like Piaget's theory, sees children as active, sense-making beings who modify their own thinking in response to environmental demands.
7. This approach views development as a process of continuous change.
8. A strength of the information-processing approach is its commitment to rigorous research methods.
9. Information processing is better at analyzing thinking into its components than at formulating a comprehensive theory. It has had little to say about imagination and creativity.

B. Developmental Cognitive Neuroscience (p. 23)
1. **Developmental cognitive neuroscience,** which has arisen over the past three decades, brings together researchers from psychology, biology, neuroscience, and medicine to study the relationship between changes in the brain and the developing child's cognitive processing and behavior patterns.
2. Neuroscientists use improved methods for analyzing brain activity while children perform various tasks, to investigate relationships between brain functioning, cognitive capacities, and behavior, including questions like these:
   a. How does genetic makeup combine with specific experiences at various ages to influence the growth and organization of the child's brain?
   b. How do changes in brain structures support rapid memory development in infancy and toddlerhood?
3. During infancy and early childhood, the brain is highly plastic. But a revolutionary finding of neuroscience research is that the brain retains considerable plasticity throughout life.
4. The final four theoretical perspectives focus on *contexts* for development.

C. Ethology and Evolutionary Developmental Psychology (pp. 23–24)
1. **Ethology** is concerned with the adaptive, or survival, value of behavior and its evolutionary history.
   a. Its modern foundations were laid by zoologists Konrad Lorenz and Niko Tinbergen, who observed behavior patterns that promoted survival in diverse animal species.
   b. The best known of these patterns is *imprinting*.
   c. Observations of imprinting led to the concept of the *critical period,* a limited time during which the child is biologically prepared to acquire certain adaptive behaviors but needs the support of an appropriately stimulating environment.
   d. The term **sensitive period,** referring to a time that is optimal for certain capacities to emerge and in which the individual is especially responsive to environmental influences, applies better to human development than the strict notion of a critical period. Its boundaries are less well-defined than those of a critical period.
   e. British psychoanalyst John Bowlby applied ethological theory to the understanding of attachment in human infants through the caregiver–infant relationship.
2. Recently, researchers have extended ethologists' observations that many aspects of children's social behavior resemble those of our primate relatives in a new area of research, **evolutionary developmental psychology,** which seeks to understand the adaptive value of species-wide cognitive, emotional, and social competencies as those competencies change with age.
   a. Evolutionary psychologists study the entire *organism–environment system.*
   b. By clarifying the origins and development of certain evolved behaviors—such as life-threatening risk taking in adolescents and male-to-male violence—that are no longer adaptive, evolutionary developmental psychology may help spark more effective interventions.

D. Vygotsky's Sociocultural Theory (pp. 24–26)
1. The field of child development has recently seen a dramatic increase in studies addressing the cultural context of children's lives, including comparisons across cultures.
2. Today, much research is examining the relationship of *culturally specific beliefs and practices* to development. The Russian psychologist Lev Vygotsky (1896–1934) played a major role in this trend.
3. Vygotsky's perspective, known as **sociocultural theory,** focuses on how *culture* is transmitted to the next generation.

Chapter 1 History, Theory, and Applied Directions

4. According to Vygotsky, *social interaction* is necessary for children to acquire the ways of thinking and behaving that make up a community's culture.
5. Like Piaget, Vygotsky viewed children as active, constructive beings. But Vygotsky saw cognitive development as a *socially mediated process,* in which children depend on assistance from adults and more-expert peers as they tackle new challenges.
6. Vygotsky believed that children undergo certain stagewise changes.
7. Cross-cultural research shows that cultures select different tasks for children's learning, and the social interactions surrounding those tasks lead to competencies essential for success in a particular culture.
8. Vygotsky said little about the role of heredity and brain growth in cognitive change.
9. Vygotsky placed less emphasis than other theorists on children's capacity to shape their own development.

E. Ecological Systems Theory (pp. 26–29)
1. The **ecological systems theory** of Urie Bronfenbrenner (1917–2005) views the child as developing within a complex *system* of relationships affected by multiple levels of the surrounding environment.
2. Bronfenbrenner calls his perspective a *bioecological model,* in which the child's biologically influenced dispositions join with environmental forces to mold development.
3. The environment is seen as a series of nested structures—*microsystem, mesosystem, exosystem,* and *macrosystem*—that include but also extend beyond home, school, and neighborhood settings.
    a. The Microsystem
        (1) The innermost level of the environment is the **microsystem,** consisting of activities and interaction patterns in the child's immediate surroundings.
        (2) All relationships are *bidirectional:* Adults affect children's behavior, but children also affect adults' behavior.
        (3) *Third parties*—other individuals in the microsystem—also affect the quality of any two-person relationship.
    b. The Mesosystem
        (1) The second level of Bronfenbrenner's model, the **mesosystem,** encompasses connections between microsystems, such as home, school, neighborhood, and child-care center.
        (2) Family–neighborhood connections are especially important for economically disadvantaged children, who, compared with affluent children, are more dependent on their immediate surroundings for social support.
        (3) Yet in dangerous, disorganized neighborhoods, high-quality activities for children and adolescents are usually scarce, and home and neighborhood obstacles often combine to reduce involvement.
    c. The Exosystem
        (1) The third level, the **exosystem,** consists of social settings that do not contain children but nevertheless affect children's experiences in immediate settings.
        (2) This level includes both formal organizations, such as parents' workplaces and religious institutions, and informal supports, such as parents' social networks.
        (3) Research confirms the negative impact of a breakdown in exosystem activities—for example, the effects of unemployment or social isolation.
        (4) When family time is at the mercy of external forces, such as parents commuting several hours a day to and from work, family routines are threatened.
    d. The Macrosystem
        (1) The outermost level of Bronfenbrenner's model, the **macrosystem,** consists of cultural values, laws, customs, and resources.
        (2) The priority that the macrosystem gives to children's needs—for example, support of high standards for child care and generous workplace benefits for employed parents—affects the experiences children have in their immediate settings.
    e. An Ever-Changing System
        (1) Bronfenbrenner sees the environment as ever-changing and calls the temporal dimension of his model the **chronosystem.**
        (2) The timing of important life events, such as the birth of a sibling, modifies relationships between children and their environments.
        (3) These changes can be imposed on the child or can arise from within the child.

F. New Directions: Development as a Dynamic System (pp. 30–31)
 1. Today's researchers, recognizing both consistency and variability in children's development, have adopted a **dynamic systems perspective**—a view in which the child's mind, body, and physical and social worlds form an *integrated system* that guides mastery of new skills.
    a. The system is *dynamic*. A change in any part of it disrupts the current organism–environment relationship.
    b. In response to change, the child actively reorganizes her behavior so the components of the system work together again but in a more complex, effective way.
 2. Researchers who adopt a dynamic systems perspective try to study children's behavior while they are in transition.
 3. Dynamic systems theorists believe that within certain universal, broad outlines of development, biological makeup and environmental factors vary greatly, leading to wide individual differences in specific skills.
 4. From this perspective, development is not a single line of change but a web of fibers.

VI. COMPARING CHILD DEVELOPMENT THEORIES (pp. 31–32)
 A. The major theoretical perspectives in child development research focus on different domains of development.
 B. Every theory contains a point of view about child development and takes a stand on the basic issues.
 C. Every theory has both strengths and limitations, allowing one to develop an *eclectic position,* or blend of several theories.

VII. APPLIED DIRECTIONS: CHILD DEVELOPMENT AND SOCIAL POLICY (pp. 32–38)
 A. In recent years, the field of child development has become increasingly concerned with applying its knowledge base to solving pressing social problems by influencing social policy.
  1. **Social policy** is any planned set of actions by a group, institution, or governing body directed at attaining a social goal.
  2. Nations attempt to solve widespread social problems through **public policy**—laws and government programs aimed to improve current conditions.
 B. U.S. public policies safeguarding children and youths have lagged behind policies in other developed nations: The United States outranks nearly all other economically advanced countries in child poverty.
  1. Nearly 21 percent of U.S. children are poor, and poverty is expected to worsen, due to the recent economic recession.
  2. Of all Western nations, the United States has the highest percentage of extremely poor children—nearly 8 percent.
  3. The United States does not rank well on any key measure of children's health and well-being.
  4. Despite improved health-care provisions signed into law in 2010, the United States remains the only industrialized nation without a universal, publicly funded health-care system.
  5. The United States has been slow to move toward national standards and funding for child care.
  6. Weak enforcement of child support payments heightens poverty in mother-headed households.
 C. Culture and Public Policies (pp. 34–35, 36)
  1. Public policies are strongly influenced by cultural variation in the extent to which *individualism* versus *collectivism* prevails.
   a. In **individualistic societies,** people think of themselves as separate entities and are largely concerned with their own personal needs.
   b. In **collectivist societies,** people define themselves as part of a group and stress group over individual goals.
  2. The United States is strongly individualistic, whereas most Western European nations lean toward collectivism.
  3. Less consensus exists among American citizens than among European citizens on issues of child and family policy, resulting in fewer and more limited programs.
  4. Good social programs must compete for a fair share of a country's economic resources.
  5. Some policies aimed at solving one social problem—for example, returning welfare recipients to the workforce—can work at cross-purposes with children's well-being, sometimes even worsening their condition.
 D. Contributions of Child Development Research (pp. 35–37)
  1. For a policy to be effective in meeting children's needs, research must guide it at every step.
  2. Research on the importance of early experiences for children's intellectual development played a major role in the founding, in 1965, of Project Head Start.
  3. Several decades of research on early rapid brain growth and plasticity and the short- and long-term benefits of early intervention helped Head Start survive.

Chapter 1 History, Theory, and Applied Directions

4. Investigators have broadened their focus to include wider social contexts that affect children's well-being and to examine the impact on children of societal changes.

E. Looking Toward the Future (p. 37)

1. Policies aimed at fostering children's development can be justified on two grounds: Children are the future, and child-oriented policies can be defended on humanitarian grounds.
2. Growing awareness of the gap between what we know and what we do to better children's lives has led experts in child development to join with concerned citizens as advocates for more effective policies, creating several influential interest groups devoted to the well-being of children:
   a. In the United States, the most vigorous children's advocacy group is the Children's Defense Fund, which engages in public education, legal action, drafting of legislation, congressional testimony, and community organizing.
   b. Another advocacy organization is the National Center for Children in Poverty, dedicated to advancing the economic security, health, and welfare of U.S. children in low-income families.
3. More researchers are collaborating with community and government agencies to enhance the social relevance of their investigations and to disseminate their findings more widely.

LECTURE ENHANCEMENTS

LECTURE ENHANCEMENT 1.1
Illustrating Domains of Development: The Relationship Between Cognitive and Emotional and Social Development (pp. 4–5)

Time: 10–15 minutes

Objective: To illustrate domains of development by examining the relationship between reading problems and internalizing behavior in school-age children.

Chapter 1 of the text notes that each domain of development—physical, cognitive, and emotional and social—influences and is influenced by the others. To highlight the relationship between reading problems (cognitive domain) and internalizing behavior (emotional and social domain), Ackerman and colleagues (2008) recruited 105 school-age children who were already participating in a longitudinal study of low-income families. The researchers collected the following information when children were in grades 3 and 5:

(1) Teachers completed the Child Behavior Checklist (CBCL), which assesses withdrawn behavior, somatic complaints, anxiety, depression, aggression, and delinquency.
(2) Statewide reading achievement test scores, which were available on all participants, were used to assess reading levels and problems. The researchers also had access to participants' scores on a vocabulary subtest from the Stanford-Binet Intelligence Scale.
(3) Children completed a self-report about emotional experiences. For example, they were asked, "How often do you feel angry, disgusted, shy, sad, or guilty?"
(4) During academic tasks, trained coders conducted direct observations to assess inattention.
(5) Parents provided demographic information, including a family disruption index. (For example, had the mother experienced any change in intimate residential partners in the past two years? Had any adult member of the household had police contact or received psychiatric treatment in the past two years?)

Results indicated that of the 105 participants, 43 percent of third graders and 39 percent of fifth graders were enrolled in a reading-assistance program. Despite their involvement in the reading program, the majority of these children scored well below average on the statewide reading achievement test. Findings also showed that reading problems in the third and fifth grades strongly predicted internalizing behavior and negative emotion, although this finding was stronger for fifth graders. That is, fifth graders experienced more distress than third graders over poor reading achievement. The relationship between reading problems, internalizing behavior, and negative emotion remained even after controlling for family disruption. Taken together, these findings highlight the negative consequences of reading problems on the psychological well-being in school-age children. According to Ackerman and colleagues, the longer reading problems persist, the more frustrated, depressed, and anxious children are likely to become.

Ask students to identify factors that may explain the relationship between reading difficulties and anxiety and depression. How might internalizing problems, in turn, contribute to reading difficulties?

Ackerman, B. P., Izard, C. E., Kobak, R., Brown, E. D., & Smith, C. (2008). Relation between reading problems and internalizing behavior in school for preadolescent children from economically disadvantaged families. *Child Development, 78,* 581–596.

LECTURE ENHANCEMENT 1.2
Risk and Resilience in Low-SES Ethnically Diverse Families (pp. 10–11)

Time: 10–15 minutes

Objective: To extend existing research on risk and resilience in low-SES ethnically diverse families.

As noted in the text, environmental risks, such as poverty, negative family interactions, parental divorce, mental illness, and drug abuse, predispose children to future problems. However, not all at-risk children experience lasting problems. To extend existing research on risk and resilience, Wadsworth and Santiago (2008) recruited 94 families living at or below the federal poverty line. Each family had at least one parent or guardian and one child or adolescent between the ages of 6 and 18 years. Thirty-three percent of the families were European American, with the remaining families being African American, Latino, Native American, or multiracial. The researchers collected the following information:

(1) The Multicultural Events Schedule for Adolescents (MESA) was used to measure family poverty-related stress. The MESA focuses on the daily hassles and life events that are common among poor, urban youths, including economic strain, family conflict, family transitions, discrimination, and victimization/violence exposure. Parents completed the MESA for children under the age of 10, whereas adolescents completed a self-report.

(2) The Economic Hardship Questionnaire (EHQ) was used to measure the number of constraints a family experienced in the past 6 months due to financial hardship. For example, in the past 6 months, We have had to sell possessions to make ends meet. We had to apply for federal assistance.

(3) Parents completed the Child Behavior Checklist (CBCL), which rates a broad range of internalizing (anxiety, somatic complaints, depression) and externalizing (aggression, impulsivity, hyperactivity) problems. Parents also completed the Adult Self Report (ASR) and the Adult Behavior Checklist (ABCL). The ASR measures one's own psychological symptoms, whereas the ABCL focuses on the partner's symptoms.

(4) Parents and adolescents completed the Responses to Stress Questionnaire, which assesses how a person responds to a stressful domain—for example, withdrawal, talking about the situation, or becoming anxious or depressed.

Results indicated that poverty-related stress (PRS) predicted psychological distress in families regardless of ethnic background. However, some individuals were more vulnerable to the effects of PRS. For example, children tended to exhibit greater behavioral difficulties and poorer coping skills than adolescents or adults. According to Wadsworth and Santiago, children may have an especially difficult time coping with PRS due to their lack of control over the family's financial situation. As a result, they may have difficulty developing effective coping strategies, which may interfere with their ability to deal with other stressful life events. And compared to males of all ages, females had higher rates of anxiety, depression, and somatic complaints, which is consistent with previous research on gender differences in stress reactions. Finally, African-American families were less affected by PRS than European-American or Latino families. This may be due to the social supports available to African-American families, such as strong extended-family relations and religious participation. Such social support may serve as a buffer against PRS.

Wadsworth, M. E., & Santiago, C. D. (2008). Risk and resiliency processes in ethnically diverse families in poverty. *Journal of Family Psychology, 22,* 399–410.

LECTURE ENHANCEMENT 1.3
Do Home and Neighborhood Characteristics Contribute to Children's Participation in Out-of-School Activities? (pp. 26–28)

Time: 10–15 minutes

Objective: To examine the influence of home and neighborhood contexts on children's participation in out-of-school activities.

According to ecological systems theory, a child's development occurs within a complex system of relationships affected by multiple levels of the environment. Moreover, each layer of the environment has a powerful impact on development. To extend existing research on how home and neighborhood contexts influence child development, Dearing and colleagues (2009) recruited 1,420 elementary school-age children who were participating in The Panel Study of Income Dynamics, Child Development Supplement (PSID–CDS), a longitudinal investigation of children's health, emotional well-being, intellectual development, academic achievement, and relationships with family and peers. The researchers collected the following information:

(1) Parents provided demographic information, including children's age, gender, ethnicity, family size, partner status, employment status, and annual income.

(2) Trained interviewers visited children's homes and completed the Home Observation for Measurement of the Environment (HOME). The HOME focuses on a range of household characteristics, such as quality of parent–child interactions, material resources, presence of children's books, affection toward child, and use of physical punishment.

(3) Using U.S. Census data, the researchers calculated neighborhood affluence using median family income, percentage of residents with a college degree, and percentage of residents in professional or managerial jobs.

(4) The researchers conducted observations of neighborhood safety and orderliness. They focused on the presence of drug-related paraphernalia, condoms, liquor containers, cigarette butts, and discarded cigarette packages in the streets or on the sidewalks.

(5) Parents provided information on their child's participation in nonschool activities during the past year, including before- and after-school programs, community center activities, lessons (e.g., music), church clubs, and summer camps.

Findings indicated that family income strongly predicted children's participation in activities outside of school. For example, a child living in a family with an annual income of $20,000 was 2.5 times as likely to participate in nonschool activities than a child living in a family with an annual income of $10,000. Neighborhood characteristics also contributed to participation rates. Children living in affluent, safe, and orderly neighborhoods had greater access to nonschool activities, which predicted higher rates of participation. One exception to this trend was participation in church clubs, with low-income children having higher participation rates than affluent children. This finding is not surprising, as churches tend to be a central source of support for low-income and ethnic minority families. Finally, the quality of the home environment had an indirect effect on children's participation in nonschool activities. Affluent families tended to provide more enrichment, which, in turn, predicted higher participation rates.

These findings support previous research on the importance of home and neighborhood contexts for children's development. Although neighborhood resources tend to have a greater impact on economically disadvantaged than on well-to-do young people, poor children often lack access to growth-enriching activities like before- and after-school programs, formal lessons, and summer camps.

According to your text, why are strong family–neighborhood ties especially important for low-income children?

Dearing, E., Wimer, C., Simpkins, S. D., Lund, T., Bouffard, S. M., Caronogan, P., Kreider, H., & Weiss, H. (2009). Do neighborhood and home contexts explain why low-income children miss opportunities to participate in activities outside of school? *Developmental Psychology, 45,* 1545–1562.

LECTURE ENHANCEMENT 1.4
Do Welfare-to-Work Programs Enhance Children's Health Outcomes? (pp. 33–37)

Time: 15 minutes

Objective: To examine the relationship between welfare reform and children's health outcomes.

A wealth of research exists on the effects of welfare reform on children's cognitive and emotional and social well-being. However, few studies have examined the relationship between welfare reform and children's physical health. In a recent study, Slack and colleagues (2008) recruited 484 families who were participating in the Illinois Families Study (IFS). To be eligible for the study, families had to have at least one child 3 years of age or younger who was used as the "focal child." The study lasted six years. The researchers collected the following information:

(1) To assess general physical health, parents completed an annual survey in which they rated the focal child's health as excellent, very good, good, fair, or poor. The researchers also had access to children's medical records for the duration of the study.

(2) Using data from the Illinois Department of Human Services and the Illinois Department of Employment, the researchers identified the following welfare and work combinations for each family: (1) mostly working, (2) mostly on cash benefits, (3) mostly combining welfare and work, and (4) neither working nor receiving welfare.

(3) To determine health care access, the researchers identified whether a focal child experienced a gap in health insurance coverage in any year (or years) of the study.

(4) Demographic information was gathered for each family and included caregiver's education and age; caregiver's age at birth of first child; number of minors in the home; race, ethnicity, and marital status of household members; focal child's age and gender; and cumulative number of months receiving welfare benefits.

Several important and unanticipated findings emerged from this study. First, children with working caregivers were no healthier than children with welfare-dependent caregivers. Slack and colleagues suggest that under current welfare reform policies, the transition from welfare-to-work may not enhance children's health as expected, particularly if children experience gaps in health insurance coverage. Findings also revealed that children were healthier in families that relied neither on welfare nor on work. It is important to note that in this study, no work/no welfare mothers were more likely than welfare-dependent or working mothers to be married or cohabitating. Thus, income from an outside source or partner may have contributed to this outcome.

Although few children in this study experienced gaps in health insurance coverage, findings suggest that the primary care setting may be an important predictor of children's health. Specifically, compared to children receiving medical care from hospital settings, those receiving care from private care settings experienced poorer health outcomes over the course of the study. The authors provide several interpretations of this finding. One possibility is that private care settings have less experience delivering services to high-risk populations, particularly those who are underinsured. Underinsured families, in turn, may be less likely to seek out health care or follow-up care from these settings. Another possibility is that private care settings may present more barriers to obtaining health care than hospital settings (for example, inconvenient hours or location). Taken together, these results suggest that current welfare-to-work programs have little impact on children's physical health. However, it is important to note that this study focused on Illinois families. Therefore, these findings may not generalize to other states' welfare-to-work programs.

Using findings from this study and research presented in the text, ask students to discuss additional reasons why welfare-to-work programs may not have a positive impact on children's health. Why is this an important public policy issue?

Slack, K. S., Holl, J. L., Yoo, J., Amsden, L. B., Collins, E., & Bolger, K. (2008). Welfare, work, and health care access predictors of low-income children's physical health outcomes. *Children and Youth Services Review, 29*, 782–801.

LEARNING ACTIVITIES

LEARNING ACTIVITY 1.1
What Is Your Stance on the Three Basic Issues of Human Development? (pp. 6–9)

To help students better understand the three basic issues of human development, present this exercise as an in-class assignment. The exercise will help students express their own viewpoints on some of the controversies in the field of human development.

Directions: The following four pairs of statements relate to basic issues about human development. Read each statement carefully. Then circle the statement in each pair that more closely reflects your own view.

1. A. Development is a continuous, gradual progression, with new abilities, skills, and knowledge gradually added at a relatively uniform pace.
   B. Development occurs at different rates, alternating between periods of little change and periods of abrupt, rapid change.
2. A. All humans follow the same general sequence of development.
   B. Each individual has a unique course of development.
3. A. Children respond to the world in much the same way as adults. The main difference is that children's thinking is less sophisticated and complex than adults'.
   B. Children have unique ways of thinking about and responding to the world that are very different from those of adults.
4. A. An individual's personality is mostly determined by heredity.
   B. An individual's personality can be modified through caregiving experiences.

Next, have students break into small groups and discuss their answers. What is their stance on the three basic issues of human development? Which theories take a stance similar to their own? If students had to choose a theory that best represents their own view of development, would they choose a single theory or would they select certain components of several theories? What aspects of their chosen theory (or theories) make it more attractive than the others?

LEARNING ACTIVITY 1.2
Interviewing a Resilient Adult (pp. 10–11)

Ask students to identify an adult they know well, such as a family member or close family friend, who experienced and overcame significant adversity as a child or adolescent. For example, the individual may have experienced the death of a parent or sibling, experienced community or school violence, had a mentally ill parent, become a teenage parent, been poor for a number of years, or been removed from the family home for some reason. If the adult is comfortable discussing the situation, have students conduct an interview with him or her. The following questions might be useful to students: Briefly describe your childhood/adolescent experience. How did you respond to the event? What factors helped you overcome the event?

Following the interview, students should compare the answers with research in the text. What factors likely contributed to the individual's resilience? For example, did he or she mention personal characteristics, a warm parental relationship, social support outside the family, or community resources? Explain, using examples from the interview.

LEARNING ACTIVITY 1.3
Keeping a Theory/Research Notebook (pp. 10–31)

Given the many developmental theories that exist, students are likely to find some more appealing and plausible than others. Encourage students to construct a systematic list of their theoretical likes and dislikes by keeping a theory/research notebook. For each theory, students should list the concepts and principles they find important and those they believe to be inadequate or incorrect. As they learn more throughout the course, they can revise their opinions, noting research that supports their changing views. At the end of the course, students should have developed a personal perspective on human development, which may emphasize one theory or blend aspects of several or many theories.

LEARNING ACTIVITY 1.4
True or False: Mid-Twentieth-Century Theories and Recent Theoretical Perspectives (pp. 14–31)

Present the following exercise to students as a quiz or in-class activity.

Directions: Read each of the following statements and indicate whether it is *True* (T) or *False* (F).

Statements:

_____ 1. According to Freud, in each stage of psychosexual development, parents walk a fine line between permitting too much or too little gratification of their child's basic needs.

_____ 2. Both Freud and Erikson pointed out that normal development must be understood in relation to each culture's life situation.

_____ 3. Behaviorism and social learning theory have been praised for acknowledging people's contributions to their own development.

_____ 4. In Piaget's theory, as the brain develops and children's experiences expand, they move through four broad stages, each characterized by qualitatively distinct ways of thinking.

_____ 5. Research indicates that Piaget underestimated the competencies of infants and preschoolers.

_____ 6. Information-processing researchers view the mind as a symbol-manipulating system through which information flows.

_____ 7. Evolutionary psychologists are solely concerned with the biological bases of development.

_____ 8. According to Vygotsky, social interaction is necessary for children to acquire the ways of thinking and behaving that make up a community's culture.

_____ 9. The mesosystem is made up of social settings that do not contain the developing persons but nevertheless affect experiences in immediate settings.

_____ 10. According to Bronfenbrenner, the environment is dynamic and ever changing.

Answers:

1. T   6. T
2. F   7. F
3. F   8. T
4. T   9. F
5. T   10. T

LEARNING ACTIVITY 1.5
Applying Ecological Systems Theory to a "Hot Topic" in Child Development (pp. 26–28)

Have students form small groups and select a "hot topic" in child or adult development, such as the effects of divorce, child abuse and neglect, quality of child care, the obesity epidemic, public policies for children, or sex education programs in the schools. Once students have selected their topic, ask them to consider how each level of the environment may affect development, including bidirectional influences and the role of third parties.

LEARNING ACTIVITY 1.6
Conducting a Survey of Attitudes Toward Government Intervention into Family Life (pp. 32–37)

Have students interview two or three family members, friends, or acquaintances and ask the following questions:
   (1) Who should be responsible for raising young children?
   (2) Should the government provide money and resources to low-income families with young children? If so, should the money come from tax dollars?

When students return to class with their responses, instruct them to classify each answer on the basis of whether parents are viewed as solely responsible for children's upbringing or whether society should play an important role. Compile the findings, and discuss them in relation to evidence that government support for children and families has been more difficult to realize in the United States than in other industrialized nations. How do students feel about their findings? Do they agree with the findings? Why or why not?

Chapter 1 History, Theory, and Applied Directions

LEARNING ACTIVITY 1.7
Researching Social Indicators of Children's Well-Being in the United States (pp. 32–37)

Although the United States is one of the wealthiest nations in the world, it does not rank among the top countries on any measure of children's health and well-being. Direct students to a website sponsored by the Children's Defense Fund: *www.childrensdefense.org*. By clicking on "State Data on Children" under the Research Library heading, students can find out their state's ranking on several leading social indicators of children's well-being. If students are not from the United States, they can choose a state to research.

Using information from the website, have students answer the following questions: How does your state rank on child poverty? How about health coverage? How are cultural values, special interests, and economic conditions reflected in these policies? Do students think that these policies reflect current research in the field of child development? How large is the gap between what we know and its application to public policy?

ASK YOURSELF ...

REVIEW: What is meant by a stage of development? Provide your own example of stagewise change. What stand do stage theorists take on the issue of continuous versus discontinuous development? (pp. 7–8)

A *stage* is a distinct period of development characterized by qualitative changes in thinking, feeling, and behaving. Stage theorists believe that development is *discontinuous*—a process in which new ways of understanding and responding to the world emerge at specific times. In this view, development is like climbing a staircase, with each step corresponding to a more mature, reorganized way of functioning. The stage concept also assumes that children undergo periods of rapid transformation as they step up from one stage to the next, alternating with plateaus during which little change occurs. For example, as children begin to represent their world through language and make-believe play in early childhood, or as they begin to think more logically in middle childhood, they are entering a new stage of development.

CONNECT: Provide an example of how one domain of development (physical, cognitive, or emotional/social) can affect development in another domain. (pp. 4–5)

Development is often divided into three broad domains: physical, cognitive, and emotional and social. Each domain influences and is influenced by the others. For example, new motor capacities, such as reaching, sitting, crawling, and walking (physical), contribute greatly to infants' understanding of their surroundings (cognitive). When babies think and act more competently, adults stimulate them more with games, language, and expressions of delight at the child's new achievements (emotional and social). These enriched experiences, in turn, promote all aspects of development.

APPLY: Anna, a high school counselor, has devised a program that integrates classroom learning with vocational training to help adolescents at risk for school dropout stay in school and transition smoothly to work life. What is Anna's position on *stability versus plasticity* in development? Explain. (pp. 8–9)

Anna's program reflects a belief that development has substantial *plasticity* throughout life. In this view, change is possible and even likely if it is supported by new experiences. First, Anna takes the position that environmental influences, not just heredity, are important. Second, by devising a program for adolescents, she rejects the view that early negative experiences establish lifelong patterns of behavior that cannot be fully overcome by later, more positive experiences. Anna takes a more optimistic view: She believes that high school students who are at risk for dropout will benefit from the program she has developed because it will provide positive experiences that will enable them to overcome the negative events of their first few years.

REFLECT: Cite an aspect of your development that differs from a parent's or grandparent's when he or she was your age. How might *contexts* explain this difference? (p. 8)

This is an open-ended question with no right or wrong answer.

REVIEW: Imagine a debate between John Locke and Jean-Jacques Rousseau on the nature–nurture controversy. Summarize the argument that each historical figure is likely to present. (p. 12)

John Locke: The child begins as a *tabula rasa,* or blank slate, neither good nor evil, whose character will be shaped entirely by experience. Parents function as rational tutors who can mold the child as they wish through careful instruction, effective example, and rewards for good behavior. In sum, nurture is the primary determinant of growth.

Jean-Jacques Rousseau: Children are not blank slates who passively respond to environmental influences. Rather, they are *noble savages,* naturally endowed with a sense of right and wrong and an innate plan for orderly, healthy growth. Environmental intervention has no value; adult training can only harm or delay a child's genetically determined, naturally unfolding course of development. In sum, nature is the primary determinant of growth.

CONNECT: What do the ideas of Rousseau, Darwin, and Hall have in common? (pp. 12–13)
Rousseau, Darwin, and Hall all emphasized the importance of nature over nurture in development. Rousseau believed that children develop according to a genetically determined, naturally unfolding course of growth. Darwin's theory emphasized the adaptive value of innate characteristics, which determine whether individuals will meet the survival requirements of their environment and, as a result, live long enough to reproduce and pass on their more beneficial characteristics to future generations. Hall, inspired by Darwin's work, saw development as a *maturational process*—a genetically determined series of events that unfold automatically.

REFLECT: Find out whether your parents read any child-rearing advice books when you were growing up. What questions most concerned them? Do you think the concerns of today's parents differ from those of your parents' generation? Explain. (p. 13)
This is an open-ended question with no right or wrong answer.

REVIEW: What aspect of behaviorism made it attractive to critics of the psychoanalytic perspective? How did Piaget's theory respond to a major limitation of behaviorism? (pp. 17–21)
The early behaviorists rejected the psychoanalytic concern with the unseen workings of the mind. They sought, instead, to create an objective science of psychology that would study directly observable events—stimuli and responses. As psychologists wondered whether behaviorism might offer a more direct and effective explanation of the development of children's social behavior than the less precise concepts of psychoanalytic theory, several kinds of social learning theory emerged. The most influential emphasized *modeling,* also known as *imitation* or *observational learning,* as a powerful source of development.

Many theorists believe that behaviorism and social learning theory offer too narrow a view of important environmental influences and that these approaches underestimate children's contributions to their own development. In response to these concerns, Piaget maintained that children's learning does not depend on reinforcers, such as rewards from adults. Rather, children actively construct knowledge as they manipulate and explore their world.

Besides investigating children's understanding of their physical environment, Piaget explored their reasoning about the social world. His cognitive-developmental perspective convinced the field that children are active learners whose minds consist of rich structures of knowledge.

CONNECT: Although social learning theory focuses on social development and Piaget's theory on cognitive development, each has enhanced our understanding of other domains. Mention an additional domain addressed by each theory. (pp. 18–20)
Albert Bandura's social learning theory emphasizes modeling, also known as *imitation* or *observational learning,* as a source of development. From its original emphasis on the emotional/social domain, the theory has evolved to stress the importance of *cognition,* or thinking. As a result, Bandura now calls it a *social-cognitive* rather than a social learning approach. In addition to explaining children's social development, social-cognitive theory provides insight into how children control their own learning and behavior through the attitudes, values, and convictions they acquire about themselves.

Piaget's cognitive-developmental theory, best known for its emphasis on the stages of cognitive development, also explores how children reason about the social world. It has sparked a great deal of research on children's conceptions of themselves, other people, and human relationships—all aspects of the social/emotional domain.

APPLY: A 4-year-old becomes frightened of the dark and refuses to go to sleep at night. How would a psychoanalyst and a behaviorist differ in their views of how this problem developed? (pp. 15, 17)
According to the psychoanalytic approach, children move through a series of stages in which they confront conflicts between biological drives and social expectations. From this perspective, fear of the dark reflects an unconscious motive or deep-seated anxiety within the child. A psychoanalyst might conclude, for example, that the child's fear really represents anxiety about nighttime separation from the parent. Once the anxiety is resolved, the fear will subside.

In contrast, behaviorists look at the effects on behavior of directly observable events, not at the inner workings of the mind. From a behaviorist perspective, a child would be afraid of the dark if previous experiences in the dark were unpleasant. Perhaps the child heard a sudden, loud noise at night or was frightened by the visual images of a nightmare. On the basis of these experiences, the child would be conditioned to respond fearfully to being in the dark.

REFLECT: Illustrate Bandura's ideas by describing a personal experience in which you observed and received feedback from another person that strengthened your self-efficacy—belief that your abilities and characteristics will help you succeed. (pp. 18–19)
This is an open-ended question with no right or wrong answer.

REVIEW: Explain how each recent theoretical perspective regards children as active contributors to their own development. (pp. 21–31)
Information processing: Like Piaget's cognitive-developmental theory, the information-processing approach views children as active, sense-making beings who modify their thinking in response to environmental demands. In this view, the human mind is a symbol-manipulating system through which information flows. From the time it is presented to the senses at input until it emerges as a behavioral response at output, information is actively coded, transformed, and organized. When presented with a task, children perform a set of mental operations and experiment with various strategies in their attempts to solve the problem.

Ethology and evolutionary developmental psychology: Both ethologists and evolutionary developmental psychologists are interested in the evolutionary history of behavior and its adaptive, or survival, value. For instance, infant smiling, babbling, grasping, and crying are built-in social signals that encourage the caregiver to approach, care for, and interact with the baby. By keeping the parent near, these behaviors help ensure that the infant will be fed, protected from danger, and provided with stimulation and affection necessary for healthy growth.

Vygotsky's sociocultural theory: Vygotsky's theory focuses on how *culture* is transmitted to the next generation. According to Vygotsky, *social interaction*—in particular, cooperative dialogues between children and more knowledgeable members of society—is necessary for children to acquire the ways of thinking and behaving that make up their community's culture. Like Piaget, Vygotsky saw children as active, constructive beings. But whereas Piaget emphasized children's independent efforts to make sense of their world, Vygotsky viewed cognitive development as a *socially mediated process,* in which children depend on assistance from adults and more-expert peers as they tackle new challenges.

Ecological systems theory: Ecological systems theory views the child as developing within a complex system of relationships affected by multiple levels of the surrounding environment. The child's biologically influenced dispositions join with environmental forces to mold development. Life changes can be imposed on the child, or they can arise from within the child, because as children get older they select, modify, and create many of their own settings and experiences. How they do so depends on their physical, intellectual, and personality characteristics and their environmental opportunities. In ecological systems theory, the child and the environment form a network of interdependent effects that, together, determine the course of development.

Dynamic systems perspective: Much like ecological systems theory, the dynamic systems perspective maintains that the child's mind, body, and physical and social worlds form an *integrated system* that guides mastery of new skills. The system is *dynamic,* or constantly in motion. A change in any part of it—from brain growth to changes in physical and social surroundings—disrupts the current organism–environment relationship. When this happens, the child actively reorganizes his or her behavior so the various components of the system work together again but in a more complex, effective way.

CONNECT: Return to the Biology and Environment box on pages 10–11. How does the story of John and Gary illustrate bidirectional influences within the microsystem, as described in ecological systems theory? (p. 27)
The microsystem consists of activities and interaction patterns in the child's immediate surroundings. Bronfenbrenner emphasizes that to understand development at this level, we must keep in mind that all relationships are *bidirectional:* Adults affect children's behavior, but children's biologically and socially influenced characteristics—their physical attributes, personalities, and capacities—also affect adults' behavior. In the example, both John and Gary experienced similar environmental stressors during their childhood and adolescence. However, Gary's personal qualities, such as his ability to make new friends and adapt to new surroundings each time his family moved, likely contributed to his resilience. In contrast, John responded to similar changes by becoming anxious and angry, picking arguments with his parents, siblings, and peers.

The story of John and Gary also illustrates how social support outside the immediate family can contribute to resilience. Gary's close relationship with his grandfather may have helped him overcome the effects of a stressful home life while also providing him with a positive role model. And unlike John, Gary had opportunities to participate in community life—for example, by volunteering for Habitat for Humanity—which likely strengthened his resilience.

APPLY: Mario wants to find out precisely how children of different ages recall stories. Anna is interested in how adult–child communication in different cultures influences children's storytelling. Which theoretical perspective has Mario probably chosen? How about Anna? Explain. (pp. 21–22, 25–26)

Mario has probably chosen an information-processing perspective. In this approach, he will break down the process by which children recall stories into the individual steps involved. Then he will analyze each step separately so that he can compare them in detail as they apply to children of different ages.

Anna is more likely to choose a sociocultural perspective, focusing on the ways in which *culture*—a social group's values, beliefs, customs, and skills—is transmitted from one generation to the next through social interaction. For example, she might compare the ways children in different cultures engage in storytelling with adults and older peers and how these interactions help them develop the ways of telling stories that are valued within their culture.

REFLECT: To illustrate the chronosystem in ecological systems theory, select an important event from your childhood, such as a move to a new neighborhood, a class with an inspiring teacher, or parental divorce. How did the event affect you? How might its impact have differed had you been five years younger? How about five years older? (p. 28)

This is an open-ended question with no right or wrong answer.

REVIEW: Explain why both strong advocacy and policy-relevant research are vital for designing and implementing public policies that meet children's needs. (pp. 35–37)

Strong advocacy for meeting children's needs is essential to ensure that policies directed at solving various social problems—for example, welfare reform—have results that also help, rather than harm, children. Because children cannot vote or speak out to protect their own interests, vigilance from child advocates is essential to make children's needs an important government priority. And for a policy to be effective in meeting children's needs, research must guide it at every step—during design, implementation, and evaluation. For example, research on the importance of early experiences for children's intellectual development were crucial to the 1965 founding of Project Head Start, the largest educational and family-services intervention program for poverty-stricken preschool U.S. children.

CONNECT: Give an example of how cultural values and economic decisions affect child-oriented public policies. What level of Bronfenbrenner's ecological systems theory contains these influences? (pp. 28, 33–35)

Cultural values and economic decisions both fall within the macrosystem in Bronfenbrenner's theory. In general, the priority that the macrosystem gives to children's needs affects the support they receive at inner levels of the environment. The culture of the United States is strongly individualistic, in contrast to most Western European nations, which lean toward collectivism. Consequently, U.S. citizens are more likely than Western Europeans to believe that the care and rearing of young children, and paying for that care, is entirely the responsibility of parents. As a result, the U.S. public has been slow to endorse government-supported benefits for all families, such as high-quality child care and paid employment leave. These cultural values have contributed to the large number of U.S. children who remain poor, even though their parent or parents are gainfully employed.

Economic decisions are another aspect of Bronfenbrenner's macrosystem that affect child-oriented public policies. For example, in times of economic difficulty, governments are unlikely to initiate new social programs and may reduce or eliminate existing ones.

APPLY: Check your local newspaper or one or two national news magazines to see how often articles on the condition of children and families appear. Why is it important for researchers to communicate with the general public about children's needs? (pp. 35–37)

When widespread social problems arise, such as poverty, homelessness, hunger, and disease, nations attempt to solve them by developing *public policies*—laws and government programs designed to improve current conditions. Growing awareness of the gap between what we know and what we do to improve children's lives has prompted experts in child development to join with concerned citizens as advocates for more effective policies.

Chapter 1 History, Theory, and Applied Directions

Besides depending on strong advocacy, public policies that enhance child development depend on policy-relevant research that documents needs and evaluates programs to spark improvements. By collaborating with community and government agencies, researchers can enhance the social relevance of their investigations. And by disseminating these findings to the public in easily understandable, compelling ways—for example, through television documentaries, newspaper and magazine articles, websites, and direct reports to government officials—researchers help to create a sense of immediacy about the conditions of children and families that, in turn, can mobilize voters to demand action from their lawmakers.

REFLECT: Do you agree with the widespread American sentiment that government should not become involved in family life? Explain. (pp. 34–35)
This is an open-ended question with no right or wrong answer.

SUGGESTED READINGS

Cabeza, R., Nyberg, L., & Park, D. (2009). *Cognitive neuroscience of aging: Linking cognitive and cerebral aging.* New York: Oxford University Press. Explores a new scientific discipline, known as the cognitive neuroscience of aging. Topics include noninvasive measures of cerebral aging; the effects of cerebral aging on cognitive functions like perception, memory, and attention; and applications of brain research.

Fraser, M. W., & Jenson, J. M. (Eds.). (2010). *Social policy for children and families: A risk and resilience model.* Newbury Park, CA: SAGE. Examines the development of social policies for at-risk children and families. Contributing authors emphasize the importance of developing policies that enhance resilience across a wide variety of domains, including family life, education, and physical and mental health.

Miller, R. (2011). *Vygotsky in perspective.* New York: Oxford University Press. Presents a contemporary view of Vygotsky's life and works, including how his concepts—such as the zone of proximal development and private, inner speech—are being applied in educational settings.

MEDIA MATERIALS

For details on individual video segments that accompany the DVD for *Child Development,* Ninth Edition, please see the DVD Guide for *Explorations in Child Development.* The DVD and DVD Guide are available through your Pearson sales representative.

Additional DVDs that may be useful in your class are listed below. They are not available through your Pearson sales representative, but you can order them directly from the distributors. (See contact information at the end of this manual.)

Bandura's Social Cognitive Theory: An Introduction (2003, Davidson Films, 38 min.). This film, narrated by Albert Bandura, uses archival materials and new footage to introduce students to the vocabulary and innovative methods of Bandura's work. Using examples from his own life, Bandura illustrates the role of chance in shaping the life course. He also describes his early work with Bobo dolls and his later research on self-efficacy. The four processes of observational learning are reviewed. A Learning Guide is available.

B. F. Skinner: A Fresh Appraisal (1999, Davidson Films, 40 min.). Using both archival and newer footage, this program takes a fresh look at Skinner and his theory. The vocabulary Skinner developed to describe his ideas and feelings is introduced in context so the student understands how the terms were intended to be used and the research that produced them. The program also lays to rest some myths about Skinner and credits him with contributions seldom attributed to him.

Child Development Theorists (2009, Insight Media, 20 min.). This program discusses the major child development theorists since Freud, explains how their theories differ, and emphasizes the value of combining approaches. It offers historical footage and photographs and discusses such theorists as Freud, Montessori, Vygotsky, Piaget, Erikson, Bowlby, Skinner, Spock, Kohlberg, and Gardner.

Endless Questions: Critical Thinking and Research (2006, Aquarius Health Care Media, 30 min.). This program, part of the *Inside Out* series, shows how researchers investigate the question, Does happiness lead to good health? using multiple methods: case study, survey, naturalistic observation, correlational studies, and controlled experiments.

Infant and Child Development (2001, Insight Media, 30 min.). This program shows how a newborn acquires the skills necessary for interacting with the environment. It presents a variety of developmental theories, including Jean Piaget's stage theory of cognitive development.

John Bowlby: Attachment Theory Across Generations (2007, Davidson Films, 40 min.). Featuring archival footage of Dr. Bowlby and a 20-year longitudinal case study of emotional development, this program examines how attachment relationships affect adult behaviors and how attachment patterns are transmitted through the generations.

John Locke (2004, Films Media Group, 21 min.). This program chronicles the life and work of the seventeenth-century English philosopher and political theorist John Locke, whose belief that human character is shaped entirely by experience served as the forerunner of the behaviorist perspective on human development.

Learning: Observational and Cognitive Approaches (2001, ACT Media, 30 min.). This program discusses observational learning and uses the research of B. F. Skinner to illustrate the cognitive processes involved in learning.

Lev Vygotsky: One Man's Legacy Through His Life and Practice (2009, PHD Lowe Productions, 3 segments, 1 hr. 53 min. total). Using interviews, commentary from family members and educators, and archival photos and film footage, this series examines the life and work of Lev Vygotsky. Key Vygotskian concepts, such as the importance of make-believe play for early cognitive development and the zone of proximal development, are also discussed.

Research Ethics (2008, Insight Media, 21 min.). This program examines ethical issues in social science, natural science, and health research, including plagiarism, crediting and citing sources, the use of human and animal subjects, informed consent, debriefing, privacy, confidentiality, and conflicts of interest.

Research Methods (2001, ACT Media, 30 min.). This program provides an overview of observational and descriptive research by illustrating how the scientific method is used to study the relationship between violent video games and aggression.

Research Methods in the Social Sciences (2005, Films Media Group, 4-part series, each segment 23 to 46 min.). Focusing primarily on research in psychology, this series explores qualitative and quantitative research methods used in a wide range of disciplines. Hosted and narrated by students, each program demonstrates how to test hypotheses, prepare experiments, and analyze data. Instructors' guides are available online.

The Developing Child (2001, WGBH Boston with the American Psychological Association, 30 min.). This program, Part 5 of the 12-part series *Discovering Psychology*, reviews the nature–nurture debate and shows how developmental psychologists study the contributions of both heredity and environment to child development.

The Developing Person: Theories of Development (2003, Insight Media, 30 min.). This film traces the history of the scientific study of human development from Locke and Rousseau to Piaget and Erikson. It explores the lifespan perspective, examines Urie Bronfenbrenner's ecological model of development, and introduces psychoanalytic theory, learning theory, behaviorism, and cognitive theory.

Theories of Human Development (2002, Insight Media, 6 segments, 30 min. each). This series of six lectures by Malcom W. Watson presents key theorists in human development: Sigmund Freud, Erik Erikson, John Bowlby, Mary Ainsworth, Albert Bandura, Jean Piaget, and Lev Vygotsky.

Why Study Human Behavior? (2001, ACT Media, 30 min.). This program introduces psychology as a science of behavior and mental processes. It explains how our lives are enhanced when we understand why we think and act as we do.

Young Minds: Is Zero-to-Three Destiny? (1999, Films Media Group, 11 min.). The idea that Mozart's music can have a lasting impact on the growth of a baby's brain captured the imagination of parents and policymakers alike. In this brief segment, *NewsHour* correspondent Betty Ann Bowser talks with advocates on both sides of the zero-to-three debate, including Yale child psychiatrist Kyle Pruett, who argues for the crucial nature of the child's first three years, and skeptics John Bruer, author of *The Myth of the First Three Years*, and Harvard child psychologist Jerome Kagan.

CHAPTER 2
RESEARCH STRATEGIES

CHAPTER-AT-A-GLANCE

Chapter Outline	Instruction Ideas	Supplements
From Theory to Hypothesis pp. 41–42	Learning Objective 2.1	Test Bank Items 1–4 Please contact your Pearson publisher's representative for a wide range of video offerings available to adopters.
Common Research Methods pp. 42–53 Systematic Observation • Self-Reports: Interviews and Questionnaires • Neurobiological Methods • The Clinical, or Case Study, Method • Methods for Studying Culture	Learning Objective 2.2 Lecture Enhancement 2.1 Learning Activities 2.1–2.2, 2.4–2.5 Ask Yourself p. 52	Test Bank Items 5–53, 125–127
Reliability and Validity: Keys to Scientifically Sound Research pp. 54–55 Reliability • Validity	Learning Objective 2.3 Learning Activity 2.5 Ask Yourself p. 55	Test Bank Items 54–63, 128
General Research Designs pp. 55–60 Correlational Design • Experimental Design • Modified Experimental Designs	Learning Objective 2.4 Lecture Enhancements 2.2–2.3 Learning Activities 2.3, 2.5 Ask Yourself p. 60	Test Bank Items 64–88
Designs for Studying Development pp. 60–66 The Longitudinal Design • The Cross-Sectional Design • Improving Developmental Designs	Learning Objective 2.5 Lecture Enhancement 2.4 Learning Activities 2.4–2.6 Ask Yourself p. 66	Test Bank Items 89–113, 129–130
Ethics in Research on Children pp. 66–69	Learning Objective 2.6 Learning Activities 2.4, 2.7 Ask Yourself p. 69	Test Bank Items 114–124, 131

BRIEF CHAPTER SUMMARY

Researchers face many challenges as they plan and implement studies of children. First, they must develop a researchable idea, either a hypothesis—a prediction drawn from a theory—or a research question. Next, they must develop a research strategy. Knowing the strengths and limitations of various research strategies is important in separating dependable information from misleading results.

Researchers must choose the research methods they will use in their investigation. Common methods include naturalistic and structured observations, self-reports, neurobiological measures, clinical, or case studies, and ethnography. Investigators must ensure that their procedures are both reliable and valid—two keys to scientifically sound research.

Next, the researcher must choose a research design. Two main types of designs, correlational and experimental, are used in all studies of human behavior. Scientists who study child development extend these approaches to special developmental research strategies—longitudinal and cross-sectional designs—that include measurements at different ages. Modified developmental designs, such as the sequential design, build on the strengths of both approaches. The microgenetic design allows researchers to track change as it occurs to gain insights into processes of development.

The ethical issues that arise in all research into human behavior are especially significant with children, who are particularly vulnerable to harm and often cannot evaluate the risks and benefits of research. To ensure that children's rights are protected, child development researchers follow special ethical guidelines and may seek advice from institutional review boards established to weigh the potential benefits of proposed studies against the costs to participants.

LEARNING OBJECTIVES

After reading this chapter, you should be able to answer the following:

2.1 Describe the role of theories, hypotheses, and research questions in the research process. (pp. 41–42)

2.2 Describe research methods commonly used to study children, noting strengths and limitations of each. (pp. 42–53)

2.3 Explain how reliability and validity apply to research methods and to the overall accuracy of research findings and conclusions. (pp. 54–55)

2.4 Distinguish correlational and experimental research designs, noting strengths and limitations of each. (pp. 55–60)

2.5 Describe designs for studying development, noting strengths and limitations of each. (pp. 60–66)

2.6 What special ethical issues arise in doing research on children? (pp. 66–69)

LECTURE OUTLINE

I. FROM THEORY TO HYPOTHESIS (pp. 41–42)
   A. Research usually begins with a prediction drawn from a theory, called a **hypothesis.**
      1. Research may pit a hypothesis taken from one theory against a hypothesis taken from another, or it may test predictions drawn from a single theory.
      2. If little or no theory exists on a topic of interest, the investigator may start with a *research question*.
      3. Hypotheses and research questions help investigators choose research methods and designs.
   B. Understanding the research process enables individuals who work directly with children to link research and practice by conducting studies, either on their own or in partnership with experienced investigators.

II. COMMON RESEARCH METHODS (pp. 42–53)
   A. Choosing a research strategy involves two main tasks.
      1. The researcher must choose from a variety of *research methods*—participants' specific activities, such as taking tests or responding to interviews.
      2. The researcher must then choose a *research design*—an overall plan for the study that will permit the best test of the research idea.
   B. Systematic Observation (pp. 42–46)
      1. Observations of the behavior of children, and of adults who are important in their lives, can be made in different ways.
      2. **Naturalistic observation:** The researcher goes into the field, or natural environment, and records the behavior of interest.
         a. The great strength of naturalistic observation is that investigators can see directly the everyday behaviors they hope to explain.
         b. A major limitation is that not all children have the same opportunity to display a particular behavior in everyday life.
      3. **Structured observations:** The investigator sets up a laboratory situation that evokes the behavior of interest so that every participant has an equal opportunity to display the response.
         a. Strengths of structured observation
            (1) It permits greater control over the research situation than does naturalistic observation.
            (2) It is useful for studying behaviors that researchers rarely have an opportunity to see in everyday life.
         b. The great disadvantage of this approach is that we cannot be certain that participants behave in the laboratory as they do in their natural environments.
      4. Collecting Systematic Observations
         a. Investigators describe everything the participant says and does over a certain time period, or they may use **event sampling,** recording all instances of a particular behavior during a specified time period.
         b. Another approach is **time sampling,** recording whether certain behaviors occur during a sample of short intervals.

5. Limitations of Systematic Observation
    a. A major problem is **observer influence**—the effects of the observer on the behavior studied.
    b. Another serious danger is **observer bias:** When observers are aware of the purposes of a study, they may see and record what they expect to see rather than what participants actually do.
C. Self-Reports: Interviews and Questionnaires (pp. 46–47)
    1. Self-reports ask research participants to provide information on their perceptions, thoughts, abilities, feelings, attitudes, beliefs, and past experiences.
    2. Clinical Interviews
        a. In a **clinical interview,** researchers use a flexible, conversational style to probe for the participant's point of view.
        b. Strengths of clinical interviews
            (1) They permit people to display their thoughts in terms that are close to the way they think in everyday life.
            (2) They can provide a large amount of information in a fairly brief period.
    3. Limitations of Clinical Interviews
        a. Participants do not necessarily report their thoughts, feelings, and experiences accurately.
        b. Because clinical interviews depend on verbal ability, they may underestimate the capacities of individuals who have difficulty putting their thoughts into words.
        c. Interviews on certain topics are particularly vulnerable to distortion.
        d. The clinical interview's flexibility means that when questions are phrased differently for each participant, variations in responses may reflect the manner of interviewing rather than real differences in thinking.
    4. Structured Interviews, Tests, and Questionnaires
        a. In a **structured interview,** each individual is asked the same set of questions in the same way.
        b. Strengths of structured interviews
            (1) They eliminate the chance that the interviewer might prompt some participants more than others.
            (2) They are more efficient than clinical interviews.
        c. Limitations of structured interviews
            (1) They can still be affected by inaccurate reporting.
            (2) They do not yield the same depth of information as clinical interviews.
D. Neurobiological Methods (pp. 47–50)
    1. Researchers seeking to uncover the biological bases of perceptual, cognitive, and motor responses use **neurobiological methods,** which measure the relationship between nervous system processes and behavior.
        a. Involuntary activities of the autonomic nervous system—such as heart rate, respiration, pupil dilation, and stress hormone levels—are highly sensitive to psychological state.
        b. Distinct patterns of autonomic activity—indicated by heart rate, levels of the hormone cortisol, and other physiological measures—are related to aspects of temperament, such as shyness and sociability.
    2. Autonomic indicators have been enriched by measures of brain functioning, especially those that detect changes in *electrical activity* in the cerebral cortex.
        a. In an *electroencephalogram (EEG)*, researchers examine brain-wave patterns for stability and organization, signs of mature functioning of the cortex. Today, researchers use an advanced tool, a geodesic sensor net (GSN) that yields improved brain-wave detection.
        b. *Event-related potentials (ERPs)* detect the general location of brain-wave activity as a child processes a particular stimulus.
        c. *Neuroimaging techniques* include *positron emission tomography (PET)* and *functional magnetic resonance imaging (fMRI)*.
            (1) Both techniques yield detailed, three-dimensional computerized pictures of the entire brain and its active areas and provide the most precise information about which brain regions are specialized for certain capacities and about abnormalities in brain functioning.
            (2) Unlike PET, which depends on X-ray photography, fMRI magnetically detects changes in blood flow and oxygen metabolism throughout the brain when a child is exposed to a stimulus.
            (3) PET and fMRI are not suitable for infants and young children because they require the child to remain motionless for a long period of time.

d. A neuroimaging technique that works well in infancy and early childhood is *near-infrared spectroscopy (NIRS),* which uses infrared light to measure blood flow and oxygen metabolism while the child attends to a stimulus. NIRS examines only the functioning of the cerebral cortex.
 e. Strengths of neurobiological methods
  (1) They can be used to infer the perceptions, thoughts, and emotions of infants and young children, who cannot report their psychological experiences clearly.
  (2) They are powerful tools for uncovering relationships between the brain and psychological development.
 f. Limitations of neurobiological methods
  (1) Researchers cannot be sure that a consistent pattern of autonomic or brain activity in response to a stimulus means that an individual has processed it in a certain way.
  (2) Extraneous factors, such as hunger, boredom, or fatigue, may influence physiological responses.
E. The Clinical, or Case Study, Method (pp. 50–51)
 1. The **clinical,** or **case study, method** brings together a wide range of information about one child, including interviews, observations, test scores, and sometimes neurobiological measures.
 2. Strengths of the clinical method
  a. It yields detailed case narratives that offer valuable insights into the many factors that affect development.
  b. It is well suited to studying the development of types of individuals who are few in number but vary widely in characteristics, such as *prodigies.*
 3. Limitations of the clinical method
  a. Because information often is collected unsystematically and subjectively, researchers' theoretical preferences may bias their interpretations.
  b. Investigators cannot assume that their conclusions apply to anyone other than the child studied.
F. Methods for Studying Culture (pp. 51–53)
 1. To study the impact of culture, researchers adjust the methods just considered or tap procedures specially devised for cross-cultural and multicultural research.
 2. To study characteristics that are believed to be universal but that vary in degree from one culture to the next, researchers adapt observational and self-report procedures so they can be understood in each cultural context.
 3. To uncover the *cultural meanings* of children's and adults' behaviors, researchers use a method called **ethnography,** borrowed from the field of anthropology.
  a. Like the clinical method, ethnographic research is a descriptive, qualitative technique.
  b. Instead of aiming to understand a single individual, ethnography is directed at understanding a culture or a distinct social group through *participant observation,* whereby the researcher spends months or years in the cultural community, participating in its daily life.
  c. A strength of ethnographic research is that by entering into close contact with a social group, researchers can understand its members' beliefs and behaviors in a way that is not possible with an observational visit, interview, or questionnaire.
  d. Limitations of ethnographic research
   (1) Investigators' own cultural values and theoretical commitments may lead them to observe selectively or misinterpret what they see.
   (2) Findings cannot be assumed to generalize beyond the people and settings in which the research was conducted.

III. RELIABILITY AND VALIDITY: KEYS TO SCIENTIFICALLY SOUND RESEARCH (pp. 54–55)
 A. To be acceptable to the scientific community, research procedures must be both *reliable* and *valid.*
 B. Reliability (p. 54)
  1. **Reliability** refers to the consistency, or repeatability, of measures of behavior.
  2. In observational research, reliability is determined by obtaining *inter-rater reliability*—agreement between different observers evaluating the same behaviors.
  3. *Test–retest reliability* measures the reliability of self-report and neurobiological data by comparing responses to the same measures on separate occasions or, for self-reports, answers on different forms of the same test or questionnaire.
  4. The reliability of qualitative methods, such as clinical and ethnographic studies, must be determined by other methods—for example, having a judge examine the qualitative records to see whether the judge agrees with the researcher's conclusions.

C. Validity (pp. 54–55)
   1. To have high **validity**, research methods must accurately measure the characteristics that the researcher set out to measure.
   2. Reliability is essential but not sufficient for valid research; methods that are implemented carelessly, unevenly, and inconsistently cannot possibly represent what an investigator intended to study.
   3. In setting up an investigation, researchers must consider two types of validity:
      a. **Internal validity** is the degree to which *conditions internal to the design of the study* permit an accurate test of the researcher's hypothesis or question.
      b. **External validity** is the degree to which researchers' *findings generalize to settings and participants outside the original study*.

IV. GENERAL RESEARCH DESIGNS (pp. 55–60)
   A. Correlational Design (pp. 55–56, 57)
      1. In a **correlational design**, researchers gather information on individuals, generally in natural life circumstances, without altering their experiences. Then they look at relationships between participants' characteristics and their behavior or development.
      2. Correlational studies have one major limitation: They do not allow researchers to infer cause and effect. Because one variable is related to another does not mean that one *causes* the other.
      3. Investigators often examine relationships using a **correlation coefficient**, a number ranging in value from +1.00 to –1.00 that describes how two measures, or variables, are associated with each other.
         a. The *magnitude, or size, of the number* shows the *strength of the relationship*.
         b. The *sign of the number* (+ or –) refers to the *direction of the relationship*.
            (1) A positive sign (+) means that as one variable *increases*, the other also *increases*.
            (2) A negative sign (–) means that as one variable *increases*, the other *decreases*.
   B. Experimental Design (pp. 56–58)
      1. An **experimental design** permits inferences about cause and effect because researchers use an evenhanded procedure to assign people to two or more treatment conditions.
      2. In an experiment, the events and behaviors of interest are divided into two types:
         a. The **independent variable** is the one the investigator expects to cause changes in another variable.
         b. The **dependent variable** is the one the investigator expects to be influenced by the independent variable.
      3. To detect cause-and-effect relationships, the researcher directly *controls* or *manipulates* changes in the independent variable by exposing participants to treatment conditions, and then compares their performance on measures of the dependent variable.
      4. A **laboratory experiment** explores cause-and-effect relationships by dividing participants into different treatment conditions.
      5. Researchers must take special precautions to control for participants' characteristics that could reduce the internal validity of their findings—for example, the problem of **confounding variables**, which are so closely associated that their effects on an outcome cannot be distinguished.
         a. To address this, researchers engage in **random assignment** of participants to treatment conditions to ensure that participants' characteristics will be equally distributed across treatment groups.
         b. Random assignment can be combined with **matching**, in which participants are measured ahead of time on the factor in question. Then children high and low on that factor are assigned in equal numbers to each treatment condition. Thus, the experimental groups are made equivalent on characteristics likely to distort the results.
   C. Modified Experimental Designs (pp. 58–60, 61)
      1. Most experiments are conducted in laboratories, where researchers can achieve the maximum control over treatment conditions. However, their findings may not apply to everyday situations.
      2. In **field experiments**, researchers capitalize on opportunities to randomly assign participants to treatment conditions in natural settings.
      3. **Natural**, or **quasi-, experiments** compare treatments that already exist, such as different family environments or preschool programs.
         a. These studies differ from correlational research only in that groups are carefully chosen to ensure that their characteristics are as much alike as possible.

b. They permit researchers to examine the impact of conditions that cannot be experimentally manipulated for ethical reasons, such as the influence of premature birth.

V. DESIGNS FOR STUDYING DEVELOPMENT (pp. 60–66)
  A. To answer questions about child development, researchers must learn how research participants change over time.
  B. To do this, they use special *developmental research* strategies in which age comparisons form the basis of the research plan.
  C. The Longitudinal Design (pp. 60–62)
    1. In a **longitudinal design,** participants are studied repeatedly at different ages, and changes are noted as they get older.
    2. Advantages of the Longitudinal Design
      a. It allows researchers to identify common patterns as well as individual differences in development.
      b. It permits investigators to examine relationships between early and later events and behaviors.
    3. Problems in Conducting Longitudinal Research
      a. A common difficulty is **biased sampling**—the failure to enlist participants who represent the population of interest.
      b. **Selective attrition** occurs when some participants move away or drop out for other reasons, and those who continue are likely to differ in important ways from those who drop out.
      c. If participants become "test-wise" with repeated testing, their performance may improve as a result of **practice effects**—better test-taking skills and increased familiarity with the test—and not because of factors associated with development.
      d. Another threat to the validity of longitudinal findings is cultural–historical change, commonly called **cohort effects.**
        (1) Longitudinal studies examine the development of *cohorts*—children developing in the same period who are influenced by particular cultural and historical conditions. Results based on one cohort may not apply to children developing in other times.
        (2) Cohort effects also occur when specific experiences influence some children but not others in the same generation.
      e. Changes within the field of child development may create problems for longitudinal research, if the theories and methods that inspired the study become outdated.
  D. The Cross-Sectional Design (pp. 62–63)
    1. A more convenient strategy for studying development is the **cross-sectional design,** in which groups of people differing in age are studied at the same point in time.
    2. Advantages of the Cross-Sectional Design
      a. It is an efficient strategy for describing age-related trends.
      b. Because participants are measured only once, difficulties such as practice effects are not a factor.
    3. Problems in Conducting Cross-Sectional Research
      a. It yields only age-group averages but does not provide evidence about development at the individual level.
      b. Because of cohort effects, comparisons of groups born and reared in different years may not really represent age-related changes but, rather, may reflect unique experiences associated with the period in which the age groups were growing up.
  E. Improving Developmental Designs (pp. 63–65)
    1. Researchers have devised ways to build on the strengths and minimize the weaknesses of the longitudinal and cross-sectional approaches.
    2. Sequential Designs
      a. In the **sequential design,** researchers conduct several similar cross-sectional or longitudinal studies, called *sequences*. The sequences might study participants over the same ages but in different years, or they might study participants over different ages but during the same years.
      b. Some sequential designs combine longitudinal and cross-sectional strategies, which is efficient and yields these other advantages.
        (1) Researchers can discover whether cohort effects are operating by comparing participants of the same age who were born in different years.
        (2) Researchers can make both longitudinal and cross-sectional comparisons and, if outcomes are similar, can be confident about their findings.

Chapter 2 Research Strategies

3. Examining Microcosms of Development
    a. The **microgenetic design,** an adaptation of the longitudinal approach, presents children with a novel task and follows their mastery over a series of closely spaced sessions.
    b. Within this "microcosm" of development, researchers observe how change occurs—an approach that is especially useful for studying cognitive development.
    c. Limitations of microgenetic studies
        (1) They are difficult to carry out because researchers must analyze each participant's behavior many times.
        (2) The time required for children to change depends on a careful match between the child's capabilities and the demands of the task.
        (3) Practice effects can distort microgenetic findings.
4. Combining Experimental and Developmental Designs
    a. Causal information, which is not provided by longitudinal or cross-sectional studies, is desirable both for testing theories and for finding ways to improve children's lives.
    b. If a developmental design indicates that children's experiences and behavior are related, researchers may be able to explore the causal link by experimentally manipulating the experiences.

VI. ETHICS IN RESEARCH ON CHILDREN (pp. 66–69)
   A. Research into human behavior creates ethical issues because of the potential for exploitation—a concern that is especially complex when children take part in research.
       1. Children are more vulnerable than adults to physical and psychological harm.
       2. Children lack the maturity to evaluate for themselves the risks of participation in research.
   B. Ethical guidelines for research on children have been developed by the federal government, by funding agencies, and by research-oriented professional associations.
       1. Special committees known as *institutional review boards (IRBs)* assess proposed studies on the basis of a **risks-versus-benefits ratio,** which involves weighing the costs to participants in terms of inconvenience and possible psychological or physical injury against the study's value for advancing knowledge and improving conditions of life.
       2. Basic rights of research participants include the following:
           a. **Protection from harm:** If there are any risks to the safety and welfare of participants that the research does not justify, preference is always given to the research participants.
           b. **Informed consent** means that people have a right to an explanation of all aspects of a study that might affect their willingness to participate. Parental consent is meant to protect the safety of children whose ability to decide is not yet fully mature.
           c. Researchers must take special precautions in the use of deception and concealment when children are research subjects.
           d. **Debriefing,** in which the researcher provides a full account and justification of the research activities after the research session is over, should be done with children as well as with adults.

LECTURE ENHANCEMENTS

LECTURE ENHANCEMENT 2.1
An Illustration of Cross-Cultural Research: Findings on Autobiographical Memory in Young Children (pp. 51–52)

Time: 10–15 minutes

Objective: To examine cross-cultural differences in maternal reminiscing style and autobiographical memories in young children.

To examine cross-cultural differences in maternal reminiscing style and autobiographical memories in young children, Wang (2008) recruited 189 3-year-olds and their mothers. The sample included three distinct populations—native Chinese in China, Chinese immigrants in the United States, and European Americans. Two female researchers visited each participant's home and conducted interviews in the language with which each family was most comfortable. At the beginning of the home visit, one researcher played with the child to establish rapport, while the other explained the procedure to the mother. Next, mothers were instructed to talk to their child about two specific, one-time events that both had experienced and that had occurred within the past two months (so children were likely to recall them), such as a trip to a museum or an amusement park. Mothers were asked to talk about one event that was emotionally positive for the child, and one was that emotionally negative. At the end of the home visit, a researcher conducted a short interview with each child to assess various aspects of self-concept (personal qualities, attributes, and beliefs). The purpose of the interview was to determine whether maternal reminiscing style also predicted self-concept in young children.

Following the mother–child conversation, the researcher again played with the child, telling him or her, "Your mom just told me that . . . (for example, you went to the museum last weekend). I've never been there before. Tell me what you did." To elicit details, the researcher used prompts like, "What else happened?" "Can you tell me more about it?" To assess various aspects of self-concept, the researcher conducted a short self-description interview with each child. She explained to the child, "I would like to write a story about you. What's the first thing I should put in the story?" She then used prompts as needed, such as "What else should I write about you?" Finally, mothers completed questionnaires about their child's self-concept and language development.

Home visits were video recorded for later coding. Mothers' utterances during the mother–child conversation were coded as elaborations or evaluations. Elaborations included introducing a topic for discussion or adding information. Evaluations included confirming, negating, questioning, or emphasizing any part of the child's previous statement. Children's utterances were coded as shared memory reports whenever they requested more information or provided new information about the event. When recounting past events to the researcher, children's utterances were coded as independent memory reports whenever they provided new information that was not discussed in the mother–child conversation.

Results indicated that European-American mothers used more elaborations and evaluations with their children than Chinese and Chinese-immigrant mothers. European-American children, in turn, demonstrated greater recall when sharing memories with their mothers and with the researcher than Chinese and Chinese-immigrant children. Regardless of cultural background, children whose mothers were more elaborative and evaluative recalled more information than children whose mothers were less elaborative and evaluative. European-American children also provided more specific information about themselves in their personal narratives—that is, included more personal qualities, attributes, and beliefs—than either group of Chinese children. Although there were no cultural differences in proportion of favorable attributes or beliefs children included in their self-concepts, once again European-American children (who were more likely to have elaborative-style mothers) provided more details about themselves compared with their Chinese counterparts.

Have students review the text discussion on individualistic and collectivist societies (Chapter 1, p. 35). How might these cultural orientations explain differences in mother–child conversations?

Wang, Q. (2008). Relations of maternal style and child self-concept to autobiographical memories in Chinese, Chinese Immigrant, and European American 3-year-olds. *Child Development, 77,* 1749–1809.

LECTURE ENHANCEMENT 2.2
Demonstrating the Correlational Design: Parents' Management of Their Teenagers' Romantic Relationships (pp. 55–56)

Time: 10–15 minutes

Objective: To illustrate the correlational design using a study of parents' management of their teenagers' romantic relationships.

To extend existing research on dating in late adolescence, Madsen (2008) recruited 104 adolescents between the ages of 17 and 19 (29 boys, 75 girls) and at least one of their parents. The majority of the participants were from middle-SES families. The researchers collected the following information:
 (1) Parents completed the Parents of Adolescents Separation Anxiety Scale (PASAC). The PASAC assesses adults' comfort with their parenting role. For example, on a scale of 1 to 5 (1 = strongly disagree; 5 = strongly agree), "I like knowing that my teenager will come to me when he/she feels upset."
 (2) Participants reported on their parents' use of psychological control. For example, on a scale of 1 to 3 (1 = not like him/her; 3 = a lot like him/her), "My mother [father] is a person who is always trying to change how I feel or think about things."
 (3) Participants completed the Network of Relationship Inventory (NRI), which measures various aspects of romantic relationships—satisfaction, intimacy, affection, admiration, conflict, and antagonism. Sample questions include: On a scale of 1 to 5 (1 = little or none; 5 = the most),

- Satisfaction: "How satisfied are you with your relationship?"
- Intimacy: "How much do you tell this person about everything?"
- Affection: "How much does this person really care about you?"
- Admiration: "How much does this person like or approve of the things you do?"
- Conflict: "How much do you and this person get upset or mad at each other?"
- Antagonism: "How much do you and this person get on each other's nerves?"

(4) Parents who were currently involved in a romantic relationship reported on their satisfaction and insecurity. For example, on a scale of 1 to 7 (1 = low; 7 = high), "How satisfied are you with your relationship?" On a scale of 1 to 7 (1 = strongly disagree; 7 = strongly agree), "I worry that my partner doesn't care as much for me as I do my partner."

(5) Parents indicated whether the family had any rules about dating. If so, they were asked to indicate who set these rules—*mostly me; me; mostly my spouse; my spouse and I set the rules together; my spouse; my child;* or *my child and I set the rules together*. There were three types of rules included in this study:
- Supervision: Rules that require the adolescent to provide information regarding his or her dating activities
- Restriction: Rules that place some limitation or constraint on the adolescent's dating activity, such as no dates on school nights or only double dates
- Prescription: Rules that specify expectations regarding how the adolescent should behave with a date or in a dating relationship, such as use good judgment, leave an uncomfortable situation

Findings indicated that most parents (64%) had dating rules for their teenager. Overall, parents were more likely to impose dating rules on daughters than sons. In addition, mothers were more involved in setting dating rules than fathers. Of the three types of rules, supervision was most common and predicted healthy parent–child relationships. That is, parents who engaged in moderate levels of supervision were more secure in their parenting role and their children tended to report healthy levels of psychological control. In contrast, adolescents who experienced high levels of restriction also reported high rates of parental psychological control. Interestingly, parents who were dissatisfied with their own romantic relationships used more prescription rules than supervision or restriction rules. According to Madsen, while supervision and restriction rules tend to focus on monitoring and safety, prescription rules provide expectations associated with more satisfying relationships. Thus, dissatisfied parents may be more likely to impose their own expectations or wishes onto their teenagers.

Finally, parents' use of dating rules had no impact on the quality of adolescents' romantic relationships. That is, relationship satisfaction, intimacy, affection, admiration, conflict, and antagonism were unrelated to the number and types of rules. Instead, dating rules were a reflection of the parent–child relationship, as well as parental satisfaction with their own romantic relationships.

Madsen, S. D. (2008). Parents' management of adolescents' romantic relationships through dating rules: Gender variations and correlates of relationship qualities. *Journal of Youth and Adolescence, 37,* 1044–1058.

LECTURE ENHANCEMENT 2.3
Illustrating Research Designs for Studying the Child: Marital Conflict, Conflict Resolution, and Children's Adjustment (pp. 56–58)

Time: 10–15 minutes

Objective: To examine the effects of marital conflict and conflict resolution on children's adjustment.

To examine the effects of marital conflict, including resolution of the conflict, on children's emotional adjustment, Goeke-Morey, Cummings, and Papp (2008) recruited 163 children between the ages of 8 and 16 years and their parents. The researchers collected the following information:

(1) For 15 consecutive days, mothers and fathers were instructed to complete separate diaries of naturally occurring marital conflict. The researchers defined marital conflict as "any major or minor interparental interaction that involved a difference of opinion, whether it was mostly negative or even mostly positive." For each entry, parents recorded how the conflict ended—for example, compromise, giving in, a spouse apologizing, agreeing to disagree, or withdrawal. Parents also recorded the degree of their own and their spouse's emotional reaction to each conflict—anger, sadness, fear, and positive emotional expression. If a target child was present during the conflict, parents recorded his or her emotional reaction as well. Because the entries for spouses were highly similar, the researchers only used the mothers' entries in the final data analyses.

(2) Target children participated in an analogue laboratory procedure. A researcher presented each child with one of two common conflict scenarios. Children were asked to visualize interparental conflict over a messy house or an expensive purchase. Specifically, they were told to imagine that their own parents had "a big fight" over the mess or purchase. Next, children were shown a video depicting two adults (who represented their own parents) ending the conflict through compromise, giving in, an apology, agreeing to disagree, or withdrawal. In some instances, the "mother" ended the conflict; in others, the "father" ended the conflict. Finally, the researcher asked each child a series of questions about the conflict scenario. For example, children were asked to answer the following questions by using a 10-point scale (1 = not at all; 10 = a whole lot): "How much do you think the problem has been worked out?" "How did that make you feel—happy, mad, scared, sad, or OK?" Children were also asked an open-ended question: "What would you do if you were in the same room with them?" The researchers were interested in children's attempts to mediate or avoid the conflict.

(3) Parents completed the Child Behavior Checklist, which rates a broad range of internalizing (anxiety, somatic complaints, depression) and externalizing (aggression, impulsivity, hyperactivity) problems.

Results indicated that parental conflict resolution is a particularly important predictor of children's psychological adjustment, perhaps more so than exposure to the initial conflict. According to the diary entries, of all possible outcomes, compromise was the most frequent end to conflict and had the greatest impact on children's reactions. Specifically, children who experienced parental compromise had fewer negative reactions like sadness and fear and rated the laboratory scenarios more positively. In contrast, withdrawing from marital conflict was associated with increased child distress. Children who frequently observed parental withdrawal were less positive and rated the laboratory scenarios more negatively. According to Goeke-Morey, Cummings, and Papp, this finding suggests that marital conflict is not a uniformly negative experience for children. In fact, marital conflicts can actually end in ways that are positive and constructive to the child. Such conflicts may also serve as a model for children's own conflict resolution strategies.

Ask students to consider the various research designs for studying development. What design was utilized in this study? What are the strengths and limitations of this design? Can students think of any special ethical considerations that might arise with this type of study? Explain.

Goeke-Morey, M. C., Cummings, E. M., & Papp, L. M. (2008). Children and marital conflict resolution: Implications for emotional security and adjustment. *Journal of Family Psychology, 21,* 744–753.

LECTURE ENHANCEMENT 2.4
An Example of the Longitudinal Research Design: The Effects of Trauma on Children (pp. 60–62)

Time: 5–10 minutes

Objective: To examine the long-term effects of trauma on children.

To examine the long-term effects of trauma on children, Mullett-Hume and colleagues (2008) recruited 204 adolescents between the ages of 12 and 16 years. The participants attended schools near "Ground Zero"—that is, within 10 blocks—of the World Trade Center attack on September 11, 2001. The participants completed the following surveys:

(1) *The New York University Child and Adolescent Stressors Checklist–Revised (NYU–CASC).* The NYU–CASC focuses on various types of trauma and life adversities. Participants were asked about exposure to domestic violence, community and school violence, significant illnesses or death of close family members, accidents or injuries to self, natural disasters, and war. The researchers were interested in the types of trauma that participants had experienced, as well as cumulative trauma.

(2) *The Child PTSD Symptom Scale (CPSS).* The CPSS assesses reactions to trauma. For example, participants were asked to answer the following questions by using a 4-point scale (0 = not at all; 3 = 5 or more times a week/almost always): "How often do you feel upset, scared, or angry when you think about or hear about the event?" "How often do you avoid activities, people, or places that remind you of the event?"

Results indicated that history of trauma exposure—rather than direct exposure to the 9/11 terrorist attack—predicted severity of stress reactions. Specifically, children who were exposed to the terrorist attack but had little or no history of other life traumas continued to experience stress symptoms 2.5 years after exposure. However, stress reactions associated with 9/11 were significantly greater for children who had experienced other traumatic events prior to the terrorist attack. According to Mullett-Hume and colleagues, these findings suggest that a history of multiple traumas may be a more potent risk factor for long-term adjustment difficulties than exposure to a single, severe traumatic event.

Have students review research on cohort effects. How might cohort effects explain why specific experiences, such as exposure to 9/11, influence some children but not others in the same generation?

Mullett-Hume, E., Anshel, D., Guevara, V., & Cloitre, M. (2008). Cumulative trauma and posttraumatic stress disorder among children exposed to the 9/11 World Trade Center attack. *American Journal of Orthopsychiatry, 78,* 103–108.

LEARNING ACTIVITIES

LEARNING ACTIVITY 2.1
Matching: Common Methods Used to Study Children (pp. 42–52)

Present the following exercise as an in-class activity or quiz.

Directions: Match each term with its description.

Terms:
_____ 1. Naturalistic observation
_____ 2. Structured observation
_____ 3. Clinical interview
_____ 4. Structured interview, questionnaires, and tests
_____ 5. Neurobiological methods
_____ 6. Clinical, or case study, method
_____ 7. Ethnography

Descriptions:
  A. To fully understand one child's psychological functioning, this method combines interviews, observations, test scores, and sometimes neurobiological assessments.
  B. Using this method, the researcher tries to capture a culture's unique values and social processes.
  C. A strength of this method is that it grants each participant an equal opportunity to display the behavior of interest.
  D. A limitation of this method is that it cannot reveal with certainty the meaning of autonomic or brain activity.
  E. Using this research method, each participant is asked the same question in the exact same way.
  F. This method comes as close as possible to the way participants think in everyday life.
  G. Using this method, researchers observe behavior in natural contexts.

Answers:

1. G   5. D
2. C   6. A
3. F   7. B
4. E

LEARNING ACTIVITY 2.2
Making Systematic Observations of Young Children (pp. 44–45)

Ask students to find a child to observe by, for example, visiting a nearby park or the home of a family they know. The procedures used to collect systematic observations vary, depending on the research problem posed. One common approach is *event sampling,* in which the observer records all instances of a particular behavior of interest during a specified time period. Another option is *time sampling*. Using this procedure, the researcher records whether certain behaviors occur during a sample of short intervals. The chart below is an example of a simple time sampling instrument:

Target Behavior: Aggression

Minute 1				Minute 2				Minute 3				Minute 4				Minute 5			
15	30	45	60	15	30	45	60	15	30	45	60	15	30	45	60	15	30	45	60

Students should choose target behaviors that are easy to identify, such as aggressive behavior (for example, hitting), prosocial behavior (for example, comforting other children, sharing toys), crying, or instances of adult–child interaction. Once students have completed their observations, ask them to share their findings with the class, including any challenges they encountered.

LEARNING ACTIVITY 2.3
True or False: General Research Designs (pp. 55–60)

Present the following activity to students as an in-class assignment or quiz.

Directions: Read each of the following statements and determine if it is *True* (T) or *False* (F).

Statements:
_____ 1. In a correlational design, researchers can infer cause and effect.
_____ 2. A researcher who finds a +.78 correlation between parent self-reports of harsh discipline and child behavior problems has found a moderate correlation.
_____ 3. The independent variable is the one the investigator expects to cause changes in the other variable.
_____ 4. In experimental research, investigators directly control or manipulate the dependent variable.
_____ 5. To protect against the effects of confounding variables, researchers engage in random assignment of participants to treatment conditions.
_____ 6. One strength of laboratory experiments is that findings often apply to everyday situations.
_____ 7. Natural, or quasi-, experiments differ from correlational research only in that groups of people are carefully chosen to ensure that their characteristics are as much alike as possible.

Answers:

1. F
2. F
3. T
4. F
5. T
6. F
7. T

LEARNING ACTIVITY 2.4
Thinking About Research Methods and Designs (pp. 42–52, 60–64, 66–69)

Pose the following questions to students for an in-class discussion:
(1) An investigator is interested in determining whether infant child care leads to an insecure attachment bond between children and their mothers during the first year of life as well as into the preschool years. What research method and design would you use for this study, and why? Would there be any special ethical considerations with this type of study? If so, what are they?

(2) An investigator is interested in determining whether sociability in children is related to school achievement and whether this relationship varies for children in preschool, grade school, and middle school. What research method and design would you use for this study, and why? Would there be any special ethical considerations with this type of study? If so, what are they?

LEARNING ACTIVITY 2.5
Critiquing Journal Articles (pp. 42–52, 55–58, 60–65)

Have students select and read two articles about child development published during the past four years. Each article should present an empirical study on a topic related to child development. Some journals to consider for this activity are *American Psychologist, Child Development, Developmental Psychology, Early Childhood Research Quarterly, Journal of Adolescence, Journal of Applied Developmental Psychology,* and *Developmental Science.*

Next, have students (1) prepare a brief summary of the problem, method, results, discussion, and conclusions of the two articles; (2) indicate the type of research method(s) and design(s) used; and (3) identify any potential problems for achieving accurate results posed by the research design(s). Students can then discuss their findings in small groups or as a class.

LEARNING ACTIVITY 2.6
Cross-Sectional, Longitudinal, and Sequential Research Designs (pp. 60–64)

Present the following exercise as an in-class activity or quiz.

Directions: The following list contains descriptions, challenges, and examples of cross-sectional, longitudinal, and sequential research designs. For each statement, determine which research design (CS = cross-sectional, L = longitudinal, or S = sequential) is being described.

_____ 1. The researcher studies groups of participants who differ in age at the same point in time.
_____ 2. The researcher is interested in whether frequent exposure to violent television in early childhood predicts aggressive and antisocial behavior in adulthood.
_____ 3. May have the same problems as longitudinal and cross-sectional strategies, but the design itself helps identify difficulties.
_____ 4. Age-related changes may be distorted because of biased sampling, participant dropout, practice effects, or cohort effects. Theoretical and methodological changes in the field can make findings obsolete.
_____ 5. The researcher follows a sequence of samples (two or more age groups), collecting data on them at the same points in time.
_____ 6. Does not permit the study of individual developmental trends. Age differences may be distorted because of cohort effects.
_____ 7. The researcher is interested in age-related changes in children's problem-solving skills. The researcher selects three samples—preschool-age children, school-age children, and adolescents—and tracks them for five years.
_____ 8. The researcher is interested in how children of different ages process traumatic events, such as terrorism or natural disasters. The researcher recruits children in grades 3, 6, 9, and 12 for the study and interviews them about the Japan earthquake and Fukushima nuclear accident, the 2011 tornado outbreaks across the U.S., and the Norway terrorist attacks.
_____ 9. The researcher studies the same group of participants repeatedly at different ages.

Answers:

1. CS   6. CS
2. L   7. S
3. S   8. CS
4. L   9. L
5. S

LEARNING ACTIVITY 2.7
Exploring Ethical Guidelines for Research with Children (pp. 66–69)

To supplement the text coverage of ethics in child research, have students visit the following website: *www.srcd.org*. On the homepage, under About SRCD, have students choose "SRCD Ethical Standards" under the "About SRCD" heading. As students review the website, have them compare ethical guidelines for children with those presented in the text. What are some special ethical considerations for research with children? Do the ethical guidelines presented on the website adequately protect child research participants from undue risk? Explain.

ASK YOURSELF . . .

REVIEW: Why might a researcher choose structured observation over naturalistic observation? How about the reverse? What might lead the researcher to opt for clinical interviewing over systematic observation? (pp. 42–44, 46)

In *naturalistic observation,* researchers go into the field, or natural environment, and record the behavior of interest. Researchers choose this approach when it is important for them to see directly the everyday behaviors they hope to explain.

In *structured observation,* the investigator sets up a laboratory situation that evokes the behavior of interest, giving every participant an equal opportunity to display the response. Structured observation permits greater control over the research situation than does naturalistic observation. It is especially useful for studying behaviors, such as parent–child or friendship interactions, that investigators rarely have an opportunity to see in everyday life. However, there is no way to ensure that participants will behave in the laboratory as they do in their natural environments.

Systematic observation provides information about how people behave but says little about the reasoning behind their responses. Therefore, researchers who are interested in exploring participants' perceptions, thoughts, feelings, attitudes, beliefs, or past experiences often use the *clinical interview*—a flexible, conversational style used to probe for the participant's point of view. The clinical interview permits people to express their thoughts in terms that are as close as possible to the way they think in everyday life. This method also provides a large amount of information in a fairly brief period—far more than could be captured by observing for the same amount of time.

CONNECT: What strengths and limitations do the clinical, or case study, method and ethnography have in common? (pp. 50–52)

Both the clinical method and ethnography are descriptive, qualitative research techniques. Whereas the clinical method is a way of obtaining as complete a picture as possible of a single individual, ethnography is directed toward understanding a culture or distinct social group through *participant observation*. A major strength of both methods is that they yield rich, detailed descriptions that offer insights into the many factors affecting development. A limitation of both methods is that investigators' cultural values and theoretical preferences may lead them to observe selectively or misinterpret what they see. Another limitation is that findings cannot be assumed to generalize to other individuals or cultures.

APPLY: A researcher wants to study the thoughts and feelings of children who have a parent on active duty in the military. Which method should she use? Why? (pp. 46–47)

Because the researcher wants to learn about children's thoughts and feelings, the best method is the *clinical interview,* which permits children to display their thoughts in terms that are as close as possible to the way they think in everyday life. This method also provides a large amount of information in a fairly brief period.

The researcher might also consider using a *structured interview,* in which each participant is asked the same set of questions in the same way. The structured interview eliminates the possibility that variations in children's responses may reflect the manner of interviewing rather than real differences in their thoughts about the question. It is also more efficient: Answers are briefer and can be gathered from an entire group at the same time. However, structured interviews do not yield the same depth of information as a clinical interview.

REVIEW: Explain why, although a research method must be reliable to be valid, reliability *does not guarantee* validity. (p. 54)

Reliability refers to the consistency, or repeatability, of measures of behavior. To be reliable, observations and evaluations of people's actions cannot be unique to a single observer. Instead, observers must agree on what they see. For research methods to have high *validity*, they must accurately measure characteristics that the researcher set out to measure. Therefore, reliability is essential for valid research. But the reliability of a study is not enough to guarantee that the researcher is actually measuring what he or she set out to measure. Even the most carefully designed experiment can be rendered invalid if the research methods do not reflect the investigator's goals.

CONNECT: Why is it better for a researcher to use multiple methods rather than just one method to test a hypothesis or answer a research question? (pp. 54–55)

To be scientifically sound, research methods must be both reliable and valid. Qualitative research methods, such as the clinical, or case study, method and ethnographic studies, do not yield quantitative scores that can be matched with those of another observer. Therefore, the reliability of these methods must be determined by using other procedures as well. Using multiple research methods also helps to ensure validity by allowing investigators to determine whether findings from one study generalize to settings and participants outside the original study.

APPLY: In studying the development of attention in school-age children, a researcher wonders whether to make naturalistic observations or structured observations. Which approach is best for ensuring internal validity? How about external validity? Why? (pp. 42–44, 54–55)

Because structured observations give each participant an equal opportunity to display the behavior of interest, they are the best option for ensuring internal validity. On the other hand, naturalistic observations are the best approach for ensuring external validity, because they reflect participants' everyday behaviors, increasing the likelihood that findings can be generalized to other individuals and settings.

REVIEW: Why are natural experiments less precise than laboratory and field experiments? (pp. 56–58, 60)

In natural, or quasi-, experiments, the researcher compares treatments that already exist, such as different family environments, schools, child-care centers, or schools. These studies differ from correlational research only in that groups of participants are carefully chosen to ensure that their characteristics are as much alike as possible.

Field experiments are more precise than natural experiments because the investigator randomly assigns participants to treatment conditions in natural settings and is therefore able to generalize experimental findings to the real world. In laboratory experiments, in addition to random assignment of participants to treatment conditions, the investigator manipulates an independent variable and looks at its effect on a dependent variable, allowing more confident inferences about cause and effect.

CONNECT: Reread the description of the study of aggressive boys and their friendships on page 44. What type of design did the researchers use, and why? (pp. 44, 56–58)

The researchers used structured observation and a correlational design. Structured observation allowed them to study behaviors—in this case, friendship interactions—that they would rarely have an opportunity to see in everyday life. The correlational design allowed them to measure the strength of the relationship between the boys' aggressiveness and the extent to which their peer interactions were angry and uncooperative. Although they were not able to infer a cause-and-effect relationship between the two variables, they found evidence that aggressive boys' close peer ties, rather than being warm and supportive, provided a context in which the boys practiced hostility and other negative behaviors.

APPLY: A researcher compares children who went to summer leadership camps with children who attended athletic camps. She finds that those who attended leadership camps are friendlier. Should the investigator tell parents that sending children to leadership camps will cause them to be more sociable? Why or why not? (pp. 55–56)

No. This study has a correlational design, in which the researcher looks at relationships between participants' characteristics and their behavior or development. Although a correlational design allows researchers to gather information on individuals in their natural life circumstances, it does not permit them to infer cause and effect. Therefore, the researcher cannot conclude that attending summer leadership camps *causes* children to be more sociable. As an alternative explanation, perhaps children who are more sociable are also more likely to choose leadership camps over athletic camps, or perhaps a third variable that the researcher did not even consider contributed to the research findings.

REFLECT: Design a study to investigate whether time devoted to adult–child picture-book reading in the preschool years contributes to reading readiness at school entry. List steps you will take to protect the internal and external validity of your investigation. (p. 55)

This is an open-ended question with no right or wrong answer.

REVIEW: Explain how cohort effects can distort the findings of both longitudinal and cross-sectional studies. How does the sequential design reveal cohort effects? (pp. 62–64)

Both longitudinal and cross-sectional studies can be influenced by *cohort effects*—the particular set of historical and cultural conditions that affect individuals born in the same time period. Therefore, results based on one cohort may not apply to children developing at other times. For example, a longitudinal study of social development carried out around the time of World War II would probably result in quite different findings than if it were carried out in the first decade of the twenty-first century, during the decade of the 1960s, or during the Great Depression of the 1930s. Similarly, a cross-sectional design comparing 5-year-old cohorts and 15-year-old cohorts—groups born and reared in different years—may not really identify age-related changes. Rather, the results may reflect unique experiences associated with the different historical time period in which each age group grew up.

In a *sequential design,* researchers overcome some of these limitations by conducting several similar longitudinal or cross-sectional studies, or *sequences,* at varying times. Sequential designs permit researchers to find out whether cohort effects are operating by comparing participants of the same age who were born in different years. If the samples do not differ on the measured variables, the researcher can rule out cohort effects.

CONNECT: Review the study on music lessons and intelligence reported in the Social Issues: Education box on page 59. Explain how it combines an experimental with a developmental design. What advantage does this approach offer? (pp. 56, 59, 60–61)

The study on music lessons and intelligence combines an experimental with a longitudinal design (a type of developmental design). The researchers experimentally manipulated participants' experiences by randomly assigning 6-year-old children to one of four experimental conditions—two groups who received music lessons (piano and voice, respectively), one group who received drama lessons, or a no-lessons control group—and then measuring changes in each child's mental-test performance over time. The two music groups consistently gained more in mental-test performance than either the drama or the no-lessons control group.

The advantage of this approach is that it allowed researchers to draw causal inferences from the results—in this case, to infer that sustained musical experiences can lead to small increases in intelligence among 6-year-olds that do not arise from comparable drama lessons.

APPLY: A researcher wants to know whether children enrolled in child-care centers in the first few years of life do as well in school as those who are not in child care. Which developmental design is appropriate for answering this question? Explain. (pp. 60–61)

A longitudinal design would be the most appropriate method for investigating this question because it would allow the researcher to track the performance of children who attend child-care centers in the first few years of life versus those who do not, to identify common patterns and differences in development between the two groups, and to examine any relationships between early child-care experiences and later school performance.

REFLECT: Suppose a researcher asks you to enroll your baby in a 10-year longitudinal study. What factors would lead you to agree and to stay involved? Do your answers shed light on why longitudinal studies often have biased samples? Explain. (pp. 61–62)

This is an open-ended question with no right or wrong answer.

REVIEW: Explain why researchers must consider children's age-related capacities to ensure that they are protected from harm and have freely consented to research. (pp. 66–68)

When children participate in research, the ethical concerns are especially complex. Children are more vulnerable than adults to physical and psychological harm. The ethical principle of *informed consent*—people's right to have all aspects of a study explained to them that might affect their willingness to participate—requires special interpretation when individuals cannot fully appreciate the research goals and activities. Parental consent is meant to protect the safety of children whose ability to decide is not yet fully mature. As soon as children are old enough to appreciate the purpose of the research, certainly by age 7, their own informed consent should be obtained in addition to parental consent. Around age 7, changes in children's thinking permit them to better understand basic scientific principles and the needs of others. Researchers should respect and enhance these new capacities by giving school-age children a full explanation of research activities in language they can understand.

CONNECT: In the experiment on music lessons and intelligence reported in the Social Issues box on page 59, why was it ethically important for the researchers to offer music lessons to the no-lessons control group during the year after completion of the study? (p. 66)

One of the research rights established by the American Psychological Association states that when researchers are investigating experimental treatments believed to be beneficial, children in control groups have the right to alternative beneficial treatments if they are available. Once researchers identified a positive relationship between music lessons and children's mental test performance, it was important to give the no-lessons control group an opportunity similar to the advantage provided to the experimental group.

APPLY: As a researcher was engaged in naturalistic observation of preschoolers' play, one child said, "Stop watching me!" Referring to the research rights listed in Table 2.5, indicate how the researcher should respond, and why. (p. 66)

Children's research rights include the right to be protected from physical or psychological harm as well as the right to discontinue participation in research at any time. Because this child has verbally expressed a desire to discontinue the observation, the researcher is ethically obligated to terminate the observation.

REFLECT: Would you approve the study on stereotyping and prejudice, in which summer-school students (without an explanation) were asked to wear colored T-shirts that identified them as members of "majority" and "minority" groups? Explain. What ethical safeguards do you believe are vital in research that requires deception of children to ensure internal validity? (pp. 66–69)

This is an open-ended question with no right or wrong answer.

SUGGESTED READINGS

Coll, C. G., & Marks, K. (2009). *Immigrant stories: Ethnicity and academics in middle childhood*. New York: Oxford University Press. A longitudinal study of first- and second-generation immigrant youths, this book examines the unique challenges and strengths of these children and their families. Topics include cultural attitudes and identity development, academic achievement, the importance of community resources, and the importance of public policies for immigrant families.

Freeman, M., & Mathison, S. (2008). *Researching children's experiences*. New York: Guilford. Presents an extensive overview of research methods commonly used to study children and adolescents. The authors also present information on recruiting minors for research, the roles and responsibilities of researchers, the importance of understanding the child's developmental level, and ethical considerations and challenges.

Stark, L. (2011). *Behind closed doors: IRBs and the making of ethical research*. Chicago, IL: University of Chicago Press. Examines the history of Institutional Review Boards (IRBs), including where our rules for the treatment of human subjects originated; the responsibilities of researchers, universities, medical facilities, and laboratories; and current guidelines for making ethical research decisions.

MEDIA MATERIALS

For details on individual video segments that accompany the DVD for *Child Development,* Ninth Edition, please see the DVD Guide for *Explorations in Child Development*. The DVD and DVD Guide are available through your Pearson sales representative.

Additional DVDs that may be useful in your class are listed below. They are not available through your Pearson sales representative, but you can order them directly from the distributors. (See contact information at the end of this manual.)

Experimental Research Methods in Psychology (2004, Films Media Group, 28 min.). Drawing on laboratory and field experiments, this program compares and contrasts experimental research methods through a study of attractiveness involving young adults. Experts also explore some of the issues common to both experimental methods, including ethical concerns and reductionism. A part of the series *Understanding Psychology*.

Exploring Qualitative Methods (2005, Films Media Group, 46 min.). Through experiments about sleep and dreams designed and conducted by students, this program provides insight into the process of collecting and using qualitative data. It covers creating effective questionnaires, preparing participant interviews, assembling case studies, and conducting observational studies. The program also explores the use of content analysis and the correlational method, employed to make qualitative data more meaningful. An instructor's guide is available online.

Nonexperimental Research Methods (2006, Films Media Group, 34 min.), Part of the series *Understanding Psychology,* this program presents nonexperimental research methods—questionnaires, interviews, and naturalistic observation—through three studies on the effects of cell phone use. Section one explains good questionnaire design and considers the advantages and limitations of this method. Section two examines the use of unstructured interviews, and section three spotlights the performance and practical difficulties of naturalistic observation.

Observation I: The Eyes Have It! (2004, Magna Systems, Inc., 27 min.). This module, part of the *Authentic Assessment* series, illustrates why, in the words of education coordinator Theresa Collado, "A good observer is a good teacher." The module explores authentic assessment techniques used in preschool settings to document children's cognitive growth. Teachers discuss systems they have developed for observing children in their own classrooms and are shown interacting with children in ways that allow them to observe children's physical, cognitive, and social and emotional development.

Observation II: Making the Connection (2004, Magna Systems, Inc., 27 min.). Teachers and education coordinators demonstrate systems they use to collate observational data gathered on young children. These data include work samples, observations, story dictation, and pictures of children engaged in activities. This module, part of the Authentic Assessment series, also demonstrates how educators use computers to collate data on children's progress throughout the year.

Parents: Our Most Important Resource (2004, Magna Systems, Inc., 27 min.). This module, part of the *Authentic Assessment* series, highlights a group parent–teacher meeting and presentation focusing on the process of developing the portfolio, the formal checklist, and the parent's reporting form. The program emphasizes the importance of communicating with parents throughout the assessment process. In a later segment, a teacher screens and observes a preschool child in the classroom and then shares her observations with the child's mother during school conferences and a home visit. The teacher and parent are seen discussing the child's progress and collaborating to set goals for him.

Research Ethics (2008, Insight Media, 21 min.). This program examines ethical issues in social science, natural science, and health research, including plagiarism, crediting and citing sources, the use of human and animal subjects, informed consent, debriefing, privacy, confidentiality, and conflicts of interest.

Research Methods in the Social Sciences (2005, Films Media Group; 4-part series, 23 to 46 min. each). Focusing primarily on research in psychology, this series explores qualitative and quantitative research methods used in a wide range of disciplines. Hosted and narrated by students, each program demonstrates how to test hypotheses, prepare experiments, and analyze data. Instructors' guides are available online.

Setting the Stage (2004, Magna Systems, Inc., 24 min.). In this module, the first in the *Authentic Assessment* series, educators discuss current research and theories on the assessment of young children. The validity of authentic assessment techniques to chart children's growth and development is contrasted with the use of standardized tests. The limits of standardized tests are discussed by center directors, education coordinators, and advocates of authentic assessment techniques. This first module of the series helps new teachers see how children can be observed in the context of their play as well as their culture, and how these observations can help teachers understand a child's overall development.

CHAPTER 3
BIOLOGICAL FOUNDATIONS, PRENATAL DEVELOPMENT, AND BIRTH

CHAPTER-AT-A-GLANCE

Chapter Outline	Instruction Ideas	Supplements
Genetic Foundations pp. 73–83 The Genetic Code • The Sex Cells • Boy or Girl? • Multiple Offspring • Patterns of Genetic Inheritance • Chromosomal Abnormalities	Learning Objectives 3.1–3.3 Learning Activities 3.1–3.3 Ask Yourself p. 83	Test Bank Items 1–37, 126–127 Please contact your Pearson publisher's representative for a wide range of video offerings available to adopters.
Reproductive Choices pp. 84–87 Genetic Counseling • Prenatal Diagnosis and Fetal Medicine	Learning Objective 3.4 Lecture Enhancement 3.1 Ask Yourself p. 87	Test Bank Items 38–45, 128
Prenatal Development pp. 88–94 Conception • Period of the Zygote • Period of the Embryo • Period of the Fetus	Learning Objective 3.5 Learning Activities 3.4–3.5, 3.8 Ask Yourself p. 94	Test Bank Items 46–64
Prenatal Environmental Influences pp. 94–107 Teratogens • Other Maternal Factors	Learning Objectives 3.6–3.7 Lecture Enhancement 3.2 Learning Activities 3.6–3.7, 3.10 Ask Yourself p. 106	Test Bank Items 65–87, 129–130
Childbirth pp. 107–109 The Baby's Adaptation to Labor and Delivery • The Newborn Baby's Appearance • Assessing the Newborn's Physical Condition: The Apgar Scale	Learning Objective 3.8 Learning Activities 3.8–3.9	Test Bank Items 88–93
Approaches to Childbirth pp. 109–112 Natural, or Prepared, Childbirth • Home Delivery • Labor and Delivery Medication	Learning Objective 3.9 Learning Enhancement 3.3 Learning Activities 3.8–3.9 Ask Yourself p. 112	Test Bank Items 94–104, 131
Birth Complications pp. 112–118, 119 Oxygen Deprivation • Preterm and Low-Birth-Weight Infants • Birth Complications, Parenting, and Resilience	Learning Objective 3.10 Learning Activity 3.10 Ask Yourself p. 117	Test Bank Items 105–114
Heredity, Environment, and Behavior: A Look Ahead pp. 118–125 The Question, "How Much?" • The Question, "How?"	Learning Objective 3.11 Learning Enhancement 3.4 Learning Activity 3.11 Ask Yourself p. 124	Test Bank Items 115–125

BRIEF CHAPTER SUMMARY

Because nature has prepared us for survival, all humans have features in common. Yet each person is also unique—a blend of genetic information and environmental influences that begin even before conception. We share some of our genetic makeup with all other organisms, and most of it with other mammals, especially primates.

A new individual is created when male and female gametes, or sex cells, combine, forming a zygote, the beginning of a new human life. The new organism inherits two forms of each gene, one from the mother and one from the father; this inheritance will determine many of the individual's traits, including hair and eye color and various disabilities and diseases. Characteristics such as height, weight, intelligence, and personality are determined by many genes through a process called polygenic inheritance.

Genetic counseling helps couples at risk for giving birth to children with genetic abnormalities consider appropriate options, and prenatal diagnostic methods allow early detection of genetic problems. Reproductive technologies, such as donor insemination, in vitro fertilization, and surrogate motherhood, enable individuals to become parents who otherwise would not, but they raise serious legal and ethical concerns.

With conception, the story of prenatal development begins to unfold. The vast changes that occur during pregnancy are divided into three periods: the period of the zygote, the period of the embryo, and the period of the fetus. The developing organism is vulnerable to the harmful effects of environmental agents called teratogens and to other risk factors in the mother, including disease, severe emotional stress, inadequate nutrition, and age.

Childbirth divides naturally into three stages: dilation and effacement of the cervix, delivery of the baby, and birth of the placenta. Childbirth practices, like other aspects of family life, are molded by the society of which mother and baby are a part. In Western nations, childbirth has typically moved from home to hospital, and family participation has declined. A natural childbirth movement has aimed to permit greater maternal control over labor and delivery, and a small number of American women choose to give birth at home. Natural, or prepared, childbirth, including special relaxation and breathing techniques and the support of a labor coach, is commonly used to reduce pain and medical intervention. The use of analgesic or anesthetic medication in childbirth is common in the United States, but the current trend is to limit the routine use of these medications. Complications of childbirth pose serious risks to development, but the development of affected infants is greatly influenced by the quality of the parent–child relationship.

The field of behavioral genetics looks at the contributions of nature and nurture to complex traits. There is a growing consensus that development is best understood as a series of complicated exchanges between nature and nurture. According to the concepts of gene–environment interaction and canalization, heredity influences children's responsiveness to varying environments. A major reason that researchers are interested in the nature–nurture issue is that they want to improve environments so that children can develop as favorably as possible. The success of any attempt to improve child development depends on the characteristics we want to change, the child's genetic makeup, and the type and timing of the intervention.

LEARNING OBJECTIVES

After reading this chapter, you should be able to answer the following:

3.1 What are genes, and how are they transmitted from one generation to the next? (pp. 74–77)

3.2 Describe various patterns of genetic inheritance. (pp. 77–81)

3.3 Describe major chromosomal abnormalities, and explain how they occur. (pp. 82–83)

3.4 What procedures can assist prospective parents in having healthy children? (pp. 84–87)

3.5 List the three periods of prenatal development, and describe the major milestones of each. (pp. 88–94)

3.6 Cite factors that influence the impact of teratogens, noting agents that are known teratogens. (pp. 94–103)

3.7 Describe the impact of additional maternal factors on prenatal development. (pp. 103–106)

3.8 Describe the three stages of childbirth, the baby's adaptation to labor and delivery, and the newborn baby's appearance. (pp. 107–109)

3.9 Describe natural childbirth and home delivery, and explain the risks of using pain-relieving drugs during labor and delivery. (pp. 109–112)

Chapter 3 Biological Foundations, Prenatal Development, and Birth

3.10 What risks are associated with oxygen deprivation and with preterm and low-birth-weight infants, and what factors can help infants who survive a traumatic birth? (pp. 112–117, 118, 119)

3.11 Explain the various ways heredity and environment may combine to influence complex traits. (pp. 118–125)

LECTURE OUTLINE

I. GENETIC FOUNDATIONS (pp. 73–83)
  A. All human beings have features in common, yet each person is also unique.
    1. Directly observable characteristics are called **phenotypes.**
    2. Phenotypes depend in part on the individual's **genotype**—the complex blend of genetic information that determines our species and influences all our unique characteristics—and in part on environmental influences that begin even before conception.
  B. Each of us is made up of trillions of *cells*.
    1. Each cell has a control center, or *nucleus*, that contains rodlike structures called **chromosomes,** which store and transmit genetic information.
    2. Human chromosomes come in 23 matching pairs (except for the XY pair in males), one inherited from the mother and one from the father.
  C. The Genetic Code (pp. 74–75)
    1. Chromosomes are made up of **deoxyribonucleic acid,** or **DNA,** a long, double-stranded molecule that looks like a twisted ladder.
    2. Each rung of the ladder consists of a pair of chemical substances called *bases*. The sequence of base pairs provides genetic instructions.
    3. A **gene** is a segment of DNA along the length of the chromosome.
    4. Humans share some of our genetic makeup with all other organisms, and most of it with other mammals, especially primates.
    5. A unique feature of DNA is that it can duplicate itself through a process called **mitosis,** during which the chromosomes copy themselves.
    6. Genes send instructions for making a rich assortment of proteins to the *cytoplasm*, the area surrounding the cell nucleus.
      a. Proteins that trigger chemical reactions throughout the body are the biological foundation on which our characteristics are built.
      b. Within the cell, environmental factors modify gene expression, so biological events, even at a microscopic level, are the result of *both* genetic and nongenetic forces.
  D. The Sex Cells (pp. 75–76)
    1. New individuals are created when two special cells called **gametes,** or sex cells—the sperm and ovum—combine.
      a. Gametes are formed through a cell division process called **meiosis,** which halves the number of chromosomes normally present in body cells, so that a gamete contains only 23 chromosomes.
      b. When sperm and ovum unite at fertilization, the resulting cell, called a **zygote,** will again have 46 chromosomes.
    2. The steps involved in meiosis are as follows:
      a. Chromosomes pair up within the original cell, and each one copies itself.
      b. In an event called **crossing over,** chromosomes next to each other break at one or more points along their length and exchange segments, so that genes from one are replaced by genes from another, creating new hereditary combinations.
      c. The chromosome pairs separate into different cells; chance determines which member of each pair will gather with others and end up in the same gamete.
      d. Each chromosome leaves its partner and becomes part of a gamete containing only 23 chromosomes instead of 46.
    3. The production of male sex cells differs from that of female sex cells.
      a. In the male, the cells from which sperm arise are produced continuously throughout life, so that a healthy man can father a child at any age after sexual maturity.

b. The female is born with all her ova already present in her ovaries, and she can bear children for only three to four decades.
E. Boy or Girl? (p. 76): The 23 pairs of chromosomes include 22 matching pairs, called **autosomes,** and one pair of **sex chromosomes,** called XX in females, XY in males.
   1. When gametes form in males, the X and Y chromosomes separate into different sperm cells.
   2. The sex of a new organism is determined by whether an X-bearing or a Y-bearing sperm fertilizes the ovum.
F. Multiple Offspring (pp. 76–77)
   1. Sometimes a zygote that has started to duplicate separates into two clusters of cells that develop into two individuals, who are called **identical,** or **monozygotic, twins** because they have the same genetic makeup.
   2. **Fraternal,** or **dizygotic, twins,** the most common type of multiple birth, result from the release and fertilization of two ova.
G. Patterns of Genetic Inheritance (pp. 77–81)
   1. Two forms of each gene, called an **allele**—one inherited from the mother and one from the father—occur at the same place on the chromosomes.
      a. If the alleles from both parents are alike, the child is **homozygous** and will display the inherited trait.
      b. If the alleles differ, the child is **heterozygous,** and relationships between the alleles determine the phenotype.
   2. Dominant–Recessive Relationships
      a. **Dominant–recessive inheritance** is a type of heterozygous pairing in which only one allele, called *dominant,* affects the child's characteristics; the second allele, called *recessive,* has no effect.
      b. Heterozygous individuals with just one recessive allele are called **carriers** of the trait, which they can pass to their children.
      c. Many disabilities and diseases are the product of recessive alleles; one of the most frequently occurring is *phenylketonuria,* or *PKU,* which affects the way the body breaks down proteins.
      d. A single gene can affect more than one trait, and the extent to which children are affected by a gene is influenced by the action of **modifier genes,** which enhance or dilute the effects of other genes.
   3. Incomplete Dominance
      a. **Incomplete dominance** is a pattern of inheritance in which both dominant and recessive alleles are expressed in the phenotype, resulting in a combined trait, or one that is intermediate between the two.
      b. An example is the *sickle cell trait,* a heterozygous condition present in 20 percent of black Africans.
      c. The sickle cell allele is common among black Africans because carriers of this allele are more resistant to malaria than individuals with two alleles for normal red blood cells.
   4. X-Linked Inheritance
      a. **X-linked inheritance** applies when a harmful allele is carried on the X chromosome.
         (1) In females, any recessive allele on one X chromosome has a good chance of being suppressed by a dominant allele on the other X.
         (2) Males are more likely to be affected by these alleles because the short Y chromosome lacks many corresponding alleles to override those on the X.
      b. A well-known example is *hemophilia,* a blood-clotting disorder.
   5. In addition to X-linked disorders, rates of miscarriage, infant and childhood deaths, birth defects, learning disabilities, behavior disorders, and mental retardation are all higher for boys.
      a. It is possible that these sex differences occur because the female, with two X chromosomes, benefits from a greater variety of genes.
      b. Nature seems to have adjusted for the male's disadvantage: Worldwide, about 107 boys are born for every 100 girls.
   6. Genomic Imprinting
      a. One exception to the rules of dominant–recessive and incomplete-dominance inheritance is seen in **genomic imprinting,** in which alleles are *imprinted,* or chemically marked, so that one pair member (either the mother's or the father's) is activated, regardless of its makeup.
      b. The imprint is often temporary and may not occur in all individuals.
      c. Imprinting helps to explain certain puzzling genetic patterns, including the inheritance of illnesses such as diabetes, asthma, and several childhood cancers.
      d. Genomic imprinting can operate on the sex chromosomes, as seen in *fragile X syndrome,* the most common inherited cause of mental retardation.

7. Mutation
   a. Harmful genes are created by **mutation,** a sudden but permanent change in a segment of DNA.
   b. Although less than 3 percent of pregnancies result in the birth of a baby with a hereditary abnormality, these children account for about 20 percent of infant deaths.
   c. *Germline mutation* takes place in the cells that give rise to gametes.
   d. In *somatic mutation,* normal body cells mutate, an event that can occur at any time of life; the DNA defect appears in every cell derived from the affected body cell.
   e. Both somatic and germline mutation may be involved in disorders that run in families.
8. Polygenic Inheritance
   a. **Polygenic inheritance** is a complex process in which many genes determine a characteristic.
   b. It is responsible for traits such as height, weight, and intelligence, which vary on a continuum.

H. Chromosomal Abnormalities (pp. 82–83)
   1. Besides harmful recessive alleles, abnormalities of the chromosomes are a major cause of serious developmental problems.
   2. Most chromosomal defects result from mistakes occurring during meiosis, when the ovum and sperm are formed.
   3. These errors usually produce many physical and mental symptoms.
   4. Down Syndrome
      a. The most common chromosomal abnormality is *Down syndrome.*
      b. In 95 percent of cases, it results from a failure of the twenty-first pair of chromosomes to separate during meiosis, so the new individual inherits three of these chromosomes rather than the normal two.
      c. Its consequences include mental retardation, speech problems, limited vocabulary, slow motor development, and distinctive physical features.
      d Children with Down syndrome develop more favorably when parents encourage them to engage with their surroundings.
      e. The risk of bearing a baby with Down syndrome rises dramatically with maternal age.
   5. Abnormalities of the Sex Chromosomes
      a. Disorders of the autosomes other than Down syndrome usually disrupt development so severely that they lead to miscarriage or to death in early childhood.
      b. Sex chromosome disorders often are not recognized until adolescence when, in some deviations, puberty is delayed. The most common problems involve the presence of an extra chromosome (either X or Y) or the absence of one X in females.
      c. Most children with sex disorders do not suffer from mental retardation; rather, their intellectual problems are usually very specific.

II. REPRODUCTIVE CHOICES (pp. 84–87)
   A. Genetic Counseling (pp. 84, 86–87)
      1. **Genetic counseling** helps couples assess their chances of giving birth to a baby with a hereditary disorder and choose the best course of action in view of the risks and family goals.
      2. Individuals likely to seek counseling include those who have had difficulties bearing children or women who delay childbearing past age 35.
      3. When a family history of mental retardation, psychological disorders, physical defects, or inherited diseases exists, the genetic counselor can prepare a *pedigree*—a picture of the family tree identifying affected relatives—which is used to estimate the likelihood that parents will have an abnormal child.
   B. Prenatal Diagnosis and Fetal Medicine (pp. 84–86)
      1. **Prenatal diagnostic methods**—medical procedures that permit detection of developmental problems before birth—are available to couples who might bear a child with abnormalities. They include *amniocentesis* and *chorionic villus sampling*.
      2. Prenatal diagnosis has led to advances in fetal medicine; however, these techniques frequently result in complications.
      3. Advances in *genetic engineering* also offer new hope for correcting hereditary defects.
         a. Researchers involved in the Human Genome Project have mapped the sequence of all human DNA base pairs and are "annotating" the genome—identifying all of its genes and their functions.
         b. A major goal is to understand human disorders, both those due to single genes and those resulting from a complex interplay of multiple genes and environmental factors.

c. New treatments are being explored for correcting genetic abnormalities—for example, *gene therapy,* the delivery of DNA carrying a functional gene to the cells.

III. PRENATAL DEVELOPMENT (pp. 88–94)
 A. Conception (pp. 88–89, 90)
  1. About once every 28 days, in the middle of a woman's menstrual cycle, an ovum bursts from one of her *ovaries*. It is drawn into one of two *fallopian tubes,* long, thin structures that lead to the uterus.
  2. The *corpus luteum*—the spot on the ovary from which the ovum was released—secretes hormones that prepare the lining of the uterus to receive a fertilized ovum.
  3. If pregnancy does not occur, the corpus luteum shrinks, and the lining of the uterus is discarded two weeks later with menstruation.
  4. In the final process of maturation of the sperm, it develops a tail that permits it to swim upstream in the female reproductive tract, through the *cervix* (opening of the uterus) and into the fallopian tube, where fertilization usually takes place.
  5. Most conceptions occur on the day of ovulation or during the 2 days preceding it.
 B. Period of the Zygote (pp. 89–91)
  1. The period of the zygote lasts about two weeks, from fertilization until the tiny mass of cells drifts down and out of the fallopian tube and attaches itself to the wall of the uterus.
  2. By the fourth day, 60 to 70 cells exist, forming a hollow, fluid-filled ball called a *blastocyst.*
   a. The cells on the inside, the *embryonic disk,* will become the new organism.
   b. The outer ring of cells, the *trophoblast,* will provide protective covering and nourishment.
  3. Implantation
   a. Between the seventh and ninth days, *implantation* occurs: The blastocyst burrows deep into the uterine lining.
   b. The trophoblast forms a membrane, the **amnion,** that encloses the developing organism in *amniotic fluid,* which helps keep the temperature of the prenatal world constant and provides a cushion against any jolts caused by the woman's movement.
   c. A *yolk sac* emerges that produces blood cells until the developing liver, spleen, and bone marrow are mature enough to take over this function.
  4. The Placenta and Umbilical Cord
   a. By the end of the second week, cells of the trophoblast form another protective membrane, the **chorion,** which surrounds the amnion.
   b. From the chorion, tiny fingerlike *villi,* or blood vessels, emerge. As the villi burrow into the uterine wall, a special organ called the *placenta* starts to develop.
    (1) By bringing the embryo's and the mother's blood close together, the **placenta** permits food and oxygen to reach the developing organism and waste products to be carried away.
    (2) The placenta is connected to the developing organism by the **umbilical cord,** which delivers blood loaded with nutrients and removes waste products.
 C. Period of the Embryo (p. 91)
  1. During the period of the **embryo,** which lasts about six weeks (from implantation through the eighth week of pregnancy), the most rapid prenatal changes take place, as the groundwork is laid for all body structures and internal organs.
  2. Last Half of the First Month
   a. In the first week of this period, the embryonic disk forms three layers of cells, which give rise to all parts of the body.
    (1) The *ectoderm* will become the nervous system and skin.
    (2) The muscles, skeleton, circulatory system, and other internal organs will develop from the *mesoderm.*
    (3) The *endoderm* will become the digestive system, lungs, urinary tract, and glands.
   b. At first, the nervous system develops fastest.
    (1) The ectoderm folds over to form a *neural tube,* or primitive spinal cord.
    (2) At 3½ weeks, the top of the neural tube swells to form a brain.
   c. While the nervous system is developing, the heart begins to pump blood, and the muscles, backbone, ribs, and digestive tract appear.
   d. At the end of the first month, the embryo consists of millions of organized groups of cells with specific functions.

Chapter 3 Biological Foundations, Prenatal Development, and Birth

3. The Second Month
    a. The eyes, ears, nose, jaw, and neck form, and tiny buds become arms, legs, fingers, and toes.
    b. Internal organs grow more distinct.
    c. At 7 weeks, production of *neurons* (nerve cells) begins deep inside the neural tube.
    d. At the end of this period, the embryo can already sense its world, and it can move.
D. Period of the Fetus (pp. 92–94)
    1. The longest prenatal period is the period of the **fetus,** lasting from the ninth week until the end of pregnancy.
    2. In this phase, the organism increases rapidly in size, especially from the ninth to the twentieth week.
    3. The Third Month
        a. In the third month, the organs, muscles, and nervous system start to become organized and connected.
        b. By the twelfth week, the external genitals are well-formed.
        c. The heartbeat can now be heard through a stethoscope.
        d. At the end of the third month, the first *trimester*—one of the three equal periods of prenatal development—is complete.
    4. The Second Trimester
        a. By the middle of the second trimester, between 17 and 20 weeks, the mother can feel the baby's movements.
        b. A white, cheeselike substance called **vernix** covers the skin, protecting it from chapping in the amniotic fluid.
        c. White, downy hair called **lanugo** also covers the entire body, helping the vernix stick to the skin.
        d. At the end of the second trimester, many organs are well-developed, and most of the brain's billions of neurons are in place.
        e. *Glial cells,* which support and feed the neurons, continue to increase rapidly throughout the remaining months of pregnancy.
        f. At the same time, neurons begin forming *synapses,* or connections, at a rapid pace.
    5. The Third Trimester
        a. The point at which the baby can first survive, called the **age of viability,** occurs sometime between 22 and 26 weeks.
        b. The brain continues to make great strides in the third trimester.
            (1) The *cerebral cortex,* the seat of human intelligence, enlarges. Convolutions and grooves in its surface appear, permitting a dramatic increase in surface area that allows for maximum prenatal brain growth.
            (2) As neurological connectivity and organization improve, the fetus spends more time awake.
            (3) By the end of pregnancy, the fetus takes on the beginnings of a personality: Higher fetal activity in the last weeks of pregnancy predicts a more active infant in the first month of life.
        c. In the final three months, the fetus gains more than 5 pounds and grows 7 inches.
        d. The fetus receives antibodies from the mother's blood to protect against illnesses.
        e. In the last weeks, most fetuses assume an upside-down position.
        f. Growth slows, and birth is about to take place.

IV. PRENATAL ENVIRONMENTAL INFLUENCES (pp. 94–107)
    A. Although the prenatal environment is far more constant than the world outside the womb, many environmental factors can affect the embryo and fetus.
    B. Teratogens (pp. 95–103)
        1. The term **teratogen** refers to any environmental agent that causes damage during the prenatal period.
        2. The harm done by teratogens depends on the following factors:
            a. *Dose:* Larger doses over longer time periods usually have more negative effects.
            b. *Heredity:* The genetic makeup of the mother and the developing organism plays an important role.
            c. *Other negative influences:* The presence of several negative factors at once can worsen the impact of a single harmful agent.
            d. *Age:* The effects of teratogens vary with the age of the organism at the time of exposure.
        3. A *sensitive period* is a limited time span in which a part of the body or a behavior is biologically prepared to develop rapidly and will be especially sensitive to its surroundings.
            a. If damage occurs during a sensitive period, recovery is difficult and sometimes impossible.
            b. Some parts of the body, such as the brain and eye, have sensitive periods that extend throughout prenatal development.
            c. Other sensitive periods, such as those for the limbs and palate, are much shorter.

4. Some general statements about the timing of harmful influences are possible:
   a. Teratogens rarely have any impact in the *period of the zygote*, before implantation.
   b. Serious defects are most likely to occur in the *embryonic period*.
   c. During the *fetal period*, teratogenic damage is usually minor.
5. The effects of teratogens go beyond immediate physical damage, and some health outcomes are delayed.
   a. Psychological consequences may occur indirectly, as a result of physical damage.
   b. Prenatally exposed children may be less resilient in the face of environmental risks, such as single parenthood or maladaptive parenting.
6. Prescription and Nonprescription Drugs
   a. Any drug with a molecule small enough to penetrate the placental barrier can enter the embryonic or fetal bloodstream.
   b. Despite the tragic lessons about drugs and prenatal development learned from experiences of pregnant women who took drugs, such as *thalidomide* in the 1960s and *diethylstilbestrol (DES)* between 1945 and 1970, many pregnant women continue to take both prescription drugs and over-the-counter medications.
      (1) Currently, the most widely used potent teratogen is a vitamin A derivative called *Accutane*, prescribed to treat severe acne and taken by hundreds of thousands of women of childbearing age in industrialized nations.
      (2) Several studies suggest that regular use of aspirin is linked to low birth weight, infant death around the time of birth, and poorer motor development, but other research fails to confirm these findings.
   c. As amounts of caffeine exceed 100 milligrams per day (equivalent to one cup of coffee), low birth weight and miscarriage increase.
   d. Antidepressant medications are linked to increased risk of premature delivery and birth complications.
7. Illegal Drugs
   a. The use of highly addictive mood-altering drugs, such as cocaine and heroin, has become more widespread, especially in poverty-stricken inner-city areas. About 4 percent of U.S. pregnant women take these substances.
   b. Babies born to users of cocaine, heroin, or methadone are at risk for a wide variety of problems, including prematurity, low birth weight, and physical defects. Also, these infants are born drug-addicted.
   c. When mothers with many problems of their own must care for these infants, who are difficult to calm, behavior problems are likely to persist.
   d. Evidence on cocaine suggests that some prenatally exposed babies have lasting problems, including an array of physical defects and perceptual, motor, and language problems.
   e. Other investigators, however, report no major negative effects of prenatal cocaine exposure.
   f. Researchers have linked prenatal marijuana exposure to attention, memory, and academic achievement difficulties and other problems, but lasting consequences are not well-established.
   g. These contradictory findings indicate how difficult it is to isolate the precise damage caused by illegal drugs.
   h. Overall, the effects of illegal drugs are far less consistent than the impact of tobacco and alcohol.
8. Tobacco
   a. An estimated 14 percent of U.S. women smoke during their pregnancies.
   b. The best-known effect of smoking during pregnancy is low birth weight.
   c. Smoking also increases the likelihood of other serious consequences, such as miscarriage, prematurity, impaired heart rate, and infant death.
   d. Even when babies born to smoking mothers seem to be in good physical condition, slight behavioral abnormalities may threaten their development.
   e. Smoking harms the fetus through the effects of nicotine, the addictive substance in tobacco.
      (1) Nicotine constricts blood vessels, lessens blood flow to the uterus, and causes the placenta to grow abnormally.
      (2) It raises the concentration of carbon monoxide in the bloodstreams of both mother and fetus.
   f. From one-third to one-half of pregnant women are "passive smokers" whose husbands, relatives, or co-workers smoke. Passive smoking is also related to low birth weight and infant death.
9. Alcohol
   a. **Fetal alcohol spectrum disorder (FASD)** encompasses a range of physical, mental, and behavioral outcomes caused by prenatal alcohol exposure.

Chapter 3 Biological Foundations, Prenatal Development, and Birth

- b. Children with FASD receive one of three diagnoses, varying in severity:
    - (1) **Fetal alcohol syndrome (FAS),** seen in children whose mothers drank heavily throughout pregnancy, is characterized by slow physical growth; a pattern of three facial abnormalities; and brain injury, evident in a small head and impairment in at least three areas of functioning.
    - (2) **Partial fetal alcohol syndrome (p-FAS),** which occurs in children whose mothers generally drank alcohol in smaller quantities, is characterized by at least two of the facial abnormalities of FAS and brain injury, evident in at least three areas of impaired functioning.
    - (3) **Alcohol-related neurodevelopmental disorder (ARND),** which occurs when prenatal alcohol exposure is less pervasive than in FAS, is characterized by impairments in at least three areas of mental functioning, despite typical physical growth and absence of facial abnormalities.
- c. Even with enriched diets, FAS babies fail to catch up in physical size during infancy or childhood.
- d. Mental impairment associated with all three FASD diagnoses is also permanent.
- e. In adolescence and early adulthood, FASD is associated with persisting attention and motor-coordination deficits, poor school performance, and lasting mental health problems.
- f. Alcohol produces its devastating effects in two ways:
    - (1) It interferes with production and migration of neurons in the primitive neural tube, causing reduced brain size, damage to many brain structures, and abnormalities in brain functioning.
    - (2) The body uses large quantities of oxygen to metabolize alcohol, drawing away oxygen that the developing organism needs for cell growth.
- g. Even mild drinking is associated with reduced head size and body growth.

10. Radiation
    - a. Ionizing radiation can cause mutation, damaging the DNA in ova and sperm.
    - b. When mothers are exposed to radiation during pregnancy, the embryo or fetus can suffer additional harm, including underdeveloped brains and physical deformities.

11. Environmental Pollution
    - a. More than 75,000 potentially dangerous chemicals are in common use in the United States.
    - b. Research suggests that many babies are "born polluted" by industrial contaminants that not only impair prenatal development but also increase the chances of health problems.
    - c. High levels of prenatal *mercury* exposure disrupt production and migration of neurons, causing widespread brain damage.
    - d. Prenatal exposure to *polychlorinated biphenyls (PCBs),* is associated with low birth weight, brain-wave abnormalities, persisting attention and memory difficulties, and lower intelligence test scores in childhood.
    - e. Exposure to high levels of *lead* is consistently related to prematurity, low birth weight, brain damage, and physical defects.

12. Maternal Disease
    - a. Certain infectious diseases caught during pregnancy can cause extensive damage.
    - b. Viruses
        - (1) *Rubella* (three-day, or German, measles) is a well-known teratogen.
            - (a) More than 50 percent of infants whose mothers become ill during the embryonic period show deafness; eye deformities; heart, genital, and urinary abnormalities; and mental retardation.
            - (b) The organ damage inflicted by prenatal rubella often leads to lifelong health problems, including severe mental illness.
            - (c) Routine vaccination in infancy and childhood has made new rubella outbreaks unlikely in industrialized nations.
        - (2) The *human immunodeficiency virus (HIV),* which can lead to *acquired immune deficiency syndrome (AIDS),* has infected increasing numbers of women over the past two decades.
            - (a) Although the incidence of AIDS has declined in industrialized nations, the disease is rampant in developing countries, where more than half of new cases affect women.
            - (b) HIV-infected pregnant women pass the deadly virus to the fetus 20 to 30 percent of the time.
            - (c) AIDS progresses rapidly in infants; by 6 months, weight loss, diarrhea, and repeated respiratory illnesses are common. The virus also causes brain damage.
            - (d) Nearly half of prenatal AIDS babies die by 1 year of age and 90 percent by age 3.
            - (e) Antiretroviral drug treatment reduces prenatal AIDS transmission by as much as 95 percent, but these drugs are not widely available in impoverished regions of the world.

(3) The developing organism is especially sensitive to the family of herpes viruses, for which no vaccine or treatment exists.
   c. Bacterial and Parasitic Diseases
      (1) Pregnant women may develop *toxoplasmosis,* caused by a parasite found in many animals, by eating raw or undercooked meat or coming into contact with the feces of infected cats.
      (2) If it strikes during the first trimester, it is likely to cause eye and brain damage.
C. Other Maternal Factors (pp. 103–107)
   1. Exercise
      a. In healthy, physically fit women, regular moderate exercise is related to increased birth weight.
      b. However, frequent, vigorous extended exercise results in lower birth weight than in healthy nonexercising controls.
   2. Nutrition
      a. A healthy diet resulting in a maternal weight gain of 25 to 30 pounds helps ensure the health of mother and baby.
      b. Consequences of Prenatal Malnutrition
         (1) Research shows that women who were affected by famine during the first trimester were more likely to have miscarriages or give birth to babies with physical defects.
         (2) Prenatal malnutrition can cause serious damage to the central nervous system.
         (3) An inadequate diet during pregnancy can also distort the structure of other organs.
         (4) Because poor nutrition suppresses development of the immune system, prenatally malnourished babies frequently catch respiratory illnesses.
         (5) In poverty-stricken families, the effects of poor nutrition combine with those of a stressful home life.
      c. Prevention and Treatment
         (1) Providing pregnant women with adequate food has a substantial impact on the health of their newborn babies.
         (2) The growth demands of the prenatal period also require vitamin–mineral enrichment.
            (a) Taking a folic acid supplement around the time of conception reduces by more than 70 percent abnormalities of the neural tube, such as *anencephaly* and *spina bifida*.
            (b) Folic acid supplementation early in pregnancy also reduces the risk of other physical defects, including cleft lip and palate and limb deformities.
            (c) Enriching women's diets with calcium helps prevent maternal high blood pressure and low birth weight.
            (d) Adequate magnesium and zinc reduce the risk of many prenatal and birth complications.
            (e) Fortifying table salt with iodine virtually eradicates *infantile hypothyroidism,* a condition of stunted growth and cognitive impairment.
         (3) When poor nutrition continues throughout pregnancy, infants may exhibit tired, restless behavior that, in turn, leads parents to be less sensitive and stimulating; successful interventions must break this cycle of apathetic caregiver–baby interaction.
   3. Emotional Stress
      a. When women experience severe emotional stress during pregnancy, their babies are at risk for a wide variety of difficulties.
      b. Intense anxiety—especially during the first two trimesters—is associated with a higher rate of miscarriage, prematurity, low birth weight, sleep disturbances, and irritability.
      c. Maternal stress hormones cross the placenta, causing a dramatic rise in fetal stress hormones and in fetal heart rate, blood pressure, blood glucose, and activity level.
      d. Excessive fetal stress may permanently alter neurological functioning as well, thereby heightening stress reactivity in later life.
      e. Stress-related prenatal complications are greatly reduced when mothers receive social support from partners, other family members, and friends.
   4. Maternal Age
      a. Over the past 30 years, first births to women in their thirties have increased more than fourfold, and those to women in their early forties have doubled.
      b. Women who delay having children until their thirties or forties face increased risk of infertility, miscarriage, and babies born with chromosomal defects.

Chapter 3 Biological Foundations, Prenatal Development, and Birth

- c. However, research indicates that healthy women in their thirties have about the same rates of other pregnancy complications as those in their twenties. Thereafter, complication rates rise.
- d. Once a girl can conceive, even in the case of teenagers, she is also physically ready to carry and give birth to a baby.

V. CHILDBIRTH (pp. 107–109)
  A. A complex series of hormonal exchanges between mother and fetus initiates the childbirth process:
    1. *Dilation and effacement of the cervix,* the longest stage of labor, lasts an average of 12 to 14 hours with a first birth and 4 to 6 hours with later births. Contractions of the uterus gradually become more frequent and powerful, causing the cervix to widen and thin to nothing, forming a clear channel from the uterus into the birth canal, or vagina.
    2. *Delivery of the baby,* the second stage, lasts about 50 minutes for a first baby and 20 minutes in later births. Strong uterine contractions continue, but the mother also feels a natural urge to squeeze and push with her abdominal muscles, forcing the baby down and out.
    3. *Birth of the placenta,* the third stage, lasts only about 5 to 10 minutes, as a few final contractions and pushes cause the placenta to separate from the wall of the uterus and be delivered.
  B. The Baby's Adaptation to Labor and Delivery (p. 108)
    1. Strong uterine contractions expose the baby's head to a great deal of pressure, and they repeatedly squeeze the placenta and the umbilical cord, temporarily reducing the baby's supply of oxygen.
    2. Healthy babies are equipped to withstand these traumas. The force of the contractions intensifies the baby's production of stress hormones, an effect that is adaptive and prepares the baby for birth.
  C. The Newborn Baby's Appearance (p. 109)
    1. The average newborn is 20 inches long and weighs 7½ pounds; boys tend to be slightly longer and heavier than girls.
    2. The combination of a large head (with its well-developed brain) and a small body means that human infants learn quickly in the first few months of life but cannot get around on their own until much later.
    3. Newborns' typical features—round faces, chubby cheeks, large foreheads, and big eyes—make adults feel like picking them up and cuddling them.
  D. Assessing the Newborn's Physical Condition: The Apgar Scale (p. 109)
    1. To assess a newborn baby's physical condition, doctors and nurses use the **Apgar Scale,** rating the newborn 0, 1, or 2 on each of five characteristics at 1 minute and again at 5 minutes after birth.
    2. A combined Apgar score of 7 or better indicates good physical condition. Babies with a score between 4 and 6 require assistance in establishing breathing and other vital signs. A score of 3 or below indicates that the infant is in serious danger and requires emergency medical attention.

VI. APPROACHES TO CHILDBIRTH (pp. 109–112)
  A. Childbirth practices are molded by the society of which mother and baby are a part.
    1. In many village and tribal cultures, expectant mothers are well-acquainted with the childbirth process.
    2. In most nonindustrialized cultures, women are assisted—though often not by medical personnel—during labor and delivery.
    3. In Western nations, childbirth moved from home to hospital in the late 1800s.
    4. Once doctors assumed responsibility for childbirth, women's knowledge of it declined.
    5. By the 1950s and 1960s, women in the West began to question routine medical procedures used during labor and delivery. A natural childbirth movement arose in Europe and North America.
    6. Today, most hospitals offer birth centers that are family-centered and homelike.
    7. A small number of American women choose to have their babies at home.
  B. Natural, or Prepared, Childbirth (pp. 110–111)
    1. **Natural, or prepared, childbirth** consists of a group of techniques aimed at reducing pain and medical intervention and making childbirth as rewarding an experience as possible.
      a. Most natural childbirth programs draw on methods developed by Grantly Dick-Read and Ferdinand Lamaze.
      b. In a typical natural childbirth program, the expectant mother and a companion participate in *classes* to learn about labor and delivery, the expectant mothers are taught *relaxation and breathing techniques,* and the companion is trained as a *labor coach.*
    2. Social Support and Natural Childbirth
      a. Social support is important to the success of natural childbirth techniques.

(1) Studies indicate that mothers who are supported during labor and delivery—either by a lay birth attendant or by a relative or friend trained as a birth companion, or *doula*—less often have instrument-assisted or cesarean (surgical) deliveries.
(2) Also, their babies' Apgar scores are higher, and they are more likely to be breastfeeding at a two-month follow-up.
    b. The continuous rather than intermittent support of a doula during labor and delivery strengthens these outcomes.
  3. Positions for Delivery
    a. When natural childbirth is combined with delivery in a birth center or at home, mothers often give birth in an upright, sitting position.
    b. When mothers are upright, labor is shortened because pushing is more effective, and the baby benefits from a richer supply of oxygen because blood flow to the placenta is increased.
    c. Water birth is a method whereby the mother sits in a warm tub of water, which supports her weight, relaxes her, and permits her to move into a comfortable position. It is associated with shorter labor.
  C. Home Delivery (pp. 111–112)
    1. Home birth has always been popular in certain industrialized nations, such as England.
    2. The mothers who choose home birth want birth to be an important part of family life and want to have greater control over their own care and that of their babies than hospitals permit.
    3. Some home births are attended by doctors, but many more are handled by *certified nurse–midwives,* who have degrees in nursing and additional training in childbirth management.
    4. For healthy women assisted by a well-trained doctor or midwife, home birth seems to be as safe as hospital birth, since complications are rare.
    5. When mothers are at risk for any kind of complication, the appropriate place for labor and delivery is the hospital, where life-saving treatment is available.
  D. Labor and Delivery Medication (p. 112)
    1. Although natural childbirth techniques lessen or eliminate the need for pain-relieving drugs, some form of medication is used in more than 80 percent of U.S. births.
    2. *Analgesics,* drugs used to relieve pain, may be given in mild doses during labor to help a mother relax.
    3. *Anesthetics* are a stronger type of painkiller that blocks sensation.
      a. Currently, the most common approach to controlling pain during labor is *epidural analgesia,* in which a regional pain-relieving drug is delivered continuously through a catheter into a small space in the lower spine.
      b. Pain-relieving drugs can also cause problems in childbirth.
        (1) Epidural analgesia weakens uterine contractions, so that labor is prolonged.
        (2) Because drugs rapidly cross the placenta, exposed newborns tend to have lower Apgar scores.
        (3) The negative impact of these drugs on the newborn's adjustment supports the current trend to limit their use.
VII. BIRTH COMPLICATIONS (pp. 112–118, 119)
  A. Oxygen Deprivation (pp. 112–113)
    1. A small number of infants experience *anoxia,* or inadequate oxygen supply, during the birth process.
    2. Brain damage is likely if regular breathing is delayed more than 10 minutes.
    3. Anoxia also may occur during labor; a common cause is squeezing of the umbilical cord, a condition that is especially likely when infants are in **breech position,** turned in such a way that the buttocks or feet would be delivered first.
    4. Another cause of oxygen deprivation is *placenta abruptio,* or premature separation of the placenta, a life-threatening event that requires immediate delivery.
    5. Anoxia can also be caused by **Rh factor incompatibility** between the mother's and baby's blood types. It can lead to mental retardation, miscarriage, heart damage, and infant death.
    6. Research suggests that the greater the oxygen deprivation during childbirth, the poorer children's cognitive and language skills will be in early and middle childhood.
  B. Preterm and Low-Birth-Weight Infants (pp. 113–117, 118, 119)
    1. Babies born three weeks or more before the end of a full 38-week pregnancy or who weigh less than 5½ pounds at birth are referred to as "premature" and are known to be at risk for many problems.

2. Although outcomes have improved over the past several decades, many newborns who weigh less than 3½ pounds experience difficulties, such as brain abnormalities, that are not overcome—an effect that strengthens as length of pregnancy and birth weight decrease.
3. About 1 in 13 American infants is born underweight, a problem that is most common among poverty-stricken mothers.
4. Prematurity is also common in multiple births. The majority of twins and triplets are born early with low birth weights.
5. Preterm versus Small-for-Date Infants
    a. **Preterm infants** are those born several weeks or more before their due date; although they are small, their weight may still be appropriate, based on time spent in the uterus.
    b. **Small-for-date infants** are below their expected weight considering the length of the pregnancy; they may be full-term babies or preterm babies who are especially underweight.
    c. The problems of small-for-date infants are usually more serious than those of preterm infants.
        (1) During the first year, they are more likely to die and catch infections.
        (2) By middle childhood, they have lower intelligence test scores and are socially immature.
        (3) In some small-for-date infants, an abnormally functioning placenta permitted ready transfer of stress hormones from mother to fetus, leading to prenatal neurological impairments that permanently weaken the ability to manage stress.
    d. Babies born at 35 weeks, compared to those born at 34 weeks, show substantially reduced rates of illness, costly medical procedures, and lengthy hospital stays.
6. Consequences for Caregiving
    a. The appearance and behavior of preterm babies can lead parents to be less sensitive and responsive in caring for them.
    b. Compared to full-term infants, preterm babies, especially those who are very ill at birth, are less often held close, touched, and talked to gently.
    c. Research reveals that distressed, emotionally reactive preterm infants are especially susceptible to the effects of parenting quality.
7. Interventions for Preterm Infants
    a. A preterm baby is cared for in a special Plexiglas-enclosed bed called an *isolette,* in which temperature is carefully controlled because these infants cannot yet regulate their own body temperature effectively.
    b. When a preterm infant is fed through a stomach tube, breathes with the aid of a respirator, and receives medication through an intravenous needle, physical needs that otherwise would lead to close contact and other human stimulation are met mechanically.
    c. Special Infant Stimulation
        (1) Certain types of stimulation can help preterm infants develop.
        (2) Touch is an especially important form of stimulation.
            (a) Preterm infants who were massaged several times each day in the hospital gained weight faster and were more advanced in mental and motor development in the first year than preterm infants not given this stimulation.
            (b) In developing countries, skin-to-skin "kangaroo care"—in which the preterm infant is placed in a vertical position between the mother's breasts or next to the father's chest—is the most readily available intervention for promoting the survival of preterm babies.
            (c) In Western nations, kangaroo care is used as a supplement to hospital intensive care.
            (d) Kangaroo skin-to-skin contact fosters improved oxygenation of the baby's body, temperature regulation, sleep, breastfeeding, alertness, and infant survival.
    d. Training Parents in Infant Caregiving Skills
        (1) For parents with adequate economic and personal resources to care for a preterm infant, a few sessions of coaching in recognizing and responding to the baby's needs are linked to enhanced parent–infant interaction.
        (2) When preterm infants live in stressed, low-income households, long-term intensive intervention is necessary.
        (3) Findings from the Infant Health and Development Program revealed that a comprehensive intervention was associated with better intellectual functioning in children who attended the program regularly over a three-year period.

- e. Very Low Birth Weight, Environmental Advantages, and Long-Term Outcomes
    - (1) In a Canadian study, participants who had weighed between 1 and 2.2 pounds at birth resembled normal-birth-weight individuals at 22 to 25 years of age—results that appeared to be due to home, school, and societal advantages.
    - (2) A better course of action would be to prevent very low birth weight by improving overall health and social conditions.
    - (3) The United Sates has made less progress in reducing **infant mortality**—the number of deaths in the first year of life per 1,000 live births—than many other countries.
    - (4) Over the past three decades, it has slipped in the international rankings, from seventh in the 1950s to twenty-eighth in 2011.
    - (5) **Neonatal mortality**—the rate of death within the first month of life—accounts for 67 percent of the infant death rate in the United States.
    - (6) Widespread poverty and weak health-care programs for mothers and young children are largely responsible for these trends.
- C. Birth Complications, Parenting, and Resilience (p. 117)
    1. Findings from a landmark study carried out in Hawaii, on Kauai, help explain how infants who survive a traumatic birth are likely to develop.
        - a. The study findings showed that the likelihood of long-term difficulties increased if birth trauma was severe.
        - b. Among mildly to moderately stressed children, the best predictor of how well they did in later years was the quality of their home environments.
    2. The Kauai study tells us that as long as birth injuries are not overwhelming, a supportive home environment can restore children's growth.
        - a. The study also found a few exceptions—children with both fairly serious birth complications and troubled families who nevertheless grew into competent adults.
        - b. These children relied on factors outside the family and within themselves to overcome stress.

VIII. HEREDITY, ENVIRONMENT, AND BEHAVIOR: A LOOK AHEAD (pp. 118–125)
- A. **Behavioral genetics** is a field devoted to uncovering the contributions of nature and nurture to the wide diversity in human traits and abilities.
- B. Researchers agree that both heredity and environment are involved in every aspect of development, but for polygenic traits, such as intelligence and personality, they do not know the precise hereditary influences involved.
- C. Some researchers believe it is useful and possible to determine *how much each factor contributes* to differences among children, but a growing consensus regards that question as unanswerable and maintains that the important question is *how nature and nurture work together*.
- D. The Question, "How Much?" (pp. 120–121)
    1. Heritability
        - a. **Heritability estimates** measure the extent to which individual differences in complex traits in a specific population are due to genetic factors.
            - (1) They are obtained from **kinship studies,** which compare the characteristics of family members.
            - (2) The most common type of kinship study compares identical twins with fraternal twins.
        - b. Although the findings of kinship studies of intelligence are controversial, most support a moderate role for heredity.
        - c. Genetic factors are also important in personality, with moderate heritability estimates for such traits as sociability, anxiety, and activity level.
        - d. Twin studies of schizophrenia consistently yield high heritabilities.
    2. Limitations of Heritability
        - a. The accuracy of heritability estimates depends on the extent to which the twin pairs studied reflect genetic and environmental variation in the population.
        - b. Heritability estimates are controversial because they can easily be misapplied, to suggest, for example, a genetic basis for ethnic differences in intelligence.
        - c. Heritability estimates have limited usefulness because they provide no precise information on how intelligence and personality develop or how children might respond to environments designed to help them develop as much as possible.

E. The Question, "How?" (pp. 121–125)
   1. Today, most researchers view development as the result of a dynamic interplay between heredity and environment.
   2. Gene–Environment Interaction
      a. According to the concept of **gene–environment interaction,** individuals differ in their responsiveness to qualities of the environment because of their genetic makeup.
      b. This concept shows that because each of us has a unique genetic makeup, we respond differently to the same environment, but sometimes different gene–environment combinations can make two children seem the same.
      c. Recently, researchers have made strides in identifying gene–environment interactions in personality development: One study shows that young children with a gene that increases their risk of an emotionally reactive temperament respond especially strongly to variations in parenting quality.
   3. Canalization
      a. **Canalization** is the tendency of heredity to restrict the development of some characteristics to just one or a few outcomes.
      b. Behaviors that are strongly canalized, such as infant perceptual development, develop similarly in a wide range of environments.
      c. Characteristics that are less strongly canalized, such as intelligence and personality, vary much more with changes in the environment.
   4. Gene–Environment Correlation
      a. According to the concept of **gene–environment correlation,** our genes influence the environments to which we are exposed.
      b. Passive and Evocative Correlation
         (1) These two types of gene–environment correlation are common at younger ages.
         (2) *Passive* correlation occurs when children are exposed to environments provided by their parents, who are influenced by their own heredity.
         (3) *Evocative* correlation occurs when children evoke responses influenced by their heredity and these responses, in turn, strengthen the child's original style.
      c. Active Correlation
         (1) *Active* gene–environment correlation becomes common in older children as they extend their experiences beyond the immediate family and make more choices, actively seeking environments that fit with their genetic tendencies.
         (2) This tendency to actively choose environments that complement our heredity is known as **niche-picking.**
      d. The influence of heredity and environment is not constant but changes with age, as genetic factors may become more important in influencing the environments we choose for ourselves.
   5. Environmental Influences on Gene Expression
      a. Some theorists regard gene–environment correlation as entirely *driven* by genetics, but others argue that heredity does not dictate children's experiences or development in a rigid way.
      b. Evidence shows that parents and other caring adults can uncouple adverse gene–environment correlations.
      c. Accumulating evidence reveals that the relationship between heredity and environment is *bidirectional*.
         (1) Genes affect children's behavior and experiences, but their experiences and behavior also affect gene expression.
         (2) Stimulation—both *internal* to the child (such as release of hormones into the bloodstream) and *external* (such as home and school)—triggers gene activity.
      d. Researchers call this view the *epigenetic framework*. **Epigenesis** means development resulting from ongoing, bidirectional exchanges between heredity and all levels of the environment.
         (1) Animal research confirms that environment can modify the genome in ways that have no impact on a gene's sequence of base pairs but nevertheless affect the operation of that gene.
         (2) Research on maternal smoking during pregnancy reveals that smoking alters the expression of a gene associated with *attention-deficit hyperactivity disorder (ADHD)*.

LECTURE ENHANCEMENTS

LECTURE ENHANCEMENT 3.1
Psychological Adjustment in Children from Embryo Donation Families (pp. 86–87)

Time: 10–15 minutes

Objective: To provide more information about the psychological adjustment of children from embryo donation families.

Since the first test-tube baby was born in 1978, numerous reproductive techniques have emerged to help infertile couples conceive. In embryo donation, an embryo created by the gametes of one couple is donated to another couple who then raise the child. Like adopted children, children conceived using donated embryos have a family structure in which the child is not genetically related to either parent. But do children conceived from donated embryos experience adjustment problems similar to those of adopted children? To find out, MacCallum and Keeley (2008) recruited 69 school-age children—17 from donated embryo families, 24 from adoptive families, and 28 from in vitro families. The researchers collected the following information:

(1) Mothers completed a marital and psychological state rating scale, which measured the quality of the marital relationship, parenting stress, anxiety, and depression.

(2) Mothers were interviewed about their perceptions of the mother–child relationship. For example, using a 4-point scale (0 = little or none; 3 = a great deal), mothers rated their enjoyment in play and age-appropriate leisure activities with the child. Mothers also rated the level of difficulty of daily routines like bedtime, frequency of disputes, intensity of disputes, overall supervision of the child, and enjoyment of motherhood. During the interviews, the researchers coded expressed warmth, such as spontaneous expressions of warmth, sympathy, and concern about the child. Finally, emotional overinvolvement was determined by the extent to which family life was focused on the child, how overprotective or overconcerned the mother was toward the child, and whether the mother had interests or activities not involving the child.

(3) Mothers and teachers completed a rating scale of children's social and emotional development, which measured hyperactivity, conduct problems, emotional difficulties, and peer problems.

(4) Mothers were asked whether they had told their children (or intended to tell them) about their assisted conception or adoption. Mothers' responses were coded into one of four categories—already told child, intending to tell child in the future, undecided about telling child, and definitely decided not to tell child.

Results indicated that children from embryo donation and in vitro families did not differ in overall outcomes. Children from embryo donation families were well-adjusted and did not demonstrate significant emotional or behavioral problems. In contrast, adopted children were more likely than children from embryo donation families to have social and emotional problems, with especially high rates of hyperactivity. According to MacCallum and Keeley, the difference between the two groups is likely due to the prenatal environments of adopted children. Research shows that compared to children living with their biological parents, adopted children are more likely to have experienced prenatal exposure to drugs and/or alcohol, poor maternal nutrition, and inadequate prenatal care.

Another important finding was that the majority of embryo donation families—59 percent—had not informed or were not planning to inform their child of his or her origins. In contrast, 89 percent of the in vitro families either had disclosed or were planning to disclose their child's origins, and all of the adoptive families had informed their child about the adoption. Thus, it seems that embryo donation is an especially private matter for many parents. Maternal overinvolvement was particularly high in embryo donation families, which may reflect a longer period of infertility in these families than in adoptive or in vitro families. When the child finally arrives, mothers may become overly involved in all aspects of the child's life. However, this overinvolvement did not predict social or emotional problems. Finally, maternal warmth and sensitivity were equally high in all three family types.

Ask students to reflect on the decision of many embryo donation families not to disclose their child's origins. Do students agree with this decision? Why or why not? What are some possible pros and cons of informing children?

MacCallum, F., & Keeley, S. (2008). Embryo donation families: A follow-up in middle childhood. *Journal of Family Psychology, 22,* 799–808.

LECTURE ENHANCEMENT 3.2
The Relationship Between Prenatal Cortisol Exposure and Infant Development During the First Year of Life
(pp. 105–106)

Time: 5–10 minutes

Objective: To extend existing research on the effects of prenatal stress on infant development during the first year of life.

To extend existing research on the effects of prenatal stress on infant development, Davis and Sandman (2010) recruited 125 newly pregnant women and followed them until 12 months postpartum. None of the women used alcohol, drugs, or tobacco during their pregnancies, and their babies were born full-term. The researchers gathered the following information:

(1) Maternal cortisol samples were collected at five separate intervals throughout pregnancy. During each interval, expectant mothers also completed stress and depression inventories. Participants were asked about how they handled day-to-day problems, how often they felt nervous or stressed, how often they felt sad or depressed, and how anxious they felt about pregnancy, labor, and delivery.

(2) During the first prenatal visit, mothers completed a structured interview that focused on pregnancy history and risk factors that might affect pregnancy outcomes, such as infection, hypertension, diabetes, and preterm labor. Follow-up interviews were conducted during subsequent visits to identify any health-related changes.

(3) When infants were 3, 6, and 12 months old, they were given the Bayley Scales of Infant Development, 2nd Edition (BSID-II), which measures mental and motor development. Sample items include:

	Mental Scale	**Motor Scale**
3 months	Eyes follow rod	Sits with support
6 months	Lifts inverted cup	Turns from back to stomach
12 months	Responds to spoken request	Squats briefly

(4) During the 3-, 6-, and 12-month postnatal visits, mothers again completed stress and depression inventories, including the Parenting Stress Index (PSI). The PSI focuses on stress within the parent–child relationship. For example, on a scale of 1 to 5 (1 = strongly disagree; 5 = strongly agree), "I find myself giving up more of my life to meet my child's needs that I ever expected." "My child rarely does things for me that make me feel good."

Results indicated that level and timing of prenatal cortisol exposure had important consequences for development in the first year of life. Specifically, fetuses that were exposed to low levels of cortisol early in pregnancy, increasing levels as pregnancy progressed, and high levels toward the end of pregnancy scored significantly higher on the BSID-II than fetuses that were exposed to high levels of maternal cortisol throughout pregnancy. According to Davis and Sandman, although the fetus is able to withstand some early cortisol exposure, excessive amounts can have long-term detrimental consequences, such as lower mental test scores. In contrast, as pregnancy progresses, increasing levels of maternal cortisol is adaptive—necessary and beneficial for development of fetal organ systems.

Findings also indicated that maternal reports of pregnancy-specific anxiety—more so than day-to-day anxiety or depression—predicted infant performance on the BSID-II. This suggests that pregnancy-specific anxiety differs from other types of anxiety and is more likely to be transmitted to the fetus. As with cortisol exposure, high levels of pregnancy-specific anxiety early in gestation were related to lower BSID-II scores at 12 months. It is important to note that women who reported high levels of pregnancy-specific anxiety also produced especially high levels of cortisol. The cortical–BSID-II relationship remained strong even after controlling for demographic variables and postnatal reports of parent–child stress.

Besides lower mental test scores, what are some additional consequences of prenatal exposure to stress? Identify several strategies for reducing excessive maternal stress during pregnancy.

Davis, E. P., & Sandman, C. A. (2010). The timing of prenatal exposure to maternal cortisol and psychosocial stress is associated with human infant cognitive development. *Child Development, 81,* 131–148.

LECTURE ENHANCEMENT 3.3
Does Childbirth Method Affect Maternal Responsiveness? (pp. 110–112)

Time: 10–15 minutes

Objective: To examine whether or not childbirth method affects maternal responsiveness to infant crying.

Although cesarean delivery is necessary for certain medical emergencies, such as Rh incompatibility or premature separation of the placenta from the uterus, there has been a dramatic increase in needless cesareans. Compared to a vaginal birth, a cesarean requires more time for recovery. Also, anesthetics may cross the placenta, making newborns sleepy and unresponsive and at increased risk for breathing difficulties. But does cesarean delivery decrease a mother's responsiveness to her newborn baby? To find out, Swain and colleagues (2009) recruited 12 first-time mothers. Six of the mothers had vaginal deliveries (VD) and six had elective cesarean section deliveries (CSD). All of the mothers were married, lived in middle- and upper-class neighborhoods, and had similar educational backgrounds.

Between 2 and 4 weeks postpartum, mothers were interviewed about their experiences as a new parent. The researchers also performed functional magnetic resonance imaging (fMRI) on each mother. Prior to conducting the fMRI, mothers were asked to record their newborn's cries during the mild discomfort of a diaper change. During the fMRI, mothers heard recordings of their own baby's cry, another baby's cry, and white noise, or static. At 10-second intervals, the mothers were asked to press a button indicating the intensity of their emotional response to the noise (0 = none, 1 = a little, 2 = a lot, 3 = maximal).

Overall, no significant differences were found between VD and CSD mothers' emotional reactions to another baby's cry or to white noise. However, the brains of VD mothers were significantly more responsive to their own infant's cry than the brains of CSD mothers. VD mothers were also more responsive to their own baby's cry than to another baby's cry. This difference was particularly noticeable in emotional centers of the brain that control empathy and emotion regulation. Swain and colleagues point out that compared to cesarean delivery, vaginal delivery involves the release of oxytocin, which increases maternal responsiveness to the newborn. In addition, VD mothers are usually able to touch and interact with their babies immediately after birth, while CSD mothers may be separated from their babies while recovering from anesthesia and surgery.

Taken together, these findings suggest that childbirth method may contribute to maternal responsiveness after birth. Increased maternal responsiveness, in turn, may lead to more accurate predictions of the baby's needs and possibly facilitate bonding.

Have students return to Chapter 2 and review research methods for studying human development. What type of research design was used in this study? What are some strengths and limitations of this study?

Swain, J. E., Tasgin, E., Mayes, L. C., Feldman, R., Constable, R. T., & Leckman, J. F. (2009). Maternal brain response to own baby-cry is affected by cesarean section delivery. *Journal of Child Psychology and Psychiatry, 49,* 1042–1052.

LECTURE ENHANCEMENT 3.4
Illustrating Gene–Environment Correlation: The Heritability of Life Events (pp. 122–124)

Time: 5–10 minutes

Objective: To extend existing research on gene–environment correlation by investigating the heritability of life events.

To extend existing research on gene–environment correlation, Bemmels and colleagues (2008) recruited 618 pairs of same-sex adolescent twins, 244 pairs of same-sex adopted adolescent and young adult siblings, and 128 pairs of same-sex biological siblings. Each participant completed the Life Events interview, which measures dependent, familial, and independent life experiences.

- An event was classified as dependent if the participant had control over or inadvertently caused it. For example, "Have you failed a course in school?" "Have you ever had a serious problem with a close friend?" "Were you ever sent to a juvenile detention facility?"
- An event was classified as familial if everyone in the family experienced it but it was independent of the participant's behavior. For example, "Are your parents divorced?" "Has a member of your family killed him- or herself?" "Has your family ever moved to a new neighborhood?"
- An event was classified as independent if it was not familial and the participant's behavior did not likely contribute to it. For example, "Has your body begun to change or develop due to puberty?" "Was a close friend of yours ever seriously hurt?" "Have you ever been mugged or robbed?"

Results indicated that individual differences in dependent life events—and only dependent life events—were strongly influenced by genetic factors. That is, compared to same-sex adopted siblings and same-sex biological siblings, identical twins were more likely to report similar stressful events that were influenced by personal actions, such as failing a course, having a serious problem with a close friend, or getting into legal trouble. Consistent with previous research, familial life events were primarily influenced by shared environmental experiences, whereas independent life events were primarily influenced by nonshared environmental experiences. These findings support the notion that events that are random and outside of one's control are not heritable, whereas those in which we have some control are influenced by genetic factors.

Using findings from this study and research in the text, how does niche-picking help explain why identical twin pairs are more likely than adopted and biological siblings to experience similar life events?

Bemmels, H. R., Burt, S. A., Legrand, L. N., Iacono, W. G., & McGue, M. (2008). The heritability of life events: An adolescent twin and adoption study. *Twin Research and Human Genetics, 11,* 257–265.

LEARNING ACTIVITIES

LEARNING ACTIVITY 3.1
Observing Similarities and Differences in Phenotypes Among Family Members (p. 73)

Have students jot down the most obvious similarities in physical characteristics and behavior for several children and parents whom they know well (for example, height, weight, eye and hair color, personality, interests, hobbies). Did they find that one child shows combined features of both parents, another resembles just one parent, or another is unlike either parent?

Next, ask students to trace a visible genetic trait (phenotype), such as hair or eye color, through as many of their family members as possible. When the genetic family tree is complete, try to determine genotypes. Note that you must begin with the most recent generation and work back. Also note that inferences must be made because homozygosity and heterozygosity cannot be determined for some dominant traits. For example, it may not be known whether someone is homozygous for dark hair or heterozygous—that is, a genetic makeup consisting of a dominant dark-hair and a recessive light-hair gene. Have students explain how differences among family members in the first activity may have occurred. Integrate the terms *phenotype, genotype, meiosis,* and *crossing over* into the discussion.

LEARNING ACTIVITY 3.2
Demonstrating Environmental Influence by Comparing Identical Twins (p. 76)

As discussed in the text, identical, or monozygotic, twins have the same genetic makeup—that is, they are genetically identical clones. Phenotypic variation of identical twins is perhaps the best evidence of the extent to which environmental influences can modify genetic expression. To demonstrate, invite a pair of identical twins (who are friends or relatives of a class member) to join your class for observation and interviews. Before the visit, have students generate a list of questions that they would like to ask each twin. These questions should be based on attributes or abilities that are thought to have a strong genetic component. For example, students may want to ask each twin questions about IQ, personality, interests, and talents. Students should also note any physical differences between the twins (for example, height, weight, handedness). After the visit, engage students in a discussion about similarities and differences among the twins, including how the environment may have contributed to differences.

LEARNING ACTIVITY 3.3
Identifying Dominant and Recessive Characteristics (p. 77)

Present the following exercise as an in-class activity or quiz.

Directions: Read each of the following sentences and indicate whether the individual has dominant (D) or recessive (R) characteristics.

_____ 1. Joe has Type A blood.
_____ 2. Raul is farsighted.
_____ 3. Megan has blond hair.
_____ 4. Jamar is double-jointed.
_____ 5. Eva has Type O blood.
_____ 6. Coral has straight hair.
_____ 7. Indria has facial dimples.
_____ 8. Grace is nearsighted.
_____ 9. Vinny has albinism.
_____ 10. Yan has Rh-positive blood.

Answers:

1. D   6. R
2. D   7. D
3. R   8. R
4. D   9. R
5. R   10. D

LEARNING ACTIVITY 3.4
True or False: Prenatal Development (pp. 88–94)

Present the following activity as an in-class assignment or quiz.

Directions: Read each of the following statements and determine whether it is *True* (T) or *False* (F).

Statements:
_____ 1. Fertilization usually takes place in the fallopian tube.
_____ 2. As many as 50 percent of zygotes do not survive the first two weeks.
_____ 3. During the period of the fetus, the most rapid prenatal changes take place.
_____ 4. At first, the nervous system develops the fastest.
_____ 5. In the second month of pregnancy, the eyes, ears, nose, jaw, and neck form.
_____ 6. The period of the fetus is the longest prenatal period.
_____ 7. Brain weight doubles from the 20th week until birth.
_____ 8. The age of viability occurs sometime between 22 and 26 weeks.
_____ 9. By 28 weeks, fetuses are awake about 30 percent of the time.
_____ 10. Higher fetal activity in the last weeks of pregnancy predicts a more passive infant in the first month of life.

Answers:

1. T   6. T
2. F   7. F
3. F   8. T
4. T   9. F
5. T   10. F

LEARNING ACTIVITY 3.5
Viewing Ultrasound Pictures and Videos (pp. 88–94)

Ultrasound examinations have become a routine screening device during pregnancy. Students may have access to their own or others' ultrasound pictures or videos. Ask students to share these pictures or videos in class, noting the observable physical features of fetuses of different prenatal ages. Videos of the ultrasounds of twins and triplets are especially interesting. Ask students to describe the types of information that can be learned through ultrasound examinations. If students bring videos to class, have them preview the footage so that they know when to "fast-forward" to a new prenatal age or physical feature.

LEARNING ACTIVITY 3.6
Examining Genetic and Environmental Vulnerability to Teratogens (pp. 95–106)

The term *teratogen* refers to any environmental agent that causes damage during the prenatal period. However, genes influence the extent to which the developing organism is affected by teratogens. In small groups, have student generate a list of genetic and environmental factors that might contribute to a developing baby's susceptibility to the effects of teratogens. Once students have completed the activity, ask them to share some examples with the class.

LEARNING ACTIVITY 3.7
Speaking to Pregnant Women About Prenatal Environmental Influences (pp. 95–106)

Present the following scenario to students:

> You have been asked by a local health department to speak to a group of newly pregnant women about prenatal environmental influences. What information would you include in your discussion? For example, what should the women know about teratogens? How about maternal disease, exercise, and nutrition? What recommendations would you give to promote a healthy pregnancy? Use research in your text to support your answers.

LEARNING ACTIVITY 3.8
Creating a Pamphlet for Expectant Fathers (pp. 88–94, 107–112)

Using research throughout the chapter, ask students to create a pamphlet detailing the process of pregnancy and childbirth for expectant fathers. For example, what changes can the father expect in his partner? What changes do the embryo and fetus undergo during each trimester? Why is nutrition so important during pregnancy? What will the newborn look like? How can he support the mother during pregnancy and childbirth? Why is social support important for both mother and baby?

LEARNING ACTIVITY 3.9
Discussing Birth Experiences (pp. 107–112)

Invite students or former students who have recently given birth to come to class to discuss their experiences. If no one is available, students often have friends or relatives who are willing to come to class. If possible, invite at least two women or couples who have recently given birth. Students in the class should prepare questions in advance to ask of the panel of guests. For example, how active was the fetus during the pregnancy? Did the mother experience morning sickness? Did the mother experience any complications during her pregnancy or delivery? Did she have the baby at home, in a birth center, or in a hospital? Who was present at the birth? What did she think about the newborn's appearance? If you can recruit more than one mother or couple, students can examine differences in birth experiences by asking questions such as: How long were you in labor? How many children have you had? What were the differences in length of each labor? Did you use medication during labor and delivery? Did you take natural childbirth classes? If so, were the classes helpful? What was the father's (or other coach's) role during labor and delivery?

LEARNING ACTIVITY 3.10
Identifying the Multiple Origins of Low Birth Weight (pp. 95–106, 113–114)

One cause of low birth weight is unpreventable physical defects. However, many other causes are preventable, such as maternal drug use, cigarette smoking, and emotional stress. In addition, mothers from poverty-stricken ethnic minority homes have increased chances of having underweight babies due to malnutrition and exposure to harmful environmental influences.

In small groups, have students list factors that increase the chances that a baby will be born underweight. Which of the factors cited could be prevented by better health care for mothers and babies? What interventions are available to babies born underweight?

LEARNING ACTIVITY 3.11
Exploring Epigenesis (p. 124)

Have students review the definition and example of epigenesis on page 124 of the text. Next, ask them to form small groups and create two scenarios—one that would likely enhance gene expression and one that would likely dampen gene expression. For example, providing an economically at-risk preschooler with intensive early intervention promotes cognitive and social and emotional growth, which translates into better academic performance and peer relations on entering school, thereby transforming gene expression. In contrast, not providing the same preschooler with early intervention and denying him or her appropriate environmental stimulation can dampen gene expression so severely that later intervention has little impact. As this example illustrates, gene–environment exchanges can contribute to vastly different outcomes in the same child.

ASK YOURSELF . . .

REVIEW: Cite evidence indicating that both heredity and environment contribute to the development of children with PKU and Down syndrome. (pp. 77–79, 82)

In *PKU* (*phenylketonuria*), one of the most frequently occurring recessive disorders, infants born with two recessive alleles lack an enzyme that converts one of the basic amino acids that make up proteins (phenylalanine) into a byproduct essential for body functioning (tyrosine). Without this enzyme, phenylalanine quickly builds to toxic levels that damage the central nervous system. By 1 year, infants born with PKU are permanently retarded. However, despite its potentially damaging effects, PKU provides an excellent illustration of the fact that inheriting unfavorable genes does not always lead to an untreatable condition. All U.S. states require that newborns be given a blood test for PKU. Affected newborns who are placed on a diet low in phenylalanine usually attain an average level of intelligence and have a normal lifespan, although they show mild deficits in certain cognitive skills.

Down syndrome, the most common chromosomal disorder, occurs in 1 out of every 770 live births. In 95 percent of cases, it results from a failure of the twenty-first pair of chromosomes to separate during meiosis, so the new individual inherits three of these chromosomes rather than the normal two. In other, less frequent forms, an extra twenty-first chromosome is attached to part of another chromosome (called a *translocation* pattern), or an error occurs during the early stages of mitosis, causing some but not all body cells to have the defective chromosomal makeup (called *mosaic* pattern). The mosaic type involves less genetic material, so symptoms may be less extreme.

Because of medical advances, fewer individuals with Down syndrome die early than was the case in the past. Many survive into their fifties and a few live even longer, although those who live past age 40 are likely to show symptoms of Alzheimer's disease, the most common form of dementia, which is linked to genes on chromosome 21. Other environmental factors also influence how well children with Down syndrome fare. These children develop most favorably when their parents encourage them to engage with their surroundings. They also benefit from infant and preschool intervention programs, although emotional, social, and motor skills improve more than intellectual performance. As with PKU, even though Down syndrome is a genetic disorder, environmental factors play a key role in how well affected children fare.

REVIEW: Using your knowledge of X-linked inheritance, explain why males are more vulnerable than females to miscarriage, infant death, genetic disorders, and other problems. (p. 80)

When a harmful allele is carried on the X chromosome, X-linked inheritance applies. Males are more likely to be affected because their sex chromosomes do not match. In females, any recessive allele on one X chromosome has a good chance of being suppressed by a dominant allele on the other X. But the Y chromosome is only about one-third as long and therefore lacks many corresponding alleles to override those on the X.

Besides X-linked disorders, many other sex differences reveal the male to be at a disadvantage. Rates of miscarriage, infant and childhood deaths, birth defects, learning disabilities, behavior disorders, and mental retardation all are greater for boys. It is possible that these sex differences can be traced to the genetic code, in that the female, with two X chromosomes, benefits from a greater variety of genes.

CONNECT: Referring to ecological systems theory (Chapter 1, pages 26–28), explain why parents of children with genetic disorders often experience increased stress. What factors, within and beyond the family, can help these parents support their children's development? (p. 82)

Ecological systems theory views the child as developing within a complex system of relationships affected by multiple levels of the surrounding environment. Caring for a disabled child can be expensive, exhausting, and stressful for parents. In addition to their daily caretaking needs, children with genetic disorders often require special medical and educational services. For example, infants with Down syndrome smile less readily, show poorer eye-to-eye contact, have weak muscle tone, and explore objects less persistently. However, when parents encourage them to engage with their surroundings, children with Down syndrome develop more favorably. From the perspective of ecological systems theory, factors in the mesosystem—for example, the availability of specialized infant and preschool intervention programs—can help these parents support their children's development, both by providing experiences that promote the child's physical and cognitive development and by relieving the parent of the sole burden of caring for the child.

APPLY: Gilbert's genetic makeup is homozygous for dark hair. Jan's is homozygous for blond hair. What color is Gilbert's hair? How about Jan's? What proportion of their children are likely to be dark-haired? Explain. (p. 77)

Because homozygous individuals inherit similar genes from both parents, they will always display the inherited trait. As a result, Gilbert will have dark hair, and Jan will have blond hair. Gilbert can pass on only the dominant dark-hair gene, so all of his and Jan's children will have dark hair. However, because Jan can only pass on the blond-hair gene, all of their children will be heterozygous and, therefore, will be carriers of the gene for blond hair.

REVIEW: Why is genetic counseling called a *communication process?* Who should seek it? (p. 84)

Genetic counseling is called a communication process because it is designed to help couples assess their chances of giving birth to a baby with a hereditary disorder and choose the best course of action in view of risks and family goals. If a family history of mental retardation, psychological disorders, physical defects, or inherited diseases exists, the genetic counselor interviews the couple and prepares a *pedigree,* a picture of the family tree in which affected relatives are identified. The pedigree is used to estimate the likelihood that parents will have an abnormal child, based on genetic principles. For many disorders, molecular genetic analyses (in which DNA is examined) can reveal whether the parent is a carrier of the harmful gene. When all the relevant information is in, the genetic counselor communicates the information to the prospective parents and helps them consider appropriate options—whether to take a chance and conceive, adopt a child, or choose from among a variety of reproductive technologies.

Individuals should seek counseling if they have had difficulties bearing children—for example, repeated miscarriages—or know that genetic problems exist in their families. In addition, women who delay childbearing past age 35 are often candidates for genetic counseling because the overall rate of chromosomal abnormalities rises sharply after that age.

REVIEW: Describe the ethical pros and cons of fetal surgery, surrogate motherhood, and postmenopausal-assisted childbearing. (pp. 84–87)

Reproductive technologies, including fetal surgery, surrogate motherhood, and postmenopausal-assisted childbearing, are evolving faster than societies can weigh the ethics of these procedures. Surgery has been performed to repair fetal heart, lung, and diaphragm malformations, urinary tract obstructions, and neural defects; blood transfusions have been given to fetuses with blood disorders and bone marrow transplants to those with immune deficiencies. These techniques frequently result in complications, the most common being premature labor and miscarriage. Currently, the medical profession is struggling with how to help parents make informed decisions about fetal surgery.

Surrogate motherhood is a controversial form of medically assisted conception in which in vitro fertilization may be used to impregnate a woman (the surrogate) with a couple's fertilized ovum, or, alternatively, sperm from a man whose partner is infertile may be used to inseminate the surrogate. The surrogate receives a fee for her childbearing services and, in return, agrees to turn the baby over to the natural father. Although most of these arrangements proceed smoothly, those that end up in court highlight the serious risks for all concerned. In one case, both parties rejected the infant with severe disabilities that resulted from the pregnancy. In several others, the surrogate mother wanted to keep the baby, or the couple changed their minds during the pregnancy. These children came into the world in the midst of conflict that threatened to last for years.

Doctors have used donor ova from younger women in combination with in vitro fertilization to help postmenopausal women become pregnant. Most recipients are in their forties, but some in their fifties and sixties, and a few at age 70, have given birth. These cases raise questions about bringing children into the world whose parents may not live to see them reach adulthood. Based on U.S. life-expectancy data, 1 in 3 mothers and 1 in 2 fathers who have a baby at age 55 will die before their child enters college.

APPLY: Imagine that you must counsel a couple considering in vitro fertilization using donor ova to overcome infertility. What medical and ethical risks would you raise? (p. 86)

The couple should be told that in vitro fertilization poses greater risks than natural conception to infant survival and healthy development. About 50 percent of in vitro procedures result in multiple births, usually twins but also triplets and higher-order multiples. Consequently, among in vitro babies, the rate of low birth weight is 2.6 times as high as in the general population. Risk of major birth defects also doubles because of many factors, including drugs used to induce ripening of ova and delays in fertilizing ova outside the womb.

Further, the couple should be told that the overall success rate of in vitro fertilization is only about 35 percent and that success declines steadily with age, from 40 percent in women younger than age 35 to just 8 percent in those age 43 and older. They should be informed that in many countries, including the United States, doctors are not required to keep records of donor characteristics, so that information about the child's genetic background may not be available in the case of serious disease. Finally, the couple should be made aware of the serious ethical concerns surrounding the in vitro "sex sorter" method, which may encourage parental sex selection.

REFLECT: Imagine that you are a carrier of fragile X syndrome and want to have children. Would you choose pregnancy, adoption, or surrogacy? If you became pregnant, would you opt for prenatal diagnosis? Explain. (pp. 84–87)

This is an open-ended question with no right or wrong answer.

REVIEW: Why is the period of the embryo regarded as the most dramatic prenatal period? Why is the period of the fetus called the "growth and finishing" phase? (pp. 91–94)

The period of the embryo lasts from implantation through the eighth week of pregnancy. During these brief six weeks, the most rapid prenatal changes take place, as the groundwork is laid for all body structures and internal organs. Because all parts of the body are forming, the embryo is especially vulnerable to interference with healthy development.

The period of the fetus is the longest prenatal period, extending from the ninth week to the end of pregnancy. It is called the "growth and finishing" phase because it is the period when the organism increases rapidly in size, especially from the ninth to the twentieth week.

CONNECT: How is brain development related to fetal capacities and behavior? What implications do individual differences in fetal behavior have for the baby's temperament after birth? (pp. 92–93)

Brain growth means new behavioral capacities. The 20-week-old fetus, for example, can be stimulated as well as irritated by sounds. If a doctor looks inside the uterus using fetoscopy, fetuses try to shield their eyes from the light with their hands, indicating that sight has begun to emerge. During the last three months of pregnancy, the brain continues to make great strides. The *cerebral cortex,* the seat of human intelligence, enlarges. As neural connectivity and organization improve, the fetus spends more time awake. At 20 weeks, fetal heart rate reveals no periods of alertness; by 28 weeks, fetuses are awake about 11 percent of the time, a figure that rises to 16 percent just before birth. Between 30 and 34 weeks, fetuses show rhythmic alternations between sleep and wakefulness that gradually increase in organization.

By the end of pregnancy, the fetus reveals the beginnings of a personality. Higher fetal activity in the last weeks of pregnancy predicts a more active infant in the first month of life. Fetal activity is linked in other ways to infant temperament. In one study, more active fetuses during the third trimester became 1-year-olds who could better handle frustration and 2-year-olds who were less fearful, in that they more readily interacted with toys and with an unfamiliar adult in a laboratory. Fetal activity level may be an indicator of healthy neurological development, which fosters adaptability in childhood.

APPLY: Amy, two months pregnant, wonders how the developing organism is being fed and what parts of the body have formed. "I don't look pregnant yet, so does that mean not much development has taken place?" she asks. How would you respond to Amy? (pp. 89–91)

The first trimester of pregnancy is the time of the most rapid prenatal changes. By the end of the second week, tiny blood vessels called villi emerge from a protective membrane called the chorion. As these villi burrow into the uterine wall, the placenta starts to develop. This special organ brings the mother's and the embryo's blood close together, permitting food and oxygen to reach the developing organism and waste products to be carried away. The placenta is connected to the developing organism by the umbilical cord, which contains one large vein that delivers blood loaded with nutrients and two arteries that remove waste products.

From the second through the eighth week of pregnancy, the period of the embryo, the foundation is laid for all body structures and internal organs. At first, the nervous system develops fastest; at the same time, the heart begins to pump blood, and muscles, backbone, ribs, and digestive tract appear. In the second month, the eyes, ears, nose, jaw, neck, arms, legs, fingers, and toes form. Internal organs become more distinct; for example, the heart develops separate chambers. The intestines grow, and the liver and spleen take over production of blood cells. At the end of this period, the embryo responds to touch and is able to move, although its tiny flutters are too light to be felt by the mother.

In these first two months—often, before the mother even knows that she is pregnant—a great deal of development has taken place: The developing organism has already become a complex being.

REVIEW: Why is it difficult to determine the prenatal effects of many environmental agents, such as drugs and pollution? (pp. 95–96)

It is difficult to determine the effects of some environmental agents on the developing organism because the harm done by teratogens is not always simple and straightforward. The effects of teratogens depend on the dose, the genetic makeup of the mother and the developing organism, other negative influences (including poor nutrition, lack of medical care, and additional teratogens), and the age of the organism at the time of exposure. Further, the effects of teratogens go beyond immediate physical damage. Some health outcomes are delayed and may not show up for decades. Psychological consequences may occur indirectly, as a result of physical damage, and prenatally exposed children may be less resilient in the face of environmental risks, such as single parenthood, parental emotional disturbance, or maladaptive parenting. As a result, their long-term adjustment may be compromised.

CONNECT: List teratogens and other maternal factors that affect brain development during the prenatal period. Using Figure 3.9 on page 95, explain why the central nervous system is often affected when the prenatal environment is compromised. (pp. 95–106)

Teratogens that affect prenatal brain growth include prescription and nonprescription drugs, illegal drugs (such as cocaine, heroin, and marijuana), tobacco, alcohol, ionizing radiation, environmental pollution, and maternal disease. Other maternal factors that affect the embryo and fetus include exercise, nutrition, emotional stress, and maternal age.

During prenatal development, each organ or body structure has a sensitive period or limited time span during which its development may be disturbed. Some parts of the body, such as the brain and eye, have sensitive periods that extend throughout prenatal development. Although teratogenic damage is usually minor during the fetal period, the brain, as well as other organs such as the ears, eyes, teeth, and genitals, can still be strongly affected.

APPLY: Nora, pregnant for the first time, believes that a few cigarettes and a glass of wine a day won't be harmful. Provide Nora with research-based reasons for not smoking or drinking. (pp. 98–100)

Nora should be told that both smoking and drinking alcohol can be harmful to the developing baby. The best-known effect of smoking during the prenatal period is low birth weight. Other serious consequences may include miscarriage, prematurity, cleft lip and palate, impaired heart rate and breathing during sleep, infant death, and asthma and cancer later in childhood. Even when a baby of a smoking mother appears to be born in good physical condition, slight behavioral abnormalities may threaten the child's development. Newborns of smoking mothers are less attentive to sounds, display more muscle tension, are more excitable when touched and visually stimulated, and more often have colic—findings that suggest subtle negative effects on brain development. Consistent with this view, prenatally exposed youngsters tend to have shorter attention spans, difficulties with impulsivity and overactivity, poorer memories, lower mental test scores, and higher levels of disruptive, aggressive behavior. Drinking during pregnancy is linked to fetal alcohol spectrum disorder (FASD), which encompasses a range of physical, mental, and behavioral outcomes that vary in severity in relation to how heavily the expectant mother drank. The most severe FASD diagnosis, fetal alcohol syndrome (FAS), is characterized by slow physical growth, distinctive facial abnormalities, and brain injury, evident in a small head and impairment in at least three areas of cognitive functioning. A less severe diagnosis, partial fetal alcohol syndrome (p-FAS), seen in children whose mothers drank alcohol in smaller quantities during pregnancy, is also characterized by facial abnormalities and brain injury, again evident in at least three areas of impaired functioning. Even the least severe FASD diagnosis, alcohol-related neurodevelopmental disorder (ARND), involves at least three areas of impaired mental functioning, despite typical physical growth and absence of facial abnormalities.

The more alcohol a woman consumes during pregnancy, the poorer the child's motor coordination, speed of information processing, attention, memory, reasoning, and intelligence and achievement test scores during the preschool and school years. In adolescence and early adulthood, FASD is associated with attention and motor-coordination deficits, poor school performance, trouble with the law, inappropriate social and sexual behaviors, alcohol and drug abuse, and lasting mental health problems, including high stress reactivity and depression.

Other genetic and environmental factors can make some fetuses more vulnerable to teratogens, and even mild drinking—less than one drink per day—is associated with some of the symptoms of FASD. Because of these risks, Nora should be advised to avoid tobacco and alcohol altogether.

REFLECT: If you had to choose five environmental influences to publicize in a campaign aimed at promoting healthy prenatal development, which ones would you choose, and why? (pp. 94–106)
   This is an open-ended question with no right or wrong answer.

REVIEW: Describe the features and benefits of natural childbirth. What aspect contributes greatly to favorable outcomes, and why? (pp. 110–111)
   Natural, or prepared, childbirth consists of a group of techniques aimed at reducing pain and medical intervention and making childbirth as rewarding an experience as possible. In a typical natural childbirth program, the expectant mother and a companion (a partner, relative, or friend) participate in three activities:
   Classes: The expectant mother and her companion attend a series of classes in which they learn about the anatomy and physiology of labor and delivery. Knowledge about the birth process reduces a mother's fear.
   Relaxation and breathing techniques: Expectant mothers are taught relaxation and breathing exercises aimed at counteracting the pain of uterine contractions.
   Labor coach: The companion learns how to help during childbirth by reminding the mother to relax and breathe, massaging her back, supporting her body, and offering encouragement and affection.
   Social support is important to the success of natural childbirth techniques. Studies have shown that mothers who had a trained lay attendant, or doula, who stayed with them throughout labor and delivery, talking to them, holding their hands, and rubbing their backs to support relaxation, had fewer birth complications and shorter labors than women who did not have supportive companionship. Other studies indicate that mothers who are supported during labor and delivery—either by a lay birth attendant or by a relative or friend with doula training—less often have instrument-assisted or cesarean (surgical) deliveries or need medication to control pain. Their babies' Apgar scores are higher, and they are more likely to be breastfeeding at a two-month follow-up.

CONNECT: Contrast the positive impact of the baby's production of stress hormones during childbirth with the negative impact of maternal stress on the fetus, discussed on pages 105–106. (p. 108)
   During pregnancy, maternal stress causes the release of stimulant hormones into the bloodstream. As a result, large amounts of blood are sent to parts of the body involved in the defensive response—the brain, the heart, and muscles in the arms, legs, and trunk. Blood flow to other organs, including the uterus, is reduced, depriving the fetus of a full supply of oxygen and nutrients. Maternal stress hormones also cross the placenta, causing a dramatic rise in fetal stress hormones and in fetal heart rate, blood pressure, blood glucose, and activity level. These processes are believed to increase the lifelong risk of serious illnesses, such as cardiovascular disease and diabetes. Excessive fetal stress also may permanently alter fetal neurological functioning, thereby heightening stress reactivity in later life.
   During childbirth, the force of the uterine contractions intensifies the baby's production of stress hormones. But in contrast to the effects of maternal stress during pregnancy, high levels of infant cortisol and other stress hormones are adaptive during childbirth. By sending a rich supply of blood to the brain and heart, they help the baby withstand oxygen deprivation. In addition, stress hormones prepare the baby to breathe by causing the lungs to absorb any remaining fluid and by expanding the bronchial tubes. Finally, stress hormones arouse infants into alertness so they are born wide awake, ready to interact with their world.

APPLY: On seeing her newborn baby for the first time, Caroline exclaimed, "Why is she so out of proportion?" What observations prompted Caroline to ask this question? Explain why her baby's appearance is adaptive. (p. 109)
   The newborn's body proportions are often surprising to first-time parents. The infant's head is large in relation to the trunk and legs, which are short and bowed. This combination of a large head (with its well-developed brain) and a small body is adaptive, equipping human infants to learn quickly in the first few months of life. And some aspects of newborns' appearance—their round faces, chubby cheeks, large foreheads, and big eyes—make adults feel like picking them up and cuddling them. This is also adaptive because, unlike most other mammals, human babies cannot get around on their own until much later.

REFLECT: If you were an expectant parent, would you choose home birth? Why or why not? (pp. 111–112)
   This is an open-ended question with no right or wrong answer.

REVIEW: Sensitive care can help preterm infants recover, but they are less likely than full-term newborns to receive such care. Explain why. (pp. 114–115)

Preterm infants have a special need for sensitive attention and for certain kinds of stimulation that can help them develop; distressed, emotionally reactive preterm infants are especially susceptible to the effects of parenting quality. However, the appearance and behavior of these babies can lead parents to be less sensitive and responsive in caring for them. Compared to full-term infants, preterm babies are less often held close, touched, and talked to gently. Preterm infants are often sleepy and unresponsive when touched and irritable during the short periods when they are awake. At times, mothers of these infants resort to interfering pokes and verbal commands, in an effort to obtain a higher level of response. This may explain why preterm babies as a group are at risk for child abuse.

In the hospital, a preterm baby is placed in a special Plexiglas-enclosed bed called an isolette, and physical needs that otherwise would lead to close contact and other human stimulation are met mechanically. As a result, preterm infants are less likely to receive sensitive care.

CONNECT: List factors discussed in this chapter that increase the chances that an infant will be born underweight. How many of these factors could be prevented by better health care for expectant mothers and babies? (pp. 113–117, 118–119)

Researchers divide low-birth-weight babies into two groups: *preterm* and *small-for-date*. Preterm infants are born several weeks or more before their due date. Although they are small, their weight may still be appropriate, based on time spent in the uterus. Small-for-date infants are below their expected weight considering length of the pregnancy. Of the two types of babies, small-for-date infants usually have more serious problems. These infants probably experienced inadequate nutrition before birth. Perhaps their mothers did not eat properly, the placenta did not function normally, or the babies themselves had defects that prevented them from growing as they should. They are especially likely to suffer from neurological impairments that permanently weaken their capacity to manage stress.

Low birth weight can result from maternal exposure to teratogens, or environmental agents that cause damage during the prenatal period, including prescription and nonprescription drugs, illegal drugs, tobacco, alcohol, ionizing radiation, environmental pollution, and infectious diseases. Other maternal factors that can lead to low birth weight include poor health, lack of exercise, malnutrition, and emotional stress.

To create a safe environment for prenatal development, it is important for a woman to make healthy lifestyle choices even before she becomes pregnant. These include regular exercise, good nutrition, and avoidance of exposure to teratogens. Although some premature births are unavoidable (for example, twins and other multiples are more likely to be born early and low birth weight), many others can be prevented by improving prenatal nutrition and prenatal health care and by avoiding teratogens before and during the pregnancy.

APPLY: Cecilia and Adena each gave birth to a 3-pound baby seven weeks preterm. Cecilia is single and poverty-stricken. Adena and her partner are happily married and earn a good income. Plan an intervention appropriate for helping each baby develop. (pp. 115–116)

Skin-to-skin "kangaroo care," in which the preterm infant is placed in a vertical position close to the chest, under the parent's clothing, would be an appropriate intervention for both Cecilia and Adena. This technique—the most readily available intervention for promoting the survival and recovery of preterm babies—is widely used in developing countries where hospitalization is not always possible. It is also widely offered in Western nations as a supplement to hospital intensive care.

Kangaroo skin-to-skin contact fosters improved oxygenation of the baby's body, temperature regulation, sleep, breastfeeding, alertness, and infant survival. The kangaroo position provides the baby with gentle stimulation of all sensory modalities: hearing, smell, touch, and visual. Parents practicing kangaroo care feel more confident about caring for their fragile babies, interact more sensitively and affectionately, and feel more attached to them. Together, these factors may explain why preterm babies given many hours of kangaroo care in their early weeks, compared to those given little or no such care, are more likely to explore novel toys and also score higher on measures of mental and motor development during the first year.

Because of Cecilia's difficult financial situation, she and her baby might also benefit from long-term intensive intervention combining medical follow-up, weekly parent training sessions, and cognitively stimulating child care from 1 to 3 years of age.

Adena and her husband, who have the economic and personal resources to care for their preterm infant, would benefit from a few sessions of coaching in recognizing and responding to their baby's needs. During the hospital stay, their fragile baby should receive special stimulation, which has been linked to faster weight gain, more predictable sleep patterns, and greater alertness in preterm infants. This intervention might include rocking in a suspended hammock or lying on a waterbed designed to replace the gentle motion the baby would have received while still in the mother's uterus, as well as exposure to other forms of stimulation, such as an attractive mobile or a tape recording of a heartbeat, soft music, or the mother's voice.

REFLECT: Many people object to the use of extraordinary medical measures to save extremely low-birth-weight babies because of their high risk of developing serious physical, cognitive, and emotional problems. Do you agree or disagree? Explain. (pp. 116–117)
   This is an open-ended question with no right or wrong answer.

REVIEW: What is epigenesis, and how does it differ from gene–environment interaction and gene–environment correlation? Provide an example of each. (pp. 121–123, 124)
   Epigenesis means development resulting from ongoing, bidirectional exchanges between heredity and all levels of the environment. For example, providing a baby with a healthy diet increases brain growth, which translates into new connections between nerve cells, which transform gene expression. This opens the door to new gene–environment exchanges—for example, advanced exploration of objects and interaction with caregivers, which further enhance brain growth and gene expression.
   Gene–environment interaction refers to the idea that because of their genetic makeup, individuals differ in their responsiveness to qualities of the environment. That is, children have unique, genetically influenced reactions to particular experiences. For example, young children with a gene that increases their risk of an emotionally reactive temperament respond especially strongly to variations in parenting quality. When parenting is favorable, these children adjust as well as or better than other children. But when parenting is unfavorable, they become poorly adjusted—more so than children not at genetic risk.
   Gene–environment correlation means that our genes influence the environments to which we are exposed. The way this happens changes with age. For young children, parents tend to provide an environment influenced by their own abilities, which their children may also have inherited. For example, parents who are good athletes are likely to provide an environment emphasizing outdoor activities and athletic skill development, and their children are likely to become good athletes for both genetic and environmental reasons—an example of *passive correlation*. In *evocative correlation,* the responses children evoke from others are also influenced by the child's heredity. For example, an active, friendly baby is likely to receive more social stimulation than a passive, quiet infant. Finally, in older children, who can actively seek environments that fit with their genetic tendencies, *active* gene–environment correlation becomes common. For example, a musically talented youngster may join his school orchestra and practice his instrument.

CONNECT: Explain how each of the following concepts supports the conclusion that genetic influences on human characteristics are not constant but change over time: somatic mutation (page 81), niche-picking (page 123), and epigenesis (page 124). (pp. 118–120)
   Somatic mutation occurs when normal body cells mutate, as happens in many cancers and other diseases. Unlike germline mutation, which occurs only in the cells that give rise to gametes, somatic mutation can take place at any time of life, perhaps reflecting a genetic susceptibility in some individuals that causes body cells to mutate easily in the presence of triggering events. Somatic mutation provides evidence that individuals do not have a single, permanent genotype but, rather, that each cell's genetic makeup can change over time.
   Niche-picking is the tendency to actively choose environments that complement our heredity. It is not seen in infants and young children, who cannot choose their own environments. But older children and adolescents are increasingly in charge of their environments and can express their preferences through niche-picking. This explains why pairs of identical twins reared apart during childhood and later reunited often discover that they share preferences in food, hobbies, and vocations.
   Epigenesis refers to development resulting from ongoing bidirectional exchanges between heredity and all levels of the environment. For example, providing a baby with a healthy diet promotes brain growth, leading to new connections between brain cells, which transform gene expression. This opens the door to new gene–environment exchanges, which, in turn, further enhance brain growth and gene expression.

APPLY: Bianca's parents are accomplished musicians. At age 4, Bianca began taking piano lessons. By age 10, she was accompanying the school choir. At age 14, she asked if she could attend a special music high school. Explain how gene–environment correlation promoted Bianca's talent. (pp. 122–123)
   According to the concept of gene–environment correlation, our genes influence the environments to which we are exposed. Early in her development, Bianca probably experienced a *passive* gene–environment correlation. Her parents, as dedicated musicians, exposed her to musical activities, such as attending concerts and listening to classical music. They also provided her first piano lessons and opportunities for other music-related experiences. Because Bianca was receptive to this abundance of musical stimulation, she undoubtedly evoked positive responses from her parents, who continued to promote her musical development—an example of *evocative* gene–environment correlation.

Chapter 3 Biological Foundations, Prenatal Development, and Birth

As Bianca grew older and became more active in choosing her own environments, she decided to accompany the school choir and, later, to attend a special music high school. Bianca's inherited musical talent led her to engage in *niche-picking*—choosing activities and environments that complemented her genetic strengths. In these ways, heredity and environment worked together to advance Bianca's musical endeavors.

REFLECT: What aspects of your own development—for example, interests, hobbies, college major, or vocational choice—are probably due to niche-picking? Explain. (p. 123)
This is an open-ended question with no right or wrong answer.

SUGGESTED READINGS

Dombrowski, S. C., & Martin, R. P. (2010). *Prenatal exposures: Psychological and educational consequences for children.* New York: Springer. A compelling look at prenatal development, this book examines the effects of teratogens on the developing organism. The authors also present research on environmental factors, such as social support, that contribute to development outcomes in prenatally exposed babies.

Flais, S. V. (2010). *Raising twins.* Washington, DC: American Academy of Pediatrics. Examines the experience of raising twins from pregnancy into early childhood. Topics include: preparing for twins, breastfeeding, sleep, establishing routines, and discipline. The author also presents real-life accounts of challenges and rewards associated with rearing multiples.

Mundy, L. (2008). *Everything conceivable: How assisted reproduction is changing men, women, and the world.* New York: Knopf. A compelling look at reproductive technologies, this book examines current research, as well as controversies, surrounding assisted reproduction. The author also includes personal narratives, myths, and the social consequences of assisted reproduction.

Simkin, P., Bolding, A., Durham, J., & McGinnis, M. (Eds.). (2010). *Pregnancy, childbirth, and the newborn.* New York: Meadowbrook Press. Presents up-to-date research on pregnancy, childbirth, and the transition to parenthood. Topics include what to expect during pregnancy, the importance of nutrition and exercise, the dangers of drugs and alcohol, prenatal care, myths and facts about childbirth, and frequently asked questions.

MEDIA MATERIALS

For details on individual video segments that accompany the DVD for *Child Development,* Ninth Edition, please see the DVD Guide for *Explorations in Child Development.* The DVD and DVD Guide are available through your Pearson sales representative.

Additional DVDs that may be useful in your class are listed below. These are not available through your Pearson sales representative, but you can order them directly from the distributors. (See contact information at the end of this manual.)

A Good Birth (2006, Fanlight Productions/Tara Young, 22 min.; includes Spanish subtitles). This film takes place in the Rio Grande Valley, along the Texas–Mexico border, where certified nurse–midwives working in both freestanding and hospital-based settings provide maternity and infant care along with emotional support and empowerment to poor and working-class mothers. Ninety percent of the families they serve fall below the poverty line or are illegal immigrants who cannot qualify for aid. From education programs for teenage mothers to attending at-home births to postnatal care, these midwives provide individualized attention to the physical and emotional needs of mothers, infants, and families during pregnancy and the birthing process and beyond.

Babyland: Infant Mortality in Memphis, TN (2008, Films Media Group, 43 min.). Noting that there are places in America where the infant mortality rate echoes that of a developing country, this *ABC News* program travels to Memphis, Tennessee—epicenter of the nation's worst infant death statistics—to investigate the issue and explore possible solutions. Viewers visit a cemetery with the epithet of "Babyland" and witness an unusual pairing of a black teen mother-to-be and a white, suburban church volunteer trying to prevent another tragic outcome. This program addresses premature birth, the main factor behind infant mortality, and profiles Memphis residents dedicated to raising awareness of, and spurring action on, our health-care system's failings.

Designer Babies: The Dangers of Corporate Genetics (2005, Films Media Group, 60 min.). This program explores the frightening implications of "market-driven" genetic engineering. Noting that the government-funded Human Genome Project has become highly lucrative for pharmaceutical companies, the program examines cases of exploitative gene harvesting in Iceland and Peru, where isolated ethnic populations contain commercially valuable DNA. Interviews with prominent scientists and activists highlight the dangers of patenting genomic data.

Fetal Alcohol Exposure: Changing the Future (2006, Films for the Humanities & Sciences, 31 min.). This program looks at the prenatal effects of maternal drinking and the primary and secondary disabilities—including neurological, cognitive, and behavioral characteristics—associated with fetal alcohol spectrum disorder (FASD). It draws on the firsthand experiences of several experts: Ann Streissguth, director of the University of Washington's Fetal Alcohol and Drug Unit; Kathy Mitchell, vice president of the National Organization on Fetal Alcohol Syndrome; Erica Lara, who works at a residential drug and alcohol treatment facility for women with young children; and Erica Gitis-Miles, a college student with FASD.

From Conception to Baby: Beginnings of Life (2011, Learning Seed, 30 min.). Outlining the complex biological processes of prenatal development, this film provides information on how chromosomes determine the gender and physical attributes of a baby, how a single cell develops into an embryo, and the stages of fetal development. It also examines the importance of prenatal care, good nutrition, and a healthy prenatal environment. An educator's guide is included.

From Conception to Birth (2005, Films Media Group/Discovery Channel, 52 min.). This program describes the beginnings of human life, from conception to birth. Following nine couples, it explores the fundamentals of egg and sperm production, cell division within the first few hours of pregnancy, the stages of gestation, and birth. State-of-the-art, reality-based animation depicts the birthing process from the inside out. Contains footage of childbirth.

Heredity & Environment: Beginnings of Life (2011, Learning Seed, 39 min.). Describing the structures and chemistry of DNA molecules, this program explains how genes are passed from parents to offspring and how they determine the traits of an individual. It also covers environmental factors, both inside and outside of the womb, that can affect a child's health later in life; genetic disorders; and the role of counseling and screening to provide health information before or during pregnancy. An educator's guide is included.

Home Birth and Alternative Medicine: Two Baby on Board Case Studies (2008, Films Media Group, 24 min.). This program focuses on a couple who are about to have their fifth child and third home birth. They want to have a water birth, and the mother plans to use the hypnobirthing technique during labor. Also profiled is a pregnant woman who does not want any labor or delivery medication and is now exploring the benefits of alternative therapies—acupuncture and prenatal yoga—to assist in pain relief.

Human Reproduction and Childbirth (2009, Insight Media, 20 min.). This program illustrates the biological functions of the male and female reproductive systems. It describes menstruation, details the process of fertilization, and traces the stages of embryonic and fetal development. The program follows a young woman's pregnancy; explains the importance of maternal nutrition, sleep, low stress levels, and avoidance of alcohol and drugs; and describes the birth process.

In the Womb (2005, National Geographic, 100 min.). Making use of striking 3-D and 4-D ultrasound imagery, this program opens a window into the delicate, dark world of the fetus, exploring each trimester of pregnancy in great detail—including a view of a fetoscope operation performed in utero to correct life-threatening complications before birth.

NOVA: Life's Greatest Miracle (2001, PBS Home Video, 60 min.). This updated version of Lennart Nilsson's world-famous *Miracle of Life* video uses the latest technological advances in microscopy and medical imaging to chronicle the inside-the-womb story of the growth of a baby from embryo to newborn.

Pregnancy in Progress: Beginnings of Life (2011, Learning Seed, 33 min.). In this program, viewers learn the early signs of pregnancy and the host of physical changes women experience during pregnancy. The program discusses common prenatal tests and what they can reveal about the organism's development. Also covered are the possible causes of infertility in women and men and common treatment options, as well as healthy prenatal care.

The Secret Life of Babies (2005, Fanlight Productions/Bernard George, 86 min.). This two-part documentary explores the extent of the baby's vast world of perceptions, from intrauterine life (Part 1) to the first months following birth (Part 2). Filmed in France, Canada, and the United States, the documentary features remarkable intrauterine footage showing the fetus's response to external stimuli. Through interviews with some of the world's leading cognitive and developmental psychologists, this program reveals what we know today about the baby's experiences before and after birth.

CHAPTER 4
INFANCY: EARLY LEARNING, MOTOR SKILLS, AND PERCEPTUAL CAPACITIES

CHAPTER-AT-A-GLANCE

Chapter Outline	Instruction Ideas	Supplements
The Organized Infant pp. 129–146 Reflexes • States • Neonatal Behavioral Assessment • Learning Capacities	Learning Objectives 4.1–4.3 Lecture Enhancement 4.1 Learning Activities 4.1–4.3, 4.7 Ask Yourself p. 146	Test Bank Items 1–60, 125–127 Please contact your Pearson publisher's representative for a wide range of video offerings available to adopters.
Motor Development in Infancy pp. 147–152 The Sequence of Motor Development • Motor Skills as Dynamic Systems • Fine-Motor Development: Reaching and Grasping	Learning Objectives 4.4–4.5 Learning Activities 4.4–4.6 Ask Yourself p. 152	Test Bank Items 61–81, 128
Perceptual Development in Infancy pp. 152–169 Touch • Taste and Smell • Hearing • Vision • Intermodal Perception • Understanding Perceptual Development	Learning Objectives 4.6–4.9 Learning Enhancements 4.2–4.3 Learning Activity 4.7 Ask Yourself p. 169	Test Bank Items 82–117, 129
Early Deprivation and Enrichment: Is Infancy a Sensitive Period of Development? pp. 169–171	Learning Objective 4.10 Lecture Enhancement 4.4 Ask Yourself p. 171	Test Bank Items 118–124

BRIEF CHAPTER SUMMARY

Infants are born with remarkable capabilities—early reflexes, an ability to learn, motor skills, and perceptual capacities. Newborns actively relate to their physical and social worlds, using capacities that are crucial for survival and that evoke care from adults. Reflexes are the newborn's most obvious organized patterns of behavior. Some have survival value; others help parents and infants establish gratifying interaction, and others form the basis for later motor skills.

Newborns move in and out of five states of arousal—degrees of sleep and wakefulness—that alternate frequently. Between birth and age 2 years, babies' sleep–wake pattern increasingly conforms to a circadian rhythm, or 24-hour schedule, as a result of brain development and the social environment. During rapid-eye-movement (REM) sleep, electrical brain-wave activity is similar to that of the waking state; in non-rapid-eye-movement (NREM) sleep, heart rate, breathing, and brain-wave activity are slow and regular. Newborns spend far more time than they ever will again in REM sleep, which provides stimulation essential for central nervous system development. Disturbed REM–NREM cycles are a sign of central nervous system abnormalities, which may lead to sudden infant death syndrome (SIDS).

Crying is the first way that babies communicate; the intensity and context of the cry help guide parents toward its cause. The sound of a baby crying stimulates feelings of discomfort in most adults, an innately programmed response that ensures that babies get care and protection. Ethological research indicates that parental responsiveness to infant crying leads to less crying over time. The most widely used instrument for assessing the organized functioning of newborns is T. Berry Brazelton's Neonatal Behavioral Assessment Scale (NBAS), which provides information about individual and cultural differences in newborn behavior.

Infants learn through classical and operant conditioning, through their natural preference for novel stimulation, and by observing and imitating others. Research on habituation and recovery has been used to assess infant perceptual and cognitive capacities, including quickness and flexibility of thinking. Specialized cells, known as mirror neurons, found in the cerebral cortex of primates may underlie the primitive ability of newborns to learn through imitation.

According to the dynamic systems theory of motor development, children acquire new motor skills by combining existing skills into increasingly complex systems of action. Each new skill is a joint product of central nervous system development, the body's movement possibilities, the child's goals, and environmental supports for the skill. Rather than being hardwired into the nervous system, behaviors are softly assembled, permitting different paths to the same skill, including effects of cultural rearing differences. Motor skills such as reaching and grasping start as gross, diffuse activity and move toward mastery of fine movements. Environments that overwhelm children with expectations beyond their current capacities can undermine development.

Studies of infant perception, including sensitivity to touch, taste, smell, and sound, reveal how babies are biologically prepared to perceive their world and how brain development and experience expand their capacities. Newborns are sensitive to touch, including pain, and can distinguish several basic tastes. They prefer complex sounds to pure tones and can detect the sounds of any human language. Vision, the least mature of the newborn's senses, develops rapidly. Depth perception emerges as infants become sensitive to motion, then binocular depth cues, and finally pictorial depth cues. Crawling experience promotes other aspects of three-dimensional understanding. Newborns respond to a facelike structure and soon come to prefer their mother's face to that of an unfamiliar woman.

Babies perceive input from different sensory systems in a unified way by detecting amodal sensory properties, information that overlaps two or more sensory systems. Infants soon master a wide range of intermodal relationships—a fundamental ability that fosters all aspects of psychological development. According to differentiation theory, infants actively search for invariant features of the environment. By acting on their environment, babies discover affordances, the action possibilities a situation offers. Development moves from a perceptual to a cognitive emphasis as babies impose meaning on what they perceive. Severe deprivation in infancy has profound effects on physical and psychological development. Evidence from natural experiments, such as babies placed in orphanages who were later adopted into families, suggests that infancy is a sensitive period.

LEARNING OBJECTIVES

After reading this chapter, you should be able to answer the following:

4.1 Explain the functions of newborn reflexes, and describe changing states of arousal during infancy, emphasizing sleep and crying. (pp. 130–138)

4.2 Why is neonatal behavioral assessment useful? (pp. 138–139)

4.3 Describe infant learning capacities, the conditions under which they occur, and the unique value of each. (pp. 139–146)

4.4 How does the dynamic systems perspective explain motor development? (pp. 147–150)

4.5 Identify factors that influence gross- and fine-motor development during the first two years. (pp. 150–152)

4.6 Describe the newborn baby's sensitivity to touch, taste, smell, and sound, noting changes during infancy. (pp. 152–158)

4.7 Describe the development of vision in infancy, with special emphasis on depth, pattern, face, and object perception. (pp. 158–166, 167)

4.8 Describe how intermodal perception develops during infancy. (pp. 166, 168)

4.9 How does differentiation theory explain perceptual development? (pp. 168–169)

4.10 How does research on early deprivation and enrichment shed light on the question of whether infancy is a sensitive period of development? (pp. 169–171)

LECTURE OUTLINE

I. THE ORGANIZED INFANT (pp. 129–146)
   A. The newborn, or *neonate,* was once considered a passive, incompetent being, but researchers have confirmed that infants display many complex abilities.
   B. Reflexes (pp. 130–132)
      1. A **reflex** is an inborn, automatic response to a particular form of stimulation.
      2. Adaptive Value of Reflexes
         a. Some reflexes have survival value. Others probably helped babies survive during our evolutionary past.
         b. Several reflexes help parents and infants establish gratifying interaction.

3. Reflexes and the Development of Motor Skills
   a. A few reflexes form the basis for complex motor skills that will develop later.
   b. Certain reflexes drop out early, but the motor functions involved are renewed later.
4. The Importance of Assessing Reflexes
   a. Testing reflexes carefully can reveal the health of a baby's nervous system.
   b. Weak or absent reflexes or overly rigid or exaggerated reflexes can signal brain damage.

C. States (pp. 132–138)
   1. Throughout the day and night, newborn infants move in and out of five **states of arousal,** or degrees of sleep and wakefulness.
   2. Newborns' sleep–wake cycles are affected more by fullness–hunger than by darkness–light.
   3. Between birth and 2 years, periods of sleep and wakefulness become fewer but longer, and the sleep–wake pattern increasingly conforms to a *circadian rhythm,* or 24-hour schedule.
   4. Changes in babies' arousal patterns are due in part to brain development, but they are also affected by culturally influenced beliefs and practices and individual parents' needs.
      a. Many Western parents try to get their babies to sleep through the night as early as age 3 to 4 months by offering an evening feeding before putting them down in a separate, quiet room.
      b. Elsewhere in the world, babies are more likely to sleep with their parents; when they do so, the baby shifts to an adultlike sleep–waking schedule only at the end of the first year.
   5. Sleep
      a. Sleep consists of at least two states: rapid-eye-movement sleep and non-rapid-eye-movement sleep.
      b. In irregular, or **rapid-eye-movement (REM) sleep,** brain-wave activity, measured with the EEG, is remarkably similar to that of the waking state. The eyes dart beneath the lids; heart rate, blood pressure, and breathing are uneven; and slight body movements occur.
      c. During regular, or **non-rapid-eye-movement (NREM) sleep,** the body is almost motionless, and heart rate, breathing, and brain-wave activity are slow and even.
      d. Newborns spend far more time in the REM state than they ever will again, and researchers believe that the stimulation of REM sleep is vital for growth of the central nervous system.
      e. Disturbed REM–NREM sleep cycles in the newborn can be a sign of central nervous system abnormalities, and mounting evidence suggests that impaired brain functioning is a major contributor to **sudden infant death syndrome (SIDS),** a major cause of infant mortality.
   6. Crying
      a. Crying is the first way that babies communicate, letting parents know that they need food, comfort, and stimulation.
      b. Young infants usually cry because of physical needs.
      c. In many cultures with vastly different infant care practices, crying typically increases during the early weeks, peaks at about 6 weeks, and then declines.
      d. Adult Responsiveness to Infant Cries
         (1) A crying baby stimulates strong feelings of discomfort in men and women, parents and nonparents alike.
         (2) The intensity and context of the cry help parents identify whether the baby is hungry, tired, or in pain.
         (3) Parents vary widely in responsiveness; parents who are high in empathy and who hold "child-centered" attitudes toward infant care are more likely to respond sensitively.
      e. Soothing a Crying Infant
         (1) Once feeding and diaper changing have been tried, lifting the infant to the shoulder and rocking or walking is highly effective.
         (2) According to *ethological theory,* parental responsiveness to infant crying is adaptive in that it ensures that the infant's basic needs will be met.
         (3) When Western parents choose to practice "proximal care" by holding their babies extensively, the amount of crying in the early months is reduced by about one-third.
         (4) Not all research indicates that prompt parental response reduces infant crying.
         (5) Parents can lessen older babies' need to cry by encouraging more mature ways of expressing their desires, such as gestures and vocalizations.
      f. Abnormal Crying
         (1) The cries of brain-damaged babies and those who have experienced prenatal and birth complications are often shrill, piercing, and shorter in duration than those of healthy babies.

(2) Neonates with *colic*, or persistent crying—a common problem, which generally subsides between 3 and 6 months—find it harder to calm down than other babies.
(3) When a baby's cry is especially unpleasant and an infant is very difficult to soothe, parents may become frustrated and angry.

D. Neonatal Behavioral Assessment (pp. 138–139)
1. A variety of instruments permit doctors, nurses, and researchers to assess the organized functioning of newborn babies.
2. T. Berry Brazelton's **Neonatal Behavioral Assessment Scale (NBAS)** evaluates the baby's reflexes, muscle tone, state changes, responsiveness to physical and social stimuli, and other reactions.
3. The *Neonatal Intensive Care Unit Network Neurobehavioral Scale (NNNS)* is specially designed for use with newborns at risk for developmental problems because of low birth weight, preterm delivery, and other conditions.
4. The NBAS has been given to many infants around the world, and researchers have learned about individual and cultural differences in newborn behavior and how child-rearing practices can affect a baby's reactions.

E. Learning Capacities (pp. 139–146)
1. *Learning* refers to changes in behavior as the result of experience.
2. Infants learn through classical and operant conditioning, through their natural preference for novel stimulation, and by observing and imitating others.
3. Classical Conditioning
   a. Newborn reflexes make **classical conditioning** possible in the young infant.
   b. Before learning can take place, an **unconditioned stimulus (UCS)** must consistently produce a reflexive, or **unconditioned, response (UCR).** For example, the stimulus of sweet breast milk (UCS) results in sucking (UCR).
   c. To produce learning, a *neutral stimulus* that does not lead to the reflex is presented just before, or at about the same time as, the UCS. For example, the mother might stroke the baby's forehead as each nursing period begins, so that the stroking is paired with the taste of milk.
   d. If learning has occurred, the neutral stimulus alone will produce a response similar to the reflexive response. The neutral stimulus is then called a **conditioned stimulus (CS),** and the response it elicits is called a **conditioned response (CR).** In this example, stroking the baby's forehead (CS) results in sucking (CR).
   e. If the CS is presented alone enough times, without being paired with the UCS, the CR no longer occurs, an outcome called **extinction.**
4. Operant Conditioning
   a. In **operant conditioning,** infants act (or *operate*) on the environment, and the stimuli that follow their behavior change the probability that the behavior will occur again.
   b. A stimulus that increases the occurrence of a response is called a **reinforcer;** for example, sweet liquid *reinforces* the sucking response in newborns.
   c. Removing a desirable stimulus or presenting an unpleasant one to decrease the occurrence of a response is called **punishment.** For example, a sour-tasting fluid *punishes* newborns' sucking response.
   d. As infants get older, operant conditioning includes a wider range of responses and stimuli; a dramatic rise in retention of operant responses occurs over the first year and a half.
   e. Infants' memory for operant responses is highly *context-dependent* at first, but after 9 months, the importance of context declines as babies move on their own.
   f. Operant conditioning plays a vital role in the formation of social relationships, as each partner's behavior reinforces the other's.
5. Habituation
   a. **Habituation** refers to a gradual reduction in the strength of a response due to repetitive stimulation.
   b. Once habituation has occurred, a new stimulus—a change in the environment—causes the habituated response to return to a high level, an increase called **recovery.**
   c. Window into Early Attention, Memory, and Knowledge
      (1) A baby who first *habituates* to a visual pattern, then *recovers* to a new one, appears to remember the first stimulus and to perceive the second one as new and different from it.
      (2) Preterm and newborn babies have long habituation times, but by 4 or 5 months, habituation occurs much more quickly.

Chapter 4 Infancy: Early Learning, Motor Skills, and Perceptual Capacities

(3) With passage of time, infants shift from a *novelty preference* to a *familiarity preference;* that is, they recover to a familiar stimulus rather than to a novel stimulus—a shift that allows researchers to use habituation to assess *remote memory*.
(4) In habituation research, infants retain certain information over much longer time spans than they do in operant conditioning studies.
(5) Examples of infants' *detection of relationships* include awareness of speech sounds that often occur together and objects that belong to the same category.

d. Habituation and Later Mental Development
(1) Habituation and recovery to visual stimuli are among the earliest available predictors of intelligence in childhood, adolescence, and early adulthood because they assess memory as well as quickness and flexibility of thinking.
(2) The simplest form of memory is *recognition;* all the baby has to do is indicate whether a new stimulus is identical or similar to a previous one.
(3) *Recall,* a more challenging form of memory, involves remembering something not present. Infants can engage in recall by the middle of the first year.

6. Newborn Imitation
a. Babies have a primitive ability to learn through **imitation**—by copying the behavior of another person.
(1) Imitation of some behaviors is also seen in chimpanzees, our closest evolutionary ancestors.
(2) Although newborns' capacity to imitate is widely accepted, a few studies have failed to reproduce the human findings.
b. Evidence exists that newborns imitate much as older children and adults do—by actively trying to match body movements they *see* with ones they *feel* themselves making.
(1) Scientists have identified specialized cells called **mirror neurons** in many areas of the cerebral cortex of primates that underlie these capacities.
(2) Mirror neurons fire identically when a primate hears or sees an action and when it carries out the same action. They are believed to be the biological basis of a variety of interrelated, complex social abilities, including imitation.
(3) Brain-imaging findings support a functioning mirror-neuron system as early as 6 months of age.
c. The view of newborn imitation as a flexible, voluntary capacity remains controversial.
d. But however limited it is at birth, imitation is a powerful means of learning—far faster than individual trial-and-error and discovery.

II. MOTOR DEVELOPMENT IN INFANCY (pp. 147–152)
A. Babies' motor achievements have a powerful impact on their social relationships.
1. Newly walking babies more actively attend to and initiate social interaction—seeking out parents for greetings and hugs.
2. Babies' delight as they work on new motor skills triggers pleasurable reactions in others, further encouraging infants' efforts.
B. The Sequence of Motor Development (pp. 147–148)
1. *Gross-motor development* refers to control over actions that help infants get around in the environment, such as crawling, standing, and walking.
2. *Fine-motor development* refers to smaller movements, such as reaching and grasping.
3. Large individual differences exist in the *rate* of motor progress.
4. Historically, researchers assumed that motor skills were separate, innate abilities that emerged in a fixed sequence. However, this view has long been discredited.
5. Many influences—both internal and external to the child—join together to influence the vast transformations in motor competencies of the first two years.
C. Motor Skills as Dynamic Systems (pp. 148–150)
1. According to **dynamic systems theory of motor development,** mastery of motor skills involves acquiring increasingly complex *systems of action*.
2. When motor skills work as a system, separate abilities blend together, each cooperating with others to produce more effective ways of exploring and controlling the environment.
3. Each new skill is a joint product of four factors: central nervous system development, movement capacities of the body, the goals the child has in mind, and environmental supports for the skill.

4. Dynamic systems theory shows why motor development cannot be genetically determined: Because it is motivated by exploration and the desire to master new tasks, heredity can map it out only at a general level.
5. Dynamic Motor Systems in Action
    a. To find out how infants acquire motor capacities, researchers conduct *microgenetic studies,* following babies from their first attempts at a skill until it becomes smooth and effortless.
    b. Findings confirm that the order in which motor skills develop does not follow a strict, predetermined cephalocaudal pattern but also depends on the anatomy of the body part being used, the surrounding environment, and the baby's efforts.
6. Cultural Variations in Motor Development
    a. Cross-cultural research illustrates how early movement opportunities and a stimulating environment contribute to motor development.
    b. Cultural variations in infant-rearing practices affect motor development.
        (1) In some cultures, including Japan, mothers believe it is unnecessary to deliberately encourage sitting, crawling, or walking.
        (2) Among the Kipsigis of Kenya, parents emphasize early motor maturity, practicing formal exercises to stimulate particular skills.
D. Fine-Motor Development: Reaching and Grasping (pp. 150–152)
    1. Of all motor skills, reaching may play the greatest role in infant cognitive development by allowing infants to explore the sights, sounds, and feel of objects.
    2. **Prereaching** by newborns—poorly coordinated swipes toward an object in front of them—suggests that babies are biologically prepared to coordinate hand with eye in the act of exploring.
    3. Development of Reaching and Grasping
        a. At 3 to 4 months, reaching reappears as purposeful, forward arm movements, gradually improving in accuracy.
        b. By 5 to 6 months, infants reach for an object in a darkened room—evidence that reaching does not depend on vision but is largely controlled by *proprioception.*
        c. Reaching improves as depth perception advances.
        d. The newborn grasp reflex is replaced by the **ulnar grasp,** a clumsy motion in which the baby's fingers close against the palm.
        e. At 4 to 5 months, both hands become coordinated in exploring objects.
        f. By the end of the first year, infants use the thumb and index finger in a well-coordinated **pincer grasp,** and the ability to manipulate objects greatly expands.
        g. Perhaps with the aid of mirror neurons, babies match their own active experience of reaching to their perception of others' actions.
    4. Early Experience and Reaching
        a. Like other motor milestones, early experience affects reaching.
        b. Because babies of Mali and Uganda spend half or more of their day held in sitting or standing positions, which facilitate reaching, they develop manual skills earlier than Western infants, who spend much of their day lying down.

III. PERCEPTUAL DEVELOPMENT IN INFANCY (pp. 152–169)
A. The union of perceptual and motor information is basic to our human nervous systems, and each domain supports development of the other.
B. Studies of infant perception reveal in what ways babies are biologically prepared to perceive their world, and how brain development and experience expand their capacities.
C. Infant perception sheds light on other aspects of development. For example, because touch, vision, and hearing permit interaction with others, they are basic to emotional and social development.
D. Touch (pp. 153–154)
    1. Sensitivity to touch is well-developed at birth; it helps stimulate early physical growth and is vital for emotional development.
    2. Measures of brain activity during painful medical procedures reveal that preterm and male babies show intense activation of sensorimotor areas in the cerebral cortex.
    3. Gentle touching enhances babies' positive responsiveness to their physical and social surroundings.

4. Parents vary their style of touching, depending on whether the goal of their interaction is to comfort, convey affection, or induce smiling, attention, or play in their baby.

E. Taste and Smell (pp. 154–155)
1. Facial expressions reveal that newborn infants can distinguish several basic tastes.
2. As with taste, certain odor preferences are present at birth.
3. In many mammals, the sense of smell plays an important role in protecting the young from predators by helping mothers and babies identify each other.
4. Immediately after birth, infants placed face down between their mother's breasts spontaneously latch on to a nipple and begin sucking within an hour.
5. Newborns' dual attraction to the odor of their mother and to that of breast milk helps them locate an appropriate food source and distinguish their caregiver from other people.

F. Hearing (pp. 155–158)
1. Newborn infants can hear a wide variety of sounds—sensitivity that improves greatly over the first few months.
2. At birth, infants prefer complex sounds to pure tones.
3. Over the first year, infants organize sounds into increasingly elaborate patterns.
4. Speech Perception
   a. Young infants listen longer to human speech than to structurally similar nonspeech sounds.
   b. Newborns make fine-grained distinctions among many speech sounds.
   c. Over the first year, infants learn to focus on meaningful sound variations and to screen out sounds not used in their native tongue.
   d. The second half of the first year may be a sensitive period in which babies acquire a range of perceptual skills for picking up socially important information.
   e. Around 7 to 9 months, infants begin to divide the speech stream into wordlike units.
5. Analyzing the Speech Stream
   a. Babies show an impressive **statistical learning capacity.** By analyzing the speech stream for patterns—repeatedly occurring sequences of sounds—they acquire a stock of speech structures for which they will later learn meanings.
   b. Once infants locate words in the speech stream, they focus on the words and detect syllable-stress regularities.
   c. Infants also attend to regularities in word sequences, apparently detecting simple word-order rules.
   d. Some researchers believe babies are born with an innate general statistical learning capacity for detecting structure in the environment.
   e. Infants' responsiveness to speech encourages parents to talk to their babies, which strengthens infants' language processing.

G. Vision (pp. 158–166, 167)
1. At birth, vision is the least developed of the senses. For example, cells in the *retina* continue to develop after birth.
2. The optic nerve that relays messages from the retina, and the visual centers in the brain that receive them, do not become adultlike for several years after birth.
3. Because visual structures are immature, newborns cannot focus well and have limited **visual acuity,** or fineness of discrimination.
4. Newborns are not yet good at discriminating colors, but by 4 months, color discrimination is adultlike.
5. Around 2 months, infants can focus on objects about as well as adults.
6. Newborns' eye movements are slow and inaccurate, but they actively scan their environment and track moving objects.
7. Depth Perception
   a. *Depth perception*—the ability to judge the distance of objects from one another and from ourselves—is important for guiding motor activity.
   b. The earliest studies of depth perception used the **visual cliff,** a Plexiglas-covered table with a platform at the center, a "shallow" side with a checkerboard pattern just under the glass, and a "deep" side with a checkerboard several feet below the glass.
      (1) Crawling babies readily crossed the shallow side of the visual cliff, but most avoided the deep side.
      (2) Recent research has looked at babies' ability to detect specific depth cues, using methods that do not require that they crawl.

c. Emergence of Depth Perception
   (1) By the age of 3 months, the depth cue of *motion* has helped infants figure out that objects are not flat but three-dimensional.
   (2) *Binocular depth cues* arise because our two eyes have slightly different views of the visual field, which the brain blends in a process called *stereopsis,* resulting in perception of depth, which emerges between 2 and 3 months.
   (3) Last to develop are *pictorial depth cues,* such as receding and overlapping lines, that create the illusion of perspective.
   (4) Around 6 months, the ability to turn, poke, and feel the surface of objects promotes sensitivity to pictorial cues as infants pick up information about size, texture, and three-dimensional shape.
d. Independent Movement and Depth Perception
   (1) From everyday experience, babies gradually figure out how to use depth cues to detect the danger of falling.
   (2) Crawling experience promotes other aspects of three-dimensional understanding, such as remembering object locations and finding hidden objects.
   (3) Crawling promotes a new level of brain organization, as indicated by more organized EEG brain-wave activity in the cerebral cortex.
   (4) Infants with severe visual impairments show broad developmental delays that reflect the impact of minimal or absent vision on their ability to explore, gain spatial understanding, and stimulate caregiver interaction.
8. Pattern Perception
   a. Even newborns prefer to look at patterned rather than plain stimuli.
   b. As infants get older, they prefer more complex patterns.
   c. Contrast Sensitivity
      (1) A general principle, **contrast sensitivity,** explains early pattern preferences.
         (a) *Contrast* refers to the difference in the amount of light between adjacent regions in a pattern.
         (b) If babies *are sensitive to* (can detect) the contrast in two or more patterns, they prefer the one with more contrast.
      (2) As babies' detection of fine-grained detail improves, around 2 months, they spend more time looking at complex patterns with greater contrast.
   d. Combining Pattern Elements
      (1) Very young infants respond to the separate parts of a pattern.
      (2) At 2 to 3 months, infants thoroughly explore a pattern's internal features.
      (3) When exposed to dynamic stimuli, such as the mother's nodding, smiling face, 6-week-olds fixate more on internal features (mouth and eyes) than on edges.
      (4) When stimuli are dynamic, thorough inspection of the entire stimulus is delayed, occurring only after 4 months.
      (5) Once babies take in all aspects of a pattern, they integrate the parts into a unified whole.
      (6) At 12 months, infants detect familiar objects represented by incomplete drawings.
9. Face Perception
   a. Newborns prefer to look at photos and simplified drawings of faces with features arranged naturally (upright) rather than unnaturally (upside down or sideways).
   b. Newborns prefer photos of faces with eyes open and a direct gaze.
   c. Some researchers claim that these behaviors reflect a built-in capacity to orient toward members of one's own species, as many newborn animals do.
   d. Others assert that newborns simply prefer any stimulus in which the most salient elements are arranged horizontally in the upper part of a pattern; however, this preference may be promoted by a bias favoring the facial pattern.
   e. Newborns cannot discriminate a complex, static image of the human face from other, equally complex configurations, but from repeated exposures to their mother's face, they learn to prefer her face to that of an unfamiliar woman.
   f. Babies quickly apply their tendency to search for pattern to face perception.
   g. Experience influences face processing, leading babies to form group biases at a young age.

Chapter 4 Infancy: Early Learning, Motor Skills, and Perceptual Capacities

   h. As early as 3 months, infants more easily discriminate among female faces than among male faces, but the greater time infants spend with female adults explains this effect, since babies with a male primary caregiver prefer male faces.
   i. Early experience promotes perceptual narrowing with respect to gender and racial information in faces.
   j. Babies' developing sensitivity to the human face supports their earliest social relationships.
10. Object Perception
   a. Perception of independently existing three-dimensional objects is essential for distinguishing the self, other people, and things.
   b. Size and Shape Constancy
      (1) Both **size constancy** (perception of an object's size as the same, despite changes in the size of its retinal image) and **shape constancy** (perception of an object's shape as stable, despite changes in the shape projected on the retina) are evident in the first week of life.
      (2) These appear to be built-in capacities that help babies detect a coherent world of objects.
   c. Perception of Object Identity
      (1) At first, infants rely heavily on motion and spatial arrangement to identify objects.
      (2) As infants become familiar with many objects and can integrate each object's diverse features into a unified whole, they rely more on shape, color, and texture and less on motion.
      (3) To perceive an object's identity, infants must keep track of its movement in and out of sight.
      (4) From 4 to 11 months, infants increasingly rely on featural information to detect the identity of an object traveling behind a screen—at first, form and later in the first year, surface features.
      (5) Experience—in particular, physically manipulating the object—boosts older infants' attention to its surface features.
H. Intermodal Perception (pp. 166, 168)
   1. *Intermodal stimulation* consists of simultaneous input from more than one modality, or sensory system. In **intermodal perception,** we make sense of these running streams of light, sound, tactile, odor, and taste information, perceiving them as integrated wholes.
   2. Babies perceive input from different sensory systems in a unified way by detecting **amodal sensory properties**—information that is not specific to a single modality but that overlaps two or more sensory systems, such as rate, rhythm, duration, intensity, and temporal synchrony.
   3. Within the first half-year, infants master a remarkable range of intermodal relationships. For example, between 4 and 6 months, infants can perceive and remember the unique face–voice pairings of unfamiliar adults.
   4. Intermodal perception develops quickly because young infants seem biologically primed to focus on amodal information.
   5. Intermodal stimulation facilitates social and language processing—for example, when an adult's gentle touch induces a baby to attend to her face.
   6. In their earliest attempts to make sense of language, infants profit from temporal synchrony between a speech sound and the motion of an object.
   7. Intermodal perception is a fundamental ability that fosters all aspects of psychological development.
   8. When caregivers provide many concurrent sights, sounds, touches, and smells, babies process more information, learn faster, and show better memory.
I. Understanding Perceptual Development (pp. 168–169)
   1. According to Eleanor and James Gibson's **differentiation theory,** infants actively search for **invariant features** of the environment—those that remain stable—in a constantly changing perceptual world.
      a. Young babies search for features that stand out and orient toward faces.
      b. As babies explore internal features and notice *stable relationships* between those features, they detect patterns, such as complex designs and individual faces.
      c. Similarly, babies analyze the speech stream for regularities, detecting words, word-order sequences, and syllable-stress patterns.
      d. The development of intermodal perception also reflects this principle, as babies seek out invariant relationships—for example, common rate and rhythm—in a voice and face, followed by more detailed associations, such as unique voice–face matches.
      e. The Gibsons describe their theory as *differentiation,* meaning analyzing or breaking down, because, over time, the baby detects increasingly fine invariant features among stimuli.

2. Perceptual development can be understood as a built-in tendency to search for order and consistency—a capacity that becomes increasingly fine-tuned with age.
3. Perception is guided by discovery of **affordances**—the action possibilities that a situation offers an organism with certain motor capabilities.
    a. By moving about and exploring the environment, babies figure out which objects can be grasped or squeezed and whether or not a surface is safe to cross.
    b. Sensitivity to these affordances makes our actions future-oriented and largely successful, rather than reactive and blundering.
4. In addition to making sense of experience by searching for invariant features and discovering affordances, babies also show the first glimmerings of a *cognitive* point of view.
    a. Babies *impose meaning* on what they perceive, constructing categories of objects.
    b. Older babies *interpret* a familiar face as a source of pleasure and affection.
    c. Many researchers regard infant development as proceeding from a perceptual to a cognitive emphasis over the first year of life.

IV. EARLY DEPRIVATION AND ENRICHMENT: IS INFANCY A SENSITIVE PERIOD OF DEVELOPMENT? (pp. 169–171)
   A. Many investigations have found that stimulating physical surroundings and warm caregiving that is responsive to infants' self-initiated efforts promote active exploration of the environment and earlier attainment of developmental milestones.
      1. The powerful effect of early experience is dramatically apparent in infants who lack the rich, varied stimulation of normal homes.
      2. Children reared in severely deprived family situations or in institutions remain substantially below average in physical and psychological development and display emotional and behavior problems throughout childhood and adolescence.
   B. Research findings indicate that early experience has a profound impact, but they do not tell us whether infancy is a *sensitive period*.
      1. Some theorists argue that early experience leaves a lasting imprint on the child's competence; others believe that most developmental delays resulting from events in the early years of life can be overcome.
      2. The best available test of whether infancy is a sensitive period comes from natural experiments, in which children were victims of deprived early environments that were later rectified.
         a. Among babies born with cataracts in both eyes, those who have corrective surgery within four to six months show rapid improvement in vision.
         b. If cataract surgery is delayed until adulthood, vision is severely and permanently impaired.
         c. Studies of children placed in orphanages and later exposed to family rearing confirm the importance of a generally stimulating physical and social environment for development.
         d. In studies of children adopted from Romanian orphanages, cognitive catch-up was impressive for children adopted before age 6 months, but those who were institutionalized for longer than the first six months showed serious intellectual deficits.
         e. Neurobiological findings indicate that early, prolonged institutionalization leads to a generalized reduction in activity in the cerebral cortex, especially the prefrontal cortex.
         f. The Bucharest Early Intervention Project—which compared institutionalized Romanian babies who received care as usual with institutionalized babies who were placed in high-quality foster families—showed that on all measures, the earlier the foster placement, the better the outcome.
      3. Environments that overwhelm children with expectations beyond their current capacities also undermine development.

LECTURE ENHANCEMENTS

LECTURE ENHANCEMENT 4.1
More on Early Infant Learning: The Effects of Looking Behavior and Previous Experience on Categorization in Young Infants (pp. 142–145)

Time: 5–10 minutes

Objective: To investigate the effects of looking behavior and previous experience on categorization in young infants.

To examine the effects of looking behavior and previous experience on categorization in young infants, Kovack-Lesh, Horst, and Oakes (2008) recruited 124 4-month-old infants. The researchers were interested in whether previous experience with dogs or cats predicted infants' ability to make a categorical distinction between the two animals. While seated on their parent's lap, infants were first presented with a series of 15-second familiarization trials. For each trial, the babies were shown two different cats on a television monitor. After viewing six trials, or 12 different types of cats, the participants were randomly assigned to one of two conditions:

(1) In the category condition, infants were shown a novel dog paired with a novel cat. If the baby learned the category of "cat" during familiarization, he should look longer at the novel dog than the novel cat.
(2) In the exemplar condition, infants were shown a previously viewed cat paired with a novel cat. If infants learned the individual cats during familiarization, they should look longer at the novel cat than the familiar one.

Results indicated that two factors contributed to infants' learning—how much they shifted their gaze back and forth during familiarization and their experience with pets in the home. Specifically, babies who engaged in high levels of switching (looking back and forth between stimuli) and who had pets at home demonstrated a strong novelty preference (a dog in the category condition, a new cat in the exemplar condition). Thus, these babies not only seemed to remember the individual items but also recognized common features among items in the same category. In contrast, babies who engaged in low levels of switching behavior and who lacked experience with pets in the home did not show a novelty preference. According to Kovack-Lesh, Horst, and Oakes, this study suggests that early categorical distinctions are likely a joint product of experience and switching speed.

Kovack-Lesh, K. A., Horst, J. S., & Oakes, L. M. (2008). The cat is out of the bag: The joint influence of previous experience and looking behavior on infant categorization. *Infancy, 13,* 285–307.

LECTURE ENHANCEMENT 4.2
More on Face Perception in Young Infants (pp. 163–164)

Time: 5–10 minutes

Objective: To examine own-race face preference in Chinese infants.

To extend existing research on young infants' preference for faces from their own ethnic group, Kelly and colleagues (2008) recruited 64 healthy 3-month-old Chinese babies. At the time of recruitment, none of the babies had been exposed to adults from other ethnic groups. All of the babies were tested in a hospital room equipped with a large-screen television. While seated on their mother's lap, the babies were presented with one of the following pairs of faces: Chinese–Caucasian, Chinese–Middle Eastern, Chinese–African, or Chinese–Chinese. Each baby was exposed to one male and one female pair. During the face presentations, researchers recorded infant eye fixations, or how long the babies stared at each pair of faces.

Results indicated that when presented with a Chinese and other-race face, 3-month-olds looked longer at the Chinese face, indicating an own-race preference. This finding is particularly important given the pairings of faces that were similar in skin tone, such as Chinese–Caucasian and Chinese–Middle Eastern. Thus, an own-race face preference is clearly evident in 3-month-olds, regardless of the ethnicity of the face with which it is paired. As noted in the text, extensive face-to-face interaction with caregivers contributes to infants' refinement of face perception. Because the babies in this study had only been exposed to Chinese caregivers, they demonstrated a robust own-race preference. Previous studies have shown that this preference is limited or absent in babies who have frequent contact with members of other races.

Using findings from this study and research presented in the text, how might face perception support infants' early social relationships?

Kelly, D. J., Liu, S., Ge, L., Quinn, P. C., Slater, A. M., Lee, K., Liu, Q., & Pascalis, O. (2008). Cross-race preferences for same-race faces extend beyond the African versus Caucasian contrast in 3-month-old infants. *Infancy, 11,* 87–95.

LECTURE ENHANCEMENT 4.3
Environmental and Social Factors Associated with Infant Stair Climbing (pp. 168–169)

Time: 10–15 minutes

Objective: To examine environmental and social factors associated with infant stair climbing.

As noted in the text, when babies crawl, and again when they walk, they gradually realize that a steeply sloping surface affords the possibility of falling. Experience in trying to keep their balance on various surfaces seems to make crawlers and walkers more aware of the consequences of their movements. However, according to Berger, Theuring, and Adolph (2008), despite the prevalence of stairs in many homes and the risk of falling associated with stairs, little research has been conducted on the environmental and social factors that influence infants' ability to navigate stairs. Instead, most studies have focused on the milestones of stair climbing, which include the average age that infants walk up and down stairs.

To extend existing research on infant stair climbing, Berger, Theuring, and Adolph (2008) recruited 732 typically developing infants and their parents who were already participating in a study about cognitive and motor development. All parents completed a survey about their infant's motor milestones, experiences on stairs (including falls), opportunities for stair climbing outside the home (child-care center, parks, friends' or relatives' homes), and locomotor methods for ascending or descending a full flight of stairs. For example, did parents specifically teach their infants how to climb stairs, or did they let them figure it out for themselves? By including questions about infants' experience on stairs and parental teaching, the researchers were able to evaluate environmental and social factors that may play an important role in infant stair climbing.

As with previous studies, results indicated that most infants mastered ascent several months after crawling and several weeks before they mastered descent. Having stairs in the home was related to age of onset for stair ascent and parental teaching of descent. Specifically, infants with stairs in the home learned to climb up staircases earlier than infants who did not have stairs in their homes. However, timing of stair descent was similar for infants with and without stairs in the home. Once infants learned to crawl up stairs, most parents carefully monitored their children's movements, often picking them up before they turned around to go down the stairs. Parents with stairs in their homes were more likely to teach their babies safe strategies for descent—such as backing down feet first—but this instruction did not affect the age of onset for stair descent.

Taken together, these findings show that both physical development and environmental supports contribute to the onset of stair climbing. Because most parents in this study monitored their babies' descent down stairs more than their ascent, social factors may be especially influential in learning to crawl or back down stairs. While babies may have effective strategies, such as backing down feet first, parental restriction may play a greater role than physical development.

Berger, S. E., Theuring, C., & Adolph, K. E. (2008). How and when infants learn to climb stairs. *Infant Behavior & Development, 30,* 36–49.

LECTURE ENHANCEMENT 4.4
The Effects of Foster-Care Placement for Institutionalized Infants and Toddlers (pp. 169–171)

Time: 10–15 minutes

Objective: To extend existing research on early intervention for institutionalized infants and toddlers.

To extend existing research on early intervention for institutionalized infants and toddlers, Smyke and colleagues (2009) recruited 208 Romanian children between the ages of 5 months and 30 months and followed them to age 54 months. Of the sample, 136 were randomly assigned into care as usual (CAU; institutionalized care) or foster care. The remaining 72 children lived with their natural families and had never been institutionalized. These children were used as a comparison group. The researchers were especially interested in the effects of high-quality foster care for children who were previously institutionalized. Foster-care families received extensive training in child development, including instruction on how to deal with developmental problems common among institutionalized infants and toddlers. For example, many of these children experience eating and sleeping difficulties; cognitive, language, and motor delays; and social/emotional problems, such as extreme withdrawal and aggression. In addition to training, social workers visited foster homes four times a year to conduct observations and provide support and guidance to participating families. Finally, a foster-parent support group was established to help families deal with the challenges of raising institutionalized children.

Researchers assessed environmental quality using the Observational Record of the Caregiving Environment at the beginning of the study and again when participants were 30 and 42 months of age. Findings indicated that quality of caregiving was significantly better in foster homes than in institutions. Perhaps more importantly, evaluations at 30 and 42 months revealed that quality of care in foster homes was indistinguishable from quality of care in comparison homes. Cognitive assessments administered at 30, 40, and 54 months indicated that foster-care children—particularly those who were placed in foster care before their second birthday—scored significantly higher than CAU children. However, neither group scored as high as children in the comparison group. Similar outcomes were found for expressive and receptive language—foster-care children scored significantly higher than CAU children, but the majority did not score as high as comparison children. The exception was children who were placed in foster care before age 15 months, who demonstrated similar language development as comparison children.

When looking at several aspects of social/emotional adjustment—emotional responsiveness and attachment—researchers found that foster-care children demonstrated significantly higher rates of positive emotion during play and social activities like peekaboo than both CAU and comparison children. Foster-care children were also significantly more likely to be classified as securely attached than CAU children (49% vs. 17.5%). To assess clinical outcomes, institutional caregivers, foster parents, and biological parents were interviewed when children were 30, 42, and 54 months of age. Results indicated that foster-care children showed declines in internalizing disorders, such as anxiety and depression, and these rates remained well below CAU children. However, foster-care placement did not have an impact on externalizing behaviors, such as aggression and attention-deficit hyperactivity disorder.

Taken together, these findings illustrate the benefits of high-quality foster care on developmental outcomes for institutionalized children. Although foster-care children lagged behind children raised by their natural parents in most aspects of development, they made significant gains in cognition, language, and some aspects of social/emotional adjustment. Consistent with previous studies, the younger children were at the time of foster-care placement, the greater the catch-up over the course of the study.

Using examples from this study and the text, do these findings support the notion that infancy is a sensitive period for development?

Smyke, A. T., Zeanah, C. H., Fox, N. A., & Nelson, C. A. (2009). A new model of foster care for young children: The Bucharest Early Intervention Project. *Child & Adolescent Clinics of North America, 18,* 721–734.

LEARNING ACTIVITIES

LEARNING ACTIVITY 4.1
True or False: Infant Reflexes and States (pp. 130–138)

Present the following activity as a quiz or in-class assignment.

Directions: Read each of the following statements and indicate whether it is *True* (T) or *False* (F).

Statements:
_____ 1. Most infant reflexes have no adaptive value, which is why they eventually disappear.
_____ 2. The tonic neck reflex may prepare the baby for voluntary reaching.
_____ 3. Because of the swimming reflex, swimming lessons should begin when babies are only a few weeks or months old.
_____ 4. Because of individual differences in development, newborn reflexes tell us very little about the health of the baby's nervous system.
_____ 5. The average newborn sleeps between 16 and 18 hours a day.
_____ 6. By age 2, the average child only needs about nine to ten hours of sleep a day.
_____ 7. Parent–infant cosleeping increases a child's risk of sudden infant death syndrome (SIDS).
_____ 8. Babies who spend more time quietly alert tend to receive more social stimulation and opportunities to explore and, therefore, may be slightly ahead in mental development.
_____ 9. Infant crying tends to peak at about 6 weeks and then declines.
_____ 10. Most researchers agree that prompt and consistent reactions to infant crying actually strengthen crying behavior.

Answers:

1. F
2. T
3. F
4. F
5. T
6. F
7. F
8. T
9. T
10. F

LEARNING ACTIVITY 4.2
Observing Habituation and Recovery in Young Infants (pp. 142–144)

Arrange for parents of a young baby to visit your class. You will need to obtain two toys of different colors ahead of time (large plastic rings available in the infant section of most toy stores work well). Place the baby in an infant seat or ask the parent to hold the baby. Next, present one of the toys to the baby (about 8 to 10 inches from the eyes). Then hold up both toys, side by side. Call students' attention to the baby's tendency to focus on the new, or unfamiliar, toy.

You may want to combine this activity with Learning Activity 4.5, which is also a classroom demonstration.

LEARNING ACTIVITY 4.3
Applying Developmental Theories to Newborn Imitation (pp. 145–146)

Have students form small groups and review the following theories of development: behaviorism, social learning theory, cognitive-developmental theory, and ethology (Chapter 1, pp. 17–21, 23–24). How might each of these theories explain the importance of newborn imitation? For instance, how can both parents and babies reinforce one another's imitation? How might newborn imitation contribute to the development of attachment? Once students have considered each theory, ask them to share their examples with the class.

LEARNING ACTIVITY 4.4
Scramble: Gross- and Fine-Motor Skills in the First Two Years (p. 148)

Present the following exercise as a quiz or in-class assignment.

Directions: Below is a list of gross- and fine-motor milestones that develop during the first two years. Place them in the order in which they typically occur (that is, average age achieved).

Milestones:
_____ 1. rolls from side to back
_____ 2. plays pat-a-cake
_____ 3. grasps a cube
_____ 4. when held upright, holds head erect and steady
_____ 5. jumps in place
_____ 6. pulls to a stand
_____ 7. walks alone
_____ 8. rolls from back to side
_____ 9. scribbles vigorously
_____ 10. stands alone
_____ 11. walks on tiptoe
_____ 12. walks up stairs with help
_____ 13. sits alone

Answers:

1.	4	8.	10
2.	1	9.	7
3.	3	10.	9
4.	8	11.	12
5.	13	12.	5
6.	6	13.	11
7.	2		

LEARNING ACTIVITY 4.5
Infant Development Demonstration: Gross- and Fine-Motor Development (pp. 147–152)

Arrange for parents of three or four babies to bring their children to your class for a demonstration of infant gross- and fine-motor milestones. Ideally, the infants should represent the following age ranges: less than 2 months, 4 to 8 months, and 8 to 14 months. Students may know parents who are willing to participate, or you may have friends or colleagues willing to attend the class for a demonstration. Before the demonstration, ask parents to bring a small selection of toys, or arrange to provide some yourself. This keeps the infants you are not focusing on at the moment occupied, and it also enables students to observe the babies' spontaneous play.

Demonstrate the following capacities discussed in the chapter:

(1) 0–2 MONTHS

Gross-motor development: Place the baby prone, and see if he or she lifts the head and looks around. From a supine position, pull the infant slowly to a sitting position and observe the ability to support the head. Infants of about 6 to 8 weeks of age, when held vertically, will hold the head erect.

Other milestones: Demonstrate the baby's ability to track an object with his or her eyes, respond to the sound of the mother's voice, and smile spontaneously (appears during the second month). You may also demonstrate prereaching (in infants under 7 weeks) by presenting a toy and observing how the infant makes poorly coordinated swipes or swings toward the toy. Alternate the toy between the infant's hands and feet to demonstrate foot reaching.

(2) 4–8 MONTHS

Gross-motor development: The following gross-motor accomplishments generally appear between 4 and 8 months of age and can be demonstrated: sitting, first with support and then alone; standing with support; and (at the end of this period) getting into a sitting position and pulling self to a standing position. To demonstrate, place the infant on his or her stomach and observe the infant's attempts to get up on all fours. Some of the older infants may even crawl a short distance.

Fine-motor development: Demonstrate the infant's ability to grasp objects using a rattle or other toy. Babies of about 4½ months should be able to grasp an object presented at the midline and on the same side as, or on the opposite side of the body from, the reaching hand (the younger 3-month-old will only grasp an object offered on the same side of the body). Point out the use of the ulnar grasp, a clumsy motion in which the fingers close against the palm. Infants of about 6 months of age can also be seen passing objects from hand to hand, and they will rake a raisin to obtain it.

(3) 8–14 MONTHS

Gross-motor development: Crawling, standing alone, and walking are gross-motor accomplishments that generally appear during this time frame.

Fine-motor development: Place a raisin before the infant to show students the well-coordinated pincer grasp. Babies of this age can put objects in and dump them out of containers. Sometimes they will build a tower of two cubes with blocks.

LEARNING ACTIVITY 4.6
Interviewing Parents about Training Infant Motor Skills (pp. 147–152)

Have students pose the following question to several parents they know: Should sitting, crawling, and walking be deliberately encouraged in infants and toddlers? Why or why not? Next, ask students to bring their answers to class for discussion. Based on their responses, did parents believe that motor development should be encouraged, or did they believe that motor skills will develop on their own? Were there any cultural differences in the answers? Are students surprised by any of the answers? Explain.

LEARNING ACTIVITY 4.7
Evaluating a Website Featuring Developmental Toys for Infants and Toddlers (pp. 139–146, 152–168)

Have students visit a website sponsored by Fisher Price, *www.fisherprice.com/us/,* which presents suggested toys and activities for babies according to their age and developmental level. Have students click on Play & Learn: Playtime Guide. Students should then select two age ranges and answer the following questions: What developmental information is presented for each age range? Is it consistent with research presented in the text? How do the recommended toys appeal to infants' and toddlers' developing learning capacities? How about perceptual development? Using what you know about stimulation, are the toys appropriate for the age range? Why or why not?

ASK YOURSELF . . .

REVIEW: Provide an example of classical conditioning, of operant conditioning, and of habituation/recovery in young infants. Why is each type of learning useful? Cite differences between operant conditioning and habituation findings on infant memory. (pp. 140–145)

Classical conditioning: Newborn reflexes make classical conditioning possible in young infants. For example, a mother who gently strokes her infant's forehead before nursing will soon notice that each time the baby's forehead is stroked, the baby makes active sucking movements, indicating that he has been classically conditioned, so the neutral stimulus alone (stroking the baby's forehead) produces a response similar to the reflexive response (sucking). Classical conditioning helps infants recognize which events usually occur together in the everyday world, so they can anticipate what will happen next. As a result, the environment becomes more orderly and predictable.

Operant conditioning: In operant conditioning, infants act, or *operate,* on the environment, and stimuli that follow their behavior change the probability that the behavior will occur again. For example, researchers have found that newborns will suck faster on a nipple when doing so produces interesting sights and sounds, including visual designs, music, or human voices. Operant conditioning allows infants to explore and control their surroundings in an effort to meet their needs for nutrition, stimulation, and social contact.

Habituation/recovery: Habituation refers to a gradual reduction in the strength of a response due to repetitive stimulation. Once this has occurred, a new stimulus—a change in the environment—causes the habituated response to return to a high level, an increase called *recovery.* By studying infants' habituation and recovery, researchers can explore babies' understanding of the world. For example, a baby who first habituates to a visual pattern (a photo of a baby) and then recovers to a new one (a photo of a bald man) appears to remember the first stimulus and perceive the second one as new and different from it. Habituation and recovery promote learning by focusing infants' attention on those aspects of the environment they know least about.

Habituation research shows that infants remember a wide range of stimuli, especially the movements of objects and people, and that they retain such information over many weeks. But some researchers argue that operant conditioning better explains infant memory because it is through their active efforts that infants learn to master their environment. In a series of studies, 3-month-olds remembered how to activate a mobile by kicking one week after training. Even after 2- to 6-month-olds had forgotten the operant response, a brief prompt was enough to reinstate the memory. A dramatic rise in retention of operant responses occurs over the first 18 months. Operant conditioning also recognizes that memory is highly context-dependent during the first six months. After 9 months, however, when babies are able to move on their own, the importance of context declines.

CONNECT: How do the diverse capacities of newborn babies contribute to their first social relationships? List as many examples as you can. (pp. 130–131, 133, 136–138)

Reflexes: Reflexes are the newborn's most obvious organized patterns of behavior. Several reflexes help parents and infants establish gratifying interaction. A baby who searches for and successfully finds the nipple, sucks easily during feedings, and grasps when her hand is touched encourages parents to respond lovingly and feel competent as caregivers. Reflexes also help parents comfort the baby because they permit infants to control distress and amount of stimulation.

States of arousal: Individual differences in babies' daily rhythms of sleep and wakefulness affect parents' attitudes toward and interactions with their baby. When newborns sleep for long periods, their well-rested parents have the energy for sensitive, responsive care. But when babies wake frequently, cry often, and are difficult to soothe, parents may feel anxious, less competent, and less positive toward their infant. Also, babies who spend more time alert probably receive more social stimulation and opportunities to explore, which may give them a slight advantage in mental development.

Crying: A baby's cry stimulates strong feelings of arousal and discomfort in adults—both men and women, parents and nonparents. This powerful response is probably innately programmed in all human beings to help ensure that babies receive the care and protection they need to survive.

APPLY: After a difficult birth, 2-day-old Kelly scores poorly on the NBAS. How would you address her mother's concern that Kelly might not develop normally? (pp. 138–139)

The Neonatal Behavioral Assessment Scale (NBAS) evaluates the newborn baby's reflexes, muscle tone, state changes, responsiveness to physical and social stimuli, and other reactions. But a single NBAS score is not a good predictor of later development. Because Kelly experienced a difficult birth, she probably needs time to recover. In addition, Kelly's behavior will combine with her mother's parenting practices to shape development. Therefore, changes in NBAS scores over the first week or two of life (rather than a single score) will provide the best estimate of Kelly's ability to recover from the stress of birth. Unlike a single score, NBAS "recovery curves" predict normal brain functioning, intelligence, and absence of emotional and behavior problems with moderate success well into the preschool years.

REFLECT: What is your attitude toward parent–infant cosleeping? Is it influenced by your cultural background? (p. 134)

This is an open-ended question with no right or wrong answer.

REVIEW: Cite evidence that motor development is a joint product of biological, psychological, and environmental factors. (pp. 148–150)

According to dynamic systems theory of motor development, mastery of motor skills involves acquiring increasingly complex systems of action. Each new skill is a joint product of four factors: (1) central nervous system development, (2) the body's movement capacities, (3) the goals the child has in mind, and (4) environmental supports for the skill. Change in any element makes the system less stable, prompting the child to explore and select new, more effective motor patterns. Because motor development is motivated by exploration and the desire to master new tasks, it cannot be genetically determined. Rather, heredity can map out motor development only at a general level. Behaviors are not *hardwired* into the nervous system but, rather, are *softly assembled,* allowing for different paths to the same motor skill.

The factors that induce change vary with age. In the early weeks of life, brain and body growth are especially important as infants achieve control over the head, shoulders, and upper torso. Later, the baby's goals (getting a toy or crossing the room) and environmental supports (parental encouragement, objects in the infants' everyday setting) play a greater role. The broader physical environment also profoundly influences motor skills. For example, infants with stairs in their home learn to crawl up stairs at an earlier age and more readily master a back-descent strategy for getting down the stairs.

Cultural variations in infant-rearing practices also affect motor development. For example, among the Kipsigis of Kenya and the West Indians of Jamaica, parents deliberately teach motor skills, such as holding the head up, sitting alone, and walking—and babies master these skills earlier than in other cultures. In contrast, the current Western practice of putting babies to sleep on their backs to protect them from sudden infant death syndrome delays gross-motor milestones of rolling, sitting, and crawling. To prevent these delays, caregivers can regularly expose babies to the tummy-lying position during waking hours. If motor development were hardwired into the brain, these striking cross-cultural differences would not exist.

CONNECT: Provide several examples of how motor development supports infants' attainment of cognitive and social competencies. (p. 147)

Babies' motor achievements have a powerful effect on their social relationships. When babies start to crawl or walk, parents begin interacting with them to restrict their movements—saying "no," expressing mild impatience, or redirecting their attention. At the same time, newly walking babies more actively attend to and initiate social interaction, seeking out parents for greetings, hugs, or games. Parents, in turn, increase their use of language, playful activities, and expressions of affection. In addition, babies' delight as they work on new motor skills triggers pleasurable reactions in others, which encourage infants' efforts further. Motor, social, cognitive, and language competencies not only develop together but also support one another.

APPLY: List everyday experiences that promote infants' mastery of reaching, grasping, sitting, and crawling. Why should caregivers place young infants in a variety of waking-time body positions? (pp. 147–148, 151–152)

Like other motor milestones, reaching is affected by early experience. For example, in cultures where mothers carry their infants on their hips or in slings for most of the day, babies have rich opportunities to explore with their hands. Infants of the !Kung of Botswana, who grasp their mothers' dangling jewelry while breastfeeding or riding along, are advanced in development of reaching and grasping. Babies of Mali and Uganda, who spend at least half of their day in sitting or standing positions, which facilitate reaching, develop manual skills earlier than Western infants, who spend much of their day lying down.

Visual stimulation also promotes early reaching. In a well-known study, institutionalized infants given a moderate amount of visual stimulation—at first, simple designs and, later, a mobile hung over the crib—reached for objects six weeks earlier than infants given nothing to look at. A third group given massive stimulation—patterned crib bumpers and mobiles at an early age—also reached sooner than unstimulated babies. But this heavy enrichment took a toll. These infants looked away and cried a great deal, and they were less advanced in reaching than the moderately stimulated group.

Reaching improves as depth perception advances and as infants gain greater control of body posture and arm and hand movements. Through practice, babies increasingly adjust their grasp to the size and shape of an object, a capacity that improves over the first year. When infants begin to sit up, around 4 to 5 months, they coordinate both hands in exploring objects, holding an object in one hand while exploring it with the other and transferring objects from hand to hand. By the end of the first year, babies use the thumb and index finger in a well-coordinated pincer grasp, greatly expanding their ability to pick up and manipulate small objects.

In similar fashion, when babies are given opportunities to sit upright, they get a new perspective on the world, which encourages them to explore further. Kicking, rocking on all fours, and reaching combine to become crawling; then crawling, standing, and stepping are united into walking. When infants spend most of the time in a single position, as happens in orphanages, where babies may spend days lying on their backs in cribs, without toys to play with, development of skills such as walking is seriously delayed. By placing young infants in a variety of waking-time body positions, caregivers create opportunities for the babies to practice and build on their developing motor skills.

REFLECT: Do you favor early, systematic training of infants in motor skills such as crawling, walking, and stair climbing? Why or why not? (pp. 148–150)

This is an open-ended question with no right or wrong answer.

REVIEW: Using examples, explain why intermodal stimulation is vital for infants' developing understanding of their physical and social worlds. (pp. 166, 168)

We receive constant *intermodal stimulation*—simultaneous input from more than one modality, or sensory system. Intermodal perception is the way we make sense of these streams of sensory information so that we perceive objects and events as unified wholes. Newborns turn in the general direction of a sound and reach for objects in a primitive way, suggesting that they expect sight, sound, and touch to go together. By 3 to 4 months, infants can match faces with voices on the basis of lip–voice synchrony, emotional expression, and even the speaker's age and gender; between 4 and 6 months, they can perceive and remember the unique face–voice pairings of unfamiliar adults.

By enabling babies to notice meaningful correlations between sensory inputs and to use these to make sense of their surroundings, intermodal perception facilitates social and language processing. When caregivers provide many concurrent sights, sounds, touches, and smells, babies process more information, learn faster, and show better memory—another example of infants' active efforts to build an orderly, predictable world.

CONNECT: According to differentiation theory, perceptual development reflects infants' active search for invariant features. Provide examples from research on hearing, pattern perception, and intermodal perception. (pp. 155–158, 161, 163, 166, 168)

Hearing: Invariant features are those that remain stable in a constantly changing perceptual world. Infants as young as 3 days old turn their eyes and head in the general direction of a sound, an ability that improves greatly over the first 6 months. At birth, infants prefer complex sounds, such as noises and voices, to pure tones. And babies only a few days old can tell the difference between a variety of sound patterns. Over the first year, infants organize sounds into increasingly elaborate patterns. Around 5 months, babies become sensitive to syllable-stress patterns in their own language; between 6 and 8 months, they start to "screen out" sounds not used in their native tongue. Soon after, they recognize familiar words in spoken passages and listen longer to speech with clear clause and phrase boundaries. Around 7 to 9 months, they extend this sensitivity to speech structure to individual words and begin to divide the speech stream into wordlike units. Overall, babies show a powerful ability to extract patterns from complex, continuous speech.

Pattern perception: Even newborns prefer to look at patterned rather than plain stimuli. At first, infants respond to the separate parts of a pattern—single, high-contrast features. At 2 to 3 months, babies thoroughly explore a pattern's internal features, pausing briefly to look at each part. Once babies take in all aspects of a pattern, they integrate the parts into a unified whole. Around 4 months, they are so good at detecting pattern organization that they perceive subjective boundaries that are not really present. At 12 months, infants detect familiar objects represented by incomplete drawings, even when as much as two-thirds of the drawing is missing.

Infants' tendency to search for a structure in a patterned stimulus applies to face perception. Newborns prefer to look at photos and simplified drawings of faces with features arranged naturally (upright) rather than unnaturally (upside down or sideways). They also track a facelike pattern moving across their visual field farther than they track other stimuli.

Intermodal perception: From the start, babies perceive input from different sensory systems in a unified way by detecting *amodal sensory properties*—information that overlaps two or more sensory systems, such as rate, rhythm, duration, intensity, temporal synchrony (for vision and hearing), and texture and shape (for vision and touch). Young infants seem biologically primed to focus on amodal information—for example, the common tempo and rhythm in concurrent sights and sounds. This precedes and seems to provide a basis for detecting more specific intermodal matches, such as the relation between a person's face and the sound of his or her voice or between an object and its verbal label. In the first half-year of life, when much input is unfamiliar and confusing, intermodal stimulation helps babies selectively attend to and make sense of their surroundings.

APPLY: After several weeks of crawling, Ben learned to avoid going headfirst down a steep incline. Now he has started to walk. Can his mother trust him not to try walking down a steep surface? Explain, using the concept of affordances. (pp. 168–169)

According to differentiation theory, developed by Eleanor and James Gibson, perception is guided by the discovery of *affordances*—the action possibilities that a situation offers an organism with certain motor capabilities. When babies crawl, and again when they walk, they gradually realize that a steeply sloping surface *affords* the possibility of falling. With added weeks of practice, they hesitate to crawl or walk down a risky incline. Experience in trying to keep their balance on various surfaces makes crawlers and walkers more aware of the consequences of their movements. Crawlers come to detect when surface slant places so much body weight on their arms that they will fall forward, and walkers come to sense when an incline shifts body weight so their legs and feet can no longer hold them upright. Because Ben is just starting to walk, he probably does not yet realize that a steep incline affords the possibility of falling. Therefore, his mother should hold his hand or support him as he walks down the incline.

REFLECT: Are young infants more competent than you thought they were before you read this chapter? List the capacities that most surprised you.

This is an open-ended question with no right or wrong answer.

REVIEW: Explain why either too much stimulation or too little stimulation over an extended time negatively disrupts early development. (pp. 169–171)

Babies reared in severely deprived family situations or in institutions remain substantially below average in physical and psychological development and display emotional and behavior problems throughout childhood. In studies of children placed in Romanian orphanages and later exposed to family rearing, those who were institutionalized for more than the first six months showed serious intellectual deficits as well as difficulty discriminating others' emotional expressions—a persistent deficiency that contributes to emotional and social adjustment problems. Abnormal development in one domain often impedes progress in others, suggesting that the more time infants and young children spend in impoverished environments, the more devastating the effects on their development.

In addition to impoverished environments, ones that overwhelm children with expectations beyond their current capacities also undermine development. Trying to create smarter "superbabies" by using stimulation for which they are not ready—such as letter and number flash cards for infants or an academic curriculum for slightly older toddlers—can cause children to withdraw, threatening their spontaneous interest and pleasure in learning and creating conditions much like those of stimulus deprivation.

CONNECT: What implications do findings on children from Eastern European orphanages have for the controversy over the lasting impact of early experiences on development? (see Chapter 1, page 9) (pp. 170–171)

Research on children from Eastern European orphanages consistently shows that the earlier infants are removed from deprived rearing conditions, the greater their catch-up in development. In one study, researchers followed the progress of a large sample of children transferred between birth and 3½ years from Romanian orphanages to adoptive families in Great Britain. On arrival, most were impaired in all domains of development. By the preschool years, catch-up in physical size was dramatic. Cognitive catch-up was impressive for children adopted before age 6 months, who consistently attained average mental test scores in childhood and adolescence when compared with a group of early-adopted British-born children. But children adopted after age 6 months showed serious intellectual deficits and mental health problems, such as inattention, overactivity, unruly behavior, and autistic-like symptoms. Below-average head size in these children suggested that early lack of stimulation permanently damaged the brain.

The fact that the early-adopted children showed recovery from early deprivation provides support for the possibility of plasticity—openness to change in response to influential experiences. Interventions that provide warm, stimulating caregiver interaction and environmental enrichment have lasting cognitive and social benefits; withdrawn, apathetic babies become active and alert and, therefore, capable of evoking positive interactions and of initiating stimulating experiences for themselves.

REFLECT: Do you think infancy is a sensitive period? Explain, using research evidence. (pp. 169–171)

This is an open-ended question with no right or wrong answer.

SUGGESTED READINGS

Nelson, K. (2010). *Young minds in social worlds: Experience, meaning, and memory.* Cambridge, MA: Harvard University Press. Presents leading research on how the social environment profoundly shapes early learning and development. The author argues that babies and young children not only strive to make sense of their world, they also create meaning through shared experiences with others.

Ottaviani, G. (2010). *Crib death: Sudden unexplained death of infants.* New York: Springer-Verlag. Examines the mystery behind sudden infant death syndrome (SIDS) by highlighting neurological and cardiac abnormalities common among babies who die unexpectedly. An excellent resource for those interested in nursing, medicine, or psychology-related professions.

Woodward, A., & Needham, A. (2009). *Learning and the infant mind.* New York: Oxford University Press. A compelling look at infant cognition, this book presents research on early learning, including knowledge of objects, categorization, and the relationship between locomotion and cognitive development.

Chapter 4 Infancy: Early Learning, Motor Skills, and Perceptual Capacities

MEDIA MATERIALS

For details on individual video segments that accompany the DVD for *Child Development,* Ninth Edition, please see the DVD Guide for *Explorations in Child Development*. The DVD and DVD Guide are available through your Pearson sales representative.

Additional DVDs that may be useful in your class are listed below. These are not available through your Pearson sales representative, but you can order them directly from the distributors. (See contact information at the end of this manual.)

Development and Discovery (2005, Magna Systems, 29 min.). Part of the *Beginnings of Life* series, this program describes how the newborn appears in the first four weeks of life and introduces tools for assessing neonates, including the Apgar scale and the revised Brazelton Clinical Neonatal Assessment Scale. It also provides information on infant reflexes, infant sleep and states of arousal, the infant's perception of pain, and how newborns bond with and respond to an adult.

Exploring and Learning (2002, Magna Systems, 25 min.). This program illustrates how the trusted caregiver is initially the child's primary mode of learning. It also discusses how the child learns to handle and arrange objects, such as blocks, in space. Infants and toddler problem solving is also demonstrated.

First Year Milestones (2006, Insight Media, 60 min.). This program features eight infants as they attain developmental milestones in the first year of life. Additional topics include bonding, brain development, memory, play, self-esteem, and communication.

Infants: Physical Development (2010, Magna Systems/Learning Seed, 29 min.). This program explores infant brain development, outlines activities that stimulate healthy brain growth, and emphasizes the importance of proper nutrition and sleep in the first year. It also describes infant reflexes and considers the emergence of gross- and fine-motor skills in children who are developing normally and in children with challenging conditions.

Interpretations: Perception (2006, Insight Media, 30 min.). This program shows how the brain selects, organizes, and interprets sensations to form the perceptions that create meaning. It explains how segmentation, grouping, depth perception, and motion allow the brain to decipher and process sensory input.

Life at One: New Experiences (2006, Insight Media, 54 min.). This program introduces a group of 1-year-olds who are participating in a longitudinal study on child development. It documents the daily routines and developmental milestones of the children and gauges each child's ability to confront new experiences.

Making Sense of Sensory Information (2008, Insight Media, 37 min.). This film explores visual perception and considers the role of human experience in determining what people perceive. It introduces the visual system, includes animated graphics and live-action footage, and uses demonstrations of optics to demonstrate the technical and philosophical challenges scientists face when attempting to explain perception.

Steps and Stages: A Caregiver's Guide to Child Development (2002, Films Media Group/A Cambridge Educational Production, 20 min.). This program provides essential information about the developmental milestones of a child's first 15 months, including infant reflexes, advances in motor development, and the beginnings of communication.

The Development of Movements in the First Year of Life (2004, Insight Media, 30 min.). This program outlines the development of motor skills during the first 15 months of an infant's life. It also considers the role of early motor development in childhood intelligence.

The Newborn: Development and Discovery (2005, Insight Media, 29 min.). This program examines methods of assessing a newborn's motor, reflex, and sensory systems. It considers changes in reflexes, bonding, and the cognitive and emotional development of the infant.

What Babies Can Do (2009, Insight Media, 52 min.). Starting out with the assumption that even young infants are capable of high-level perception and cognition, this program demonstrates simple studies that assess what infants of different ages do and do not know about their environment.

CHAPTER 5
PHYSICAL GROWTH

CHAPTER-AT-A-GLANCE

Chapter Outline	Instruction Ideas	Supplements
The Course of Physical Growth **pp. 176–184** Changes in Body Size • Changes in Body Proportions • Changes in Muscle–Fat Makeup • Skeletal Growth • Gains in Gross-Motor Skills • Hormonal Influences on Physical Growth • Worldwide Variations in Body Size • Secular Trends	Learning Objectives 5.1–5.3 Lecture Enhancement 5.1 Learning Activities 5.1–5.2, 5.4–5.5 Ask Yourself p. 184	Test Bank Items 1–30, 126–127 Please contact your Pearson publisher's representative for a wide range of video offerings available to adopters.
Brain Development pp. 184–192 Development of Neurons • Development of the Cerebral Cortex • Advances in Other Brain Structures • Brain Development in Adolescence • Sensitive Periods in Brain Development	Learning Objectives 5.4–5.5 Learning Activity 5.3 Ask Yourself p. 192	Test Bank Items 31–59, 128
Factors Affecting Physical Growth **pp. 192–202** Heredity • Nutrition • Infectious Disease • Emotional Well-Being	Learning Objective 5.6 Lecture Enhancement 5.2 Learning Activity 5.4 Ask Yourself p. 202	Test Bank Items 60–91, 129
Puberty: The Physical Transition to Adulthood pp. 203–205 Sexual Maturation in Girls • Sexual Maturation in Boys • Individual and Group Differences in Pubertal Growth	Learning Objective 5.7 Learning Activities 5.6–5.7	Test Bank Items 92–96
The Psychological Impact of Pubertal Events pp. 205–210 Is Puberty Inevitably a Period of Storm and Stress? • Reactions to Pubertal Changes • Pubertal Change, Emotion, and Social Behavior • Pubertal Timing	Learning Objectives 5.8–5.9 Lecture Enhancement 5.3 Learning Activities 5.5–5.7 Ask Yourself p. 210	Test Bank Items 97–105, 130
Puberty and Adolescent Health **pp. 210–221** Eating Disorders • Sexuality • Sexually Transmitted Disease • Adolescent Pregnancy and Parenthood • A Concluding Note	Learning Objectives 5.10–5.13 Lecture Enhancement 5.4 Learning Activities 5.7–5.9 Ask Yourself p. 221	Test Bank Items 106–125, 131

BRIEF CHAPTER SUMMARY

Primates, including humans, experience a prolonged period of physical growth. Physical growth in infancy and childhood follows the cephalocaudal and proximodistal trends. During puberty, growth proceeds in the reverse direction, and sex differences in body proportions appear.

The best estimate of a child's physical maturity is skeletal age, a measure of development of the bones. In early childhood, body growth causes the child's center of gravity to shift toward the trunk, which paves the way for new gross-motor skills. As they develop, children integrate previously acquired motor skills. In childhood, boys' advantage over girls in many gross-motor skills largely reflects parental expectations and practice.

The endocrine glands control the physical changes of childhood and adolescence through a complex set of hormonal secretions released by the pituitary gland and regulated by the hypothalamus. Sexual maturation is controlled by pituitary secretions that stimulate the release of the sex hormones, estrogens and androgens.

Worldwide variations in body size are the combined result of heredity and environment. Secular trends in physical growth have occurred in industrialized nations as a result of improved health and nutrition. Consequently, most children are taller and heavier than their ancestors and reach puberty earlier.

The human brain reaches its adult size earlier than any other organ. Stimulation of the brain is vital during periods in which it is growing most rapidly. Although some lateralization, or specialization of the cerebral hemispheres, exists at birth, brain plasticity remains high for the first few years.

Both heredity and nutrition affect physical growth. Breastfeeding is especially well-suited to meeting infants' growth needs. The importance of adequate nutrition is evident in the most severe forms of malnutrition—marasmus and kwashiorkor. Infectious disease can combine with poor nutrition to undermine healthy physical development. Growth faltering and psychosocial dwarfism illustrate the role of parental love and stimulation in children's healthy physical growth. In industrialized countries, and increasingly in developing countries as well, overweight and obesity are growing problems, with health, psychological, and social consequences.

Puberty brings dramatic physical changes leading to an adult-sized body and sexual maturity. Whereas many tribal and village societies celebrate the onset of puberty with an adolescent initiation ceremony, Western societies grant little formal recognition to puberty. Although adolescents' physical changes and growing powers of reasoning may lead to a rise in family strife, such conflict is generally mild. The timing of puberty has a major impact on psychological adjustment. For some adolescent girls, cultural ideals of thinness play a role in producing the serious eating disorders of anorexia nervosa and bulimia.

Biological factors, including heredity and prenatal hormone levels, play an important role in homosexuality. Lesbian, gay, and bisexual teenagers face special challenges in establishing a positive sexual identity. American adolescents receive mixed messages from adults and the social environment about sexual activity, which contributes to high rates of teenage pregnancy, abortion, and parenthood. The best approach to teenage pregnancy is prevention, but when babies are born to adolescents, young mothers need school programs that provide job training, instruction in parenting and life-management skills, and child care.

LEARNING OBJECTIVES

After reading this chapter, you should be able to answer the following:

5.1 Describe the course of physical growth, including changes in body size, proportions, muscle–fat makeup, and skeleton, and their relationship to gains in gross-motor skills. (pp. 176–181)

5.2 Describe hormonal influences on physical growth. (pp. 181–183)

5.3 Discuss factors that contribute to worldwide variations and secular trends in physical growth. (pp. 183–184)

5.4 Cite major milestones in brain development, at the level of individual brain cells and at the level of the cerebral cortex. (pp. 184–189)

5.5 Describe changes in other brain structures and in the adolescent brain, and discuss evidence on sensitive periods in brain development. (pp. 189–192)

Chapter 5 Physical Growth

5.6 How do heredity, nutrition, infectious disease, and parental affection contribute to physical growth and health? (pp. 192–202)

5.7 Describe sexual maturation in girls and boys, noting genetic and environmental influences on pubertal timing. (pp. 203–205)

5.8 What factors influence adolescents' reactions to the physical changes of puberty? (pp. 205–208)

5.9 Describe the impact of pubertal timing on adolescent adjustment, noting sex differences. (pp. 208–210)

5.10 What factors contribute to eating disorders in adolescence? (pp. 210–212)

5.11 Discuss cultural, social, and personal influences on adolescent sexual attitudes and behavior. (pp. 212–215)

5.12 Cite factors involved in the development of homosexuality. (pp. 215–216)

5.13 Discuss factors related to sexually transmitted disease and teenage pregnancy and parenthood, noting prevention and intervention strategies. (pp. 217–220)

LECTURE OUTLINE

I. THE COURSE OF PHYSICAL GROWTH (pp. 176–184)
   A. All primates, including humans, experience a prolonged period of physical growth compared with other animals.
      1. Prolonged physical immaturity ensures that children remain dependent on adults long enough to acquire the knowledge and skills essential for life in a complex social world.
      2. Physical and psychological development are closely linked, but disagreement exists about how they are related, especially in *puberty*.
   B. Changes in Body Size (pp. 176, 177)
      1. During infancy, body size changes rapidly; growth slows in early and middle childhood and then accelerates sharply at puberty.
      2. Two types of growth curves are used to track overall changes in body size:
         a. The **distance curve,** which plots the average size of a sample of children at each age, indicates typical yearly progress toward maturity.
         b. The **velocity curve,** which plots the average amount of growth at each yearly interval, reveals the exact timing of growth spurts.
   C. Changes in Body Proportions (pp. 176–177)
      1. After birth, growth follows the **cephalocaudal trend,** with the head and chest having a growth advantage over the trunk and legs, and the **proximodistal trend,** with growth from the center of the body outward.
      2. During puberty, the hands, legs, and feet accelerate first, followed by the torso, and large differences between girls and boys appear.
   D. Changes in Muscle–Fat Makeup (p. 177)
      1. Body fat increases prenatally and also after birth, reaching a peak at about 9 months of age.
      2. Girls have slightly more body fat than boys at birth, a difference that persists into the early school years and then magnifies.
      3. Muscle accumulates slowly in infancy and childhood, with a dramatic rise at adolescence, especially for boys.
   E. Skeletal Growth (p. 178)
      1. The best estimate of a child's physical maturity is **skeletal age,** a measure of development of the bones.
      2. The embryonic skeleton is first formed of soft, pliable tissue called cartilage; during pregnancy, cartilage cells begin to harden into bone, a process that continues throughout childhood and adolescence.
      3. Growth centers called **epiphyses** appear at the extreme ends of the long bones of the body just before birth and continue to produce cartilage cells throughout childhood but eventually disappear, at which point bone growth stops.
      4. Girls are considerably ahead of boys in skeletal age and in development of other organs at birth and over infancy and childhood.
   F. Gains in Gross-Motor Skills (pp. 178–181)
      1. Changes in size, proportions, and muscle strength support an explosion of new gross-motor skills.

2. Advances in Early and Middle Childhood
   a. By age 2, preschoolers' gaits become smooth and rhythmic, allowing them to run and jump, and then, between 3 and 6 years, to hop, gallop, and skip.
   b. During the school years, improved balance, strength, agility, and flexibility support refinements in running, jumping, hopping, and ball skills.
3. In childhood and adolescence, children integrate previously acquired motor skills into more complex *dynamic systems of action,* which they revise as their bodies grow larger and their central nervous systems develop.
4. Size and strength contribute to boys' superior athletic performance in adolescence, whereas in childhood, the social environment plays a prominent role.
5. Organized Youth Sports
   a. Today's school-age children devote less time to outdoor, informal physical play than children in previous generations.
   b. At the same time, about half of U.S. youngsters participate in organized sports at some time between the ages of 5 and 18.
      (1) For most children, playing on an athletic team is associated with increased self-esteem and social skills.
      (2) However, critics argue that youth sports overemphasize competition and substitute adult control for children's natural experimentation with rules and strategies.
   c. Despite the growth of organized sports, only 49 percent of school-age boys and 35 percent of girls are active enough for good health. In adolescence, these rates drop.

G. Hormonal Influences on Physical Growth (pp. 181–183)
   1. The vast physical changes of childhood and adolescence are controlled by the body's endocrine glands, which manufacture *hormones,* chemical substances secreted by specialized cells.
   2. The most important hormones for human growth are released by the **pituitary gland,** located at the base of the brain near the **hypothalamus,** a structure that initiates and regulates pituitary secretions.
   3. **Growth hormone (GH),** the only pituitary secretion produced continuously throughout life, affects the development of all tissues except the central nervous system and the genitals.
   4. GH acts directly on the body and also stimulates the liver and epiphyses to release another hormone, *insulin-like growth factor 1 (IGF-1),* which triggers cell duplication throughout the body.
   5. A second pituitary hormone, **thyroid-stimulating hormone (TSH),** prompts the thyroid gland to release *thyroxine,* necessary for brain development and for GH to have its full impact on body size.
   6. Sexual maturation is controlled by pituitary secretions that stimulate the release of sex hormones.
   7. Although **estrogens** are thought of as female hormones and **androgens** as male hormones, both are present in each sex, but in different amounts.
      a. Androgens, especially *testosterone* for boys (secreted by the testes), exert a GH-enhancing effect, contributing greatly to gains in body size.
      b. In both sexes, estrogens increase GH secretion, adding to the growth spurt and stimulating gains in bone density.
      c. Estrogens released by girls' ovaries cause the breasts, uterus, and vagina to mature and the body to take on feminine proportions; they also help regulate the menstrual cycle.
      d. *Adrenal androgens* influence girls' height spurt but have little impact on boys.

H. Worldwide Variations in Body Size (p. 183)
   1. Worldwide, a 9-inch gap exists between the smallest and the largest 8-year-olds.
   2. Because ethnic variations in growth rate are common, *growth norms* must be applied cautiously.
   3. Both heredity and environment contribute to these differences.
      a. Body size sometimes reflects evolutionary adaptations to a particular climate.
      b. Children who grow tallest usually reside in developed countries, where food is plentiful.

I. Secular Trends (p. 184)
   1. Over the past 150 years, **secular trends in physical growth**—changes in body size from one generation to the next—have occurred in industrialized nations, largely as a result of improved health and nutrition.
   2. The pattern of secular gain suggests that the larger size of today's children is mostly due to a faster rate of physical development.
   3. Secular trends are smaller for low-income children, who have poorer diets.

Chapter 5 Physical Growth

II. BRAIN DEVELOPMENT (pp. 184–192)
   A. Development of Neurons (pp. 185–186)
      1. The human brain has 100 to 200 billion **neurons,** or nerve cells, that store and transmit information, many of which have thousands of direct connections with other neurons.
      2. Between the neurons are **synapses,** tiny gaps where fibers from different neurons come close together but do not touch.
      3. Neurons send messages to one another by releasing chemicals called **neurotransmitters,** which cross synapses.
      4. Neurons are produced in the embryo's primitive neural tube and then migrate to form the major parts of the brain.
      5. Neurons then differentiate, establishing their unique functions by forming synaptic connections with neighboring cells.
      6. Because space is needed for these connective structures, **programmed cell death** occurs: As synapses form, many surrounding neurons die.
      7. As neurons form connections, *stimulation* becomes vital to their survival; neurons that are seldom stimulated soon lose their synapses in a process called **synaptic pruning.**
      8. About half of the brain's volume consists of **glial cells,** which are responsible for **myelination,** the coating of neural fibers with an insulating fatty sheath, *myelin,* that improves the efficiency of message transfer.
   B. Development of the Cerebral Cortex (pp. 186–189)
      1. The **cerebral cortex** surrounds the rest of the brain and is the largest brain structure—accounting for 85 percent of the brain's weight and containing the greatest number of neurons and synapses.
      2. Because it is the last brain structure to stop growing, it is sensitive to environmental influences for longer than any other part of the brain.
      3. Regions of the Cerebral Cortex
         a. Different regions of the cerebral cortex have specific functions.
         b. The cortical regions with the most extended period of development are the *frontal lobes.* The **prefrontal cortex,** lying in front of areas controlling body movement, is responsible for thought—including consciousness, attention, inhibition of impulses, reasoning, and planning.
         c. It undergoes especially rapid myelination and formation and pruning of synapses during the preschool and school years, followed by another period of accelerated growth in adolescence.
      4. Lateralization and Plasticity of the Cerebral Cortex
         a. The cerebral cortex has two *hemispheres,* or sides, that differ in their functions.
         b. For most of us, the left hemisphere is largely responsible for verbal abilities and for positive emotion; the right hemisphere handles spatial abilities and negative emotion.
         c. In left-handed people, the cortex may be less clearly specialized.
         d. Specialization of the two hemispheres, or **lateralization,** may have evolved because it enabled humans to cope with changing environmental demands.
         e. Brain Plasticity
            (1) Before lateralization, many areas of the cerebral cortex are not yet committed to specific functions.
            (2) This high level of **brain plasticity** gives the cortex a high capacity for learning.
            (3) An overabundance of synaptic connections supports brain plasticity, ensuring that young children will acquire certain capacities even if some areas are damaged.
         f. Lateralization and Handedness
            (1) By the end of the first year, most children display a right-handed bias.
            (2) Handedness reflects the greater capacity of one side of the brain—the individual's **dominant cerebral hemisphere**—to carry out skilled motor action.
            (3) For right-handed people—90 percent of the population in Western nations—language is housed in the left hemisphere with hand control.
            (4) Although a hereditary *bias* for right-handedness may exist, this bias may not be strong enough to overcome experiences, including prenatal events.
            (5) Unusual lateralization, such as that of left-handers, may have certain advantages, possibly as a result of more even distribution of cognitive functions across hemispheres.
   C. Advances in Other Brain Structures (pp. 189–190)
      1. The **cerebellum,** at the rear and base of the brain, aids in balance and control of body movement.
         a. Development of connections between the cerebellum and the cerebral cortex contributes to dramatic gains in motor coordination and supports thinking.

      b. Damage to the cerebellum is associated with both motor and cognitive deficits.
   2. The **reticular formation,** a structure in the brain stem that maintains alertness and consciousness, generates synapses and myelinates from early childhood into adolescence.
   3. The **hippocampus,** an inner-brain structure that plays a vital role in memory and in images of space that help us find our way, undergoes rapid formation of synapses and myelination in the second half of the first year.
   4. Adjacent to the hippocampus is the **amygdala,** a structure that plays a central role in processing emotional information. Throughout childhood and adolescence, connections between the amygdala and the prefrontal cortex, which governs regulation of emotion, form and myelinate.
   5. The **corpus callosum,** a large bundle of fibers connecting the two cerebral hemispheres, supports smooth coordination of movements and integration of perception, attention, and language.
D. Brain Development in Adolescence (pp. 190–191)
   1. In adolescence, the prefrontal cortex becomes more effective at managing integrated functioning, but the *prefrontal cognitive-control network* still requires fine-tuning, and teenagers' performance on tasks requiring self-restraint and planning is not yet fully mature.
   2. Adolescence also brings changes in the brain's *emotional/social network*. As a result, adolescents react more strongly to stressful events and experience pleasurable stimuli more intensely.
   3. Because the cognitive-control network is not yet functioning optimally, most teenagers find it hard to manage these powerful influences.
   4. The surge in sex hormones at puberty heightens sensitivity of the prefrontal cortex and inner brain structures to the hormone *oxytocin,* which increases responsiveness to emotional and social stimuli.
E. Sensitive Periods in Brain Development (pp. 191–192)
   1. Stimulation of the brain is vital when it is growing most rapidly.
   2. Animal and human studies reveal that early, extreme sensory deprivation results in permanent brain damage and loss of functions, findings that verify the existence of sensitive periods in brain development.
   3. **Experience-expectant brain growth** refers to the young brain's rapidly developing organization, which depends on ordinary experiences to grow normally.
   4. **Experience-dependent brain growth,** a lifelong process, consists of additional growth and refinement of established brain structures as a result of specific learning experiences.

III. FACTORS AFFECTING PHYSICAL GROWTH (pp. 192–202)
   A. Heredity (pp. 192, 194)
      1. Because identical twins are much more alike in body size than fraternal twins, we know that heredity contributes considerably to physical growth.
      2. As long as negative environmental influences like poor nutrition and illness are not severe, deprived children typically show *catch-up growth*—a return to a genetically influenced growth path—once conditions improve.
      3. Genes influence growth by controlling the body's production of and sensitivity to hormones, and genetic makeup also affects body weight.
   B. Nutrition (pp. 194–200)
      1. Nutrition is especially crucial during the first two years, because the baby's brain and body are growing so rapidly.
      2. Breastfeeding versus Bottle-Feeding
         a. In early infancy, breast milk is ideally suited to babies' needs, and bottled formulas try to imitate it.
         b. Breastfed babies in poverty-stricken regions are much less likely to be malnourished and far more likely to survive the first year of life than bottle-fed babies, but many mothers in these areas do not know about the benefits of breastfeeding.
         c. Breastfeeding has become more common in industrialized nations; today, 75 percent of American mothers breastfeed.
         d. Breastfed and bottle-fed children in industrialized nations do not differ in emotional adjustment.
      3. Nutrition in Childhood and Adolescence
         a. At around 1 year, infants' diets should include all the basic food groups.
         b. Children tend to imitate the eating practices of people they admire—both adults and peers.
         c. At puberty, rapid body growth leads to a dramatic rise in food intake, which comes at a time when eating habits are the poorest.
         d. Frequency of family meals is a powerful predictor of healthy eating.

4. Malnutrition
    a. About 27 percent of the world's children suffer from malnutrition before age 5, primarily in developing countries and war-torn areas, where food resources are limited.
    b. The most seriously affected suffer from two dietary diseases:
        (1) **Marasmus,** a wasted condition of the body caused by a diet low in all essential nutrients, usually appears in the first year of life when a baby's mother cannot produce enough breast milk and bottle-feeding is also inadequate.
        (2) **Kwashiorkor,** caused by a diet very low in protein, usually strikes between ages 1 and 3, in regions where children get just enough calories from starchy foods but little protein.
    c. Children who survive these extreme forms of malnutrition often grow to be smaller and suffer from lasting damage to the brain, heart, liver, or other organs.
    d. Malnutrition seriously affects learning and behavior.
    e. The passivity and irritability of malnourished children worsen the impact of poor diet and also accompany *iron-deficiency anemia,* a condition affecting about 25 percent of infants and children worldwide that interferes with many central nervous system processes.
    f. Withdrawal, listlessness, and inability to be soothed when upset reduce the iron-deficient baby's capacity to pay attention, explore, and evoke sensitive caregiving from parents.
    g. Because government-sponsored supplementary food programs do not reach all families in need, an estimated 21 percent of U.S. children suffer from *food insecurity*—uncertain access to enough food for a healthy, active life.
5. Obesity
    a. Today, 32 percent of U.S. children and adolescents are overweight; 17 percent suffer from **obesity**—a greater-than-20-percent increase over healthy weight, based on *body mass index (BMI)*—a ratio of weight to height associated with body fat.
    b. A rise in overweight and obesity has also occurred in many Western nations, such as Canada and Germany, and obesity rates are increasing rapidly in some developing countries, such as China.
    c. Besides serious emotional and social difficulties, obese children are at risk for lifelong health problems.
    d. Causes of Obesity
        (1) Although identical twins are more likely to share the disorder than fraternal twins, heredity accounts for only a *tendency* to gain weight.
        (2) In industrialized nations, a consistent relationship exists between low education and income and overweight and obesity, especially among ethnic minorities.
        (3) Factors responsible include lack of knowledge about healthy diet; a tendency to buy high-fat, low-cost foods; and neighborhoods that lack convenient access to affordable, healthy foods.
        (4) Children who were undernourished in their early years are at risk for later excessive weight gain.
        (5) Parental feeding practices also contribute to childhood obesity, and parents may fail to help children learn to regulate their own food intake.
        (6) Insufficient sleep is consistently associated with weight gain.
        (7) Overweight children are less physically active than their normal-weight peers.
        (8) The broader food environment affects the incidence of obesity.
    e. Consequences of Obesity
        (1) In Western societies, both children and adults rate obese youngsters as unlikable.
        (2) In school, obese children and adolescents are often socially isolated.
        (3) Psychological consequences of obesity combine with discrimination to result in reduced life chances.
    f. Treating Obesity
        (1) The most effective interventions for obesity are family-based and focus on changing behaviors.
        (2) Schools can help reduce obesity by serving healthier meals and ensuring regular physical activity.
C. Infectious Disease (pp. 201–202)
    1. Infectious Disease and Malnutrition
        a. When children are poorly fed, ordinary childhood illnesses interact with malnutrition in a vicious spiral:
            (1) Poor diet depresses the body's immune system.
            (2) Disease, in turn, contributes to malnutrition by reducing appetite and limiting the body's ability to absorb foods.

b. In developing countries, widespread diarrhea, resulting from unsafe water and contaminated foods, causes nearly three million childhood deaths annually.
c. Most developmental impairments and deaths due to diarrhea can be prevented with a nearly cost-free treatment, *oral rehydration therapy (ORT),* which quickly replaces lost body fluids.
      2. Immunization
         a. Widespread immunization of infants and young children in industrialized nations has led to a dramatic decline in childhood diseases in the past half-century.
         b. However, 30 percent of U.S. preschoolers lack essential immunizations.
         c. Inability to pay for vaccines is one cause of inadequate immunization. Another is that some parents believe there is a link between vaccines and a rise in the number of children diagnosed with autism, despite studies showing no consistent effects.
   D. Emotional Well-Being (p. 202)
      1. **Growth faltering** is a term applied to infants whose weight, height, and head circumference are substantially below age-related growth norms and who are withdrawn. In as many as half such cases, a disturbed parent–infant relationship contributes to the failure to grow normally.
      2. Extreme emotional deprivation can lead to **psychosocial dwarfism,** a growth disorder that usually appears between 2 and 15 years of age.

IV. PUBERTY: THE PHYSICAL TRANSITION TO ADULTHOOD (pp. 203–205)
   A. During **puberty,** young people attain an adult-sized body and become capable of producing offspring; along with rapid body growth are changes in physical features related to sexual functioning.
      1. **Primary sexual characteristics** involve the reproductive organs directly.
      2. **Secondary sexual characteristics,** such as breast development, are visible on the outside of the body.
   B. Sexual Maturation in Girls (pp. 203, 204)
      1. Female puberty begins with the budding of the breasts and the growth spurt.
      2. **Menarche,** or first menstruation, typically occurs relatively late in the sequence of pubertal events, between ages 10½ and 15½, when the girl's body is large enough for childbearing.
   C. Sexual Maturation in Boys (pp. 203–204)
      1. The first sign of puberty in boys is the enlargement of the testes.
      2. Pubic hair emerges soon after, about the same time the penis begins to enlarge.
      3. The growth spurt occurs much later in the sequence of pubertal events for boys than for girls. At about age 14, the height gain peaks, facial and body hair emerges, and the voice deepens.
      4. **Spermarche,** or first ejaculation, occurs around age 13½.
   D. Individual and Group Differences in Pubertal Growth (pp. 204–205)
      1. Heredity contributes substantially to the timing of puberty, but nutrition and exercise also make a difference.
      2. Variations in pubertal growth also exist between regions of the world and between income and ethnic groups. Physical health plays a major role.
      3. Early family experiences may also affect pubertal timing. Research indicates that girls and boys with a history of harsh parenting or parental separation tend to reach puberty early.

V. THE PSYCHOLOGICAL IMPACT OF PUBERTAL EVENTS (pp. 205–210)
   A. Is Puberty Inevitably a Period of Storm and Stress? (pp. 205–206)
      1. Although certain emotional problems occur more often in adolescence than earlier, the rate of serious psychological disturbance rises only slightly from childhood to adolescence.
      2. Today we know that biological, psychological, and social forces combine to influence adolescent development.
      3. Most tribal and village societies have a briefer transition to adulthood, but adolescence is not absent.
      4. Because this stage is greatly extended in industrialized nations, adolescents confront a wider array of psychological challenges.
   B. Reactions to Pubertal Changes (p. 206)
      1. Today, girls typically report a mixture of positive and negative emotions.
      2. Overall, boys get much less social support than girls for the physical changes of puberty.
      3. Both girls and boys react more positively to pubertal changes when they are better prepared.
      4. Many tribal and village societies celebrate the onset of puberty with an *adolescent initiation ceremony*.
      5. Western societies grant little formal recognition to the movement from childhood to adolescence.

Chapter 5 Physical Growth

6. Because Western adolescents are granted partial adult status at many different ages, the process of becoming an adult is more confusing.
- C. Pubertal Change, Emotion, and Social Behavior (pp. 207–208)
    1. Adolescent Moodiness
        a. Higher pubertal hormone levels are related to greater moodiness, but only modestly so.
        b. Negative moods are linked to a greater number of negative life events, which increase steadily from childhood to adolescence.
        c. Another contributor to adolescent moodiness is change in sleep schedules.
        d. Frequent reports of negative mood level off in late adolescence.
    2. Parent–Child Relationships
        a. Research in diverse cultures shows a rise in parent–child conflict at puberty.
        b. From an evolutionary perspective, the separation from parents at puberty may be adaptive.
        c. As the teenage years conclude, parent–adolescent interactions are less hierarchical.
- D. Pubertal Timing (pp. 208–210)
    1. The timing of puberty has a major impact on psychological adjustment.
    2. Early-maturing boys are viewed as relaxed and physically attractive, whereas early-maturing girls tend to be unpopular, withdrawn, and prone to depression.
    3. The Role of Physical Attractiveness
        a. The societal image of a good-looking male fits the early-maturing boy.
        b. Early-maturing Caucasian girls tend to report a less positive **body image**—conception of and attitude toward their physical appearance—than their on-time and late-maturing agemates.
    4. The Importance of Fitting in with Peers
        a. Early-maturing girls and late-maturing boys have difficulty because they fall at the extremes in physical development and feel "out of place" with their agemates.
        b. The young person's context greatly increases the likelihood of negative outcomes related to early pubertal timing.
    5. Long-Term Consequences
        a. Unlike early-maturing boys, early-maturing girls are prone to lasting difficulties.
        b. Since childhood family conflict and harsh parenting are linked to earlier pubertal timing, many early-maturing girls may enter adolescence with emotional and social difficulties.

VI. PUBERTY AND ADOLESCENT HEALTH (pp. 210–221)
- A. Eating Disorders (pp. 210–212)
    1. Anorexia Nervosa
        a. **Anorexia nervosa** is an eating disorder in which young people starve themselves because of a compulsive fear of getting fat.
        b. Individuals with anorexia have an extremely distorted body image, seeing themselves as too heavy even after becoming severely underweight.
        c. The physical consequences of anorexia are severe.
        d. Forces within the person, the family, and the larger culture give rise to anorexia nervosa.
        e. Because individuals with anorexia typically deny or minimize their problem, treating the disorder is difficult.
    2. Bulimia Nervosa
        a. In **bulimia nervosa,** young people, mainly girls, engage in strict dieting and excessive exercise accompanied by binge eating, often followed by deliberate vomiting and purging with laxatives.
        b. Bulimia is more common than anorexia and is influenced by heredity as well as by personal and family factors.
        c. Young people with bulimia usually feel depressed and guilty about their abnormal eating habits and want help.
- B. Sexuality (pp. 212–216)
    1. The Impact of Culture
        a. Sexual attitudes in North America are relatively restrictive; typically, parents give children little or no information about sex.
        b. Adolescents who do not get information about sex from their parents are likely to learn from friends, books, magazines, movies, TV, and the Internet.

- c. In several studies, teenagers' media exposure to sexual content positively predicted current sexual activity and intentions to be sexually active in the future.
- d. The contradictory messages delivered by adults and the social environment leave many young people with little sound advice on how to conduct their sex lives responsibly.
2. Adolescent Sexual Attitudes and Behavior
   a. The sexual attitudes of U.S. adolescents and adults have become more liberal over the past 40 years.
   b. Rates of extramarital sex among U.S. young people rose for several decades but have recently declined.
   c. A substantial percentage of young people are sexually active by ninth grade.
3. Characteristics of Sexually Active Adolescents
   a. Early and frequent sexual activity is linked to many personal, family, peer, and educational characteristics that are also associated with growing up in a low-income family.
   b. Early, prolonged father absence predicts higher rates of intercourse and pregnancy among adolescent girls.
4. Contraceptive Use
   a. Although adolescent contraceptive use has increased in recent years, about 20 percent of sexually active teenagers in the United States do not use contraception consistently.
   b. Both adolescent cognition and the social environment play a role in adolescents' reluctance to use contraception.
5. Sexual Orientation
   a. About 4 percent of U.S. 15- to 44-year-olds identify as lesbian, gay, or bisexual.
   b. The evidence to date indicates that genetic and prenatal biological influences are largely responsible for homosexuality.

C. Sexually Transmitted Disease (p. 217)
1. Sexually active adolescents, both homosexual and heterosexual, are at risk for sexually transmitted diseases (STDs).
2. One-fifth of U.S. AIDS cases occur in people between the ages of 20 and 29.
3. School courses and media campaigns have made many young people aware of basic facts about AIDS, but most have limited understanding of other STDs.

D. Adolescent Pregnancy and Parenthood (pp. 217–220)
1. About 740,000 U.S. teenage girls become pregnant annually.
2. The U.S. adolescent pregnancy rate is higher than that of most other industrialized countries.
3. Factors that heighten the risk of adolescent pregnancy are a lack of effective sex education for many teenagers; a scarcity of convenient, low-cost contraceptive services; and the effects of living in poverty, which encourage young people to take risks.
4. Because nearly one-third of U.S. adolescent pregnancies end in abortion, the number of American teenage births in North America is lower than it was 50 years ago, but teenage parenthood is a much greater problem today.
5. Correlates and Consequences of Adolescent Parenthood
   a. Life conditions and personal attributes interfere with teenage mothers' ability to parent effectively.
   b. The lives of expectant teenagers tend to worsen with respect to educational attainment, marital patterns, and economic circumstances.
   c. Teenage girls often experience complications of pregnancy and birth.
   d. Compared with adult mothers, adolescent mothers know less about child development, perceive their babies as more difficult, and interact less effectively with them.
   e. Adolescent parenthood frequently is repeated in the next generation.
6. Prevention Strategies
   a. Effective sex education programs combine several key elements:
      (1) They teach techniques for handling sexual situations—including refusal skills.
      (2) They deliver clear, accurate messages that are appropriate for participating adolescents' culture and sexual experience.
      (3) They last long enough to have an impact.
      (4) They provide specific information about contraceptives and ready access to them.
   b. Sex education programs focusing on abstinence have little or no impact on delaying teenage sexual activity or on preventing pregnancy.
   c. Efforts to prevent adolescent pregnancy and parenthood must go beyond sex education and access to contraception to build academic and social competence.

Chapter 5 Physical Growth

7. Intervening with Adolescent Parents
   a. Young mothers need health care, encouragement to stay in school, job training, instruction in parenting and life-management skills, and high-quality, affordable child care.
   b. Home visiting programs are also helpful. The Nurse–Family Partnership aims to reduce pregnancy and birth complications, promote competent parenting, and improve family conditions for first time, low-income expectant mothers, many of them teenagers.

E. A Concluding Note (p. 221)
   1. Adolescents' unhealthy behaviors are not an irrational response to inner turmoil, as theorists once believed; rather, every level of the ecological system affects teenagers' well-being.
   2. To design more powerful interventions, researchers must deal with simultaneous risks and the multiple factors that contribute to them.
   3. Families, schools, and nations must create conditions that permit adolescents to expand their capacity for positive health practices.

LECTURE ENHANCEMENTS

LECTURE ENHANCEMENT 5.1
Motivational Climate of Youth Sports and Children's Achievement-Related Attributions (pp. 179, 181)

Time: 10–15 minutes

Objective: To examine the effects of motivational climate on children's mastery-oriented versus ego-oriented attributions.

To extend existing research on the effects of sports participation on school-age children, Smith, Smoll, and Cumming (2009) recruited 243 children between ages 9 and 13 years (145 boys, 98 girls) who were participating in community basketball programs. The researchers were primarily interested in factors that contribute to children's mastery-oriented versus ego-oriented motives for sports participation. For example, mastery-oriented children focus on skill development, effort, and self-improvement in sports, just as they do in academics. Ego-oriented children, in contrast, focus more on social comparison and outperforming others and place a high value on recognition and status, regardless of effort. The researchers collected the following information:

(1) During the first week of practice and again during the final week of the competitive season (approximately 12 weeks apart), participants completed the Achievement Goal Scale for Youth Sports (AGSYS), which measures both mastery and ego orientations. Sample mastery-oriented questions included: On a scale of 1 to 5 (1 = not at all true; 5 = very true), "I feel successful when I do my best." "The most important thing is to improve my skills." Ego-related questions included: On a scale of 1 to 5 (1 = not at all true; 5 = very true), "I want to do better than others at my sport." "I want to show that I am better than others."

(2) During the final week of the competitive season, participants completed the Motivational Climate Scale for Youth Sports (MCSYS), which assesses athlete perceptions of coach-initiated motivational climate. Sample mastery-oriented questions included: On a scale of 1 to 5 (1 = not at all true; 5 = very true), "The coach made players feel good when they improved a skill." "The coach said that all of us were important to the team's success." Ego-oriented questions included: On a scale of 1 to 5 (1 = not at all true; 5 = very true), "Winning games was the most important thing for the coach." "The coach paid the most attention to the best players."

Results indicated that coach-initiated motivational climate had important consequences for children's achievement-related motives. Specifically, children whose coaches emphasized cooperation, effort, and improvement scored significantly higher in mastery orientation, whereas children whose coaches emphasized competition and winning scored higher in ego orientation. Moreover, children who rated their coaches as high in ego orientation tended to become more ego oriented over the course of the sports season. Although boys were slightly more ego oriented than girls, particularly at the end of the sports season, coach-initiated motivational climate had a significant impact on both male and female athletes.

Ask students to share their experiences with youth sports. Did their coaches emphasize cooperation and effort or competition and winning? How did the motivational climate affect students' attitudes toward sports?

Smith, R. E., Smoll, F. L., & Cumming, S. P. (2009). Motivational climate and changes in young athletes' achievement goal orientations. *Motivation and Emotion, 33,* 173–183.

Instructor's Resource Manual for Berk / Child Development, 9e

LECTURE ENHANCEMENT 5.2
Does Early Weaning Predict Rapid Weight Gain in Infancy? (pp. 194–195)

Time: 5–10 minutes

Objective: To examine if early weaning predicts rapid weight gain in infancy.

As discussed in the text, one way parents can prevent their infants from becoming overweight children and adults is to breastfeed for the first six months, which is associated with slower early weight gain. But does early weaning predict rapid weight gain in infancy? To find out, Sloan and colleagues (2009) recruited 210 mother–infant pairs. A series of interviews were conducted with the mothers in their homes. When the infants were between 10 and 18 months, the mothers provided information about the length of time they breastfed and when they started introducing solid foods. The researchers also collected demographic information, including household income and the mother's current or most recent occupation. Infant weight was recorded at birth, 8 weeks, 7 months, and 14 months.

Results indicated that babies who were weaned before 4 months of age were heavier at 7 and 14 months than babies who were weaned after 4 months. Both groups—those weaned before 4 months and those weaned after 4 months—started out with similar birth weights. According to Sloan and colleagues, these findings may have important implications for preventing obesity in children and adults. Previous studies have shown that rapid weight gain in infancy and early childhood is related to overweight and obesity, which, in turn, contributes to elevated blood pressure, impaired glucose tolerance (a risk factor for adult-onset diabetes), and coronary heart disease. Thus, a helpful intervention may be to encourage mothers to breastfeed for a minimum of four months.

Sloan, S., Gildea, A., Stewart, M., Sneddon, H., & Iwaniec, D. (2009). Early weaning is related to weight and rate of weight gain in infancy. *Child: Care, Health and Development, 34,* 59–64.

LECTURE ENHANCEMENT 5.3
Pubertal Timing, Adolescent Dating, and Depressed Mood from Adolescence to Early Adulthood (pp. 208–210)

Time: 10–15 minutes

Objective: To examine the effects of pubertal timing and adolescent dating on depressed mood from adolescence to early adulthood.

To examine the effects of pubertal timing and adolescent dating on depressed mood from adolescence to early adulthood, Natsuaki, Biehl, and Ge (2009) recruited 15,170 12-year-olds who were participating in the National Longitudinal Study of Adolescent Health. Participants were followed to age 23. The researchers collected the following information:

(1) At three separate intervals—early adolescence, middle adolescence, and early adulthood—participants completed a depression inventory.
(2) Between ages 12 and 16, participants completed an assessment of pubertal development. Girls provided information on breast development, curviness of the body, and age at menarche. Boys provided information on growth of underarm hair, thickness of facial hair, and lowering of voice.
(3) At early and mid-adolescence, participants were asked, "In the past 18 months, have you had a special romantic relationship with anyone?" If they answered no, participants were then asked if they had kissed and/or told someone that they loved them in the last 18 months. If they answered yes to both questions, they were coded as having a romantic relationship.

Overall, findings indicated that depressed mood tended to increase from ages to 12 to 14, peaking between ages 15 and 16, and then gradually declining into early adulthood. Consistent with previous research, girls scored higher in depression than boys, regardless of age. Results also showed that pubertal timing contributed to depressed mood. Specifically, early-maturing girls were at greatest risk for depression, followed by late-maturing boys.

For both boys and girls, dating at age 12 was a risk factor for depression in early and mid-adolescence, although girls were more vulnerable to the negative consequences of early dating than boys. According to Natsuaki, Biehl, and Ge, one explanation for the negative consequences of early adolescent dating is that romantic relationships require high levels of emotional involvement, energy, motivation, and time, which may interfere with academic achievement, same-sex friendships, and other commitments. Younger adolescents may have an especially difficult time balancing romantic relationships with other developmental tasks, which can lead to emotional problems. Early dating may also lead to increased parent–child conflict. Moreover, girls may be especially vulnerable to the effects of early dating due to their growing preoccupation with intimacy.

Because boys are less concerned with intimacy in interpersonal relationships, they may have a slight buffer against the adverse effects of early romantic involvement. Finally, the negative consequences of early pubertal timing and adolescent dating tended to decline with age for both boys and girls.

According to the text, why are early-maturing girls and late-maturing boys at risk for emotional problems? What factors determine whether the effects of pubertal timing persist?

Natsuaki, M. N., Biehl, M. C., & Ge, X. (2009). Trajectories of depressed mood from early adolescence to young adulthood: The effects of pubertal timing and adolescent dating. *Journal of Research on Adolescence, 19,* 47–74.

LECTURE ENHANCEMENT 5.4
Parental Knowledge, Family Time, and Adolescent Sexual Risk Behaviors (pp. 212–215)

Time: 10–15 minutes

Objective: To extend existing research on how parenting practices contribute to adolescent sexual risk behaviors.

To extend existing research on parenting practices and adolescent sexual risk behaviors, Coley, Votruba-Drzal, and Schindler (2009) recruited 3,206 adolescents who were participating in the National Longitudinal Survey of Youth. Participants were between the ages of 13 and 18 years. The researchers collected the following information at four separate intervals throughout the study:

(1) Participants completed a questionnaire focusing on maternal knowledge, paternal knowledge, and family activities. For example:
- Maternal and paternal knowledge: On a scale of 0 to 4 (0 = knows nothing; 4 = knows everything), "How much does s/he know about whom you are with when you are not at home?"
- Family activities: On a scale of 0 to 7 (0 = no days per week; 7 = seven days per week), "How often do you eat dinner with your family?" "Have fun with your family?" "Participate in some religious activity with your family?"

(2) Participants reported on their involvement in risky sexual behavior. Questions included: "How many times have you had sexual intercourse in the last 12 months?" "How many partners have you had in the last 12 months?" "Thinking about all of the times you have had sexual intercourse in the last 12 months, how many times did you or your partner use a method of birth control?" "Which method did you use most often?"

(3) Participants and their families provided demographic information, including adolescent gender and ethnicity, mother's age at first birth, number of minors in the household, parental education, family income, parental employment status, and family structure (single-parent household, dual-parent household, or blended-family household).

Findings indicated that both parental knowledge and family activities predicted adolescent sexual risk behaviors. Specifically, young people whose parents—particularly fathers—were knowledgeable about their friends and activities and who regularly spent time with their families engaged in lower rates of risky sexual behavior. In contrast, young people who engaged in high rates of risky sexual behavior reported low levels of parental knowledge and family activities. The researchers also found that family structure predicted adolescents' sexual behavior. Youths from single-parent homes or stepfamilies engaged in higher-than-average levels of sexual behavior. In addition, adolescents in stepfamily arrangements reported lower levels of parental involvement and family time.

Taken together, these findings underscore the importance of parent involvement during adolescence. Although adolescents desire increased autonomy and separation from the family, they still benefit from supervision, monitoring, and family activities. According to Coley, Votruba-Drzal, and Schindler, parents can help protect their teenagers from risky sexual behaviors by becoming more knowledgeable about time spent away from home and increasing the frequency of family time, such as eating more meals together and planning fun activities.

Coley, R. L., Votruba-Drzal, E., & Schindler, H. S. (2009). Fathers' and mothers' parenting predicting and responding to adolescent sexual risk behaviors. *Child Development, 80,* 808–827.

LEARNING ACTIVITIES

LEARNING ACTIVITY 5.1
Observing Children's Gross-Motor Skills (pp. 178–179)

Early and middle childhood are a time of rapidly developing motor skills. Preschool bodies become more streamlined, and children have a better sense of balance. Running, jumping, hopping, and skipping become common activities. Coordination also improves, as is evident in children's throwing and catching balls, riding and steering tricycles, and playing on the rings and bars of playground equipment. During the school years, improved balance, strength, agility, and flexibility support refinements in running, jumping, hopping, and ball skills. Children sprint across the playground, play hopscotch in intricate patterns, kick and dribble soccer balls, and swing bats at pitched balls.

Ask students to visit a playground at a neighborhood park or school and select several children between the ages of 2 and 12 for observation. Students should jot down descriptions of the children's activities and movements, paying special attention to differences between younger and older children. Students should also note any sex differences that they observe. (The Milestones table on text page 179 offers an overview of gross-motor skills that can serve as a convenient observation guide.)

LEARNING ACTIVITY 5.2
Interviewing Parents and Grandparents About Secular Trends in Physical Growth (p. 184)

Have students interview parents and grandparents about their height and weight and the approximate age at which they reached adult stature. Girls might also ask their mothers and grandmothers to report how old they were when menarche occurred. To help interpret their findings, students should ask about diet and health during the childhood years and any other factors that parents and grandparents think might have influenced secular change. Data from the entire class can be pooled for an overall look at secular trends in physical growth.

LEARNING ACTIVITY 5.3
Matching: Brain Development (pp. 184–192)

Present the following exercise as an in-class activity or quiz.

Directions: Match each of the following terms with its correct description.

Terms:

_____ 1. Neurons
_____ 2. Synapses
_____ 3. Neurotransmitters
_____ 4. Programmed cell death
_____ 5. Synaptic pruning
_____ 6. Glial cells
_____ 7. Myelination
_____ 8. Cerebral cortex
_____ 9. Prefrontal cortex
_____ 10. Lateralization
_____ 11. Brain plasticity
_____ 12. Dominant cerebral hemisphere
_____ 13. Cerebellum
_____ 14. Experience-expectant brain growth
_____ 15. Experience-dependent brain growth

Descriptions:

A. Neurons send messages to one another by releasing these chemicals, which cross synapses.
B. Neurons that are seldom stimulated soon lose their synapses.
C. Handedness reflects the greater capacity of one side of the brain to carry out skilled motor action.
D. The coating of neural fibers with an insulating fatty sheath that improves the efficiency of message transfer.
E. These are tiny gaps where fibers from different neurons come close together but do not touch.
F. About half of the brain's volume consists of these.
G. As synapses form, many surrounding die—20 to 80 percent, depending on the brain region.
H. These are nerve cells that store and transmit information.
I. Term for specialization of the two hemispheres.
J. It is the largest brain structure, accounting for 85 percent of the brain's weight and containing the greatest number of neurons and synapses.
K. If part of the cortex is damaged, other parts can take over the tasks it would have handled.
L. This consists of additional growth and refinement of established brain structures as a result of specific learning experiences that occur throughout our lives, varying widely across individuals and cultures.
M. This refers to the young brain's rapidly developing organization, which depends on ordinary experiences.
N. Lying in the front of areas controlling body movement, this structure is responsible for various aspects of thought, such as consciousness, attention, integration of information, and use of memory.
O. A structure that aids in balance and control of body movement.

Answers:

1. H
2. E
3. A
4. G
5. B
6. F
7. D
8. J
9. N
10. I
11. K
12. C
13. O
14. M
15. L

LEARNING ACTIVITY 5.4
Creating a Pamphlet on the Importance of Nutrition and Exercise in Childhood and Adolescence (pp. 179–181, 194–196, 198–200)

Ask students to pretend they have been asked to create a pamphlet for a local health department about the importance of nutrition and exercise during childhood and adolescence. Students should list and briefly describe topics they would include in their presentation. For example, what factors contribute to obesity in children? How can parents and schools reduce obesity rates? What are the benefits of physical activity and exercise? How can schools structure physical education so that it appeals to young people of varying skill levels?

LEARNING ACTIVITY 5.5
Making Naturalistic Observations of Young Adolescents (pp. 179–181, 209)

To better understand the various aspects of adolescent physical development, students can visit a junior high school before or after school. Instruct them to watch for examples of developmental patterns discussed in the text—for example, sex differences in athletic skill, changes in body proportions during early adolescence, and the tendency among teenagers to seek companions whose level of biological maturity is similar to their own. After students have completed the activity, spend some class time discussing their observations.

LEARNING ACTIVITY 5.6
True or False: "Facts on Puberty" Quiz (pp. 203–210)

Before introducing the text discussion on puberty, present students with the following exercise.

Directions: Read each of the following statements and indicate whether it is *True* (T) or *False* (F).

Statements:
_____ 1. Menarche takes place immediately before the peak of the height spurt.
_____ 2. In the sequence of pubertal events, the growth spurt occurs at approximately the same age for both boys and girls.
_____ 3. Both heredity and physical health contribute to pubertal growth.
_____ 4. Research indicates that adolescence is a period of storm and stress for most teenagers.
_____ 5. Both biological and social forces contribute to the experience of adolescence.
_____ 6. Girls adjust especially well to puberty when their fathers are aware of pubertal changes.
_____ 7. Compared to girls, boys tend to get less social support for the physical changes of puberty.
_____ 8. Most researchers agree that high sex hormone levels are primarily responsible for adolescent moodiness.
_____ 9. Psychological distancing between parents and children is normal during adolescence, and most parent–child conflict is mild.
_____ 10. Late-maturing boys and early-maturing girls tend to be popular, self-confident, and sociable.

Answers:

1. F   6. T
2. F   7. T
3. T   8. F
4. F   9. T
5. T   10. F

LEARNING ACTIVITY 5.7
Critiquing an Adolescent Magazine (pp. 203–217)

Have students locate and critique a magazine geared toward adolescents using the following questions: Does the magazine primarily target teenage boys or girls? Is there an advice column in the magazine? If so, does the column provide advice about puberty or sexuality? Is the information consistent with research in the text? What types of images are portrayed in the magazines? Are the images supportive of healthy development? Why or why not? As a parent, would you encourage your children to read such magazines? Explain.

LEARNING ACTIVITY 5.8
Advice from the Popular Press Regarding Parent–Child Communication About Sexuality (pp. 212–217)

Parents in the United States tend to give their children little information about sex. Although both parents and adolescents express a desire for open communication about sexual issues, parents often feel that they lack the knowledge and communication skills to talk openly about sex. One source of information for parents is the popular press. Magazines such as *Parents, Ladies' Home Journal, Working Mother, Family Circle,* and *Parent & Child* sometimes offer information on adolescent sexuality and advice for discussing sex with adolescents and younger children.

Ask students to locate one or two articles in the popular press that give parents information on adolescent sexuality or advice on discussing sex with their children. Next, have students critique the articles they find. For example, what topics are covered? Are values discussed in addition to the biological details of sex? Are the more difficult topics, such as homosexuality, contraception, and STDs, discussed? What is the quality of the information in the articles? Does the information seem accurate (supported by research in the text)? What specific advice, if any, is given for improving communication between parents and children? Are the articles culturally sensitive? Explain.

Chapter 5 Physical Growth

LEARNING ACTIVITY 5.9
Critiquing an Episode of *16 and Pregnant* or *Teen Mom* (pp. 217–221)

As noted in the text, becoming a parent is especially challenging for adolescents, who have not established a clear sense of direction in their own lives. MTV currently produces two programs—*16 and Pregnant* and *Teen Mom*—that highlight the effects of adolescent pregnancy and parenthood on young people and their families. Ask students to view an episode of either program and answer the following questions: Briefly describe the episode. What kind of relationship does the teenage mother have with the child's father? How about her own family? What challenges do the teenagers face? For instance, is the mother still in school? How about the father? Who provides financial support to the baby? What types of social support are available? Did the mother experience any pregnancy complications? Using research in the text to support your answer, do you think the mother and baby will fare well in the long run? What role do you see the father playing in the mother's and baby's life? Explain, citing examples from the episode.

ASK YOURSELF . . .

REVIEW: What aspects of physical growth account for the long-legged appearance of many 8- to 12-year-olds? (pp. 176–177)

As the child's overall size increases, parts of the body grow at different rates. During infancy and childhood, physical growth follows the cephalocaudal and proximodistal trends: The head, chest, and trunk grow first, then the arms and legs, and finally the hands and feet. During puberty, growth proceeds in the reverse direction: The hands, legs, and feet accelerate first, followed by the torso. This pattern explains why young adolescents often appear out of proportion—long-legged, with giant feet and hands.

CONNECT: Relate secular trends in physical growth to the concept of cohort effects, discussed on page 62 in Chapter 2. (p. 184)

Cohort effects are the specific set of cultural and historical conditions that influence the development of children growing up in the same time period and may not apply to children developing at other times. For example, over the past 150 years, secular trends in physical growth—changes in body size from one generation to the next—have occurred in industrialized nations, including Australia, Canada, Japan, New Zealand, the United States, and nearly all European countries. Improved health and nutrition are largely responsible. Secular trends are smaller for low-income children, who tend to have poor diets and are more likely to suffer from growth-stunting illnesses. And in regions with widespread poverty, famine, and disease, either no secular change or a secular decrease in body size has occurred.

APPLY: Nine-year-old Allison dislikes physical education and thinks she isn't good at sports. What strategies can be used to improve her involvement and pleasure in physical activity? (pp. 179–181)

Allison's teacher should provide a physical education program that emphasizes enjoyable games and individual exercise rather than competition. This approach is particularly motivating for girls and is associated with lasting positive consequences. Educating Allison's parents about the minimal differences between school-age boys' and girls' physical capacities may also be helpful. Her parents can be encouraged to seek out opportunities for her to participate in individual and team sports in the community, especially endurance sports, such as running and cycling, which are especially likely to carry over into adulthood. If her parents, coaches, and teachers emphasize effort, improvement, participation, and teamwork, Allison is likely to enjoy sports more, exert greater effort to improve her skills, and perceive herself as more competent.

REFLECT: How does your height compare with that of your parents and grandparents when they were your age? Do your observations illustrate secular trends? (p. 184)

This is an open-ended question with no right or wrong answer.

REVIEW: How does stimulation affect brain development? Cite evidence at the level of neurons and at the level of the cerebral cortex. (pp. 185–186)

As neurons form connections, stimulation is vital to their survival. Neurons that are stimulated by input from the surrounding environment continue to establish synapses, forming increasingly elaborate systems of communication that support more complex abilities. Neurons that are seldom stimulated soon lose their synapses and return to an uncommitted state so they can support future development.

The cerebral cortex, which surrounds the rest of the brain, is the largest brain structure and contains the greatest number of neurons and synapses. Because it is also the last brain structure to stop growing, the cerebral cortex is sensitive to environmental influences for much longer than any other part of the brain. And although the cortex is programmed from the start for hemispheric specialization, early experience greatly influences the rate and success of its advancing organization.

CONNECT: What stance on the nature–nurture issue does evidence on development of handedness support? Document your answer with research findings. (p. 189)

Research on handedness supports the joint contribution of nature and nurture to brain lateralization. Handedness reflects the greater capacity of one side of the brain—the individual's dominant cerebral hemisphere—to carry out skilled motor action. Left-handed parents show only a weak tendency to have left-handed children. One genetic theory proposes that most children inherit a gene that biases them for right-handedness and a left dominant cerebral hemisphere, but the bias is not strong enough to overcome experiences that might sway a child toward a left-hand preference. These influential experiences can include prenatal events—for example, orientation of the fetus within the uterus. The orientation of most singleton fetuses—facing toward the left—is believed to promote greater control over movements on the body's right side. Because twins, both identical and fraternal, usually lie in opposite directions in the uterus, they are more likely than ordinary siblings to differ in handedness.

Handedness also involves practice. It is strongest for complex skills requiring extensive training, such as eating with utensils, writing, and engaging in athletic activities. Finally, wide cultural differences exist in rates of left-handedness. In Tanzania, Africa, where children are physically restrained and punished for favoring the left hand, less than 1 percent of adults are left-handed.

APPLY: Lucia experienced damage to the left hemisphere of her cerebral cortex shortly after birth. As a first grader, she shows impressive recovery of language and spatial skills, but she lags behind her peers in academic progress. What accounts for her recovery of skills? How about her cognitive deficits? (p. 188)

Children who experience injuries to the cerebral cortex either before birth or in the first six months of life show delays in language development, regardless of whether the injury occurred in the left or right cerebral hemisphere, indicating that at first, language functioning is broadly distributed in the brain. By age 5, however, these children catch up in vocabulary and grammatical skills, as undamaged areas of the brain—in either the right or the left hemisphere—take over these language functions. This accounts for Lucia's recovery of language skills. Compared with language, spatial skills are more impaired after early brain injury. But with spatial skills as with language skills, early brain injury has far less impact than later injury, because of the remarkable plasticity of the young brain.

This high brain plasticity comes at a price. When healthy brain regions take over the functions of damaged ones, a "crowding effect" occurs. Multiple tasks must be done by a smaller than usual volume of brain tissue. Consequently, the brain processes information less quickly and accurately than it would if it were intact. For Lucia, complex mental abilities of all kinds are likely to suffer into middle childhood or longer, because performing them well requires considerable space in the cerebral cortex.

REFLECT: Which infant enrichment program would you choose: one that emphasizes social games and gentle talking and touching, or one that includes reading and number drills and classical music lessons? Explain. (pp. 191–192)

This is an open-ended question with no right or wrong answer.

REVIEW: Explain why breastfeeding can have lifelong consequences for the development of babies born in poverty-stricken regions of the world. (pp. 194–195)

In early infancy, breast milk is ideally suited to babies' needs. It provides the correct balance of fat and protein, includes iron that is easily absorbed by the baby's system, and helps ensure healthy physical growth. As a result, breastfed babies in poverty-stricken regions of the world are much less likely to be malnourished and 6 to 14 times more likely to survive the first year of life. Even breastfeeding for just a few weeks offers some protection against respiratory and intestinal infections, which are devastating to young children in developing countries. Also, a nursing mother is less likely to get pregnant; although breastfeeding is not a reliable method of birth control, it does help increase spacing among siblings—a major factor in reducing infant and childhood deaths in nations with widespread poverty.

Unfortunately, many mothers in the developing world do not know about the benefits of breastfeeding. Although most babies get some breastfeeding, fewer than 40 percent are exclusively breastfed for the first six months. In place of breast milk, mothers may give their babies commercial formula or low-grade nutrients, such as rice water or highly diluted cow or goat milk. Contamination of these foods as a result of poor sanitation is common and often leads to illness and infant death.

CONNECT: How are bidirectional influences between parent and child involved in the impact of malnutrition on psychological development? (pp. 196–197)

Animal evidence reveals that a deficient diet alters the production of neurotransmitters in the brain, an effect that can disrupt all aspects of development. Children with marasmus show poor fine-motor coordination, have difficulty paying attention, and display a more intense stress response to fear-arousing situations, perhaps caused by the constant gnawing pain of hunger. The passivity and irritability of malnourished children worsen the impact of poor diet; these behaviors also accompany iron-deficiency anemia, which affects about 25 percent of infants and children worldwide and interferes with many central nervous system processes. Withdrawal, listlessness, and inability to be soothed when upset reduce these babies' ability to pay attention, explore, and evoke sensitive caregiving from parents. For this reason, interventions for malnourished children must foster development by supporting the parent–child relationship as well as the child's nutrition.

APPLY: Ten-month-old Shaun is below average in height and painfully thin. He has a serious growth disorder. List possibilities, and indicate what clues you would look for to tell which one Shaun has. (pp. 196, 202)

One possibility is marasmus, a wasted condition of the body caused by a diet low in all essential nutrients. It usually appears in the first year of life when a baby's mother is too malnourished to produce enough breast milk and bottle-feeding is also inadequate. As a result, the baby becomes painfully thin and is in danger of dying.

A second possibility is growth faltering, a term applied to infants whose weight, height, and head circumference are substantially below age-related growth norms and who are withdrawn and apathetic, although no biological cause can be found for the baby's failure to grow. In as many as half such cases, a disturbed parent–infant relationship contributes to the failure to grow normally.

Unless Shaun's mother is seriously malnourished or lacks access to infant formula, he probably does not suffer from marasmus. If Shaun suffers from growth faltering, his behavior and that of his mother will provide strong clues to its diagnosis. For example, during feeding, diaper changing, and play, his mother may seem cold and distant, and at other times impatient and hostile. Shaun may try to keep track of her whereabouts at all times but avoid her gaze when she approaches. He is also likely to be irritable and to display abnormal feeding behaviors, such as poor sucking or vomiting, which disrupt growth and also stress the parent–infant relationship further by leading Shaun's mother to feel anxious and helpless.

REFLECT: In rearing a child, which feeding and other child-rearing practices would you use, and which would you avoid, to prevent overweight and obesity? (pp. 198–200)

This is an open-ended question with no right or wrong answer.

REVIEW: Summarize the impact of pubertal timing on adolescent development. (pp. 208–210)

The timing of puberty has a major impact on adolescent psychological adjustment, largely as a result of two factors: how closely the adolescent's body matches cultural ideas of physical attractiveness and how well the young person fits in physically with agemates.

In several studies, both adults and peers viewed early-maturing boys as relaxed, independent, self-confident, and physically attractive. These boys tended to be popular with agemates, to hold leadership positions in school, and to be athletic stars. In contrast, late-maturing boys expressed more anxiety and depressed mood than their on-time counterparts. However, early-maturing boys, though viewed as well-adjusted, reported slightly more psychological stress, depressed mood, and problem behaviors than their on-time and late-maturing agemates.

Early-maturing girls tended to be unpopular, withdrawn, lacking in self-confidence, anxious, and prone to depression, and they held few leadership positions and achieved less well in school. Like early-maturing boys, they were more involved in deviant behavior (smoking, drinking, early sexual activity). In contrast, their later-maturing counterparts were regarded as physically attractive, lively, sociable, and leaders at school.

Follow-ups revealed that early-maturing girls were especially prone to lasting difficulties. Whereas early-maturing boys' depression subsided by age 13, depressed early-maturing girls tended to remain depressed, reporting poorer-quality relationships with family and friends, smaller social networks, and lower life satisfaction into early adulthood than their on-time counterparts.

CONNECT: How might adolescent moodiness contribute to the psychological distancing between parents and children that accompanies puberty? (*Hint:* **Think about bidirectional influences in parent–child relationships.) (pp. 207–208)**

Research indicates that the moods of younger adolescents are less stable than those of older adolescents and adults, and also that puberty is related to a rise in parent–child conflict, which persists into the mid-teenage years. Reports from adolescents who tracked their daily moods and activities revealed that mood swings were strongly related to situational changes, with low points typically occurring in adult-structured settings and high points coinciding with peer activities, such as going out with friends on weekends, and self-chosen leisure activities. Adult efforts to direct and control undoubtedly induce negative moods in teenagers. At the same time, teenage withdrawal probably evokes controlling and critical behavior from adults, leading to cycles of adult control–adolescent negative mood/withdrawal that contribute to the psychological distancing between parents and children that accompanies puberty.

APPLY: As a school-age child, Chloe enjoyed leisure activities with her parents. Now, as a 14-year-old, she spends hours in her room and resists going on weekend family excursions. Explain Chloe's behavior. (p. 208)

Among nonhuman primates and in many nonindustrialized cultures, the young typically leave the family around the time of puberty. Departure of young people is adaptive in that it discourages sexual relations between close blood relatives. But adolescents in industrialized societies, who remain economically dependent on parents, cannot physically leave the family. Consequently, a modern substitute seems to have emerged: psychological distancing. This may explain why Chloe prefers to spend so much time alone and no longer wants to join in weekend family activities.

REFLECT: Recall your own reactions to the physical changes of puberty. Are they consistent with research findings? Explain. (p. 206)

This is an open-ended question with no right or wrong answer.

REVIEW: Compare risk factors for anorexia nervosa and bulimia nervosa. How do treatments and outcomes differ for the two disorders? (pp. 210–212)

Forces within the person, the family, and the larger culture give rise to anorexia nervosa. Identical twins share the disorder more often than fraternal twins, indicating a genetic influence. Abnormalities in neurotransmitters in the brain, linked to anxiety and impulse control, may make some individuals more susceptible. Problem eating behavior in early childhood is also linked to anorexia in adolescence. Furthermore, the societal image of "thin is beautiful" contributes to the poorer body image of early-maturing girls, who are at greatest risk for anorexia nervosa. In addition, many young people with anorexia have unrealistically high standards for their own behavior and performance, are emotionally inhibited, and avoid intimate ties outside the family. Consequently, they are often excellent students who are responsible and well-behaved. But parent–adolescent interactions reveal problems related to autonomy. Often the mothers of these girls have high expectations for physical appearance, achievement, and social acceptance and are overprotective and controlling; fathers tend to be emotionally distant.

Twin studies show that bulimia, like anorexia, is influenced by heredity. Overweight and early menarche increase the risk. Although some adolescents with bulimia, like those with anorexia, are perfectionists, most are impulsive, sensation-seeking young people who lack self-control in many areas, engaging in a variety of risky behaviors. And although young people with bulimia, like those with anorexia, are pathologically anxious about gaining weight, they may have experienced their parents as disengaged and emotionally unavailable rather than overcontrolling.

Because individuals with anorexia typically deny or minimize the seriousness of the problem, treating the disorder is difficult. Hospitalization is often necessary to prevent life-threatening malnutrition. The most successful treatment combines family therapy with medication to reduce anxiety and neurotransmitter imbalances; behavior modification may be helpful as a supplementary approach. Even with treatment, only 50 percent of young people with anorexia recover fully. For many, eating problems continue in less extreme form. In contrast, individuals with bulimia usually feel depressed and guilty about their abnormal eating habits and desperately want help. As a result, bulimia is usually easier to treat than anorexia, through support groups, nutrition education, training in changing eating habits, and anti-anxiety, antidepressant, and appetite-control medication.

CONNECT: Explain how unfavorable life experiences and personal attributes associated with teenage parenthood increase the chances that it will be repeated in the next generation. (pp. 214–215, 217–218)

Early and frequent sexual activity is linked to personal, family, peer, and educational characteristics. These include childhood impulsivity, weak sense of personal control over life events, early pubertal timing, parental divorce, single-parent and stepfamily homes, large family size, little or no religious involvement, weak parental monitoring, disrupted parent–child communication, sexually active friends and older siblings, poor school performance, lower educational aspirations, and tendency to engage in norm-violating acts, including alcohol and drug use and delinquency. Many of these factors are associated with growing up in a low-income family, so it is not surprising that early sexual activity is more common among young people from economically disadvantaged homes, who are especially likely to engage in irresponsible sex, to be reluctant to use contraception, and to have unrealistic expectations about the impact of early parenthood on their current and future lives. For low-income minority teenagers in particular, early parenthood may present a way to move into adulthood when educational and career avenues are unavailable.

Adolescent parents' lives tend to worsen in several respects after the baby is born. For teenage mothers, the likelihood of earning a high school diploma is reduced, as are the chances of marriage; for those who do marry, divorce is more likely than for peers who delay childbearing. For teenage mothers and fathers alike, reduced educational and occupational attainment often persists well into adulthood. As a result, their children's life experiences, like their own, are likely to promote early sexual activity and a repetition of adolescent parenthood in the next generation.

APPLY: At age 17, Veronica dropped out of school, moved in with her boyfriend Todd, and gave birth to Ben. A few months later, Todd left Veronica, saying he couldn't stand being tied down with the baby. Suggest interventions likely to protect Veronica and Ben from lasting hardships. (p. 220)

Adolescent parents benefit from relationships with family members and other adults who are sensitive to their developmental needs. For Veronica, a long-term "mentor" relationship with a relative, neighbor, or teacher who would provide emotional support and guidance might increase her likelihood of remaining in school until graduation. Veronica also could benefit from a home visiting program such as the Nurse–Family Partnership. In this program, a registered nurse would visit the home regularly during Ben's first two years to offer intensive social support, providing Veronica with a sympathetic ear; assistance in accessing community services and help from family members; and encouragement to finish high school, find work, and engage in family planning in the future.

Todd would benefit from a program focused on adolescent fathers, which would attempt to increase his financial and emotional commitment to Ben. If Todd provides Veronica with financial and child-care assistance, as well as emotional support, she will be more likely to sustain a relationship with him. And for Ben, a lasting tie to his father is likely to mean that he will receive warmer, more stimulating caregiving and will show better long-term adjustment.

REFLECT: Describe sex education classes that you experienced in school. Did they help you postpone early sex and engage in more responsible sexual behavior? Explain. (pp. 219–220)

This is an open-ended question with no right or wrong answer.

SUGGESTED READINGS

Blyth, D., & Simmons, R. G. (2009). *Moving into adolescence: The impact of pubertal change and school context*. Piscataway, NJ: Rutgers. Examines the pubertal experience for young people in Western societies. The authors discuss the developmental milestones associated with the transition to adulthood, including how parents and schools can support adolescents during this exciting and challenging time of life.

Heinberg, L. J., & Thompson, J. K. (2009). *Obesity in youth: Causes, consequences, and cures*. Washington, DC: American Psychological Association. Presents leading research on the obesity epidemic among American children, including genetic and environmental contributions; psychological and social consequences, such as poor body image and peer rejection; treatment options; and strategies for preventing overweight and obesity.

Stiles, J. (2008). *The fundamentals of brain development: Integrating nature and nurture*. Boston, MA: Harvard University Press. A compelling look at brain development in infancy and early childhood, this book highlights milestones of neurological development, biological and environmental influences on brain development, typical and atypical development, and plasticity in the young brain.

MEDIA MATERIALS

For details on individual video segments that accompany the DVD for *Child Development,* Ninth Edition, please see the DVD Guide for *Explorations in Child Development*. The DVD and DVD Guide are available through your Pearson sales representative.

Additional DVDs that may be useful in your class are listed below. These are not available through your Pearson sales representative, but you can order them directly from the distributors. (See contact information at the end of this manual.)

Battling Eating Disorders (2006, Films Media Group/A Meridian Production, 29 min.). This program examines the impact of anorexia and other eating disorders on teenagers, especially young women, and how body image and self-esteem contribute to maladaptive eating habits. Hosted by *The Sopranos'* Jamie-Lynn Sigler, a survivor of teenage anorexia, the program looks at the rise of so-called Pro-Ana websites, which promote anorexia, bulimia, and binge eating. It emphasizes the importance of identifying these disorders as actual diseases, not simply misguided lifestyle choices—a realization that is essential for effective treatment.

Body Image for Boys (2002, Films Media Group/A Cambridge Educational Production, 18 min.). This program explores how young men are affected by media depictions of the ideal male physique and how such images have contributed to a preoccupation with appearance and to a rise in anorexia and body dysmorphic disorder among young men. The program includes interviews with experts and young men dealing with problems like steroid abuse, eating disorders, and exercise addiction.

Diet: A Look at Processed Food, Nutrition, and Obesity in the 20th Century (2010, Films Media Group, 52 min.). This program examines how attitudes about the industrialization of food have changed greatly over the past several decades. It traces the rise and fall of attitudes about processed food, from being considered a promising cure for malnourishment to eventually being linked to obesity, heart disease, and cancer. Using archival footage from BBC's *Horizon* television series, the program also reviews twentieth-century theories about the causes of obesity, and the diets and "miracle cures" designed to combat weight gain. Original BBC title: *Diet: A Horizon Guide*.

Fat Like Me: How to Win the Weight War (2003, Films Media Group, 40 min.). This *ABC News* special looks at the causes of obesity from the viewpoint of nutritionists, psychologists, pediatricians, and other experts. The program explores the physical and emotional damage resulting from obesity and offers ideas for parents and schools to use as they work together to help children improve their health. Hidden-camera coverage documents a social experiment in which a slim teen who has been professionally made up to look obese is subjected to the type of abuse that is often directed at overweight people. The hidden-camera segment is followed by a discussion of the stigmatizing effects of intolerance. A teacher's guide is included.

Fear of Fat: Eight Stories of Eating and Weight (2006, Films Media Group, 60 min.). This program features eight ordinary people who tell, in a chillingly matter-of-fact way, about their life-scarring—and even severely life-threatening—experiences with body weight and self-image. Bouts with eating disorders are described in detail, as well as feelings of hurt, anger, and alienation. The program also explores society's unhealthy focus on thinness, emphasizing the emotional and physical consequences.

Fixing My Brain: Neuroplasticity and the Arrowsmith Program (2008, Films Media Group, 52 min.). This film profiles Barbara Arrowsmith, who struggled with severe learning difficulties as a child until she designed a self-improvement regimen aimed at strengthening areas of her brain. The program takes viewers inside the school Arrowsmith founded and follows the progress of four students with cognitive challenges. Psychology and special-education experts voice diverging opinions on Arrowsmith's methods.

Food and Obesity: What We Eat (2006, Films Media Group, 46 min.). This program explores a glaring paradox in North America's food-obsessed culture—that our knowledge of nutrition has never been better, while our collective health has never been worse. This program outlines what food means to us socially and psychologically, as well as how the media influence our eating habits. It also examines organic foods, diabetes, and the value of vegetables, and profiles a family of modest means to show the real-world challenges of healthy eating.

Human Brain Development: Nature and Nurture (2006, Insight Media, 30 min.). This program illustrates how genetic predisposition combines with experience to shape early brain development. The program also addresses brain plasticity and language development from infancy through late adulthood.

Inside the Lives of Children Having Children (2009, Films Media Group, 42 min.) This *ABC News* program features four families coping with the day-to-day challenges of teenage pregnancy and parenthood. It also examines two disparate schools of thought on combating teen pregnancy—one highlighting abstinence, the other safe sex.

Middle Childhood: Physical Growth and Development (2008, Magna Systems, Inc., 22 min.). This program illustrates physical milestones that occur between ages 6 and 12. It also presents educator insights and classroom strategies for promoting healthy physical development. Topics covered include gross- and fine-motor milestones, how technology affects physical growth, reasons for the rise in childhood obesity and asthma, accidental injuries, the importance of nutrition and adequate sleep, and special concerns for children with physical challenges.

Nutrition for Infants and Children (2006, Films Media Group, 26 min.). Designed for parents, expectant parents, and caregivers, this program explains the importance of good nutrition for healthy growth and development in newborns, infants, and toddlers. It explores the relative merits of breastfeeding and bottle-feeding, potential food allergies, the importance of a balanced diet and exercise even for very young children, and the implications of special dietary preferences, such as vegetarianism.

Preschoolers: Physical Development (2008, Magna Systems/Learning Seed, 21 min.). This program features children ages 2 to 5. It covers the physical characteristics of preschoolers, how gross- and fine-motor skills develop, and physical milestones most children reach during this stage. This program also covers the physical challenges that some children experience, activity modifications to help children with these challenges, and why good nutrition and sleep are crucial.

Sexually Transmitted Infections (2003, Films Media Group, 27 min.). This program demonstrates how teens can protect themselves from sexually transmitted infections (STIs) through an emphasis on prevention, including both abstinence and safe sex. Topics covered include the ways these infections are carried and spread, their symptoms, current testing procedures, available treatments, and advice for talking with a sexual partner about STIs. A 15-page facilitator's guide is included.

Silence Ain't Sexy (2008, Insight Media, 27 min.). In this program, teenagers talk about their sexual experiences, which include abstinence, sexual intercourse within committed relationships, and casual hook-ups. The program also discusses media messages about sex, STDs, and pregnancy.

Smart Nutrition (2009, Films Media Group, 21 min.). Exploring the question of what adolescents should eat, the host of this program and two teenagers discuss the importance of breakfast, body image, portion size, physical activity, beverages, the value of fruits and vegetables, late-night snacking, vegetarian diets, and acne. Educational resources are available online.

Teen Sex (2004, Films Media Group/ Discovery Channel, 45 min.). This program explores contemporary changes in sexual mores through interviews with teens ages 13 to 19, who talk about peer pressure, the double standard, media influence, sexual intercourse, oral sex, sexually transmitted diseases, birth control, and pregnancy—and how these issues affect them and their families. The program, which contains mature themes and explicit language and imagery, presents onscreen statistics from the Kaiser Family Foundation to highlight important trends. It also includes interviews with parents and commentary by experts, including adolescent medicine specialist Gale Burstein, Leslee Unruh of the National Abstinence Clearinghouse, and *Seventeen* magazine editor Atoosa Rubenstein.

CHAPTER 6
COGNITIVE DEVELOPMENT: PIAGETIAN, CORE KNOWLEDGE, AND VYGOTSKIAN PERSPECTIVES

CHAPTER-AT-A-GLANCE

Chapter Outline	Instruction Ideas	Supplements
Piaget's Cognitive-Developmental Theory pp. 226–227 Basic Characteristics of Piaget's Stages • Piaget's Ideas About Cognitive Change	Learning Objective 6.1 Learning Activities 6.1, 6.10	Test Bank Items 1–13 Please contact your Pearson publisher's representative for a wide range of video offerings available to adopters.
The Sensorimotor Stage: Birth to 2 Years pp. 228–239 Sensorimotor Development • Follow-Up Research on Infant Cognitive Development • Evaluation of the Sensorimotor Stage	Learning Objectives 6.2–6.3 Learning Activities 6.2–6.3, 6.10 Ask Yourself p. 239	Test Bank Items 14–46, 131
The Preoperational Stage: 2 to 7 Years pp. 239–249 Advances in Mental Representation • Limitations of Preoperational Thought • Follow-Up Research on Preoperational Thought • Evaluation of the Preoperational Stage	Learning Objectives 6.4–6.5 Lecture Enhancements 6.1–6.2 Learning Activities 6.4–6.5, 6.10 Ask Yourself p. 249	Test Bank Items 47–68, 132–133
The Concrete Operational Stage: 7 to 11 Years pp. 249–253 Concrete Operational Thought • Limitations of Concrete Operational Thought • Follow-Up Research on Concrete Operational Thought	Learning Objectives 6.6–6.7 Learning Activities 6.5, 6.10 Ask Yourself p. 253	Test Bank Items 69–80
The Formal Operational Stage: 11 Years and Older pp. 253–259 Hypothetico-Deductive Reasoning • Propositional Thought • Consequences of Adolescent Cognitive Changes • Follow-Up Research on Formal Operational Thought	Learning Objectives 6.8–6.9 Lecture Enhancement 6.3 Learning Activities 6.6, 6.10 Ask Yourself p. 259	Test Bank Items 81–96, 134
Piaget and Education pp. 259–260	Learning Objective 6.10 Learning Activity 6.10	Test Bank Item 97
Overall Evaluation of Piaget's Theory pp. 260–261 Is Piaget's Account of Cognitive Change Clear and Accurate? • Does Cognitive Development Take Place in Stages? • Piaget's Legacy	Learning Objective 6.11 Learning Activity 6.10 Ask Yourself p. 261	Test Bank Items 98–100
The Core Knowledge Perspective pp. 261–266 Infancy: Physical and Numerical Knowledge • Children as Naïve Theorists • Evaluation of the Core Knowledge Perspective	Learning Objectives 6.12–6.13 Learning Activities 6.7, 6.10 Ask Yourself p. 266	Test Bank Items 101–107, 135
Vygotsky's Sociocultural Theory pp. 266–269 Children's Private Speech • Social Origins of Cognitive Development • Vygotsky's View of Make-Believe Play	Learning Objectives 6.14–6.15 Lecture Enhancement 6.4 Learning Activities 6.8–6.10	Test Bank Items 108–121, 132, 136
Vygotsky and Education pp. 269–272 Reciprocal Teaching • Cooperative Learning	Learning Objective 6.16 Learning Activity 6.10	Test Bank Items 122–127, 137
Evaluation of Vygotsky's Theory pp. 272–273	Learning Objective 6.17 Learning Activity 6.10 Ask Yourself p. 272	Test Bank Items 128–130

Copyright © 2013 Pearson Education, Inc. All Rights Reserved.

BRIEF CHAPTER SUMMARY

Cognitive development is the process by which the intellectual capacities of infants change into those of the child, adolescent, and adult. Three key perspectives on cognitive development are Piaget's cognitive-developmental theory, the core knowledge perspective, and Vygotsky's sociocultural theory.

Swiss cognitive theorist Jean Piaget viewed children as discovering, or constructing, virtually all knowledge of the world through their own activity. His findings have inspired a wealth of research on cognitive development, including studies that have called some of his own findings into question.

Piaget believed that children move through four invariant, universal stages during which the exploratory behaviors of infants evolve into the abstract, logical intelligence of adolescence and adulthood. Later researchers have challenged Piaget's belief that infants construct all mental representations out of sensorimotor activity. Studies suggest that the cognitive attainments of infancy do not develop in the neat, stepwise fashion that Piaget predicted, and that young babies have more built-in cognitive equipment for making sense of experience than Piaget believed.

Piaget's preoperational stage, from 2 to 7 years, is characterized by rapid advances in mental representation, notably language, make-believe play, and drawing. In contrast to Piaget's belief that language is important primarily as an expression of children's internal images, later research supports a view of language as a powerful source of cognitive development, not merely an indicator of it.

With the appearance of sociodramatic play—make-believe with others, rather than alone—children show awareness that make-believe is a representational activity. The development of children's drawings, from scribbles to representational pictures, reflects both cognitive advances and the emphasis that the child's culture places on artistic expression.

Piaget believed that young children's thought is preoperational: They are not capable of mental representations that obey logical rules. Evidence suggests that Piaget was only partly right about young children's cognitive capacities. When given simplified tasks based on familiar experiences, preschoolers show the beginnings of logical thinking, and they appear to acquire operational reasoning gradually, challenging Piaget's stage concept.

Piaget's concrete operational stage, from 7 to 11 years, is characterized by thought that is increasingly flexible and logical, with greater awareness of classification hierarchies. Spatial reasoning also improves, as indicated by children's understanding of cognitive maps. But children at this stage can think logically only about concrete information they perceive directly, not about abstract ideas. Culture and schooling appear to play an important role in attainment of the concrete operational stage.

Around age 11, children enter Piaget's formal operational stage, becoming capable of abstract, systematic, scientific thinking, including the ability to form hypotheses based on a general theory and to evaluate the logic of verbal propositions. Language is increasingly important at this stage. However, many college students and even many adults are not fully formal operational. People are most likely to think abstractly in situations in which they have had extensive experience while relying on intuitive judgments in other situations. Cultural influences also play a major role in whether people develop the ability to solve hypothetical problems.

Piaget has had a major impact on education. Teacher training and classroom practices widely reflect three educational principles derived from his view: discovery learning, sensitivity to children's readiness to learn, and acceptance of individual differences. But critics have challenged Piaget's insistence that young children learn mainly through acting on the environment and his neglect of other important avenues, such as verbal teaching and corrective feedback.

Some researchers argue for a core knowledge perspective—the view that infants are born with several innate, special-purpose knowledge systems referred to as core domains of thought that jump-start vital aspects of cognition. This perspective continues to be hotly debated.

Lev Vygotsky believed that infants are born with basic perceptual, attention, and memory capacities that develop in the first two years through direct contact with the environment. Vygotsky viewed human cognition as inherently social and saw language as the foundation for all higher cognitive processes. He believed that children's learning occurs within the zone of proximal development—tasks too difficult to do alone but possible with help from others—and saw make-believe play as a key zone of proximal development for preschoolers.

Vygotsky's theory has given us new visions of teaching and learning that emphasize social context and collaboration; specific Vygotsky-inspired innovations include reciprocal teaching and cooperative learning. Vygotsky's emphasis on social experience helps us understand the wide cultural variation in cognitive skills and underscores the vital role of teaching in cognitive development.

Chapter 6 Cognitive Development: Piagetian, Core Knowledge, and Vygotskian Perspectives

LEARNING OBJECTIVES

After reading this chapter, you should be able to answer the following:

6.1 According to Piaget, how does cognition develop? (pp. 226–227)

6.2 Describe major cognitive attainments of Piaget's sensorimotor stage. (pp. 228–230)

6.3 What does follow-up research reveal about infant cognitive development and the accuracy of Piaget's sensorimotor stage? (pp. 230–238)

6.4 Describe advances in mental representation and cognitive limitations during the preoperational stage. (pp. 239–245)

6.5 What does follow-up research reveal about preschoolers' cognitive development and the accuracy of Piaget's preoperational stage? (pp. 245–249)

6.6 What are the major characteristics of Piaget's concrete operational stage? (pp. 249–252)

6.7 Discuss follow-up research on concrete operational thought. (pp. 252–253)

6.8 Describe major characteristics of the formal operational stage and typical consequences of adolescents' advancing cognition. (pp. 253–257)

6.9 What does follow-up research reveal about formal operational thought? (pp. 257–259)

6.10 Describe educational implications of Piaget's theory. (pp. 259–260)

6.11 Summarize contributions and shortcomings of Piaget's theory. (pp. 260–261)

6.12 Explain the core knowledge perspective on cognitive development, noting research that supports its assumptions. (pp. 261–265)

6.13 What are the strengths and limitations of the core knowledge perspective? (pp. 265–266)

6.14 Explain Vygotsky's view of cognitive development, noting the importance of social experience and language. (pp. 266–269)

6.15 According to Vygotsky, what is the role of make-believe play in cognitive development? (p. 269)

6.16 Describe educational implications of Vygotsky's theory. (pp. 269–272)

6.17 Cite strengths and limitations of Vygotsky's theory. (pp. 272–273)

LECTURE OUTLINE

I. INTRODUCTION (pp. 225–226)
   A. **Cognition** refers to the inner processes and products of the mind that lead to "knowing."
      1. It includes all mental activity—attending, remembering, symbolizing, categorizing, planning, reasoning, problem solving, creating, and fantasizing.
      2. Mental processes make their way into virtually everything human beings do.
   B. Researchers studying cognitive development address three main issues: its *typical course, individual differences* in cognitive development, and the *mechanisms* of cognitive development.
   C. This chapter addresses three perspectives on how cognitive development occurs.
      1. *Piaget's cognitive-developmental theory* and the *core knowledge perspective* have a biological emphasis.
      2. *Vygotsky's sociocultural theory* stresses social and cultural contributions.

II. PIAGET'S COGNITIVE-DEVELOPMENTAL THEORY (pp. 226–227)
   A. Because Piaget viewed children as discovering, or *constructing*, virtually all knowledge about their world through their own perceptual and motor activities, his theory is described as a **constructivist approach** to cognitive development.

B. Basic Characteristics of Piaget's Stages (p. 226)
1. Piaget believed that children move through four stages—sensorimotor, preoperational, concrete operational, and formal operational—during which infants' exploratory behaviors transform into the abstract, logical intelligence of adolescence and adulthood.
2. Piaget's stage sequence has three important characteristics:
   a. The stages provide a *general theory* of development, in which all aspects of cognition change in an integrated fashion, following a similar course.
   b. The stages are *invariant;* they always occur in a fixed order, and no stage can be skipped.
   c. The stages are *universal;* they are assumed to characterize children everywhere.
3. Piaget emphasized that individual differences in genetic and environmental factors affect the speed with which children move through the stages.
C. Piaget's Ideas About Cognitive Change (pp. 226–227)
1. Specific psychological structures called **schemes**—organized ways of making sense of experience—change with age.
2. The infant's first schemes are sensorimotor action patterns.
3. The toddler makes a transition from a sensorimotor approach to the world to a cognitive approach based on **mental representations**—internal depictions of information that the mind can manipulate.
4. Our most powerful mental representations are *images*—mental pictures—and *concepts,* categories in which similar objects or events are grouped together.
5. Adaptation
   a. **Adaptation,** which involves building schemes through direct interaction with the environment, consists of two complementary activities: *assimilation* and *accommodation*.
      (1) In **assimilation,** we use our current schemes to interpret the external world.
      (2) In **accommodation,** we create new schemes or adjust old ones.
   b. Piaget used the term **equilibration** to describe the changing balance between assimilation and accommodation, from a state of cognitive *equilibrium,* when children are not changing much, to a state of *disequilibrium* during times of rapid cognitive change.
6. Organization
   a. Schemes also change through **organization,** a process that occurs internally, apart from direct contact with the environment.
   b. Once children form new schemes, they rearrange them and link them with other schemes to create a strongly interconnected cognitive system.

III. THE SENSORIMOTOR STAGE: BIRTH TO 2 YEARS (pp. 228–239)
A. Piaget referred to the stage spanning the first two years of life as the **sensorimotor stage,** reflecting his belief that infants and toddlers "think" with their eyes, ears, hands, and other sensorimotor equipment but cannot yet carry out many activities mentally.
B. The **circular reaction** is Piaget's term for the way newborn infants adapt their first schemes.
1. It involves stumbling onto a new experience caused by the baby's own motor activity.
2. The reaction is "circular" because, as the infant tries to repeat the event again and again, a sensorimotor response that originally occurred by chance becomes strengthened into a new scheme.
C. Sensorimotor Development (pp. 228–230)
1. Piaget divided this stage into six substages, covering development over the first two years.
   a. Substage 1: Reflexive schemes (birth to 1 month)
   b. Newborn reflexes are the building blocks of sensorimotor intelligence.
   c. Babies suck, grasp, and look in much the same way, whatever experiences they have.
2. Repeating Chance Behaviors
   a. Substage 2: Primary circular reactions (1 to 4 months)
      (1) Babies start to gain voluntary control over their actions through the *primary circular reaction,* by repeating chance behaviors largely motivated by basic needs.
      (2) They begin to vary their behavior in response to environmental demands.
   b. Substage 3: Secondary circular reactions (4 to 8 months)
      (1) Infants sit up and become skilled at reaching for and manipulating objects.

Chapter 6 Cognitive Development: Piagetian, Core Knowledge, and Vygotskian Perspectives

(2) Babies use the *secondary circular reaction* to try to repeat interesting events caused by their own actions; they can imitate others' behavior more effectively.
3. Intentional Behavior
   a. Substage 4: Coordination of secondary circular reactions (8 to 12 months)
      (1) Babies can engage in **intentional, or goal-directed, behavior,** coordinating schemes deliberately to solve simple problems, such as finding hidden objects.
      (2) Retrieving hidden objects shows that infants have begun to master **object permanence,** the understanding that objects continue to exist when they are out of sight.
      (3) However, this awareness is not yet complete, because babies make the **A-not-B search error:** If they reach several times for an object at one hiding place (A), then see it moved to another (B), they still search for it at the first hiding place (A).
      (4) Infants in Substage 4 can better anticipate events and may use their capacity for intentional behavior to try to change those events.
   b. Substage 5: *Tertiary circular reactions* (12 to 18 months)
      (1) Toddlers repeat behaviors with variation, provoking new outcomes.
      (2) Toddlers develop the capacity to experiment, which makes them better problem solvers.
      (3) More flexible action patterns permit toddlers to imitate many more behaviors.
4. Mental Representation
   a. Substage 6: Mental representation (18 months to 2 years)
   b. Sensorimotor development culminates in mental representation, which allows toddlers to arrive at solutions to problems suddenly rather than through trial and error.
   c. They are capable of **deferred imitation**—the ability to remember and copy the behavior of models who are not present.
   d. They can also engage in **make-believe play,** in which they act out everyday and imaginary activities.
D. Follow-Up Research on Infant Cognitive Development (pp. 230–236, 237)
   1. Many studies suggest that infants display a variety of understandings earlier than Piaget believed.
      a. To investigate babies' understanding of physical reality, researchers use the **violation-of-expectation method,** in which they *habituate* babies to a physical event (expose them to the event until their looking declines) or show them an *expected event* (one that follows physical laws) and an *unexpected event* (a variation of the first event that violates physical laws) and then determine whether infants recover to the expected or the unexpected event.
      b. Recovery to the unexpected event suggests that the infant is "surprised" by a deviation from physical reality—and, therefore, is aware of that aspect of the physical world.
      c. Some critics believe that this method indicates only limited, nonconscious awareness of physical events, or reveals only babies' perceptual preference for novelty.
   2. Object Permanence
      a. Researchers Renée Baillargeon and her collaborators, using the violation-of-expectation method, claimed to have found evidence for object permanence in the first few months of life, although several other researchers have failed to confirm some of these findings.
      b. Four- and 5-month-olds will track a ball's path of movement as it disappears and reappears from behind a barrier, suggesting awareness that objects persist when out of view.
      c. Consistent with the idea that a young infant's notion of object permanence strengthens with age is research showing that infants solve some object-hiding tasks before others: Eight- to 10-month-olds remove the cover from a partially hidden object before they are able to do so from a fully covered object.
   3. Searching for Objects Hidden in More Than One Location
      a. Poor memory cannot account for why babies make the A-not-B search error.
      b. Research suggests that a complex, dynamic system of factors increases the chances that the baby will make the A-not-B search error; disrupting any one of these factors increases 10-month-olds' accurate searching at B.
      c. Mastery of object permanence is a gradual achievement. Crucial to success are a wide variety of experiences perceiving, acting on, and remembering objects.

4. Mental Representation
    a. Evidence that 8- to 10-month-olds can recall the location of hidden objects after delays of more than a minute, and that 14-month-olds can recall location after delays of a day or more, indicate that babies construct mental representations of objects and their whereabouts much earlier than 18 months, as Piaget believed.
    b. Deferred and Inferred Imitation
        (1) Laboratory research suggests that deferred imitation is present at 6 weeks of age.
        (2) Between 12 and 18 months, toddlers use deferred imitation skillfully, retain modeled behaviors for several months, and copy the actions of peers as well as adults.
        (3) The ability to recall modeled behaviors in the order in which the actions occurred also strengthens over the second year.
        (4) Toddlers even imitate rationally, by *inferring* others' intentions.
        (5) Between 14 and 18 months, toddlers become increasingly adept at imitating actions an adult *tries* to produce, even if these are not fully realized.
        (6) Though advanced in terms of Piaget's predictions, toddlers' ability to represent others' intentions seems to have roots in earlier sensorimotor activity.
    c. Categorization
        (1) Young infants can *categorize,* grouping similar objects and events into a single representation.
        (2) Categorization helps infants make sense of experience by reducing the enormous amount of new information they encounter every day so they can learn and remember.
        (3) Habituation findings show that, in the second half of the first year, infants can group objects into an impressive array of categories.
        (4) As they gain experience in comparing to-be-categorized items in varied ways and as their store of verbal labels expands, toddlers start to categorize flexibly.
        (5) Researchers agree that infants' and toddlers' exploration of objects and expanding knowledge of the world contribute to advances in categorization, eventually enriching conceptual understanding.
        (6) Variations among languages lead to cultural differences in the development of categories.
    d. Problem Solving
        (1) As Piaget indicated, around 7 to 8 months, infants develop intentional means–end action sequences and use these to solve simple problems.
        (2) Soon after, infants' representational skills permit more effective problem solving than Piaget's theory would suggest.
        (3) By 10 to 12 months, infants can engage in **analogical problem solving**—applying a solution strategy from one problem to other relevant problems.
    e. Symbolic Understanding
        (1) The realization that words can be used to cue mental images of things not physically present—a symbolic capacity called **displaced reference**—emerges around the first birthday.
        (2) Although toddlers at first have difficulty using language to acquire new information about an absent object, as memory and vocabulary improve, skill at displaced reference expands.
        (3) The capacity to use language as a flexible symbolic tool—to modify an existing mental representation—improves from the end of the second into the third year.
        (4) Awareness of the symbolic function of pictures also emerges in the second year.
        (5) Studies have shown poorer performance after a video than a live demonstration—a **video deficit effect:** Children asked to retrieve an object after watching a video of an adult hiding it had more trouble than those who had watched a live demonstration.
        (6) This effect has also been found for 2-year-olds' deferred imitation and word learning.
        (7) One- to 3-year-old heavy television viewers tend to have attention, memory, and reading difficulties in the early school years.
E. Evaluation of the Sensorimotor Stage (pp. 236–238)
    1. Recent research raises questions about Piaget's view of how infant development takes place.
        a. Some aspects of infants' and toddlers' cognitive development, such as actively searching for hidden objects, occur within Piaget's time frame.
        b. Other capacities, such as deferred imitation and categorization, emerge earlier than Piaget expected.
        c. The cognitive attainments of infancy and toddlerhood do not develop in the neat, stepwise fashion Piaget predicted.

Chapter 6 Cognitive Development: Piagetian, Core Knowledge, and Vygotskian Perspectives

    d. Recent research provides evidence that infants comprehend a great deal before they are capable of the motor behaviors that Piaget assumed led to those understandings.

  2. Unlike Piaget, most researchers now believe that young babies have more built-in cognitive equipment for making sense of experience, but intense disagreement exists over the extent of this initial understanding.

IV. THE PREOPERATIONAL STAGE: 2 TO 7 YEARS (pp. 239–249)
  A. In Piaget's **preoperational stage,** from ages 2 to 7, children show an extraordinary increase in representational, or symbolic, activity.
  B. Advances in Mental Representation (pp. 239–243)
    1. Piaget acknowledged that language is our most flexible means of mental representation but did not regard language as the primary ingredient in childhood cognitive change.
    2. In Piaget's view, sensorimotor activity leads to internal images of experience, which children then label with words. Still, Piaget underestimated the power of language to spur children's cognition.
    3. Make-Believe Play
      a. Piaget believed that through pretending, children practice and strengthen newly acquired representational schemes.
      b. Development of Make-Believe Play
        (1) *Play detaches from the real-life conditions associated with it.*
        (2) *Play becomes less self-centered.*
        (3) *Play includes more complex combinations of schemes,* and children combine pretend schemes with those of peers in **sociodramatic play,** the make-believe with others that is under way by the end of the second year and increases rapidly in complexity during early childhood.
      c. Children as young as age 2 display awareness that make-believe is a representational activity.
      d. Benefits of Make-Believe
        (1) Piaget's view of make-believe as mere practice of representational schemes is now regarded as too limited.
        (2) Play not only reflects but also contributes to children's cognitive and social skills.
        (3) Make-believe strengthens a variety of mental abilities, including sustained attention, memory, language and literacy, and the ability to reflect on one's own thinking.
    4. Drawings
      a. Cognitive factors, including the realization that pictures can serve as symbols, influence the development of children's artful representations.
      b. From Scribbles to Pictures
        (1) At first, children's intended representation is contained in their gestures rather than in the resulting marks on the page, *scribbles*.
        (2) Around age 3, scribbles start to become pictures, the child's *first representational forms*.
        (3) When children begin using lines to represent the boundaries of objects, around age 3 or 4, they can draw their first picture of a person.
        (4) Children create *more realistic drawings* as perception, language, memory, and fine-motor capacities gradually improve.
      c. Cultural Variations in Development of Drawing
        (1) In cultures with rich artistic traditions, children create elaborate drawings that reflect the conventions of their culture.
        (2) In cultures with little interest in art, even older children and adolescents produce only simple forms.
    5. Symbol–Real World Relations
      a. Around age 3, children become capable of **dual representation**—viewing a symbolic object (for example, a scale model of a room) as both an object in its own right and a symbol.
      b. With age, children come to understand a wide range of symbols that have little similarity to what they represent, a prerequisite for more advanced knowledge.
  C. Limitations of Preoperational Thought (pp. 243–245)
    1. According to Piaget, young children are not capable of **operations**—mental representations of actions that obey logical rules.

2. Egocentric and Animistic Thinking
   a. Piaget saw the most fundamental deficiency of preoperational thinking as **egocentrism**—failure to distinguish others' symbolic viewpoints from one's own.
   b. He regarded egocentrism as responsible for preoperational children's *animistic thinking,* the belief that inanimate objects have lifelike qualities, such as feelings—a belief that results in magical thinking among preschoolers.
   c. Piaget argued that young children's egocentric bias prevents them from *accommodating,* or reflecting on and revising their faulty reasoning in response to their physical and social worlds.
3. Inability to Conserve
   a. **Conservation** refers to the idea that certain physical characteristics of objects remain the same, even when their outward appearance changes—for example, the amount of water in a tall glass and the same amount in a short, wide container.
   b. Preoperational children's inability to conserve highlights the fact that their thinking is characterized by **centration.** They focus on one aspect of a situation, neglecting other important features.
4. The most important illogical feature of preoperational thought is its lack of **reversibility,** the ability to go through a series of steps in a problem and then mentally reverse direction, returning to the starting point—an ability that is part of every logical operation.
5. Lack of Hierarchical Classification
   a. Preoperational children have difficulty with **hierarchical classification**—the organization of objects into classes and subclasses on the basis of similarities and differences.
   b. In Piaget's *class inclusion problem,* preoperational children illustrate this limitation by centering on an overriding feature but failing to think reversibly.

D. Follow-Up Research on Preoperational Thought (pp. 245–248)
   1. Researchers have challenged Piaget's account of preschoolers as cognitively deficient.
   2. Egocentric, Animistic, and Magical Thinking
      a. When researchers adapt Piaget's three-mountains problem to include familiar objects and use methods other than picture selection, 4-year-olds show clear awareness of others' vantage points.
      b. Nonegocentric responses also appear in young children's conversations.
      c. Piaget overestimated preschoolers' animistic beliefs. Even infants and toddlers have begun to distinguish animate from inanimate, as indicated by their remarkable categorical distinctions between living and nonliving things.
      d. Preschoolers think that magic accounts for events they cannot otherwise explain, but their notions of magic are flexible and appropriate.
      e. Between ages 4 and 8 years, as children gain familiarity with physical events and principles, magical beliefs decline.
   3. Logical Thought
      a. Many studies show that when preschoolers are given tasks that are simplified and made relevant to their everyday lives, they do not display the illogical characteristics that Piaget saw in the preoperational stage but, rather, show some ability to reason about transformations.
      b. Preschoolers can engage in impressive *reasoning by analogy* about physical changes—evidence of thinking logically about cause and effect.
      c. Preschoolers seem to use illogical reasoning only when they must grapple with unfamiliar topics, too much information, or contradictory facts.
   4. Categorization
      a. Despite their difficulty with Piagetian class inclusion tasks, preschoolers organize their everyday knowledge into nested categories.
      b. Two- to 5-year-olds readily draw inferences about nonobservable characteristics shared by category members.
      c. During the second and third year, children form many *basic-level* categories; by the third year, preschoolers easily move back and forth between these categories and *general categories*.
      d. As preschoolers learn more about their world, they devise theories about underlying characteristics shared by category members, which help them identify new instances.
      e. Adults' explanations are a major source of young children's categorical learning.

Chapter 6 Cognitive Development: Piagetian, Core Knowledge, and Vygotskian Perspectives

E. Evaluation of the Preoperational Stage (pp. 248–249)
1. Evidence indicates that Piaget was partly wrong and partly right about young children's cognitive capacities.
2. When given simplified tasks based on familiar experiences, preschoolers do show the beginnings of logical thinking, suggesting that they acquire operational reasoning gradually, not all at once as Piaget believed.

V. THE CONCRETE OPERATIONAL STAGE: 7 TO 11 YEARS (pp. 249–253)
A. According to Piaget, the **concrete operational stage,** from about 7 to 11 years, marks a major turning point in cognitive development, when thought becomes far more logical, flexible, and organized.
B. Concrete Operational Thought (pp. 249–251)
1. Conservation
a. The ability to pass *conservation tasks* provides clear evidence of *operations* — mental actions that obey logical rules.
b. Older children are capable of *decentration,* focusing on several aspects of a problem and relating them, rather than centering on only one.
2. Classification
a. Between ages 7 and 10, children pass Piaget's *class inclusion problem,* indicating they are more aware of classification hierarchies.
b. Collections become common in middle childhood.
3. Seriation
a. Six- to 7-year-olds are able to order items along a quantitative dimension, such as length or weight — an ability known as **seriation.**
b. The concrete operational child can also seriate mentally, an ability called **transitive inference.**
4. Spatial Reasoning
a. Piaget found that school-age children's understanding of space is more accurate than that of preschoolers.
b. Children's mental representations of familiar large-scale spaces, such as their neighborhood or school, are called **cognitive maps.**
c. Preschoolers and young school-age children include *landmarks* on the maps they draw, but their arrangement is not always accurate.
d. Around age 8 to 10, children organize their maps better, and they are able to give clear, well-organized directions for getting from one place to another by using a "mental walk" strategy.
e. By the end of middle childhood, children combine landmarks and routes into an *overall view of a large-scale space*.
f. Cultural frameworks — for example, the extent to which people use maps for way-finding, as opposed to other sources of information — also influence children's map making.
C. Limitations of Concrete Operational Thought (p. 252)
1. The important limitation of concrete operational thinking is that children think in an organized, logical fashion only when dealing with concrete information that they can perceive directly, but until age 11 or 12, their mental operations work poorly with abstract ideas.
2. School-age children master Piaget's concrete operational tasks step by step, not all at once, following a *continuum of acquisition* (or gradual mastery) of logical concepts — another indication of the limitations of concrete operational thinking.
D. Follow-Up Research on Concrete Operational Thought (pp. 252–253)
1. Piaget believed that brain development combined with experience in a rich and varied external world should lead children everywhere to reach the concrete operational stage.
2. Yet specific cultural and teaching practices affect children's task performance.
a. In tribal and village societies, where children rarely attend school, conservation is often delayed.
b. The very experience of going to school seems to promote mastery of Piagetian tasks.
c. Certain informal, nonschool experiences can also foster operational thought.
3. Some investigators have concluded that the forms of logic required by Piagetian tasks do not emerge spontaneously but are heavily influenced by training, context, and cultural conditions.

VI. THE FORMAL OPERATIONAL STAGE: 11 YEARS AND OLDER (pp. 253–259)
A. According to Piaget, around age 11, young people enter the **formal operational stage,** in which they develop the capacity for abstract, systematic, scientific thinking.

B. Hypothetico-Deductive Reasoning (pp. 253–254)
   1. At adolescence, young people become capable of **hypothetico-deductive reasoning.** When faced with a problem, they start with a *hypothesis,* or prediction about variables that might affect an outcome, from which they *deduce* logical, testable inferences.
   2. Then they systematically isolate and combine variables to see which of these inferences are confirmed in the real world.
C. Propositional Thought (pp. 254–255)
   1. Another characteristic of the formal operational stage is **propositional thought**—adolescents' ability to evaluate the logic of propositions (verbal statements) without referring to real-world circumstances.
   2. Although Piaget did not view language as playing a central role in cognitive development, he acknowledged its importance during adolescence.
D. Consequences of Adolescent Cognitive Changes (pp. 255–257)
   1. Self-Consciousness and Self-Focusing
      a. Piaget believed that in adolescence, a new form of egocentrism arises, in which adolescents have difficulty distinguishing their own and others' perspectives, so that they develop two distorted images of the relationship between self and others.
         (1) **Imaginary audience** is adolescents' belief that they are the focus of everyone else's attention and concern, which makes them extremely self-conscious.
         (2) The **personal fable** is teenagers' belief that others are observing and thinking about them, which leads to an inflated opinion of their own importance.
      b. Imaginary-audience and personal-fable ideation do not result from egocentrism, as Piaget suggested, but are partly an outgrowth of advances in perspective taking, which cause young teenagers to be more concerned with what others think.
      c. In one study, the sense of omnipotence associated with the personal fable predicted self-esteem and overall positive adjustment.
   2. Idealism and Criticism
      a. In adolescence, the capacity for abstract thinking opens up the world of the ideal.
      b. Envisioning a perfect family against which theirs falls short, adolescents become fault-finding critics.
      c. Teenage idealism and criticism lead to a greater capacity to work constructively for social change.
   3. Decision Making
      a. Teenagers perform less well than adults in planning and decision making, where they must inhibit emotion and impulses in favor of thinking rationally.
      b. Research indicates that teenagers are less effective than adults at decision making even under "cool," unemotional conditions.
      c. Over time, young people learn from their successes and failures, gather information from others about decision making, and reflect on the decision-making process.
E. Follow-Up Research on Formal Operational Thought (pp. 257–259)
   1. Are Children Capable of Hypothetico-Deductive and Propositional Thinking?
      a. School-age children show glimmerings of hypothetico-deductive reasoning.
      b. Children's capacity for propositional thought is also limited; they often fail to grasp the logical **necessity** of propositional reasoning—that the accuracy of conclusions drawn from premises rests on the rules of logic, not on real-world confirmation.
      c. In early adolescence, young people become better at analyzing the *logic* of propositions, regardless of their *content*.
   2. Do All Individuals Reach the Formal Operational Stage?
      a. Even many well-educated adults fail hypothetico-deductive tasks and have trouble reasoning with sets of propositions that contradict real-world facts.
      b. People are most likely to think abstractly and systematically on tasks in which they have had extensive guidance and practice in using such reasoning.
      c. Individuals in tribal and village societies rarely do well on tasks typically used to assess formal operational reasoning.

Chapter 6 Cognitive Development: Piagetian, Core Knowledge, and Vygotskian Perspectives

VII. PIAGET AND EDUCATION (pp. 259–260)
   A. Three educational principles derived from Piaget's theory continue to influence teacher training and classroom practices:
      1. *Discovery learning:* Children are encouraged to discover for themselves through spontaneous interaction with the environment.
      2. *Sensitivity to children's readiness to learn:* Teachers build on children's current thinking and do not try to speed up development by imposing new skills before children indicate they are ready.
      3. *Acceptance of individual differences:* Teachers plan activities for individual children and small groups, not just for the whole class.
   B. Critics have challenged Piaget's insistence that young children learn mainly through acting on the environment and his neglect of other important avenues, such as verbal teaching and corrective feedback.

VIII. OVERALL EVALUATION OF PIAGET'S THEORY (pp. 260–261)
   A. Piaget's contributions to the field of child development are greater than those of any other theorist.
      1. He awakened psychologists and educators to a view of children as curious knowledge seekers who contribute actively to their own development.
      2. His pioneering efforts inspired the current focus on *mechanisms of cognitive change*.
      3. Piaget's theory offers a useful "road map" of cognitive development that is accurate in many respects, though incorrect in others.
   B. Is Piaget's Account of Cognitive Change Clear and Accurate? (p. 260)
      1. Piaget focused on broad transformations in thinking, but he was vague about exactly what the child does to equilibrate.
      2. Piaget was not explicit about how the diverse achievements of each stage are bound together by a single, underlying form of thought, and efforts to confirm this coherence have not succeeded.
      3. Today, researchers agree that the child's efforts to assimilate, accommodate, and reorganize structures cannot adequately explain observed patterns of change.
      4. Piaget's belief that infants and young children must act on the environment to revise their thinking is too narrow a notion of how learning takes place.
   C. Does Cognitive Development Take Place in Stages? (pp. 260–261)
      1. Many cognitive changes proceed slowly and gradually.
      2. Periods of cognitive equilibrium are rare; rather, children are constantly acquiring new skills.
      3. Today, virtually all experts agree that children's cognition is less broadly stagelike than Piaget believed.
         a. Some theorists, while agreeing with Piaget that development is a *general process* that follows a similar course across diverse cognitive domains, reject his idea of stages; their belief that thought processes are alike at all ages—just present to a greater or lesser extent—forms the basis of the *information-processing perspective*.
         b. Other researchers think that the stage notion is valid but must be modified.
         c. The *neo-Piagetian perspective* combines Piaget's stage approach with information-processing ideas.
         d. Still other researchers adopt a *core knowledge perspective*—the belief that infants are born with several basic, built-in types of knowledge, each of which jump-starts vital aspects of cognition.
   D. Piaget's Legacy (p. 261)
      1. Although Piaget's description of development is no longer fully accepted, researchers are far from consensus on how to modify or replace it.
      2. Research into children's thinking is far more fragmented today than several decades ago.
      3. Researchers continue to draw inspiration from Piaget's vision of the child as an active, constructive learner—the starting point for most research on cognitive development.

IX. THE CORE KNOWLEDGE PERSPECTIVE (pp. 261–266)
   A. According to the **core knowledge perspective,** infants begin life with innate, special-purpose knowledge systems, referred to as *core domains of thought.*
      1. Each of these "prewired" understandings permits a ready grasp of new, related information and therefore supports early, rapid development of certain aspects of cognition.
      2. Core knowledge theorists argue that infants could not make sense of the multifaceted stimulation around them without having been genetically "set up" to comprehend crucial aspects of it.
   B. Two core domains have been studied extensively in infancy: *physical knowledge* and *numerical knowledge.*

C. The core knowledge perspective asserts that an inherited foundation makes possible remarkably advanced knowledge systems in early childhood.
   1. Domains of core knowledge appear to include *linguistic knowledge, psychological knowledge,* and *biological knowledge.*
   2. Core knowledge theorists see development as *domain-specific* and uneven.
   3. Children are viewed as *naïve theorists,* building on core knowledge concepts to explain their everyday experiences.
D. Infancy: Physical and Numerical Knowledge (pp. 262–264)
   1. Core knowledge theorists point to evidence indicating that young children are aware of basic object properties and build on this knowledge quickly.
   2. For example, at 9½ months, babies expect an object placed inside a transparent container to be visible through that container.
   3. Research also suggests that young infants have basic number concepts and that 6-month-olds can discriminate ratios.
   4. These impressive findings suggest that some notion of quantity is present in the first year. But like other violation-of-expectation results, they are controversial.
E. Children as Naïve Theorists (pp. 264–265)
   1. A growing number of researchers believe that children form naïve theories, or explanations of events, that differ between core domains.
   2. According to this **theory theory** (meaning *theory of children as theorists*), after children observe an event, they draw on innate concepts to explain, or theorize about, its cause. Then they test their naïve theory against experience, revising it when it cannot adequately account for new information.
   3. These revisions often lead to dramatic stagelike changes similar to those described by Piaget, but theory theorists claim that because children start with innate knowledge, their reasoning advances more quickly than Piaget believed.
   4. Researchers have extensively investigated children's *theory of mind*—the psychological knowledge of self and others that forms rapidly during the preschool years.
   5. Children's explanations in different domains develop at different rates, starting with physical and psychological explanations.
F. Evaluation of the Core Knowledge Perspective (pp. 265–266)
   1. Critics take issue with the core knowledge assumption that infants are endowed with *knowledge.*
   2. The core knowledge perspective acknowledges that experience is essential for children to elaborate their initial knowledge, but it has not offered greater clarity than Piaget's theory about how heredity and environment jointly produce cognitive change.

X. VYGOTSKY'S SOCIOCULTURAL THEORY (pp. 266–269, 270)
   A. Lev Vygotsky, while viewing children as active seekers of knowledge, emphasized the effect on their thinking of rich social and cultural contexts.
   B. Vygotsky believed that infants are endowed with basic perceptual, attention, and memory capacities that develop during the first two years through direct contact with the environment.
      1. Rapid growth of language leads to a profound change in thinking, broadening preschoolers' participation in social dialogues with more knowledgeable individuals, who encourage them to master culturally important tasks.
      2. Through this process, the infant's basic mental capacities are transformed into uniquely human, higher cognitive processes.
   C. Children's Private Speech (pp. 266–267)
      1. Piaget gave the name *egocentric speech* to the utterances of young children who talk aloud to themselves as they play; the name reflected his belief that young children have difficulty taking the perspectives of others.
      2. Vygotsky believed that children speak to themselves for self-guidance. He believed that language is the foundation for all higher cognitive processes.
      3. As a result of studies supporting Vygotsky's perspective, children's self-directed speech is now called **private speech** instead of egocentric speech; children who freely use private speech during a challenging activity are more attentive and involved in the activity.

Chapter 6 Cognitive Development: Piagetian, Core Knowledge, and Vygotskian Perspectives

   D. Social Origins of Cognitive Development (pp. 267–269)
      1. Vygotsky believed that children's learning occurs within the **zone of proximal development**—a range of tasks too difficult for the child to do alone but possible with the help of adults and more skilled peers.
      2. To promote cognitive development, social interaction must have certain features:
         a. **Intersubjectivity** is the process whereby two participants who begin a task with different understandings arrive at a shared understanding, which creates a common ground for communication.
         b. **Scaffolding** means adjusting the support offered during a teaching session to fit the child's current level of performance.
         c. **Guided participation,** a broader concept than scaffolding, refers to shared endeavors between more expert and less expert participants but allows for variations in the precise features of communication.
         d. A wealth of research evidence supports Vygotsky's ideas and indicates that when adults establish intersubjectivity by being stimulating, responsive, and supportive, they foster many competencies in children.
         e. Children of effective scaffolders use more private speech, are more successful when attempting difficult tasks on their own, and are advanced in overall cognitive development.
         f. However, research shows that effective scaffolding can take different forms in different cultures.
   E. Vygotsky's View of Make-Believe Play (pp. 269, 270)
      1. Vygotsky regarded make-believe play as a broadly influential zone of proximal development in which *children advance themselves* as they try out a wide variety of challenging skills.
      2. Vygotsky saw make-believe as the central source of development in the preschool years.
         a. As children create imaginary situations, they learn to act in accord with internal ideas, not just in response to external stimuli.
         b. The rule-based nature of make-believe strengthens children's capacity to think before they act.
      3. Make-believe enhances an array of cognitive and social skills and is also rich in private speech.

XI. VYGOTSKY AND EDUCATION (pp. 269–272)
   A. Educators today are eager to use the ideas of Vygotsky, whose theory emphasizes the importance of social context and collaboration in teaching and learning.
   B. Going beyond independent discovery, a Vygotskian classroom promotes *assisted discovery,* as teachers tailor their interventions to each child's zone of proximal development.
   C. *Peer collaboration* also fosters assisted discovery.
   D. Vygotsky believed that preschoolers need socially rich, meaningful activities in their zones of proximal development, as well as ample opportunity for make-believe play.
   E. Two Vygotsky-based educational innovations are reciprocal teaching and cooperative learning.
   F. Reciprocal Teaching (p. 271)
      1. In **reciprocal teaching,** a teacher and two to four students form a collaborative group and take turns leading dialogues on the content of a text passage.
      2. Within the dialogues, group members apply four cognitive strategies: questioning, summarizing, clarifying, and predicting.
      3. Reciprocal teaching creates a zone of proximal development in which children gradually learn to scaffold one another's progress.
   G. Cooperative Learning (pp. 271–272)
      1. Vygotsky believed that more expert peers can spur children's development, as long as they adjust the help they provide to fit the less mature child's zone of proximal development.
      2. Peer collaboration appears to promote development only under certain conditions; a crucial factor is **cooperative learning,** in which small groups of classmates work toward common goals.
      3. Because working in groups comes more easily to children reared in collectivist than in individualistic cultures, Western children usually require extensive guidance for cooperative learning to succeed.
      4. When teachers prompt, explain, model, and have children role-play how to work together effectively, cooperative learning results in achievement gains across a wide range of school subjects.

XII. EVALUATION OF VYGOTSKY'S THEORY (pp. 272–273)
   A. Vygotsky's theory helps us understand the wide cultural variation in cognitive skills because it grants social experience a fundamental role in cognitive development.
   B. The theory also underscores the vital role of teaching in cognitive development.

C. Vygotsky elevated language to highest importance compared with other symbol systems, such as pictures and maps, an emphasis that is applicable in Western culture but less so in some other cultures.
D. Vygotsky focused on social and cultural influences but said little about biological contributions to children's cognition.

LECTURE ENHANCEMENTS

LECTURE ENHANCEMENT 6.1
Can Children's Drawings Help Identify Adjustment Difficulties at School? (pp. 241–242)

Time: 10–15 minutes

Objective: To highlight how children's drawings can help identify adjustment difficulties at school.

As noted in the text, a variety of factors—the realization that pictures can serve as symbols, improved planning and spatial understanding, and the emphasis the child's culture places on artistic expression—influence the development of children's artful representations. According to Harrison, Clarke, and Ungerer (2008), drawings can also provide insight into relationships with adults, as well as children's overall adjustment. In one study, researchers recruited 125 6-year-olds and collected the following information:

(1) Participants completed a 30-minute interview that addressed general perceptions of themselves, their school, and their teachers.
(2) Participants completed the School Liking and Avoidance Scale. Using a three-point scale (yes = 3, no = 2, sometimes = 1), children were asked such questions as, "Is school fun?" "Do you enjoy school?" "Do you ask your parents to let you stay home from school?" "Does school make you feel like crying?" To assess participants' feelings about their teacher, they were asked: "Do you like to see your teacher when you get to school?" "Is your teacher nice to you?" "Does your teacher smile at you?" "Does your teacher play or read with you?"
(3) Participants were asked to draw a picture of themselves and their teacher at school. Drawing materials were provided but no further instructions were given. Researchers recorded any spontaneous comments, and once participants completed their drawings, they were asked to identify the people and objects in the picture. Pictures were scored on the following dimensions, which are commonly used to assess child–family drawings:
    - Creativity—going beyond the instructions and adding lively, colorful, or imaginative features
    - Pride/happiness—showing an emotional connectedness to the teacher, such as holding hands or doing something fun with the teacher
    - Vulnerability—using overwhelming, exaggerated, distorted, or displaced body images
    - Emotional distance/isolation—using expressions of anger, negative affect, physical distance from the teacher, or physical barriers between the child and teacher
    - Tension/anger—showing rigid and constricted features or scribbling out the teacher's face
    - Role reversal—representing the child as larger, more powerful, or more potent than the teacher
    - Bizarreness/disassociation—including unusual signs or symbols, angry facial features, or morbid fantasy themes
(4) Teachers rated their relationship quality with each child on five dimensions: conflict/anger, warmth/positive emotions, open communication, dependency, and troubled feelings.
(5) Teachers rated participants' overall school adjustment by identifying the prevalence of problem behaviors (for example, acting out, aggression, learning problems) and strengths/competencies (for example, leadership, frustration tolerance, social skills).

Findings revealed significant relationships among children's reports, children's drawings, teacher-rated relationship quality, and teacher-rated school adjustment. That is, children who reported negative feelings about their teacher also included negative themes in their drawings, such as scribbling out the teacher's face. Their teachers, in turn, were likely to report strained teacher–child relationships and problematic classroom behavior. Taken together, these findings suggest that children's artistic representations of relationships with teachers are an important tool for identifying adjustment difficulties at school.

Harrison, L. J., Clarke, L., & Ungerer, J. A. (2008). Children's drawings provide a new perspective on teacher–child relationship quality and school adjustment. *Early Childhood Research Quality, 22,* 55–71.

LECTURE ENHANCEMENT 6.2
Using Gestures to Facilitate Children's Learning of Piagetian Tasks (pp. 244–245)

Time: 10–15 minutes

Objective: To examine how gestures facilitate young children's learning.

Research shows that gestures are an important aspect of communication. For example, we often use gestures to reiterate information expressed in speech and to clarify ambiguities. Teachers also frequently use gestures when providing instruction to children. To examine how gestures contribute to young children's learning, Ping and Goldin-Meadow (2008) conducted two experiments with kindergarten and first-grade students.

Experiment 1: Sixty-one children were presented with a pretest that included eight conservation tasks—two conservation-of-liquid tasks, two conservation-of-number tasks, two conservation-of-length tasks, and two conservation-of-matter tasks. Because the goal of the study was to teach children conservation, those who solved all of the tasks correctly were eliminated from the study. Next, children were given instruction in how to solve liquid and number conservation. In one condition, the researcher used speech only to explain how to solve a problem. Children were given verbal instructions with the objects on the table (e.g., glasses) or with the objects off the table. For example, in the conservation-of-liquid task, the researcher presented the child with two identical glasses of water and said, "I think these two glasses have the same amount of water." After pouring water from one glass into a shorter, wider glass, she said, "One of the glasses is taller and the other one is shorter, but the shorter glass is wider and the taller glass is skinnier." In a second condition, the researcher used both speech and gesture to explain how to solve the problem, again with objects on or off the table. In the conservation-of-liquid task, for instance, the researcher used her hands to illustrate the height and width of the glasses. As with the speech-only condition, children were given instruction with the objects on the table or with the objects off the table. After determining if the two glasses had the same or different amounts of water, the child was asked to explain his or her answer.

Results indicated that children in the speech-plus-gesture condition improved more from pretest to posttest than children in the speech-only condition. Children in the speech-plus-gesture condition also gave more details when explaining their answers. Children performed similarly on tasks where the objects were visible or off the table. This suggests that gestures can facilitate children's learning even when they do not direct attention to concrete objects.

Experiment 2: Fifty-two children were presented with the same pretest and posttest as in Experiment 1, except a second researcher was also in the room and sat at a table behind the child. In the conservation-of-liquid task, the first researcher told the child, "I think these two glasses have the same amount of water." She then poured the water from one glass into a shorter, wider glass, and repeated the same sentence. Next, the first researcher handed the glasses to the second researcher who then put the glasses on the table or out of the child's view. The child was instructed to face the second researcher, who provided instructions with the objects on the table or with the objects off the table. The purpose of the second researcher was to determine if gesture requires a spatial connection to props to be an effective teaching tool. As with Experiment 1, children were given instructions with speech only or with both speech and gesture. After the child indicated whether the two glasses had the same or different amounts of water, the second researcher asked the child to explain his or her answer.

Similar to findings in Experiment 1, children in the speech-plus-gesture condition improved more from pretest to posttest than children in the speech-only condition. They also provided more details when explaining their answers. Even when gestures were produced in a neutral space (on the table by the second researcher, but with the glasses out of view), children in the speech-plus-gesture condition performed better than children in the speech-only condition. Thus, according to Ping and Goldin-Meadow, gesture does not necessarily require a spatial connection to props to be an effective teaching tool.

Ping, R. M., & Goldin-Meadow, S. (2008). Hands in the air: Using ungrounded iconic gestures to teach children conservation of quantity. *Developmental Psychology, 44,* 1277–1287.

LECTURE ENHANCEMENT 6.3
Improved Proportional Reasoning Affects Gains in Decision Making Through Adolescence into Early Adulthood (pp. 256–257)

Time: 5–10 minutes

Objective: To examine the contribution of increasingly complex proportional reasoning to developmental gains in decision making.

Research shows that with age, young people become increasingly skilled at decision making, which is supported by the development of proportional reasoning—the ability to use ratios to solve mathematical problems. According to Piaget, proportional reasoning emerges as young people transition from concrete to formal operational thinking.

To examine developmental differences in decision making as they relate to proportional reasoning, Huizenga, Crone, and Jansen (2008) recruited 241 participants and divided them into four age groups: 6- to 9-year-olds, 10- to 12-year-olds, 13- to 15-year-olds, and 18- to 25-year-olds. Each participant completed the "hungry donkey task," which was designed to mimic real-life decision making. A display was presented that consists of four doors—A, B, C, and D—and a donkey sitting in front of the doors. Participants were told to help the hungry donkey collect as many apples as possible by pressing a key in front of each door. The door would then open, showing the outcome of their decision (number of apples gained and number of apples lost). The goal was to figure out how to maximize gains and minimize losses. For example, Door A resulted in four apples per trial but in half of the trials, a loss of 10 apples occurred. In a reversed task, Door A resulted in a loss of four apples per trial with a gain of 10 apples half the time. Each participant completed 200 trials.

Compared to children, adolescents and adults increasingly made more effective decisions. Specifically, the younger participants were more likely to guess or rely solely on one-dimensional reasoning: frequency of gains. In contrast, with age, the older participants more often engaged in two-dimensional proportional reasoning, making decisions that maximized gains while minimizing losses. Because they attempted to reconcile the two dimensions in favor of an ultimately more favorable outcome, older participants were also less distracted by initial gains if a large loss followed. That is, if a door choice had large gains for several trials, followed by a significant loss, older participants were more likely to select doors with smaller gains *and* smaller losses. This strategy resulted in significantly more apples at the end of the task than the guessing or frequency of gains strategy used by younger individuals. Although adolescents were more adept than children at applying strategies that maximized gains while minimizing losses, adults engaged in more effective strategy use than adolescents.

According to Huizenga, Crone, and Jansen, limitations in information-processing capacity may prevent younger individuals from experimenting with or considering how combinations of different doors can maximize gains and minimize losses. Instead, they rely on guessing or mere frequency of gains. Over adolescence and into early adulthood, effective strategy use—based on more complex proportional reasoning—increases gradually.

In addition to gains in information processing, what other factors contribute to adolescents' improved decision making? Under what circumstances are adolescents likely to make poor decisions?

Huizenga, H. M., Crone, E. A., & Jansen, B. J. (2008). Decision-making in healthy children, adolescents and adults explained by the use of increasingly complex proportional reasoning rules. *Developmental Science, 10,* 814–825.

LECTURE ENHANCEMENT 6.4
More on Vygotsky's Sociocultural Theory: The Relationship Between Language and Self-Regulation in Young Children (pp. 266–267)

Time: 10–15 minutes

Objective: To examine the relationship between language and self-regulation in young children.

If you spend much time around the parents of young children, you may hear the phrase, "Use your words." This phrase reflects a common belief that children can better regulate their behavior when they use words to express their desires, needs, and feelings. To examine the relationship between language and self-regulation, Vallotton and Ayoub (2011) recruited 120 14-month-olds and followed them to age 36 months. The researchers collected the following information in three waves—when participants were 14, 24, and 36 months old:

    (1) Self-regulation was assessed using the Bayley Behavior Rating Scale. During home visits, a trained observer rated children on their ability to maintain attention on tasks, degree of negativity, and adaptation to changes in the environment.

(2) Language skills were assessed using the Child Language Data Exchange System (CHILDES). During each home visit, participants and their mothers participated in a 10-minute dyadic play episode. The researchers were interested in children's spoken vocabulary. Specifically, observers coded for number of unique vocabulary words spoken. For instance, "dog" and "cat" are two unique words, whereas "dog" and "dogs" are considered the same word. Observers also coded for total number of words spoken during the mother–child interaction.

(3) Because mothers' use of language likely contributes to children's language and self-regulation, observers also coded mothers' spoken language during each dyadic play episode.

(4) Because cognitive development is related to both verbal skills and behavior, children were given a cognitive assessment at each wave of data collection.

Findings indicated that language skills, even as early as 14 months, contributed to children's ability to regulate their own behavior. Specifically, compared to children with low spoken language scores, those with higher scores were better at maintaining attention on tasks, were less negative, and adapted more easily to changes in the environment. However, spoken vocabulary was a better predictor of self-regulation than overall talkativeness (i.e., total number of words spoken). According to Vygotsky, symbols, such as spoken words, are important mental tools for regulating our thoughts, emotions, and behavior. While talkativeness may help children communicate and control their environment, vocabulary may be a better indicator of a child's symbolic skills and, thus, a better predictor of self-regulation. Finally, the relationship between language skills and self-regulation remained strong even after controlling for maternal language and cognitive development. Taken together, these findings suggest that language skills have a unique and positive impact on the development of self-regulation in early childhood.

Vallotton, C., & Ayoub, C. (2011). Use your words: The role of language in the development of toddlers' self-regulation. *Early Childhood Research Quality, 26,* 169–181.

LEARNING ACTIVITIES

This chapter provides a number of concepts that can easily be demonstrated in the classroom. You may want to consider inviting a panel of parents and children to your class and combining some of the suggested observations presented below. (Ideally, you will want children of various ages for the demonstration.)

LEARNING ACTIVITY 6.1
Applying Piaget's Concepts of Assimilation and Accommodation (p. 227)

Piagetian concepts can be complex and challenging to grasp. Often, new ideas are best understood when they are applied to one's personal experiences. Ask students to consider their own learning in relation to Piaget's theory. For example, each semester students find themselves in a challenging state of *disequilibrium* as they enroll in new courses. They have to *accommodate* quickly, creating new *schemes* so they can make sense of new realms of knowledge (that is, course material). Once they do so, their new cognitive structures enable them to *assimilate,* or see the world in a different light, and they experience the thrill of mastery. And when students combine new concepts into *organized* wholes, their sense of equilibrium is enhanced. Under these conditions, they probably do best on exams.

Suggest that students illustrate Piaget's concepts of cognitive change through one of their own learning experiences. Then ask them to imagine themselves in the place of the young infant, for whom creating and organizing schemes are awesome tasks. The baby does not just enroll in a new course of study that is similar to ones he has taken before. Instead, many aspects of the environment are strange and mysterious, and thousands of schemes must be created, revised, and put together.

LEARNING ACTIVITY 6.2
Testing Infants for Object Permanence (pp. 229–232)

Arrange for several infants to visit your class for a demonstration of object permanence. If possible, infants should range in age from 6 to 24 months of age.

(1) *Successive object-hiding task.* After attracting the baby's attention, hide a rattle or other attractive toy beneath a cup or under a cloth. See if the baby will set aside the obstacle and retrieve the object. Infants between 8 and 12 months generally succeed at this task; younger ones have difficulty.

(2) *Hiding-by-cloth and hiding-by-hand task*. Place the toy on a table or desk, next to a folded cloth. Then unfold the cloth over the toy. By 10 months, babies will usually retrieve the toy. Next, using your hand, carry the toy toward and under the cloth, and bring your hand out without the toy (leave the toy under the cloth). Not until age 14 months will most babies search for the toy. In the second, more difficult task, younger infants seem to expect the object to appear in the hand because that is where the object initially disappeared.

(3) *Successive object-hiding task*. This time, set two cups on the table. Place the toy under one cup (A) and then move it beneath the other (B). Infants between 12 and 18 months of age easily find the object in the second location; younger ones frequently make the well-known A-not-B search error by looking in the first hiding place.

(4) *Invisible object-hiding task*. Hide the toy in a small box, place the box under a cover, and, while out of the baby's sight, dump the toy out of the box. Then show the baby the empty box. With the capacity to represent sensorimotor actions internally, infants between 18 months and 2 years of age can solve this problem.

LEARNING ACTIVITY 6.3
Observing Early Categorization Skills (pp. 233–235)

This demonstration can be combined with Learning Activity 6.2, or you can suggest that students locate a toddler for observation. Place a set of objects, such as four boxes and four balls, in front of the child. Research indicates that 12-month-olds will touch objects that belong together, but they do not yet group them. A little later, single-category grouping can be seen. For example, 16-month-olds are likely to put all the balls together but not the boxes. Finally, around 18 months, children sort the objects exhaustively into two classes. Advanced categorization skills are believed to contribute to the vocabulary spurt that typically occurs between 18 months and 2 years.

LEARNING ACTIVITY 6.4
Observing Young Children's Make-Believe Play (pp. 239–241)

Have students arrange to visit a child-care center or the home of a friend or family member with young children. Ask students to briefly describe the setting, age(s) of the children, and play behaviors. In addition, students can classify the children's make-believe play based on observations of symbolic mastery:

(1) *Play detaches from the real-life conditions associated with it*. In early pretending, toddlers use only realistic objects—for example, a toy telephone to talk into or a cup to drink from. Gradually, children can flexibly imagine objects and events, without any support from the real world.

(2) *Play becomes less self-centered*. At first, make-believe is directed toward the self—for example, children pretend to feed or wash only themselves. A short time later, pretend actions are directed toward other objects, as when the child feeds a doll. And early in the third year, children become detached participants who make a doll feed itself or a parent doll feed a baby doll.

(3) *Play includes more complex combinations of schemes*. The toddler can pretend to drink from a cup but does not yet combine pouring and drinking. Later, children combine schemes with those of peers, especially in sociodramatic play, the make-believe play with others that is under way by age 2½ and increases rapidly during the next few years.

LEARNING ACTIVITY 6.5
Interviewing the Preoperational or Concrete Operational Child (pp. 243–248, 249–252)

Depending on your access to children of different ages, you can select one of the activities below for a classroom demonstration, or you may decide to combine the activities to illustrate developmental differences in cognitive development.

(1) Arrange for a group of preschool-age children to visit your class for an interview and demonstration of Piagetian tasks. With class sizes of 35 students or fewer, you can bring children into the classroom and have groups of 3 to 5 students sit on the floor and work with a single child, taking turns, asking questions, and recording responses. Then, the children's answers and explanations, as well as any problems that arose in the course of interviewing, can be discussed at the end of the class period. Alternatively, you can demonstrate a short Piagetian interview, or students can find and interview a child on their own. Piagetian tasks appropriate for this demonstration include (1) conservation problems (see text pages 244–245) and (2) the class inclusion problem (page 245). For tasks that children fail, have students simplify and then readminister them. Examples of how to simplify Piagetian tasks can be found in the text discussion of follow-up research on preoperational thought (page 246).

(2) To demonstrate cognitive attainments during the concrete operational stage, ask several school-age children between the ages of 6 and 10 to come to class to be interviewed by small groups of your students. Alternatively, demonstrate a short Piagetian interview, or students can find and interview a child on their own. The Piagetian tasks listed above are also appropriate for this activity. Following the activity, ask students to reflect on the experience. For example, what challenges arose during the activity? Did the children perform as Piaget would have expected? Was their performance consistent with research presented in the text? Explain.

LEARNING ACTIVITY 6.6
Assessing Propositional Thinking (pp. 254–255, 257–258)

Have students locate two children (preferably a child under the age of 10 and an adolescent) and present the following statement: "If dogs are bigger than elephants and elephants are bigger than mice, then dogs are bigger than mice." Students should record each child's answer and compare it with research in the text. Did the younger child judge the statement to be false? What factors allow older children and adolescents to grasp the logical necessity of propositional reasoning?

LEARNING ACTIVITY 6.7
Matching: The Core Knowledge Perspective (pp. 261–266)

Present the following exercise as an in-class assignment or quiz.

Directions: Match each of the following terms with the appropriate description.

Terms:
_____ 1. Core knowledge perspective
_____ 2. Physical knowledge
_____ 3. Numerical knowledge
_____ 4. Psychological knowledge
_____ 5. Biological knowledge
_____ 6. Theory theory

Descriptions:
A. The capacity to keep track of multiple objects and to add and subtract small quantities.
B. Ideas about inheritance of characteristics and understanding of bodily processes, such as birth, growth, illness, and death.
C. Infants begin life with innate, special-purpose knowledge systems referred to as core domains of thought.
D. After observing an event, children draw on innate concepts to explain, or theorize about, its cause. Then they test their theory against experience, revising it when it cannot adequately account for new information.
E. Understanding of people as agents who have mental states that influence their behavior, which is vital for surviving in human groups.
F. Understanding of objects and their effects on one another.

Answers:

1. C   4. E
2. F   5. B
3. A   6. D

LEARNING ACTIVITY 6.8
Observing Examples of Private Speech and Scaffolding (pp. 267, 268)

While visiting a child-care center or the home of a friend or family member with young children (see Learning Activity 6.4), have students jot down instances of private speech. Students are likely to observe private speech as children play with puzzles, books, and other construction toys, and as they engage in other challenging tasks, such as drawing, literacy, and math pursuits. What activities were children engaged in when they demonstrated private speech? Did private speech seem to help children focus on certain tasks? Explain.

In addition to observing private speech, ask students to note and briefly describe examples of scaffolding. What kinds of support did adults offer when children attempted difficult tasks (for example, direct instruction, breaking the task down into manageable units, suggesting strategies)? Did adults gradually withdraw support as children gained competence with the task? Explain.

LEARNING ACTIVITY 6.9
Speaking to Parents and Teachers About the Importance of Make-Believe Play (p. 269)

Tell students to pretend they have been asked to speak to a group of parents and teachers of preschool-age children. Both the parents and teachers are concerned that too much classroom time is being devoted to play and wonder if they should incorporate more academics into the curriculum. Have students list information they would include in their discussion. For example, what are some benefits of make-believe play in early childhood? Will an emphasis on academics promote greater cognitive development than an emphasis on make-believe play? Why or why not?

LEARNING ACTIVITY 6.10
The Impact of Culture on Cognitive Development

Throughout Chapter 6, there are numerous examples of how cultural experiences contribute to cognitive development. In small groups, have students list some major cognitive milestones of infancy, childhood, and adolescence. For each milestone, students should explain how cultural factors contribute to it. Once students complete their lists, have them share some examples with the class.

ASK YOURSELF . . .

REVIEW: Using the discussion on pages 230–236, construct your own summary table of infant and toddler cognitive development. Which entries in your table are consistent with Piaget's sensorimotor stage? Which ones develop earlier than Piaget anticipated?

This is an open-ended question. Students should be encouraged to be creative but accurate and thorough in constructing the table.

CONNECT: Recall from Chapter 4 (page 163) that by the middle of the first year, infants identify objects by their features and paths of movement, even when they cannot observe the entire path. How might these attainments contribute to understanding of object permanence? (pp. 229–231)

Infants are fascinated by moving objects. As they observe objects in motion, they pick up additional information about the objects' boundaries, such as shape, color, and texture. Young infants need all of these cues to infer object unity. But as infants become familiar with many objects, they rely more on shape, color, and texture and less on motion. In the second half of the first year, as infants become better able to distinguish objects on the basis of their features, experience in watching objects move in and out of view contributes to their development of object permanence—the understanding that objects continue to exist when they are out of sight.

APPLY: Several times, after her father hid a teething biscuit under a red cup, 10-month-old Mimi retrieved it easily. Then Mimi's father hid the biscuit under a nearby yellow cup, but Mimi persisted in searching for it under the red cup. What factors might be contributing to Mimi's inaccurate search behavior? (pp. 230–231)

Searching for hidden objects seems to represent a true advance in object permanence understanding because infants solve some object-hiding tasks before others. Ten-month-olds like Mimi search for an object placed on a table and covered by a cloth before they search for an object that a hand deposits under a cloth. In the second, more difficult task, infants seem to expect the object to reappear in the hand from which it initially disappeared. When the hand emerges without the object, they conclude that there is no other place the object could be. At 12 months, Mimi is not yet able to infer that her father would put the biscuit under a different cup—an understanding that typically develops later, around 14 months.

REFLECT: What advice would you give the typical U.S. parent about permitting an infant or toddler to watch as much as 1 to 1½ hours of TV or video per day? Explain. (p. 238)

This is an open-ended question with no right or wrong answer.

Chapter 6 Cognitive Development: Piagetian, Core Knowledge, and Vygotskian Perspectives

REVIEW: Select two of the following features of preoperational thought: egocentrism, a focus on perceptual appearances, difficulty reasoning about transformations, and lack of hierarchical classification. Present evidence indicating that preschoolers are more capable thinkers than Piaget assumed. (pp. 244–248)

Egocentrism: For Piaget, the most serious deficiency of preoperational thought is *egocentrism*—failure to distinguish others' symbolic viewpoints from one's own. He believed that when children first mentally represent the world, they tend to focus on their own viewpoint and assume that others perceive, think, and feel the same way they do. For example, in Piaget's three-mountains problem, preoperational children cannot select a picture that shows the mountains from a doll's perspective that differs from their own. Instead, they simply choose the photo that reflects their own vantage point.

Focus on perceptual appearances: Piaget believed that preoperational children are easily distracted by the *perceptual appearance* of objects. For example, in a conservation-of-liquid task, most preoperational children believe that a short, wide container has less water than a tall, narrow container, even when they have seen the water poured from one container into the other.

Difficulty reasoning about transformations: In the conservation-of-liquid task in which water is poured from one container into another, preoperational children treat the initial and final states of the water as unrelated events, ignoring the *dynamic transformation* (pouring of water) between one state and the other. Piaget also believed that preoperational thought is characterized by *irreversibility*—the inability to go through a series of steps in a problem and then mentally reverse direction, returning to the starting point, which is part of every logical operation.

Lack of hierarchical classification: In Piaget's famous *class inclusion problem,* children are shown 16 flowers, 4 of which are blue and 12 of which are red. Asked, "Are there more red flowers or more flowers?" the preoperational child responds, "More red flowers." The child centers on the overriding feature, red, and fails to realize that both red and blue flowers are included in the category "flowers."

Research shows that when Piagetian tasks are modified to include familiar objects in familiar contexts, young children are much more competent problem solvers than Piaget assumed. For example, when the nature of Piaget's three-mountains problem is changed to include familiar objects and use methods other than picture selection, children as young as 4 years show a clear awareness of others' vantage points. Similarly, when conservation tasks are simplified and made relevant to their everyday lives, preschoolers can overcome perceptual appearances and think logically about transformations. They recognize, for example, that a substance that has been dissolved in water continues to exist even though it is invisible in the water. And despite their difficulty with Piagetian class inclusion tasks, preschoolers organize their everyday knowledge into nested categories at an early age, recognizing that objects with very different perceptual features may go together because of their common function, behavior, and natural kind.

CONNECT: Make-believe play promotes both cognitive and social development (see page 240). Explain why this is so. (pp. 239–241)

Research reveals that make-believe play strengthens a wide variety of cognitive abilities, including sustained attention, memory, logical reasoning, language and literacy, imagination, creativity, understanding of emotions, and the ability to reflect on one's own thinking and take another's perspective. Through pretending, young children practice and strengthen newly acquired representation schemes. Reflecting preschool children's growing symbolic mastery, their pretend play, compared with toddlers' pretending, increasingly detaches from the real-life conditions associated with it, becomes less self-centered, and includes more complex combinations of schemes. By the end of the second year, children begin to combine schemes with those of peers in *sociodramatic play.* Gradually, they become able to create and coordinate several roles in an elaborate plot.

Social skills also benefit from make-believe play. Compared with social nonpretend activities, such as drawing or putting puzzles together, preschoolers' interactions during sociodramatic play last longer, show more involvement, draw more children into the activity, and are more cooperative. As a result, preschoolers who devote more time to sociodramatic play are seen as more socially competent by their teachers.

APPLY: Three-year-old Will understands that his tricycle isn't alive and can't feel or move on its own. But watching the setting sun, Will exclaimed, "The sun is tired. It's going to sleep!" Explain this apparent contradiction in Will's reasoning. (pp. 244, 245–246)

Will is displaying animistic thinking—the belief that inanimate objects have lifelike qualities, such as thoughts, wishes, feelings, and intentions. Will has had enough experience with everyday objects, such as his tricycle, to know that these are not alive. But Will does not know much about the solar system, so he does not understand why the setting sun appears to dip below the horizon. Because the sun appears to move, and because movement is a characteristic associated with living things, it is not surprising that Will assumes that the sun is alive.

REFLECT: Did you have an imaginary companion as a young child? If so, what was your companion like, and why did you create it? Were your parents aware of your companion? What was their attitude toward it? (pp. 240–241)

This is an open-ended question with no right or wrong answer.

REVIEW: Children's performance on conservation tasks illustrates a continuum of acquisition of logical concepts. Review the preceding sections, and list additional examples of gradual development of operational reasoning. (pp. 249–252)

Children's ability to pass *conservation tasks* provides clear evidence of *operations*—mental actions that obey logical rules. For example, in conservation of liquid, concrete operational children understand that the amount of liquid does not change when it is poured into a different container. This understanding is evidence of *decentration*—focusing on several aspects of a problem and relating them, rather than centering on only one—and of *reversibility*—the capacity to imagine the water being returned to the original container as proof of conservation.

Between ages 7 and 10, children also pass Piaget's *class inclusion problem*. This indicates that they are more aware of classification hierarchies and can focus on relations between a general category and two specific categories at the same time—that is, on three relations at once. Another example is seen in children's capacity for *seriation*—ordering items along a quantitative dimension, such as length or weight. At age 6 to 7, children can create a series efficiently, in an orderly sequence.

Concrete operational children can also seriate mentally, an ability called *transitive inference*. When shown pairings of sticks of unequal length, children 7 years and older understand that if stick *A* is longer than stick *B* and stick *B* is longer than stick *C*, then stick *A* is longer than stick *C*. But school-age children think in an organized, logical fashion only when dealing with concrete information they can perceive directly. Until age 11 or 12, they have difficulty with a hypothetical version of a transitive inference task: "Susan is taller than Sally and Sally is taller than Mary. Who is the tallest?" Their difficulty with hypothetical problems illustrates that their mastery of logical concepts is a gradual process.

CONNECT: Using research on cognitive maps, conservation, and class inclusion, explain how tasks not adapted to children's cultural contexts can underestimate their cognitive competencies. (pp. 250–252)

Piaget believed that brain development combined with rich and varied experiences should lead children everywhere to reach the concrete operational stage. But specific cultural and teaching practices affect children's performance on Piagetian tasks.

Cognitive maps: Children's cultural frameworks influence their map making. Compared with their Western agemates, non-Western children ride in cars less often and walk more often, developing intimate knowledge of their neighborhoods as a result. When 12-year-olds in small cities in India and in the United States drew maps of their neighborhoods, the Indian children represented many landmarks and aspects of social life in a small area near their home, whereas the U.S. children drew a more formal, extended space and included few landmarks—a difference that reflected cultural interpretations of the task.

Conservation: In tribal and village societies in which children rarely attend school, even basic conservation tasks (number, length, and liquid) are not understood until age 11 or later. This suggests that participation in relevant everyday activities helps children master conservation and other Piagetian problems. In Western nations, for example, children think about fairness in terms of equal distribution, a value that is emphasized in their culture. Because they often see the same quantity arranged in different ways, they grasp conservation early.

Class inclusion: Brazilian 6- to 9-year-old street vendors, who seldom attend school, do poorly on Piaget's class inclusion tasks but excel on versions relevant to street vending—for example, "If you have 4 units of mint chewing gum and 2 units of grape chewing gum, is it better to sell me the mint gum or [all] the gum?"

On the basis of such findings, some investigators have concluded that the forms of logic required by Piagetian tasks do not emerge spontaneously but are heavily influenced by training, context, and cultural conditions.

APPLY: Nine-year-old Adrienne spends many hours helping her father build furniture in his woodworking shop. How might this experience facilitate Adrienne's advanced performance on Piagetian seriation problems? (p. 250)

Seriation refers to the ability to order items along a quantitative dimension, such as length or weight. To build furniture, it is necessary to make components of appropriate lengths and to compare and adjust them while building each piece. According to Piaget, children learn best by acting directly on their world. Through her hands-on experience with furniture making, Adrienne will learn to judge lengths of wood, which will foster her ability to solve seriation problems. She will also develop *transitive inference*—the ability to seriate mentally.

Chapter 6 Cognitive Development: Piagetian, Core Knowledge, and Vygotskian Perspectives

REFLECT: Which aspects of Piaget's description of the concrete operational stage do you accept? Which do you doubt? Explain, citing research evidence. (pp. 249–252)

This is an open-ended question with no right or wrong answer.

REVIEW: Describe research findings that challenge Piaget's notion of a new stage of cognitive development at adolescence. (pp. 253–255, 257–259)

Piaget believed that around age 11, young people enter the *formal operational stage,* in which they develop the capacity for abstract, systematic, scientific thinking. Unlike concrete operational children, formal operational adolescents no longer require concrete things or events as objects of thought but, rather, can "operate on operations," coming up with new, more general logical rules through internal reflection.

Research on formal operational thought challenges some of Piaget's ideas. School-age children already show the glimmerings of hypothetico-deductive reasoning, although they are less competent at it than adolescents. In simplified situations involving no more than two possible causal variables, 6-year-olds understand that hypotheses must be confirmed by appropriate evidence. And when a simple set of premises runs contrary to real-world knowledge, even 4- to 6-year-olds can use propositional thought to reason logically in make-believe play.

In early adolescence, young people become better at both hypothetico-deductive reasoning and propositional thought. As they get older, they handle problems that require increasingly complex sets of mental operations. In justifying their reasoning, they move from simply giving a concrete example to explaining the logical rules on which it is based. However, these capacities do not appear suddenly at puberty. Rather, gains occur gradually from childhood on—findings that call into question the emergence of a discrete new stage of cognitive development at adolescence.

CONNECT: How does evidence on adolescent decision making help us understand teenagers' risk taking in sexual activity and drug use? (pp. 256–257)

Adolescents handle many cognitive tasks more effectively than they did when younger. But changes in the brain's emotional/social network outpace development of the prefrontal cortex's cognitive-control network. Consequently, teenagers perform less well than adults in planning and decision making, where they must inhibit emotion and impulses in favor of thinking rationally. In the heat of the moment, when making a good decision depends on inhibiting "feel-good" behavior and the appeal of immediate rewards, the brain's emotional/social network tends to prevail, and adolescents are far more likely than adults to emphasize short-term over long-term goals.

As "first-timers" in many situations, adolescents do not have sufficient knowledge to consider pros and cons and predict likely outcomes. They are more likely than adults to fall back on well-learned intuitive judgments. And after engaging in risky behavior without experiencing negative consequences, teenagers rate its benefits higher and its risks lower than peers who have not tried it. And even under "cool," unemotional conditions, teenagers are less effective than adults at decision making. In a study of responses to challenging hypothetical real-world dilemmas, adults outperformed adolescents, more often considering alternatives, weighing benefits and risks, and suggesting advice seeking, especially in areas where they had little experience.

APPLY: Clarissa, age 14, is convinced that no one appreciates how hurt she feels at not being invited to the homecoming dance. Meanwhile, 15-year-old Justine, alone in her room, pantomimes being sworn in as student body president with her awestruck parents, teachers, and peers looking on. Which aspect of the personal fable is each girl displaying? Which girl is more likely to be well-adjusted, which poorly adjusted? Explain. (pp. 255–256)

Clarissa's thinking illustrates the aspect of the personal fable in which adolescents view themselves as sinking to unusual depths of despair, which others cannot possibly understand. She does not believe that anyone can possibly imagine how hurt she feels at not being invited to the dance. Justine's pantomime of being sworn in as student body president illustrates another aspect of the personal fable, in which she views herself as reaching great heights of omnipotence. This sense of omnipotence has been found to predict self-esteem and overall positive adjustment in adolescents, perhaps because seeing oneself as highly capable and influential helps young people cope with the challenges of adolescence. Therefore, Justine is more likely to be well-adjusted than Clarissa, whose sense of personal uniqueness is modestly associated with depression and suicidal thinking, and may interfere with forming the type of close relationships that provide social support during stressful times.

REFLECT: Cite examples of your own idealistic thinking or poor decision making as a teenager. How has your thinking changed? (pp. 256–257)

This is an open-ended question with no right or wrong answer.

REVIEW: Cite examples of findings that have led contemporary researchers to challenge Piaget's account of cognitive change. (pp. 260–261)

Many cognitive changes proceed slowly and gradually. Few abilities are completely absent in one period and suddenly present in another. Also, periods of cognitive equilibrium are rare. Instead, children are constantly modifying structures and acquiring new skills. Today, virtually all experts agree that children's cognition is less broadly stagelike than Piaget believed. Further, contemporary researchers disagree on how general or specific cognitive development actually is.

Some theorists agree with Piaget that development is a *general* process, following a similar course across the diverse cognitive domains of physical, numerical, and social knowledge. But they reject the existence of stages, believing instead that thought processes are alike at all ages—just present to a greater or lesser extent—and that variations in children's knowledge and experience largely account for uneven performance across domains. Other researchers think that the stage notion is still valid but that it must be modified. While pointing to strong evidence for certain stagelike changes, they also recognize many smaller developments that lead up to these transformations.

Still others deny not only Piaget's stages but also his belief that the human mind is made up of general reasoning abilities that can be applied to any cognitive task. They argue that the remarkable competencies of infants and young children indicate that cognitive development begins with far more than sensorimotor reflexes; rather, infants come into the world with several basic, built-in types of knowledge, each of which jump-starts vital aspects of cognition.

CONNECT: How are educational principles derived from Piaget's theory consistent with his emphasis on an active child who takes responsibility for her own learning? (pp. 259–260)

Three educational principles derived from Piaget's theory continue to influence teacher training and classroom practices, especially during early childhood:

In a classroom based on *discovery learning,* children are encouraged to discover for themselves through spontaneous interaction with the environment. Instead of presenting ready-made knowledge verbally, teachers provide a rich variety of activities designed to promote exploration and discovery.

Sensitivity to children's readiness to learn means that teachers in a Piagetian classroom do not try to hasten children's development by imposing new skills before children are interested or ready but, rather, introduce learning experiences that build on children's current level of thinking, challenging their incorrect ways of viewing the world.

The belief in *acceptance of individual differences* is based on Piaget's assumption that all children go through the same sequence of development, but at different rates. Therefore, teachers must plan activities for individuals and small groups, not just for the class as a whole. In addition, teachers evaluate educational progress in relation to the child's previous development, rather than on the basis of normative standards, or average performance of same-age peers.

REFLECT: Which aspects of Piaget's theory do you accept? Which do you doubt? Explain, citing research evidence. (pp. 260–261)

This is an open-ended question with no right or wrong answer.

REVIEW: What are core domains of thought? Cite examples of innate knowledge in the physical and numerical domains. Why do some researchers question the existence of innate knowledge? (pp. 261–264)

According to the core knowledge perspective, infants begin life with innate, special-purpose knowledge systems referred to as core domains of thought, each of which permits a ready grasp of new, related information. Two domains have been studied extensively in infancy. The first is *physical knowledge*—in particular, understanding of objects and their effects on one another. For example, 2½-month-olds seem to recognize that one solid object cannot move through another solid object. Furthermore, in the first half-year, infants are sensitive to basic principles of object support, staring intently at a box that rests in midair with nothing holding it in place.

The second core domain is *numerical knowledge*—the capacity to keep track of multiple objects and to add and subtract small quantities. Research suggests that young infants have basic number concepts. In the best-known study, 5-month-olds saw a screen raised to hide a single toy animal, then watched a hand place a second toy behind the screen. Finally the screen was removed to reveal either one or two toys. Infants looked longer at the impossible, one-toy display, suggesting that they kept track of the two objects, which would require them to add one object to another.

These findings—like other violation-of-expectation results—are controversial. Critics question whether other aspects of object displays, rather than numerical sensitivity, are responsible for the findings. These investigators cite research indicating that before 14 to 16 months, toddlers have difficulty making less-than and greater-than comparisons between small sets. Core knowledge theorists respond that infant looking behaviors may be a more reliable indicator of understanding than older children's verbal and motor behaviors, which may not always display their true competencies. Proponents of core knowledge point to studies of cultures with no verbal counting routines in which, nevertheless, adults demonstrate primitive number knowledge that resembles findings on infants. But critics continue to argue that such knowledge is not built-in but, rather, constructed over an extended time period.

CONNECT: Describe similarities and differences between Piaget's theory and the theory theory. (pp. 264–266)

According to theory theory (theory of children as theorists), after children observe an event, they draw on innate concepts to explain, or theorize about, its cause. They then test their naïve theory against experience, revising it when it cannot adequately account for new information. These revisions often lead to stagelike changes in cognitive development resembling those described by Piaget—dramatic, qualitative shifts in the complexity of concepts and explanations. However, theory theorists claim that because children start with innate knowledge, their reasoning advances quickly, with sophisticated cause-and-effect explanations evident much earlier than Piaget proposed.

REVIEW: Describe features of social interaction that support children's cognitive development. How does such interaction create a zone of proximal development? (pp. 267–269)

Intersubjectivity—the process by which two participants who begin a task with different understandings arrive at a shared understanding—is one ingredient of effective social interaction. Intersubjectivity creates a common ground for communication, as each partner adjusts to the other's perspective. The capacity for intersubjectivity is present early, in parent–infant mutual gaze, exchange of vocal and emotional signals, imitation, and joint play with objects. Later, language facilitates it, as preschoolers increasingly seek others' help and direct that assistance to ensure that it is beneficial. Between ages 3 and 5, children strive for intersubjectivity in dialogues with peers, as when they affirm a playmate's message or add new ideas, and contribute to ongoing play to sustain it.

Another important feature of social interaction is *scaffolding*—adjusting the support offered during a teaching session to fit the child's current level of performance. As the child's competence increases, effective scaffolders gradually and sensitively withdraw support, turning over responsibility to the child. The children take the language of these dialogues, make it part of their private speech, and use this speech to organize their independent efforts. *Guided participation,* a broader term than scaffolding, refers to shared endeavors between more expert and less expert participants without specifying the precise features of communication, thereby allowing for variations across situations and cultures.

Intersubjectivity and scaffolding interact to create a *zone of proximal development,* a range of tasks too difficult for a child to do alone but possible with the help of adults and more skilled peers, as adults tailor their efforts to the child's current level of functioning. Make-believe play is a unique, broadly influential zone of proximal development in which children advance themselves as they try out a wide variety of challenging skills and acquire many new competencies.

CONNECT: Explain how Piaget's and Vygotsky's theories complement each other. How would classroom practices inspired by these theories be similar? How would they be different? (pp. 267–268, 269–270)

Both Piaget and Vygotsky viewed children as active seekers of knowledge, and both regarded the emergence of play as an important developmental milestone, although they differed in their explanations of the role of make-believe play in cognitive development.

Piaget paid far more attention than Vygotsky to the development of basic cognitive processes, while deemphasizing language as a source of cognitive development. For example, Piaget regarded children's self-directed speech as *egocentric speech,* or "talk for self," which would eventually decline as a result of cognitive maturity and certain social experiences. In contrast, Vygotsky regarded language as the foundation for all higher cognitive processes, including controlled attention, deliberate memorization and recall, categorization, planning, problem solving, abstract reasoning, and self-reflection. In Vygotsky's view, children speak to themselves for self-guidance, and this *private speech* plays a positive role in cognitive development.

Both Piagetian and Vygotskian classrooms emphasize active participation and acceptance of individual differences. But whereas a Piagetian classroom promotes *discovery learning* through spontaneous interaction with the environment, a Vygotskian classroom goes beyond independent discovery to promote *assisted discovery.* Teachers guide children's learning, tailoring their interventions to each child's zone of proximal development. Assisted discovery is aided by *peer collaboration,* as children work in groups, teaching and helping one another.

Piaget, too, believed that peer interaction contributes to cognitive change. But in line with his view that children learn mainly through acting on the environment, he saw this as occurring primarily through certain social experiences, such as disagreements with peers, through which children came to see that others hold viewpoints different from their own.

APPLY: Tanisha sees her 5-year-old son Toby talking aloud to himself as he plays. She wonders whether she should discourage this behavior. Use Vygotsky's theory and related research to explain why Toby talks to himself. How would you advise Tanisha? (p. 267)

Vygotsky believed that children speak to themselves for self-guidance. Because language helps children think about mental activities and behavior and select courses of action, Vygotsky viewed it as the foundation for all higher cognitive processes, including controlled attention, deliberate memorization and recall, categorization, planning, problem solving, abstract reasoning, and self-reflection. As children get older and find tasks easier, their self-directed speech is internalized as silent, *inner speech*—the internal verbal dialogues we carry on while thinking and acting in everyday situations. Children who freely use self-guiding private speech during a challenging activity are more attentive and involved and show better task performance than their less talkative agemates. Because private speech helps children overcome difficulties and fosters task mastery, Tanisha should not discourage Toby from talking to himself.

REFLECT: When do you use private speech? Does it serve a self-guiding function for you, as it does for children? Explain. (p. 267)

This is an open-ended question with no right or wrong answer.

SUGGESTED READINGS

Johnson, S. (2010). *Neoconstructivism: The new science of cognitive development*. New York: Oxford University Press. A compelling look at cognitive development in infants and young children, this book explores a diverse range of topics, including historical accounts of early learning, current theories, language acquisition, the importance of play, and the relationship between cognition and social understanding.

Miller, R. (2011). *Vygotsky in perspective*. New York: Cambridge. An extensive look at the life and works of Lev Vygotsky. The author presents key Vygotskian concepts, as well as contemporary applications of sociocultural theory for understanding child development.

Singer, D., Hirsh-Pasek, K., & Golinkoff, R. (Eds.). (2006). *Play = Learning: How play motivates and enhances children's cognitive and social–emotional growth*. New York: Oxford University Press. A collection of chapters highlighting the diverse benefits of play for children's learning. The authors argue that in trying to create a generation of "Einsteins," many parents and educators are overlooking the importance of play in early child development.

MEDIA MATERIALS

For details on individual video segments that accompany the DVD for *Child Development,* Ninth Edition, please see the DVD Guide for *Explorations in Child Development*. The DVD and DVD Guide are available through your Pearson sales representative.

Additional DVDs that may be useful in your class are listed below. These are not available through your Pearson sales representative, but you can order them directly from the distributors. (See contact information at the end of this manual.)

Adolescent Cognition: Thinking in a New Key (2004, Insight Media, 30 min.). This program, featuring David Elkind, addresses the cognitive changes that occur during adolescence. Elkind cites the work of Piaget, Erikson, and Goffman as he examines the intellectual, emotional, and social consequences of the changes in thinking that characterize this period of life.

Growing Minds: Cognitive Development in Early Childhood (1996, Davidson Films, 25 min.). This program, which examines the work of Lev Vygotsky and Jean Piaget, illuminates the similarities and differences in their theories of early cognitive development. David Elkind uses their research, as well as his own work, to explore three aspects of intellectual growth: reasoning, visual perception, and language use.

Infants: Cognitive Development (2010, Magna Systems, 28 min.). This Learning Seed program discusses Piaget's sensorimotor stage and traces cognitive development from simple reflexes to the beginnings of thought. It explores infant intelligence, information processing, and memory, and follows the progression of infant communication from crying to babbling to actual word usage.

Learning from Others: Learning in a Social Context (2003, Annenberg/CPB, 30 min.). This program, part of *The Learning Classroom: Theory into Practice* series, examines the role of communication and interaction with others in learning, with an emphasis on Vygotsky's work. The program features an elementary teacher and a high school teacher, along with expert commentary from Tufts University professor David Elkind, Yale University professor James P. Comer, and University of California at Santa Cruz professor Roland Tharp.

Lev Vygotsky Documentary (2009, PDH Lowe Productions, 1 hr. 53 min.). This three-part program, which covers Vygotsky's life, theory, and practice, highlights a range of Vygotskian concepts. These include the role of learning through internalization of culture and social relationships, language development and thought, mediated learning, zone of proximal development, inclusion of special needs children in a school setting, play, and the role of collaborative dialogue and communication.

Middle Childhood: Cognitive & Language Development (2008, Magna Systems, 20 min.). This program explores how the mind expands and how thinking becomes more logical and organized in middle childhood. It presents educator insights and classroom strategies for fostering cognitive development and language in school-age children. Topics include the characteristics of concrete operational thinking, how to measure intelligence, the stages of learning how to read and write, methods used in bilingual education, and the role of memory.

Preschoolers: Cognitive Development (2008, Magna Systems, 24 min.). Using footage of preschoolers in the classroom, dynamic graphics, and interviews with teachers and caregivers, this program delivers a detailed overview of cognitive development in 3- to 5-year-olds. It examines how preschoolers begin to use language, mental imagery, and symbolic thinking, how they perceive past and future events, and what they understand about their own thinking. This program also discusses how the brain grows neural bridges and examines widely studied theories of cognitive development, including characteristics of preoperational thought.

The Teenage Brain: A Work in Progress (2007, Insight Media, 43 min.). This program focuses on the social, emotional, cognitive, and linguistic developments of the adolescent years and shows how these developments influence the actions and attitudes of teenagers.

Windows on the Mind: Children's Drawings (1993, Insight Media, 25 min.). Challenging Piaget's belief that children go through a universal developmental process that is clearly reflected in their drawings, researchers in this program compare the drawings of children from an urban area in Dundee, Scotland, with those of Aboriginal children in Australia.

CHAPTER 7
COGNITIVE DEVELOPMENT: AN INFORMATION-PROCESSING PERSPECTIVE

CHAPTER-AT-A-GLANCE

Chapter Outline	Instruction Ideas	Supplements
The Information-Processing Approach p. 278	Learning Activity 7.8	Test Bank Items 1–3 Please contact your Pearson publisher's representative for a wide range of video offerings available to adopters.
A General Model of Information Processing pp. 278–282 Components of the Mental System • Implications for Development	Learning Objective 7.1 Lecture Enhancement 7.1 Learning Activities 7.1, 7.8	Test Bank Items 4–21, 124
Developmental Theories of Information Processing pp. 282–286 Case's Neo-Piagetian Theory • Siegler's Model of Strategy Choice	Learning Objective 7.2 Learning Activity 7.8 Ask Yourself p. 286	Test Bank Items 22–35, 125
Attention pp. 286–292, 293 Sustained, Selective, and Adaptable Attention • Planning	Learning Objective 7.3 Lecture Enhancement 7.2 Learning Activity 7.8 Ask Yourself p. 292	Test Bank Items 36–48
Memory pp. 292–302 Strategies for Storing Information • Retrieving Information • Knowledge and Semantic Memory • Episodic Memory • Eyewitness Memory	Learning Objectives 7.4–7.6 Learning Activities 7.2–7.6, 7.8 Ask Yourself p. 302	Test Bank Items 49–90, 126–129
Metacognition pp. 303–307 Metacognitive Knowledge • Cognitive Self-Regulation	Learning Objective 7.7 Learning Activity 7.8 Ask Yourself p. 307	Test Bank Items 91–104
Applications of Information Processing to Academic Learning pp. 307–314 Reading • Mathematics • Scientific Reasoning	Learning Objective 7.8 Lecture Enhancements 7.3–7.4 Learning Activities 7.7–7.8	Test Bank Items 105–121, 130
Evaluation of the Information-Processing Approach pp. 314–315	Learning Objective 7.9 Learning Activity 7.8 Ask Yourself p. 315	Test Bank Items 122–123

BRIEF CHAPTER SUMMARY

Information-processing theorists view the mind as a complex, symbol-manipulating system through which information flows, often using the metaphor of a computer. One general model of information processing, the store model, assumes that information is stored in three parts of the mental system for processing: the sensory register, the short-term memory store, and the long-term memory store. To manage the cognitive system's activities, the central executive directs the flow of information and engages in activities that enable complex, flexible thinking.

Developmental models of information processing include Case's neo-Piagetian perspective, which starts with Piaget's stages but attributes change within and between stages to increases in the efficiency with which children use their limited working-memory capacity. Siegler's model of strategy choice, another developmental model, views children's cognition from an evolutionary perspective, suggesting that children generate a variety of strategies for solving challenging problems and that, with experience, some strategies are selected and survive, whereas others die off. This model overcomes deficiencies of the stage approach in accounting for both diversity and continuous change in children's thinking.

Attention is fundamental to human thinking because it determines which information will be considered in any task. Children acquire selective, adaptable attention through gains in inhibition and attentional strategies. Inhibition gains free working-memory resources and, thus, promotes effective strategy use. With age, children become more capable of planning, which involves the coordination of attention with other cognitive processes.

We retrieve information from our long-term knowledge base in three ways—through recognition, recall, and reconstruction. Recognition, the simplest form, is fairly automatic and reaches a near-adult level during the preschool years. Recall lags behind recognition and shows much greater improvement with age. Reconstruction is a constructivist approach that involves selecting and interpreting new information in terms of existing knowledge.

Fuzzy-trace theory suggests that when we first encode information, we reconstruct it automatically, creating a gist—a vague, fuzzy version that preserves essential meaning without details. Gists can serve as enduring retrieval cues, contributing to improved recall with age.

Our taxonomically organized, hierarchically structured general knowledge system is referred to as semantic memory. Children's expanding knowledge promotes improved memory by making new, related information more meaningful so that it is easier to store and retrieve. Semantic memory contributes vitally to episodic memory, recollections of personally experienced events that occurred at a specific time and place. Both children and adults remember familiar events in terms of scripts, general descriptions of what occurs and when it occurs in a particular situation. Young children also develop autobiographical memory—representations of personally meaningful one-time events.

The accuracy and completeness of children's episodic memories are central to their ability to recount relevant experiences when testifying in court cases. Compared with preschoolers, school-age children are better at giving accurate and detailed eyewitness accounts in court and resisting adults' misleading questions. But when a biased adult repeatedly asks leading questions, children are far more likely to give false information.

Metacognition—awareness and understanding of various aspects of thought—expands greatly in early and middle childhood as children construct a naïve theory of mind—a coherent understanding of people as mental beings. Unlike preschoolers, who view the mind as a passive container of information, older children see it as an active, constructive agent that selects and transforms information. Young children are not yet good at cognitive self-regulation, the process of continually monitoring progress toward a goal, checking outcomes, and redirecting unsuccessful outcomes.

Fundamental discoveries about information processing have been applied to children's mastery of academic skills, particularly in reading and mathematics. Children's active efforts to construct literacy knowledge through informal experiences are known as emergent literacy. Phonological awareness—the ability to reflect on and manipulate the sound structure of spoken language—is a strong predictor of later reading achievement. Children learn to read most effectively when taught with a mixture of a whole-language approach, which exposes children to meaningful text, and phonics, which emphasizes the basic rules for translating written symbols into sounds. Similarly, in learning mathematics, children do best with a blend of frequent practice, reasoning about number concepts, and teaching that conveys effective strategies. The capacity to engage in scientific reasoning improves with age, as children develop the ability to distinguish between theory and evidence.

Major strengths of the information-processing approach are its explicitness and precision in breaking down cognitive activities into their components. But information processing has difficulty reassembling these components of cognition into a broad, comprehensive theory of development. Computer models of cognitive processing do not reflect the richness of real-life learning experiences and overlook aspects of cognition that are not linear and logical, such as creativity. The near future is likely to bring new breakthroughs in understanding mechanisms of cognitive development and neurological changes that underlie various mental activities.

Chapter 7 Cognitive Development: An Information-Processing Perspective

LEARNING OBJECTIVES

After reading this chapter, you should be able to answer the following:

7.1 Describe the store model of the human information processing system, noting implications for cognitive development and related findings. (pp. 278–282)

7.2 How do Case's neo-Piagetian theory and Siegler's model of strategy choice explain changes in children's thinking? (pp. 282–286)

7.3 Describe the development of attention, including sustained, selective, and adaptable strategies. (pp. 286–291, 293)

7.4 Describe the development of strategies for storing and retrieving information from memory. (pp. 292–296)

7.5 Explain the development of episodic memory and its relationship to semantic memory. (pp. 296–300, 301)

7.6 How does eyewitness memory change with age, and what factors influence the accuracy of children's reports? (pp. 300, 302)

7.7 Describe the development of metacognitive knowledge and cognitive self-regulation. (pp. 303–306)

7.8 Discuss the development of reading, mathematics, and scientific reasoning, noting the implications of research findings for teaching. (pp. 307–314)

7.9 Summarize the strengths and limitations of the information-processing approach. (pp. 314–315)

LECTURE OUTLINE

I. THE INFORMATION-PROCESSING APPROACH (p. 278)
   A. Information processing is an approach to the study of cognition that attempts to uncover *mechanisms of change*—how children and adults operate on information as it moves through the cognitive system.
   B. Information-processing theorists are interested both in internal, self-generated cognitive changes and in how external influences, such as teaching techniques, affect children's thinking.
   C. Most information-processing theorists view the mind as a complex symbol-manipulating system through which information from the environment flows, often using the metaphor of a computer.
      1. First, information is *encoded*—taken in and retained in symbolic form.
      2. Internal processes operate on the information, *recoding* it and then *decoding* it.
      3. Individuals use the information to make sense of their experiences and to solve problems.
   D. Researchers use computer-like diagrams and flowcharts to try to map the exact series of steps children and adults follow when faced with a task or problem.

II. A GENERAL MODEL OF INFORMATION PROCESSING (pp. 278–282)
   A. The s*tore model*—a computer-like view of the cognitive system—assumes that we store information in three parts of the mental system for processing: the *sensory register*, the *short-term memory store*, and the *long-term memory store*.
   B. As information flows sequentially through each, we can use *mental strategies* to operate on and transform it.
   C. Components of the Mental System (pp. 278–280)
      1. First, information enters the **sensory register,** where sights and sounds are represented directly but stored only momentarily.
      2. In the second part of the mind, the **short-term memory store,** we retain attended-to information briefly so we can actively "work" on it to reach our goals.
         a. The short-term store can be looked at in terms of its *basic capacity*, or *short-term memory:* how many pieces of information it can hold at once for a few seconds.
         b. A more meaningful indicator of this capacity is called **working memory**—the number of items that can be briefly held in mind while also engaging in some effort to manipulate them.
            (1) Children's performance on working-memory tasks is a good predictor of their capacity to learn.
            (2) By engaging in a variety of basic cognitive procedures, such as focusing attention on relevant items, we increase the chances that information will be retained.

c. To manage the cognitive system's activities, the **central executive** directs the flow of information, implementing the basic procedures and also engaging in more sophisticated activities that enable complex, flexible thinking.
    (1) The central executive coordinates incoming information with information already in the system, and it selects, applies, and monitors strategies.
    (2) The more effectively the central executive joins with working memory to process information, the better learned those cognitive activities will be.
    (3) **Automatic processes** are so well-learned that they require no space in working memory and permit us to focus on other information while simultaneously performing them.
3. The third and largest storage area is **long-term memory,** our permanent knowledge base, which is unlimited.
    a. To aid retrieval of information, we apply strategies.
    b. Information in long-term memory is *categorized* by its contents, allowing us to retrieve items by following the same network of associations used to store them in the first place.

D. Implications for Development (pp. 280–282)
  1. The store model suggests that several aspects of the cognitive system improve with age: the *basic capacity* of its stores, the *speed* with which children work on information, and *executive function*.
  2. Working-Memory Capacity
    a. Short-term and working-memory spans increase steadily with age.
    b. Still, individual differences are evident at all ages; they are of concern because working-memory capacity predicts academic achievement in middle childhood and adolescence.
    c. Compared to their economically advantaged agemates, children from poverty-stricken families are more likely to score low on working-memory span tasks.
  3. Speed of Processing
    a. With age, children process information more efficiently.
    b. Increased processing speed enables older children and adults to scan information more quickly, to transform it more rapidly, and to hold more information in working memory.
  4. Executive Function
    a. The **executive function** is the set of cognitive operations and strategies—such as controlling attention and organizing thought and behavior—necessary for self-initiated, purposeful behavior in relatively novel, challenging situations.
    b. Some investigators view executive function as a unitary capacity; others see it as made up of multiple, distinct cognitive abilities that collaborate in goal-directed action.
    c. Heritability evidence suggests substantial genetic contributions to individual differences in working-memory capacity and attentional processing, but the environment also influences executive function.

III. DEVELOPMENTAL THEORIES OF INFORMATION PROCESSING (pp. 282–286)
  A. *Developmental* approaches to information processing aim to explain how children's thinking changes.
  B. Case's Neo-Piagetian Theory (pp. 283–284)
    1. Robbie Case's **neo-Piagetian theory** accepts Piaget's stages but attributes change within each stage, and movement from one stage to the next, to increases in the efficiency with which children use their limited working-memory capacity.
    2. Each stage involves a distinct type of cognitive structure: in infancy, sensory input and physical actions; in early childhood, internal representations of events and actions; in middle childhood, simple transformations of representations; and in adolescence, complex transformations of representations.
    3. In Case's theory, three factors contribute to cognitive change:
      a. *Brain development:* Neurological changes, including synaptic growth and synaptic pruning, improve the efficiency of thought, leading to readiness for each stage.
      b. *Practice with schemes and automization:* Case saw Piagetian schemes as the child's mental strategies, which become automatic through repeated use, freeing working memory to combine existing schemes and generate new ones.
      c. *Formation of central conceptual structures:* Once the schemes of a Piagetian stage become automatic and brain development further increments processing speed, enough space in working memory is available to consolidate schemes into an improved representational form.

Chapter 7 Cognitive Development: An Information-Processing Perspective

(1) As a result, children generate **central conceptual structures**—networks of concepts and relations that permit them to think about a wide range of situations in more advanced ways.
(2) When children form new central conceptual structures, they move to the next stage of development.
4. Case's theory offers an information-processing account of the *continuum of acquisition*—that many understandings appear in specific situations at different times rather than being mastered all at once.
C. Siegler's Model of Strategy Choice (pp. 284–286)
1. Robert Siegler's **model of strategy choice** uses an evolutionary metaphor—"natural selection"—to describe cognitive change.
   a. When given challenging problems, children generate a *variety* of strategies.
   b. With experience, some strategies are *selected;* they become more frequent and "survive," while others become less frequent and "die off."
   c. Children's mental strategies display *variation* and *selection,* yielding adaptive problem-solving techniques—ones best suited to solving the problems at hand.
2. Siegler used the microgenetic research design to study children's strategy use.
   a. He found that strategy use for basic math facts—and many other types of problems—follows an *overlapping-waves pattern,* in which children observe how well strategies work and gradually select strategies on the basis of two adaptive criteria: *accuracy* and *speed*.
   b. As children home in on effective strategies, correct solutions become more strongly associated with problems, and eventually children display the most efficient strategy—automatic retrieval of the answer.
3. Siegler's model reveals that no child thinks in just one way, even on a single task.
4. The model of strategy choice overcomes deficiencies of the stage approach in accounting for both diversity and continuous change in children's thinking.

IV. ATTENTION (pp. 286–292, 293)
A. Attention is fundamental to human thinking because it determines which information will be considered in any task.
B. Sustained, Selective, and Adaptable Attention (pp. 286–289)
1. As children make the transition to toddlerhood, attraction to novelty declines and *sustained attention* improves, especially during play.
   a. Many skills, including language, exploration, and problem solving, benefit from this improved ability to concentrate.
   b. As sustained attention increases, children become better at focusing on only those aspects of a situation that are relevant to their goals.
2. Children acquire selective, adaptable attention through gains in inhibition and attentional strategies.
3. Inhibition
   a. Selective attention requires **inhibition**—the ability to control internal and external distracting stimuli.
   b. By controlling irrelevant stimuli, inhibition frees working-memory resources for the task at hand and, therefore, supports many information-processing skills.
4. Attentional Strategies
   a. Development of an efficient attentional strategy occurs in four phases:
      (1) **Production deficiency:** Preschoolers rarely engage in attentional strategies: They usually fail to *produce* strategies when these could be helpful.
      (2) **Control deficiency:** Young elementary school children sometimes produce strategies, but not consistently, and have difficulty *controlling,* or executing, strategies effectively.
      (3) **Utilization deficiency:** Slightly later, children execute strategies consistently, but their performance either does not improve or improves less than that of older children.
      (4) **Effective strategy use:** By the mid-elementary school years, children use strategies consistently, and performance improves.
   b. This sequence also characterizes children's use of memory strategies.
C. Planning (pp. 289–291)
1. **Planning** involves thinking out a sequence of acts ahead of time and allocating attention accordingly to reach a goal.
2. The seeds of effective planning are present in infancy.
3. On relatively simple tasks requiring reasoning about how best to implement a future action, preschoolers have great difficulty generating a plan.

4. Marked gains in planning take place around 5 years of age, and further improvement occurs during middle childhood.
5. Planning in most everyday tasks requires children to coordinate attention skills with other cognitive processes.
6. Executive-function difficulties may underlie the symptoms of **attention-deficit hyperactivity disorder (ADHD),** which involves inattention, impulsivity, and excessive motor activity resulting in academic and social problems.

V. MEMORY (pp. 292–302)
   A. *Memory strategies* are deliberate mental activities we use to increase the likelihood of holding information in working memory and transferring it to our long-term knowledge base.
   B. Strategies for Storing Information (pp. 292–294)
      1. Rehearsal, Organization, and Elaboration
         a. **Rehearsal** is a memory strategy that involves repeating information to ourselves; **organization** is a strategy that involves grouping related items.
         b. Older children are more likely to apply several memory strategies at once.
         c. By the end of middle childhood, children start to use a third memory strategy, **elaboration,** which involves creating a relationship between two or more pieces of information that do not belong to the same category.
         d. While older-school-age children and adolescents are adept at strategic memorizing, they frequently engage in other pursuits—such as text messaging and e-mailing friends—while doing schoolwork. Research confirms that media multitasking greatly reduces learning.
      2. Culture, Schooling, and Memory Strategies
         a. People usually use memory strategies when they need to remember information for its own sake, in contrast to many times when memory occurs as a natural byproduct of daily activities.
         b. People in non-Western cultures who lack formal schooling rarely use or benefit from instruction in memory strategies because they see no practical reason to use them.
         c. The development of memory strategies is not just a matter of a more competent information-processing system. It is also a product of task demands and cultural circumstances.
   C. Retrieving Information (pp. 294–296)
      1. To use information that has entered our long-term knowledge base, we must *retrieve* (or recover) it using recognition, recall, or reconstruction.
      2. Recognition and Recall
         a. **Recognition**—noticing that a stimulus is identical or similar to one previously experienced—is the simplest form of retrieval.
         b. **Recall**—generating a mental representation of an absent stimulus—begins in the second half of the first year for memories that are strongly cued, but development of recall lags behind recognition from infancy on.
         c. Compared with recognition, recall shows far greater improvement with age, because older children make use of a wider range of retrieval cues.
      3. Reconstruction
         a. To remember complex, meaningful material, we select and interpret the information we encounter in terms of our existing knowledge.
         b. Constructive processing can involve **reconstruction** of information, or recoding it while it is in the system or is being retrieved.
         c. Children, like adults, reconstruct stored information.
         d. Over time, children make more inferences about past events, a process that increases the coherence—and, therefore, the memorableness—of reconstructed information but also may lead to inaccurate recall.
      4. Another View of Reconstruction: Fuzzy-Trace Theory
         a. According to Brainerd and Reyna's **fuzzy-trace theory,** when we first encode information, we reconstruct it automatically, creating a vague, fuzzy version called a **gist.**
         b. The gist, which preserves essential meaning without details, is especially useful for reasoning.
         c. Because gist requires less working-memory capacity, it frees attention for the steps involved in thinking.
         d. Since fuzzy traces are less likely than verbatim memories to be forgotten, gists can serve as enduring retrieval cues, contributing to improved recall with age.

D. Knowledge and Semantic Memory (pp. 296–297)
   1. Our vast, taxonomically organized and hierarchically structured general knowledge system consisting of concepts, language meanings, facts, and rules (such as memory strategies and arithmetic procedures) is often referred to as **semantic memory.**
   2. Children's expanding knowledge promotes improved memory by making new, related information more meaningful so that it is easier to store and retrieve.
   3. Children with expert knowledge of a topic show greater organization at retrieval, suggesting that they apply memory strategies in their area of expertise with little or no effort, by rapidly associating new items with the large number they already know.
E. Episodic Memory (pp. 297–300, 301)
   1. Because knowledge that makes up semantic memory does not require storage of when or where the information was acquired, it differs from **episodic memory**—recollections of personally experienced events that occurred at a specific time and place.
   2. Semantic memory develops earlier than episodic memory, and semantic knowledge contributes vitally to the development of episodic memory.
   3. Children who have acquired substantial knowledge for interpreting personally experienced events are better able to recall those events than children with less knowledge.
   4. Children develop two types of episodic memory: memory for recurring events and memory for significant one-time events.
   5. Scripts
      a. Preschoolers, like adults, remember repeated events in terms of **scripts,** general descriptions of what occurs and when it occurs in a particular situation.
      b. Scripts are a special form of reconstructive memory, which help children and adults organize and interpret everyday experiences.
      c. Some researchers believe that the general event structures of scripts provide a foundation for organizing memory for unique events, such as a special birthday party.
   6. Autobiographical Memory
      a. Each of us has a unique **autobiographical memory,** made up of representations of one-time events that are long-lasting because they are imbued with personal meaning.
      b. To form an autobiographical memory, children must have a sufficiently clear self-image to serve as an anchor for personally significant events—a milestone reached around age 2 years—and must integrate their experiences into a meaningful, time-organized life story.
      c. The style parents use to elicit children's autobiographical narratives may be either *elaborative* or *repetitive;* preschoolers who experience the elaborative style recall more information about past events.
      d. Differences in autobiographical narratives reflect variations in parent–child conversations and in cultural values.
      e. **Infantile amnesia,** an inability to retrieve events that happened to us before age 3, may reflect the nonverbal nature of infants' and toddlers' memory processing.
F. Eyewitness Memory (pp. 300, 302)
   1. The accuracy and completeness of children's episodic memories are central to their ability to recount relevant experiences when testifying in court cases involving child abuse and neglect, child custody, and other legal matters.
   2. Compared with school-age children, preschoolers are more prone to memory errors when giving descriptions of past experiences and inferring others' motives, for several reasons:
      a. Responding to interview questions is challenging for preschoolers whose language competence is not well-developed.
      b. Preschoolers are poor at *source-monitoring*—identifying where they got their knowledge.
      c. Accurately reporting certain temporal information is difficult for younger children.
      d. Younger children are less skilled at ignoring irrelevant information, which makes them more willing to accept adult suggestions.
      e. Younger children are more likely to agree with adults' yes-or-no questions.
      f. Preschoolers forget more easily than older children.
      g. Younger children are less competent at reporting autobiographical memories completely.

3. Suggestibility
    a. Inaccurate reporting by children and adolescents in court is more likely to occur when adults repeat questions, use a confrontational questioning style, suggest incorrect "facts," or provide reinforcement for giving desired answers.
    b. One study of 4- to 7-year-olds showed that after a high-pressure interview, children were far more likely to give false information—even fabricating quite fantastic events.
    c. The more distinctive and personally relevant an event is, the more likely children are to recall it accurately over time.
4. Interventions
    a. Adults must prepare child witnesses so they understand the courtroom process and know what to expect.
    b. Even children as young as 3 or 4 can be trained to monitor the source of their memories and to reject misleading source information.
    c. Legal professionals must use interviewing procedures that increase children's accurate reporting.
    d. Courtroom procedures can be adapted to protect children who may be at risk for trauma or punishment for answering questions.

VI. METACOGNITION (pp. 303–307)
  A. **Metacognition** refers to awareness and understanding of various aspects of thought.
    1. During early and middle childhood, metacognition expands greatly as children construct a naïve **theory of mind,** a coherent understanding of people as mental beings, which they revise as they encounter new evidence.
    2. A second facet of metacognitive research concerns children's knowledge of mental activity, or *what it means to think*.
  B. Metacognitive Knowledge (pp. 303–304)
    1. Knowledge of Cognitive Capacities
      a. By age 3, children realize that thinking takes place inside their heads.
      b. But children younger than age 6 focus on outcomes of thought and not the *process* of thinking.
      c. School-age children realize that people can extend their knowledge by making *mental inferences*.
      d. By age 10, children grasp the interrelatedness of cognitive processes.
      e. Understanding of cognitive capacities changes greatly during childhood.
        (1) Preschoolers view the mind as a passive container of information.
        (2) Older children regard the mind as an active, constructive agent.
      f. Language development (especially mental-state vocabulary) and capacity for more complex thinking contribute greatly to school-age children's more process-oriented view of the mind.
    2. Knowledge of Strategies
      a. School-age children are far more conscious of mental strategies than preschoolers.
      b. By the end of middle childhood, children start to consider how *interactions* among multiple variables—such as motivation of the learner and difficulty of the task—affect cognitive performance.
  C. Cognitive Self-Regulation (pp. 304–306)
    1. School-age children and adolescents are not yet proficient at **cognitive self-regulation,** the process of continually monitoring and controlling progress toward a goal—planning, checking outcomes, and redirecting unsuccessful efforts.
    2. Parents and teachers can foster self-regulation by suggesting strategies for problem solving and explaining their effectiveness.

VII. APPLICATIONS OF INFORMATION PROCESSING TO ACADEMIC LEARNING (pp. 307–314)
  A. Discoveries about the development of information processing have been applied to children's mastery of academic skills.
  B. Reading (pp. 307–310)
    1. Because reading uses many skills at once, it taxes all aspects of the information-processing system.
    2. Becoming a proficient reader is a complex process that begins in the preschool years.
    3. Early Childhood
      a. Children's active efforts to construct literacy knowledge through informal experiences are called **emergent literacy.**

b. **Phonological awareness**—the ability to reflect on and manipulate the sound structure of spoken language, as indicated by sensitivity to changes in sounds within words, to rhyming, and to incorrect pronunciation—is a strong predictor of emergent literacy knowledge.
c. The more informal literacy experiences preschoolers have, the better their language and emergent literacy development and their later literacy skills.
d. On average, a preschooler from a low-income family is read to for a total of 25 hours during early childhood, a middle-income child for 1,000 hours. The gap in experiences translates into large differences in skills vital for reading readiness.
4. Middle Childhood
    a. During middle childhood, phonological awareness continues to predict reading (and spelling) progress; other information-processing skills also contribute.
    b. Many studies show that children learn best with a mixture of two very different approaches to reading:
        (1) A **whole-language approach** is the view that from the beginning, children should be exposed to text in its complete form—stories, poems, letters, posters, and lists.
        (2) A **phonics approach** is the view that children should first be coached on *phonics*—the basic rules for translating written symbols into sounds—and should not get complex reading material until they have mastered these skills.
5. Adolescent readers use efficient decoding and comprehension skills as they actively engage with the text, adjusting the way they read to fit their current purpose.

C. Mathematics (pp. 310–313)
1. Mathematical reasoning, like reading, builds on informally acquired knowledge.
2. Early Childhood
    a. Between 14 and 16 months, toddlers display a beginning grasp of **ordinality**—order relationships between quantities.
    b. By age 3½ to 4, most children have grasped the principle of **cardinality**—that the last word in a counting sequence indicates the quantity of items in a set.
    c. Children experiment with various strategies to solve arithmetic problems and eventually master the efficient *min* strategy.
    d. Arithmetic knowledge emerges in many cultures around the world, but children construct these understandings sooner when adults provide many occasions for counting, comparing quantities, and talking about number concepts.
3. Middle Childhood
    a. In elementary school, written notation systems and formal computational techniques enhance children's ability to represent numbers, compute, and estimate.
    b. Arguments about how to teach math resemble those in reading, pitting drill in computing against "number sense," or understanding; a blend of the two approaches is most beneficial.
    c. Solid mastery of basic math is promoted by encouraging students to apply strategies and making sure they understand why certain strategies work well.

D. Scientific Reasoning (pp. 313–314)
1. The heart of scientific reasoning is coordinating theories with evidence—a capacity that improves with age.
2. Age-Related Change
    a. Younger children often blend evidence and theory into a single representation of "the way things are."
    b. The ability to distinguish theory from evidence and use logical rules to examine their relationship improves from childhood into adolescence, continuing into adulthood.
3. How Scientific Reasoning Develops
    a. Factors that support skill at coordinating theory with evidence include greater working memory resources, permitting simultaneous comparison of a theory and the effects of several variables, and exposure to increasingly complex problems through schooling.
    b. The ability to *think about* theories, *deliberately isolate* variables, *consider all influential* variables, and *actively seek* disconfirming evidence is rarely present before adolescence.
    c. Reasoning scientifically requires the metacognitive capacity to evaluate one's objectivity.
    d. Information-processing findings reveal that scientific reasoning develops gradually out of many specific experiences with different types of problems.

VIII. EVALUATION OF THE INFORMATION-PROCESSING APPROACH (pp. 314–315)
   A. A major strength of the information-processing approach is its explicitness and precision in breaking down complex cognitive activities into their components.
      1. It has provided detailed evidence on how individuals at different ages and different skill levels attend, remember, reason, and solve problems.
      2. It has contributed greatly to the design of teaching techniques to advance children's thinking.
   B. The information-processing approach also has several limitations.
      1. Information processing has had difficulty reassembling the components of cognition into a broad, comprehensive theory of development.
      2. Computer models of cognitive processing do not reflect the richness of real-life learning experiences.
      3. Information processing has not told us much about the links between cognition and other areas of development.
   C. The near future is likely to bring new breakthroughs in understanding mechanisms of cognitive development and neurological changes underlying various mental activities, and in identifying teaching techniques that support children's learning.

LECTURE ENHANCEMENTS

LECTURE ENHANCEMENT 7.1
Working Memory and Academic Achievement (p. 280)

Time: 5–10 minutes

Objective: To extend existing research on the relationship between working memory and learning in children.

To examine the relationship between working memory and learning in children who have been diagnosed with learning disabilities, Alloway (2009) recruited 37 children between the ages of 7 and 11 years and followed them for two years. All of the participants were receiving special education support at the time of the study.

At Time 1, participants completed the Working Memory Test Battery for Children (WMTB–C). The WMTB–C consists of the following tasks:
- *Digit recall.* Participants were presented with a sequence of digits and then asked to recall the digits in the correct order.
- *Word recall.* Participants were presented with a sequence of one-syllable words and then asked to recall the words in the correct order.
- *Listening recall.* Participants were presented with a series of spoken sentences, asked to verify if each sentence was true or false, and then instructed to recall the last word of each sentence.
- *Backward digit recall.* Participants were presented with a sequence of digits and then asked to recall the digits in reverse order.
- *Block recall test.* Participants were shown nine cubes randomly arranged on a board. They were then instructed to tap a specific sequence in the correct order.
- *Visual patterns test.* Participants were shown a two-dimensional grid of black-and-white squares for three seconds. They were then instructed to mark the location of the black squares on an empty grid.

Participants also completed a standardized intelligence test at Time 1. At Time 1 and Time 2, participants completed a standardized reading (basic reading skills, reading comprehension, and spelling) and math (mathematical reasoning and numerical operations) assessment.

Findings indicated that significant impairments in working memory at Time 1 predicted reading and math difficulties at Time 2. That is, compared to children with higher scores on working-memory tasks at the onset of the study, those with low scores were significantly more likely to score below grade level on reading and math assessments two years later. Reading and math scores at Time 1 were also predictive of scores at Time 2. Intelligence test scores, however, did not predict reading and math performance at Time 2. According to Alloway, these findings suggest that working-memory capacity and domain-specific knowledge are unique predictors of academic outcomes in children with learning difficulties.

According to research presented in the text, what can educators do to reduce memory loads in children with learning difficulties?

Alloway, T. P. (2009). Working memory, but not IQ, predicts subsequent learning in children with learning difficulties. *European Journal of Psychological Assessment, 25*, 92–98.

Chapter 7 Cognitive Development: An Information-Processing Perspective

LECTURE ENHANCEMENT 7.2
Long-Term Consequences of Attention Problems in Childhood (pp. 286–288)

Time: 10–15 minutes

Objective: To examine the long-term consequences of attention problems in childhood.

To examine the long-term consequences of attention problems in childhood, Friedman and colleagues (2009) used data on 866 twins who were participating in the Colorado Longitudinal Twin Study. Participants were followed from age 7 to age 17. Using archival data, the researchers gathered the following information:

(1) Each year, teachers completed the Attention Problems Scale, which measures impulsivity, overactivity, organization, learning, and attention.
(2) When participants were 16 years old, they were given an intelligence test.
(3) When participants were 17 years old, they completed an attentional control task, which measures participants' ability to inhibit automatic responses, ignore irrelevant information, and shift from one task to another.
- Example of Inhibition Task: The individual is presented with a list of color words in a different colored font. Instead of reading the word, the individual is told to name the font color.
- Example of Ignoring Irrelevant Stimuli Task: The individual is presented with a series of letters or words of unpredictable length. The goal is to read only the final three letters of each series, while ignoring all of the other letters.
- Example of Shifting Task: The individual is presented with a series of shapes of different colors and, for each, must name either the shape or the color, based on the cue given.

Results indicated that attention problems were fairly stable over childhood and into adolescence. That is, teacher ratings of attention problems at age 7 moderately predicted attention problems at older ages. In addition, participants who were identified as having attention problems in childhood scored lower on the attentional control task at age 17 than participants who were not identified as having attention problems. Interestingly, attention problems were more strongly related to inhibition than to the ability to ignore irrelevant stimuli and shift attention from one task to another. It is possible that the inhibition task required more attentional control than the other tasks, although the study did not specifically address this. Also, attention problems were more strongly related to inhibition than to IQ. According to Friedman and colleagues, this suggests that the relationship between attention problems and inhibition cannot simply be explained by lower levels of cognitive ability. It is important to note, however, that children who were identified as having attention problems had lower IQ scores than children who were not identified as having attention problems.

Taken together, these results support the notion that attention problems arise primarily from a deficit in inhibition. Moreover, attention problems seem to have a differential impact on various aspects of attentional control.

Ask students to think of ways in which adults can foster attentional control in children. What activities or experiences are likely to enhance attentional control? Can students think of activities or experiences that might compromise the development of attentional control?

Friedman, N. P., Haberstick, B. C., Willcutt, E. G., Miyake, A., Young, S. E., Corley, R. P., & Hewitt, J. K. (2009). Greater attention problems during childhood predict poorer executive functioning in late adolescence. *Psychological Science, 18,* 893–900.

LECTURE ENHANCEMENT 7.3
Developmental Changes in Literacy Skills (pp. 307–310)

Time: 5–10 minutes

Objective: To examine developmental changes in literacy skills from kindergarten through third grade.

To extend existing research on developmental changes in literacy skills, Foster and Miller (2008) used data on 12,621 children who were participating in the Early Childhood Longitudinal Study (ECLS). The ECLS follows children from kindergarten through the end of third grade. The researchers collected the following information:

(1) In the fall of the kindergarten year, participants completed a reading assessment that focuses on basic literacy skills and reading comprehension. For example, participants were asked to identify upper- and lowercase letters, associate letters with sounds at the beginning and end of common words, identify words that are embedded within sentences, and determine the meaning of sentences.

(2) On the basis of their scores on the kindergarten reading assessment, participants were assigned to one of three literacy readiness groups:
- Low readiness: Students who scored at least one standard deviation below the mean.
- Average readiness: Students who scored within one standard deviation of the mean.
- High readiness: Students who scored at least one standard deviation above the mean.

(3) In first and third grades, participants completed a reading measure that assesses phonics and text comprehension.

(4) Parents provided information on annual household income and their highest level of educational attainment.

Results indicated that by the end of first grade, children in the average readiness group scored similarly to those in the high readiness group in phonics proficiency. In contrast, children in the low readiness group did not achieve this level of phonics proficiency until the end of third grade. Children in the average and high readiness groups also scored higher on text comprehension than participants in the low readiness group. This finding makes sense, given that a strong foundation in phonics is necessary to transition to higher-level reading skills, such as text comprehension.

Results also showed that low readiness children were more likely than average or high readiness children to come from low-income families with lower levels of parent education. This finding is consistent with previous research showing that poverty-stricken children often enter school with deficits in basic literacy skills and that, without intensive intervention, they remain behind agemates in reading achievement throughout the school years.

According to Foster and Miller, if schools wait until second or third grade to initiate aggressive reading instruction for poor readers, it becomes extremely difficult to close the achievement gap between low-income children and their more economically advantaged counterparts. Thus, early identification and intervention are critical for preventing long-term deficits in reading achievement.

Foster, W. A., & Miller, M. (2008). Development of the literacy achievement gap: A longitudinal study of kindergarten through third grade. *Language, Speech, and Hearing Services in Schools, 38,* 173–181.

LECTURE ENHANCEMENT 7.4
Cross-Cultural and Gender Differences in Exceptional Mathematical Talent (pp. 310–313)

Time: 10–15 minutes

Objective: To examine cross-cultural and gender differences in exceptional mathematical talent.

The male advantage in mathematical ability is evident in virtually every country where males and females have equal access to secondary education, though the difference is declining. Heredity contributes to the gender gap in math, but social pressures are also influential. To examine cross-cultural trends in mathematical achievement among high school students, Andreescu and colleagues (2008) analyzed two decades of data from the International Mathematical Olympiad (IMO) and USA Mathematical Olympiad (USAMO). The IMO and USAMO are competitions that require individuals to write rigorous proofs for extremely difficult math problems. Although the USAMO consists only of North American students, the IMO includes students from 95 countries around the world. Top scorers in these competitions have truly exceptional skills in mathematical problem solving, at the one-in-a-million level. Data on the IMO indicates that 12 countries have ranked among the top 15 in the world in at least 10 of the past 14 years. All of the countries, with the exception of the United States, are located in Asia or Eastern Europe. However, between 1995 to 2008, half of the U.S. students were immigrants or children of immigrants from Asia or Eastern Europe. In addition, the number of girls sent to the IMO competition varies widely from country to country. Bulgaria, for instance, has sent teams with girls since 1959, whereas the U.S. did not have teams with girls until 1998. These findings illustrate how some countries identify and nurture both boys' and girls' mathematical talent, while countries like the U.S. identify exceptional girls far less often.

Results from the USAMO also show that girls are underrepresented in the math competition. Between 2005 and 2007, only one girl made the list of top-12 teams, and that girl made the list three years in a row. As with the IMO findings, half of the top scorers were immigrants or children of immigrants from Asia or Eastern Europe. In the USAMO, Caucasian students—both boys and girls—tend to be underrepresented in the competition. The authors point out that compared to many Asian and Eastern European countries, North American high schools rarely teach the advanced mathematical skills (for example, writing rigorous proofs) required for the IMO and USAMO. Therefore, native-born American students of both genders tend to be underrepresented in these competitions. The makeup of IMO and USAMO teams indicate that top-scoring students tend to come from Asian or Eastern European countries—countries committed to identifying and nurturing mathematical talent. When girls do participate in the competitions, they often serve on the 15 top-scoring teams. Thus, if genetic factors were primarily responsible for exceptional mathematical talent, we would not expect to see females performing at such a high level. According to Andreescu and colleagues, the "myth that females cannot excel in mathematics must be put to rest. Teachers, guidance counselors, parents...and, most importantly, girls themselves need to be informed about the fact that females *can* excel in mathematics, even at the very highest level."

Andreescu, T., Gallian, J. A., Kane, J. M., & Mertz, J. E. (2008). Cross-cultural analysis of students with exceptional talent in mathematical problem solving. *Notices of the American Mathematical Society, 55,* 1248–1260.

LEARNING ACTIVITIES

LEARNING ACTIVITY 7.1
Matching: A General Model of Information Processing (pp. 278–282)

Present the following exercise to students as an in-class assignment or quiz.

Directions: Match each of the following terms with its correct description.

Terms:
_____ 1. Sensory register
_____ 2. Short-term memory store
_____ 3. Working memory
_____ 4. Central executive
_____ 5. Automatic processes
_____ 6. Long-term memory
_____ 7. Executive function

Descriptions:
- A. The number of items that can be briefly held in mind while also engaging in some effort to monitor or manipulate those items.
- B. These are so well-learned that they require no space in working memory and, therefore, permit us to focus on other information while simultaneously performing them.
- C. The part of the mind where we retain attended-to information briefly so we can actively "work" on it to reach our goals.
- D. Here, a broad panorama of sights and sounds are represented directly but stored only momentarily.
- E. This structure directs the flow of information, engaging in more sophisticated activities that enable complex, flexible thinking.
- F. The set of cognitive operations and strategies necessary for self-initiated, purposeful behavior in relatively novel, unchanging situations.
- G. This represents a permanent knowledge base, which is unlimited.

Answers:

1. D   5. B
2. C   6. G
3. A   7. F
4. E

LEARNING ACTIVITY 7.2
Memory Strategies (pp. 292–293)

The website *www.mindtools.com/memory.html* contains a number of articles on various memory strategies and their applications. Have students select a memory strategy that they think would be useful for a school-age child. What cognitive advances enable a school-age child to benefit from this memory strategy? Explain. Next, have students review the article "*Memory Improvement Techniques,*" which lists eight ways to make memory strategies memorable. Briefly define these strategies, and give examples of how teachers can adapt them for classroom instruction. Students may want to use a particular subject area, such as reading or math, to demonstrate their points.

LEARNING ACTIVITY 7.3
Demonstration of Organization Strategies (pp. 292–293)

This activity can be presented in class to demonstrate strategies for storing and retrieving information. Tell students to write their answers on a sheet of paper, which will be used for discussion following the activity.

Instructions: Read aloud the following set of 12 words. Begin at the top of the left-hand column and read to the bottom of the column. Then read the second column, proceeding from top to bottom. Reread the words a second time. Then cover the words, and write them in any order:

cake	clock
book	fish
shoe	tree
car	chair
ball	bike
dish	egg

Now do the same thing for the following list:

dog	orange
cat	peach
pig	shirt
cow	pants
grape	shoe
pear	socks

In this activity, most people remember more words from the second list than from the first. Typically, this is because people divide the words in the second list into three categories—animals, fruits, and clothes—and use these categories to facilitate remembering. In contrast, the words on the first list cannot be grouped easily into categories. It is important to note that even though students are experienced with organizational strategies, younger children often organize inconsistently. Skillful use of organization requires extensive experience with strategies.

LEARNING ACTIVITY 7.4
Comparing Recognition and Recall Memory in Young Children (pp. 294–295)

Invite several 3- to 5-year-old children and their parents to your classroom for a demonstration of recognition and recall memory in early childhood. If this is not an option, ask students to locate a 3- to 5-year-old child whom they can observe outside of class. Prior to the demonstration, instruct students to gather an assortment of ten items (pictures or toys), which will be used for a memory game. Arrange the items on a table where the child can clearly see them. After the child has had a chance to take a good look (approximately 30 seconds), remove the items and mix them with six unfamiliar items (pictures or toys that were not included in the original set). After all 16 items are returned to the table, ask the child to point to those that he or she has seen before. Next, remove all of the items, and ask the child to name as many as he or she can remember. Once students have completed the activity, ask them to discuss their findings. Did most children demonstrate better recognition than recall? Did students notice children using any memory strategies during the task?

LEARNING ACTIVITY 7.5
Observing Adult–Child Conversations About the Past: Building an Autobiographical Memory (pp. 298–300)

According to the text, by conversing with adults, young children learn to structure personally significant events into an autobiographical memory. Have students ask the parent of a young child (3- to 5-year-old) to discuss with the child a recent, significant event, such as a summer vacation, a birthday party, or a trip to the dentist or doctor. Another option is to have students observe a preschool teacher discussing with one or more children an important classroom experience, such as a class visitor, a field trip, or a holiday celebration. Students should describe which style of communication the adult uses to elicit autobiographical narratives (that is, elaborate or repetitive). Why is the elaborative style more effective in eliciting autobiographical memories?

LEARNING ACTIVITY 7.6
Children's Eyewitness Memory (pp. 300, 302)

Present students with the following scenario:

> A good friend of yours recently experienced a robbery at her home. Her 5-year-old daughter, Skye, was sleeping on the couch at the time and woke up as the robbers were exiting the house. A lamp was on in an adjoining room and Skye saw one of the robber's faces. When the police arrived, Skye was able to give a description of the robber and "thought" he was a teenager in her neighborhood. The police arrested the teenager, and the case is headed to court. Your friend is unsure if Skye's testimony will be accurate, given her young age and the fact that the room Skye was in was not well-lit. Using research in the text as a guide, how would you advise your friend? If your friend decides to allow Skye to testify, what should she do to prepare Skye for the experience? What should she avoid, and why?

LEARNING ACTIVITY 7.7
True or False: Applications of Information Processing to Academic Learning (pp. 307–314)

Present the following activity as an in-class assignment or quiz.

Directions: Read each of the following statements and determine if it is *True* (T) or *False* (F).

Statements:
_____ 1. By age 3, children fully understand the symbolic function of the elements of print.
_____ 2. Phonological awareness is a relatively weak predictor of emergent literacy knowledge.
_____ 3. One reason children from low-income families lag behind their economically advantaged peers in reading achievement is that they have fewer home and preschool literacy learning opportunities.
_____ 4. Many studies show that children learn to read best with a mixture of whole-language and phonics instruction.
_____ 5. Children as young as 14 months display a beginning grasp of ordinality.
_____ 6. Most researchers agree that drill and repetition of math facts is the best approach for teaching school-age children.
_____ 7. Compared with North America, math lessons in Asian classrooms devote less time to exploring math concepts and strategies and more to drill and repetition.
_____ 8. When reasoning scientifically, children are especially likely to overlook evidence that does not match their prior beliefs when a causal variable is implausible and when task demands are high.
_____ 9. The ability to think about theories, deliberately isolate variables, and actively seek disconfirming evidence is well-developed by middle childhood.
_____ 10. Like Piaget, information-processing theorists believe that scientific thinking results from abrupt, stagewise change.

Answers:

1. F   6. F
2. F   7. F
3. T   8. T
4. T   9. F
5. T   10. F

LEARNING ACTIVITY 7.8
Supporting Advances in Information Processing

Throughout Chapter 7, there are numerous examples of how adults contribute to advances in children's information processing. In small groups, have students select one aspect of information processing, such as attention or memory, and list ways in which adults can support development in this area. Students should also consider developmental differences. For example, adolescents will need different types of adult support than school-age children. Once students have completed the activity, ask them to share some examples with the class.

ASK YOURSELF . . .

REVIEW: Summarize evidence indicating that speed of information processing increases with age, contributing to gains in working-memory capacity. In Case's neo-Piagetian theory, how do gains in processing efficiency contribute to development? (pp. 281, 282–283)

Developmental increases in working-memory capacity in part reflect gains in processing speed. Efficient processing releases working-memory resources to support storage of information. The faster children can repeat to-be-learned information either aloud or silently to themselves, the larger their memory spans. Research confirms that with age, children process information more efficiently. Robert Kail gave 7- to 22-year-olds a variety of cognitive tasks in which they had to respond as quickly as possible. For example, in a name-retrieval task, they had to judge whether parts of pictures were physically identical or had the same name (for example, two umbrellas, one opened and one closed). In a mental addition task, they were given addition problems and answers, and they had to indicate whether the solutions were correct. And in a visual search task, they were shown a single digit and asked to signal if it was among a set of digits that appeared on a screen. On all tasks, processing time decreased with age. More important, the rate of change—a fairly rapid decline in processing time, trailing off around age 12—was similar across many activities. These changes in processing speed have been found in Canada, Korea, and the United States; similarity across diverse tasks in several cultures implies a fundamental change in efficiency of the information-processing system. Increased processing speed enables older children and adults to scan information more rapidly and also transform it more rapidly. As a result, they can hold more information in working memory at once.

Case's neo-Piagetian theory accepts Piaget's stages but attributes change within each stage, and movement from one stage to the next, to increases in the efficiency with which children use their limited working-memory capacity. As children become more efficient processors, the amount of information they can hold and combine in working memory expands, making movement to a higher stage possible. Within each stage, as the child's schemes become automatic, working-memory resources are freed for combining existing schemes and generating new ones. In this view of Piaget's concepts of assimilation and accommodation, *practicing schemes* (assimilation) leads to *automatization,* which *releases working memory* for other activities, permitting *scheme combination and construction* (accommodation). Once the schemes of a Piagetian stage become automatic and brain development further increases processing speed, enough space in working memory is available to consolidate schemes into an improved representational form. As a result, children generate new *central conceptual structures,* which permit them to move to the next stage of development.

CONNECT: Recall the dynamic systems perspective, which assumes that periods of instability precede a reorganized, more effectively functioning, stable system (see pages 30–31 in Chapter 1 and pages 148–149 in Chapter 4). How are findings on children's strategy development consistent with this idea? (pp. 284–286)

Siegler found that children's strategy use for a variety of problems follows an *overlapping-waves pattern*. Performance tends to progress from a single incorrect approach, to a highly variable state in which they try different strategies, to use of a more advanced procedure. Children's use of many different strategies is an example of a period of instability, characteristic of the dynamic systems perspective, in which changes in some aspects of the system—the child's cognitive capacities and the problems with which they are presented—lead children to actively reorganize their behavior, eventually reintegrating the components of the dynamic system in a more complex, effective way as they realize that certain problem-solving strategies are consistently effective.

APPLY: Five-year-old Kayla used several strategies to solve conservation-of-number problems involving rows of pennies. On one, she said, "The rows aren't the same." On the next, she said, "The rows have the same number because you didn't add any." On the third, she said, "I counted the pennies. The rows have the same number." Did she move from a more to a less mature strategy? Explain. Why is it beneficial for Kayla to experiment with strategies? (pp. 284–286)

To study children's strategy use, Robert Siegler used the microgenetic research design, presenting children with problems over an extended time period. He found that children experiment with diverse strategies on many types of problems, including conservation of number. As they try strategies, children observe which work best, which work less well, and which are ineffective. Gradually they select strategies on the basis of two adaptive criteria: *accuracy* and *speed*. As children home in on effective strategies, they learn more about the problems at hand. As a result, correct solutions become more strongly associated with problems, and children display the most efficient strategy—automatic retrieval of the answer.

Strategy variability is vital for devising new, more adaptive ways of thinking, which "evolve" through extensive experience solving problems. By experimenting with various strategies, Kayla is developing essential problem-solving skills. Over time, she will likely select the third strategy, counting, which will gradually become automatic, yielding a correct answer very quickly.

REFLECT: Think of a challenging task that you recently completed successfully. Describe executive skills you implemented, explaining how each contributed to your success. (pp. 281–282)
This is an open-ended question with no right or wrong answer.

REVIEW: How does inhibition support development of attention and other information-processing skills? (p. 288)
The ability to inhibit thoughts and behaviors improves from infancy on. Between ages 3 and 4, for example, preschoolers perform considerably better in situations in which they must follow some commands but not others, as in the game "Simon Says." On more complex tasks requiring children to inhibit distracting stimuli, marked gains occur from early to middle childhood. These gains are linked to a steady age-related increase in activation of the prefrontal cortex while children engage in these inhibitory tasks. By clearing unnecessary stimuli, inhibition increases available space in working memory, which, in turn, opens the door to higher-level strategy use—working more effectively with information held in mind.

CONNECT: What other components of executive function likely contribute to improved planning in middle childhood? What can adults do to scaffold children's planning skills? (pp. 290–291)
During middle childhood, children become better at planning, which involves reasoning about a sequence of acts ahead of time and allocating attention accordingly in order to reach a goal. The development of planning illustrates how attention becomes coordinated with other cognitive processes. To solve problems involving multiple steps, children must postpone action in favor of weighing alternatives, organizing task materials, and remembering the steps of their plan so they can attend to each one in sequence. Along the way, they must monitor how well the plan works and revise it if necessary. Planning clearly places heavy demands on working memory.
  Children learn much from cultural tools that support planning—directions for playing games, patterns for construction, recipes for cooking—especially when they collaborate with more expert planners, such as parents and teachers. While collaborating on projects, parents can provide basic information about the usefulness of plans and how to implement specific steps. Parents can also foster planning by encouraging it in everyday activities. In school, the demands of academic tasks—and teachers' explanations for how to plan—contribute to gains in planning. Having many opportunities to practice planning helps children understand its components and use that knowledge to guide future activities.

APPLY: At age 7, Jonah played his piano pieces from beginning to end instead of spending extra time on the hard sections. Around age 8, he devoted more time to sections he knew least well, but his performance did not improve for several months. What explains Jonah's gradual gains in strategy use and performance? (pp. 288–289)
The development of a selective attentional strategy follows a predictable four-phase sequence. During the first phase, *production deficiency,* preschoolers fail to *produce* attentional strategies in situations where they could be helpful. At phase 2, *control deficiency,* young elementary school children sometimes produce strategies, but not consistently. They fail to *control*, or execute, strategies effectively. Jonah, at age 7, is unaware that he should spend more time practicing the hard sections to improve his piano playing. During phase 3, *utilization deficiency,* slightly older children execute strategies consistently, but their performance either does not improve or improves less than that of older children, as is the case with Jonah at age 8. Once he starts using the strategy consistently, Jonah enters phase 4, *effective strategy use,* and his performance improves.

REFLECT: Describe an instance in which you applied a strategy for the first time but experienced a utilization deficiency. Why do you think the deficiency occurred, and how did you overcome it? (p. 289)
This is an open-ended question with no right or wrong answer.

REVIEW: According to fuzzy-trace theory, why do we encode information in gist form? Describe the development of gist and verbatim representations, and explain how gist contributes to improved reasoning and more detailed recall—but also to certain memory errors—with age. (p. 296)
According to fuzzy-trace theory, when we first encode information, we reconstruct it automatically, creating a vague, fuzzy version called a *gist,* which preserves essential meaning without details and is especially useful for reasoning. Although we can also retain a literal, verbatim version, we have a bias toward gist because it requires less space in working memory, freeing attention for the steps involved in thinking.

Fuzzy-trace theorists take issue with the assumption that all reconstructions are transformations of verbatim memory. Instead, they believe that both verbatim and gist memories are present but are stored separately to be used for different purposes. With age, children rely less on verbatim memory and more on fuzzy, reconstructed gists. For example, in one study, preschoolers were better at answering verbatim- than gist-dependent questions, whereas the reverse was true for second graders.

Fuzzy-trace research reveals that although memory is vital for reasoning, getting bogged down in details can interfere with effective problem solving. And because fuzzy traces are less likely than verbatim memories to be forgotten, gists can serve as enduring retrieval cues, contributing to improved recall of details with age. In such recall, however, gists heighten the chances of reporting false items that are consistent with the fuzzy meaning of an experience. In this way, fuzzy-trace theory helps explain why some memory inaccuracies decrease with age, while others increase.

CONNECT: Using what you know about development of autobiographical memory, explain why preschoolers' eyewitness testimony usually is less accurate than that of older children. What situational factors make children's reporting more inaccurate? (pp. 297, 300, 302)

Autobiographical memory is a type of *episodic memory*—recollections of personally experienced events that occurred at a specific time and place. The accuracy and completeness of children's episodic memories are central to their ability to recount relevant experiences when testifying in court cases. Because preschoolers are more prone to memory errors than school-age children, their eyewitness testimony is usually less accurate than that of older children. Several factors are involved.

First, responding to interview questions is challenging for children whose language competence is not well-developed. Preschoolers often are unaware when they do not understand, and they answer the question anyway. Preschoolers are especially poor at identifying where they got their knowledge, often confusing what they heard or saw on TV with what actually happened. Children younger than age 8 to 10 have difficulty reporting certain temporal information—for example, saying how often and on which dates an event occurred. And because younger children are less skilled at *inhibition*—ignoring irrelevant information—they are more willing to accept adult suggestions that are inconsistent with experienced events.

When an adult asks a yes-or-no question, preschoolers are more likely than older children to agree, perhaps out of a desire to please. In addition, preschoolers' bias toward verbatim representations (encoding specifics) leads them to forget more easily than older children, whose gist memories persist over time and serve as retrieval cues for details. Finally, because younger children are less competent at using narratives to report their autobiographical memories systematically and completely, they may omit information that they actually remember.

As the specifics of what actually occurred fade, young children may substitute a script reflecting what typically happens, reporting features that are consistent with the original situation but were not actually part of it. A number of situational factors also make children's reporting more inaccurate. Court testimony often involves repeated questioning, which, by itself, negatively affects children's response consistency and accuracy. A high-pressure interview, in which an adult says, for example, that a child's friends have already said "yes" in response to leading questions, or praises the child for agreeing, can influence young children's answers. Children who have constructed a false memory often continue to give false reports when later questioned by an impartial interviewer. When biased interviewing is combined with stereotyping of the accused, children can easily be misled into giving false information.

APPLY: When asked what happens at kindergarten, 5-year-old Ali replies, "First, you have center time and circle time. Sometimes you listen to a story. Next you eat your snack and go outdoors." But Ali can't remember what she did during center time two days ago. Explain Ali's memory performance. Why is this type of memory useful? (p. 298)

Like adults, preschoolers remember familiar events—what you do when you go to child care or get ready for bed—in terms of *scripts,* general representations of what occurs and when it occurs in a particular situation. Scripts are a special form of reconstructive memory. When we experience repeated events, we fuse them into the same script representation, and any specific instance of a scripted experience becomes hard to recall. Ali has constructed a script for what happens at kindergarten. Because nothing out of the ordinary occurred two days ago, she cannot recall exactly what happened. This type of reconstructive memory is helpful in organizing and interpreting everyday experiences, while preventing long-term memory from being cluttered with unimportant information.

REFLECT: Describe your earliest autobiographical memory. How old were you when the event occurred? Do your responses fit with research on infantile amnesia? (pp. 298–300, 301)

This is an open-ended question with no right or wrong answer.

REVIEW: What evidence indicates that preschoolers view the mind as a passive container of information, whereas school-age children view it as an active, constructive agent? (pp. 303–304)

Unlike preschoolers, who view the mind as a passive container of information, older children regard it as an active, constructive agent that selects and transforms information. Six- and 7-year-olds realize, for example, that doing well on a task depends on paying attention—concentrating and exerting effort. By age 10, children distinguish mental activities on the basis of *certainty of knowledge*. They are aware that if you "remember," "know," or "understand," you are more certain than if you "guess," "estimate," or "compare." They also grasp the interrelatedness of cognitive processes—for example, that remembering is crucial for understanding, which, in turn, strengthens memory.

Consistent with their more active view of the mind, school-age children are far more conscious of mental strategies than preschoolers. When shown video clips depicting two children using different recall strategies and asked which one is likely to produce better memory, kindergarten and young elementary school children knew that rehearsing or categorizing is better than looking or naming. Older children recognize more subtle differences—that organizing is better than rehearsing. And between third and fifth grade, children develop a much better understanding of how and why strategies work, so that they become better able to discriminate good from bad reasoning, regardless of whether the outcome is correct.

CONNECT: How does research on adolescent brain development contribute to our understanding of the gradual development of cognitive self-regulation and the special self-regulatory challenges of the teenage years (see pages 190–191 in Chapter 5)? (pp. 304–305)

As the prefrontal cortex becomes more efficient at overseeing and managing the integrated functioning of various areas of the cerebral cortex, adolescents gradually gain in diverse cognitive skills, including speed of thinking, attention, memory, planning, capacity to integrate information, and regulation of cognition and emotion. But because the prefrontal cognitive-control network still requires fine-tuning, teenagers' performance on tasks requiring self-restraint, planning, and future orientation is not yet fully mature.

School-age children and adolescents often have difficulty putting what they know about thinking into action because they are not yet proficient at cognitive self-regulation, the process of continually monitoring and controlling progress toward a goal—planning, checking outcomes, and redirecting unsuccessful efforts. Cognitive self-regulation develops gradually because monitoring and controlling task outcomes is highly demanding, requiring constant evaluation of effort and progress. In addition, because of changes in the brain's emotional/social network, adolescents react more strongly to stressful events and experience pleasurable stimuli more intensely. Because the cognitive-control network is not yet functioning optimally, teenagers find it hard to manage these powerful influences.

APPLY: Although 9-year-old Melody knows she should look over her homework, she nevertheless often turns in assignments with careless mistakes. What might account for the gap between what Melody knows and what she does? (pp. 304–305)

School-age children, like Melody, are not yet good at cognitive self-regulation, the process of continually monitoring progress toward a goal—planning, checking outcomes, and redirecting unsuccessful efforts. For example, although most third to sixth graders know that they should group items when memorizing, reread a complicated paragraph to make sure they understand it, and relate new information to what they already know, they do not always do so. Cognitive self-regulation develops gradually because monitoring learning outcomes is cognitively demanding, requiring constant evaluation of effort and progress. Parents and teachers promote children's self-regulation when they patiently point out important features of a task, suggest strategies, and explain why the strategies are effective—telling children not just what to do but why to do it, which provides them with a rationale for future action. When children apply a strategy consistently, their knowledge of strategies strengthens, resulting in a bidirectional relationship between metacognition and strategic processing that enhances self-regulation.

REFLECT: Suppose you had the opportunity to help a second grader with the following assignment: Write a five-sentence paragraph comparing and contrasting fruits and vegetables. What would you do to promote cognitive self-regulation? (pp. 304–305)

This is an open-ended question with no right or wrong answer.

REVIEW: Why are gains in metacognition important for the development of scientific reasoning? How can teachers promote the development of scientific reasoning? (pp. 313–314)

In her research into the development of scientific reasoning, Deanna Kuhn found that the capacity to reason like a scientist improves with age. The ability to distinguish theory from evidence and use logical rules to examine their relationship—rather than seeing both theory and evidence as a single representation of "the way things are"—improves from childhood through adolescence, continuing into adulthood. Among other factors, researchers believe that sophisticated *metacognitive understanding* is vital for scientific reasoning. Microgenetic research shows that when children regularly pit theory against evidence over many weeks, they experiment with various strategies, reflect on and revise them, and become aware of the nature of logic. Then they apply their abstract appreciation of logic to a wide variety of situations. The ability to *think about* theories, *deliberately isolate* variables, and *actively seek* disconfirming evidence is rarely present before adolescence; even among adolescents and adults, wide variation in scientific reasoning skills exists. To promote development of scientific reasoning, teachers should give students numerous opportunities to experiment with scientific tasks, exposing them to increasingly complex problems and instruction that highlights features of scientific reasoning—for example, pointing out inconsistencies between a scientist's expectations in a particular situation and everyday beliefs.

APPLY: Review Heidi's reasoning about the impact of several variables on the bounce of tennis balls on page 313. What features of her thinking suggest that she is beginning to reason scientifically? (pp. 313–314)

The heart of scientific reasoning is coordinating theories with evidence. By hypothesizing about what factors might affect the bounce of tennis balls, Heidi is experimenting with evidence that might support or refute her theory that certain characteristics of the tennis balls influence the outcome of her serves. Her thinking indicates that Heidi is beginning to reason like a scientist, viewing evidence as separate from and bearing on a theory.

CONNECT: Using mechanisms of cognitive development discussed in this chapter, explain why teaching both basic skills and understanding of concepts and strategies is vital for children's progress in reading and mathematics. (pp. 310–312)

Most experts believe that children learn best when they receive a balanced mixture of basic skills and conceptual understanding. When teachers combine real reading and writing with teaching of phonics and engage in other excellent teaching practices—encouraging children to tackle reading challenges and integrating reading into all school subjects—first graders show far greater literacy progress than do their agemates in classrooms without this blend of teaching approaches. Learning relations between letters and sounds enables children to decode words they have never seen before, freeing working memory for higher-level activities involved in comprehending the text's meaning. But an emphasis on basic skills alone may cause children to lose sight of the goal of reading: understanding. The most beneficial instruction also aims to increase children's use of effective strategies for reading comprehension, preparing them to make the shift from "learning to read" to "reading to learn," which occurs around age 7 to 8.

Similarly, mathematics instruction in elementary school both builds on and greatly enriches children's informal knowledge of number concepts and counting. For instance, teaching basic skills, such as written notation systems and formal computational techniques, provides the foundation for later mastery of more complex tasks. And understanding of basic arithmetic computation makes possible *estimation*—the ability to generate approximate answers, which can be used to evaluate the accuracy of exact answers. Again, the most effective approach blends drill in computing with "number sense," or understanding, so that students understand why certain strategies work well. Once these skills are well-learned, working memory is freed up, allowing children to focus on more advanced concepts and strategies.

REFLECT: Describe early, informal experiences important for literacy and math development that you experienced while growing up. How do you think those experiences contributed to your academic progress after you started school? (pp. 307–309, 310–311)

This is an open-ended question with no right or wrong answer.

SUGGESTED READINGS

DuPaul, G. J., & Kern, L. (2011). *Young children with ADHD: Early identification and intervention*. Washington, DC: American Psychological Association. Written by leading experts in the field, this book examines assessment and identification of ADHD in school-age children, as well as treatment options, academic interventions, strategies for preventing injuries in hyperactive children, and the importance of family support.

Henry, L. (2011). *The development of working memory in children*. Thousand Oaks, CA: Sage. Explores the development of working memory in both typically developing children and in those with learning difficulties. The author also examines how working memory contributes to children's learning and academic achievement.

McGee, L. M., & Richgels, D. J. (2011). *Literacy's beginnings: Supporting young readers and writers*. Boston: Allyn and Bacon. An excellent resource for anyone interested in education, child development, or related professions, this book presents developmentally appropriate strategies for teaching reading and writing.

MEDIA MATERIALS

For details on individual video segments that accompany the DVD for *Child Development,* Ninth Edition, please see the DVD Guide for *Explorations in Child Development*. The DVD and DVD Guide are available through your Pearson sales representative.

Additional DVDs that may be useful in your class are listed below. These are not available through your Pearson sales representative, but you can order them directly from the distributors. (See contact information at the end of this manual.)

Attention Deficit Disorder (2004, Insight Media, 20 min.). Featuring counselor Barbara Berg, who was diagnosed with ADHD at the age of 42, this program offers insights into the effects of ADHD on children and teachers. It covers such common symptoms as hypersensitivity to sound, touch, and smell; withdrawal; and a variety of less obvious behaviors. The program also presents strategies for designing manageable routines for children.

How Does Your Memory Work? (2008, Insight Media, 50 min.). This program explores the mechanisms of human recollection and presents case studies and medical findings that reveal the complexity of the brain's systems that enable memory. It features neuroscientists Randy Buckner and Faraneh Vargha-Khadem and the psychologist Alain Brunet.

Living with ADHD (2004, Films Media Group/BBCW Production, 50 min.). This program describes new medical strategies designed for parents who are raising children with ADHD. It also focuses on the challenges of parents who, in addition to their children, are diagnosed with the disorder. While presenting concerns that Ritalin and other drugs have led to overmedication, the program suggests that clinical advances are enabling children to learn constructive behavior, build relationships, and lay the foundations of a rewarding life.

Loftus Speaks: The Malleability of Memory (2009, Films Media Group, 81 min.) In this program, Elizabeth Loftus—a highly regarded expert on memory—lectures on her research on the malleability of memory. Topics include memory paradigms; memory distortion; growing evidence of criminal convictions based on false memories; repressed memory accusations and implanted memories; induced memory and misinformation studies; and how psychotherapy techniques such as guided imagination, dream interpretation, and hypnosis can lead to false memories.

Lost for Words: Literacy in America (2006, Insight Media, 20 min.). Explaining that 10 million students in the United States will never meet their age-specific reading levels, this program examines the ways in which a child's struggle with literacy affects his or her life. It also looks at innovative methods that parents and schools are using to help children improve their reading skills.

Memory: Brain and Body (2008, Films Media Group, 22 min.). Is there such a thing as a perfect recollection or photographic memory? This program examines that question and others related to the brain's ability to store knowledge. Using a wide range of examples, the program demonstrates that even the sharpest mental recording is subjective, selective, incomplete, and even faulty. It also shows how the performance of elite athletes may be tied to muscle memory, which facilitates previously learned actions and circumvents conscious thought. Neuroscientist Dr. Lawrence Farwell discusses a technique he invented, called brain fingerprinting, that measures the brain's electrical signals when it references previously stored information.

Middle Childhood: Cognitive and Language Development (2007, Insight Media, 24 min.). This program reviews Piaget's theory of concrete operational development and the information-processing perspective. It describes characteristics of language usage in school-age children and examines the role of schools in cognitive development.

The Drugging of Our Children: Inside the ADHD Controversy (2005, Films Media Group, 104 min.). This program challenges the reliance on psychotropic drugs to treat attention-deficit hyperactivity disorder. The program, which includes interviews with psychiatrists, neurologists, and education experts, as well as with parents and children, raises questions about how ADHD is diagnosed. It also analyzes the relationship between school procedures, the medical establishment, and the pharmaceutical industry.

The Mind's Storehouse: Memory (2006, Insight Media, 30 min.) Asking the question of whether memory is reliable, this program includes interviews with memory researchers that cover such topics as encoding, storage, and retrieval of memory. It also provides demonstrations of short-term memory. The program features Elizabeth Loftus, who discusses her extensive research on the creation of false memories.

Toddlers: Cognitive Development (2009, School Media Associates/Learning Seed, 26 min.). This program explores theories of cognitive development and discusses the toddler's daily acquisition of knowledge and development of language. It shows children working on, and learning from, cause-and-effect experiments. Viewers can observe toddlers as they engage in activities that foster memory development and the retrieval of information.

CHAPTER 8
INTELLIGENCE

CHAPTER-AT-A-GLANCE

Chapter Outline	Instruction Ideas	Supplements
Definitions of Intelligence pp. 320–322 Alfred Binet: A Holistic View • The Factor Analysts: A Multifaceted View	Learning Objective 8.1	Test Bank Items 1–19, 125–126 Please contact your Pearson publisher's representative for a wide range of video offerings available to adopters.
Recent Advances in Defining Intelligence pp. 323–326, 327 Combining Psychometric and Information-Processing Approaches • Sternberg's Triarchic Theory • Gardner's Theory of Multiple Intelligences	Learning Objective 8.2 Lecture Enhancement 8.1 Learning Activities 8.1, 8.4 Ask Yourself p. 326	Test Bank Items 20–34, 127
Measuring Intelligence pp. 326–330 Some Commonly Used Intelligence Tests • Aptitude and Achievement Tests • Tests for Infants • Computation and Distribution of IQ Scores	Learning Objectives 8.3–8.4 Learning Activities 8.2–8.3 Ask Yourself p. 330	Test Bank Items 35–51
What Do Intelligence Tests Predict, and How Well? pp. 330–333 Stability of IQ Scores • IQ as a Predictor of Academic Achievement • IQ as a Predictor of Occupational Attainment • IQ as a Predictor of Psychological Adjustment	Learning Objective 8.5 Learning Activity 8.4 Ask Yourself p. 333	Test Bank Items 52–66, 128
Ethnic and Socioeconomic Variations in IQ pp. 334–335	Learning Objective 8.6 Learning Activity 8.5	Test Bank Items 67–71
Explaining Individual and Group Differences in IQ pp. 335–346 Genetic Influences • Adoption Studies: Joint Influence of Heredity and Environment • Race and Ethnicity: Genetic or Cultural Groupings? • Cultural Bias in Testing • Reducing Cultural Bias in Testing • Home Environment and Mental Development	Learning Objectives 8.7–8.9 Lecture Enhancements 8.2–8.3 Learning Activities 8.5–8.7 Ask Yourself p. 346	Test Bank Items 72–110, 129
Early Intervention and Intellectual Development pp. 347–350, 351 Benefits of Early Intervention • Strengthening Early Intervention	Learning Objective 8.10 Lecture Enhancement 8.4	Test Bank Items 111–116
Giftedness: Creativity and Talent pp. 350, 352–355 The Psychometric View • A Multifaceted View	Learning Objective 8.11 Learning Activity 8.8 Ask Yourself p. 355	Test Bank Items 117–124, 130

BRIEF CHAPTER SUMMARY

The psychometric approach to cognitive development is the basis for the various intelligence tests available for assessing children's mental abilities. This approach focuses on outcomes and results. Psychometric researchers seek to determine the factors, or dimensions, that make up intelligence and how these change with age. They are interested in discovering how intelligence can be measured so that scores will be useful for predicting future academic achievement, career attainment, and other aspects of intellectual success. Finally, they are interested in individual differences in intelligence.

Today, most people think of intelligence as a complex combination of attributes, including verbal ability, practical problem solving, and social competence, though experts lack consensus on its ingredients. And whereas some people view the various abilities that make up intelligence as closely interconnected, others expect them to be relatively distinct—to correlate weakly.

The first intelligence tests were developed to measure general ability as a way of predicting school performance. To investigate whether intelligence is a single trait or an assortment of abilities, researchers used a complicated correlational procedure called factor analysis to identify the underlying mental abilities that contribute to successful intelligence test performance.

To overcome the limitations of factor analysis, some researchers, combining psychometric and information-processing approaches, conduct componential analyses of children's test scores to find relationships between components of information processing and children's intelligence test performance. Sternberg's triarchic theory of successful intelligence extends these efforts, identifying three broad, interacting intelligences: analytical, creative, and practical. Gardner's theory of multiple intelligences proposes at least eight independent intelligences, each defined by a distinct set of processing operations.

Standardized intelligence tests use the scores of a large, representative sample of individuals as a standard for interpreting individual scores. Although they sample only a narrow range of cognitive capacities, these tests have some value in predicting future academic, vocational, and life success. Group-administered tests are useful for instructional planning; individually administered tests are especially valuable in identifying highly intelligent children as well as those with learning problems. Related types of tests include aptitude tests, which assess an individual's potential to learn a specialized activity, and achievement tests, which assess actual knowledge and skill. Measures of infants' intelligence typically measure perceptual and motor responses, but infant tests predict later intelligence poorly. The stability of IQ scores depends on the age of the child at the time of first testing and the elapsed time between two testings.

The relationship of socioeconomic status to intellectual development has sparked a debate over the roles of nature versus nurture in determining IQ. Heritability estimates support a moderate role for heredity in accounting for individual differences in IQ but cannot be used to explain ethnic or socioeconomic variations in test scores. Environmental factors, such as communication styles, lack of familiarity with test content, reactions to testing conditions, and fear of being judged on the basis of negative stereotypes, can lead test scores to underestimate minority children's intelligence. Dynamic assessment, measuring what the child can achieve with social support, can reduce this cultural bias. Both shared and nonshared environmental influences also contribute to individual differences in intelligence, as do family beliefs about intellectual success and expectations for children's educational attainment.

Research on preschool early intervention programs indicates that gains in IQ and achievement test scores vanish with time. However, when high-quality intervention starts in infancy and extends through early childhood, children display cognitive and academic achievement advantages throughout childhood and adolescence.

Recognition that intelligence tests do not sample the entire range of human mental skills has led to an expanded conception of giftedness, which includes creativity: the ability to produce work that is both original and appropriate. High creativity is usually manifested as talent in one field or a few related fields. A multifaceted view of creativity holds that it depends on personality and motivation, as well as cognitive resources.

LEARNING OBJECTIVES

After reading this chapter, you should be able to answer the following:

8.1 Describe changing definitions of intelligence on which mental tests are based. (pp. 320–322)

8.2 How do contemporary researchers use and expand componential analyses of intelligence test scores to define intelligence? (pp. 323–326, 327)

8.3 Describe commonly used intelligence tests for children, distinguish between aptitude and achievement tests, and discuss the usefulness of infant tests. (pp. 326–329)

8.4 How are IQ scores computed and distributed in large, representative samples? (p. 330)

8.5 Discuss the stability of IQ and its prediction of academic achievement, occupational attainment, and psychological adjustment. (pp. 330–333)

8.6 Describe ethnic and socioeconomic variations in IQ. (pp. 334–335)

8.7 Discuss the contributions of heredity and environment to individual and group differences in IQ. (pp. 335–339)

8.8 Evaluate evidence on whether ethnic differences in IQ result from test bias, and discuss efforts to reduce cultural bias in testing. (pp. 339–343)

8.9 Summarize the impact of shared and nonshared environmental influences on IQ. (pp. 344–346)

8.10 Discuss the impact of early intervention on intellectual development. (pp. 347–350, 351)

8.11 Evaluate theories of creativity, and discuss ways to nurture creativity and talent. (pp. 350–355)

LECTURE OUTLINE

I. INTRODUCTION (pp. 319–320)
   A. The **psychometric approach** to cognitive development is the basis for the wide variety of intelligence tests available for assessing children's mental abilities.
   B. The psychometric perspective is *product*-oriented, largely concerned with outcomes and results and with developing ways of measuring intelligence so that scores will predict future achievement.
   C. This approach raises questions of nature versus nurture and whether intelligence tests are biased.

II. DEFINITIONS OF INTELLIGENCE (pp. 320–322)
   A. Most people think of intelligence as a complex combination of attributes, including verbal ability, practical problem solving, and social competence, but little consensus exists among experts.
   B. Alfred Binet: A Holistic View (pp. 320–321)
      1. Interest in testing mental ability developed in response to the beginning of universal public education in Europe and North America, as educators sought methods to identify students who were unable to benefit from regular classroom instruction.
      2. The first successful intelligence test was constructed by French psychologist Alfred Binet and his colleague Theodore Simon in 1905.
      3. The Binet test was so successful in predicting school performance that it became the basis for new intelligence tests.
   C. The Factor Analysts: A Multifaceted View (pp. 321–322)
      1. To find out whether intelligence is a single trait or an assortment of abilities, researchers used a complicated correlational procedure called **factor analysis** that involves identifying clusters of test items, or *factors*.
      2. Early Factor Analysts
         a. British psychologist Charles Spearman was the first influential factor analyst.
            (1) Finding that all test items he examined correlated with one another, he proposed that a common underlying **general intelligence,** called *g,* influenced each of them.
            (2) Spearman concluded that the test items varied in the extent to which *g* contributed to them and that each set of similar items also measured a **specific intelligence** unique to the task.
         b. American psychologist Louis Thurstone declared the supremacy of separate, unrelated factors, which he called *primary mental abilities*.
      3. Contemporary Extensions
         a. Current theorists combine the approaches of Spearman and Thurstone and propose *hierarchical models* of mental abilities, with *g* at the highest level, assumed to be present in all factors.
         b. Crystallized versus Fluid Intelligence
            (1) According to Raymond B. Cattell, intelligence consists of two broad factors, in addition to *g*.
            (2) **Crystallized intelligence** refers to skills that depend on accumulated knowledge and experience, good judgment, and mastery of social customs.

(3) **Fluid intelligence** depends more on basic information-processing skills and is assumed to be influenced more by conditions in the brain and less by culture.
(4) Cattell's theory has important implications for the issue of *cultural bias* in intelligence testing.
  c. The Three-Stratum Theory of Intelligence
  (1) John Carroll's **three-stratum theory of intelligence** represents the structure of intelligence as having three tiers, with *g* at the top.
  (2) In the second tier are *broad abilities,* which Carroll considered the basic biological components of intelligence.
  (3) In the third tier are *narrow abilities*—specific behaviors through which people display the second-tier factors.

III. RECENT ADVANCES IN DEFINING INTELLIGENCE (pp. 323–326, 327)
  A. Combining Psychometric and Information-Processing Approaches (p. 323)
    1. **Componential analyses** of children's test scores combine the psychometric and information-processing approaches, looking for relationships between aspects (or components) of information processing and children's intelligence test performance.
    2. Processing speed, measured in terms of reaction time on diverse cognitive tasks, is moderately related to general intelligence and to gains in mental test performance over time.
    3. fMRI research reveals that the metabolic rate of the cerebral cortex is lower for high-scoring individuals, suggesting that they require less mental energy for thinking.
    4. Other factors, including flexible attention, memory, and reasoning strategies, are as important as basic processing efficiency in predicting IQ.
    5. Identifying relationships between cognitive processing and mental test scores brings us closer to isolating the cognitive skills that contribute to high intelligence.
  B. Sternberg's Triarchic Theory (pp. 323–324)
    1. Robert Sternberg's **triarchic theory of successful intelligence** is made up of three broad, interacting intelligences: (1) *analytical intelligence,* (2) *creative intelligence,* and (3) *practical intelligence*.
    2. Intelligent behavior involves balancing all three intelligences to achieve success in life, according to one's personal goals and the requirements of one's cultural community.
      a. *Analytical* intelligence consists of information-processing components.
      b. *Creative* intelligence is the capacity to solve novel problems.
      c. *Practical* intelligence is the application of intellectual skills in everyday situations.
    3. The triarchic theory emphasizes the complexity of intelligent behavior.
  C. Gardner's Theory of Multiple Intelligences (pp. 325–326, 327)
    1. Howard Gardner's **theory of multiple intelligences** defines intelligence in terms of distinct sets of processing operations that permit individuals to solve problems and discover new knowledge.
    2. Gardner proposes at least eight independent intelligences—linguistic, logico-mathematical, musical, spatial, bodily-kinesthetic, naturalist, interpersonal, and intrapersonal—each with a unique biological basis, a distinct course of development, and different expert, or "end-state," performances.
    3. Gardner's view is reminiscent of the *core knowledge perspective,* which posits the existence of innately specified, core domains of thought, present at birth or emerging early in life.
    4. Gardner's theory has stimulated innovations in education extending from kindergarten through college in many countries.
    5. Critics of Gardner's theory, however, question the independence of his intelligences.
    6. Nonetheless, Gardner calls attention to several intelligences—interpersonal and intrapersonal—not tapped by intelligence tests.
    7. Related to Gardner's interpersonal and intrapersonal intelligences, and brought to the public's attention through popular books, is the concept of **emotional intelligence,** a set of emotional abilities that enable individuals to process and adapt to emotional information.

IV. MEASURING INTELLIGENCE (pp. 326–330)
  A. Although intelligence tests sample only a narrow range of human cognitive capacities, they are modest to good predictors of future success—academic, vocational, and in other aspects of life.
    1. *Group-administered tests* given in classrooms are useful for instructional planning and for identifying students who require more extensive evaluation.

Chapter 8 Intelligence

2. *Individually administered tests,* given to children who require more extensive evaluation, demand considerable training and experience to give well.
- B. Some Commonly Used Intelligence Tests (pp. 327–328)
    1. The Stanford-Binet Intelligence Scales
        a. The **Stanford-Binet Intelligence Scales, Fifth Edition,** the modern descendant of Binet's first successful intelligence test, is designed for individuals from age 2 to adulthood.
        b. The latest edition (the fifth) measures general intelligence and five intellectual factors: fluid reasoning, quantitative reasoning, knowledge, visual-spatial reasoning, and working memory.
        c. The knowledge and quantitative reasoning factors emphasize crystallized intelligence (culturally loaded, fact-oriented information).
        d. The other factors tap fluid intelligence and are assumed to be less culturally biased.
        e. A special edition is tailored for assessing children between ages 2 years and 7 years 3 months.
    2. The Wechsler Intelligence Scale for Children
        a. The **Wechsler Intelligence Scale for Children–IV (WISC–IV),** the fourth edition of a widely used test for 6- through 16-year-olds, includes four broad intellectual factors: verbal reasoning, perceptual reasoning, working memory, and processing speed.
        b. A downward extension of the test is for children 2 years 6 months through 7 years 3 months.
        c. Only verbal reasoning emphasizes crystallized, culture-dependent intelligence; the other three factors focus on fluid, information-processing skills.
        d. The Wechsler tests were the first to use samples representing the total population of the United States to devise standards for interpreting test scores.
- C. Aptitude and Achievement Tests (p. 328)
    1. **Aptitude tests** assess an individual's potential to learn a specialized activity.
    2. **Achievement tests** aim to assess actual knowledge and skill attainment.
    3. Differences among intelligence, aptitude, and achievement tests are not clear-cut.
- D. Tests for Infants (p. 329)
    1. Accurately measuring infants' intelligence is a challenge because babies cannot answer questions or follow directions.
    2. Most infant measures emphasize perceptual and motor responses.
    3. New tests, such as the *Bayley Scales of Infant and Toddler Development,* suitable for children between 1 month and 3½ years, also tap early language, cognition, and social behavior.
    4. The *Bayley-III* has three main subtests: the Cognitive Scale, the Language Scale, and the Motor Scale.
    5. Two additional Bayley-III scales depend on parental report: the Social-Emotional Scale and the Adaptive Behavior Scale.
    6. Infant tests predict later intelligence poorly. Because most infant scores do not tap the same dimensions of intelligence assessed in older children, they are conservatively labeled **developmental quotients (DQs)** rather than IQs.
    7. Infant tests are largely used for *screening*—helping to identify infants who are at risk for future developmental problems.
    8. Speed of habituation and recovery to visual stimuli is among the best infant correlates of later intelligence.
- E. Computation and Distribution of IQ Scores (p. 330)
    1. Scores on intelligence tests are arrived at by computing an **intelligence quotient (IQ),** indicating the extent to which the raw score (number of items passed) deviates from the typical performance of same-age individuals.
    2. To make this comparison possible, test designers engage in **standardization**—giving the test to a large, representative sample and using the results as the *standard* for interpreting scores.
    3. Within the standardization sample, scores at each age level form a **normal distribution,** in which most scores cluster around the mean, or average, with progressively fewer falling toward each extreme.
        a. This *bell-shaped distribution* results whenever researchers measure individual differences in large samples.
        b. When an intelligence test is standardized, the mean IQ is set at 100.

V. WHAT DO INTELLIGENCE TESTS PREDICT, AND HOW WELL? (pp. 330–333)
- A. Stability of IQ Scores (pp. 330–331)
    1. To study stability—how effectively IQ at one age predicts itself at the next—researchers rely on longitudinal studies, testing the same children repeatedly.

2. Correlational Stability
   a. Researchers have identified two generalizations about the stability of IQ.
      (1) *The older the child at time of first testing, the better the prediction of later IQ.*
      (2) *The closer in time two testings are, the stronger the relationship between the scores.*
   b. Preschool scores predict less well than later scores.
      (1) With age, test items focus less on concrete knowledge and more on complex reasoning and problem solving, which require different skills.
      (2) Once schooling is under way, IQ may become more stable because daily classroom activities and test items become increasingly similar, and then the quality of school experiences may help sustain individual differences in IQ.
3. Stability of Absolute Scores
   a. Stability can also be viewed in *absolute* terms by examining each child's profile of IQ scores over repeated testings.
      (1) The majority of children show substantial IQ fluctuations, typically 10 to 20 points or more, during childhood and adolescence.
      (2) Profiles of change tend to be orderly, with scores either increasing or decreasing with age, in each case reflecting distinct personality traits and life experiences.
   b. According to the **environmental cumulative deficit hypothesis,** the negative effects of underprivileged rearing conditions increase the longer children remain in these conditions; as a result, early cognitive deficits lead to more deficits.
B. IQ as a Predictor of Academic Achievement (pp. 331–332)
   1. Beginning at age 7, IQ is moderately correlated with adult educational attainment.
      a. Some researchers believe that both IQ and achievement depend on the abstract reasoning processes that underlie *g*.
      b. Others argue that both IQ and achievement tests draw on the same pool of culturally specific information.
   2. Although IQ predicts achievement better than any other tested measure, other factors, such as motivation and personality characteristics that lead some children to try hard in school, are at least as important as IQ in accounting for differences in school performance.
C. IQ as a Predictor of Occupational Attainment (pp. 332–333)
   1. Research indicates that childhood IQ predicts adult occupational attainment about as well as it correlates with academic achievement.
   2. Occupational achievement also depends on factors related to family background, personality, and **practical intelligence,** which includes mental abilities apparent in the real world but not in testing situations.
D. IQ as a Predictor of Psychological Adjustment (p. 333)
   1. IQ is moderately correlated with emotional and social adjustment.
   2. Research indicates that low IQ in early and middle childhood is associated with later antisocial behavior only when children also score high in emotional and behavior problems and when poor intellectual functioning persists.
   3. Lower childhood mental test scores are also associated with psychological disorders, including high anxiety and depression in adolescence and adulthood, but the relationships are modest.

VI. ETHNIC AND SOCIOECONOMIC VARIATIONS IN IQ (pp. 334–335)
A. **Socioeconomic status (SES),** an index used by researchers in industrialized nations to assess a family's social position and economic well-being, combines three interrelated but not completely overlapping variables: (1) years of education, (2) the prestige of one's job and the skill it requires, both of which measure social status, and (3) income, which measures economic status.
B. Because certain ethnicities are heavily represented at lower-SES levels and others at higher levels, researchers searching for the roots of socioeconomic disparities have compared the IQ scores of SES and ethnic groups.
C. Although the difference has been shrinking, American black children and adolescents score, on average, 10 to 12 IQ points below American white children. Hispanic children fall midway between black and white children.
D. Ethnicity and SES account for only about one-fourth of total variation in IQ, which also varies greatly *within* each ethnic and SES group.
E. The IQ nature–nurture controversy escalated in the 1970s with the controversial claims of psychologist Arthur Jensen, who asserted—and still maintains—that heredity is largely responsible for group differences in IQ, and was rekindled in the 1990s with the publication of *The Bell Curve,* which made similar claims.

Chapter 8 Intelligence

VII. EXPLAINING INDIVIDUAL AND GROUP DIFFERENCES IN IQ (pp. 335–346)
   A. Research aimed at explaining individual, ethnic, and SES differences in mental abilities falls into three broad types:
      1. Some investigations address the importance of heredity.
      2. Others look at whether IQ scores are biased measures of the abilities of low-SES and minority children.
      3. Still others examine the influences of children's home environments.
   B. Genetic Influences (pp. 335–337)
      1. Behavioral geneticists examine the relative contributions of heredity and environment to complex traits by conducting *kinship studies*.
      2. Heritability of Intelligence
         a. Researchers derive a *heritability estimate* by correlating the IQs of family members who vary in the extent to which they share genes, and then arriving at an index of heritability, ranging from 0 to 1, indicating the proportion of variation in a population that is due to genetic factors.
         b. The greater the genetic similarity between family members, the more they resemble one another in IQ.
         c. The correlation for identical twins reared apart is much higher than for fraternal twins reared together.
         d. Evidence also exists for the role of environment: Correlations for twin, nontwin sibling, and parent–child pairs living together are stronger than for those living apart.
         e. Heritability estimates, typically about .50 in Western industrialized nations, may be too high, because twins reared together often experience similar overall environments.
      3. Do Heritability Estimates Explain Ethnic and SES Variations in IQ?
         a. Jensen relied on the heritability estimate to support his argument that ethnic and SES differences in IQ have a strong genetic basis, but this line of reasoning, which applies to individual comparisons *within* groups, is widely regarded as inappropriate in making between-group comparisons.
         b. Heritability of IQ is *higher* under advantaged rearing conditions than under disadvantaged conditions, because factors associated with poverty prevent children from attaining their genetic potential.
   C. Adoption Studies: Joint Influence of Heredity and Environment (pp. 337–338)
      1. In adoption studies, researchers gather two types of information:
         a. They examine IQ correlations between adopted children and their biological and adoptive parents for insight into genetic and environmental influences.
         b. They look at changes in the absolute value of IQ as a result of growing up in an advantaged adoptive family, for evidence on the power of the environment.
      2. Adoption research confirms that both environment and heredity contribute significantly to IQ.
         a. Children adopted in the early years attain IQs that, on average, match the scores of their adoptive parents' biological children, suggesting a sizable role for environment.
         b. Adoption studies also reveal stronger correlations between the IQ scores of biological relatives than between those of adoptive relatives, evidence of a genetic contribution.
         c. Studies have shown that African-American children adopted in the first year of life into well-off white homes score high on intelligence tests, consistent with other evidence that poverty severely depresses scores.
         d. Dramatic gains in IQ from one generation to the next, called the **Flynn effect,** support the conclusion that, given new experiences and opportunities, members of oppressed groups can move far beyond their current test performance.
   D. Race and Ethnicity: Genetic or Cultural Groupings? (p. 339)
      1. DNA analyses reveal wide genetic variation *within* races and minimal genetic variation *between* them.
      2. Members of ethnic groups that have been the focus of the IQ nature–nurture controversy are far more similar in cultural values, experiences, and opportunities than in genetic makeup.
   E. Cultural Bias in Testing (pp. 339–341)
      1. A controversial question about ethnic differences in IQ is whether they result from *test bias*.
         a. Tests are biased if they sample knowledge that not all groups have had equal opportunity to learn, or if the testing situation impairs the performance of some groups but not others.
         b. Some experts claim that tests are intended to represent success in the common culture and, thus, are fair to both minority and majority children.
         c. Others believe that lack of exposure to certain communication styles and knowledge, along with negative stereotypes about the test-taker's ethnic group, can undermine children's performance.

2. Communication Styles
    a. Ethnic minority families often foster unique language skills that do not match the expectations of most classrooms and testing situations.
    b. Ethnic minority parents without extensive schooling may prefer a *collaborative style of communication* when completing tasks with children, in contrast to the *hierarchical style* typical of tests.
3. Knowledge
    a. Many researchers argue that IQ scores are affected by specific information acquired as part of majority-culture upbringing, which is reflected in verbal, fact-oriented (crystallized) test items.
    b. Knowledge affects ability to reason effectively, and even nonverbal test items, such as spatial reasoning, depend on learning opportunities.
    c. The sheer amount of time a child spends in school predicts IQ.
4. Stereotypes
    a. **Stereotype threat**—fear of being judged on the basis of a negative stereotype—can trigger anxiety that interferes with performance in children and adults.
    b. Over middle childhood, children from stigmatized groups often start to devalue academic achievement and to engage in self-protective disengagement, sparked by stereotype threat.

F. Reducing Cultural Bias in Testing (pp. 342–343)
1. Many experts acknowledge that IQ scores can underestimate the intelligence of children from ethnic minority groups.
2. To avoid incorrectly labeling minority children as slow learners and assigning them to remedial classes, test scores should be combined with assessments of children's adaptive behavior—their ability to cope with the demands of their everyday environments.
3. Minority children's performance is enhanced by culturally relevant testing procedures, such as **dynamic assessment,** an innovation consistent with Vygotsky's *zone of proximal development,* in which the adult introduces purposeful teaching into the testing situation to find out what the child can attain with social support.
4. Dynamic assessment often follows a pretest–intervene–retest procedure.
5. Research shows that "static" assessments, such as IQ scores, frequently underestimate how well children do on test items after receiving adult assistance.
6. Dynamic assessment is time-consuming and as yet has not been more effective than traditional tests in predicting academic achievement.
7. Rather than adapting testing to support high-quality classroom learning experiences, U.S. education is placing greater emphasis on traditional test scores.
    a. A *high-stakes testing* movement has arisen, making progress through the school system contingent on test performance. The U.S. No Child Left Behind Act broadens high-stakes testing to the identification of "passing" and "failing" schools.
    b. The emphasis on passing standardized tests has narrowed the focus of instruction in many classrooms to test preparation, and it may widen SES and ethnic group differences in educational attainment.
8. Despite limitations, intelligence tests continue to be valid measures of school learning potential.

G. Home Environment and Mental Development (pp. 344–346)
1. Factors in the home environment contribute to variation in mental test scores between children of the *same* ethnic and SES background.
2. Researchers divide home influences into two broad types:
    a. **Shared environmental influences** pervade the atmosphere of the home and *similarly* affect siblings living in it.
    b. **Nonshared environmental influences,** such as birth order and spacing, make siblings *different* from one another.
3. Shared Environmental Influences
    a. These influences are observed using (1) studies relating home environmental qualities to IQ and (2) studies examining the impact on student performance of family beliefs about intellectual success on student performance.
    b. Observations of Home Environmental Qualities
        (1) The **Home Observation for Measurement of the Environment (HOME)** is a checklist for gathering information about the quality of children's home lives through observation and parental interview.

(2) Evidence on HOME confirms research findings of links between stimulation provided by parents and mental development, regardless of SES and ethnicity.
(3) The HOME–IQ relationship declines in middle childhood, as children spend more time away from home.
(4) Because all of the children studied were reared by their biological parents, *genetic–environmental correlation* may be a factor.
(5) Family living conditions—both HOME scores and resources in the surrounding neighborhood—continue to predict children's IQ beyond the contribution of parental IQ and education.
   c. Family Beliefs About Intellectual Success
(1) Newly arrived immigrant parents from Asia and Latin America emphasize intellectual success, and their children do well in school, regardless of SES.
(2) Parental beliefs are also linked to academic performance among nonimmigrant children from various ethnic groups.
  4. Nonshared Environmental Influences
   a. The experiences of children growing up in the same family are similar in some ways but differ in others. Parents may favor one child or assign children special roles.
   b. Kinship research suggests that these nonshared environmental influences are more powerful than shared influences on IQ.
   c. The impact of the shared environment on IQ is greatest in childhood but later gives way to nonshared influences.
   d. Some researchers believe that the most potent nonshared environmental influences are unpredictable, unique events.

VIII. EARLY INTERVENTION AND INTELLECTUAL DEVELOPMENT (pp. 347–350, 351)
  A. **Project Head Start,** begun by the U.S. government in 1965, is the most extensive of the early intervention programs initiated in the 1960s as part of the War on Poverty in the United States.
    1. The goal of these programs was to address learning problems early, before formal schooling begins, to offset the declines in IQ and achievement common among low-SES children.
    2. Currently, Head Start serves about 904,000 children and their families.
    3. Parent involvement is central to the Head Start philosophy, and parents also receive services.
  B. Benefits of Early Intervention (pp. 347–349)
    1. Extensive research has established the long-term benefits of early intervention.
    2. The most extensive of these studies showed that poverty-stricken children who attended programs had higher IQ and achievement test scores than controls during the first two or three years of elementary school.
    3. That study also showed that, although differences in test scores declined after that time, these children and adolescents remained ahead on real-life measures of school adjustment.
    4. A report on one early intervention program, the High/Scope Perry Preschool Project, revealed benefits lasting well into adulthood.
    5. Gains in school adjustment for participants in Head Start and other community-based preschool interventions are similar, though not as strong.
     a. Head Start preschoolers, who are more economically disadvantaged than children in other programs, have more severe learning and behavior problems.
     b. Quality of services in Head Start often does not equal that of model university-based programs.
    6. A consistent finding is that gains in IQ and achievement test scores from attending Head Start and other interventions quickly dissolve.
     a. The Head Start Impact Study, comparing a group of Head Start preschoolers against controls attending other preschool programs, found that the Head Start 3- and 4-year-olds gained in vocabulary, emergent literacy, and other skills relative to the controls.
     b. However, the study found that, except for language skills, academic test-score advantages were no longer evident by end of first grade.
     c. Head Start children typically enter inferior public schools in poverty-stricken neighborhoods, which undermine the benefits of preschool education.
     d. When high-quality intervention starts in infancy and extends through early childhood, children display cognitive and academic achievement advantages throughout childhood and adolescence.

7. **Early Head Start,** providing services for infants and toddlers and their families, was funded by the U.S. Congress in 1995 in recognition of the greater power of intervening as early as possible.
    a. Currently, 700 Early Head Start sites serve 63,000 low-income families.
    b. The strongest effects have occurred at sites mixing center and home-visiting services.
8. Even when intervention is delayed until age 3 or 4, impressive improvements in school adjustment from attending a one- or two-year Head Start program result.

C. Strengthening Early Intervention (pp. 349–350, 351)
    1. Excellent early intervention is highly cost effective when compared with the later cost of providing special education, treating criminal behavior, and supporting unemployed adults.
    2. Economists estimate a lifetime return to society of $300,000 to $500,000 on an investment of about $17,000 per preschool child.
    3. According to research, outstanding programs shared the following critical features, among others:
        a. They employ well-educated, well-compensated teachers and have generous teacher–child ratios.
        b. They offer intensive intervention and emphasize parent involvement, education, and support.
        c. They focus on the whole child.
    4. Because of limited funding, only 60 percent of poverty-stricken 3- and 4-year-olds attend some type of preschool program.
    5. Supplementary programs, such as Jumpstart, deliver intervention to children in child-care centers and strengthen intervention in Head Start and other preschool classrooms.
    6. The Head Start REDI (Research-based Developmentally Informed) program, an enrichment curriculum designed to be integrated into existing Head Start learning activities, is remarkably successful at strengthening Head Start children's school readiness.

IX. GIFTEDNESS: CREATIVITY AND TALENT (pp. 350, 352–355)
    A. **Gifted** children—those who display exceptional intellectual strengths—have diverse characteristics.
        1. Some have IQ scores above 130 and have keen memories and an exceptional capacity to solve challenging academic problems.
        2. Recognition that intelligence tests do not sample the entire range of human mental skills has led to an expanded conception of giftedness, which includes creativity.
    B. **Creativity** is the ability to produce work that is *original* yet *appropriate*.
        1. In addition to its value on the job and in daily life, creativity is vital for societal progress.
        2. Ideas about creativity have changed radically during the past two decades.
    C. The Psychometric View (pp. 350, 352)
        1. Until recently, research on creativity was dominated by a purely cognitive perspective based on tests of **divergent thinking**—the generation of multiple or unusual possibilities when faced with a task or problem—in contrast to **convergent thinking,** emphasized on intelligence tests, which involves arriving at a single correct answer.
        2. Critics note that the tests of divergent thinking are poor predictors of creative accomplishment in everyday life, because they tap only one of the complex cognitive contributions to creativity.
        3. Still, divergent-thinking tests have been the major focus of research on creativity in children.
    D. A Multifaceted View (pp. 352–355)
        1. Recent theories of creativity agree that many elements must converge for creativity to occur.
        2. Sternberg and Lubart's **investment theory of creativity** is one influential multifaceted approach.
            a. In this view, pursuing a novel project increases the chances of arriving at a creative, highly valued product.
            b. But whether a person initiates an original project and brings it to fruition depends on that person's cognitive, personality, motivational, and environmental resources.
        3. Cognitive Resources
            a. Creative work depends on a variety of high-level cognitive skills:
                (1) It requires *problem finding* and *the ability to define* a problem clearly.
                (2) The creator must be able to *alternate between divergent and convergent thinking*.
                (3) To narrow the range of possibilities, creative individuals rely on *insight processes*—combining and restructuring elements in sudden but useful ways.
                (4) Creativity requires the ability to *evaluate competing ideas*.

b. Because of its cognitive ingredients, high creativity is usually manifested as **talent**—outstanding performance in one or a few related fields.
c. IQ and creativity correlate only modestly; other factors are essential for creative giftedness.
4. Personality Resources
   a. Creative people have an *innovative style of thinking*.
   b. They have a high *tolerance of ambiguity* and the patience and persistence to *persevere*.
   c. They have a *willingness to take risks* and the *courage of their convictions*.
5. Motivational Resources
   a. Motivation for creativity must be *task-focused* (motivated by a desire to meet a high standard), not *goal-focused* (motivated by extrinsic rewards, such as grades and prizes).
   b. Although extrinsic rewards are not always detrimental to creativity, creativity can suffer if they are overemphasized.
6. Environmental Resources
   a. Studies of talented children and accomplished adults often reveal a family life focused on the child's needs and parents who are devoted to developing their child's abilities.
   b. Extreme giftedness often results in social isolation, so gifted children and adolescents often benefit from classrooms in which they can interact with like-minded peers.
   c. In classrooms where knowledge acquisition is stressed over using knowledge originally, children's thinking becomes *entrenched*, and talented students may lose their drive to excel.
   d. Gardner's theory of multiple intelligences has inspired several model school programs that provide enrichment to all students in diverse disciplines.
   e. This approach has been successful in highlighting the strengths of students who had previously been considered unexceptional or at risk for school failure.

LECTURE ENHANCEMENTS

LECTURE ENHANCEMENT 8.1
Emotional Intelligence, Successful Intelligence, and Leadership Skills (p. 327)

Time: 5–10 minutes

Objective: To examine the link between emotional intelligence, successful intelligence, and leadership skills in gifted students.

As noted in the text, emotional intelligence is positively associated with self-esteem, empathy, prosocial behavior, cooperation, leadership skills, and life satisfaction. In addition, Sternberg's theory underscores the importance of analytical, creative, and practical skills—skills that are often overlooked on intelligence tests—for life success. To examine the relationship among emotional intelligence, successful intelligence, and leadership skills, Chan (2008) recruited 498 gifted students in grades 4 through 12 and collected the following information:
   (1) Participants completed a leadership rating scale, which measures leadership self-efficacy, leadership flexibility, and goal orientation (related to leadership and achievement).
   (2) Participants completed an emotional intelligence scale that assesses social skills, empathy, management of emotions, and utilization of emotions.
   (3) Participants completed Sternberg's Successful Intelligence Questionnaire, which measures analytical, creative, and practical abilities.

Results indicated that both emotional intelligence and successful intelligence predicted leadership skills. Participants who scored high in emotional and successful intelligence scored higher in overall leadership skills than participants who scored low in these areas. When looking at specific aspects of emotional and successful intelligence, practical abilities and management of emotions were especially strong predictors of leadership skills. These findings suggest that the ability to apply intellectual skills in everyday situations and the ability to manage and regulate emotions are important leadership qualities. No significant age or gender differences were found.

Engage students in a discussion about emotional and successful intelligence. Do students believe that emotional intelligence is a more important predictor of academic and/or vocational success than IQ? Why or why not?

Chan, D. W. (2008). Leadership and intelligence. *Roeper Review, 29,* 183–189.

LECTURE ENHANCEMENT 8.2
Reducing Stereotype Threat in School-Age Children (p. 341)

Time: 5–10 minutes

Objective: To extend existing research on stereotype threat.

To extend existing research on stereotype threat, Alter and colleagues (2010) recruited 49 African-American middle school students, ranging in age from 9 to 13 years. Prior to completing a 10-item math exam, participants were randomly assigned to one of four treatment conditions—threat or challenge and high racial salience or low racial salience. The threat condition emphasized the diagnostic nature of the test. Specifically, the experimenter told participants that the exam would "show how good [they] were right now on this type of work" and that "it would measure [their] ability at solving math problems." In contrast, the challenge condition emphasized the role of the test in improving participants' general mathematical ability. The experimenter explained that they "would learn a lot of new things" and that "working on these problems might be a big help in school because it sharpens the mind and learning to do math well could help [them] in [their] studies." Because research shows that reporting one's race can heighten susceptibility to stereotype threat, participants reported their race either before (high racial salience) or after (low racial salience) completing the math exam. It is important to note that participants completed a math exam that was designed for their grade level.

Findings indicated that stereotype threat had a negative impact on performance in the threat condition but not in the challenge condition. Specifically, participants in the high racial salience condition performed significantly better on the math exam when it was framed as a challenge rather than a threat. When asked to report their race prior to beginning the math exam, African-American children in the threat condition performed more poorly than those in the challenge condition. In contrast, when asked to report their race after the exam, children performed at grade level, or on a level commensurate with their peers. According to Alter and colleagues, by simply reframing threatening tests as challenges, educators may ameliorate the effects of stereotype threat in academically marginalized students.

Alter, A. L., Aronson, J., Darley, J. M., Rodriguez, C., & Ruble, D. N. (2010). Rising to the threat: Reducing stereotype threat by reframing the threat as a challenge. *Journal of Experimental Social Psychology, 46,* 166–171.

LECTURE ENHANCEMENT 8.3
More on Shared Environmental Influences: Do Age Differences Between Siblings Predict IQ? (pp. 344–346)

Time: 5–10 minutes

Objective: To examine the relationship between age and IQ in nontwin siblings.

To extend existing research on shared environmental influences on intelligence, Sundet, Eriksen, and Tambs (2008) used existing data on 334,361 pairs of brothers (ages 18 to 21) identified through Norway's National Conscript Service, a mandatory military registration. All participants were administered a standardized intelligence test during the registration process. In addition to gathering IQ test scores, the researchers also recorded the number of male siblings and classified the age difference for each pair of brothers into one of six categories: 1–2 years, 3–4 years, 5–6 years, 7–8 years, 9–10 years, or 11+ years. Information on parent education was also collected. No twin pairs were included in the study. Focusing on age differences between siblings to identify the presence of shared environmental effects (for example, the closer in age, the greater the likelihood of experiencing shared environments) is an alternative to twin and adoption studies, which are often criticized for both overestimating and underestimating the effects of shared environments.

Findings revealed that correlations between siblings' IQ test scores decreased as the age gap increased. That is, siblings who were closer in age had more similar IQ scores than siblings who were farther apart in age. This relationship remained significant even after controlling for parent education. According to Sundet, Eriksen, and Tambs, this finding provides additional support for the role of shared family influences on intelligence. For example, siblings who are closer in age likely influence each other more than siblings who are farther apart in age. They are also more likely to share more family experiences that tend to change over time—family resources, stressful events, and routine transitions.

Sundet, J. M., Eriksen, W., & Tambs, K. (2008). Intelligence correlations between brothers decrease with increasing age difference: Evidence of shared environmental effects in young adults. *Psychological Science, 19,* 843–847.

LECTURE ENHANCEMENT 8.4
More on Head Start Outcomes: Does Maternal Education Contribute? (pp. 347–349)

Time: 10–15 minutes

Objective: To extend existing research on short- and long-term benefits of Head Start attendance.

To extend existing research on both short- and long-term benefits of community-based early intervention, Lee (2010) recruited 603 children who were participants in the National Longitudinal Survey of Youth. All of the children attended Head Start preschool programs. The researchers gathered the following information:

(1) When children were between the ages of 5 and 6 and 11 and 12, they were administered biannual reading and math assessments from the Peabody Individual Achievement Test (PIAT). The reading recognition assessment focuses on word recognition and pronunciation ability, with items increasing in difficulty from preschool to high school. Sample tasks include matching letters and reading single words aloud. The math assessment focuses on a range of basic and advanced skills, ranging from recognizing numerals to solving geometry and trigonometry problems.

(2) In addition to math and achievement assessments, the Children's Behavior Problems Index (CBI) was also administered biannually. Mothers were asked to rate children on six behavioral subscales—antisocial, anxious/depressed, headstrong, hyperactive, immature dependency, and peer conflict/social withdrawal.

(3) Mothers provided family background information, including their own education, child characteristics (e.g., low birth weight, gender, birth order, Head Start entry age, special needs), ethnicity, marital status, number of children in the home, nonmaternal child care, family income, and native language/language used in the home.

Findings indicated that Head Start children who made significant short-term gains in reading, math, and behavior were more likely to maintain those gains over time than children who made minimal short-term gains. However, these outcomes were moderated by maternal education. Specifically, mothers who had at least a high school education had children with higher reading scores at ages 5 to 6 and also at ages 11 to 12. In addition, maternal education predicted child behavior problems. Mothers with more education had children with lower rates of behavioral problems than mothers who had not completed high school. Taken together, these findings indicate that maternal education contributes to both short- and long-term outcomes of community-based early intervention programs like Head Start. Mothers with more education not only had children who made significant short-term gains in reading, math, and behavior, their children were more likely to maintain these gains into middle childhood.

Lee, K. (2010). Do early academic achievement and behavior problems predict long-term effects among Head Start children? *Children and Youth Services Review, 32*, 1690–1703.

LEARNING ACTIVITIES

LEARNING ACTIVITY 8.1
Matching: Gardner's Multiple Intelligences (pp. 325–326)

Present the following activity as an in-class assignment or quiz.

Directions: Match each of Gardner's multiple intelligences with its end-state performance possibilities.

Intelligences:

_____ 1. Linguistic intelligence
_____ 2. Logico-mathematical intelligence
_____ 3. Musical intelligence
_____ 4. Spatial intelligence
_____ 5. Bodily-kinesthetic intelligence
_____ 6. Naturalist intelligence
_____ 7. Interpersonal intelligence
_____ 8. Intrapersonal intelligence

End-state performance possibilities:

A. Sculptor, navigator
B. Mathematician
C. Person with detailed, accurate self-knowledge
D. Therapist, salesperson
E. Dancer, athlete
F. Poet, journalist
G. Instrumentalist, composer
H. Biologist

Answers:

1. F
2. B
3. G
4. A
5. E
6. H
7. D
8. C

LEARNING ACTIVITY 8.2
An Online Intelligence Test (pp. 326–328)

Have students visit the following website: *www.iqtest.com,* which contains an online intelligence test. Please note that the test and results are free. The site provides an option of a full IQ profile, which requires a $10 fee. However, the full profile is not required for this activity. After taking the test, have students answer the following questions: Do you think your performance on the IQ test is an accurate assessment of your intellectual ability? Why or why not? How might your educational experiences, culture, and home environment have influenced your performance? Do you believe this test would accurately predict academic achievement? Explain, using examples from the IQ test and research presented in the text.

LEARNING ACTIVITY 8.3
Assessing Emotional Intelligence (p. 327)

Direct students to the following website: *testyourself.psychtests.com/testid/3038,* which presents a free emotional intelligence test designed by leading researchers in the field. The assessment takes approximately 20 minutes to complete. Students will be asked about their personal approaches to dealing with emotional and social situations and will be presented with a variety of vignettes that require them to predict what characters are thinking or feeling. After completing the test, students should record their emotional IQ and summarize the feedback provided by the website. Do students agree with the results of the test? Explain, using examples from the test and research presented in the text.

LEARNING ACTIVITY 8.4
Identifying Factors Related to Academic and Vocational Success (pp. 323–326, 331–333)

In small groups, have students list all of the qualities and skills that they believe are important for academic and vocational success. How many of these qualities and skills are assessed by traditional intelligence tests? Are any consistent with Sternberg's triarchic theory of successful intelligence or Gardner's theory of multiple intelligences? Do students think these qualities and skills are important for people in different cultures? Why or why not?

LEARNING ACTIVITY 8.5
Ethnic and Socioeconomic Variations in IQ (pp. 334–342)

Present students with the following questions for discussion:

> Why should the IQ scores of ethnic minority children be interpreted with caution? What environmental factors contribute to ethnic and SES variations in IQ? What is test bias, and how might it undermine children's performance? Be sure to mention research on communication styles, test content, and stereotypes.

LEARNING ACTIVITY 8.6
True or False: Explaining Individual and Group Differences in IQ (pp. 335–346)

Present the following exercise to students as a quiz or in-class activity.

Directions: Read each of the following statements and indicate whether it is *True* (T) or *False* (F).

Statements:
_____ 1. The IQ correlation for identical twins reared apart is much lower than for fraternal twins reared together.
_____ 2. Children adopted in the early years attain IQs that, on average, match the scores of their adoptive parents' biological children and the scores of nonadopted peers in their schools and communities.
_____ 3. Research shows that African-American children's language emphasizes emotional and social concerns rather than facts about the world.
_____ 4. Contrary to popular belief, stereotype threat has little impact on children's mental test scores.
_____ 5. Research indicates that "static" assessments, such as IQ scores, frequently underestimate how well children do on test items after receiving adult assistance.
_____ 6. Despite their limitations, IQ scores continue to be valid measures of school learning potential for the majority of Western children.
_____ 7. The HOME–IQ relationship increases in middle childhood and then declines in adolescence.
_____ 8. In immigrant families, IQ is primarily responsible for the high valuing of intellectual endeavors and children's superior academic performance.
_____ 9. Kinship research suggests that nonshared environmental factors are more powerful than shared influences on IQ.
_____ 10. Most researchers agree that birth order and spacing predict IQ scores.

Answers:

1. F   6. T
2. T   7. F
3. T   8. F
4. F   9. T
5. T   10. F

LEARNING ACTIVITY 8.7
Supporting Mental Development in Infants and Toddlers (pp. 344–346)

Tell students to pretend that they have been asked to speak to a group of parents with very young children. Using research in the text as a guide, have students describe environmental factors that promote favorable mental development in infants and toddlers. What environmental factors tend to undermine mental development? Why are high-quality child care and/or early intervention especially important for low-income infants and toddlers?

LEARNING ACTIVITY 8.8
Nurturing the School-Age Child's Creativity and Talent (pp. 350, 352–355)

Have students form small groups and respond to one of the following scenarios:
(1) Provide advice to parents who want to nurture their child's creativity and special talents. What general approaches to child rearing should parents adopt? Describe research findings that support your recommendations.
(2) Provide advice to teachers who want to nurture students' creativity and special talents. What general approaches to instruction should teachers adopt? Describe research findings that support your recommendations.

Once students have responded to the scenarios, ask them to share their recommendations with the class. How might parents and teachers work together to support children's creativity and talent?

ASK YOURSELF . . .

REVIEW: Using Sternberg's triarchic theory, explain the limitations of current mental tests in assessing the complexity of human intelligence. (pp. 323–324)

Sternberg's triarchic theory of successful intelligence identifies three broad, interacting intelligences: *analytical intelligence,* or information-processing skills; *creative intelligence,* the capacity to solve novel problems; and *practical intelligence,* application of intellectual skills in everyday situations. Intelligent behavior, in Sternberg's view, involves balancing all three intelligences to achieve success in life, according to one's personal goals and the requirements of one's cultural community. This theory emphasizes the complexity of intelligent behavior and the limitations of current intelligence tests in assessing that complexity. For example, out-of-school, practical forms of intelligence are vital for life success and help explain why cultures vary widely in the behaviors they regard as intelligent. When researchers asked ethnically diverse parents to describe an intelligent first grader, Caucasian Americans mentioned cognitive traits. In contrast, ethnic minorities (Cambodian, Filipino, Vietnamese, and Mexican immigrants) saw noncognitive capacities—motivation, self-management, and social skills—as especially important. According to Sternberg, mental tests can easily underestimate, and even overlook, the intellectual strengths of some children, especially ethnic minorities.

CONNECT: Describe similarities between Gardner's theory of multiple intelligences and the core knowledge perspective on cognitive development (see Chapter 6, pages 261–262). What questions raised about this view also apply to Gardner's theory? (p. 326)

Like the core knowledge perspective, Gardner's theory of multiple intelligences accepts the existence of innately specified, core domains of thought that are present at birth or emerge very early in life, permitting a ready grasp of new, related information. As children respond to the demands of their culture, they transform those intelligences to fit the activities they are called on to perform.

However, critics point out that excellence in most fields requires a combination of intelligences. This is similar to the questions raised about the core knowledge view by its critics, who question the assumption that infants are endowed with ready-made knowledge. Critics of Gardner's theory also note that current mental tests suggest common features among several of Gardner's intelligences. Also, some exceptionally gifted individuals have abilities that are broad rather than limited to a particular domain.

APPLY: Eight-year-old Charya, an immigrant from Cambodia, had difficulty responding to test items asking for word definitions and general information. But she solved puzzles easily, and she quickly figured out which number comes next in a complex series. How does Charya score in crystallized and fluid intelligence? What might explain the difference? (pp. 321–322)

Crystallized intelligence refers to skills that depend on accumulated knowledge and experience, good judgment, and mastery of social customs—abilities acquired because they are valued by the individual's culture. On intelligence tests, vocabulary, general information, and arithmetic problems are examples of items that emphasize crystallized intelligence. In contrast, *fluid intelligence* depends more heavily on basic information-processing skills—the ability to detect relationships among stimuli, the speed with which the individual can analyze information, and the capacity of working memory. Fluid intelligence is assumed to be influenced more by conditions in the brain and less by culture.

Charya's difficulty in supplying word definitions and general information would result in a low score on crystallized intelligence; in contrast, her ability to solve number series problems and puzzles would result in a high score on fluid intelligence. The differences in Charya's scores are most likely associated with differences in culture and learning opportunities, which would affect scores on items testing crystallized intelligence but not on those reflecting fluid intelligence.

REFLECT: Select one of your intellectual strengths from Gardner's multiple intelligences, listed in Table 8.1 on page 325. How do you display that intelligence? What other intelligences contribute to your strong performance? (pp. 325–326)

This is an open-ended question with no right or wrong answer.

REVIEW: Why are aptitude and achievement tests closely related to intelligence tests and to each other? (pp. 326, 328)

Aptitude tests assess an individual's potential to learn a specialized activity. In contrast, achievement tests aim to assess not potential to learn but actual knowledge and skill attainment. Intelligence tests assess the widest array of skills. However, differences among intelligence, aptitude, and achievement tests are not clear-cut. Certain items on each, especially those assessing verbal and math skills, are similar. Most tests tap both aptitude and achievement, though in different balances.

CONNECT: Both the Stanford-Binet and the Wechsler tests provide a measure of general intelligence and an array of subtest scores. What evidence presented earlier in this chapter supports the use of these hierarchical models of intelligence? (pp. 321, 327–328)

To find out whether intelligence is a single trait or an assortment of abilities, researchers have used a correlational procedure called *factor analysis,* which identifies sets of test items that cluster together, meaning that test-takers who do well on one item in a cluster tend to do well on the others. The first influential factor analyst, British psychologist Charles Spearman, found that all test items he examined correlated with one another. As a result, he proposed that a common underlying *general intelligence,* called *g,* influenced each of them. Both the Stanford-Binet and the Wechsler tests reflect this hierarchical approach by measuring both general intelligence and a variety of separate factors. These factors are measured by subtests—groups of related items that provide information about a child's strengths and weaknesses.

APPLY: Assia's score on the Stanford-Binet Intelligence Scales is 115; Leila's score is 145. Using Figure 8.4, explain how well each child performed in relation to other children her age. (p. 330)

The percentage of same-age individuals in the population a person with a certain IQ outperformed is determined by adding the percentage figures to the left of that IQ score. Assia, with an IQ score of 115, scored better than 84.1 percent of her agemates. Leila, with a score of 145, outperformed 99.9 percent of her agemates.

REVIEW: Provide two competing explanations for the correlation between IQ and academic achievement. (pp. 331–332)

Researchers offer different explanations for the correlation between IQ and academic achievement. Some believe that both IQ and achievement depend on the same abstract reasoning processes that underlie *g*. Consistent with this interpretation, IQ correlates best with achievement in the more abstract school subjects, such as English, mathematics, and science. Other researchers argue that both IQ and achievement tests draw on the same pool of culturally specific information. From this perspective, an intelligence test is, in fact, partly an achievement test, and a child's past experiences affect performance on both measures. Support for this view comes from evidence that crystallized intelligence (which reflects acquired knowledge) is a better predictor of academic achievement than is its fluid counterpart.

CONNECT: Describe evidence from previous chapters that non-Western children with little or no formal schooling display considerable practical intelligence, despite poor performance on tasks commonly used to assess Western children's cognitive skills. (*Hint:* See Chapter 6, page 252, and Chapter 7, page 294.) (pp. 332–333)

In Western societies, where children are largely excluded from participation in adult work, the role of equipping them with the skills they need to become competent workers is assigned to school. In many non-Western societies, in contrast, children observe and participate in adult work from an early age. This difference is reflected in practical intelligence—for example, in the use of memory strategies that employ cues available in everyday life. Western children are unlikely to use such practical cues; instead, they get a great deal of practice with using memory strategies to remember isolated bits of information. Their development of such memory strategies does not represent a more competent information-processing system but, rather, is a product of task demands and culture.

As another example, cognitive maps are used to assess perspective taking because children must infer the map's overall layout by relating its separate parts. In many non-Western communities, however, people rarely use maps for way finding but rely on information from neighbors, street vendors, and shopkeepers. When a researcher asked 12-year-olds in small cities in India and the United States to draw maps of their neighborhoods, the Indian children represented many landmarks and aspects of social life, such as people and vehicles, in a small area near their home—an approach reflecting practical intelligence that is meaningful within their culture.

APPLY: When 5-year-old Paul had difficulty adjusting to kindergarten, his teacher arranged for special testing. Paul's IQ turned out to be below average, at 95. When discussing Paul's score with his parents and teacher, what should the psychologist say about the stability of IQ? (pp. 330–331)

Researchers have identified two generalizations about the *correlational stability* of IQ: First, the older the child at time of first testing, the better the prediction of later IQ. Second, the closer in time two testing sessions are, the stronger the relationship between the scores. Preschool IQs do not predict school-age scores well; correlations are typically weak until age 6. One reason is that with age, test items focus less on concrete knowledge and more on complex reasoning and problem solving, which require different skills. Also, during periods of rapid development, children frequently change places in a distribution. Finally, IQ may become more stable after schooling is under way because daily classroom activities are increasingly similar to test items. In terms of the *stability of absolute scores,* the majority of children show substantial IQ fluctuations (typically 10 to 20 points or more) during childhood and adolescence. Therefore, the psychologist should inform Paul's parents and teacher that Paul's IQ score at age 5 does not necessarily predict future poor school performance.

REFLECT: How do James's experiences, described in the opening to this chapter, fit with findings on children who show mental test score gains with age? (pp. 330–331)

This is an open-ended question with no right-or-wrong answer.

REVIEW: Why can't heritability estimates explain ethnic differences in IQ? Using research findings, describe environmental factors that contribute to these differences. (pp. 336–337, 339)

Heritability estimates usually are derived from comparisons of identical and fraternal twins. Because these estimates are typically computed *within* a single ethnic group, they provide no direct evidence on what accounts for between-group differences. DNA analyses reveal wide genetic variation *within* races but only minimal genetic variation *between* them. Furthermore, heritability of IQ is higher under advantaged (higher-SES) than disadvantaged rearing conditions. Factors associated with low income and poverty, including weak or absent prenatal care, family stress, low-quality schools, and lack of community supports for effective child rearing, prevent children from attaining their genetic potential.

CONNECT: Explain how dynamic assessment is consistent with Vygotsky's zone of proximal development and with scaffolding (see Chapter 6, pages 267–268). (pp. 342–343)

Dynamic assessment is a testing procedure in which the adult introduces purposeful teaching into the testing situation to find out what the child can attain with social support. It is consistent with Vygotsky's zone of proximal development in that it is tailored to the child's individual ability and emphasizes the importance of assistance from more expert adults. The teacher intervenes on tasks carefully selected to help the child move beyond her current level of development, seeking the teaching style best suited to the child and communicating strategies the child can apply in new situations. This allows the teacher to gradually turn over responsibility to the child, an approach consistent with scaffolding.

APPLY: Josefina, a Hispanic fourth grader, does well on homework assignments. But when her teacher announces, "It's time for a test to see how much you've learned," Josefina usually does poorly. How might stereotype threat explain this inconsistency? (p. 341)

Stereotype threat—the fear of being judged on the basis of a negative stereotype—can trigger anxiety that interferes with performance. Mounting evidence confirms that stereotype threat undermines test taking in children who are aware of ethnic stereotypes about their group. Josefina is likely to be aware of ethnic stereotypes, such as "Hispanics aren't good at academic work." Although she does well on homework assignments (which are "not a test"), when Josefina is told that she is being tested, she performs poorly, in line with this negative ethnic stereotype.

REFLECT: Do you think that intelligence tests are culturally biased? What evidence and observations influenced your conclusions? (pp. 342–343)

This is an open-ended question with no right or wrong answer.

REVIEW: Summarize the benefits of early intervention programs, such as Head Start, for poverty-stricken children. What program characteristics might contribute to and strengthen those benefits? (pp. 347–350)

More than two decades of research have established the long-term benefits of early intervention. The most extensive of these studies, which combined data from seven interventions implemented by universities or research foundations, found that poverty-stricken children who attended programs scored higher in IQ and achievement than controls during the first two to three years of elementary school. After that, differences declined, but children and adolescents who had received intervention remained ahead on real-life measures of school adjustment. They were less likely to be placed in special education or retained in grade, and a greater number graduated from high school. They also showed lasting benefits in attitudes and motivation and were more likely to give achievement-related reasons for being proud of themselves.

The extent of these gains is related to program characteristics and other aspects of the environment. For example, when Head Start children typically enter inferior public schools in poverty-stricken neighborhoods, this may undermine the benefits of preschool education. But when high-quality intervention starts in infancy and extends through early childhood, children display cognitive and academic achievement advantages throughout childhood and adolescence. And even when intervention is delayed until age 3 or 4, improved school adjustment is seen. The comprehensiveness of Head Start, along with its emphasis on parent involvement, may be responsible. The more involved parents are in Head Start, the better their child-rearing practices and the more stimulating their home learning environments. These factors are positively related to preschoolers' independence, task persistence, and academic, language, and social skills.

CONNECT: Using what you learned about brain development in Chapter 5 (see pages 186–192), explain why intensive intervention for poverty-stricken children starting in infancy and continuing through early childhood has a greater impact on IQ than intervention starting later. (pp. 347–350)

The first two years of life are critical in terms of brain growth—a prime reason that early intervention is necessary to help disadvantaged children reach their cognitive potential. During the first two years, brain growth occurs at an astounding pace. Connections between neurons, myelination of neural fibers, development of the prefrontal cortex, and lateralization of the hemispheres of the brain are under way. By age 2, brain weight is 70 percent of its adult weight, and by age 6, it is 90 percent, as a result of gains in neural fibers and myelination.

Furthermore, infancy and early childhood are periods of high brain *plasticity*, in which many areas of the cerebral cortex are not yet committed to specific functions. A highly plastic cortex has a high capacity for learning and is especially responsive to stimulation. Research on children adopted from Romanian orphanages reveals that early, extreme sensory deprivation results in brain damage and impairments in all domains of psychological development.

This evidence supports the view that infancy and early childhood constitute a sensitive period in brain development. This may help to explain why intensive intervention for poverty-stricken children, starting in infancy and continuing through the preschool years, has an especially profound impact on IQ.

CONNECT: How is high-stakes testing likely to affect encouragement of creativity in classrooms? Explain. (p. 355)

To promote children's creativity, classrooms should offer opportunities for divergent thinking, even when some ideas have little value; encourage sensible risk taking through assignments and activities that include choices and have more than one right answer; encourage tolerance of ambiguity; and model creative thinking by demonstrating that creative insights often result from integrating material across fields, not from memorizing information. Unfortunately, high-stakes testing emphasizes convergent thinking aimed at coming up with a single correct answer. In classrooms where the focus is on preparation for such tests, knowledge acquisition is likely to take precedence over using knowledge in original ways. As a result, children's thinking tends to become entrenched, or limited to commonplace associations that produce correct answers.

REFLECT: Describe several childhood experiences that you believe enhanced your creativity, along with ones that might have discouraged it. In the latter instances, what would you do differently to foster children's creative potential? Use research to justify your recommendations. (pp. 354–355)

This is an open-ended question with no right or wrong answer.

SUGGESTED READINGS

Cartledge, G. Y., Gardner, R., & Ford, D. Y. (2008). *Teaching diverse learners*. Newark, NJ: Prentice Hall. A collection of chapters focusing on the educational needs of culturally and racially diverse learners, including children with special needs. Other topics include research on gifted and talented students, assessment and testing, and strategies for enhancing social and academic skills.

Colverd, S., & Hodgkin, B. (2011). *Developing emotional intelligence in the primary school*. Philadelphia, PA: Taylor & Francis. Examines the relationship between emotional intelligence and academic achievement in school-age children. The authors present leading research on emotional intelligence, teaching practices that promote social/emotional competence, and behavior management strategies for working with difficult children.

Johnson, A. W. (2009). *Objectifying measures: The dominance of high-stakes testing and the politics of schooling*. Philadelphia, PA: Temple University Press. A compelling look at the high-stakes testing movement, this book examines the effects of standardized testing on educational quality in the United States. The author also presents research on how high-stakes testing affects minority students from low-SES backgrounds.

MEDIA MATERIALS

For details on individual video segments that accompany the DVD for *Child Development,* Ninth Edition, please see the DVD Guide for *Explorations in Child Development.* The DVD and DVD Guide are available through your Pearson sales representative.

Additional DVDs that may be useful in your class are listed below. These are not available through your Pearson sales representative, but you can order them directly from the distributors. (See contact information at the end of this manual.)

Battle of the Brains: The Case for Multiple Intelligences (2007, Films Media Group/BBCW Production, 50 min.). This program questions whether IQ tests are an adequate assessment of students' knowledge. It advocates taking a different approach, involving the creation of an array of unusual challenges to assess brainpower, and it argues for the interplay of multiple intelligences. Assisted by the insights of Harvard's Howard Gardner and experts using brain scanning technology at the UC Davis MIND Institute, the program brings together a group of highly intelligent people and presents them with trials of all types. The results establish the validity of measuring not just what people know but also the important ways in which they exercise their practical, creative, emotional, and kinesthetic IQs.

Child Genius: A Longitudinal Look at Young Prodigies (2008, Films Media Group, 3-part series, 48–75 min. each). This three-part series documents the childhood experiences of several prodigiously intelligent boys and girls, revisiting them at regular stages and observing their evolving relationships and attitudes. The program focuses on the parent–child dynamic, as well as the intellectual achievements of the children.

Emotional Intelligence in the Classroom (2008, Insight Media, 31 min.). In this program, Karen Hansen compares definitions and models of emotional intelligence and offers practical techniques that educators can use to nurture emotional intelligence. The film considers adolescents' ability to deepen their emotional intelligence and highlights the role of secondary schools in promoting emotional intelligence.

Killing Creativity: Are Schools or Parents to Blame? (2007, Films Media Group/BBC–Open University co-production, 60 min.). Focusing on the study of childhood creativity, this program invites viewers to observe a group of 25 7-year-olds and their families. It asks: Why does childhood creativity frequently fade? Why does it matter? Exploring the impact of school and whether it dampens the creative impulse, the program looks at ways adults can encourage and promote imagination, curiosity, and originality.

Psychometrics I: Intelligence and Ability Assessment (2011, Insight Media, 25 min.). This program explores the history of intelligence testing from Galton and Binet to Gardner, Sternberg, and Goleman. It examines the types and functions of psychometric instruments and considers their uses in education and employment screening. The program looks at the concepts of validity, reliability, and factor analysis, and it defines general, static, and fluid intelligences.

Speaking of Creativity (2005, Insight Media, 48 min.). In this program, various actors, artists, musicians, and filmmakers discuss their experiences with the creative process.

The Einstein Effect: Savants and Creativity (2006, Films Media Group, 54 min.). Mute until the age of 9, Stephen Wiltshire learned to communicate through realistic, richly detailed drawings. Alonzo Clemens sculpts clay animal figures with great precision, even though he can barely form a sentence. Matt Savage faced extraordinary developmental problems as a child but has become a teen prodigy among jazz musicians. This program asks: What is the relationship between creativity and autistic behavior? Why does slow learning—such as what the young Albert Einstein experienced—sometimes conceal genius? This program attempts to answer these questions and highlights other aspects of brain research, revealing links between the realms of savants and prodigies.

The Search for Intelligence: Intelligence (2006, Aquarius Health Care Media, 30 min.). What is intelligence? Can the standardized exams of today actually measure it? This program investigates Sternberg's triarchic theory of intelligence, Gardner's theory of multiple intelligences, and a newer area of research—emotional intelligence. The nature–nurture influence on intelligence is explored, as well as the phenomenon of stereotype threat. This film is part of the *Inside Out* series.

What Makes a Genius? (2010, Films Media Group/BBC–Science Channel co-production, 51 min.). This program examines innovative research that might help determine what makes a person a genius, or whether such a label even makes sense. Interviewed are Dr. Manuel Casanova of the University of Louisville, who has detected differences in brain structure that may account for extreme intelligence; Dr. Justin Halberda of Johns Hopkins University, who has administered a color-coded computer test that measures latent mathematical ability in children; and Dr. Elly Nedivi of MIT, who has found a gene associated with learning. Artists and savants are also featured.

CHAPTER 9
LANGUAGE DEVELOPMENT

CHAPTER-AT-A-GLANCE

Chapter Outline	Instruction Ideas	Supplements
Components of Language p. 360	Learning Objective 9.1 Learning Activity 9.8	Test Bank Items 1–6 Please contact your Pearson publisher's representative for a wide range of video offerings available to adopters.
Theories of Language Development pp. 360–368 The Nativist Perspective • The Interactionist Perspective	Learning Objective 9.2 Learning Activities 9.1, 9.8 Ask Yourself p. 368	Test Bank Items 7–40, 126
Prelinguistic Development: Getting Ready to Talk pp. 368–373 Receptivity to Language • First Speech Sounds • Becoming a Communicator	Learning Objective 9.3 Lecture Enhancement 9.1 Learning Activities 9.2, 9.5, 9.8 Ask Yourself p. 373	Test Bank Items 41–61, 127
Phonological Development pp. 373–375 The Early Phase • Phonological Strategies • Later Phonological Development	Learning Objective 9.4 Lecture Enhancement 9.2 Learning Activity 9.8 Ask Yourself p. 375	Test Bank Items 62–65
Semantic Development pp. 376–384 The Early Phase • Later Semantic Development • Ideas About How Semantic Development Takes Place	Learning Objectives 9.5–9.6 Learning Activities 9.3–9.6, 9.8 Ask Yourself p. 384	Test Bank Items 66–89, 128–129
Grammatical Development pp. 384–390 First Word Combinations • From Simple Sentences to Complex Grammar • Development of Complex Grammatical Forms • Later Grammatical Development • Ideas About How Grammatical Development Takes Place	Learning Objectives 9.7–9.8 Lecture Enhancement 9.3 Learning Activities 9.4, 9.8 Ask Yourself p. 390	Test Bank Items 90–106, 130
Pragmatic Development pp. 390–393 Acquiring Conversational Skills • Communicating Clearly • Narratives • Sociolinguistic Understanding	Learning Objective 9.9 Lecture Enhancement 9.4 Learning Activities 9.6, 9.8 Ask Yourself p. 393	Test Bank Items 107–118, 131
Development of Metalinguistic Awareness pp. 394, 395	Learning Objective 9.10 Learning Activity 9.8	Test Bank Items 119–120
Bilingualism: Learning Two Languages in Childhood pp. 394, 396–397	Learning Objective 9.11 Learning Activities 9.7–9.8 Ask Yourself p. 397	Test Bank Items 121–125, 132

BRIEF CHAPTER SUMMARY

Language—the most awesome of universal human achievements—develops with extraordinary speed during early childhood. Children must master four components of language—phonology, semantics, grammar (which includes two main parts, syntax and morphology), and pragmatics—and combine them into a flexible communication system.

The nativist theory of language development proposes that all children have an innate language acquisition device containing a universal grammar—a built-in storehouse of rules that apply to all human languages. Interactionist theories of language development emphasize interactions between inner capacities and environmental influences.

Newborns prefer speech to other sounds and make fine-grained distinctions between human-language sounds, a skill that may support them in learning their native language. By the second half of the first year, babies have begun to analyze the internal structure of sentences and words. They are capable of a statistical analysis of sound patterns that helps them locate words in speech. Caregiver–child interaction, including infant-directed speech and joint attention, supports early language learning.

Phonological development is a complex process that depends on the child's ability to attend to sound sequences, produce sounds, and combine them into understandable words and phrases. Pronunciation improves greatly over the preschool years as the vocal tract matures and as preschoolers engage in active problem solving and use a variety of phonological strategies.

Children's language comprehension develops ahead of production. Toddlers show a steady, continuous increase in rate of word learning that persists through the preschool years, when children add as many as nine new words per day. Although children produce their first word at an average age of 12 months, complex genetic and environmental influences contribute to the age at which children produce their first word. The properties of the child's native language are influential, and 2-year-olds' spoken vocabularies vary substantially across languages. Vocabulary continues to increase rapidly during the elementary school years, as children engage in conversation with more expert speakers. They also learn to read and are exposed to a diverse and complex vocabulary. Ideas about how semantic development takes place include the role of the phonological store (a special part of working memory), word-learning strategies such as mutual exclusivity bias and shape bias, syntactic bootstrapping, and adult influences. The emergentist coalition model proposes that children expand their vocabularies using the same cognitive strategies they apply to nonlinguistic stimuli. To decipher language, children draw on a coalition of cues—perceptual, social, and linguistic—that shift in importance with age.

Between 1½ and 2½ years, children combine two words to express a variety of meanings. Some researchers believe this telegraphic speech reflects a more complete, consistent grammar in the child's mind. In the third year, three-word sentences appear, following word orders of adult speech in the child's language. Gradually, preschoolers refine and generalize grammatical forms, eventually mastering negatives, questions, and other complex constructions. By the end of the preschool years, children use most of the grammatical structures of their native language competently, but grammatical development continues into middle childhood.

Debate continues over how children's grammatical development takes place. In one view, children rely on techniques such as semantic bootstrapping, using word meanings to decipher sentence structure. Others believe children master grammar through direct observation. Adults inform children about grammar through recasts and expansions.

Besides phonology, vocabulary, and grammar, children must learn pragmatics—the rules for engaging in appropriate and effective communication. During early and middle childhood, children acquire conversational strategies, including the turnabout, shading, and an understanding of illocutionary intent. Conversations with adults about past experiences contribute to gains in children's ability to produce well-organized, detailed, expressive narratives. Children also learn speech registers—language adaptations to social expectations, as parents teach their culture's social routines, such as politeness.

Preschoolers show the beginnings of metalinguistic awareness, but major advances do not occur until middle childhood. Bilingual children are advanced in metalinguistic awareness and, like bilingual adults, may engage in code switching—using "guest" words from one language within an utterance in the other language. Research shows that children fluent in two languages are advanced in cognitive development.

LEARNING OBJECTIVES

After reading this chapter, you should be able to answer the following:

9.1 What are the four components of language? (p. 360)

9.2 Describe and evaluate major theories of language development. (pp. 360–367)

9.3 Discuss receptivity to language, development of speech sounds, and conversational skills during infancy. (pp. 368–373)

9.4 Describe the course of phonological development. (pp. 373–375)

9.5 Summarize the course of semantic development, noting individual differences. (pp. 376–381)

9.6 Discuss ideas about how semantic development takes place, including the influence of memory and strategies for word learning. (pp. 381–383)

9.7 Describe the course of grammatical development. (pp. 384–388)

9.8 Discuss ideas about how grammatical development takes place, including strategies and communicative support for mastering new structures. (pp. 388–390)

9.9 Describe the course of pragmatic development. (pp. 390–393)

9.10 Describe the development of metalinguistic awareness and its role in language-related attainments. (pp. 394, 395)

9.11 How do children become bilingual, and what are the advantages of bilingualism? (pp. 394, 396–397)

LECTURE OUTLINE

I. COMPONENTS OF LANGUAGE (p. 360)
   A. Language consists of several subsystems, which are interdependent.
   B. **Phonology** refers to the rules governing the structure and sequence of speech sounds.
   C. **Semantics** involves vocabulary—the way underlying concepts are expressed in words and word combinations.
   D. **Grammar** consists of two main parts: **syntax,** the rules by which words are arranged into sentences, and **morphology,** the use of grammatical markers that indicate number, tense, case, person, gender, active or passive voice, and other meanings.
   E. **Pragmatics**—the rules for engaging in appropriate and effective communication.

II. THEORIES OF LANGUAGE DEVELOPMENT (pp. 360–368)
   A. The Nativist Perspective (pp. 360–366)
      1. Linguist Noam Chomsky proposed a *nativist* theory that regards language as a uniquely human accomplishment, etched into the structure of the brain.
      2. Chomsky proposed that all children have a **language acquisition device (LAD)**—an innate system that permits them, once they have acquired sufficient vocabulary, to combine words into grammatically consistent, novel utterances and to understand the meaning of sentences they hear.
      3. The LAD contains a **universal grammar,** a built-in storehouse of rules that apply to all human languages, which young children use to decipher grammatical categories and relationships.
      4. The LAD ensures that language will be acquired early and swiftly.
      5. Evidence Relevant to the Nativist Perspective
         a. Research reveals that deaf children can generate an intricate natural language, even when reared in linguistically deficient environments.
         b. Can Animals Acquire Language?
            (1) Members of many species can acquire a vocabulary from several dozen to several hundred symbols.
            (2) Common chimpanzees have been taught artificial languages and American Sign Language, yet are unable to produce strings of three or more symbols that conform to a rule-based structure.
            (3) The linguistic attainments of a bonobo chimp, Kanzi, are especially impressive.
            (4) Nonetheless, the findings support Chomsky's assumption of a uniquely human capacity for an elaborate grammar.
         c. Language Areas in the Brain
            (1) Studies of communication disorders in adults with brain damage suggest that **Broca's area,** located in the left frontal lobe, supports grammatical processing and language production, while **Wernicke's area,** located in the left temporal lobe, plays a role in comprehending word meaning.
            (2) However, if the left hemisphere is injured in the first few years, other regions take over language functions.

(3) Grammatical competence may depend more on specific brain structures than the other components of language.
    d. A Sensitive Period for Language Development
       (1) Evidence for a sensitive period coinciding with brain lateralization would support the nativist position that language development has unique biological properties.
       (2) Studies of deaf adults who acquired their first language (American Sign Language) at different ages support the existence of a sensitive period.
       (3) Research confirms an age-related decline beginning around age 5 to 6 in capacity to acquire a second language with a native accent.
  6. Limitations of the Nativist Perspective
    a. Researchers have had difficulty specifying Chomsky's universal grammar, and critics doubt that one set of rules can account for all grammatical forms.
    b. The assumption that grammatical knowledge is innately determined does not fit with certain observations of language development.
    c. Chomsky's theory lacks comprehensiveness.
    d. The nativist perspective does not regard children's cognitive capacities as important.
B. The Interactionist Perspective (pp. 366–367)
  1. Recent ideas about language development emphasize *interactions* between inner capacities and environmental influences.
  2. Information-Processing Theories
    a. The most influential information-processing accounts are derived from research with *connectionist,* or *artificial neural network, models.*
    b. Connectionists assume that children make sense of their complex language environments by applying powerful, analytic cognitive capacities of a general kind, rather than capacities especially tuned to language.
    c. Other theorists blend the nativist perspective with the information-processing idea that the human brain is extraordinarily skilled at detecting patterns.
    d. Proponents of information-processing approaches point out that the regions of the brain housing language also govern other similar perceptual, motor, and cognitive abilities.
  3. Social Interactionist Theories
    a. According to the social interactionist perspective, native capacity, a strong desire to understand others and to be understood by them, and a rich language environment combine to help children discover the functions and regularities of language.
    b. As the child strives to communicate, she cues her caregivers to provide appropriate language experiences, which, in turn, help her relate the content and structure of language to its social meanings.

III. PRELINGUISTIC DEVELOPMENT: GETTING READY TO TALK (pp. 368–373)
  A. Receptivity to Language (pp. 368–369)
    1. Newborns' ability to make fine-grained distinctions among virtually all human-language sounds is a skill that may help them crack the phonological code of their native tongue.
    2. Learning Native-Language Sound Categories and Patterns
      a. As adults, we analyze the speech stream into **phonemes,** the smallest sound units that signal a change in meaning.
      b. The tendency to perceive as identical a range of sounds that belong to the same phonemic class is called **categorical speech perception.** Newborns, like adults, are capable of it.
      c. Humans, as well as other primates and chinchillas, categorize not only speech but also nonspeech sounds. This indicates that categorical perception is a property of the auditory system, and human languages take advantage of it.
      d. In the second half of the first year, infants have begun to detect the internal structure of sentences and words—information that will be vital for linking speech units with their meanings.
      e. Infants acquire a great deal of language-specific knowledge before they start to talk around 12 months of age.
    3. Adult Speech to Young Language Learners
      a. Adults in many countries speak to babies in **infant-directed speech (IDS),** which is made up of short sentences with high-pitched, exaggerated expression, clear pronunciation, distinct pauses between speech segments, clear gestures to support verbal meaning, and repetition of new words in a variety of contexts.

       b. From birth on, infants prefer IDS over other kinds of adult talk.
       c. Parents fine-tune IDS, adjusting the length and content of their utterances to fit babies' changing needs—adjustments that foster language progress in the second and third years.
   B. First Speech Sounds (p. 370)
       1. Around 2 months, babies begin to make vowel-like noises, known as **cooing.**
       2. Around 6 months, babies add consonants and begin **babbling**—repeating consonant–vowel combinations in long strings, such as "babababababa."
       3. As caregivers respond contingently to infant babbles, infants modify their babbling to include sound patterns like those in the adult's speech.
   C. Becoming a Communicator (pp. 370–373)
       1. At birth, infants are already prepared for some aspects of conversational behavior—for example, initiating interaction by making eye contact.
       2. By 3 to 4 months, infants start to gaze in the same direction adults are looking—a skill that becomes more accurate at 10 to 11 months.
       3. This **joint attention,** in which the child attends to the same object or event as the caregiver, contributes greatly to early language development.
       4. Around the first birthday, babies *point* toward objects and locations, and they grasp the communicative function of others' pointing.
       5. Infant pointing leads to two communicative gestures:
           a. In **protodeclarative** gestures, the baby points to, touches, or holds up an object while looking at others to make sure they notice.
           b. In **protoimperative** gestures, the baby gets another person to do something by reaching, pointing, and often making sounds at the same time.
       6. The earlier toddlers form word–gesture combinations, and the greater number they use, the sooner they produce two-word utterances at the end of the second year.

IV. PHONOLOGICAL DEVELOPMENT (pp. 373–375)
   A. Between 1 and 4 years, children make great progress in phonological development.
   B. The Early Phase (pp. 373–374)
       1. Children's first words are influenced, in part, by the small number of sounds they can pronounce.
       2. All languages cater to young children's phonological limitations through the use of simplified words.
       3. One-year-olds first learning to talk know how familiar words are supposed to sound, even when they mispronounce them, and toddlers are sensitive to mispronunciations of new words.
   C. Phonological Strategies (pp. 374–375)
       1. By the middle of the second year, children start trying to pronounce each individual sound within a word.
       2. Children apply systematic strategies to challenging words so that these words fit with their pronunciation capacities yet resemble adult utterances.
       3. Although individual differences exist in the precise strategies children adopt, they follow a general developmental pattern.
           a. At first, children produce *minimal words,* focusing on the stressed syllable and its consonant–vowel combination.
           b. Next, they add ending consonants, adjust vowel length, and add unstressed syllables.
           c. Finally, they produce the full word with a correct stress pattern.
   D. Later Phonological Development (p. 375)
       1. Phonological development is largely complete by age 5, but a few syllable stress patterns signaling subtle differences in meaning are not acquired until middle childhood or adolescence.
       2. These late attainments are probably affected by the semantic complexity of the words.

V. SEMANTIC DEVELOPMENT (pp. 376–384)
   A. Word comprehension begins in the middle of the first year, and, on average, children say their first word around 12 months.
   B. By age 6, they understand the meaning of about 10,000 words.
   C. Children's **comprehension,** the language they understand, develops ahead of **production,** the language they use.
       1. This discrepancy is related to the development of two types of memory: *recognition* and *recall*.

2. Comprehension requires only *recognition* of a word's meaning, while production requires children to *recall* both the word and the concept for which it stands.
D. The Early Phase (pp. 376–380)
1. Children's first words build on the sensorimotor foundations Piaget described and on categories infants have formed.
2. Investigations concur that earliest words usually include people, objects that move, foods, familiar actions, and social terms.
3. Young toddlers add to their vocabularies slowly, at a pace of one to three words per week.
4. Most children show a steady, continuous increase in rate of word learning that persists through the preschool years.
5. Research shows that children can connect a new word with an underlying concept after only a brief encounter, a process called **fast-mapping.** As toddlers form networks of related concepts and words, these help them fast-map new words.
6. Individual and Cultural Differences
   a. Children produce their first word at an average age of 12 months, with a range from 8 to 18 months, depending on a complex blend of genetic and environmental influences.
   b. The properties of the child's native language are influential, and 2-year-olds' spoken vocabularies vary substantially across languages.
   c. For example, the early vocabularies of children acquiring Mandarin Chinese are relatively large because the language has many short words with easy-to-pronounce initial consonants.
   d. Children have unique styles of early language learning.
      (1) Most toddlers use a **referential style,** with vocabularies consisting mainly of words that refer to objects.
      (2) Some toddlers use an **expressive style,** producing many more social formulas and pronouns.
      (3) Language style is linked to temperament and to the type of language parents use.
      (4) Language style is also linked to culture. Nouns are particularly common in the vocabularies of English-speaking toddlers, but Chinese, Japanese, and Korean toddlers have more words for social routines.
7. Types of Words
   a. Object, action, and state words are most common in young children's vocabularies.
   b. Object and Action Words
      (1) Young language learners in many cultures have more object than action words in their beginning vocabularies.
      (2) Nevertheless, young children learning Chinese, Japanese, and Korean—languages in which nouns are often omitted from adults' sentences, while verbs are stressed—acquire verbs more readily than their English-speaking agemates.
   c. State Words
      (1) Between 2 and 2½ years, children's use of *state* (modifier) words expands to include labels for attributes of objects.
      (2) General distinctions appear before more specific ones.
8. Underextensions and Overextensions
   a. When young children first learn words, they may apply them too narrowly, an error called **underextension.**
   b. A more common error between 1 and 2½ years is **overextension,** applying a word to a broader collection of objects and events than is appropriate.
9. Word Coinages and Metaphors
   a. Children as young as age 2 coin new words based on ones they already know.
   b. Preschoolers also extend language meanings through metaphors, which permit them to communicate in vivid and memorable ways.
E. Later Semantic Development (pp. 380–381)
1. During the elementary school years, vocabulary increases fourfold.
   a. Older school-age children enlarge their vocabularies by fast-mapping, by analyzing the structure of complex words, and by figuring out word meanings from context.
   b. Reading contributes enormously to vocabulary growth.
   c. By the end of elementary school, synonyms and explanations of categorical relationships appear.
2. As they transition to adolescence, young people add a variety of abstract words to their vocabularies and also master sarcasm and irony.

F. Ideas About How Semantic Development Takes Place (pp. 381–383)
  1. Adult feedback facilitates semantic development, but the child's cognitive processing also plays a major role.
  2. The Influence of Memory
     a. Young children's fast-mapping is supported by a special part of working memory, a **phonological store** that permits us to retain speech-based information.
     b. By the end of the second year, toddlers can recognize familiar words on the basis of their initial sounds.
     c. This ability frees working memory for other language tasks, such as comprehending more complex strings of words.
     d. After age 5, semantic knowledge also influences the speed with which children form phonological traces, and both factors affect vocabulary growth.
  3. Strategies for Word Learning
     a. Young children figure out the meanings of words by contrasting them with words they already know and assigning the new label to a gap in their vocabulary.
     b. Early in vocabulary growth, children may adopt a **mutual exclusivity bias**—the assumption that words refer to entirely separate (nonoverlapping) categories.
     c. Once toddlers have acquired about 75 words, a **shape bias** is clearly evident: Previous learning of nouns based on shape heightens attention to the shape properties of additional objects.
     d. According to a hypothesis called **syntactic bootstrapping,** preschoolers discover many word meanings by observing how words are used in *syntax,* or the structure of sentences.
  4. Explaining Vocabulary Development
     a. Some theorists believe children are innately biased to induce word meanings using principles such as mutual exclusivity and syntactic bootstrapping.
     b. Critics observe that a small set of built-in, fixed principles cannot account for the varied, flexible manner in which children master vocabulary.
     c. An alternative perspective, the **emergentist coalition model,** proposes that word-learning strategies *emerge* out of children's efforts to decipher language. Children draw on a *coalition* of cues—perceptual, social, and linguistic—that shift in importance with age.

VI. GRAMMATICAL DEVELOPMENT (pp. 384–390)
  A. First Word Combinations (pp. 384–385)
    1. Between 1½ and 2½ years, children transition from word–gesture combinations to combining words into two-word utterances called **telegraphic speech,** which focuses on high-content words, omitting smaller, less important ones.
    2. Because children the world over use two-word utterances, one view is that a more complete, and perhaps adultlike, grammar lies behind these two-word sentences.
    3. Other researchers argue that two-word sentences are largely made up of simple formulas and that young children do not yet grasp subject–verb and verb–object relations.
  B. From Simple Sentences to Complex Grammar (pp. 385–386)
    1. In the third year, three-word sentences appear, following the word order of the adult speech to which the child is exposed.
    2. Between 2½ and 3 years, children create sentences in which adjectives, articles, nouns, verbs, and prepositional phrases start to conform to an adult structure.
    3. Gradual Mastery of Grammatical Structures
       a. Studies of children acquiring diverse languages reveal that their first use of grammatical rules is piecemeal—applied to only one or a few verbs, not across the board.
       b. Only gradually do preschoolers refine and generalize their early grammatical forms.
    4. Development of Grammatical Morphemes
       a. Once children form three-word sentences, they add **grammatical morphemes**—small markers that change the meaning of sentences.
       b. English-speaking 2- and 3-year-olds acquire these morphemes in a regular sequence.
       c. Once children apply a regular morphological rule, they extend it to words that are exceptions, a type of error called **overregularization.**
  C. Development of Complex Grammatical Forms (pp. 387–388)
    1. Negatives

a. Three types of negation appear in the following order in 2½- to 3-year-olds learning a wide variety of languages: (1) *nonexistence* (remarking on the absence of something); (2) *rejection* (expressing opposition to something); and (3) *denial* (denying the truthfulness of something).
b. These early constructions probably result from imitating parental speech.
2. Questions
   a. Questions first appear during the early preschool years and develop in an orderly sequence.
   b. English-speaking children, as well as those who speak many other languages, can use rising intonation to convert an utterance into a yes/no question.
   c. Children seem to produce accurate questions piecemeal and gradually.
3. Other Complex Constructions
   a. Between ages 3½ and 6, children produce more complex constructions, including sentences joined by connectives, embedded sentences, and passive sentences.
   b. By the end of the preschool years, children use most of the grammatical structures of their native language competently.
D. Later Grammatical Development (p. 388)
   1. During the school years, children's mastery of complex constructions improves.
   2. School-age children apply the passive voice to a wider range of nouns and verbs, and they develop advanced understanding of infinitive phrases.
E. Ideas About How Grammatical Development Takes Place (pp. 388–390)
   1. Strategies for Acquiring Grammar
      a. Evidence that grammatical development is an extended, learned process has raised questions about Chomsky's nativist account, and debate continues over just how children master grammar.
      b. In one view, children use **semantic bootstrapping,** relying on other properties of language to detect basic grammatical regularities—for example, using word meanings to figure out sentence structure.
      c. Some theorists believe that children master grammar through direct observation of the structure of language.
      d. Other theorists agree with the essence of Chomsky's position.
         (1) One idea accepts semantic bootstrapping but proposes that the grammatical categories into which children group word meanings are innate.
         (2) Another theory holds that children start not with innate knowledge but with a special *language-making capacity*.
   2. Communicative Support for Grammatical Development
      a. Parents often correct grammatical errors *indirectly,* by reformulating the child's erroneous expressions, using two techniques:
         (1) **Recasts** restructure inaccurate speech into correct form.
         (2) **Expansions** elaborate on children's speech, increasing its complexity.
      b. Other grammatical prompts ask children to clarify what they mean so interaction can continue.
      c. The impact of such feedback has been challenged because the techniques are not used in all cultures.

VII. PRAGMATIC DEVELOPMENT (pp. 390–393)
A. Acquiring Conversational Skills (pp. 390–391)
   1. Young children in conversation are able to make eye contact, respond appropriately to their partner's remarks, and take turns.
   2. In early childhood, children add more conversational strategies.
      a. In the **turnabout,** the speaker not only comments on what has just been said but also adds a request to get the partner to respond again.
      b. Between ages 5 and 9, more advanced conversational strategies appear, including **shading,** in which a speaker initiates a change of topic gradually by modifying the focus of discussion.
      c. By age 3, children have some understanding of **illocutionary intent**—what a speaker means to say, even if the form of the utterance is not perfectly consistent with it.
   3. Adults' patient, sensitive interactions with young children encourage and sustain advanced conversational ability, and the presence of a sibling also enhances those skills.
B. Communicating Clearly (pp. 391–392)
   1. To communicate effectively, we must master **referential communication skills**—the ability to produce clear verbal messages and to recognize when messages we receive are unclear.

2. Young children's referential communication is less mature in highly demanding situations in which they cannot see their listeners' reactions or rely on typical conversational aids, such as gestures and objects to talk about.
3. Around age 3, preschoolers begin asking others to clarify ambiguous messages.
C. Narratives (pp. 392–393)
1. Conversations with adults about past experiences contribute to dramatic gains in children's ability to produce well-organized, detailed, expressive narratives.
    a. Four-year-olds typically produce *leapfrog narratives,* brief renditions that jump from one event to another in a disorganized fashion.
    b. Between 4½ and 5 years, children start to produce *chronological narratives.*
    c. Around age 6, chronological narratives extend into *classic narratives,* in which children add a resolution.
2. Preschoolers' narratives are restricted in part by their limited working memories; also, young children often presume more shared knowledge than their listener has.
3. During middle childhood, orienting information, detailed descriptions, connectives, and evaluative comments rise dramatically.
4. Make-believe play and narrative competence support each other.
5. Children's narrative forms vary widely across cultures.
    a. African-American children often use a *topic-associating style,* blending several anecdotes and producing longer, more complex narratives than those of American white children.
    b. Japanese children also connect events with a common theme, using a structure that resembles the culturally valued poetic form *haiku.*
D. Sociolinguistic Understanding (p. 393)
1. Even preschool children are sensitive to language adaptations to social expectations, known as **speech registers.**
2. The importance of register adjustments is evident in how often parents teach their culture's social routines, such as politeness.
3. Adolescence brings dramatic gains in capacity to adapt language style to social context.

VIII. DEVELOPMENT OF METALINGUISTIC AWARENESS (pp. 394, 395)
A. Researchers are especially interested in **metalinguistic awareness**—the ability to think about language as a system.
B. Early metalinguistic understandings are good predictors of vocabulary and grammatical development, but full flowering of metalinguistic skills does not occur until middle childhood, as cognition advances and teachers point out features of language in reading and writing activities.
1. Between ages 4 and 8, children make great strides in *phonological awareness,* becoming able to identify all the phonemes in a word.
2. School-age children also make strides in morphological awareness.
C. Bilingual children are advanced in metalinguistic awareness, as well as other cognitive skills.

IX. BILINGUALISM: LEARNING TWO LANGUAGES IN CHILDHOOD (pp. 394, 396–397)
A. Many children grow up *bilingual,* learning two or more languages.
B. Children can become bilingual by acquiring both languages at the same time in early childhood or by learning a second language after mastering the first.
C. Children of bilingual parents who teach them both languages in infancy and early childhood show no special problems with language development but separate the language systems from the start.
1. Preschoolers acquire normal native ability in the language of their surrounding community and good-to-native ability in the second language, depending on exposure.
2. When school-age children acquire a second language, they generally take five to seven years to attain speaking and writing skills on par with those of native-speaking agemates.
D. Bilingual children and adults sometimes engage in **code switching,** producing an utterance in one language that contains one or more "guest" words from the other.
E. Compared to their monolingual agemates, bilingual children have somewhat smaller vocabularies in each language. But the difference seems largely due to opportunity to acquire certain words.
F. Research shows that children who become fluent in two languages are advanced in cognitive development. They are also advanced in certain aspects of metalinguistic awareness.
G. The advantages of bilingualism provide strong justification for bilingual education programs in schools.

LECTURE ENHANCEMENTS

LECTURE ENHANCEMENT 9.1
Temperament, Joint Attention, and Early Language Development (pp. 371–372)

Time: 10–15 minutes

Objective: To examine the relationship among temperament, joint attention, and early language development.

To examine the relationship among temperament, joint attention, and early language development, Salley and Dixon (2008) recruited 51 21-month-old toddlers and collected the following information:

(1) To assess children's temperament, parents completed the Early Childhood Behavior Questionnaire (ECBQ). The ECBQ measures a diverse range of temperamental traits, including attention, inhibitory control, intensity of mood, activity level, shyness, sociability, discomfort, fear, motor activity, frustration, and soothability.

(2) To measure children's language development, parents completed the MacArthur–Bates Communicative-Developmental Inventory (MBCDI). The MBCDI presents a series of word lists that are organized into categories, such as nouns, verbs, and pronouns. Using the word lists, parents are asked to identify the words that their child produces.

(3) To measure parent–child joint attention, trained examiners completed the Early Social Communication Scales (ESCS) as children and their mothers participated in two laboratory tasks. The researchers were primarily interested in two categories of joint attention: responding to joint attention (RJA) and initiating joint attention (IJA). RJA was coded when a child followed the direction of his or her mother's eye gaze, head turn, or pointing. IJA was coded when a child pointed to or looked at an object while alternating his or her gaze between the object and the mother. In the first task, children sat on their mother's lap while a female experimenter presented a large, brightly colored picture book. If a child did not spontaneously point out pictures in the book after 20 seconds, the experimenter said the child's name and began pointing out pictures. In the second task, children were shown a large windup toy that ran across a table that was outside of their reach. The experimenter then put the toy in a sealed plastic container, gave the container to the child, and left the room. The experimenter's absence gave children an opportunity to engage in IJA with their mothers.

Consistent with previous studies, temperament was a strong predictor of language development. Children who were identified as having an easy temperament (that is, able to maintain and shift attention, positive mood, sociable, easy to soothe) scored higher on the MBCDI than children who were identified as having a difficult temperament. Fear, frustration, sadness, and discomfort were especially predictive of slow language development. Similarly, children who scored high in negative affect engaged in slightly lower levels of joint attention—both RJA and IJA—than children who scored low in negative affect. According to Salley and Dixon, although temperament was a stronger predictor of language development than joint attention, joint attention continues to be a vital feature of early communication skills.

Ask students to look ahead to Chapter 10 and review research on the goodness-of-fit model. Using research on temperament and strategies for supporting early language development in this chapter, how can parents facilitate toddlers' emotional well-being and language skills at the same time?

Salley, B. J., & Dixon, W. E. (2008). Temperamental and joint attentional predictors of language development. *Merrill-Palmer Quarterly, 53,* 131–154.

LECTURE ENHANCEMENT 9.2
Cross-Cultural Similarities and Differences in First Words (pp. 373–374)

Time: 10–15 minutes

Objective: To examine cultural similarities and differences in early vocabulary development.

To examine cultural similarities and differences in early vocabulary development, Tardif and colleagues (2008) recruited 970 infants between 8 and 16 months of age. The participants were from families that spoke one of three languages: American English, Mandarin Chinese, or Cantonese Chinese. To be eligible for participation, all babies had to be able to produce 1 to 10 words. Parents completed the MacArthur–Bates Communicative Development Inventory, which contains approximately 400 words that are divided into 20 semantic categories, such as animals, vehicles, food and drink, sounds, common nouns, people, household items, and action words. Parents were instructed to indicate which words their baby had spoken.

Results indicated that across all three languages, the majority of first words fell within the people (e.g., "daddy," "mommy") and sounds (e.g., "Uh oh") categories. In addition, common nouns tended to be animals or manipulative objects that children encountered in their homes. However, there were some differences between the groups, particularly when vocabulary size was taken into account. By the time children had a vocabulary size of 7 to 10 words, most produced at least one "people term." But Mandarin- and Cantonese-speaking children produced more "people terms" than English-speaking children—for example, referring to siblings, grandparents, uncles and aunts, and other family members. According to Tardif and colleagues, socialization practices common among Chinese families may explain this finding. Specifically, in Chinese culture, barely verbal children are expected to address others (even nonrelatives) using kinship terms. In contrast, American children often greet others with "hi" or a proper name. The Chinese language also includes many more kinship terms than the English language.

When looking at children's first 3 words, Mandarin- and Cantonese-speaking children were 20 times less likely to produce common nouns than English-speaking children. Instead, Chinese speakers were more likely to produce people terms or verbs. This difference may reflect Chinese parents' tendency to emphasize actions over common object terms. Taken together, these findings indicate that some cross-cultural similarities exist in early word learning. In all three groups, people and sounds were among the first 10 words. However, experience—particularly parental input—also plays an important role in vocabulary development.

Tardif, T., Fletcher, P., Liang, W., Zhang, Z., Kaciroti, N., & Marchman, V. A. (2008). Baby's first 10 words. *Developmental Psychology, 44,* 929–938.

LECTURE ENHANCEMENT 9.3
More on Early Grammatical Development (pp. 384–390)

Time: 5–10 minutes

Objective: To extend existing research on early grammatical development.

To extend existing research on early grammatical development, Bannard and Matthews (2009) recruited 38 2- and 3-year-old children and their parents. Participants were brought to a laboratory room equipped with a computer for testing. With the child seated on his or her parent's lap in front of the computer, a researcher showed the child a picture of a tree with stars on the branches. The goal was for the child to earn stickers to cover each star on the tree. To earn a sticker, the child had to listen to a four-word sentence presented by the computer and then repeat the sentence. Sentences included both frequently appearing chunks of words and less frequently appearing chunks of words. For example:

Frequently appearing: Sit in your chair.   Less frequent: Sit in your truck.
Frequently appearing: Up in the air.   Less frequent: Up in the bath.

Each child was presented with 32 sentences. Participants' responses were coded for accuracy and duration (how long it took the child to repeat the sentence). The researchers were interested in whether or not children produced frequently appearing chunks of words with greater speed and accuracy than less frequently appearing chunks of words.

Results indicated that participants were significantly more likely to produce frequent sentences correctly than infrequent sentences. In addition, compared to 2-year-olds, 3-year-olds were much faster at repeating the first three words of a sentence if the fourth word represented a familiar chunk. For example, they were quicker to repeat, "Sit in your" when the following word was *chair* rather than *truck*. Thus, age and previous experience (or knowledge) have a significant impact on the accuracy and rate in which young children produce words and sentences. Moreover, it appears that children store familiar utterances as wholes, and they use this information in the course of grammatical development.

Bannard, C., & Matthews, D. (2009). Stored word sequences in language learning: The effect of familiarity on children's repetition of four-word combinations. *Psychological Science, 19,* 241–248.

LECTURE ENHANCEMENT 9.4
The Effects of Context on Early Conversational Skills (pp. 390–393)

Time: 10–15 minutes

Objective: To examine the effects of context on early conversational skills.

To extend existing research on the effects of context on young children's conversational skills, Hoff (2010) conducted the following two studies:

(1) In the first study, 20 children between the ages of 1 year 5 months and 2 years 2 months were recruited. Participants and their mothers were videotaped at home as they interacted during a mealtime (breakfast or lunch), toy play, and book reading. A researcher provided books and toys for the home observations. Following each observation, researchers coded children's speech using the Systematic Analysis of Language Transcripts (SALT). The researchers were interested in verbal output (total number of utterances produced), vocabulary use (total number of word types used), discourse cohesion (percentage of child utterances that were topic-continuing replies to maternal speech), and grammatical complexity (mean length of utterances).

Findings indicated that total number of utterances produced and grammatical complexity did not differ according to context. However, vocabulary use and discourse cohesion was significantly greater during mother–child book reading than during mealtime or toy play. That is, children produced a greater variety of words and answered more questions during book reading than during the other dyadic activities.

(2) In the second study, 16 children between the ages of 1 year 9 months and 3 years were recruited. All of the children had at least two siblings. Participants were recorded at home during joint toy play with three different family members—a sibling between 4 and 5 years of age, a sibling between 7 and 8 years of age, and their mothers. Older siblings and mothers were instructed to play with the participants using toys provided by the researcher. Each family member played with the child for a total of 20 minutes on two separate days. As with the first study, researchers coded children's speech using the SALT.

Findings indicated that children used a richer vocabulary and were more likely to answer questions when playing with their mothers rather than their older siblings. They were also more likely to reply to questions posed by their 7- to 8-year-old siblings than their 4- to 5-year-old siblings. It is important to note that mothers provided more opportunities for children to answer questions than siblings, which likely explains greater discourse cohesion during mother–child than sibling–child interactions. Total number of utterances and grammatical complexity did not differ significantly based on the child's play partner.

Taken together, these studies highlight the importance of context—specifically, conversational setting and developmental level of the conversational partner—for various aspects of young children's language use. Compared with other mother–child activities, book reading seems to promote richer conversation. According to Hoff, book reading introduces a wider range of topics than meal- or playtime, which prompts children to use a larger vocabulary. In addition, when playing with toys, mother–child conversations are richer in vocabulary and discourse cohesion than sibling conversations. Both studies suggest that context has little impact on total utterances or grammatical complexity.

Have students return to Chapter 6 and review Vygotsky's sociocultural theory. How might scaffolding and the zone of proximal development help explain how young children acquire conversation skills?

Hoff, E. (2010). Context effects on young children's language use: The influence of conversational setting and partner. *First Language, 30,* 461–472.

LEARNING ACTIVITIES

LEARNING ACTIVITY 9.1
True or False: Theories of Language Development (pp. 360–367)

Present the following exercise to students as a quiz or in-class activity.

Directions: Read each of the following statements and indicate whether it is *True* (T) or *False* (F).

Statements:
_____ 1. Because reinforcement and imitation contribute to early language development, most of today's researchers advocate the behaviorist perspective.
_____ 2. Noam Chomsky was the first individual to convince the scientific community that children assume much responsibility for their own language learning.
_____ 3. Like the behaviorist view, the nativist perspective regards deliberate training by parents as unnecessary for language development.
_____ 4. With extensive training, many animals can acquire language skills similar to those of a preschool-age child.
_____ 5. Contrary to long-held belief, Broca's and Wernicke's areas are not solely or even mainly responsible for specific language functions.
_____ 6. Left-hemispheric localization is necessary for effective language processing.
_____ 7. Research shows that the typical right-hemispheric localization of ASL functions, which require visual–spatial processing of hand, arm, and facial movements, is greatly reduced in individuals who learned ASL after puberty.
_____ 8. Connectionists assume that children make sense of their complex language environments by applying powerful analytic cognitive capacities of a general kind rather than capacities especially tuned to language.
_____ 9. All social interactionist theorists agree that children make sense of their complex language environments by applying general cognitive capacities.
_____ 10. During the preschool years, children with Williams syndrome have larger vocabularies and produce grammatically more complex sentences than children with Down syndrome.

Answers:

1.	F	6.	F
2.	T	7.	T
3.	F	8.	T
4.	F	9.	F
5.	T	10.	T

LEARNING ACTIVITY 9.2
Matching: Prelinguistic Development: Getting Ready to Talk (pp. 368–373)

Present the following exercise as an in-class activity or quiz.

Directions: Match each of the following terms with its correct description.

Terms:
_____ 1. Phonemes
_____ 2. Categorical speech perception
_____ 3. Infant-directed speech
_____ 4. Cooing
_____ 5. Babbling
_____ 6. Joint attention
_____ 7. Protodeclarative
_____ 8. Protoimperative

Descriptions:

A. A form of communication made up of short sentences with high-pitched, exaggerated expression, clear pronunciation, distinct pauses between speech segments, clear gestures to support verbal meaning, and repetition of new words in a variety of contexts.
B. The baby points to, touches, or holds up an object while looking at others to make sure they notice.
C. The child attends to the same object or event as the caregiver.
D. The smallest sound units that signal a change in meaning, such as the difference between the consonant sounds in "pa" and "ba."
E. Around 2 months, babies begin to make vowel-like noises.
F. The tendency to perceive as identical a range of sounds that belong to the same phonemic class.
G. Around 6 months, babies repeat consonant–vowel combinations, often in long strings.
H. The baby gets another person to do something by reaching, pointing, and often making sounds at the same time.

Answers:

1. D   5. G
2. F   6. C
3. A   7. B
4. E   8. H

LEARNING ACTIVITY 9.3
Comprehension versus Production (p. 376)

At all ages, language comprehension develops ahead of language production. To illustrate this concept, have students discuss their own learning experiences. For example, when acquiring a second language, students comprehend words, phrases, and conversations with greater ease and accuracy than when asked to produce the same words, phrases, and conversations. In addition, although students may comprehend the key elements in a lecture or assigned reading, they may have difficulty reproducing these elements in a testing situation. Furthermore, as pointed out in the text, recall is more difficult than recognition. Therefore, if we rely solely on what children or students produce or recall, we may greatly underestimate what they actually know or comprehend.

LEARNING ACTIVITY 9.4
Interviewing Parents About Their Toddler's Early Vocabulary (pp. 376–380)

Ask students to interview the parent of a toddler about early vocabulary development. During the interview, parents can be asked to list the words their child produces and the contexts in which the child uses them. Students should note examples of object words, action words, and state words and of early two-word combinations. Once students have completed the activity, ask them to share their findings with the class. Use their findings to discuss individual differences in early language development.

LEARNING ACTIVITY 9.5
Supporting Language Development in Infants and Children (pp. 368–373, 378–379)

Present the following scenario to students:

> You have been asked to speak to a group of parents, child-care workers, and teachers about children's language development. What are some major milestones of language development in infancy and early childhood? How can adults support language development in infants and toddlers? How about in school-age children? Are there any cultural factors that should be considered? What strategies can adults use with deaf children? What strategies should adults avoid, and why?

LEARNING ACTIVITY 9.6
Observing Adolescent Communication Skills (pp. 380–381, 393)

Ask students to visit a location in which adolescents are likely to congregate (a mall, fast-food restaurant, arcade, high school sporting event). As they observe adolescents interacting with peers, students should note examples of vocabulary, grammar, and pragmatics. For instance, did students notice any abstract words or sarcasm being used? How about the use of slang? Did adolescents modify their language at all? (For example, if an adult approached, did they speak differently to the adult than to their peers?) Once students have completed their observation, spend some class time discussing their findings.

LEARNING ACTIVITY 9.7
Conducting an Interview on Attitudes Toward Bilingual Education (pp. 394–397)

Have students interview at least two people (friends, parents, relatives) regarding their attitudes toward bilingual education, using the following questions: Do you believe bilingual education should be offered in public schools? Why or why not? Should schools use an immersion approach to teaching a country's dominant language to immigrant children, or should schools teach both the child's native tongue and the new national language? Explain. Do you speak more than one language? If so, how did you acquire your second language, and how fluent are you? Students are free to think of additional questions they would like to ask. Following the interview, ask students to compare the answers with research reported in the text. Did their interviewees provide answers that resemble contemporary attitudes toward bilingual education? Explain.

LEARNING ACTIVITY 9.8
Examining Genetic and Environmental Influences on Language Development

Chapter 9 presents a wealth of research on factors contributing to children's language development. In small groups, have students list genetic and environmental influences on language development. Students should consider advances in vocabulary, grammar, and pragmatics. How does this information support the interactionist perspective on language development?

ASK YOURSELF . . .

REVIEW: Summarize outcomes of attempts to teach language to animals. Are results consistent with the nativist assumption that human children are uniquely endowed with an LAD? Explain. (p. 361)

To determine whether the ability to master a grammatically complex language system is unique to humans, many attempts have been made to teach language to animals, including dolphins, parrots, gorillas, orangutans, and chimpanzees. With extensive training, members of each of these species can acquire a vocabulary ranging from several dozen to several hundred symbols and can produce and respond to short, novel sentences, although they do so less consistently than a preschool child.

Chimpanzees are closest to humans in the evolutionary hierarchy. Common chimps, the species studied most often, have been taught artificial languages (in which a computer keyboard generates visual symbols) and American Sign Language. Yet even after years of training, common chimps are unable to produce strings of three or more symbols that conform to a rule-based structure.

Bonobo chimps are more intelligent and social than common chimps. The linguistic attainments of a bonobo named Kanzi are especially impressive. While young, Kanzi picked up his mother's artificial language by observing trainers interact with her. Through listening to his caregivers' fluent speech, Kanzi acquired remarkable comprehension of English, including the ability to discriminate hundreds of English words and to act out unusual sentences he had not heard before. But Kanzi rarely combined words, preferring to join a word to a gesture. And his comprehension of grammar does not exceed that of a human 2-year-old, who is not far along in grammatical development. Overall, these findings support the assumption of a uniquely human capacity for an elaborate grammar.

REVIEW: How do the two types of interactionist theories of language development differ from nativist views and from each other? (pp. 365, 366–367)

One type of interactionist theory applies the information-processing perspective to language development on the basis of research with connectionist, or artificial neural network, models. Connectionist researchers design computer systems to simulate the multilayered networks of neural connections in the brain, program them with basic learning procedures, then expose the artificial network to various types of language input and provide feedback about the accuracy of its responses.

Designers of artificial neural networks assume that children make sense of their complex language environments by applying powerful, analytic cognitive capacities of a general kind rather than capacities especially tuned to language.

In contrast, according to the social interactionist perspective, native capacity, a strong desire to understand others and be understood by them, and a rich language environment combine to help children discover the functions and regularities of language. The social interactionists' central premise is that children's social competencies and language experiences greatly affect language development.

CONNECT: Cite research in this chapter and in Chapter 5 indicating that with age, areas of the cortex become increasingly specialized for language. Relate these findings to the concept of brain plasticity. (pp. 362–364)

Humans have evolved specialized regions in the brain that support language skills. As mentioned in Chapter 5, for most individuals, language is housed largely in the left hemisphere of the cerebral cortex. Rather than being fully formed at birth, dedicated language areas in the brain develop over time as children acquire language. In addition, at birth, the brain is not yet fully lateralized; it is highly plastic. Although the left hemisphere is biased for language processing, if it is injured in the first few years, other regions take over language functions, and most such children eventually attain normal language competence. Thus, left-hemispheric localization is not necessary for effective language processing. Indeed, as noted in Chapter 5, deaf adults who as children learned sign language depend more on the right hemisphere than hearing individuals do. Additional research reveals that many parts of the brain participate in language activities to differing degrees, depending on the language skill and the individual's mastery of that skill.

APPLY: Describe evidence for the existence of a sensitive period for language learning. What are the practical implications of these findings for teaching children a second language? (pp. 364–365)

To investigate whether acquiring a second language is harder after a sensitive period has passed, researchers in one study examined U.S. census data, selecting immigrants from Spanish- and Chinese-speaking countries who had resided in the United States for at least 10 years. The census form had asked the immigrants to rate how competently they spoke English, from "not at all" to "very well"—self-reports that correlate strongly with objective language measures. As age of immigration increased from infancy and early childhood into early adulthood, English proficiency declined, regardless of respondents' level of education. Other research confirms an age-related decline beginning around age 5 to 6 in capacity to acquire a second language with a native accent. Furthermore, ERP and fMRI measures of brain activity indicate that second-language processing is less lateralized, and also overlaps less with brain areas devoted to first-language processing, in older than in younger learners. But second-language competence does not drop sharply at a certain age. Rather, a continuous, age-related decrease occurs. The more "committed" the brain is to native-language patterns, the better children's mastery of their native language and the less effectively they acquire foreign languages. Although the sensitive period boundary for second-language acquisition remains unclear, these results suggest that the earlier second-language instruction begins, the better the outcome.

REVIEW: Cite findings indicating that both infant capacities and caregiver communication contribute to prelinguistic development. (pp. 368–371)

From the very beginning, infants are prepared to acquire language. Newborns are capable of categorical speech perception—the tendency to perceive as identical a range of sounds that belong to the same phonemic class—but are sensitive to a much wider range of speech categories than exists in their own language. As infants listen actively to the talk of people around them, they focus on meaningful sound variations. Between 6 and 8 months, they start to organize speech into the phonemic categories of their own language; that is, they stop attending to sounds that will not be useful in mastering their native tongue. Visual language discrimination—by monitoring a speaker's face and lip movements—changes similarly. At 4 to 6 months, infants can distinguish their native language from an unfamiliar language merely by watching silent video clips of adult speakers in each language. In the second half of the first year, infants have begun to detect the internal structure of sentences and words. They become vigilant *statistical analyzers* of sound patterns, able to distinguish adjacent syllables that frequently occur together from those that seldom occur together.

Adults in many countries speak to infants in *infant-directed speech (IDS),* a form of communication made up of short sentences with high-pitched, exaggerated expression, clear pronunciation, distinct pauses between speech segments, clear gestures to support verbal meaning, and the repetition of new words in a variety of contexts. Parents fine-tune IDS, adjusting the length and content of their utterances to fit babies' changing needs. These adjustments enable toddlers to join in and foster language progress in the second and third years. In addition, toddlers' first words and phrases are usually ones they hear often in their caregivers' IDS.

By 3 to 4 months, infants start to gaze in the same general direction adults are looking, and around their first birthday, babies realize that a person's visual gaze signals a vital connection between the viewer and his or her surroundings. *Joint attention,* in which the child attends to the same object or event as the caregiver, who often labels it, contributes greatly to early language development, enabling babies to establish a "common ground" with the adult through which they can discern the meaning of the adult's verbal labels. Also around the first birthday, babies *point* toward an object or location while looking back toward the caregiver. Caregivers who respond sensitively and involve infants in dialogue-like exchanges encourage early language progress.

CONNECT: Explain how parents' use of infant-directed speech illustrates Vygotsky's zone of proximal development (see Chapter 6, pages 267–268). (p. 369)

Research suggests that infant-directed speech (IDS) is not a deliberate effort to teach infants to talk but, rather, arises from adults' desire to hold young children's attention and ease their task of understanding. Parents fine-tune IDS, adjusting the length and content of their utterances to fit children's changing needs. By modifying IDS in line with the baby's changing competencies, parents create a zone of proximal development for language learning. The more effectively parents modify their verbal input to suit their infants' learning needs, the better their children's language comprehension during the second year.

APPLY: Fran frequently corrects her 17-month-old son Jeremy's attempts to talk and—fearing that he won't use words—refuses to respond to his gestures. How might Fran be contributing to Jeremy's slow language progress? (pp. 371–372)

Around the first birthday, babies extend their joint attention and social interaction skills. They point toward an object or location while looking back toward the caregiver in an effort to direct the adult's attention. One-year-olds also grasp the communicative function of others' pointing, interpreting pointing to indicate the location of a hidden toy only when the adult also makes eye contact. This infant pointing leads to two communicative gestures—the *protodeclarative,* in which the baby points to, touches, or holds up an object while looking at others to make sure they notice, and the *protoimperative,* in which the baby gets another person to do something by reaching, pointing, and often making sounds at the same time. Over time, some of these gestures become explicitly symbolic. Soon toddlers integrate words with gestures, using the gesture to expand their verbal message, as in pointing to a toy while saying "give." Gradually, gestures recede, and words become dominant. Toddlers' use of preverbal gestures predicts faster vocabulary growth in the second and third years. The earlier toddlers form word–gesture combinations and the greater number they use, the sooner they produce two-word utterances at the end of the second year and the more complex their sentences at age 3½.

Thus, rather than nurturing Jeremy's language development, Fran's refusal to respond to his gestures is probably contributing to his slow language progress. Research shows that during the second year, caregiver–child interaction contributes greatly to the transition to language. Fran should take advantage of opportunities to engage in dialogue-like exchanges with Jeremy, joining in his activity, offering verbal prompts, and initiating and expanding on his vocalizations—responses that are associated with children's earlier attainment of major language milestones.

REFLECT: Find an opportunity to speak to an infant or toddler. How did your manner of speaking differ from the way you typically speak to an adult? What features of your speech are likely to promote early language development, and why? (pp. 370–373)

This is an open-ended question with no right or wrong answer.

REVIEW: Why do young toddlers often fail to pick up the fine details of a new word's sounds, even though they can perceive those sounds? (p. 374)

Toddlers are sensitive to speech sounds, including mispronunciations of new words. But when learning a new word, they often do not pick up the fine details of its sounds, which contributes to their pronunciation errors. Associating words with their referents places extra demands on toddlers' limited working memories. Intent on communicating, they focus on the word–referent pairing while sacrificing the word's sounds, which they encode imprecisely.

APPLY: As his father placed a bowl of pasta on the dinner table, 2-year-old Luke exclaimed, "So 'licious!" Explain Luke's phonological strategy. (pp. 374–375)

In attempting to pronounce the word *delicious,* Luke uses a phonological strategy typical of 2-year-olds. By the middle of the second year, children move from trying to pronounce whole syllables and words to trying to pronounce each individual sound within a word—an intermediate phase of development in which pronunciation is partly right and partly wrong. At first, children produce *minimal words,* focusing on the stressed syllable and trying to pronounce its consonant–vowel combination.

Soon, they add ending consonants, adjust vowel length, and add unstressed syllables. Luke has added one unstressed syllable (*cious*) to the stressed syllable (*li*). Eventually, he will produce the full word, "delicious," with its correct stress pattern, although he may still need to refine its sounds.

REFLECT: For one week, keep a log of words you mispronounce or do not pronounce fluently (you slow down to say them). Are they words that convey complex concepts or words with sounds that are relatively infrequent in English or in your native tongue? Research indicates that these factors, which affect children's pronunciation, also affect the pronunciation of adults. (p. 375)

This is an open-ended question with no right or wrong answer.

REVIEW: Using your knowledge of phonological and semantic development, explain why "Mama" and "Dada" are usually among children's first words. (pp. 373–375, 376)

Phonological development depends on the child's ability to attend to sound sequences, produce sounds, and combine them into understandable words and phrases. Children's first words are influenced in part by the small number of sounds they can pronounce. The easiest sound sequences start with consonants, end with vowels, and include repeated syllables, as in "Mama" and "Dada." To learn words, children also must identify which concept each label picks out in their language community—a process known as *semantic development*. Throughout the world, sounds resembling "Mama," "Dada," and "Papa" refer to parents, so it is not surprising that these are among the first words produced by children everywhere.

CONNECT: Explain how children's strategies for word learning support an interactionist perspective on language development. (pp. 380–383)

According to the interactionist perspective, language development is the product of interactions between the child's inner capacities and environmental influences. A rich social environment builds on children's natural readiness to acquire language, as children's cognitive capacities join with diverse patterns of information in the environment to guide word learning. For example, drawing on their ability to infer others' intentions and perspectives, preschoolers often rely on social cues to identify word meanings. Adults also inform children directly about word meanings—for example, by using a new adjective with several objects, which helps the child infer that the word refers to an object property. To fill in for words they have not yet learned, children as young as age 2 coin new words using ones they already know, such as "crayoner" for a child using crayons. And they extend language meanings through metaphor ("Clouds are pillows") and eventually to nonsensory comparisons ("Friends are like magnets").

Some theorists believe that children acquire vocabulary efficiently and accurately because they are innately biased to induce word meanings using certain principles, such as mutual exclusivity (the assumption that words refer to entirely separate and nonoverlapping categories) and syntactic bootstrapping, the hypothesis that preschoolers discover many word meanings by observing how words are used in the structure of sentences. But others point out that these built-in principles are not sufficient to account for the varied, flexible manner in which children draw on any useful information to master vocabulary. An alternative perspective is that word learning is governed by the same cognitive strategies that children apply to nonlinguistic stimuli. The *emergentist coalition model* proposes that children's word-learning strategies *emerge* out of their efforts to decipher language, in which they draw on a *coalition* of perceptual, social, and linguistic cues that shift in importance with age. When several kinds of information are available, children's inner capacities join with diverse patterns of information in the environment to yield the phenomenal pace of semantic development.

APPLY: Katy's first words included "see," "give," and "thank you," and her vocabulary grew slowly during the second year. What style of language learning did she display, and what factors might have contributed to it? (pp. 378–379)

Katy's first words reflect an *expressive style* of early language learning, which emphasizes social formulas and pronouns, reflecting a belief that words are for talking about people's feelings and needs. Most toddlers, in contrast, use a *referential style*, which focuses on using words to label things. Because all languages contain many more object labels than social phrases, the vocabularies of referential-style toddlers grow faster than those of children who use an expressive style. This accounts for Katy's slow vocabulary growth in the second year.

Both biological and environmental factors seem to account for a toddler's choice of language style. Expressive-style children tend to be highly sociable, and their parents more often use verbal routines ("How are you?" "It's no trouble.") that support social relationships. Culture also plays a role. Nouns are particularly common in the vocabularies of English-speaking toddlers, but Chinese, Japanese, and Korean toddlers, perhaps because of a cultural emphasis on the importance of group membership, have more words for social routines.

APPLY: At age 20 months, Nathan says "candy" when he sees buttons, pebbles, marbles, cough drops, and chocolate kisses. Are Nathan's naming errors random or systematic? Why are they an adaptive way of communicating? (p. 380)

Nathan is making a systematic error known as *overextension*—applying a word to a wider collection of objects and events than is appropriate. Toddlers' overextensions reflect their remarkable sensitivity to categorical relations. Children often overextend deliberately because they have difficulty recalling or have not acquired a suitable word. In addition, when a word is hard to pronounce, toddlers frequently substitute a related one they can say. As vocabulary and pronunciation improve, overextensions disappear.

REVIEW: To what extent do children use a consistent grammar in their early two- and three-word utterances? Explain, using research evidence. (pp. 384–385)

Researchers disagree regarding the use of a consistent grammar in children's telegraphic speech. According to one view, a more complete, and perhaps adultlike, grammar lies behind these two-word sentences. Consistent with this idea, children often use the same construction to express different propositions. For example, a child might say, "Mommy cookie" when he sees his mother eating a cookie and also when he wants her to give him a cookie. Other researchers argue that toddlers' two-word sentences do not follow a consistent, flexible grammar but are largely made up of simple formulas, such as "more + X" and "eat + X," with many different words inserted in the X position. When children entering the two-word phase were taught several noun and verb nonsense words, they easily combined the new nouns with words they knew. But they seldom produced word combinations with the new verbs, suggesting that they did not yet grasp subject–verb and verb–object relations, which are the foundation of grammar.

CONNECT: Provide several examples of how children's cognitive development influences their mastery of grammar. (pp. 384–390)

Sometime between 1½ and 2½ years, as productive vocabulary approaches 200 to 250 words, children transition from word–gesture combinations to joining two words: "Mommy shoe," "go car," "more cookie." As they begin to combine words, children are absorbed in figuring out word meanings and using their limited vocabularies in whatever way possible to get their thoughts across. In the third year, three-word sentences appear in which English-speaking children clearly follow a subject–verb–object word order. Between ages 3½ and 6, children produce more intricate constructions, beginning with connectives, such as *and*. Over time, their usage increasingly conforms to the rules of their language. By the end of the preschool years, children use most grammatical structures of their native language competently. During the school years, children's mastery of complex construction improves, as seen in use of the passive voice and in advanced understanding of infinitive phrases, such as the difference between "John is eager to please" and "John is easy to please." Appreciation of these subtle grammatical distinctions in middle childhood and adolescence is supported by an improved capacity to analyze and reflect on language and to attend to multiple linguistic and situational cues. Evidence that grammatical development is an extended, learned process, beginning with knowledge of specific instances and building toward general categories and rules, has lent support to those researchers who have concluded that grammar is a product of general cognitive development—children's tendency to search for consistencies and patterns of all sorts.

APPLY: Three-year-old Jason's mother told him that the family would take a vacation in Miami. The next morning, Jason announced, "I gotted my bags packed. When are we going to Your-ami?" How do language researchers explain Jason's errors? (pp. 386–387)

Jason's errors are an example of *overregularization*, which occurs when children extend a regular morphological rule to words that are exceptions. To change many verbs to the past tense, the ending *-ed* is added to the verb form. Thus, Jason knew that the past tense of "get" is "got," but he added the regular ending *-ed* to that form. Similarly, Jason knew that the word "my" refers to the self and that when responding to someone else's "my" statement, the speaker should change the pronoun to "your."

Children show an inconsistent pattern of overregularization, more often overregularizing infrequently used than frequently used words. Because they hear frequently used irregular forms often in adult speech, they probably learn them by rote memory. For less common irregulars, children alternate between correct and overregularized forms for months or even years. In one view, as children hear more instances in others' speech, the irregular form eventually wins out. At times, however, preschoolers overregularize frequently used exceptions, saying "ated," "felled," or "feets." In these instances, perhaps their memory for the irregular morpheme fails, so they call on the *-ed* or *-s* rule, and overregularization results.

REFLECT: Do you favor a nativist, an information-processing, or a social interactionist account of grammatical development, or some combination? Use research evidence to support your position. (pp. 388–390)

This is an open-ended question with no right or wrong answer.

REVIEW: Summarize findings indicating that adult–child conversations promote preschoolers' pragmatic skills. (pp. 390–391)

Surprisingly advanced conversational abilities are present early, and adults' patient, sensitive interactions with young children encourage and sustain them. Whether observed at home or in preschool, adult–child conversation is consistently related to general measures of language progress. Dialogues with caregivers about storybooks are particularly effective. They expose children to great breadth of language knowledge, including how to communicate in a clear, coherent narrative style—a skill that undoubtedly contributes to the association between joint storybook reading and literacy development. The presence of a sibling also enhances young children's conversational skills. As they listen to conversations between a twin or older sibling and a parent, toddlers pick up important skills. And older siblings' remarks to their younger siblings, which tend to focus on regulating interaction ("OK, your turn"), probably contribute to younger siblings' skill at conversing with others.

CONNECT: What cognitive advances contribute to the development of referential communication? (pp. 391–392)

The ability to understand another's perspective greatly contributes to the development of referential communication skills. In contrast to older children, preschoolers have difficulty taking the perspective of others. However, when they are given simpler tasks or engage in face-to-face interaction with familiar people, they adjust their speech to their listener's perspective quite well. Preschoolers' referential communication is less mature in highly demanding situations—for example, telephone conversations—in which they cannot see their listener's reactions or rely on typical conversational aids, such as gestures and objects to talk about. Between ages 4 and 8, both conversing and giving directions over the phone improve greatly. Telephone talk provides an excellent example of how preschoolers' communication skills depend on the demands of the situation.

Children's ability to evaluate the adequacy of messages they receive also improves with age. Around age 3, preschoolers start to ask others to clarify ambiguous messages. At first, children recognize when a message provides a poor description of a concrete object. Only later can they tell when a message contains inconsistencies. To succeed at tasks requiring them to attend to and integrate two competing representations, children must be able to inhibit attention from being drawn to the distracting representation.

APPLY: What pragmatic skills are evident in Erin's utterances, presented in the introduction to this chapter? How did Erin's parents and brother encourage her pragmatic development? (pp. 390–393)

For a conversation to go well, participants must take turns, stay on topic, state their messages clearly, and conform to cultural rules governing how individuals are supposed to interact. At age 1 year, Erin was already able to state her message clearly when she exclaimed, "Done!" as she wiggled in her high chair. In addition, at 2½, Erin used referential communication skills when she talked about the trip to the aquarium in response to Marilyn's prompting.

By engaging in dialogues about picture books and conversing about daily activities, Oscar and Marilyn encouraged Erin's pragmatic development. The presence of her older brother also contributed to Erin's conversational skills. Toddlers closely monitor interactions between their twin or older siblings and parents, and they often try to join in. When they do, these verbal exchanges last longer, with each participant taking more turns.

REFLECT: List examples of speech registers you use in daily life. What childhood experiences might have influenced your mastery of these registers? (p. 393)

This is an open-ended question with no right or wrong answer.

REVIEW: Explain why metalinguistic awareness expands greatly in middle childhood. What might account for bilingual children's advanced metalinguistic skills? (pp. 394, 396)

The beginnings of metalinguistic awareness are present in early childhood. Around age 4, children also know that word labels are arbitrary and not part of the objects to which they refer. Nevertheless, full flowering of metalinguistic skills does not occur until middle childhood, as cognition advances and teachers point out features of language in reading and writing activities. Metalinguistic knowledge is evident in elementary school children's improved ability to define words and appreciate their multiple meanings in puns, riddles, and metaphors. Bilingual children who become proficient in two languages earlier in life and to greater proficiency develop denser neuronal connections in language areas of the left hemisphere, perhaps accounting for their advanced metalinguistic awareness, as well as their advanced performance on tests of other cognitive skills.

CONNECT: How can bilingual education promote ethnic minority children's cognitive and academic development? (pp. 394, 396–397)

Research shows that bilingualism has positive consequences for development. Children who become fluent in two languages outperform others on tests of selective attention, inhibition of irrelevant information, analytical reasoning, concept formation, and cognitive flexibility. They are also advanced in certain aspects of metalinguistic awareness, such as detection of errors in grammar, meaning, and conventions of conversation. These capacities enhance reading achievement. For ethnic minority children, providing instruction in their native tongue as well as in the majority language lets them know that their heritage is respected. It also prevents the problems of inadequate proficiency in both languages, which can result when minority children gradually lose their first language as a result of being taught the second. This circumstance leads to serious academic difficulties and is believed to contribute to high rates of school failure and dropout among low-SES Hispanic young people in the United States. Finally, in classrooms where two languages are integrated into the curriculum, minority children are more involved in learning, participate more actively in class discussions, and acquire speaking and reading skills in the second language more easily than in classrooms where teachers speak only in a language these children can barely understand.

APPLY: Reread the examples of Erin's language at the beginning of this chapter. Were Marilyn and Oscar wise to teach Erin both English and Spanish? Does Erin's mixing of the two languages indicate confusion? Justify your answers with research findings. (pp. 394, 396)

Children of bilingual parents who teach them both languages in infancy and early childhood separate the language systems from the start, distinguishing their sounds, saying their first word, and attaining other early language milestones according to a typical timetable. Preschoolers acquire normal native ability in the language of their surrounding community and good-to-native ability in the second language, depending on their exposure to it. A large body of research now shows that children who become fluent in two languages at an early age are advanced in cognitive development, outperforming others on tests of selective attention, inhibition of irrelevant information, analytical reasoning, concept formation, and cognitive flexibility.

Bilingual children, like bilingual adults, sometimes engage in *code switching*—producing an utterance in one language that contains one or more "guest" words from the other, as Erin sometimes does. But from the start, these children separate the language systems, distinguishing their sounds, mastering equivalent words in each, and attaining language milestones according to a typical timetable. Their metalinguistic skills are particularly well-developed. Given these findings, Marilyn and Oscar were wise to teach Erin both English and Spanish.

REFLECT: Did you acquire a second language at home or study one in school? If so, when did you begin, and how proficient are you in the second language? Considering research on bilingualism, what changes would you make in your second-language learning, and why? (pp. 394–397)

This is an open-ended question with no right or wrong answer.

SUGGESTED READINGS

Columbo, J., McCardle, P., & Freund, L. (Eds.). (2008). *Infant pathways to language*. New York: Psychology Press. Presents the leading research on early language development, including contemporary theories, genetic and environmental contributions, the importance of gestures, language disorders, and intervention strategies for young children with language delays.

Enfield, N. J. (2009). *The anatomy of meaning: Speech, gesture, and composite utterances*. New York: Cambridge University Press. A compelling look at language development, this book examines how gestures, utterances, and social experiences interact in our day-to-day communication. The author presents research from various cultures throughout the world, including original case studies of speech–gesture fieldwork.

Garcia, O. (2009). *Bilingual education in the 21st century: A global perspective*. New York: John Wiley & Sons. A comprehensive overview of bilingual education throughout the world, this book examines traditional and contemporary views about bilingualism, including theories, misconceptions, and public policies. Strategies for implementing bilingual education programs in various settings are also presented.

MEDIA MATERIALS

For details on individual video segments that accompany the DVD for *Child Development*, Ninth Edition, please see the DVD Guide for *Explorations in Child Development*. The DVD and DVD Guide are available through your Pearson sales representative.

Additional DVDs that may be useful in your class are listed below. These are not available through your Pearson sales representative, but you can order them directly from the distributors. (See contact information at the end of this manual.)

Baby Sign Language (2005, Films Media Group, 10 min.). This program demonstrates how a preverbal child can communicate using American Sign Language. Presenting the work of researcher Joseph Garcia, founder of the business Sign with Your Baby, this program illustrates the benefits and positive implications of introducing ASL to children regardless of whether they are hearing-impaired.

Language Development (2004, Insight Media, 29 min.). This program examines language development from infancy through adolescence, including social factors that contribute to language acquisition. The program also provides educational strategies for enhancing children's language development.

Let There Be Words: The Origin of Human Language (2007, Films Media Group, 48 min.). This program looks back to prehistoric times in its examination of two major questions: What is language, and how did humans acquire it? Noam Chomsky and others defend their theoretical perspectives on the origins of language.

Multilingual Hong Kong: A Sociolinguistic Case Study of Code-Switching (2005, Films Media Group, 32 min.). Focusing on multilingual Hong Kong, this program uses interviews with Hong Kong residents to illuminate the phenomenon of code-switching. Their explanations of why and when they mix Cantonese and English reveal much about cultural identity in cosmopolitan populations and the effects of globalization. Scholarly analysis is provided by specialists from The University of Hong Kong and the City University of Hong Kong. Portions are in Chinese with English subtitles.

Promoting Language and Literacy (2003, Magna Systems, Inc., 29 min.). This program follows caregivers of infants and toddlers to illustrate early language acquisition and preparation for literacy. The program also shows the processes that skilled caregivers use to respond to a child's communication, from nonverbal expressions to phrases and sentences. Caregivers talk about ways to assist children who show language delays and those whose home language is not English.

Read My Lips: Learning Language (2004, Films Media Group/BBC–Open University coproduction, 60 min.). This program explores how we develop the arts of speech and physical expression to make ourselves understood and to understand others. The film observes a group of 25 3-year-olds as they learn as many as 10 new words a day. The body language that supplements verbal skills is also explored, and the program demonstrates that children with verbal disadvantages can compensate through other techniques. Part of the series *Child of Our Time*.

Sound Insight: Breaking the Sound Barrier in a Deaf World (2004, Aquarius Health Care Media/Primary Focus, 28 min.). This program is about Sue Thomas, who became deaf at 18 months and grew up at a time when the world had little to offer those who suffered from deafness. Sue eventually learned sign language, and also became so adept at lip reading that the FBI, recognizing her skills, hired her for undercover investigations.

Storytelling: A Pathway to Literacy (2003, Insight Media, 30 min.). Proposing that storytelling is a critical tool for encouraging a love for reading, this program features professional storytellers and demonstrates practical ways to use storytelling to support children's language and literacy development.

The Mind of Noam Chomsky (2008, Insight Media, 60 min.). Hosted by psychologist Howard Gardner, this program examines the career of Noam Chomsky, including his theory of language development and his seminal contributions to the study of cognition.

Thinking and Language: Language Acquisition (2006, Aquarius Health Care Media, 30 min.). In this program, part of the *Inside Out* series, Daniel Kahneman discusses his research in cognitive psychology, and linguist Noam Chomsky and others present their theories of language acquisition. The program also tells the story of Genie, a young girl who, as a result of severe neglect and abuse, did not learn language.

Why Do We Talk? The Science of Speech (2009, Films Media Group/BBC–Science Channel coproduction, 53 min.). Spotlighting speech researchers, this program discusses the structures—sociological, anatomical, developmental, and intellectual—that underlie speech. Included in this program are Deb Roy, who is uncovering the effect of daily life on language; Tecumseh Fitch, who is researching vocal-tract positioning in animals; Cathy Price, who is piecing together a speech-related map of the brain; William Fifer, who is examining the roots of language reception in babies; Ofer Tchernichovski, who is conducting experiments with zebra finches; Faraneh Vargha-Khadem, who is working on the isolation of a speech gene, FOXP2; and Simon Kirby, whose experiment allows him to observe the evolution of made-up language. Noam Chomsky also appears.

CHAPTER 10
EMOTIONAL DEVELOPMENT

CHAPTER-AT-A-GLANCE

Chapter Outline	Instruction Ideas	Supplements
Functions of Emotions pp. 401–405 Emotions and Cognitive Processing • Emotions and Social Behavior • Emotions and Health • Other Features of the Functionalist Approach	Learning Objective 10.1 Learning Activity 10.1 Ask Yourself p. 405	Test Bank Items 1–18, 131 Please contact your Pearson publisher's representative for a wide range of video offerings available to adopters.
Development of Emotional Expression pp. 405–413 Basic Emotions • Self-Conscious Emotions • Emotional Self-Regulation • Acquiring Emotional Display Rules	Learning Objectives 10.2–10.3 Learning Activities 10.2–10.4 Ask Yourself p. 413	Test Bank Items 19–44, 132–133
Understanding and Responding to the Emotions of Others pp. 414–418, 419 Social Referencing • Emotional Understanding in Childhood • Empathy and Sympathy	Learning Objectives 10.4–10.5 Ask Yourself p. 418	Test Bank Items 45–61
Temperament and Development pp. 418–428 The Structure of Temperament • Measuring Temperament • Stability of Temperament • Genetic and Environmental Influences • Temperament as a Predictor of Children's Behavior • Temperament and Child Rearing: The Goodness-of-Fit Model	Learning Objectives 10.6–10.7 Lecture Enhancement 10.1 Learning Activity 10.5 Ask Yourself p. 428	Test Bank Items 62–88, 134
Development of Attachment pp. 428–441 Bowlby's Ethological Theory • Measuring the Security of Attachment • Stability of Attachment • Cultural Variations • Factors That Affect Attachment Security • Multiple Attachments • Attachment and Later Development	Learning Objectives 10.8–10.10 Lecture Enhancements 10.2–10.4 Learning Activities 10.6–10.7 Ask Yourself p. 441	Test Bank Items 89–124, 135–136
Attachment, Parental Employment, and Child Care pp. 441–444	Learning Objective 10.11 Learning Activity 10.8 Ask Yourself p. 444	Test Bank Items 125–130

BRIEF CHAPTER SUMMARY

Emotion—a rapid appraisal of the personal significance of a situation—prepares us for action. The functionalist approach to emotion emphasizes that the broad function of emotions is to energize behavior aimed at attaining personal goals. In this view, emotions are central in all human endeavors; emotions also contribute to the emergence of self-awareness and help babies forge a sense of self-efficacy. Emotional self-regulation is essential for adaptation to the child's physical and social worlds.

Emotional reactions lead to learning that is essential for survival, as seen in the impact of anxiety levels on performance. In early infancy, a bidirectional relationship between emotion and cognition is already under way. Children's emotional signals affect others' behavior, and the emotional responses of others, in turn, regulate children's social behavior.

Emotions influence children's physical well-being, as seen in two childhood growth disorders—growth faltering and psychosocial dwarfism—that result from emotional deprivation. Children exposed to chronic stress as a result of prolonged early rearing in deprived orphanages show extreme reactivity to stress. However, stress reactivity can be reduced by sensitive adult care.

Basic emotions—happiness, interest, surprise, fear, anger, sadness, disgust—are universal in humans and other primates and have a long evolutionary history of promoting survival. The infant's early arousal states of attraction and withdrawal gradually become clear, well-organized signals as the central nervous system develops and the child's goals and experiences change. Happiness, first expressed in the baby's smiles, binds parent and child into a warm, supportive relationship that fosters the infant's developing competence. Angry reactions, which increase with age into the second year, motivate caregivers to ease a baby's distress. Sadness occurs in response to deprivation of a familiar, loving caregiver. Fear, most frequently expressed as stranger anxiety, arises in the second half of the first year but eventually declines. Higher-order self-conscious emotions, including shame, embarrassment, guilt, envy, and pride, involve injury to our sense of self and appear at the end of the second year, varying in expression from culture to culture. Children must develop emotional self-regulation—strategies for adjusting emotional states to a comfortable level of intensity, which requires effortful management of emotions—and must learn to follow the emotional display rules of their society.

Children's emotional expressiveness begins with an infant's social referencing—relying on another person's emotional reaction to appraise an uncertain situation. Emotional understanding expands rapidly in the preschool years. Gradually, children develop empathy, which leads to the development of sympathy. Temperament and parenting both play a role in the development and expression of empathy.

Temperament includes early-appearing, stable individual differences in emotional reactivity and self-regulation. Thomas and Chess identified three types of children—easy, difficult, and slow-to-warm-up—based on nine dimensions of temperament. Rothbart developed a second model of temperament that looks at effortful control, the self-regulatory aspect of temperament, which involves suppressing a dominant response in favor of a more adaptive one. Temperament is only moderately stable; it develops with age and is affected by both genetic and environmental influences. The goodness-of-fit model describes how temperament and environment together can produce favorable outcomes.

Attachment is the strong affectionate tie that develops between infants and the familiar people who respond to their needs. Bowlby's ethological theory of attachment recognizes the infant's emotional tie to the caregiver as an evolved response that promotes survival. As attachment develops, babies display separation anxiety when the primary caregiver leaves. Eventually, children depend less on the physical proximity of caregivers. Instead, an image of the caregiver serves as an internal working model, which becomes a vital part of the child's personality, guiding future close relationships.

Attachment security is influenced by several factors, including early availability of a consistent caregiver, quality of caregiving, infant characteristics, and the parents' own internal working models. Sensitive caregiving by fathers, like that of mothers, predicts secure attachment. Today, nearly 2.4 million U.S. children live with their grandparents but apart from parents, in so-called skipped-generation families. Warm grandparent–grandchild bonds help protect children from adjustment problems. Contrary evidence exists about the relationship between secure attachment in infancy and later cognitive, emotional, and social competence. Continuity of caregiving appears to be a key factor in this relationship.

As mothers of young children have increasingly entered the workforce, controversy has emerged over the impact of child care on attachment. Evidence suggests that quality of care is crucially important.

LEARNING OBJECTIVES

After reading this chapter, you should be able to answer the following:

10.1 Describe the functionalist approach to emotional development. (pp. 401–405)

Chapter 10 Emotional Development

10.2 How does the expression of basic emotions change during infancy? (pp. 405–408)

10.3 Describe the development of self-conscious emotions, emotional self-regulation, and conformity to emotional display rules. (pp. 408–413)

10.4 Describe the development of emotional understanding from infancy through middle childhood. (pp. 414–416)

10.5 Describe the development of empathy from infancy into adolescence, noting individual differences. (pp. 416–418, 419)

10.6 What is temperament, and how is it measured? (pp. 418–423)

10.7 Discuss the roles of heredity and environment in the stability of temperament, the relationship of temperament to cognitive and social functioning, and the goodness-of-fit model. (pp. 423–427)

10.8 What are the unique features of ethological theory of attachment? (pp. 428–430)

10.9 Describe how researchers measure the security of attachment, and discuss the stability of attachment patterns. (pp. 430–437)

10.10 Discuss infants' formation of multiple attachments and the role of early attachment quality in later development. (pp. 437–441)

10.11 Discuss the implications of parental employment and child care for attachment security and early psychological development. (pp. 441–443)

LECTURE OUTLINE

I. FUNCTIONS OF EMOTIONS (pp. 401–405)
   A. **Emotion** is a rapid appraisal of the personal significance of a situation, which prepares you for action.
      1. Happiness, for example, leads you to approach a situation and sadness to passively withdraw.
      2. An emotion expresses your readiness to establish, maintain, or change your relation to the environment on a matter of importance to you.
   B. The **functionalist approach to emotion** emphasizes that the broad function of emotions is to energize behavior aimed at attaining personal goals.
      1. Emotions arise from ongoing exchanges between the person and the environment.
      2. In this view, emotions are central in all our endeavors.
   C. Emotions and Cognitive Processing (p. 402)
      1. Emotional reactions can lead to learning that is essential for survival.
      2. The emotion–cognition relationship is evident in the impact of anxiety on performance.
      3. The emotion–cognition relationship is bidirectional—an interplay already under way in early infancy.
   D. Emotions and Social Behavior (pp. 402–403, 404)
      1. Children's emotional signals powerfully affect the behavior of others, whose emotional reactions, in turn, regulate children's social behavior.
      2. By age 3 months, a complex caregiver–infant communication system is in place in which each partner responds in an appropriate and carefully timed fashion to the other's cues.
      3. With age, infants begin to initiate, as well as respond to, emotional expressions.
      4. When faced with unfamiliar people, objects, or events, older infants engage in *social referencing*, using their caregiver's affect as a guide to how to respond.
   E. Emotions and Health (p. 403)
      1. Research indicates that emotions influence children's physical well-being.
         a. Two childhood growth disorders resulting from emotional deprivation are *growth faltering* and *psychosocial dwarfism*.
         b. Persistent psychological stress is associated with a variety of health difficulties.
      2. Children adopted into Canadian homes who were exposed to chronic stress as a result of at least 8 months of early rearing in deprived Romanian orphanages and who were physically ill showed extreme reactivity to stress, as indicated by high concentrations of the stress hormone *cortisol*.

3. Sensitive adult care helps normalize cortisol production, but many institutionalized children adopted after much of their first year in deprived institutions suffer from lasting adjustment difficulties.
F. Other Features of the Functionalist Approach (p. 405)
1. Emotions contribute to the emergence of self-awareness.
2. Babies' interest and excitement when acting on novel objects help them forge a *sense of self-efficacy*—confidence in their own ability to control events in their surroundings.
3. By the middle of the second year, children begin to experience *self-conscious emotions* that have to do with evaluations of the self's goodness or badness.
4. To adapt to their physical and social worlds, children must develop *emotional self-regulation*.

II. DEVELOPMENT OF EMOTIONAL EXPRESSION (pp. 405–413)
A. Facial expressions offer researchers the most reliable cues to infant emotions.
1. People around the world associate photographs of different facial expressions with emotions in the same way.
2. In line with the *dynamic systems perspective*, emotional expressions vary with the person's developing capacities, goals, and context.
B. Basic Emotions (pp. 406–408)
1. Happiness, interest, surprise, fear, anger, sadness, disgust—the **basic emotions**—are universal in humans and other primates and have a long evolutionary history of promoting survival.
2. Babies' earliest emotional life consists mainly of attraction to pleasant stimulation and withdrawal from unpleasant stimulation.
3. According to the dynamic systems perspective, children coordinate separate skills into more effective systems as the central nervous system develops and the child's goals and experiences change.
4. In one view, sensitive, contingent caregiver communication helps infants construct emotional expressions that more closely resemble those of adults.
5. Gradually, emotional expressions become well-organized and specific.
6. Happiness
    a. Happiness contributes to many aspects of development.
    b. Babies smile and laugh when they achieve new skills.
    c. As the smile encourages caregivers to be affectionate and stimulating, the baby smiles more.
        (1) In the early weeks, babies smile when full, during REM sleep, and in response to gentle touches and sounds.
        (2) Between 6 and 10 weeks, the parent's communication evokes a broad grin called the **social smile.**
        (3) These changes parallel the development of infant perceptual capacities.
        (4) Around 3 to 4 months, laughter appears, reflecting faster processing of information.
        (5) Like adults, 10- to 12-month-olds have several smiles, which vary with context.
        (6) At the end of the first year, the smile has become a deliberate social signal.
7. Anger and Sadness
    a. Newborn babies respond with generalized distress to a variety of unpleasant experiences—including hunger, painful medical procedures, and changes in body temperature.
    b. From 4 to 6 months into the second year, angry expressions increase in frequency and intensity.
    c. As infants become capable of intentional behavior, they want to control their own actions and the effects they produce and will purposefully try to change an undesirable situation.
    d. Older infants are better at identifying who caused them pain or removed a toy.
    e. Babies' rise in anger is adaptive: anger motivates caregivers to relieve a baby's distress.
    f. Sadness occurs often when infants are deprived of a familiar, loving caregiver or when caregiver–infant communication is seriously disrupted.
8. Fear
    a. Fear rises during the second half of the first year into the second year.
    b. The most frequent expression of fear is **stranger anxiety**—wariness in response to unfamiliar adults.
        (1) Stranger anxiety is not universal; it depends on temperament, past experiences with strangers, and the current situation.
        (2) In cultures that practice a collective caregiving system, infants show little stranger anxiety.
    c. The rise in fear after age 6 months keeps newly mobile babies' enthusiasm for exploration in check.

Chapter 10   Emotional Development

(1) Infants use the familiar caregiver as a **secure base** from which to explore, venturing into the environment and then returning for emotional support.
(2) Infants' behavior in response to encounters with strangers is a balance between approach and avoidance.
(3) As cognitive development permits toddlers to discriminate more effectively between threatening and nonthreatening people and situations, stranger anxiety and other fears of the first two years decline.

C. Self-Conscious Emotions (pp. 408–409)
   1. Besides basic emotions, humans are capable of a higher-order set of feelings, including guilt, shame, embarrassment, envy, and pride, which are called **self-conscious emotions** because each involves injury to or enhancement of our sense of self.
   2. These emotions appear at the end of the second year, as toddlers become firmly aware of the self as a separate, unique individual.
   3. Self-conscious emotions require adult instruction in when to feel proud, ashamed, or guilty.
      a. In Western individualistic nations, most children are taught to feel pride over personal achievements.
      b. In collectivist cultures, such as China and Japan, calling attention to purely personal success evokes embarrassment and self-effacement.
   4. As their self-concepts develop, children become increasingly sensitive to praise and blame or to the possibility of such feedback from parents.
   5. Among Western children, intense shame is associated with feelings of personal inadequacy and is linked to maladjustment; but guilt, when it occurs in appropriate circumstances and is neither excessive nor accompanied by shame, is related to good adjustment.
   6. The consequences of shame for children's adjustment may vary across cultures.
   7. School-age children experience pride in a new accomplishment and guilt over a transgression even when no adult is present.

D. Emotional Self-Regulation (pp. 409–412)
   1. **Emotional self-regulation** refers to the strategies we use to adjust emotional state to a comfortable level of intensity so we can accomplish our goals.
   2. Emotional self-regulation requires voluntary, effortful management of emotions, or *effortful control,* which improves gradually as a result of brain development and the assistance of caregivers.
   3. Individual differences in effortful control are evident in infancy and play such a vital role in children's adjustment that effortful control is considered a major dimension of temperament.
   4. Infancy
      a. Young infants have only a limited capacity to regulate their emotional states.
      b. Between 2 and 4 months, caregivers build on the baby's increased tolerance for stimulation by initiating interactions that arouse pleasure in the baby but do not overwhelm the infant.
      c. By 4 to 6 months, the ability to shift attention and self-soothe helps infants control emotion.
      d. At the end of the first year, crawling and walking enable infants to regulate emotion by approaching or retreating from various situations.
      e. Infants whose parents respond contingently and sympathetically to their emotional cues tend to be less fussy and to be easier to soothe.
      f. Parents who respond impatiently or angrily reinforce the baby's rapid rise to intense distress.
      g. In the second year, gains in representation and language give children new ways of regulating emotion, including a vocabulary for talking about feelings.
      h. Toddlers whose parents are emotionally sympathetic but set limits and who offer the child acceptable alternatives to the prohibited activity display more effective anger-regulation strategies and social skills during the preschool years.
   5. Early Childhood
      a. After age 2, children frequently talk about their feelings, and language becomes a major means of actively trying to control the feelings.
      b. By age 3 to 4, they verbalize a variety of emotional self-regulation strategies.
      c. Warm, patient parents who use verbal guidance, including suggesting and explaining strategies, strengthen children's capacity to handle stress.
      d. Such children are more likely to use private speech to regulate emotion.
      e. Preschoolers who experience negative emotion intensely have greater difficulty shifting their attention away from disturbing events and inhibiting their feelings.

6. Middle Childhood and Adolescence
   a. After school entry, emotion regulation strategies become more varied, sophisticated, and flexible.
   b. Between ages 6 and 8, children increasingly reserve the full performance of emotional expressions for communicating with others.
   c. School-age children's developing sense of self-worth and expanding knowledge of the wider world pose new challenges in regulating negative emotion.
   d. Common fears of the school years—including poor academic performance, rejection by classmates, and threats to parental health—are shaped, in part, by culture.
   e. By age 10, most children shift adaptively between two general strategies for managing emotion.
      (1) In **problem-centered coping,** they appraise the situation as changeable, identify the difficulty, and decide what to do about it.
      (2) If problem solving does not work, they engage in **emotion-centered coping,** which is internal, private, and aimed at controlling distress when little can be done about an outcome.
   f. When emotional self-regulation has developed well, young people acquire a sense of *emotional self-efficacy,* a feeling of being in control of their emotional experience.

E. Acquiring Emotional Display Rules (pp. 412–413)
   1. In addition to regulating internal emotional states, children must learn to control what they communicate to others.
   2. All societies have **emotional display rules** that specify when, where, and how it is appropriate to express emotion.
      a. Parents encourage infants to suppress negative emotions by imitating their positive emotional expressions (interest, happiness, surprise) more often than their negative ones (anger, sadness).
      b. Boys get more such training than girls—social pressure that promotes the well-known sex difference whereby females are emotionally expressive and males are emotionally controlled.
      c. To foster harmonious relationships, most cultures teach children to communicate positive feelings and inhibit unpleasant ones.
      d. Gradually, children learn how to express negative emotion in ways likely to evoke a desired response from others.
      e. Collectivist versus individualistic values affect a culture's specific emotional display rules.

III. UNDERSTANDING AND RESPONDING TO THE EMOTIONS OF OTHERS (pp. 414–418, 419)
   A. Some researchers claim that young babies respond in kind to others' emotions through a built-in, automatic process of *emotional contagion*. Others believe that infants acquire these emotional contingencies through operant conditioning.
      1. Around 3 to 4 months, infants become sensitive to the structure and timing of face-to-face interactions and expect their social partner to respond in kind to their gaze, smile, or vocalization.
      2. From 5 months on, infants perceive facial expressions as organized patterns and can match the emotion in a voice with the appropriate face of a speaking person.
      3. Between 7 and 12 months, ERPs recorded while infants attend to facial expressions reveal reorganized brain-wave patterns resembling those of adults, suggesting enhanced processing of emotional cues.
   B. Social Referencing (pp. 414–415)
      1. **Social referencing**—relying on another person's emotional reaction to appraise an uncertain situation—begins at 8 to 10 months.
      2. The caregiver's voice is more effective than a facial expression alone because it conveys both emotional and verbal information.
      3. Social referencing helps toddlers move beyond simply reacting to others' emotional messages, allowing them to use those signals to guide their own actions and to find out about others' intentions.
   C. Emotional Understanding in Childhood (pp. 415–416)
      1. During the preschool years, children's emotional understanding expands rapidly.
      2. Cognitive Development and Emotional Understanding
         a. Children begin referring to causes, consequences, and behavioral signs of emotion early in the preschool years.
         b. By age 4 to 5, children correctly judge the causes of many basic emotions; after age 4, they appreciate that both desires and beliefs motivate behavior.
         c. Preschoolers can also predict what a playmate expressing a certain emotion might do next and can come up with effective ways to relieve others' negative feelings.

Chapter 10 Emotional Development

        d. Ability to appreciate mixed emotions improves in middle childhood.
        e. As with metacognition, or thinking about thought, striking gains in thinking about emotion occur in middle childhood.
    3. Social Experience and Emotional Understanding
        a. The more mothers label emotions, explain them, and express warmth and enthusiasm in conversing with preschoolers, the more "emotion words" children use and the better developed their emotional understanding—an example of *scaffolding*.
        b. Attachment security is related to warmer and more elaborative parent–child narratives, including discussions of feelings.
        c. As preschoolers learn more about emotion from interacting with adults, they engage in more emotion talk with siblings and friends, especially during make-believe play.
        d. Knowledge about emotions helps children greatly in their efforts to get along with others.
  D. Empathy and Sympathy (pp. 416–418, 419)
    1. **Empathy** involves a complex interaction of cognition and affect: the ability to detect different emotions, to take another's emotional perspective, and to *feel with* that person, or respond emotionally in a similar way.
        a. Beginning in the preschool years, empathy is an important motivator of **prosocial, or altruistic, behavior**—actions that benefit another person without any expected reward for the self.
        b. In some children, empathy does not lead to **sympathy**—feelings of concern or sorrow for another's plight—but escalates into *personal distress,* so that the child focuses on his own anxiety rather than on the person in need.
    2. Development of Empathy
        a. Newborn babies tend to cry in response to the cry of another baby.
        b. In sensitive, face-to-face communication, infants "connect" emotionally with their caregivers—experiences believed to be the foundation of empathy.
        c. Children do not begin to empathize until self-awareness strengthens, near age 2 years.
        d. Older toddlers seem to be able to engage in basic *affective perspective-taking*—inferring how another feels by imagining themselves in that person's place.
        e. Empathy increases over the elementary school years as children understand a wider range of emotions.
        f. In late childhood and adolescence, advances in perspective taking permit an empathic response not just to people's immediate distress but also to their general life condition.
    3. Individual Differences
        a. Temperament plays a role in whether empathy occurs and in whether it prompts sympathetic, prosocial behavior or a personally distressed, self-focused response.
        b. Children who are sociable, assertive, and good at regulating emotion are more likely than poor emotion regulators to empathize with others' distress and engage in prosocial behavior,
        c. Individual differences in empathy and sympathy are evident in children's facial and neurobiological responses to watching videotapes of people in need.
        d. Parenting profoundly influences empathy and sympathy.
           (1) Children whose parents are warm and show empathic concern for their feelings are likely to show empathy toward others.
           (2) Angry, punitive parenting disrupts empathy and sympathy at an early age.

IV. TEMPERAMENT AND DEVELOPMENT (pp. 418–428)
  A. **Temperament** refers to early-appearing, stable individual differences in reactivity and self-regulation.
    1. *Reactivity* refers to variations in quickness and intensity of emotional arousal, attention, and motor action.
    2. *Self-regulation* refers to strategies that modify reactivity.
  B. Thomas and Chess's New York Longitudinal Study, initiated in 1956, was a groundbreaking investigation of the development of temperament in children.
    1. Results showed that temperament can increase a child's chances of experiencing psychological problems or can protect a child from the negative effects of a stressful home life.
    2. The study also showed that parenting practices can modify children's temperaments considerably.
  C. The Structure of Temperament (pp. 420–421)
    1. Thomas and Chess identified three types of children based on parents' descriptions of their behavior on nine dimensions of temperament.

- a. The **easy child** (40 percent of the sample) quickly establishes regular routines in infancy, is generally cheerful, and adapts easily to new experiences.
- b. The **difficult child** (10 percent) has irregular daily routines, is slow to accept new experiences, and tends to react negatively and intensely.
- c. The **slow-to-warm-up child** (15 percent) is inactive, shows mild, low-key reactions to environmental stimuli, is negative in mood, and adjusts slowly to new experiences.
  2. The remaining 35 percent of children do not fit any one category.
  3. The difficult pattern places children at high risk for adjustment problems in early and middle childhood.
  4. Slow-to-warm-up children tend to show excessive fearfulness and slow, constricted behavior in the late preschool and school years.
  5. Today, the most influential model of temperament is Mary Rothbart's. It combines related traits proposed by others, yielding a list of just six dimensions.
  6. Rothbart's dimensions represent the three underlying components included in the definition of temperament: *emotion, attention,* and *action.*
  7. Rothbart found that individuals differ not only in reactivity on each dimension but also in the self-regulatory dimension of temperament, **effortful control**—the capacity to voluntarily suppress a dominant response in order to plan and execute a more adaptive response.
- D. Measuring Temperament (pp. 421–422)
  1. Temperament can be assessed through parent interviews and questionnaires and laboratory observations by researchers.
  2. Although information from parents has been criticized as being biased, parental reports are moderately related to researchers' observations of children's behavior.
  3. Observations by researchers avoid subjectivity but can lead to other inaccuracies.
  4. Most neurobiological research has focused on children at the extremes of the positive-affect and fearful-distress dimensions of temperament.
     - a. **Inhibited,** or **shy, children** react negatively to and withdraw from novel stimuli.
     - b. **Uninhibited,** or **sociable, children** display positive emotion to and approach novel stimuli.
- E. Stability of Temperament (p. 423)
  1. The overall stability of temperament is low in infancy and toddlerhood and only moderate from the preschool years on, partly because temperament itself develops with age.
  2. Long-term prediction from early temperament is best achieved after age 3, when children's styles of responding are better established.
  3. In the third year, children perform more consistently across a wide variety of tasks requiring effortful control.
  4. The low to moderate stability of temperament confirms that experience can modify biologically based temperamental traits, although children rarely change from one extreme to another.
- F. Genetic and Environmental Influences (pp. 423–425)
  1. The word *temperament* implies a genetic foundation for individual differences in personality.
     - a. Identical twins are more similar than fraternal twins across a wide range of temperamental traits.
     - b. Heritability estimates suggest a moderate role for genetic factors in temperament and personality, with differences in genetic makeup accounting for about half of individual differences.
     - c. Environment also has a powerful influence on temperament.
       - (1) Persistent nutritional and emotional deprivation profoundly alters temperament.
       - (2) Children who spent their infancy in deprived orphanage conditions are easily overwhelmed by stressful events.
     - d. Heredity and environment often jointly contribute to temperament, since a child's approach to the world affects the experiences to which she is exposed.
  2. Cultural Variations
     - a. Compared with North American Caucasian infants, Chinese and Japanese babies tend to be less active, irritable, and vocal and better at quieting themselves.
     - b. These variations may have genetic roots, but they are supported by cultural beliefs and practices.
  3. Nonshared Environment
     - a. In families with several children, *nonshared environmental influences*—those that make siblings different from one another—affect both temperament and intelligence.
     - b. *Shared environmental influences*—those that affect all siblings similarly—also play a role.

Chapter 10 Emotional Development

G. Temperament as a Predictor of Children's Behavior (pp. 425–426)
 1. Children's temperamental traits consistently predict their cognitive and social functioning.
 2. Young children's attention span forecasts their learning and cognitive development.
 3. Temperament is also related to social behavior, as seen in observations of shy children and irritable, anger-prone children.
 4. Children's capacity for effortful control is linked to favorable development and adjustment in cultures as diverse as China and the United States. Positive outcomes include persistence, task mastery, and moral maturity.
H. Temperament and Child Rearing: The Goodness-of-Fit Model (pp. 426–427)
 1. Thomas and Chess proposed a **goodness-of-fit model** to explain how temperament and environment together can produce favorable outcomes.
 2. Goodness of fit, which involves creating child-rearing environments that recognize each child's temperament while encouraging more adaptive functioning, helps explain why difficult children are at risk for later adjustment problems.
  a. These children frequently experience parenting that fits poorly with their dispositions and, as a result, are less likely to receive sensitive caregiving.
  b. When parents are positive and sensitive, difficultness declines by age 2 to 3, and parental sensitivity, support, and clear expectations foster effortful control, reducing the likelihood that difficultness will persist.
  c. In one study, preschoolers with a chromosome 17 gene that interferes with functioning of the inhibitory neurotransmitter serotonin (and, thus, greatly increases the risk of negative mood and self-regulation difficulties) benefited, especially, from positive parenting.
 3. Effective parenting of challenging children also depends on life conditions—good parental mental health, marital harmony, and favorable economic conditions—and cultural values.

V. DEVELOPMENT OF ATTACHMENT (pp. 428–441)
 A. **Attachment** is the strong, affectionate tie we have with special people in our lives that leads us to experience pleasure and joy when we interact with them and to be comforted by their nearness during times of stress.
  1. Both the *psychoanalytic perspective* and *behaviorism* emphasize the importance of feeding in promoting this close emotional bond, though for different reasons.
  2. Research has shown that attachment does not depend on hunger satisfaction.
  3. Both psychoanalytic and behaviorist accounts of attachment emphasize the caregiver's contribution to the attachment relationship but pay little attention to the importance of the infant's characteristics.
 B. Bowlby's Ethological Theory (pp. 428–430)
  1. **Ethological theory of attachment,** which recognizes the infant's emotional tie to the caregiver as an evolved response that promotes survival, is the most widely accepted view today.
   a. John Bowlby first applied this idea to the infant–caregiver bond.
   b. Bowlby believed that attachment can best be understood in an evolutionary context in which survival of the species is of utmost importance.
  2. Attachment develops in four phases:
   a. *Preattachment phase* (birth to 6 weeks): Babies recognize their own mother's smell and voice but are not yet attached to her and do not mind being left with an unfamiliar adult.
   b. *"Attachment-in-the-making" phase* (6 weeks to 6–8 months): Infants begin to develop a *sense of trust*—the expectation that the caregiver will respond when signaled—but still do not object to separation.
   c. *"Clear-cut" attachment phase* (6–8 months to 18 months–2 years): Babies display **separation anxiety,** becoming upset when the primary caregiver leaves.
   d. *Formation of a reciprocal relationship* (18 months to 2 years and on): Rapid growth in language enables toddlers to understand some of the factors that influence the parent's coming and going and to predict her return; separation protest declines.
  3. Out of their experiences during these four phases, children construct an enduring affectionate tie that they use as a secure base in the parents' absence.
   a. This image serves as an **internal working model,** or set of expectations about the availability of attachment figures, their likelihood of providing support during times of stress, and the self's interaction with them.
   b. The internal working model becomes a vital part of personality, serving as a guide for all future close relationships.

c. As early as the second year, toddlers form attachment-related expectations about parental comfort and support.
C. Measuring the Security of Attachment (pp. 430–432)
1. A widely used laboratory technique for measuring the quality of attachment between 1 and 2 years of age is the **Strange Situation,** designed by Mary Ainsworth and her colleagues, which takes the baby through eight short episodes, each involving a brief separation from and reunion with the parent.
2. Using the Strange Situation, researchers have identified a secure attachment pattern and three patterns of insecurity:
    a. **Secure attachment** (about 60 percent; percentages are for North American infants in middle-SES families): These infants use the parent as a secure base. They may or may not cry when separated from the parent; when she returns, they seek contact, and their crying is reduced.
    b. **Avoidant attachment** (15 percent): These infants seem unresponsive to the parent when she is present and usually are not distressed when she leaves. During reunion, they avoid or are slow to greet the parent.
    c. **Resistant attachment** (10 percent): Before separation, these infants seek closeness to the parent and often fail to explore. When the parent leaves, they are usually distressed; on her return, they combine clinginess with angry, resistive behavior.
    d. **Disorganized/disoriented attachment** (15 percent): This pattern reflects the greatest insecurity; at reunion, these infants show confused, contradictory behaviors.
3. The **Attachment Q-Sort,** an alternative method suitable for children between 1 and 4 years of age, permits attachment to be assessed through home observations.
D. Stability of Attachment (p. 432)
1. Quality of attachment is usually secure and stable for middle-SES babies experiencing favorable life conditions.
2. Infants who move from insecurity to security typically have well-adjusted mothers with positive family and friendship ties.
3. In low-SES families with many daily stresses and little social support, attachment generally moves away from security or changes from one insecure pattern to another.
4. Securely attached babies more often maintain their attachment status than insecure babies.
5. Disorganized/disoriented attachment is as stable as attachment security.
E. Cultural Variations (pp. 432–433)
1. Attachment patterns may have to be interpreted differently in certain cultures.
2. Nevertheless, the secure pattern is still the most common attachment quality in all societies studied to date.
F. Factors That Affect Attachment Security (pp. 433–437)
1. Four important influences on attachment security are (1) early availability of a consistent caregiver, (2) quality of caregiving, (3) the baby's characteristics, and (4) family context, including parents' internal working models.
2. Early Availability of a Consistent Caregiver
    a. Research shows that institutionalized infants experience emotional difficulties because they are prevented from forming a close bond with one or a few adults.
    b. Children who spent their first year or more in deprived Eastern European orphanages—though able to bond with their adoptive or foster parents—show elevated rates of attachment insecurity.
3. Quality of Caregiving
    a. **Sensitive caregiving**—responding promptly, consistently, and appropriately to infants and holding them tenderly and carefully—is moderately related to attachment security.
    b. In studies of Western babies, **interactional synchrony**—best described as a sensitively tuned "emotional dance" in which the caregiver responds to infant signals in a well-timed, rhythmic, appropriate fashion—separated the experiences of secure and insecure babies.
    c. Cultures vary in their view of which behaviors represent sensitivity toward infants.
    d. Compared with securely attached infants, avoidant babies tend to receive overstimulating care, whereas resistant infants often experience inconsistent care.
    e. Highly inadequate caregiving is a powerful predictor of disruptions in attachment.
4. Infant Characteristics
    a. Because attachment results from a *relationship* between two partners, infant characteristics should affect how easily it is established.
    b. Prematurity and other complications that make caregiving more taxing are linked to attachment insecurity, but at-risk newborns fare well when parents have the time and patience to care for them.

Chapter 10 Emotional Development

      c. The role of infant temperament in attachment security has been intensely debated.
      d. The evidence suggests that infant difficultness and maternal anxiety perpetuate each other, impairing caregiving and the security of the parent–infant bond.
      e. Other research focusing on disorganized/disoriented attachment has uncovered gene–environment interactions.
      f. However, twin comparisons reveal that the heritability of attachment is virtually nil.
      g. The influence of children's characteristics on attachment quality depends on goodness of fit; interventions that teach parents to interact sensitively with difficult-to-care-for infants are highly successful in enhancing attachment security.
    5. Family Circumstances
      a. Family stressors, such as job loss or a failing marriage, can undermine attachment indirectly, by interfering with the sensitivity of parental care.
      b. The availability of social supports predicts greater attachment security.
    6. Parents' Internal Working Models
      a. To assess parents' "state of mind" with respect to attachment, Mary Main and her colleagues devised the *Adult Attachment Interview*.
      b. Quality of parents' internal working models is clearly related to their children's attachment security in infancy and early childhood.
      c. However, our early rearing experiences do not destine us to become either sensitive or insensitive parents.
  G. Multiple Attachments (pp. 437–439)
    1. Babies develop attachments to a variety of familiar people.
    2. Fathers
      a. Fathers' sensitive caregiving and interactional synchrony with infants, like mothers', predict attachment security.
      b. Mothers and fathers in many cultures interact differently with their babies: Mothers devote more time to physical care and expressing affection, fathers to playful interaction.
      c. Play is a vital context in which fathers build secure attachments.
      d. Today, nearly one-third of U.S. employed women say that their spouse or partner shares equally in or takes most responsibility for child-care tasks.
    3. Grandparent Primary Caregivers
      a. Nearly 2.4 million U.S. children live with their grandparents but apart from parents, in so-called *skipped-generation families*.
      b. Grandparents generally step in when parents' troubled lives threaten children's well-being and, thus, tend to assume the parenting role under highly stressful life circumstances.
      c. Many report feeling emotionally drained, depressed, and worried about what will happen to the children if their own health fails.
      d. Nonetheless, warm grandparent–grandchild bonds help protect children from worsening adjustment problems.
  H. Attachment and Later Development (pp. 439–441)
    1. According to psychoanalytic and ethological theories, the inner feelings of affection and security that result from a healthy attachment relationship support all aspects of psychological development.
    2. Findings are mixed on the relationship between secure attachment in infancy and improved cognitive, emotional, and social competence in later years.
    3. Mounting evidence indicates that *continuity of caregiving* determines whether attachment security is linked to later development.
    4. A child whose parental caregiving improves or who has other compensating affectionate ties outside the immediate family may show *resilience*, bouncing back from adversity, whereas a child who experiences tender care in infancy but lacks sympathetic ties later on is at risk for problems.

VI. ATTACHMENT, PARENTAL EMPLOYMENT, AND CHILD CARE (pp. 441–444)
  A. More than 60 percent of U.S. mothers of a child under 2 are employed, giving rise to questions about the impact on the attachment bond of child care and daily separations of infant from parent.
  B. The weight of evidence suggests that *quality of care* is crucially important.
    1. Exposure to long hours of mediocre to poor nonparental care has been shown to have negative effects on the cognitive and social development of infants and young children.

2. Good child care can reduce the negative impact of a stressed, poverty-stricken home life.
3. In contrast to most European countries, where child care is nationally regulated and funded to ensure its quality, reports on U.S. child care raise serious concerns.
   a. Many children from low-income families experience inadequate child care.
   b. The settings providing the worst care tend to serve middle-SES families, who are especially likely to use for-profit centers, where quality tends to be the lowest.
   c. Low-SES children are more likely to attend publicly subsidized, nonprofit centers with smaller group sizes and lower teacher–child ratios.
4. The U.S. National Association for the Education of Young Children has devised standards for **developmentally appropriate practice** with respect to high-quality child care for infants and toddlers, specifying program characteristics that meet the developmental and individual needs of young children, based on current research and consensus among experts.

LECTURE ENHANCEMENTS

LECTURE ENHANCEMENT 10.1
The Relationship Among Child Rearing, Shyness in Preschool, and Social Withdrawal in Middle Childhood (p. 422)

Time: 10–15 minutes

Objective: To extend existing research on child-rearing practices that contribute to shyness in preschoolers and social withdrawal in middle childhood.

As noted in the text, child-rearing practices affect the chances that an emotionally reactive baby will become a fearful child. Warm, supportive parenting reduces shy infants' and preschoolers' intense physiological reaction to novelty, whereas cold, intrusive parenting heightens anxiety. To extend existing research on child-rearing practices that contribute to shyness, as well as the long-term consequences of social reticence in early childhood, Hane and colleagues (2008) recruited 80 preschool-age children and their mothers who were participating in a longitudinal study of temperament and social behavior. The researchers collected the following information:

(1) When children were 4 years old, their mothers completed the Colorado Child Temperament Inventory (CCTI), which measures multiple dimensions of temperament, including emotionality, distractibility, activity level, shyness, and sociability.
(2) When children were 4 and again when they were 7, they participated in a 15-minute free-play session with their mothers and three unfamiliar peers. Using 10-second intervals, trained observers coded for social participation (for example, onlooking, solitary play, parallel play, conversation, group play) and cognitive quality (for example, functional, sociodramatic, constructive, games with rules).
(3) During the free-play session and cleanup at ages 4 and 7, observers recorded quality of maternal behavior, including negative affect, positive affect, negative control, and guidance. Quality of maternal behavior was also coded during a difficult origami paper-folding task at age 7.

Overall, social reticence at age 4 predicted social withdrawal at age 7. That is, children who engaged in high rates of onlooking behavior, solitary play, or functional play at age 4 tended to engage in similar behaviors at age 7. This finding was particularly strong for preschoolers who experienced negative and controlling parenting—for example, having a mother who "took over" during cleanup or the origami paper-folding task. In contrast, maternal positive affect and guidance at age 4 predicted more favorable social outcomes at both ages 4 and 7. According to Hane and colleagues, children with a history of extreme shyness and social withdrawal may elicit more negativity from parents, which, in turn, exacerbates their reticence. Not surprisingly, maternal reports of shyness on the CCTI were highly correlated with social reticence and social withdrawal during the free-play sessions.

Reflecting on research presented in the text, besides child-rearing practices, what other environmental factors might contribute to shyness and sociability in young children? What parenting practices might help offset early shyness and social withdrawal?

Hane, A. A., Cheah, C., Rubin, K. H., & Fox, N. A. (2008). The role of maternal behavior in the relation between shyness and social reticence in early childhood and social withdrawal in middle childhood. *Social Development, 4,* 795–811.

LECTURE ENHANCEMENT 10.2
A Longitudinal Study of Maternal Sensitivity and Adopted Children's Social Development (p. 434)

Time: 15–20 minutes

Objective: To illustrate the effects of early and later maternal sensitivity on children's social development.

Research shows that sensitive caregiving is moderately related to attachment security in both biological and adoptive mother–infant pairs and in diverse cultures and SES groups. To examine the effects of early and later maternal sensitivity on children's social development, Jaffari-Bimmel and colleagues (2006) followed 160 internationally adopted children from infancy to age 14. All of the children were placed in adoptive families by age 6 months, and the families were predominantly middle to upper-middle class. The researchers collected the following information:

(1) When the children were 5 months old, their adoptive mothers rated their health condition on arrival (that is, at the time of adoption)—birth weight, incidence of prematurity, and health problems.

(2) When the children were 12 months old, attachment security was assessed using Ainsworth's Strange Situation.

(3) At ages 12, 18, and 30 months, maternal sensitivity was assessed at home and in the laboratory. While the children and their mothers completed age-appropriate tasks, like putting together puzzles and building with blocks, trained researchers coded for emotional support, respect for the child's autonomy, structure- and limit-setting, hostility, and quality of instruction.

(4) At ages 7 and 14 years, maternal sensitivity was again assessed in the home. While the children and their mothers worked on a difficult, age-appropriate puzzle, trained researchers coded for supportive presence, intrusiveness, sensitivity, timing, and clarity of instruction.

(5) When the children were ages 12, 18, and 30 months and ages 7 and 14 years, their adoptive mothers completed a temperament questionnaire. In infancy, the researchers were primarily interested in mood and resistance. In middle childhood and adolescence, the researchers focused on aggression, reactivity, and restlessness.

(6) When children were ages 7 and 14 years, adoptive mothers and teachers completed a measure of social development. The questionnaire focused on social acceptance, social rejection, prosocial competence, friendliness, and social esteem.

(7) When the children were ages 7 and 14 years, their adoptive mothers reported on the degree to which the family had experienced stressful life events during the past two years. The instrument included physical health problems of relatives, bereavement, unemployment, divorce, financial problems, marital problems, problems at work, and conflict with relatives and/or neighbors.

Findings indicated that developmental history and sensitive caregiving from infancy through middle childhood predicted social development at age 14. Participants who were healthy at the time of adoption and who experienced few stressful life events and received sensitive caregiving in both infancy and middle childhood were rated as higher in social development (by adoptive mothers and teachers) than agemates who were unhealthy at the time of adoption, experienced a large number of stressful life events, or received less-sensitive caregiving in infancy and middle childhood. Another important finding was that maternal sensitivity in middle childhood and adolescence helped buffer against the negative effects of a difficult temperament, as measured at 12, 18, and 30 months and ages 7 and 14 years.

Children with a difficult temperament who experienced high levels of maternal sensitivity in middle childhood and adolescence had more favorable social development at age 14 than children with a difficult temperament who experienced insensitive caregiving. Finally, consistent with previous studies, attachment security in infancy was moderately related to social development at ages 7 and 14. It is important to note that securely attached infants were more likely to receive sensitive caregiving throughout infancy and childhood than insecure infants. Compared to their insecurely attached counterparts, secure children scored higher in social acceptance, prosocial competence, friendliness, and social esteem. Taken together, these findings show that both early and later maternal sensitivity is important for children's social development.

Jaffari-Bimmel, N., Juffer, F., van IJzendoorn, M. H., Bakermans-Kraneburg, M. J., & Mooijaart, A. (2006). Social development from infancy to adolescence: Longitudinal and concurrent factors in an adoption sample. *Developmental Psychology, 42,* 1143–1153.

LECTURE ENHANCEMENT 10.3
Early Parent–Child Interaction: Is There a Spillover Effect Between Mothers and Fathers? (pp. 436, 437–438)

Time: 5–10 minutes

Objective: To examine a possible spillover effect between mother–infant and father–infant interaction styles.

To determine if a spillover effect exists between mothers' and fathers' interactions with their babies, Barnett and colleagues (2008) recruited 97 middle-class families in which both the mother and the father resided in the home. When infants were 6 months old, researchers conducted home visits with each family. Mothers and fathers were filmed separately as they participated in a free-play session with their infants. The researchers were interested in parental sensitivity/responsiveness, positive regard toward the child (smiling, touching, laughing), negative regard toward the child (disapproving, harsh, or hostile vocalizations; tense or abrupt movements of the baby), and animation (quantity and intensity of parental vocal, physical, and affective energy). Infants' positive and negative affect was also coded.

Next, mothers and fathers completed a questionnaire assessing emotional intimacy and conflict. For example: On a 5-point scale (1 = strongly disagree; 5 = strongly agree), "My spouse/partner really understands my hurts and joys." On a 9-point scale (1 = not at all; 9 = very much), "How often do you feel angry or resentful toward your spouse/partner?"

Results indicated that mothers tended to be more sensitive when interacting with their babies, while fathers engaged in higher levels of animation during free play. The researchers also observed a spillover effect in caregiving behaviors. That is, positive interactions in the mother–infant dyad predicted positive interactions in the father–infant dyad. Similarly, when mothers engaged in negative, intrusive interactions, fathers tended to engage in negative, intrusive interactions. Because mothers' and fathers' interaction styles with their babies were similar, for the most part one parent did not offer a buffer against the other parent's negative interactions. The researchers also found that parents who reported high levels of intimacy and low levels of conflict with their spouse/partner engaged in more sensitive and positive caregiving. Not surprisingly, low levels of intimacy and high levels of conflict were associated with negative and hostile interactions in both mothers and fathers. Finally, sensitive parent–child interactions predicted higher levels of positive infant affect, whereas negative, intrusive interactions predicted higher levels of negative infant affect.

Have students return to Chapter 1 and review ecological systems theory (pp. 26–29). How might bidirectional influences affect quality of caregiving? Ask students to think of factors that might contribute to a spillover effect between mothers and fathers.

Barnett, M. A., Deng, M., Mills-Koonce, W. R., Willoughby, M., & Cox, M. (2008). Interdependence of parenting behavior of mothers and fathers of infants. *Journal of Family Psychology, 22,* 561–573.

LECTURE ENHANCEMENT 10.4
Attachment Relationships in Middle Childhood (pp. 439–441)

Time: 5–10 minutes

Objective: To examine attachment relationships in middle childhood.

To extend existing research on attachment relationships in middle childhood, Seibert and Kerns (2009) recruited 114 children between the ages of 7 and 12 years. As participants viewed a drawing with three concentric circles, they were instructed to "Nominate three people who are important in your life right now, and place these people in the three circles based on how close you feel to that person." Participants were then asked to provide demographic information (age, gender, and relationship to child) for each person they nominated. Finally, participants were presented with various scenarios and based on their nominations, asked who they would go to first, second, and last. The scenarios focused on multiple aspects of attachment, such as general attachment, companionship needs, and emotion-eliciting situations. Sample questions included:

- General attachment: "If you felt really sad, who would you go to first?"
- General companionship: "If you wanted someone to play with, who would you go to first?"
- Context-specific attachment: "Imagine that you get into a fight with one of your best friends and you feel lonely and sad. Who would you most want to talk to about this?"
- Context-specific companionship: "Imagine that you want to go see a new movie. Who would you most want to go with you?"
- Emotion-eliciting situations at school: "Imagine that you are at school and one of your friends says something really mean to you. Who would you want to talk to about this first?"

Overall, children tended to nominate parents first for general attachment questions and peers first for companionship questions. For emotion-eliciting situations, children were equally likely to seek out parents and peers for support. Because the emotion-eliciting situations occurred at school, many children indicated that they would seek out a peer first and then a parent. According to Seibert and Kerns, rather than taking the place of parents, peers may function as temporary stand-ins when parents are not immediately available. Another interesting finding was that when participants identified a sibling as a significant attachment figure, they almost always selected an older, rather than a younger, sibling. Like peers, older siblings may function as temporary stand-ins when children lack immediate access to a parent.

Although participants were more likely to identify parents for general attachment needs and peers for companionship needs, older children were more likely than younger children to turn to their peers first for support. This finding is consistent with research on the transition to adolescence, during which peers become increasingly important.

Seibert, A. C., & Kerns, K. A. (2009). Attachment figures in middle childhood. *International Journal of Behavioral Development, 33,* 347–355.

LEARNING ACTIVITIES

LEARNING ACTIVITY 10.1
True or False: Function of Emotions (pp. 401–405)

Present the following exercise as an in-class activity or quiz.

Directions: Read each of the following statements and indicate whether each is *True* (T) or *False* (F).

Statements:

1. Functionalist theorists believe that emotions have little impact on overall development.
2. In both children and adults, high anxiety impairs thinking, especially on complex tasks.
3. As early as the first month of life, a complex caregiver–infant communication system is in place in which each partner responds in an appropriate and carefully timed fashion to the other's cues.
4. By 9 months, infants become initiators of positive emotional exchanges, smiling before the caregiver smiles.
5. Young children often rely on social referencing to learn how to behave in everyday situations.
6. Most research confirms that psychological stress has little impact on children's growth and development.
7. Extremely high cortisol interferes with release of growth hormone and, thus, can stunt children's physical growth.
8. Sensitive parenting can protect the young brain from both excessive and inadequate stress-hormone exposure.
9. Babies' interest and excitement when acting on novel objects help them forge a sense of self-efficacy.
10. By late childhood, most emotions are expressed as openly and freely as they were in the early years of life.

Answers:

1. F   6. F
2. T   7. F
3. F   8. T
4. T   9. T
5. T   10. F

LEARNING ACTIVITY 10.2
Classroom Demonstration: Development of Emotional Expression (pp. 405–409)

Arrange for a group of babies, ranging in age from several weeks to 18 months, to visit your classroom for a demonstration of emotional expression during infancy. Students may have friends or family members who are willing to participate in the demonstration. Alternatively, you may have friends or colleagues who are available for a class period.

During the demonstration, have students carefully observe the infants' facial, body, and vocal expressions and record any examples of basic emotions, including events that may have elicited these emotions. For example, a baby may smile in response to his or her parent's facial expression and/or voice. In addition, interview parents about their infants' range of emotional expressions (happiness, interest, surprise, fear, anger, sadness, and disgust). Are their answers consistent with research in the text—that infants' precise emotions are difficult to detect in the early months but become more recognizable with age?

Using a baby between 2 and 4 months of age, demonstrate the social smile by nodding, smiling, and talking softly to the infant. Also, illustrate parental responsiveness to infant smiling to underscore the adaptive role of the smile in promoting positive interactions between parent and child. For babies 3 months of age and older, ask parents to describe and, if possible, demonstrate stimuli that elicit laughter, and note their dynamic quality (for example, kissing the baby's tummy). For infants over 7 months of age, point out the rise in fear reactions that generally occurs around this time and that is reflected in the baby's wariness of strange adults, hesitancy to reach for novel objects, and tendency to keep track of the parent's whereabouts in an unfamiliar environment. Finally, ask students to look for instances of social referencing and use of the secure base in older infants. Point out that after 10 months of age, babies often rely on the caregiver's emotional response to form an appraisal of an uncertain situation.

LEARNING ACTIVITY 10.3
Supporting Emotional Self-Regulation in Infants and Toddlers (pp. 409–411)

Tell students to pretend they have been asked to speak to a group of parents on the importance of helping young children manage their emotional experiences. Using research in the text as a guide, have students list the information they would include in their presentation. For example, why is emotional self-regulation important? What infant and toddler behaviors reflect the beginnings of effortful control and emotional self-regulation? How can parents help their infants and toddlers regulate emotion? What caregiving behaviors should parents avoid, and why?

LEARNING ACTIVITY 10.4
Evaluating Coping Styles (p. 412)

Instruct students to interview at least one school-age child and one adolescent about their reactions to emotional situations. For example, "How do you typically respond when your mother or father is angry with you?" "Assume that you just got a D on a class assignment or test. How would you feel/react?" Students should then determine if the responses illustrate a problem-centered or emotion-centered coping style. Next, ask students to share some examples, along with the age and gender of each respondent. Did any patterns emerge? That is, do there seem to be age or gender differences?

LEARNING ACTIVITY 10.5
Matching: The Rothbart Model of Temperament (p. 420)

Present the following exercise as an in-class activity or quiz.

Directions: Match each of the following terms with its correct description.

Terms:

_____ 1. Activity level
_____ 2. Attention span/persistence
_____ 3. Fearful distress
_____ 4. Irritable distress
_____ 5. Positive affect
_____ 6. Effortful control

Descriptions:

A. Wariness and distress in response to intense or novel stimuli, including time to adjust to new situations.
B. Extent of fussing, crying, and distress when desires are frustrated.
C. Frequency of expression of happiness and pleasure.
D. Level of gross motor activity.
E. Capacity to voluntarily suppress a dominant, reactive response in order to plan and execute a more adaptive response.
F. Duration of orienting or interest.

Answers:

1. D   4. B
2. F   5. C
3. A   6. E

LEARNING ACTIVITY 10.6
Observing the Attachment Relationship During the First Two Years (pp. 428–429, 431)

This activity can be included as an extension of Learning Activity 10.2. If you have access to a baby 6 weeks of age or younger, demonstrate and/or describe the built-in signals of the preattachment phase—grasping, smiling, crying, and gazing into the adult's eyes. Next, show students that babies under 6 months old are generally willing to be held and soothed by unfamiliar adults, although from 2 to 8 months, they respond preferentially to familiar caregivers. For example, when held by familiar adults, babies smile and vocalize more consistently and quiet more readily when picked up. At around 6 to 8 months, "clear-cut" attachment is evident. To illustrate, ask the parent of a baby between 8 and 18 months old to leave the room briefly, as is done in Ainsworth's Strange Situation.* Securely attached infants generally try to follow; if they cannot, they become distressed at the parent's departure but are quickly comforted by physical proximity when he or she returns. By the end of the second year, growth in mental representation and language enables children to tolerate parental absences more easily. After participants have had sufficient time to become comfortable in the classroom, ask the parent of an 18- to 24-month-old to explain to the child that he or she is going to leave the room for a moment but will be back shortly. Students should note the reaction of the child and compare it to research in the text.

For demonstrations in which the parent leaves the room, make sure the parent immediately returns if the child becomes distressed.

LEARNING ACTIVITY 10.7
Investigating Threats to Attachment Security (pp. 430–432, 433–437)

Present the following scenario to students:

> As part of a large research study, you have been asked to conduct home visits for infants and toddlers who may be at risk for insecure attachment. What clues would you look for to distinguish among avoidant, resistant, and disorganized/disoriented attachment? What caregiving behaviors might signal a threat to attachment security? How about infant characteristics? What questions would you ask to identify important contextual influences on the infant–parent relationship (for example, recent divorce, financial difficulties)?

LEARNING ACTIVITY 10.8
Attachment, Parent Employment, and Child Care (pp. 441–443)

In small groups, have students respond to the following scenario:

> Paul and Ava are parents to 3-month-old Kevin. After giving birth, Ava decided to spend several months at home caring for the baby. Although Ava enjoys being a stay-at-home mother, she would like to return to her full-time job in the near future. Friends and family members have expressed concerns about Ava returning to work so soon, and Paul's parents are worried that Kevin may experience learning and behavioral problems if he attends child care at such a young age.

Using research in the text as a guide, what advice would you give Paul and Ava? Do their friends and family have valid concerns? Why or why not? If Ava does decide to return to work, how can she and Paul ensure that Kevin develops favorably?

ASK YOURSELF . . .

REVIEW: Using research findings, provide an example of the impact of emotions on children's (1) cognitive processing, (2) social behavior, and (3) physical health. (pp. 402–403)

Cognitive processing: The relationship between emotion and cognition, which is evident in the impact of anxiety on performance, is bidirectional—a dynamic interplay already under way in early infancy. In one study, researchers taught 2- to 8-month-olds to pull a string to activate pleasurable sights and sounds. As the infants learned the task, they responded with interest, happiness, and surprise. Then, for a short period, pulling the string no longer turned on the attractive stimuli. The babies' emotional reactions quickly changed—mostly to anger but occasionally to sadness. Once the contingency was restored, the infants who had reacted angrily showed renewed interest and enjoyment, whereas the sad babies turned away. Here, emotions were interwoven with cognitive processing, serving as outcomes of mastery and as the energizing force for continued involvement in learning.

Social behavior: Children's emotional signals, such as smiling, crying, and attentive interest, powerfully affect the behavior of others. Similarly, the emotional reactions of others regulate children's social behavior. Careful analyses of caregiver–infant interactions reveal that by 3 months, a complex communication system is in place in which each partner responds in an appropriate and carefully timed fashion to the other's cues. In several studies, researchers disrupted this exchange of emotional signals by having the parent assume either a still-faced, unreactive pose or a depressed emotional state. Two- to 7-month-olds tried facial expressions, vocalizations, and body movements to get the parent to respond again. When these efforts failed, they turned away, frowned, and cried. Clearly, when engaged in face-to-face interaction, even young infants expect their partners to be emotionally responsive.

Physical health: Much research indicates that emotions influence children's physical well-being. Two childhood growth disorders that involve emotional deprivation were discussed in Chapter 5—growth faltering and psychosocial dwarfism. Many other studies indicate that persistent psychological stress, manifested in anxiety, depressed mood, anger, and irritability, is associated with a variety of health difficulties from infancy to adulthood. Stress elevates heart rate and blood pressure and depresses immune response—reactions that may explain the relationship with cardiovascular disease, infectious illness, and several forms of cancer.

CONNECT: Does the still-face reaction help us understand infants' responses to parental depressed mood, reviewed in the Biology and Environment box on page 404? Explain. (pp. 402, 404)

Depressed parents typically view their infants and children more negatively than independent observers do. Depressed parents rarely smile at, comfort, or talk to their babies, and babies respond to the parent's sad, vacant gaze by turning away, crying, or looking sad or angry themselves. This response is similar to the *still-face reaction* seen in studies in which researchers observed 2- to 7-month-olds' responses to parents who deliberately assumed a still-faced, unreactive pose. The babies tried a variety of tactics—facial expressions, vocalizations, and body movements—to get the parent to respond again. When these efforts failed, the babies—much like babies with depressed parents—turned away, frowned, and cried. This response occurs only when natural human communication is disrupted—not to a still-faced doll or to the mother wearing a still-faced mask. The still-face reaction is seen in babies from diverse cultures, suggesting that it is a built-in withdrawal response to caregivers' lack of communication, as occurs when a parent is depressed.

APPLY: Recently divorced, Jeannine—mother of 3-month-old Jacob—feels lonely, depressed, and anxious about finances. How might Jeannine's emotional state affect Jacob's emotional and social adjustment? What can be done to help Jeannine and Jacob? (p. 404)

Maternal depression can have devastating effects on the parent–child relationship. Depressed mothers rarely smile at, comfort, or talk to their babies, and their babies often respond by turning away, crying, and looking sad or angry. Research suggests that if Jeannine's depression persists, her relationship with Jacob will likely worsen, putting Jacob at increased risk for serious adjustment problems during childhood. He may respond by withdrawing into a depressed mood himself or, alternatively, by becoming impulsive and aggressive.

Early treatment is vital to prevent Jeannine's depression from interfering with her relationship with Jacob. Jeannine should first seek counseling aimed at reducing stress and treating her depression, as well as therapy specifically focused on improving her relationship with Jacob by teaching her to engage in emotionally positive, responsive caregiving. If Jeannine does not respond easily to treatment, a warm relationship with his father or another caregiver can safeguard Jacob's well-being.

REFLECT: Using one of your own experiences, illustrate the bidirectional relationship between emotion and cognition. (p. 402)

This is an open-ended question with no right or wrong answer.

REVIEW: Why do many infants show stranger anxiety in the second half of the first year? What factors can increase or decrease wariness of strangers? (pp. 407–408)

Like anger, fear rises during the second half of the first year into the second year. Older infants hesitate before playing with a new toy, and newly crawling infants soon back away from heights. But the most frequent expression of fear is *stranger anxiety* in response to unfamiliar adults, seen in many, though not all, infants and toddlers. The response depends on several factors: temperament (some babies are generally more fearful), past experiences with strangers, and the current situation. When an unfamiliar adult picks up the infant in a new situation, stranger anxiety is likely. But if the adult sits still while the baby moves around and a parent is nearby, infants often show positive and curious behavior. The stranger's style of interaction—expressing warmth, holding out an attractive toy, playing a familiar game, and approaching slowly rather than abruptly—reduces the baby's fear. As cognitive development permits toddlers to discriminate more effectively between threatening and nonthreatening people and situations, stranger anxiety declines. This change is adaptive because adults other than caregivers will soon be important in children's development.

Cross-cultural research shows that infant-rearing practices can modify stranger anxiety. Among the Efe hunters and gatherers of Congo, West Africa, where the maternal death rate is high, infant survival is safeguarded by a collective caregiving system in which, from birth, Efe babies are passed from one adult to another. Consequently, Efe infants show little stranger anxiety.

CONNECT: Why do children of depressed parents have difficulty regulating emotion (see page 404)? What implications do their weak self-regulatory skills have for their response to cognitive and social challenges? (pp. 409–412)

Infants whose parents "read" and respond contingently and sympathetically to their emotional cues tend to be less fussy and fearful, to express more pleasurable emotion, to be more interested in exploration, and to be easier to soothe. In contrast, depressed parents are more likely to respond impatiently or angrily, or to be unresponsive, waiting to intervene until the infant has become extremely agitated. These responses reinforce the baby's rise to intense distress, making it harder for parents to soothe the baby in the future, and also for the baby to learn to calm herself. When caregivers fail to regulate stressful experiences for infants who cannot yet regulate them for themselves, brain structures that buffer stress may fail to develop properly, resulting in an anxious, emotionally reactive child who has a reduced capacity for managing emotional problems.

Later, as preschoolers, children learn strategies for regulating emotion by watching adults handle their own feelings. Because a depressed mother rarely expresses positive emotions and has difficulty with her own emotional regulation, her preschooler is likely to have continuing problems managing emotion that will seriously interfere with psychological adjustment.

APPLY: At age 14 months, Reggie built a block tower and gleefully knocked it down. But at age 2, he called to his mother and pointed proudly to his tall block tower. What explains this change in Reggie's emotional behavior? (pp. 408–409)

In the middle of the second year, as 18- to 24-month-olds become firmly aware of the self as a separate, unique individual, self-conscious emotions appear. These higher-order emotions, including guilt, shame, embarrassment, envy, and pride, all involve injury to or enhancement of our sense of self. At 14 months, Reggie had not yet developed a clear sense of himself as a separate person, so he simply enjoyed the experience of building the block tower and then knocking it down. But at age 2, Reggie experienced pride in his achievement at stacking the blocks into a tower and wanted to share his accomplishment with his mother.

Development of pride and other self-conscious emotions also depends on adult instruction in *when* to feel proud, ashamed, or guilty. The situations in which adults encourage self-conscious emotions vary from culture to culture. In Western individualistic nations, children are generally taught to feel pride in personal achievement, as Reggie is expressing.

REFLECT: How do you typically manage negative emotion? Describe several recent examples. How might your early experiences, gender, and cultural background have influenced your style of emotional self-regulation? (pp. 409–413)

This is an open-ended question with no right or wrong answer.

REVIEW: What do preschoolers understand about emotion, and how do cognition and social experience contribute to their understanding? (pp. 415–416)

Early in the preschool years, children refer to causes, consequences, and behavioral signs of emotion, and over time their understanding becomes more accurate and complex. By age 4 to 5, they correctly judge the causes of many basic emotions, but their explanations tend to emphasize external factors over internal states—a balance that changes with age. Preschoolers can predict what a playmate expressing a certain emotion might do next, and they realize that thinking and feeling are interconnected and come up with effective ways to relieve others' negative feelings, such as hugging a friend who is sad.

In middle childhood, children's ability to consider conflicting cues when explaining others' emotions improves, and children recognize that people can experience more than one emotion at a time, unlike preschoolers, who deny that two emotions can occur at once, much as they do not integrate two variables (height and width) in a Piagetian conservation-of-liquid task.

Social experience also contributes to emotional understanding. The more mothers label emotions, explain them, and express warmth and enthusiasm when conversing with preschoolers, the more "emotion words" children use and the better developed their emotional understanding. Preschoolers whose parents frequently acknowledge their emotional reactions and explicitly teach them about diverse emotions are better able to judge others' emotions when tested at later ages. As preschoolers learn more about emotion from interacting with adults, they engage in more emotion talk with siblings and friends, especially during make-believe play. Make-believe, in turn, contributes to emotional understanding, especially when children play with siblings. The intense nature of the sibling relationship, combined with frequent acting out of feelings, makes pretending an excellent context for early learning about emotions. As early as 3 to 5 years of age, children seem to recognize that acknowledging others' emotions and explaining their own enhance the quality of relationships.

CONNECT: Why is good emotional self-regulation vital for empathy to result in sympathy and prosocial behavior? (pp. 416–418)

Empathy involves a complex interaction of cognition and affect—the ability to detect different emotions, to take another's emotional perspective, and to respond emotionally in a similar way. Temperament plays a role in whether empathy occurs and whether it prompts sympathetic, prosocial behavior or a personally distressed, self-focused response. Children who are sociable, assertive, and good at regulating emotion are more likely than poor emotion regulators to help, share, and comfort others in distress, and these children are also more likely to empathize with others' positive emotions of joy and happiness. In contrast, aggressive children's high hostility, weakened capacity to take another's perspective, and impulsive acting out of negative feelings blunt their capacity for empathy and sympathy. And shy children may not display sympathetic concern because they are easily overwhelmed by anxiety when others are distressed.

CONNECT: Cite ways that parenting contributes to emotional understanding, self-conscious emotions, empathy, and sympathy. Do you see any patterns? Explain. (pp. 408–409, 416–418)

Parents promote children's development of emotional understanding when they label emotions, explain them, and express warmth and enthusiasm when conversing with preschoolers. Preschoolers whose parents frequently acknowledge their children's emotions and explicitly teach them about diverse emotions are better able to judge others' emotions when tested at later ages.

Self-conscious emotions develop as 18- to 24-month-olds become firmly aware of the self as a separate individual, but children also require adult instruction in *when* to feel proud, ashamed, or guilty. Quality of adult feedback influences children's early self-evaluative reactions. For example, when parents repeatedly comment on the worth of the child and her performance, their children experience self-conscious emotions intensely. In contrast, when parents focus on how to improve performance, they induce moderate, more adaptive levels of shame and pride and greater persistence on difficult tasks.

Parenting also profoundly influences the development of empathy and sympathy. When parents are warm, encourage their child's emotional expressiveness, and show a sensitive, empathetic concern for the child's feelings, their children are likely to react in a concerned way to the distress of others—relationships that persist into adolescence and emerging adulthood.

By watching adults handle their own feelings, preschoolers pick up strategies for regulating their own emotion, including negative emotion that threatens their sense of self-worth. Children who experience angry, punitive parenting, or receive praise and blame that focus on the child's worth rather than on performance, are likely to have greater difficulty in developing effective emotion-regulation skills. Because these emotionally reactive children become increasingly difficult to rear, they often are targets of ineffective parenting, a bidirectional effect that compounds their poor emotional self-regulation. In contrast, when parents are warm, acknowledge emotion and encourage emotional expressiveness, and demonstrate emotional understanding, empathy, and sympathy, their children are likely to develop these capacities.

Chapter 10 Emotional Development

APPLY: When 15-month-old Ellen fell down while running, she looked at her mother, who smiled and exclaimed, "Oh, wasn't that a funny tumble!" How is Ellen likely to respond emotionally, and why? (pp. 414–415)

Beginning at 8 to 10 months, as babies start to evaluate unfamiliar people, objects, and events in terms of their own safety and security, they often engage in *social referencing*—relying on another person's emotional reaction to appraise an uncertain situation. Many studies show that a caregiver's emotional expression (happy, angry, or fearful) influences an infant's or toddler's social referencing. This means that parents can use social referencing to teach their youngster how to react to everyday events. As recall memory and language skills improve, babies retain these emotional messages over longer time intervals. By the middle of the second year, social referencing also permits toddlers to compare their own and others' assessments of events. When Ellen fell down, she looked to her mother for an emotional reaction. Her mother's smile and exclamation revealed that she viewed the situation in a positive light, and Ellen will be likely to respond in similar fashion. In this way, Ellen's mother is helping to regulate her daughter's emotional experience.

REVIEW: How do genetic and environmental factors work together to influence temperament? Cite examples from research on nonshared environmental influences, cultural variations in temperament, and goodness of fit. (pp. 423–425, 426)

The word *temperament* implies a genetic foundation for individual differences in personality. Research indicates that identical twins are more similar than fraternal twins across a wide range of temperamental traits and personality measures. Heritability estimates derived from kinship studies suggest that genetic factors account for about half of individual differences in temperament and personality. But environment also plays a powerful role. For example, persistent nutritional and emotional deprivation profoundly alters temperament, resulting in maladaptive emotional reactivity. Heredity and environment often jointly contribute to temperament, in that a child's approach to the world affects the experiences to which he or she is exposed.

Nonshared environmental influences: Nonshared environmental influences—those that make siblings different from one another—play an important role in personality development. Parents' tendency to emphasize each child's unique qualities affects their child-rearing practices. In a study of 3-year-old identical twins, mothers' differential treatment of each twin predicted differences between twins in psychological adjustment. The twin who received more warmth and less punitive parenting was more positive in mood and prosocial behavior and less likely to have behavior problems. Each child, in turn, evokes responses from caregivers that are consistent with parental beliefs and the child's developing temperament. Siblings' distinct experiences with teachers, peers, and others outside the family also affect personality development.

Cultural variations: Variations in temperament between infants in different cultures may have genetic roots, but they are supported by cultural beliefs and practices. For example, Japanese mothers usually say that babies come into the world as independent beings who must learn to rely on their parents through close physical contact. American mothers typically believe just the opposite—that they must wean the baby away from dependency toward autonomy. These cultural beliefs influence the ways in which parents interact with their children. As another example, Chinese and Japanese adults discourage babies from expressing strong emotion, which contributes to their infants' tranquility. These differences in child rearing enhance early ethnic variations in temperament.

Goodness of fit: Thomas and Chess proposed a *goodness-of-fit model* to describe how temperament and environment together can produce favorable outcomes. Goodness of fit involves creating child-rearing environments that recognize each child's temperament while encouraging more adaptive functioning. If a child's disposition interferes with learning or getting along with others, adults must gently but consistently counteract the child's maladaptive style.

CONNECT: Do findings on ethnic differences in temperament illustrate genetic–environmental correlation, discussed on pages 122–123 in Chapter 3? Explain. (p. 424)

Because parents provide their child with an environment that reflects their own heredity, ethnic differences in children's temperament are, first, an example of *passive* genetic–environmental correlation. The child has no control over the choice of environment but is likely to take on certain ethnic characteristics for both genetic and environmental reasons. For example, compared with North American Caucasian infants, Asian babies tend to be less active, irritable, and vocal, more easily soothed when upset, and better at quieting themselves. Chinese and Japanese toddlers are also more fearful and inhibited, remaining closer to their mothers in an unfamiliar playroom and displaying more anxiety when interacting with a stranger. They are also more emotionally restrained, smiling, laughing, and crying less than Caucasian-American babies.

Although these variations may have genetic roots, they are supported by cultural beliefs and practices. Japanese mothers usually say that newborn babies come into the world as independent beings who must learn to rely on their mothers through close physical contact. American mothers typically believe just the opposite—that they must wean the baby away from dependence toward autonomy. Consistent with these beliefs, Asian mothers interact gently, soothingly, and gesturally with their babies, whereas Caucasian mothers use a more active, stimulating, verbal approach—differences that enhance early ethnic variations in temperament.

APPLY: Mandy and Jeff are parents of 2-year-old inhibited Sam and 3-year-old difficult Maria. Explain the importance of effortful control to Mandy and Jeff, and suggest ways they can strengthen it in each of their children. (pp. 421–423, 426–427)

Effortful control, the self-regulatory dimension of temperament, is the capacity to voluntarily suppress a dominant response in order to plan and execute a more adaptive response. Variations in effortful control are evident in how effectively a child can focus and shift attention, inhibit impulses, and manage negative emotion. Beginning in the preschool years, children's capacity for effortful control—their ability to restrain negative emotion and impulsive action—is linked to favorable development and adjustment in diverse cultures. Positive outcomes include persistence, task mastery, academic achievement, cooperation, moral maturity, empathy, sympathy, prosocial behaviors of sharing and helpfulness, and resistance to stress.

Both inhibited and difficult children benefit from warm, accepting parenting that makes firm but reasonable demands for mastering new experiences. With a reserved, inactive toddler like Sam, highly stimulating parenting—questioning, instructing, and pointing out objects—is likely to foster exploration. Preschoolers who were high in such fearful reactivity as 2-year-olds tended to score slightly better than agemates in effortful control as 4-year-olds. But if Mandy and Jeff overprotect Sam, they will make it harder for him to overcome his urge to retreat from new stimuli.

A difficult child, like Maria, will also withdraw from new experiences but will react negatively and intensely. Mandy and Jeff should be aware that in toddlerhood and childhood, parental sensitivity, support, clear expectations, and limits foster effortful control, reducing the likelihood that Maria's difficultness will persist and lead to emotional and social difficulties. Recent evidence indicates that temperamentally difficult children function much worse than other children when exposed to inept parenting, yet benefit most from good parenting.

Infants are born with unique dispositions, but parenting practices can impede or promote children's effortful control, thereby profoundly altering the link between early temperament and development.

REFLECT: How would you describe your temperament as a young child? Do you think it has remained stable, or has it changed? What factors might be involved? (p. 423)

This is an open-ended question with no right or wrong answer.

REVIEW: What factors explain stability in attachment pattern for some children and change for others? Are these factors also involved in the link between attachment in infancy and later development? Explain. (p. 432)

Quality of attachment is usually secure and stable for middle-SES babies experiencing favorable life conditions. And infants who move from insecurity to security typically have well-adjusted mothers with positive family and friendship ties. In contrast, in low-SES families with many daily stresses and little social support, attachment generally moves away from security or changes from one insecure pattern to another. These findings indicate that securely attached babies more often maintain their attachment status than insecure babies, whose relationship with the caregiver is, by definition, fragile and uncertain. In one poverty-stricken sample, however, many securely attached infants ended up insecure when reassessed in early adulthood. Child maltreatment, maternal depression, and poor family functioning in adolescence distinguished these young people from the few who stayed securely attached. Disorganized/disoriented attachment is the only insecure pattern that is as stable as attachment security, with nearly 70 percent retaining this classification over the second year and the majority remaining highly insecure over the long run.

CONNECT: Review research on emotional self-regulation on page 410. How do the caregiving experiences of securely attached infants promote the development of emotional self-regulation? (p. 434)

Sensitive caregiving—responding promptly, consistently, and appropriately to infants and holding them tenderly and carefully—is moderately related to attachment security in both biological and adoptive mother–infant pairs and in diverse cultures and SES groups. In studies of Western infants, a special form of communication called *interactional synchrony* separated the experiences of secure from insecure babies. It is best described as a sensitively tuned "emotional dance," in which the caregiver responds to infant signals in a well-timed, rhythmic, appropriate fashion, and both partners match emotional states, especially the positive ones. Sensitive face-to-face play, in which interactional synchrony occurs, helps infants regulate emotion. Infants whose parents read and respond contingently and sympathetically to their emotional cues tend to be less fussy, to express more pleasurable emotion, to be more interested in exploration, and to be easier to soothe.

Chapter 10 Emotional Development

APPLY: In evaluating her childhood attachment experiences, Monica recalls her mother as tense and distant. Is Monica's newborn daughter likely to develop an insecure attachment? Explain, using research on adults' internal working models. (p. 437)

It is important not to assume any direct transfer of parents' childhood experiences to quality of attachment with their own children. Parental internal working models are *reconstructed memories* affected by many factors, including relationship experiences over the life course, personality, and current life satisfaction. Our early rearing experiences do not destine us to become sensitive or insensitive parents. Rather, the way we *view* our childhoods—our ability to come to terms with negative events, to integrate new information into our working models, and to look back on our own parents in an understanding, forgiving way—appears to be much more influential in how we rear our children than the actual history of care we received. Monica needs to come to terms with her memories of her own childhood and resolve her negative feelings toward her mother. As long as Monica regards her childhood with objectivity and balance, neither idealizing her mother nor feeling angry about the past, her daughter should develop a secure infant–mother attachment.

REFLECT: How would you characterize your internal working model? What factors, in addition to your early relationship with your parents, might have influenced it? (p. 437)

This is an open-ended question with no right or wrong answer.

REVIEW: Cite evidence that high-quality infant and toddler child care supports development, whereas poor-quality care undermines it. (pp. 441–443)

Good child care can reduce the negative impact of a stressed, poverty-stricken home life and sustain the benefits of growing up in an economically advantaged family. Evidence from the U.S. National Institute of Child Health and Development (NICHD) Study of Early Child Care, a longitudinal study of more than 1,300 infants and their families, confirms that use of nonparental care by itself does not affect attachment quality, although spending many hours in poor-quality child care, especially when combined with risk factors in the home, contributed to attachment insecurity. In contrast, when children reached age 3, a history of higher-quality child care predicted better social skills. In sum, among NICHD participants, those in both poor-quality home and child-care environments fared worst in social skills and problem behaviors, whereas those in both high-quality home and child-care environments fared best. In between were those preschoolers who were in high-quality child care but poor-quality homes; these children benefited from the protective influence of high-quality child care.

APPLY: Randi and Mike are worried that placing their 6-month-old baby, Lucinda, in child care may disrupt Lucinda's sense of security. List steps that Randi and Mike can take to ensure that Lucinda's experiences—at home and in child care—support her emotional and social development. (pp. 441–443)

Research suggests that quality of caregiving is crucially important to young children's development. Randi and Mike can help support Lucinda's attachment security by engaging in sensitive, warm parenting. In addition, they should select a high-quality child-care center for Lucinda to attend. For child care to foster attachment security, the professional caregiver's relationship with the baby is vital. When caregiver–child ratios are generous, group sizes are small, and caregivers are educated about child development and child rearing, caregivers' interactions are more positive and children develop more favorably—cognitively, emotionally, and socially. Child care with these characteristics, by relieving rather than intensifying parental and child stress, can promote healthy attachment and development.

SUGGESTED READINGS

Read, V. (2009). *Developing attachment in early years settings: Nurturing secure relationships from birth to five years*. New York: Taylor & Francis. Presents research-based strategies for fostering secure attachment in infants and young children. Topics include measuring attachment; individual differences in attachment; the importance of high-quality child care; and the relationship between attachment, emotional growth, and learning.

Sokol, B.W., Müller, U., Carpendale, J. M., Young, A. R., & Iarocci, G. (2010). (Eds.). *Social interaction and the development of social understanding and executive functions*. New York: Oxford University Press. A collection of chapters examining the complex relationship between social interaction, behavior, and cognitive development. The authors emphasize how child rearing, family background, education, and culture contribute to the development of self-control and social understanding in children and adolescents.

Strelau, J. (2008). *Temperament as a regulator of behavior: After fifty years of research*. New York: Percheron Press. Drawing on 50 years of research, this book examines the relationship between temperament and diverse aspects of behavior, including learning styles, physiological aspects of temperament, self-regulation, and the role of temperament in moderating the effects of stress. The author also provides an overview of assessment instruments used to measure temperament.

MEDIA MATERIALS

For details on individual video segments that accompany the DVD for *Child Development*, Ninth Edition, please see the DVD Guide for *Explorations in Child Development*. The DVD and DVD Guide are available through your Pearson sales representative.

Additional DVDs that may be useful in your class are listed below. These are not available through your Pearson sales representative, but you can order them directly from the distributors. (See contact information at the end of this manual.)

Childcare Basics (2008, Films Media Group, 18 min.). When dual-earner couples and single parents are at work, who takes care of their children? This program describes the child-care industry—its goals, policies, procedures, and licensing and accreditation standards—and presents the advantages and disadvantages of a variety of child-care options, including preschool, daycare, nannies, parent's-day-out programs, and government-funded programs. Educational resources are available online.

Families Talk About...Grandparents as Parents (2008, Insight Media, 15 min.). In this program, grandparents discuss their experiences with and the challenges of becoming the primary caregivers of their grandchildren.

Fatherhood: The Influence in the First Two Years (2003, Insight Media, 30 min.). Examining the evolving role of the father, this program shows how a father's contribution to child rearing affects the development of a child.

Getting to Know You: The First Two Years of Psychosocial Development (2003, Insight Media, 30 min.). This program examines social and emotional development during the first two years of life, including factors that shape the emotions and personality, the development of temperament, social referencing, and Mary Ainsworth's research on attachment.

Infants: Social & Emotional Development (2010, Magna Systems/Learning Seed, 23 min.). This program examines the range of emotions—from distress to enjoyment—that infants express in the first year of life. It shows babies as they learn to distinguish others' expressions, as well as their ability to imitate. The program also examines the stages of emotional development, how children form attachments, and the influence of personality and temperament on an infant's social and emotional growth.

John Bowlby: Attachment Theory Across Generations (2007, Insight Media, 35 min.). Featuring the work of John Bowlby, this program examines the impact that attachment relationships have on adult behavior, including the transmission of attachment patterns to subsequent generations.

Life at 1: A Longitudinal Study in Child Development (2006, Films Media Group, 2 parts, 55 min. each). Marking the first phase of a seven-year project, this two-part series invites viewers into the lives of a group of 1-year-olds and their families. The joys, traumas, and challenges in each child's first year create a set of informative case studies that shed light on the impact on children of marital stress, career pressures, medical issues, and the interplay of nature and nurture.

Life with Dad (2002, Films Media Group, 44 min.). This program provides an intimate look at the daily challenges facing three single fathers and their children. It addresses societal acceptance of single dads and the concepts of maleness, fatherhood, and family.

Mary Ainsworth: Attachment and the Growth of Love (2005, Davidson Films, 38 min.). This film discusses how Mary Ainsworth's observations of mothers and babies in Uganda and in Baltimore supported the theoretical work of John Bowlby. The film includes footage of the Strange Situation and discusses the four major attachment patterns. The film emphasizes the lifetime importance of attachment and describes assessing attachment in adults.

Parents and Children (2007, Insight Media, 30 min.). This program explores the factors that influence parenting choices, including social class. It also looks at the growing impact of child care outside of the home.

Secure Attachments: The Foundation of Relationships in Child Care Programs (2005, Child Development Media, 21 min.). Part of the series *Relationship-Based Child Care for Babies and Toddlers,* this program is designed to give child-care professionals an understanding of attachment theory and research. The components of a secure attachment relationship are explored, along with examples of behaviors that indicate insecure attachment. Set in a busy infant room in a child-care center, the program highlights practical steps that caregivers can take to create links between home and child care, including suggestions for fostering secure attachment relationships.

The Mommy Mystique: The Anxiety of Modern Motherhood (2005, Films Media Group, 23 min.). Featuring an interview with author and cultural observer Judith Warner, this *ABC News* program conveys the perspective of an American mother who has done much of her parenting outside the United States. Warner discusses her book, *Perfect Madness,* and its observations about the hectic, competitive lifestyle embraced by many American moms.

The Temperament Program (2005, Child Development Media, 4 films, each 20–22 min.). This four-part series is based on the research of Stella Chess and Alexander Thomas as well as the work of the Temperament Program at Kaiser Permanente Northern California. The series includes *Using Temperament Concepts to Prevent Behavior Problems; Understanding the High-Intensity, Slow-Adapting Child; Understanding the High-Activity, Slow-Adapting Child with Low Rhythmicity;* and *Understanding the Withdrawn Child with High Sensitivity and Intensity.* Students will have an opportunity to observe children of diverse temperaments interacting in their natural environments. The series discusses child-rearing strategies.

CHAPTER 11
SELF AND SOCIAL UNDERSTANDING

CHAPTER-AT-A-GLANCE

Chapter Outline	Instruction Ideas	Supplements
Emergence of Self and Development of Self-Concept pp. 448–460 Self-Awareness • The Categorical, Remembered, and Enduring Selves • The Inner Self: Children's Theory of Mind • Self-Concept • Cognitive, Social, and Cultural Influences on Self-Concept	Learning Objectives 11.1–11.4 Lecture Enhancements 11.1–11.2 Learning Activities 11.1–11.3 Ask Yourself p. 460	Test Bank Items 1–51, 120–124 Please contact your Pearson publisher's representative for a wide range of video offerings available to adopters.
Self-Esteem: The Evaluative Side of Self-Concept pp. 461–468, 469 The Structure of Self-Esteem • Changes in Level of Self-Esteem: The Role of Social Comparisons • Influences on Self-Esteem • Achievement-Related Attributions	Learning Objectives 11.5–11.6 Lecture Enhancement 11.3 Learning Activities 11.2–11.4 Ask Yourself p. 468	Test Bank Items 52–81, 125
Constructing an Identity: Who Should I Become? pp. 468–475 Paths to Identity • Identity Status and Psychological Well-Being • Factors Affecting Identity Development	Learning Objective 11.7 Learning Activities 11.5–11.6 Ask Yourself p. 474	Test Bank Items 82–102, 126
Thinking About Other People pp. 476–480 Understanding People as Personalities • Understanding Social Groups: Race and Ethnicity	Learning Objective 11.8 Lecture Enhancement 11.4 Learning Activity 11.7	Test Bank Items 103–112, 127
Understanding Conflict: Social Problem Solving pp. 480–482 The Social Problem-Solving Process • Enhancing Social Problem Solving	Learning Objective 11.9 Learning Activity 11.8 Ask Yourself p. 482	Test Bank Items 113–119

BRIEF CHAPTER SUMMARY

Social cognition involves thinking about the self and other people. Although nonsocial and social cognition share many features, social cognition is more complex because behavior is affected by inner states that cannot be directly observed.

Self-awareness begins at birth, when infants sense that they are physically distinct from their surroundings. During the second year, toddlers become consciously aware of the self's physical features, and self-recognition is well under way. Sensitive caregiving and secure attachment promote early self-development.

By the end of the second year, language becomes a powerful tool in self-development. Between 18 and 30 months, children develop a categorical self, beginning to classify themselves and others on the basis of age, physical characteristics, goodness and badness, and competencies. Adult–child conversations about the past grant the child a remembered self, and preschoolers gradually develop an enduring self—a view of themselves as persisting over time.

As children think about themselves and others, they form a naïve theory of mind—a coherent understanding of their own and others' mental lives. Children's developing theory of mind contributes vitally to perspective taking. At the end of the second and continuing over the third year, children display a clearer grasp of people's emotions and desires, but their understanding is limited to a simplistic desire theory of mind. But from age 4 on, they exhibit a more advanced belief–desire theory of mind where both beliefs and desires determine actions. Children's understanding of false beliefs—ones that do not represent reality accurately—strengthens over the preschool years. Factors contributing to the development of theory of mind include language and verbal reasoning, executive function, parent–child conversations about mental states, make-believe play, and social interaction with siblings, friends, and adults.

As children think more intently about themselves, they construct a self-concept. Preschoolers' self-concepts are very concrete, but in middle childhood, children organize their observations of typical behaviors and internal states into general dispositions and make social comparisons between themselves and others. Adolescents can generalize about the self but often do so in contradictory ways in response to social pressures. From mid- to late adolescence, teenagers combine their traits into an organized system. The changing content of the self is a product of cognitive capacities, feedback from others, the development of perspective-taking skills, parental support, and the values of the child's culture.

Another component of self-concept is self-esteem—judgments of self-worth and feelings associated with those judgments. Self-esteem originates early, based on evaluative information available to children and their ability to process that information. It is profoundly influenced by the child's culture and by the family's child-rearing practices. As children become able to view themselves in terms of stable dispositions, they combine separate self-evaluations into an overall sense of self-esteem to which they add several new dimensions in adolescence. From middle childhood to adolescence, individual differences in self-esteem become increasingly stable.

Around age 3, children begin making attributions about their successes and failures, which affect their beliefs about whether or not greater effort can lead to success. Children who make mastery-oriented attributions credit their successes to ability and take an incremental view of ability, believing they can improve it through effort and focusing on learning goals. In contrast, children who develop learned helplessness attribute their failures, not their successes, to ability. They hold an entity view of ability and, as a result, focus on performance goals and tend to give up easily. Parents' and teachers' communications play an important role in children's attributions, as do cultural values.

Adolescents' self-descriptions provide the cognitive foundation for forming an identity, first recognized by Erikson as a crucial step toward becoming a productive, content adult. Identity achievement refers to exploration followed by commitment; moratorium involves exploration without having reached commitment. Less desirable identity statuses are foreclosure (commitment without exploration) and diffusion (lack of both exploration and commitment). For teenagers who are members of minority groups, a sense of ethnic identity is central to the quest for identity.

Children's person perception begins with concrete descriptions of others' behaviors; in adolescence, these are drawn together into organized character sketches. Basic concepts of race, ethnicity, and social class emerge in the preschool years, and school-age children absorb prevailing societal attitudes toward various social groups. However, prejudice can be greatly reduced through long-term intergroup contact and collaboration among groups.

Social problem-solving skills—generating and applying strategies that prevent or resolve disagreements in ways that are acceptable to both the self and others—improve over early and middle childhood and predict socially competent behavior. Interventions that teach effective social problem-solving skills improve peer relations and reduce the risk of adjustment difficulties.

Chapter 11 Self and Social Understanding

LEARNING OBJECTIVES

After reading this chapter, you should be able to answer the following:

11.1 Describe the development of self-awareness in infancy and toddlerhood, along with the emotional and social capacities it supports. (pp. 448–450)

11.2 Describe the development of the categorical, remembered, and enduring selves. (pp. 450–451)

11.3 Discuss theory-of-mind development from early to middle childhood, citing social consequences and contributing factors. (pp. 451–456, 457)

11.4 Discuss the development of self-concept from early childhood through adolescence, noting cognitive, social, and cultural influences. (pp. 456–460)

11.5 Discuss development of and influences on self-esteem from early childhood through adolescence. (pp. 461–464)

11.6 Discuss achievement-related attributions, and suggest ways to foster a mastery-oriented approach in children. (pp. 464–468, 469)

11.7 Describe the four identity statuses, along with factors affecting identity development. (pp. 468–475)

11.8 Discuss changes in children's appreciation of others' attributes and understanding of social groups, including factors that contribute to prejudice and ways to reduce it. (pp. 476–480)

11.9 Discuss the development of social problem-solving skills, noting ways to enhance social problem solving in children. (pp. 480–481)

LECTURE OUTLINE

I. INTRODUCTION (pp. 447–448)
   A. **Social cognition** refers to the way children come to understand their multifaceted social world—the development of thinking about the self and other people.
   B. The trends identified for cognitive development also apply to social understanding:
      1. Social-cognitive development proceeds *from concrete to abstract*.
      2. Social cognition becomes *better organized* with *age*.
      3. Children revise their ideas about the causes of behavior from *simple, one-sided explanations* to *complex, interacting relationships* that take into account both person and situation.
      4. Social cognition moves toward *metacognitive understanding* as children develop the ability to think about their own and other people's social thoughts.
   C. Social cognition is more complex than nonsocial cognition, but it develops as rapidly.

II. EMERGENCE OF SELF AND DEVELOPMENT OF SELF-CONCEPT (pp. 448–460)
   A. Self-Awareness (pp. 448–450)
      1. Beginnings of Self-Awareness
         a. At birth, infants sense that they are physically distinct from their surroundings.
         b. Newborns' remarkable capacity for *intermodal perception* supports the beginnings of self-awareness.
         c. Over the first few months, infants distinguish their own visual image from other stimuli, but their self-awareness is limited.
         d. Research shows that by 4 months, infants view another person as a potential social partner.
      2. Explicit Self-Awareness
         a. During the second year, toddlers become consciously aware of the self's physical features.
         b. Around age 2, **self-recognition**—identification of the self as a physically unique being—is well under way.
         c. As self-recognition takes shape, older toddlers also construct an explicit body self-awareness:
            (1) At the end of the second year, they realize that their own body can serve as an obstacle.
            (2) Nevertheless, toddlers lack an objective understanding of their own body dimensions. They make **scale errors,** attempting to do things that their body size makes impossible.

3. Influences on Self-Awareness
    a. During the first year, as infants act on the environment, they probably notice effects that help them sort out self, other people, and objects.
    b. Sensitive caregiving seems to play a role.
        (1) Securely attached toddlers display more complex self-related actions during play.
        (2) Eighteen-month-olds who often establish joint attention with their caregivers are advanced in mirror self-recognition.
    c. Cultural variations in early self-development include differences between children reared with a *distal parenting style,* common in cultures that value *independence,* versus a *proximal parenting style,* which is typical in cultures that value *interdependence*.
4. Self-Awareness and Early Emotional and Social Development
    a. Self-awareness leads to first efforts to understand another's perspective.
    b. Mirror self-awareness precedes the appearance of sustained, mutual peer imitation.
    c. Two-year-olds' self-recognition leads to a sense of ownership; the stronger their self-definitions, the more possessive 2-year-olds tend to be.

B. The Categorical, Remembered, and Enduring Selves (pp. 450–451)
    1. Because language permits children to represent and express the self more clearly, it greatly enhances self-awareness.
    2. Between 18 and 30 months, children develop a **categorical self** as they classify themselves and others on the basis of perceptually distinct attributes and behaviors and physical characteristics.
    3. Adult–child conversations about the past lead to an autobiographical memory, a life-story narrative that grants the child a **remembered self**—a more coherent portrait than is offered by the isolated, episodic memories of the first few years.
    4. These narratives are a major means through which caregivers imbue the young child's sense of self with cultural values.
    5. As they talk about personally significant events and as their cognitive skills advance, preschoolers gradually develop an **enduring self**—a view of themselves as persisting over time.

C. The Inner Self: Children's Theory of Mind (pp. 451–456, 457)
    1. As children think more about themselves and others, they form a naïve *theory of mind*—a coherent understanding of their own and others' rich mental lives.
    2. Young preschoolers are clearly aware of an **inner self** of private thoughts and imaginings.
    3. Children's developing theory of mind contributes vitally to **perspective taking**—the capacity to imagine what others may be thinking and feeling and to distinguish those viewpoints from one's own.
    4. Early Understandings of Mental States
        a. Over the first year of life, infants build an implicit appreciation of people as animate beings whose behavior is governed by intentions, desires, and feelings.
        b. At the end of the second year and continuing over the third year, children display a clearer grasp of people's emotions and desires and begin to realize that people differ from one another.
        c. Toddlers and young preschoolers comprehend mental states that can be readily inferred from their own and others' actions.
        d. But their understanding is limited to a simplistic **desire theory of mind:** They think that people always act in ways consistent with their desires and do not understand that behavior is also affected by less obvious, more interpretive mental states, such as beliefs.
    5. Development of Belief–Desire Reasoning
        a. Between ages 3 and 4, children increasingly refer to their own and others' thoughts and beliefs.
        b. From age 4 on, children exhibit a **belief–desire theory of mind,** a more advanced view in which both beliefs and desires determine actions, and they understand the relationship between these inner states.
        c. Evidence for preschoolers' belief–desire reasoning comes from games that test whether they realize that *false beliefs*—ones that do not represent reality accurately—can guide people's behavior.
            (1) Research shows that only a handful of 3-year-olds, but many 4-year-olds, can explain false beliefs.
            (2) Some researchers claim that procedures for false-belief tasks require verbal explanations, and they have made the controversial assertion that children comprehend others' false beliefs by age 15 months.
            (3) False-belief understanding strengthens gradually after age 3½, becoming more secure between ages 4 and 6.

6. Reasoning About Beliefs in Middle Childhood
   a. School-age children extend false-belief understanding further with the realization that people can increase their knowledge by making *mental inferences*.
   b. By age 6 to 7, children are aware that people form beliefs about other people's beliefs and that these *second-order beliefs* can also be wrong.
   c. Appreciation of *second-order false belief* requires the ability to view a situation from at least two perspectives—that is, to reason simultaneously about what two or more people are thinking, a form of perspective taking called **recursive thought.**
   d. At around age 7 to 8, children grasp that two people are likely to interpret the same event differently.
7. Social Consequences
   a. Preschoolers' capacity to use both beliefs and desires to predict people's behavior is a powerful tool for reflecting on thoughts and emotions and a good predictor of social skills.
   b. False-belief understanding is linked to gains in young children's capacity to discuss thoughts and feelings in conversations with friends, and it predicts quality of sociodramatic play.
   c. School-age children's capacity for recursive thought leads to further, dramatic gains in social skills: They now understand that conflicts often arise because of multiple yet legitimate interpretations of the same reality.
   d. Theory-of-mind development from early to middle childhood promotes children's reasoned attempts to change others' beliefs.
8. Factors Contributing to Children's Theory of Mind
   a. Language and Verbal Reasoning
      (1) The prefrontal cortex seems to play a crucial role in theory-of-mind development.
      (2) Understanding the mind requires the ability to reflect on thoughts, which language makes possible.
   b. Executive Function
      (1) Aspects of preschoolers' executive function—such as the ability to think flexibly and plan—predict current performance on false-belief tasks as well as improvements over time.
      (2) These cognitive skills enhance children's capacity to reflect on their experiences and mental states.
   c. Security of Attachment and Maternal "Mind-Mindedness"
      (1) Mothers of securely attached babies are more likely to comment appropriately on their infants' mental states and to continue to do so when their children reach preschool age.
      (2) This maternal "mind-mindedness" exposes infants and young children to concepts and language that help them think about their own and others' mental lives.
      (3) Children's reflections on inner states may be among the representations that make up their internal working models of close relationships.
   d. Make-Believe Play
      (1) Make-believe offers a rich context for thinking about the mind.
      (2) Preschoolers who are deeply absorbed in creating make-believe characters are more advanced than agemates in their understanding of false belief and other aspects of the mind.
   e. Social Interaction
      (1) Children with older siblings are exposed to and participate in more family talk about thoughts, beliefs, and emotions.
      (2) At age 4, elaborative, well-connected conversations, in which the parent builds on the child's contributions, is associated with children's theory-of-mind progress.
      (3) Core knowledge theorists believe that to profit from these social experiences, children must be biologically prepared to develop a theory of mind, and that children with *autism* are deficient in the brain mechanism that enables humans to detect mental states.

D. Self-Concept (pp. 456, 458–459)
   1. During early childhood, children begin to construct a **self-concept**—the set of attributes, abilities, attitudes, and values that an individual believes defines who he or she is.
   2. Early Childhood
      a. Preschoolers' self-concepts largely consist of observable characteristics.
      b. By age 3½, children also describe themselves in terms of typical emotions and attitudes.
      c. And by age 5, children's degree of agreement with statements about their psychological characteristics coincides with maternal reports of their personality traits.

3. Middle Childhood
   a. Over time, children organize their observations of typical behaviors and internal states into general dispositions.
   b. Between ages 8 and 11, a major shift occurs: When 11-year-olds describe themselves, they emphasize competencies, and they mention both positive and negative traits.
   c. These evaluative self-descriptions result from school-age children's **social comparisons**—judgments of their own appearance, abilities, and behavior in relation to those of others.
4. Adolescence
   a. Young adolescents unify separate traits into more abstract descriptors, but their generalizations about the self are not interconnected and are often contradictory.
   b. From middle to late adolescence, teenagers combine their traits into an organized system.
   c. Compared with school-age children, teenagers place more emphasis on social virtues.
   d. Adolescents move toward the kind of unity of self that is central to identity development.

E. Cognitive, Social, and Cultural Influences on Self-Concept (pp. 459–460)
   1. Cognitive development affects the changing *structure* of the self.
      a. School-age children combine typical experiences and behaviors into stable psychological dispositions.
      b. In middle childhood, children gain a clearer understanding of traits as causes of behavior.
      c. Formal operational thought transforms the adolescent's vision of the self into a complex and well-organized picture.
   2. The changing *content* of the self is a product of both cognitive capacities and feedback from others.
      a. Sociologist George Herbert Mead described the self as a **generalized other**—a blend of what we imagine important people in our lives think of us—and proposed that a psychological self emerges when children adopt a view of the self that resembles others' attitudes toward the child.
      b. Mead's ideas indicate that an improved ability to infer what other people are thinking is crucial for developing a self-concept based on personality traits.
      c. In middle childhood and adolescence, young people become better at "reading" messages they receive from others and internalizing others' expectations, forming an *ideal self* that they use to evaluate their real self; a large discrepancy between the two can greatly undermine self-esteem.
      d. The content of self-concept varies from culture to culture.

III. SELF-ESTEEM: THE EVALUATIVE SIDE OF SELF-CONCEPT (pp. 461–468, 469)
   A. **Self-esteem** refers to the judgments we make about our own worth and the feelings associated with those judgments.
   B. Self-esteem is important because evaluations of our own competencies affect emotional experiences, future behavior, and long-term psychological adjustment.
   C. The Structure of Self-Esteem (pp. 461–462)
      1. Researchers have studied self-esteem by applying *factor analysis* to children's ratings of the truth of various self-evaluative statements.
      2. The structure of self-esteem depends on evaluative information available to children and their ability to process that information.
      3. Around age 6 to 7, children in diverse Western cultures have formed at least four broad self-evaluations: academic competence, social competence, physical/athletic competence, and physical appearance.
      4. School-age children combine their separate self-evaluations into a general psychological image of themselves—an overall sense of self-esteem, so that self-esteem takes on a hierarchical structure.
      5. During childhood and adolescence, perceived physical appearance correlates more strongly with global self-esteem than any other self-esteem factor.
      6. The arrival of adolescence adds new dimensions of self-esteem—close friendship, romantic appeal, and job competence—reflecting important concerns of this period.
   D. Changes in Level of Self-Esteem: The Role of Social Comparisons (p. 462)
      1. Preschoolers have difficulty distinguishing between desired and actual competence, usually rating their own ability as very high and often underestimating the difficulty of tasks.
      2. Self-esteem declines over the first few years of elementary school as children evaluate themselves in various areas and become cognitively capable of social comparison.
      3. Because most children protect their self-esteem by eventually balancing social comparisons with personal achievement goals, this decline is seldom harmful.

4. From fourth grade on, self-esteem rises and remains high for the majority of young people.
5. A major exception is a decline in self-worth for some adolescents after transition to middle and high school.
E. Influences on Self-Esteem (pp. 463–464)
1. From middle childhood to adolescence, individual differences in self-esteem become increasingly stable.
2. Across age, sex, SES, and ethnic groups, individuals with mostly favorable self-esteem profiles tend to be well-adjusted, whereas low self-esteem in all areas is linked to adjustment difficulties.
3. Certain self-esteem factors are strongly related to poor adjustment. For example, those who view their peer relationships negatively are likely to be anxious and depressed.
4. Culture
   a. Cultural forces profoundly affect self-esteem.
      (1) A strong emphasis on social comparison in school may underlie the finding that despite their higher academic achievement, Chinese and Japanese children score lower than U.S. children in self-esteem.
      (2) At the same time, Asian children, whose culture values modesty and social harmony, rely less on social comparisons to promote their own self-esteem.
   b. Gender-stereotyped expectations also affect self-esteem.
      (1) By adolescence, girls feel less confident than boys about their physical appearance and athletic abilities.
      (2) Boys are somewhat advantaged in academic self-esteem, but girls exceed boys in self-esteem dimensions of close friendship and social acceptance.
   c. Compared with Caucasian agemates, African-American children tend to have slightly higher self-esteem.
   d. Children and adolescents who attend schools or live in neighborhoods where their SES and ethnic groups are well-represented have fewer self-esteem problems.
5. Child-Rearing Practices
   a. Children and adolescents whose parents are warm and accepting and provide reasonable expectations for mature behavior feel especially good about themselves.
   b. Controlling parents, who too often help or make decisions for their child, communicate a sense of inadequacy to children.
   c. Overly tolerant, indulgent parenting is linked to unrealistically high self-esteem. These children, whom researchers label *narcissistic,* are vulnerable to temporary, sharp drops in self-esteem when their overblown self-images are challenged.
   d. The best way to foster a good self-image is to encourage children to strive for worthwhile goals.
F. Achievement-Related Attributions (pp. 464–468, 469)
1. **Attributions** are our common, everyday explanations for the causes of our own and others' behavior.
   a. We group attributions into two broad categories: external, environmental causes and internal, psychological causes.
   b. Then we divide the category of psychological causes into *ability* and *effort.*
   c. Individual differences in **achievement motivation**—the tendency to persist at challenging tasks—are as important as intelligence in predicting school achievement.
2. Emergence of Achievement-Related Attributions
   a. Around age 3, children begin making attributions about their successes and failures; these affect their *expectancies of success,* which influence their willingness to try hard in the future.
   b. Preschoolers are "learning optimists" who rate their own ability very high and often underestimate task difficulty.
   c. By age 3, some children become nonpersisters, who give up easily when faced with a challenge and express shame and despondency after failing.
      (1) Nonpersisters have a history of parental criticism of their worth and of excessive control.
      (2) Persisters, in contrast, have parents who patiently support the child's initiative.
3. Mastery-Oriented versus Learned-Helpless Children
   a. School-age children gradually become able to distinguish among ability, effort, and external factors in explaining their performance.
   b. Mastery-oriented children:
      (1) Children who are high in achievement motivation make **mastery-oriented attributions,** crediting their successes to ability, a characteristic they can improve through trying hard and can count on when faced with new challenges.

(2) As a result of this **incremental view of ability,** mastery-oriented children attribute both failure and success to factors that can be changed or controlled.
- c. Learned-helpless children:
  - (1) Children who develop **learned helplessness** attribute their failures to lack of ability but their successes to external events, such as luck.
  - (2) These children hold an **entity view of ability**—a belief that it cannot be improved by trying hard.
- d. Mastery-oriented children focus on how best to increase their ability through effort.
- e. Learned-helpless children focus on obtaining positive and avoiding negative evaluations of their fragile sense of ability.
- f. Over time, learned-helpless children's ability no longer predicts how well they do.
- g. When adolescents view their own ability as fixed and low, they conclude that mastering a challenging task is not worth the cost—extremely high effort.

4. Influences on Achievement-Related Attributions
   - a. Adult communication plays a key role in children's development of mastery-oriented versus learned-helpless attributions.
     - (1) Parents' trait statements, even when positive, encourage children to adopt an entity view of ability that leads them to question their competence in the face of setbacks.
     - (2) Teachers who attribute children's failures to effort and who are caring and helpful tend to have mastery-oriented students.
   - b. For members of certain groups, such as girls and some ethnic minority children, performance is especially likely to be undermined by adult feedback, with the message that poor performance reflects inherently low ability.
   - c. Cultural values affect the development of learned helplessness: Asian parents and teachers are more likely than their American counterparts to hold an incremental view of ability.

5. Fostering a Mastery-Oriented Approach
   - a. **Attribution retraining** gives learned-helpless children repeated feedback to help them revise their attributions and believe that they can overcome failure by exerting more effort.
   - b. Another approach is to encourage low-effort students to focus less on grades and more on mastering a task for its own sake.
   - c. Attribution retraining is most effective when begun early.

IV. CONSTRUCTING AN IDENTITY: WHO SHOULD I BECOME? (pp. 468–475)
   A. Forming an **identity,** first recognized by psychoanalyst Erik Erikson as a major personality achievement and a crucial step toward becoming a productive, content adult, involves defining who you are, what you value, and the directions you choose to pursue in life.
   1. The search for identity drives many choices, such as vocation and expression of one's sexual orientation, as well as moral, political, and religious ideals.
   2. Erikson believed that successful psychosocial outcomes of infancy and childhood pave the way toward a coherent, positive identity.
      - a. In this view, teenagers in complex societies experience an *identity crisis*—a temporary period of confusion and distress as they experiment with alternatives before settling on values and goals.
      - b. Through this process of soul-searching, they develop a solid inner core that provides a sense of sameness as they move through different roles in daily life.
      - c. Although current theorists agree that questioning of values, plans, and priorities is necessary for a mature identity, they no longer describe this process as a "crisis."
      - d. For most young people, identity development is a process of *exploration* followed by *commitment*.
   3. Erikson described the negative outcome of adolescence as *identity confusion,* which occurs when young people's earlier conflicts were resolved negatively or when society limits their choices to ones that do not match their limits and desires.
   B. Paths to Identity (pp. 470–471)
   1. Progress in identity development can be evaluated on two key criteria derived from Erikson's theory: *exploration* and *commitment,* which, in various combinations, yield four *identity statuses:*
      - a. **Identity achievement** involves commitment to values, beliefs, and goals following a period of exploration.
      - b. **Identity moratorium** consists of exploration without reaching commitment.

Chapter 11 Self and Social Understanding

      c. **Identity foreclosure** is commitment in the absence of exploration.
      d. **Identity diffusion** is an apathetic state characterized by lack of both exploration and commitment.
   2. The pattern of identity development often varies across *identity domains,* such as sexual orientation, vocation, and religious, political, and other worldviews.
   3. Many young people change from "lower" statuses (foreclosure or diffusion) to "higher" statuses (moratorium or achievement) between their mid-teens and mid-twenties.
   4. Because attending college provides opportunities to explore educational and career options and lifestyles, college students are increasingly engaged in focused, in-depth consideration of potential commitments.
   5. Those who go to work immediately after high school graduation often settle on a self-definition earlier.
   6. Researchers once thought that adolescent girls postponed establishing an identity, focusing instead on Erikson's next stage, intimacy development. However, adolescents of both sexes typically make progress on identity concerns before experiencing genuine intimacy in relationships.
  C. Identity Status and Psychological Well-Being (pp. 471–472, 473)
   1. Individuals who move away from foreclosure and diffusion toward moratorium and achievement build a well-structured identity that integrates various domains.
   2. Identity achievement and moratorium are both psychologically healthy routes to a mature self-definition, whereas long-term foreclosure and diffusion are maladaptive.
   3. Adolescents who get stuck in either foreclosure or diffusion are passive in the face of identity concerns and have adjustment difficulties.
      a. Foreclosed individuals display a *dogmatic, inflexible cognitive style,* internalizing others' values and beliefs and resisting information that threatens their position.
      b. Long-term diffused teenagers are the least mature in identity development.
        (1) They typically use a *diffuse-avoidant* cognitive style, avoiding dealing with personal decisions and problems.
        (2) Of all young people, they are the most likely to commit antisocial acts and to use and abuse drugs.
  D. Factors Affecting Identity Development (pp. 472–475)
   1. Personality
      a. Adolescents who assume that absolute truth is always attainable tend to be foreclosed.
      b. Those who doubt that they will ever feel certain about anything are more often identity-diffused.
      c. Those who appreciate that they can use rational criteria to choose among alternatives are more likely to be in a state of moratorium or identity achievement.
   2. Family
      a. Teenagers' identity development is enhanced when their families serve as a "secure base" from which they can confidently move out into the wider world.
      b. Foreclosed teenagers usually have close bonds with parents but lack opportunities for healthy separation.
      c. Diffused young people report the lowest levels of parental support.
   3. Peers
      a. Interaction with diverse peers encourages adolescents to explore values and role possibilities.
      b. Close friends provide emotional support, assistance, and models of identity development.
   4. School, Community, and Culture
      a. Identity development also depends on schools and communities that offer rich and varied opportunities for exploration.
      b. Culture strongly influences an aspect of mature identity not captured by the identity-status approach: constructing a sense of self-continuity despite major personal changes.
      c. Societal forces are also responsible for the special challenges faced by gay, lesbian, and bisexual youths and by ethnic minority adolescents in forming a secure identity.
      d. For teenagers who are members of minority groups, **ethnic identity**—a sense of ethnic group membership and attitudes and feelings associated with that membership—is central to the quest for identity.
      e. Minority youths often feel caught between the standards of two cultures. The result is **acculturative stress**—psychological distress resulting from conflict between the minority and the host culture.
      f. Forming a **bicultural identity**—by exploring and adopting values from both the adolescent's subculture and the dominant culture—can be beneficial.

V. THINKING ABOUT OTHER PEOPLE (pp. 476–480)
　A. Understanding People as Personalities (p. 476)
　　1. Researchers study **person perception**—the way we size up the qualities of people with whom we are familiar—by asking children to describe people they know.
　　2. Young children's descriptions of others focus on concrete activities, behaviors, and commonly experienced emotions and attitudes.
　　3. In adolescence, inferences about others' personalities are drawn together into organized character sketches that integrate physical traits, typical behaviors, and inner dispositions.
　B. Understanding Social Groups: Race and Ethnicity (pp. 476–480)
　　1. At an early age, children begin to acquire stereotypes about social groups, and those stereotypes can easily overwhelm their capacity to size up people as individuals.
　　2. Most 3- and 4-year-olds have formed basic concepts of race and ethnicity.
　　3. By the early school years, children absorb prevailing societal attitudes, associating power and privilege with white people and poverty and inferior status with people of color.
　　4. Children pick up much information about group status from (1) social contexts that present a world sorted into groups and (2) experiences involving explicit labeling of groups, even when the group distinctions presented are neutral rather than stereotypic.
　　5. Children are especially likely to form biased attitudes when an authority figure validates a status hierarchy by labeling, sorting, or treating groups differently.
　　6. In-Group and Out-Group Biases: Development of Prejudice
　　　a. By age 5 to 6, white children in diverse Western nations generally evaluate their own racial group more favorably than other racial groups—biases that also characterize many adults.
　　　b. *In-group favoritism* emerges first; children simply prefer their own group, generalizing from self to similar others.
　　　c. *Out-group prejudice* requires a more challenging social comparison between in-group and out-group. But it does not take long for white children to acquire negative attitudes toward ethnic minority out-groups.
　　　d. Many ethnic minority children show *out-group favoritism,* in which they assign positive characteristics to the privileged ethnic majority and negative characteristics to their own group.
　　　e. School-age children understand that people who look different need not think, feel, or act differently; as a result, their voicing of negative attitudes toward minorities declines.
　　　f. Yet, even in children and adolescents who are aware of the injustice of discrimination, prejudice can operate subtly, unintentionally, and without awareness.
　　　g. Research suggests that, at least to some degree, older school-age children's desire to present themselves in a socially acceptable light may contribute to reduced expressions of out-group prejudice.
　　　h. The extent to which children hold racial and ethnic biases depends on the following personal and situational factors: a fixed view of personality traits, overly high self-esteem, and a social world in which people are sorted into groups.
　　7. Reducing Prejudice
　　　a. An effective way to reduce prejudice is through intergroup contact, in which ethnically different individuals have equal status, work toward common goals, and become personally acquainted, and in which authority figures expect them to engage in such interaction.
　　　b. Long-term contact and collaboration among neighborhood, school, and community groups may be the best ways to reduce ethnic prejudices.
　　　c. Classrooms that expose children to broad ethnic diversity, teach them to understand and value differences, and encourage perspective taking prevent children from forming negative biases and reduce already acquired biases.
　　　d. School integration in the United States has receded dramatically since the late 1980s as courts returned desegregation authority to states and cities.
　　　e. Today's U.S. schools seldom offer exposure to diversity but, instead, largely perpetuate prejudices.
　　　f. Attending integrated classrooms leads to higher achievement, educational attainment, and occupational aspirations among ethnic minority students.

Chapter 11 Self and Social Understanding

VI. UNDERSTANDING CONFLICT: SOCIAL PROBLEM SOLVING (pp. 480–482)
   A. From the preschool to the school years, conflicts among children shift from material concerns, such as play objects, to psychological and social issues.
   B. Resolution of conflict, rather than conflict per se, promotes development.
   C. Social conflicts provide repeated occasions for **social problem solving**—generating and applying strategies that prevent or resolve disagreements, resulting in outcomes that are both acceptable to others and beneficial to the self.
   D. The Social Problem-Solving Process (pp. 480–481)
      1. An *information-processing approach* permits the identification of processing deficits, so intervention can be tailored to meet individual needs.
      2. Children who get along well with agemates interpret social cues accurately and have a repertoire of effective problem-solving strategies.
      3. Children with peer difficulties often hold biased social expectations.
      4. Children improve greatly in social problem solving over the preschool and early school years, largely as a result of gains in perspective-taking capacity—in particular, recursive thought.
   E. Enhancing Social Problem Solving (p. 481)
      1. Intervening with children who have weak social problem-solving skills can improve peer relations, give children a sense of mastery in the face of stressful life events, and reduce the risk of adjustment difficulties in children from low-SES and troubled families.
      2. In one intervention—the *Promoting Alternative Thinking Strategies* (PATHS) curriculum for preschool children—teachers provide children with weekly lessons in the ingredients of social problem solving.
      3. In evaluations of PATHS, preschoolers scored higher than no-intervention controls in accurately "reading" others' thoughts and emotions, selecting competent solutions to social conflicts, and cooperating and communicating verbally with peers.
      4. Practice in enacting responses may strengthen intervention outcomes.
      5. Because children with social difficulties often have parents who model poor social skills and use ineffective child-rearing practices, intensive family intervention may be necessary.

LECTURE ENHANCEMENTS

LECTURE ENHANCEMENT 11.1
Attachment Security, Maternal Mind-Mindedness, and Development of Theory of Mind (pp. 451–456)

Time: 15–20 minutes

Objective: To examine the contributions of infant attachment security and maternal mind-mindedness to early theory of mind development.

To examine the contributions of infant attachment security and maternal mind-mindedness to early theory of mind development, Laranjo and colleagues (2010) recruited 61 mother–child dyads and collected data at three time periods—when participants were 12 to 13 months old (Time 1), 15 to 16 months old (Time 2), and 26 months old (Time 3). The researchers gathered the following information during three home visits:

  (1) During Time 1 and Time 3, mothers completed a demographic questionnaire and provided information about their child's language development.
  (2) In addition to providing demographic information and completing a language inventory at Time 1, mothers and children also participated in two 10-minute play sequences. In the first sequence, researchers provided a standard set of toys. In the second sequence, no toys were used. Instead, mothers had to maintain infants' attention verbally through one-to-one interaction. Each play sequence was filmed and researchers coded mothers' comments based on the following categories, which were used to determine maternal mind-mindedness:
     • Comments on the infant's mental state, such as thoughts, desires, and knowledge. For example, "You want this book." "You know this game."
     • Comments on mental processes. For example, "Where do you think the block goes?" "You find this game difficult."
     • Comments on the infant's emotional engagement. For example, "You've had enough." "You're excited."

- Comments on the infant's attempts to manipulate other people's thoughts. For example, "You're making fun of me."
- Comments that involve the mother speaking for the infant. For example, "See, Mom, it's easier this way."

(3) During Time 2, researchers assessed attachment security using the Attachment Q-Sort (AQS). They filmed mother–toddler interactions during free play and later coded for the child's attachment behaviors toward the mother.

(4) During Time 3, researchers presented two tasks to assess early theory of mind (ToM).
- *Discrepant desires*. Participants were presented with two piles of books—one pile consisted of colorfully illustrated children's books, whereas the other pile consisted of colorless, boring-looking academic books. The researcher asked, "Do you want to look at some books?" Nearly all of the children played with the colorfully illustrated books, which were considered their favorites. The researcher then took the preferred books from the child and made vocalizations and facial expressions indicating disgust and disinterest. When looking at the academic books, the researcher expressed interest and excitement. Finally, the researcher told the child that she would like to read and asked the child to select a book. As she pretended to read with a neutral expression, she asked for a second book. A correct response was coded each time the child selected a book that was consistent with the researcher's preference.
- *Visual perspectives*. As the mother sat with her eyes closed, the child was presented with four toys and told to show the toy to his or her mother. As each toy was presented, the child had to modify its position in order for the mother to see it. For example, one toy had only one side. Therefore, the child had to turn the toy toward the mother so she could view it.

Findings indicated that maternal mind-mindedness during Time 1 strongly predicted ToM performance at Time 3. Specifically, mothers who frequently commented on their 1-year-old's mental references during free play and one-on-one interactions had children who performed better on the ToM tasks at age 2 than mothers who made less frequent mental references. While maternal mind-mindedness made a significant contribution to ToM performance, the relationship between attachment security and ToM performance was much weaker. In fact, attachment quality was only marginally related to performance on the visual perspectives task. Thus, it appears that mental-state talk between mothers and infants makes an important and unique contribution to early theory of mind development.

Laranjo, J., Bernier, A., Meins, E., & Carlson, S. M. (2010). Early manifestations of children's theory of mind: The roles of maternal mind-mindedness and infant security of attachment. *Infancy, 15,* 300–323.

LECTURE ENHANCEMENT 11.2
Early Self-Concept, Self-Other Differentiation, and the Development of Prosocial Behavior (p. 456)

Time: 10–15 minutes

Objective: To examine the contributions of early self-concept and self-other differentiation to the development of prosocial behavior.

Research indicates that early prosocial behavior emerges in the second year of life. For instance, in response to another person's distress, many 2-year-olds attempt to provide comfort in the form of a hug or by offering a favorite toy. To experience such empathic concern, children must be able to differentiate what happens to others and what happens to themselves. In a recent study examining aspects of self-development that contribute to early prosocial behavior, Kartner, Keller, and Chaudhary (2010) recruited 77 19-month-olds representing two different cultures—38 from Berlin, Germany, and 39 from Delhi, India. The researchers collected the following information:

(1) Mothers answered a series of questions about their socialization goals. The researchers were particularly interested in autonomous socialization (promotion of self-confidence and assertiveness) and relational socialization (promotion of prosocial behavior, such as learning to help others, and obedience).

(2) Toddlers completed a "rouge test," which assesses self-recognition. They were first presented with a mirror. After three minutes, mothers distracted the children and rubbed a dot of red lipstick on their nose. The children were then allowed to look in the mirror a second time. If the children touched their nose while looking in the mirror, the researchers noted this as a display of self-recognition.

(3) A distress simulation was presented to assess toddlers' prosocial behavior. An adult first presented several toys, including two teddy bears, and engaged in 10 minutes of free play with the toddler. One of the bears was modified

so that an arm would fall off when its jacket was removed. After the free-play episode, the researcher removed the bear's jacket and exclaimed, "Look! The arm fell off! The arm broke, my teddy is broken!" The adult then covered her face and pretended to cry. For the next 2½ minutes, the adult looked up and repeated the statement every 15 to 20 seconds. Afterward, she explained to the child that she would take the bear home to repair it and then continued to play with the child for 5 minutes. The researchers were interested in instances of prosocial behavior (providing physical comfort like a hug or kiss or offering an alternative toy), gaze (instances of looking at the adult during the distress simulation and subsequent play time), distress indicators (freezing or body tension, pulling on clothes, rubbing or scratching self, and stereotypic movements like turning a toy around and around without looking at it), and exploratory behavior (examining the broken bear or gazing back and forth between the adult and the bear).

Results indicated that mothers from each culture tended to emphasize different socialization goals for their toddlers. Specifically, Berlin mothers placed a stronger emphasis on autonomous socialization goals, whereas Delhi mothers were more likely to emphasize relational socialization goals. These socialization goals, in turn, predicted toddlers' prosocial behavior. Mothers who emphasized relational socialization—particularly obedience—had more prosocial children than those who emphasized autonomous socialization. Interestingly, mirror self-recognition only predicted prosocial behavior in the Berlin sample.

Kartner, J., Keller, H., & Chaudhary, N. (2010). Cognitive and social influences on early prosocial behavior in two sociocultural contexts. *Developmental Psychology, 46,* 905–914.

LECTURE ENHANCEMENT 11.3
The Relationship Between Adolescent Self-Esteem and Psychological Well-Being in Adulthood (pp. 461–463)

Time: 10–15 minutes

Objective: To examine the relationship between adolescent self-esteem and psychological well-being in adulthood.

To examine the relationship between adolescent self-esteem and psychological adjustment in adulthood, Boden, Fergusson, and Horwood (2008) recruited 1,000 15-year-olds and followed them to age 25. The researchers collected the following information:

(1) At age 15, participants completed a self-esteem inventory.
(2) At ages 16, 18, 21, and 25 years, participants completed an anxiety and depression inventory.
(3) At age 16, participants completed a self-report of delinquency, which focused on a diverse range of conduct problems and antisocial behavior (for example, alcohol and drug abuse, fire-starting, stealing).
(4) At ages 16, 18, 21, and 25 years, participants were asked about suicidal ideation. For example, "Have you ever thought about killing yourself?" "How often do you think about killing yourself?"
(5) At ages 16, 18, 21, and 25 years, participants reported on their substance use, including alcohol, tobacco, and illegal drugs.
(6) At ages 18, 21, and 25 years, participants reported on their life satisfaction. Using a four-point scale, ranging from very happy to very unhappy, participants answered questions about work, family, friends, and leisure.
(7) At ages 21 and 25 years, participants completed a relationship quality inventory, which focused on their current or most recent romantic relationship. The inventory includes four subscales—love, maintenance, conflict, and ambivalence.
(8) At ages 18 and 21 years, participants completed a peer attachment inventory, which included attachment to same-sex and opposite-sex friends.
(9) Because life experiences and demographic variables may influence the relationship between adolescent self-esteem and adult outcomes, the researchers also collected information on family SES, maternal education, experiences with physical discipline, parental substance abuse, and family instability (for example, divorce).

Results indicated that low self-esteem at age 15 predicted anxiety, depression, antisocial behavior, suicidal ideation, substance abuse, lower levels of life satisfaction, and dissatisfaction with peers and romantic partners at age 25. These findings were especially strong for low-SES participants, those who experienced family instability (such as divorce), and those who reported high levels of physical discipline in childhood. These findings are consistent with previous research showing that self-esteem has important and long-lasting implications for psychological well-being, with low self-esteem predicting a diverse range of negative outcomes.

In small groups, have students list factors that contribute to self-esteem in adolescence. Next, ask students to review Bronfenbrenner's ecological systems theory (Chapter 1, pp. 26–29). For each factor listed, have students identify the level of the environment to which it belongs. How might third parties contribute to adolescent self-esteem?

Boden, J. M., Fergusson, D. M., & Horwood, L. J. (2008). Does adolescent self-esteem predict later life outcomes? A test of the causal role of self-esteem. *Development and Psychopathology, 20,* 319–339.

LECTURE ENHANCEMENT 11.4
The Impact of Race and Gender on School-Age Children's Conversational Styles and Friendship Choices (pp. 479–480)

Time: 15–20 minutes

Objective: To examine the influence of race and gender on school-age children's conversational styles and friendship choices.

To examine the influence of ethnicity and gender on children's conversations and friendship choices, Leman and Lam (2008) recruited 428 school-age children. Two minority groups (African-Caribbean and South Asian) and one majority group (European) were included in the sample. Each participant was paired with a same-sex peer, with five types of pairings for both boys and girls: Both African-Caribbean (AC–AC), both South Asian (SA–SA), both European (Eu–Eu), African-Caribbean and European (AC–Eu), and South Asian and European (SA–Eu). A research assistant interviewed each pair by presenting eight pictures that included target children of the same age and race as the participants. After presenting the pictures, the research assistant said, "Imagine that these children were going to be new children in your class. Now, if you had to pick just one of them you both would most want to play with, which would that be? Do think about it together before picking." Each dyad had 3 minutes to select a playmate.

In addition to examining how race influenced choice of playmate, Leman and Lam were interested in whether assertion and affiliation contributed to children's conversational style as they selected a playmate. As each dyad discussed which playmate to choose, researchers coded personal assertion and interpersonal affiliation. For example:
- High assertion: Giving commands or demands, strong disagreement, dominance, aggression
- Unassertive: Sitting passively, withdrawing from conversation
- High affiliation: Joining in, clear cooperation
- Unaffiliation: Distant behavior, active resistance, outright rejection, strong disagreement

Results indicated that same-race pairs were more likely to select a playmate from their own racial group. Cross-race pairs had more difficulty selecting a playmate but when they did agree, they tended to select a European child. Overall, boys were more assertive than girls, which is consistent with previous research findings.

Findings also indicated that European children were more assertive than South Asian and African-Caribbean children. Specifically, when interacting with minority children, majority children were more likely to offer their opinions or disagree with their partner's choice. However, while they had a more assertive conversational style generally, European children did not dominate minority children or use aggression to persuade their partner. It is important to note that participants came from ethnically diverse neighborhoods and schools. Based on previous research with less diverse samples, one would expect majority children in any culture to be more dominant than minority children. Thus, it seems that children's experiences with diversity could possibly affect their conversational styles with children from other ethnic backgrounds. Finally, South Asian children were more affiliative than European children, but there were no differences in affiliation between European and African-Caribbean children.

According to Leman and Lam, socialization experiences with parents, teachers, and peers likely explain racial and gender differences in conversational styles. It is possible that European children are more often reinforced for an assertive conversational style, whereas South Asian children learn to be more affiliative than European or African-Caribbean children. One of the most important findings of this study—that majority children did not dominate discussions with minority children—has practical implications. Frequent contact between children varying in race and ethnicity is likely to improve intergroup relations. When majority children are given opportunities to interact with and learn from minority children, they may be more inclined to view minorities as equals and, therefore, avoid using dominance and aggression in their interactions.

Ask students to reflect on their own experiences with children from different racial and ethnic backgrounds. Did they primarily attend racially diverse schools or racially homogonous schools? Were students encouraged to interact with children from other races? Based on this study, research presented in the text, and their own experiences, what strategies should parents and educators use to foster favorable intergroup relations?

Leman, P. J., & Lam, V. L. (2008). The influence of race and gender on children's conversations and playmate choices. *Child Development, 79,* 1329–1343.

LEARNING ACTIVITIES

LEARNING ACTIVITY 11.1
Matching: Emergence of Self and Development of Self-Concept (pp. 448–460)

Present the following activity as a quiz or an in-class assignment.

Directions: Match each of the following terms with its description.

Terms:

_____ 1. Social cognition
_____ 2. Self-recognition
_____ 3. Categorical self
_____ 4. Remembered self
_____ 5. Enduring self
_____ 6. Inner self
_____ 7. Desire theory of mind
_____ 8. Belief–desire theory of mind
_____ 9. Self-concept
_____ 10. Social comparisons

Descriptions:

A. A view of oneself as persisting over time.
B. The set of attributes, attitudes, and values that an individual believes defines who he or she is.
C. How children come to understand their multifaceted social world.
D. Judging one's own appearance, abilities, and behavior in relation to those of others.
E. Identification of the self as a physically unique being.
F. Private thoughts and imaginings.
G. Children classify themselves on the basis of age, physical characteristics, and goodness and badness.
H. Thinking that people always act in ways consistent with their desires and do not understand that less obvious, more interpretive mental states, such as beliefs, also affect behavior.
I. A more coherent portrait than is offered by the isolated, episodic memories of the first few years.
J. A more sophisticated view of the mind in which both beliefs and desires determine actions.

Answers:

1. C   6. F
2. E   7. H
3. G   8. J
4. I   9. B
5. A   10. D

LEARNING ACTIVITY 11.2
Self-Concept and Self-Esteem in Early and Middle Childhood (pp. 456, 461)

To examine self-concept and self-esteem in early and middle childhood, have students interview a preschooler or school-age child. The following questions can help guide the interview: "Hi [child's name]. Can you tell me a little about yourself?" "What are some things that you like to do?" For each activity mentioned, ask the child to rate his or her competence. For example, if the child mentions baseball, ask "How good are you at baseball?"

Once students have completed their interviews, compile the results for a class discussion. What traits did children emphasize? Were there age-related differences in children's self-descriptions? Did younger children rate their own ability as extremely high? Did older school-age children describe separate evaluations? Were there any gender differences? Explain.

LEARNING ACTIVITY 11.3
Evaluating Spelling Bees (and Other Competitive School Activities) (pp. 456–460, 461–468)

Ask students what they think about competitive academic activities, such as spelling bees. For example, how are children affected by participation in these types of events? Do they encourage or discourage working hard? What are the effects on self-concept and self-esteem for the many losers and for the few winners? Do these events encourage a mastery orientation or a learned-helpless approach, or both? Do students think that competitive school activities should be modified? Why or why not? Are there ways to change the structure of spelling bees and other competitive school activities so that they encourage cooperation, rather than competition, among children?

LEARNING ACTIVITY 11.4
Promoting Self-Esteem in Children and Adolescents (pp. 461–467)

Tell students to pretend they have been asked to speak to a group of parents and teachers about promoting self-esteem in children and adolescents. What information would students include in their presentation? For example, how does the level of self-esteem change from early childhood to adolescence, and what factors contribute to this change? What are some influences on self-esteem? What are the consequences of low self-esteem? How about extremely high self-esteem? What are some strategies for promoting self-esteem? Students should include research on mastery-oriented attributions and learned helplessness.

LEARNING ACTIVITY 11.5
The Four Identity Statuses (pp. 470–471)

Present the following exercise as an in-class activity or quiz.

Directions: Read each of the following scenarios. Based on the information provided, indicate which identity status (IA = identity achievement, ID = identity diffusion, IF = identity foreclosure, or IM = identity moratorium) best describes the adolescent.

_____ 1. Jacob's father, grandfather, and two of his uncles are all accountants. Since he was in junior high, Jacob has indicated that he plans to be an accountant just like the rest of his family. During his first semester of college, Jacob declared a major in accounting.

_____ 2. Janessa spent her junior and senior years of high school exploring career options within the field of education. She attended career fairs and shadowed a social worker, school principal, special education teacher, and speech and language pathologist. After her first semester in college, Janessa declared her major in special education.

_____ 3. Yuri is about to finish high school. Although she plans to attend college, Yuri has not decided what she wants to do with her life. She has considered medicine, law, and business. Yuri has volunteered at a nursing home and currently works part-time as a secretary for a small law firm. Yuri plans to spend her first year or two of college exploring her options before settling on a major.

_____ 4. Ashton is a junior in high school and seems uninterested in college or trade school. He has worked several part-time jobs but usually quits within a few weeks. When asked what he wants to do with his life, Ashton usually says, "It really doesn't matter to me what I do. I'm not in any hurry to go to college or start a career. There's plenty of time for that later."

Answers:

1. IF   3. IM
2. IA   4. ID

LEARNING ACTIVITY 11.6
Supporting Adolescent Identity Development (pp. 472–474)

Have students respond to one of the following scenarios:
(1) Provide advice to parents who want to nurture their teenager's identity development. In addition, cite parenting practices that are associated with a foreclosed or diffused identity status. Reflecting on your own adolescence, in what ways did your parents support or hinder your identity development?
(2) Provide advice to high school personnel for nurturing students' identity development. What teaching practices, school services, and activities would be helpful? Reflecting on your own adolescence, in what ways did your high school experience foster or hinder your identity development?

LEARNING ACTIVITY 11.7
Diversity and Inequality in Children's Media (pp. 479–480)

For this activity, you will need to gather a variety of children's magazines, books, and/or videos of television programs. Divide students into small groups and provide them with one or two media items. Ask students to describe any images that represent racial, ethnic, or economic diversity. Next, have students evaluate these images. For example, do the images portray any stereotyped traits? Are males perceived more positively than females? Are positive attributes more evident in images of Caucasians than in images of racial or ethnic minorities? Explain.

LEARNING ACTIVITY 11.8
Observing Social Problem Solving (pp. 480–481)

Have students arrange to visit a kindergarten or early elementary classroom to observe a free-play period. If students do not have access to a classroom, they can go to a park to observe children playing. As they observe, students should take notes on children's behavior, noting disputes over objects; entry into and control over play activities; and disagreements over facts, ideas, and beliefs. Once students have finished their observations, have them evaluate children's social problem-solving skills. (Students may find Figure 11.10 helpful.) If adults are present during the observation, how did they respond to children's disputes? How did children respond to adult intervention?

ASK YOURSELF . . .

REVIEW: How does cognitive development affect changes in self-concept from early childhood to adolescence? (pp. 456, 458–460)

Cognitive development affects both the changing *structure* and the changing *content* of the self. In early childhood, children's self-concepts largely consist of observable characteristics but also include typical emotions and attitudes, suggesting a beginning understanding of their unique psychological characteristics. In middle childhood, as children are better able to coordinate several aspects of a situation in reasoning about their physical world, they do so in the social realm as well, combining typical experiences and behaviors into stable psychological dispositions. In adolescence, the development of formal operational thought transforms the teenager's vision of the self into a complex, well-organized, internally consistent picture.

The changing *content* of the self is a product of both cognitive capacities and feedback from others. The sociologist George Herbert Mead believed that a psychological self emerges when children adopt a view of the self that resembles others' attitudes toward the child. In this view, *perspective-taking skills*—in particular, an improved ability to infer what others are thinking—are crucial for developing a self-concept based on personality traits. During middle childhood and adolescence, young people become better at "reading" these messages from others, and as school-age children internalize others' expectations, they form an *ideal self* that they use to evaluate their real self.

CONNECT: Recall from Chapter 6 (page 246) that between ages 4 and 8, children figure out who is really behind the activities of Santa Claus and the Tooth Fairy, and they realize that magicians use trickery. How might these understandings relate to their developing theory of mind? (pp. 452–454)

Toddlers and young preschoolers comprehend mental states that they can readily infer from their own and others' actions. But their understanding is limited to a *desire theory of mind:* They think that people always act in ways consistent with their desires and do not understand that behavior is also affected by less obvious, more interpretive mental states, such as beliefs. From age 4 on, children exhibit a *belief–desire theory of mind,* in which they realize that both beliefs and desires determine actions, and they understand the relationship between these inner states. Dramatic evidence for preschoolers' belief–desire reasoning comes from games that test whether they realize that *false beliefs*—ones that do not represent reality accurately—can guide people's behavior. Mastery of false belief signals a change in representation—the ability to view beliefs as *interpretations,* not just reflections, of reality. Once children grasp the relation between beliefs and behavior, they apply their understanding to a wider range of situations, including the magical thinking that leads young children to believe in Santa Claus and the Tooth Fairy.

APPLY: Suggest ways that parents can promote a sturdy sense of self in infants and toddlers. (pp. 448–451)

During the first year, as infants act on the environment, they notice effects that help them sort out self, other people, and objects. For example, smiling and vocalizing at a caregiver who smiles and vocalizes back helps infants build an image of the self as separate from, but vitally connected to, external reality. Sensitive caregiving promotes this early self-development. Compared to their insecurely attached agemates, securely attached toddlers display more complex self-related actions during play and also show greater knowledge of their own and their parents' physical features—for example, in labeling of body parts. And joint attention seems to offer toddlers many opportunities to compare their own and others' reactions to objects and events, which may enhance their awareness of their own physical uniqueness.

Self-awareness quickly becomes a central part of children's emotional and social lives and leads to children's first efforts to understand another's perspective. They become increasingly sensitive to variations in caregivers' emotional messages, which sets the stage for social referencing and later emergence of self-conscious emotions.

Parents can promote development of another aspect of self-concept—the *remembered self,* which develops through adult–child conversations about the past. By participating in personal storytelling, children come to view the self as a unique, continuously existing individual embedded in a world of others. As early as age 2, parents use these discussions to impart rules, standards, and evaluative information about the child. These narratives are a major means through which caregivers imbue the young child's sense of self with cultural values.

REVIEW: Describe and explain changes in the structure and level of self-esteem from early childhood to adolescence. (pp. 461–462)

Self-esteem is the component of self-concept that includes our judgments about our own worth and the feelings associated with those judgments. The structure of self-esteem changes from early childhood to adolescence based on the evaluative information available to children and their ability to process that information.

Children become self-evaluative beings around age 2, as soon as a categorical self with features that can be judged positively or negatively is in place. By age 4, preschoolers have several self-judgments—for example, about learning things in school, making friends, getting along with parents, and feeling physically attractive. Compared with that of older children, however, their understanding is limited.

Around age 6 to 7, children in diverse Western cultures have formed at least four broad self-evaluations: academic competence, social competence, physical/athletic competence, and physical appearance. Furthermore, school-age children's newfound ability to view themselves in terms of stable dispositions enables them to combine their separate self-evaluations into a general psychological image of themselves—an overall sense of self-esteem. Consequently, self-esteem takes on a hierarchical structure. The arrival of adolescence adds several new dimensions of self-esteem—close friendship, romantic appeal, and job competence—that reflect important concerns of this period.

Self-esteem is high among preschoolers, who have trouble distinguishing between their desired and their actual competence. It declines over the first few years of elementary school as children receive more competence-related feedback, as their performances are increasingly judged in relation to those of others, and as they become cognitively capable of social comparison. However, this drop in self-esteem in the early school years is seldom harmful. Then, from fourth grade on, self-esteem rises and remains high for the majority of young people, who report feeling especially good about their peer relationships and athletic capabilities. Some adolescents experience a decline in self-worth after transition to middle and high school, but for most, becoming an adolescent leads to feelings of pride and self-confidence.

CONNECT: What cognitive changes support the transition to a self-concept emphasizing competencies, personality traits, and social comparisons? (*Hint:* See page 283 in Chapter 7.) (pp. 459–460)

The cognitive changes of middle childhood promote a self-concept emphasizing competencies, personality traits, and social comparisons. According to Case's neo-Piagetian theory, change within each of Piaget's stages depends on increases in the efficiency with which children use their limited working-memory capacity. As children become more efficient processors, the amount of information they can hold and combine in working memory expands, making movement to a higher stage possible. To think about the self in terms of competencies and personality traits (descriptors that integrate many specific behaviors) and to make social comparisons, children need to have developed central conceptual structures that integrate multiple dimensions, as they do around age 9 to 11. School-age children apply these structures to many problems—both those in the nonsocial realm (such as conservation, classification, and seriation) and those in the social domain that involve thinking about themselves and other people.

APPLY: Should parents try to promote children's self-esteem by telling them they're "smart" or "wonderful"? Are children harmed if they do not feel good about everything they do? Why or why not? (p. 464)

Research confirms that children do not benefit from compliments, such as "You're terrific," that have no basis in real attainment. American cultural values have increasingly emphasized a focus on the self that may lead parents to indulge children and boost their self-esteem too much. Such overly tolerant, indulgent parenting is linked to unrealistically high self-esteem, which undermines development. Children who combine an inflated sense of superiority with obsessive worry about what others think of them are vulnerable to temporary, sharp drops in self-esteem when their overblown self-images are challenged. They tend to lash out at peers who express disapproval and to display adjustment problems, including meanness and aggression. In contrast, when school-age children are encouraged to strive for worthwhile goals, a bidirectional relationship emerges between achievement and self-esteem: Achievement fosters self-esteem, which contributes to further effort and gains in performance.

Warm, positive parenting combined with firm but appropriate expectations, backed up with explanations, lets young people know that they are accepted as competent and worthwhile, while also helping them make sensible choices and evaluate themselves against reasonable standards.

REFLECT: Recall your own attributions for academic successes and failures when you were in elementary school. What are those attributions like now? What messages from others may have contributed to your attributions? (pp. 464–468)

This is an open-ended question with no right or wrong answer.

REVIEW: List personal and contextual factors that promote identity development. (pp. 472–474)

Personality: Identity status is both cause and consequence of personality characteristics. Adolescents who are conformist and obedient and who assume that absolute truth is always attainable tend to be foreclosed, whereas those who are self-indulgent and doubt they will ever feel sure about anything are more often identity-diffused. Young people who are curious and open-minded and who appreciate that they can use rational criteria to choose among alternatives are more likely to be in a state of moratorium or identity achievement.

Family: Families can enhance teenagers' identity development by serving as a "secure base" from which adolescents can confidently move out into the wider world. Adolescents who feel attached to their parents and look to them for guidance while also feeling free to voice their own opinions tend to be in a state of moratorium or identity achievement. In contrast, foreclosed teenagers usually have close bonds with parents but lack opportunities for healthy separation, and diffused young people report the lowest levels of parental support.

Peers: Interaction with diverse peers through school and community activities encourages adolescents to explore values and role possibilities. Close friends, like parents, can act as a secure base, providing emotional support, assistance, and models of identity development.

School, community, and culture: Identity development depends on schools and communities that offer rich and varied opportunities for exploration. Supportive experiences that foster identity development include classrooms that promote high-level thinking, teachers and counselors who encourage low-SES and ethnic minority students to attend college, extracurricular and community activities that offer teenagers responsible roles consistent with their interests and talents, and vocational training that immerses adolescents in the real world of work. Culture strongly influences an aspect of mature identity that is not captured by the identity-status approach: constructing a sense of self-continuity despite major personal changes. Finally, societal forces are responsible for the special challenges faced by gay, lesbian, and bisexual youths and by ethnic minority adolescents in forming a secure identity.

CONNECT: Explain the close link between adolescent identity development and cognitive processes. (pp. 468–469)
   Adolescents' well-organized self-descriptions and differentiated sense of self-esteem provide the cognitive foundation for forming an identity, which involves defining who one is, what one values, and the directions one chooses to pursue in life—an explicit theory of oneself as a rational agent.
   In early adolescence, young people unify separate traits into more abstract descriptors of the self. By middle to late adolescence, they combine these traits into an organized system. For example, their use of qualifiers in describing traits ("I have a *fairly* quick temper") reveals their awareness that psychological qualities can vary from one situation to another. Older adolescents also add integrating principles that resolve formerly troublesome contradictions—for example, "When I'm around my friends, who think what I say is important, I'm very talkative, but around my family I'm quiet because they're never interested enough to really listen to me." As they revise their self-concepts to include enduring beliefs and plans, adolescents move toward the kind of unity of self that is central to identity development. Adolescence adds several new dimensions of self-esteem—close friendship, romantic appeal, and job competence—as well as an increasing ability to balance social comparison information with personal achievement goals.

APPLY: Eighteen-year-old Brad's parents worry that he will waste time at college because he is unsure about his major and career goals. Explain why Brad's uncertainty might be advantageous for his identity development. (pp. 470–471)
   In the course of identity development, some young people remain in one status, whereas others experience many status transitions. Many young people change from lower to higher status between their mid-teens and mid-twenties. Brad's uncertainty about his college major and career goals indicates that he is in an identity status of *moratorium*. Although adolescents in moratorium are often anxious about the challenges they face, they resemble identity-achieved individuals in using an active, information-gathering cognitive style to make personal decisions and solve problems—seeking out relevant information, evaluating it carefully, and critically reflecting on and revising their views. Attending college will give Brad many opportunities to explore career options and lifestyles. As a result, he is likely to make more progress toward formulating an identity than he did in high school.

REFLECT: Does your identity status vary across the domains of sexuality, close relationships, vocation, religious beliefs, and political values? Describe factors that may have influenced your identity development in an important domain. (p. 470)
   This is an open-ended question with no right or wrong answer.

REVIEW: Explain how improved perspective taking contributes to gains in social problem solving from early to middle childhood. (p. 481)
   Children improve greatly in social problem solving over the preschool and early school years, largely as a result of gains in perspective taking—the capacity to imagine what other people may be thinking and feeling. Instead of grabbing, hitting, or insisting that another child obey, 5- to 7-year-olds tend to rely on friendly persuasion and compromise, to think of alternative strategies when an initial one does not work, and to resolve disagreements without adult intervention. Sometimes they suggest creating new, mutual goals, reflecting awareness that how they solve problems will influence the future of the relationship. By kindergarten, the accuracy and effectiveness of each component of social problem solving are related to socially competent behavior.

CONNECT: How might school integration contribute to social–cognitive capacities that reduce prejudice, including perspective taking and empathy? (p. 479)
   Children's developing theory of mind contributes vitally to perspective taking, the capacity to imagine what others may be thinking and feeling, which develops rapidly throughout childhood and adolescence. Perspective taking, in turn, is crucial for a wide variety of social–cognitive achievements, including understanding others' emotions. Advances in perspective taking permit an empathic response not just to people's immediate distress but also to their general life conditions. To empathize with individuals in life conditions that differ greatly from their own, young people must have attained an advanced form of perspective taking in which they come to understand that people lead continuous emotional lives beyond the current situation.
   Research confirms that an effective way to reduce prejudice, in children and adults alike, is through intergroup contact. Classrooms that expose children to broad ethnic diversity, teach them to understand and value ethnic and racial differences, directly address the damage caused by prejudice and discrimination, emphasize moral values of justice and fairness, and encourage perspective taking and empathy prevent children from forming negative biases and also reduce already acquired biases.

APPLY: Ten-year-old Marla believes her classmate Becky will never get good grades because she's lazy. Jane believes that Becky tries but can't concentrate because her parents are divorcing. Why is Marla more likely than Jane to develop prejudices? (p. 478)

Children who believe that people's personality traits are fixed rather than changeable tend to judge others as either "good" or "bad," ignoring the motives and circumstances behind their behavior, as Marla does when she says that Becky is "lazy." Because of her tendency to view personality traits as stable, Marla is more likely to develop prejudices than a child like Jane, who sees personality as changeable and, therefore, is more likely to consider various factors that may contribute to another person's behavior. In this case, Jane is able to take into account situational conditions (a disrupted home life) that may explain Becky's poor grades.

REFLECT: Describe several efforts by schools, religious institutions, and youth organizations in your community to combat racial and ethnic prejudices in children. (pp. 479–480)

This is an open-ended question with no right or wrong answer.

SUGGESTED READINGS

Apperly, I. (2010). *Mindreaders: The cognitive basis of theory of mind*. Philadelphia, PA: Taylor & Francis. An interdisciplinary look at theory of mind, this book examines cognitive and developmental contributions to our ability to understand beliefs, desires, knowledge, and intentions. The author presents research on both children and adults, as well as practical applications of this body of research.

Deutsch, N. (2008). *Pride in the projects: Teens building identities in urban contexts*. New York: New York University Press. Based on four years of field research, this book examines identity development in inner-city youth. Although many of these young people encounter significant obstacles in their daily life, such as exposure to gangs and violence, discrimination, and poverty, having access to community resources and high-quality after-school programs can help foster resilience and favorable identity development.

Dweck, C. (2007). *Mindset*. New York: Random House. Written by a leading expert in motivation and personality development, this book examines diverse aspects of self-development across the lifespan, including aspects of parent–child communication that foster creativity, academic motivation, and mastery-oriented attributions.

Wagner, B. (2009). *Suicidal behavior in children and adolescents*. New Haven, CT: Yale University Press. Examines developmental factors that contribute to suicidal thoughts and behavior in children and adolescents, including the capacity for emotional self-regulation, changes and stressors within peer and family networks, romantic difficulties, and academic challenges. The author also addresses controversies surrounding use of antidepressant medication in children and teenagers.

MEDIA MATERIALS

For details on individual video segments that accompany the DVD for *Child Development*, Ninth Edition, please see the DVD Guide for *Explorations in Child Development*. The DVD and DVD Guide are available through your Pearson sales representative.

Additional DVDs that may be useful in your class are listed below. These are not available through your Pearson sales representative, but you can order them directly from the distributors. (See contact information at the end of this manual.)

Cultural Identity vs. Acculturation: Implications for Theory, Research, and Practice (2002, Insight Media, 45 min.). Featuring psychology professor Manuel Ramirez, this program questions whether acculturation to mainstream culture means the inevitable relinquishment of ethnic identity. The program provides historical and contemporary perspectives.

Finding the Words: Case Studies in Autism Treatment (2005, Films Media Group/ABC News; 2-part series, 22 min. each). This program introduces Jake and Andrew, two young boys with autism, and examines their progress while discussing the benefits and apparent limits of applied behavior analysis, a technique that has been used with both boys for several years, with mixed results.

Healing with Animals: Autism (2004, Aquarius Health Care Media, 30 min.). This program, which focuses on children with autism and their therapeutic encounters with animals, documents the healing power that animals can provide to humans. A young boy with autism is seen emerging from his isolated world during horseback riding lessons, and a teenage girl gains confidence as she leads a llama at a local fair.

Identity Crisis: Self-Image in Childhood (2005, Films Media Group/BBC–Open University coproduction, 60 min.). This program examines emotional and psychological development in 25 5-year-old boys and girls, who reveal the ways in which nationality, gender, skin color, economic class, and the presence or absence of either parent influence their sense of self-worth and their expectations for the future.

Middle Childhood: Social & Emotional Development (2008, Magna Systems, 24 min.). This program explores the social and emotional milestones of middle childhood, including advances in self-concept and self-esteem, the stages of friendship, the development of coregulation between parents and children, and peer victimization.

Prejudice: More Than Black and White (2008, Films Media Group, 35 min.). In this program, psychology professors Susan Fiske and Mahzarin Banaji—representatives of the Council on American-Islamic Relations and other protolerance groups—and victims of prejudice share their insights and experiences about what makes people prone to irrational hate, and what steps individuals and society can take to eradicate it. It also features a pro-gay Baptist minister who formerly took a stance against homosexuality and an ex-Imperial Wizard of the Ku Klux Klan who now speaks out for tolerance. Contains inflammatory language and images.

Real Life Teens: Self-Esteem (2009, Films Media Group, 18 min.). This program discusses the results of low self-esteem among teens: feelings of inferiority, poor academic achievement, poor lifestyle choices, and withdrawal from relationships and activities. It also examines how teens can reinforce—or, if necessary, rebuild—their belief in themselves. Subjects covered include social and societal causes of low self-esteem, how parents and teachers fit into the picture, and more.

Refrigerator Mothers (2002, Fanlight Productions/Kartemquin Films, 53 min.). This program looks back to the 1950s through the 1970s and examines the then-common belief, posited by the influential psychologist Bruno Bettelheim, that cold and rejecting mothers were to blame for their children's autism. Through the stories of seven mothers and their children, the film explores the devastating impact of this misdiagnosis.

Self-Esteem and Identity in the Digital Age (2007, Insight Media, 27 min.). Featuring a family therapist, an adolescent psychologist, and students, this program explores the technology-related pitfalls associated with growing up in the digital age. It covers such topics as body image and antisocial behaviors.

Teen Suicide: It Shouldn't Be a Secret (2005, Insight Media, 23 min.). This program examines ways in which friends, schools, and parents can help prevent teen suicide. It features a teenager who attempted suicide, national teen suicide experts, and a panel of articulate teens, including a boy who saved his friend from suicide.

Voices of Pain, Voices of Hope (2005, Insight Media, 43 min.) Emphasizing that the only way to overcome prejudice is to admit to personal biases, this program features ethnically and culturally diverse students confronting their attitudes toward and experiences with prejudice. It explores issues associated with self-worth, self-image, cultural pride, and personal worldview and shows how to create a dialogue about identity and culture.

Who Am I? Psychosocial Development During Adolescence (2003, Insight Media, 30 min.). This program illustrates how adolescents navigate the task of forging an identity, while simultaneously transitioning into adulthood. It examines the process by which values, beliefs, attitudes, and aspirations are integrated into a stable self-definition.

CHAPTER 12
MORAL DEVELOPMENT

CHAPTER-AT-A-GLANCE

Chapter Outline	Instruction Ideas	Supplements
Morality as Rooted in Human Nature pp. 486–488	Learning Objective 12.1	Test Bank Items 1–9, 123 Please contact your Pearson publisher's representative for a wide range of video offerings available to adopters.
Morality as the Adoption of Societal Norms pp. 488–496 Psychoanalytic Theory and the Role of Guilt • Social Learning Theory • Limitations of "Morality as the Adoption of Societal Norms" Perspective	Learning Objectives 12.2–12.4 Lecture Enhancement 12.1 Learning Activities 12.1–12.2 Ask Yourself p. 496	Test Bank Items 10–38, 124–126
Morality as Social Understanding pp. 496–514 Piaget's Theory of Moral Development • Evaluation of Piaget's Theory • Kohlberg's Extension of Piaget's Theory • Research on Kohlberg's Stages • Are There Sex Differences in Moral Reasoning? • Influences on Moral Reasoning • Moral Reasoning and Behavior • Religious Involvement and Moral Development • Further Challenges to Kohlberg's Theory • The Domain Approach to Moral Understanding	Learning Objectives 12.5–12.9 Lecture Enhancements 12.2–12.3 Learning Activities 12.3–12.6 Ask Yourself p. 514	Test Bank Items 39–93, 124, 127–128
Development of Morally Relevant Self-Control pp. 514–516, 517 Toddlerhood • Childhood and Adolescence • Individual Differences	Learning Objective 12.10 Learning Activity 12.7	Test Bank Items 94–102
The Other Side of Self-Control: Development of Aggression pp. 516–526 Emergence of Aggression • Aggression in Early and Middle Childhood • Aggression and Delinquency in Adolescence • Stability of Aggression • The Family as Training Ground for Aggressive Behavior • Social-Cognitive Deficits and Distortions • Community and Cultural Influences • Helping Children and Parents Control Aggression	Learning Objective 12.11 Lecture Enhancement 12.4 Learning Activities 12.8–12.9 Ask Yourself p. 526	Test Bank Items 103–122, 129

BRIEF CHAPTER SUMMARY

All cultures promote morality through an overarching social organization that specifies rules for good conduct. Morality is rooted in our psychological makeup and is grounded in our genetic heritage, perhaps through prewired emotional reactions. We share many morally relevant behaviors with other species, and areas within the prefrontal cortex are vital for emotional responsiveness to others' suffering.

In addition to their biological underpinnings, morally relevant emotions, such as empathy, sympathy, and guilt, require cognitive development and strong caregiving supports in order to develop. Both psychoanalytic theory and social learning theory regard moral development as a matter of internalization—adopting societal standards for right action as one's own.

Most researchers today disagree with Freud's view of moral development as a process of internalizing hostility toward the same-sex parent. Conscience development is supported by a type of discipline called induction, in which an adult motivates the child's active commitment to moral norms by helping the child notice the effects of misbehavior on others. Discipline that relies heavily on threats of punishment or withdrawal of love does not lead children to internalize moral norms.

From the social learning perspective, morality is acquired like any other set of competencies, through reinforcement and modeling. Children are most willing to imitate models who display warmth and responsiveness, competence and power, and consistency between assertions and behavior. Harsh punishment has undesirable side effects; positive disciplinary alternatives, such as time out, are more effective in promoting moral development.

Personal commitment to societal standards of good conduct is essential but not sufficient for moral development, because prevailing societal standards may be at odds with ethical principles and social goals. Cognitive-developmental theorists believe that individuals develop morally through construction—actively thinking about situations in which social conflicts arise and attaining new moral understandings.

Piaget identified two broad stages of moral understanding. Young children (ages 5 to 8 years) exhibit heteronomous morality, viewing rules as handed down by authorities and as permanent and unchangeable. Older children (ages 9 to 10 years and older) make the transition to autonomous morality, seeing rules as flexible, socially agreed-on principles that are subject to revision.

Critics believe that Piaget underestimated the moral capacities of young children. Research reveals that by age 4, children recognize the difference between truthfulness and lying. Further, preschool and early school-age children have differentiated notions about the legitimacy of authority figures.

Kohlberg's Moral Judgment Interview examines how individuals resolve hypothetical moral dilemmas. In Kohlberg's system, maturity of moral judgment is determined on the basis of the way a person reasons about the dilemma, not the content of the response. Kohlberg identified six stages of moral reasoning, which he organized into three general levels: preconventional, conventional, and postconventional.

Progress through Kohlberg's stages is slow and gradual. Researchers have challenged Kohlberg's claim that the stages are organized wholes; they have found that Kohlberg's moral stages are loosely organized and overlapping, and that situational factors play a role in people's responses to real-life moral dilemmas.

Maturity of moral reasoning is only modestly related to moral behavior. Moral action is also influenced by the individual's emotions, temperament, history of morally relevant experiences and intuitions, and moral identity.

The most important challenge to Kohlberg's theory concerns his conception of moral maturity, the applicability of his stage model to moral reasoning and behavior in everyday life, and the appropriateness of his stages for characterizing children's moral reasoning. Some researchers have argued for a pragmatic approach to morality, in which an individual's moral maturity varies based on context.

Even young children can distinguish between moral imperatives, social conventions, and matters of personal choice; older children make further distinctions within these domains. Moral behavior depends on the ability to resist temptation, which children begin to develop in the second year. During the school years, children become better at devising strategies for resisting temptation.

All children display aggression at times, but some show abnormally high rates of hostility as early as the preschool years. Aggression comes in three forms: physical, verbal, and relational. Physical aggression decreases between ages 3 and 6, whereas verbal aggression increases. Boys are more physically aggressive than girls, but only small sex differences exist in verbal and relational aggression. In adolescence, delinquent acts increase, especially for boys.

Children who are products of strife-ridden families and harsh, inconsistent discipline develop social-cognitive deficits and distortions that contribute to long-term maintenance of aggression. Training parents in effective child-rearing techniques and teaching children alternative ways of resolving conflict help reduce aggression.

Chapter 12 Moral Development

LEARNING OBJECTIVES

After reading this chapter, you should be able to answer the following:

12.1 Describe and evaluate the biological perspective on morality. (pp. 486–488)

12.2 Describe and evaluate the psychoanalytic perspective on moral development. (pp. 488–490)

12.3 Describe and evaluate the social learning perspective on moral development. (pp. 490–494, 495)

12.4 Cite central features of the cognitive-developmental approach to moral development. (pp. 494–495)

12.5 Describe and evaluate Piaget's theory of moral development. (pp. 496–499)

12.6 Describe Kohlberg's theory of moral development, and discuss research on his stages. (pp. 499–504)

12.7 Describe influences on moral reasoning and its relationship to moral behavior. (pp. 504–509)

12.8 Discuss challenges to Kohlberg's theory. (pp. 509–510)

12.9 How do children distinguish moral imperatives from social conventions and matters of personal choice? (pp. 510–513)

12.10 Discuss the development of morally relevant self-control, noting implications of individual differences for cognitive and social competencies. (pp. 514–516, 517)

12.11 Discuss the development of aggression, noting various influences, and describe successful interventions. (pp. 516–525)

LECTURE OUTLINE

I. INTRODUCTION (pp. 485–486)
   A. Morality is rooted in our psychological makeup; also, in all cultures, it is promoted by an overarching social organization that specifies rules for good conduct.
   B. Morality has as an *emotional component,* a *cognitive component,* and a *behavioral component;* a growing body of research reveals that these three facets of morality are interrelated.

II. MORALITY AS ROOTED IN HUMAN NATURE (pp. 486–488)
   A. In the 1970s, biological theories of human social behavior suggested that many morally relevant behaviors and emotions have roots in our evolutionary history.
   B. In other species, most self-sacrificing acts occur within family groups; humans, too, are biased to aid family members but also have an unmatched capacity to make sacrifices for nonrelatives.
      1. Evolutionary theorists believe this capacity originated in hunting-and-gathering bands, which limited selfishness by developing informal systems of social exchange.
      2. Because willingness to aid others ensures survival of the majority of the group, traits that foster altruism are adaptive and become increasingly prominent through natural selection.
   C. Many researchers believe that genes encourage prosocial acts and, thereby, promote survival of the species through prewired emotional reactions.
   D. Researchers have identified areas within the prefrontal cortex that are vital for emotional responsiveness to the suffering of others and to one's own misdeeds.
   E. Humans' mirror neuron systems are also believed to support empathic responding, as reflected in heightened cortical activity in response to pain experienced by another, which is positively correlated with self-reported empathy.
   F. In addition to the biological foundations of morality, strong caregiving and cognitive development also play a vital role.

III. MORALITY AS THE ADOPTION OF SOCIETAL NORMS (pp. 488–496)
   A. Both psychoanalytic theory and social learning theory regard moral development as a matter of **internalization:** adopting societal standards for right action as one's own.
      1. Morality moves from society to individual as children acquire norms, or prescriptions for good conduct, widely held by members of their social group.

2. Factors jointly affecting the child's willingness to adopt societal standards include parental discipline style, child and parent characteristics, and the child's view of both the misdeed and the reasonableness of parental demands.
B. Psychoanalytic Theory and the Role of Guilt (pp. 488–490)
1. Freud believed that morality emerges between ages 3 and 6, the period of the Oedipus and Electra conflicts, and is largely complete by age 5 or 6.
    a. Young children desire to possess the parent of the other sex but give up this wish because they fear punishment and loss of parental love.
    b. To maintain their parents' affection, children form a *superego,* or conscience, by *identifying* with the same-sex parent, whose moral standards they adopt.
    c. Freud believed that children turn the hostility previously aimed at the same-sex parent toward themselves, which evokes feelings of guilt when they disobey the superego.
2. Today, most researchers disagree with Freud's ideas about conscience development.
    a. School-age children feel guilt when they intentionally engage in acts that harm others.
    b. Contrary to Freud's beliefs, children whose parents frequently use threats, commands, or physical force tend to violate standards often and to feel little guilt, whereas parental warmth and responsiveness predict greater guilt following transgression.
3. Inductive Discipline
    a. In **induction,** a type of discipline that promotes conscience development, an adult helps the child notice others' feelings by pointing out the effects of the child's misbehavior on others, noting their distress and making clear that the child caused it.
    b. Induction is effective as early as age 2.
    c. Induction remains powerfully effective at older ages. In one study, the more adolescents reported that their mothers used induction, the stronger their **moral identity**—endorsement of moral values (such as fairness, kindness, and generosity) as central to their self-concept.
    d. The success of induction may lie in its power to cultivate children's active commitment to moral norms.
        (1) By emphasizing the impact of the child's actions on others, induction encourages empathy and sympathetic concern, which motivate prosocial behavior.
        (2) Children and adolescents who view discipline as fair are more likely to listen to, accept, and internalize the parent's message.
    e. Discipline that relies heavily on threats of punishment or withdrawal of love does not get children to internalize moral norms and interferes with empathy and prosocial responding.
4. The Child's Contribution
    a. Empathy is moderately heritable, and more empathic children are more responsive to induction.
    b. Because temperament influences a child's response to parents' inductive tactics, parents should tailor their disciplinary strategies to the child's personality.
5. The Role of Guilt
    a. Although little support exists for Freudian ideas about conscience development, Freud was correct that guilt is an important motivator of moral action.
    b. To influence children without coercion, parents can induce *empathy-based guilt* by explaining that the child's behavior is causing someone distress.
    c. Contrary to Freud's view, guilt is not the only force that compels us to act morally, and moral development is a gradual process beginning in the preschool years and extending into adulthood.
C. Social Learning Theory (pp. 490–494, 495)
1. From a social learning perspective, moral behavior is acquired like any other set of responses: through reinforcement and modeling.
2. Importance of Modeling
    a. Operant conditioning is not enough to enable children to acquire moral responses.
    b. In this view, children learn to behave morally largely through *modeling*—observing and imitating adults who demonstrate appropriate behavior.
    c. Certain characteristics of the model affect children's willingness to imitate:
        (1) *Warmth and responsiveness:* Preschoolers are more likely to copy the prosocial actions of an adult who is warm and responsive rather than one who is cold and distant.
        (2) *Competence and power:* Children tend to select competent, powerful models to imitate.

Chapter 12 Moral Development

- (3) *Consistency between assertions and behavior:* When models say one thing and do another, children generally choose the most lenient standard of behavior demonstrated by the adults.
- d. At the end of early childhood, children who have had consistent exposure to caring adults tend to behave prosocially whether or not a model is present.
3. Effects of Punishment
    - a. Disciplinary tactics involving yelling at, slapping, or spanking children are ineffective.
    - b. To foster long-term goals, such as acting kindly toward others, most parents rely on warmth and reasoning.
    - c. Frequent punishment promotes only immediate compliance, not lasting changes in behavior.
    - d. Harsh punishment has several undesirable side effects.
        - (1) When parents spank a child in response to the child's aggression, the punishment models aggression.
        - (2) Harshly treated children react with anger and resentment, which prompts a focus on their own distress rather than a sympathetic orientation to others' needs.
        - (3) Children, adolescents, and adults whose parents used *corporal punishment* are more accepting of such discipline, so that its use may transfer to the next generation.
    - e. Although corporal punishment spans the SES spectrum, its frequency and harshness are elevated among less educated, economically disadvantaged parents.
    - f. Parents with mental health problems are more likely to be punitive and also to have hard-to-manage children, whose disobedience evokes more parental harshness.
        - (1) These findings suggest that heredity contributes to the link between punitive discipline and children's adjustment difficulties.
        - (2) However, good parenting can shield children who are genetically at risk for aggression and antisocial activity from developing these behaviors.
        - (3) In a longitudinal study extending from 15 months to 3 years, early corporal punishment predicted emotional and behavior problems in children of diverse temperaments.
    - g. Among countries differing widely in characteristics, such as economic well-being, increased use of yelling and corporal punishment is positively associated with child anxiety and aggression.
    - h. The use of corporal punishment in the Unites States increases from infancy to age 5 and then declines, but it is high at all ages, even in the case of infants.
4. Alternatives to Harsh Punishment
    - a. One alternative is a technique called **time out,** which involves removing children from the immediate setting until they are ready to act appropriately.
    - b. Another is *withdrawal of privileges,* such as playing outside or watching a favorite TV program.
    - c. Parents increase the effectiveness of punishment through *consistency* in disciplinary responses, by maintaining a generally *warm parent–child relationship,* and by offering *explanations* that help the child relate the misdeed to expectations for future behavior.
5. Positive Relationships, Positive Parenting
    - a. Effective discipline encourages good behavior by building a mutually respectful bond with the child, letting the child know ahead of time how to act, and praising mature behavior.
    - b. When sensitivity, cooperation, and shared positive emotion are evident in joint activities between mothers and their young children, children show firmer conscience development.
    - c. Parents who use positive parenting strategies, such as providing reasons for rules, focus on long-term social and life skills—cooperation, problem solving, and consideration for others.
- D. Limitations of "Morality as the Adoption of Societal Norms" Perspective (pp. 494–495)
    1. Both psychoanalytic and social learning theories view moral development as a process of adopting societal norms.
    2. But theories that regard morality as entirely a matter of internalizing norms have been criticized because prevailing standards may be at odds with important ethical principles and humanitarian goals.
    3. Cognitive-developmental theorists believe that individuals develop morally through **construction**—actively attending to and interrelating multiple perspectives on situations in which social conflicts arise and thereby deriving new moral understandings.

IV. MORALITY AS SOCIAL UNDERSTANDING (pp. 496–514)
- A. Piaget's Theory of Moral Development (pp. 496–497)
    1. Piaget's early work on children's moral judgments originally inspired the cognitive-developmental perspective. Studying children through clinical interviews, Piaget identified two broad stages of moral understanding.

2. Heteronomous Morality (about 5 to 8 Years)
   a. Children in Piaget's first stage, **heteronomous morality,** view rules as handed down by authorities (God, parents, and teachers), as having a permanent existence, as unchangeable, and as requiring strict obedience.
   b. According to Piaget, two factors limit children's moral understanding: (1) cognitive immaturity, especially a limited capacity to imagine other perspectives and **realism**—the tendency to view mental phenomena, including rules, as fixed external features of reality; and (2) the power of adults to insist that children comply, which promotes unquestioning respect for rules and those who enforce them.
   c. As a result, in judging an act's wrongness, younger children focus on impressive consequences rather than on intent to do harm.
3. Morality of Cooperation (about 9 to 10 Years and Older)
   a. Through cognitive development, gradual release from adult control, and peer interaction, children make the transition to the second stage, **morality of cooperation,** in which they no longer view rules as fixed but see them as flexible, socially agreed-on principles that can be revised to suit the will of the majority.
   b. By interacting as equals with peers, children learn to settle conflicts in mutually beneficial ways, following a standard of fairness called *reciprocity,* in which they express the same concern for the welfare of others as they do for themselves.
   c. Older children and adolescents move beyond younger children's crude payback morality to a grasp of the importance of mutuality of expectations, called **ideal reciprocity,** as expressed in the Golden Rule.
B. Evaluation of Piaget's Theory (pp. 497–499)
   1. Follow-up research indicates that Piaget's theory accurately describes the general direction of change in moral judgment: With age, outer features, such as physical damage or getting punished, give way to subtler considerations, such as the actor's intentions or the needs and desires of others.
   2. Several aspects of Piaget's theory have been questioned because they underestimate the moral capacities of young children.
   3. Intentions and Moral Judgments
      a. When questioned about moral issues in a way that makes a person's intention as obvious as the harm done, preschool and early school-age children are capable of judging ill-intentioned people as more deserving of punishment than well-intentioned ones.
      b. By age 4, children recognize the difference between truthfulness and lying, and they approve of telling the truth and disapprove of lying.
      c. By age 7 to 8, they evaluate very negatively certain types of truthfulness—for example, blunt statements that are especially likely to have negative social consequences.
      d. Children from collectivist cultures more often rate lying favorably when the intention is modesty.
   4. Reasoning About Authority
      a. Research indicates that young children do not regard adults with unquestioning respect, as Piaget assumed.
      b. By age 4, children have differentiated notions about the legitimacy of authority figures, which they refine during the school years.
      c. In reasoning about authority, preschool and young elementary school children place greater weight than older children on power, status, and consequences for disobedience.
   5. Stagewise Progression
      a. Many children display both heteronomous and cooperative moral reasoning, raising doubts about whether each stage represents a general, unifying organization of moral judgment responses.
      b. Moral development is currently viewed as a more extended process than Piaget believed, as seen in Kohlberg's six-stage sequence.
C. Kohlberg's Extension of Piaget's Theory (pp. 499–502)
   1. Like Piaget, Kohlberg used clinical interviews to study moral reasoning, but he used a more open-ended approach.
   2. The Clinical Interview
      a. In Kohlberg's *Moral Judgment Interview,* individuals resolve dilemmas that present conflicts between two moral values and justify their decisions.
      b. The best known of these, the "Heinz dilemma," pits the value of obeying the law (not stealing) against the value of human life (stealing a drug to save the life of a dying person).
      c. Moral judgment maturity is determined by the *way an individual reasons about the dilemma,* not by *the content of the response.*

d. Given a choice between obeying the law and preserving individual rights, the most advanced moral thinkers support individual rights (stealing a drug to save a life).
3. A Questionnaire Approach
   a. For more efficient gathering and scoring of moral reasoning, researchers have devised short-answer questionnaires, most recently the *Sociomoral Reflection Measure–Short Form (SRM–SF)*.
   b. Like Kohlberg's clinical interview, the SRM–SF asks individuals to evaluate the importance of moral values and produce moral reasoning.
   c. SRM–SF scores correlate well with those obtained from the Moral Judgment Interview and show similar age trends, but they are far less time-consuming to obtain.
4. Kohlberg's Stages of Moral Understanding
   a. In his initial investigation, Kohlberg, extending the age range Piaget studied, administered the Moral Judgment Interview to 10-, 13-, and 16-year-old boys.
   b. He reinterviewed participants at three- to four-year intervals over the next 20 years and generated his six-stage sequence by analyzing age-related changes in their moral judgments.
   c. Kohlberg's first three stages characterize children as moving from a morality focused on outcomes to one based on ideal reciprocity.
   d. Inclusion of older adolescents yielded the fourth stage, in which young people expand their notion of ideal reciprocity to encompass the need for societal rules and laws.
   e. Kohlberg also posited the fifth and sixth stages, which have remained infrequent in subsequent research.
   f. Kohlberg organized his six stages into three general levels and made stronger claims than Piaget about a fixed order of moral change:
      (1) He regarded his moral stages as universal and invariant.
      (2) He viewed each new stage as building on reasoning of the preceding stage.
      (3) He saw each stage as an organized whole—a qualitatively distinct structure of moral thought that a person applies across a wide range of situations.
   g. Kohlberg believed that moral understanding is promoted by disequilibrium, or awareness of weaknesses in one's current thinking, and gains in perspective taking.
   h. The Preconventional Level
      (1) At the **preconventional level,** morality is externally controlled. Children accept the rules of authority figures and judge actions by their consequences: Behaviors that result in punishment are viewed as bad, those that lead to rewards as good.
      (2) *Stage 1: The punishment and obedience orientation:* Children find it difficult to consider two points of view in a moral dilemma, so they overlook people's intentions and focus on fear of authority and avoidance of punishment as reasons for behaving morally.
      (3) *Stage 2: The instrumental purpose orientation:* Children realize that people can have different perspectives in a moral dilemma. They view right action as flowing from self-interest and understand reciprocity as equal exchange of favors.
   i. The Conventional Level
      (1) At the **conventional level,** individuals regard conformity to social rules as an important way of actively maintaining the current social system to ensure positive human relationships and societal order.
      (2) *Stage 3: The "good boy–good girl" orientation, or the morality of interpersonal cooperation:* The individual understands *ideal reciprocity,* as expressed in the Golden Rule.
      (3) *Stage 4: The social-order-maintaining orientation:* The individual believes that societal laws should be enforced in an evenhanded fashion, and each member of society has a personal duty to uphold them.
   j. The Postconventional or Principled Level
      (1) At the **postconventional level,** individuals move beyond unquestioning support for the rules and laws of their own society, defining morality in terms of abstract principles and values that apply to all situations and societies.
      (2) *Stage 5: The social-contract orientation:* Individuals regard laws and rules as flexible instruments for furthering human purposes.
      (3) *Stage 6: The universal ethical principle orientation:* Right action is defined by self-chosen ethical principles of conscience that are valid for all humanity.

D. Research on Kohlberg's Stages (pp. 502–503)
    1. Kohlberg's original research and other longitudinal studies using hypothetical dilemmas provide convincing evidence for his stage sequence.
    2. Development of moral reasoning is slow and gradual.
    3. Among college-educated young adults, Stage 4 reasoning is typical; few people move beyond it.
    4. Are Kohlberg's Stages Organized Wholes?
        a. If they are, individuals should use the same level of moral reasoning for everyday moral problems as for hypothetical dilemmas.
        b. In fact, real-life conflicts often elicit moral reasoning below a person's actual capacity because they involve practical considerations and intense emotion as well as cognition.
        c. Like Piaget's cognitive and moral stages, Kohlberg's moral stages are loosely organized and overlapping.
    5. Cognitive Influences on Moral Reasoning
        a. Moral maturity is positively correlated with IQ, performance on Piagetian cognitive tasks, and perspective-taking skill.
        b. But Kohlberg argued that cognitive and perspective-taking attainments are not sufficient to ensure moral advances, which also require reorganization of thought unique to the moral domain.
        c. So far, the domain in which the cognitive ingredients required for more mature moral judgment first emerges—cognitive, social, or moral—remains unclear.
E. Are There Sex Differences in Moral Reasoning? (pp. 503–504)
    1. Carol Gilligan and others have argued that Kohlberg's theory does not adequately represent the morality of girls and women, which emphasizes an "ethic of care" that Kohlberg's system devalues but that, in this view, is a *different* but no less valid basis for moral judgment than a focus on impersonal rights.
    2. Most studies that have tested Gilligan's claim do not support her conclusion. Although Kohlberg emphasized justice rather than caring as the highest of moral ideals, his theory taps both sets of values.
    3. Nevertheless, some evidence indicates that although the morality of males and females includes both orientations, females tend to stress care, or empathic perspective taking, whereas males either stress justice or focus equally on justice and care.
    4. Both cultural and situational contexts profoundly affect use of a care orientation.
F. Influences on Moral Reasoning (pp. 504–506)
    1. Factors affecting the maturity of moral understanding include personality and social experiences, such as child-rearing practices and aspects of culture.
    2. Personality
        a. A flexible, open-minded approach to new information and experiences is linked to gains in moral reasoning.
        b. Open-minded young people are more socially skilled and, therefore, have more opportunities for social participation, which exposes them to others' perspectives.
    3. Child-Rearing Practices
        a. Children who develop mature moral reasoning are likely to have parents whose child-rearing style combines warmth, exchange of ideas, and appropriate demands for maturity.
        b. Children whose parents lecture, use threats, or make sarcastic remarks show little or no change in moral reasoning over time.
    4. Schooling
        a. Moral reasoning advances in late adolescence and early adulthood only as long as a person remains in school.
        b. Higher education introduces young people to social issues extending beyond personal relationships to entire political or cultural groups, promoting advances in moral reasoning.
    5. Peer Interaction
        a. Research supports Piaget's belief that interaction among peers who confront one another with differing viewpoints promotes moral understanding.
        b. Adolescents who report more close friendships and who more often participate in conversations with their friends are advanced in moral reasoning.
        c. Peer discussions and role playing of moral problems can provide a basis for interventions aimed at improving high school and college students' moral understanding.

6. Culture
   a. Individuals in industrialized nations advance to a higher level of Kohlberg's stages than individuals in village societies, who rarely move beyond Stage 3. One explanation is that reasoning at Stages 4 to 6, which depends on appreciating the role of larger structures, such as laws, in resolving moral conflict, cannot develop in these societies.
   b. In cultures where young people participate in the institutions of their society at early ages, such as Israeli *kibbutzim,* moral reasoning is advanced.
   c. Another possible reason for cultural variation is that responses to moral dilemmas in collectivist cultures (including village societies) are often more other-directed than in Western Europe and North America.
      (1) In one study, Japanese adolescents, who almost always integrate care- and justice-based reasoning, placed greater weight on caring, which they regarded as a communal responsibility.
      (2) In research conducted in India, even highly educated people viewed solutions to moral dilemmas as the responsibility of the entire society, not of a single person.
   d. These findings raise the question of whether Kohlberg's highest level represents a culturally specific way of thinking, but a common morality of justice and care is clearly evident in the responses of people from vastly different cultures.
G. Moral Reasoning and Behavior (pp. 506–507, 508)
   1. A central assumption of the cognitive-developmental perspective is that moral understanding should affect moral motivation.
   2. Yet the connection between more mature moral reasoning and action is only modest.
   3. Moral behavior is also influenced by many factors besides cognition, including emotions and temperament.
   4. *Moral identity* also affects moral behavior: When moral goals are personally important, individuals are more likely to feel obligated to act on their moral judgments.
   5. Researchers have begun to identify the origins of moral identity in hopes of capitalizing on it to promote moral commitment.
      a. Parenting strategies that launch conscience development and empathy on an early, favorable path may contribute vitally to moral identity and action.
      b. *Just educational environments*—in which teachers guide students in democratic decision making and rule setting and taking responsibility for others' welfare—enhance moral commitment.
      c. Schools can expand students' opportunities to experience and explore moral emotions, thoughts, and actions by promoting civic engagement.
H. Religious Involvement and Moral Development (pp. 507, 509)
   1. For many people, morality and spirituality are inseparable; their moral values, judgments, and behaviors are deeply embedded in their faith.
   2. Religion is especially important in U.S. family life.
      a. Nearly two-thirds of Americans report being religious, far more than in Europe.
      b. By middle childhood, children whose parents regularly attend religious services have begun to formulate complex religious and spiritual ideas that serve as moral forces in their lives.
      c. A national survey reveals that 81 percent of U.S. teenagers identify with one religion, although formal religious involvement declines in adolescence.
      d. Adolescents who remain part of a religious community are advantaged in moral values and behavior compared with nonaffiliated youths.
      e. Religious institutions may be uniquely suited to foster moral and prosocial commitments in young people and to discourage risky behaviors. For inner-city youth with few good sources of social support, outreach by religious institutions can lead to life-altering involvement.
I. Further Challenges to Kohlberg's Theory (pp. 509–510)
   1. Despite wide support, Kohlberg's theory continues to face challenges.
   2. A key controversy has to do with Kohlberg's belief that moral maturity is not achieved until the postconventional level.
      a. If people had to reach Stages 5 and 6 to be considered truly morally mature, few individuals would measure up.
      b. John Gibbs argues that maturity is found in a revised understanding of Stages 3 and 4 that emphasizes ideal reciprocity.

- c. Gibbs views "postconventional" moral reasoning as a highly reflective metacognitive endeavor in which people grapple with existential issues.
3. Other researchers favor abandoning Kohlberg's stages for a *pragmatic approach to morality* that, they assert, better accounts for morality in everyday life.
    - a. In this view, each person makes moral judgments at varying levels of maturity, depending on the individual's current context and motivations.
    - b. Everyday moral judgments, rather than being efforts to arrive at just solutions, are practical tools that people use to achieve their goals.
    - c. This pragmatism, according to Krebs and Denton, accounts for the lack of a strong association between moral judgment maturity and behavior.
4. Gibbs challenges the pragmatic approach on several grounds.
    - a. Despite their mixed motives in everyday situations, people often rise above self-gratification to support others' rights.
    - b. People's awareness of the greater adequacy of higher-stage moral judgments can influence their behavior even in highly corrupt environments.
5. Kohlberg's stages tell us more about moral understanding in adolescence and adulthood than in early and middle childhood.
    - a. When children are given moral dilemmas relevant to their everyday lives, their responses indicate that their *prosocial moral reasoning* is more advanced than Kohlberg's stages suggest.
    - b. Because Kohlberg focused on young children's tendency to center on prominent external features in their social world, he underestimated their potential for deeper moral understanding.

J. The Domain Approach to Moral Understanding (pp. 510–513)
1. Researchers taking a *domain approach to moral understanding* focus on children's developing capacity to distinguish **moral imperatives** from **social conventions** and **matters of personal choice.**
2. Research reveals that children display more advanced moral reasoning than assumed by the externally controlled vision of Kohlberg's preconventional morality.
3. Moral versus Social-Conventional Distinctions
    - a. In interviews, 3- and 4-year-olds reveal that they judge moral violations as more wrong than violations of social conventions.
    - b. Young children also say that a moral violation is wrong regardless of the setting in which it is committed, even if no authority figure saw them commit the violation and no rules existed prohibiting it.
    - c. While realizing that moral transgressions are worse than social-conventional violations, preschool and young school-age children reason rigidly *within* the moral domain, making judgments based on salient features and consequences while neglecting other important information.
    - d. As they construct a flexible appreciation of moral rules, children clarify and link moral imperatives and social conventions.
    - e. School-age children distinguish social conventions with a clear *purpose* from ones with no obvious justification.
    - f. With age, children realize that *intentions* and *context* also affect the moral implications of violating a social convention.
4. Relation of Personal and Moral Domains
    - a. As children's grasp of moral imperatives and social conventions strengthens, so does their conviction that certain choices are up to the individual.
    - b. Concern with matters of personal choice intensifies during the teenage years, and young people increasingly insist that parents not encroach on the personal arena (such as dress).
    - c. In contrast, adolescents typically say that parents have a right to tell them what to do in moral and social-conventional situations.
    - d. Notions of personal choice, in turn, enhance children's moral understanding.
        - (1) As early as age 6, children view freedom of speech and religion as individual rights, even if laws exist denying those rights.
        - (2) At the same time, older school-age children place limits on individual choice, depending on circumstances.
    - e. Adolescents are increasingly mindful of the overlap among moral imperatives, social conventions, and personal choice.

5. Culture and Moral, Social-Conventional, and Personal Distinctions
   a. Children and adolescents in diverse Western and non-Western cultures use similar criteria to reason about moral, social-conventional, and personal concerns.
   b. Certain behaviors, however, are regarded as morally wrong in one culture but only as an arbitrary convention in another.
   c. When children are asked about acts that obviously lead to harm or violate rights, cross-cultural similarity prevails.

V. DEVELOPMENT OF MORALLY RELEVANT SELF-CONTROL (pp. 514–516, 517)
   A. Whether children and adults act in accord with their beliefs and good intentions depends in part on willpower, or self-control.
   B. *Effortful control* refers to the extent to which children can manage their reactivity, including the ability to inhibit urges to act in ways that violate moral standards, sometimes called *resistance to temptation*.
   C. Toddlerhood (pp. 514–515)
      1. To behave in a self-controlled fashion, children must have the representational, memory, and inhibitory skills to recall a caregiver's directive and apply it to their own behavior.
      2. Between 12 and 18 months, the first glimmerings of self-control appear in the form of **compliance:** toddlers' clear awareness of caregivers' expectations and ability to obey simple requests.
      3. At first, self-control depends heavily on caregiver support.
      4. Compliance quickly leads to toddlers' first consciencelike verbalizations.
      5. Researchers often study self-control by giving children tasks that require **delay of gratification**—waiting for an appropriate time and place to engage in a tempting act.
      6. Children who are advanced in development of attention and language tend to be better at delaying gratification.
      7. Young children's capacity to delay gratification is influenced by both biologically based temperament and quality of caregiving.
   D. Childhood and Adolescence (pp. 515–516)
      1. By the third year, the capacity for self-control is in place, though not yet complete.
      2. Cognitive development enables children to use a variety of effective self-instructional strategies to improve resistance to temptation.
      3. Strategies for Resisting Temptation
         a. When preschoolers were shown two rewards, a highly desirable one that they would have to wait for and a less desirable one that they could have anytime, the most self-controlled children used any technique they could to divert their attention from the desired objects.
         b. Teaching preschoolers to transform a stimulus in ways that de-emphasize its arousing qualities enables them to shift attention and inhibit emotional reactivity, promoting delay of gratification.
         c. Having something interesting to do while waiting also helps preschoolers resist temptation.
         d. During the school years, self-control becomes a flexible capacity for **moral self-regulation**—the ability to monitor and adjust one's own conduct as necessary.
      4. Knowledge of Strategies
         a. Metacognitive knowledge, or awareness of strategies, contributes to self-regulation.
         b. In the late elementary school years, children start to use techniques involving transformations of rewards or their own arousal states, which greatly facilitates moral self-regulation.
   E. Individual Differences (pp. 516, 517)
      1. In research studies, 4-year-olds who were better at delaying gratification were especially adept as adolescents in applying metacognitive skills to their behavior and in inhibiting impulsive responding.
      2. Children who are better at delaying gratification can wait long enough to interpret social cues accurately, which supports effective social problem solving and positive peer relations.
      3. Mischel proposes that the interaction of two processing systems, *hot* and *cool,* governs the development of self-control and accounts for individual differences.
         a. With age, the emotional, reactive hot system is increasingly subordinated to the cognitive, reflective cool system, as a result of improved functioning of the prefrontal cortex.
         b. Throughout childhood and adolescence, temperament and parenting jointly influence the extent to which cool-system representations gain control over hot-system reactivity.

VI. THE OTHER SIDE OF SELF-CONTROL: DEVELOPMENT OF AGGRESSION (pp. 516–526)
   A. Beginning in late infancy, all children display aggression from time to time.
      1. As interactions with siblings and peers increase, aggressive outbursts occur more often.
      2. Although at times aggression serves prosocial ends, most human aggressive acts are clearly antisocial.
      3. As early as the preschool years, some children show abnormally high rates of hostility.
      4. If allowed to continue, this belligerent behavior can lead to lasting delays in moral development, deficits in self-control, and ultimately an antisocial lifestyle.
   B. Emergence of Aggression (pp. 517–518)
      1. In the second half of the first year, infants develop the cognitive capacity to identify sources of anger and frustration and the motor skills to lash out at them.
      2. By the second year, two general types of aggression emerge:
         a. In **proactive** (or *instrumental*) **aggression,** children act to fulfill a need or desire—obtain an object, privilege, space, or social reward—and unemotionally attack a person to achieve their goal.
         b. The other type, **reactive** (or *hostile*) **aggression,** is an angry, defensive response to a provocation or blocked goal and is meant to hurt another person.
      3. Proactive and reactive aggression come in three forms.
         a. **Physical aggression** harms others through physical injury.
         b. **Verbal aggression** harms others through threats of physical aggression, name calling, or hostile teasing.
         c. **Relational aggression** damages another's peer relationships through social exclusion, malicious gossip, or friendship manipulation.
         d. Although verbal aggression is always direct, physical and relational aggression can be either *direct* or *indirect*.
   C. Aggression in Early and Middle Childhood (p. 518)
      1. Between ages 3 and 6, physical aggression decreases, whereas verbal aggression increases.
      2. Proactive aggression declines as preschoolers' improved capacity to delay gratification enables them to resist grabbing others' possessions.
      3. Reactive aggression in verbal and relational forms tends to rise over early and middle childhood.
      4. By age 17 months, boys are considerably more physically aggressive than girls—a difference found throughout childhood in many cultures.
      5. Although girls have a reputation for being verbally and relationally more aggressive than boys, the sex difference is small.
   D. Aggression and Delinquency in Adolescence (pp. 518–519)
      1. Most young people decline in teacher- and peer-reported aggression in adolescence, but both police arrests and self-reports show that delinquency rises over early and middle adolescence and then declines.
      2. Over time, decision making, emotional self-regulation, and moral reasoning improve; peers become less influential; and young people enter social contexts (such as higher education) that are less conducive to lawbreaking.
      3. For most adolescents, a brush with the law does not forecast long-term antisocial behavior. A small percentage become recurrent offenders, and some enter a life of crime.
      4. In adolescence, the gender gap in physical aggression widens, and serious violent crime is mostly the domain of boys.
      5. SES and ethnicity are strong predictors of arrests but are only mildly related to teenagers' self-reports of antisocial acts, a difference due to the tendency to arrest, charge, and punish low-SES ethnic minority youths more often than their higher-SES white and Asian counterparts.
   E. Stability of Aggression (pp. 519–520, 521)
      1. Children high in either physical or relational aggression relative to their agemates tend to remain so over time.
      2. Longitudinal research shows that high physical aggression that diminished over the school years was often replaced with indirect relational aggression. Although the trend applied to both genders, girls displayed it more often than boys.
      3. For both boys and girls, persistently high physical or relational aggression predicts later internalizing and externalizing difficulties and social skills deficits, including antisocial activity.
      4. Aggressive behavior that emerges in childhood and endures is far more likely to translate into long-term adjustment difficulties than aggression that first appears in adolescence.

a. Some children, especially those who are irritable, fearless, impulsive, and overactive, are at risk for aggression, but whether or not they become aggressive largely depends on child-rearing conditions.
b. Strife-ridden families, poor parenting practices, aggressive peers, and televised violence strongly predict both antisocial activity and reduced sensitivity to others' suffering.

F. The Family as Training Ground for Aggressive Behavior (pp. 520–522)
1. Parenting behaviors that undermine moral internalization and self-control—such as love withdrawal, power assertion, and inconsistent discipline—are linked to aggression from early childhood through adolescence in diverse cultures.
2. Anger and punitiveness quickly create a conflict-ridden family atmosphere and an "out-of-control" child.
3. Preschool siblings with critical, punitive parents are more aggressive toward one another, and conflict spreads to peer relationships.
4. Boys are more likely than girls to be targets of harsh physical discipline and parental inconsistency because they are more active and impulsive and, therefore, harder to control.
5. When children extreme in these characteristics are exposed to emotionally negative, inept parenting, their capacity for emotional self-regulation, empathic responding, and guilt after transgressions is severely disrupted, and they lash out when disappointed or frustrated.
6. Parents can also foster aggression indirectly through poor supervision of children, including a failure to limit out-of-home activities and association with antisocial friends.

G. Social-Cognitive Deficits and Distortions (pp. 522–523)
1. Children who are products of these family processes acquire a violent, callous view of the social world, and those who are high in reactive aggression often see hostile intent where it does not exist.
2. When such children feel threatened, they are especially likely to interpret accidental mishaps as hostile and, as a result, to make unprovoked attacks.
3. Compared with nonaggressive agemates, children high in proactive aggression believe there are more benefits and fewer costs for engaging in hostile acts.
4. Thus, they callously use aggression to advance their own goals and are relatively unconcerned about causing suffering in others—an aggressive style associated with later, more severe conduct problems.
5. Another biased social-cognitive attribute of proactively aggressive children is overly high self-esteem.
6. Antisocial adolescents are delayed in maturity of moral judgment, and they tend to view aggression as within the social-conventional and personal domains rather than the moral domain.
7. They minimize the harmful impact of their antisocial acts, rationalizing their behavior as acceptable or even admirable. These youths also score low in moral identity.

H. Community and Cultural Influences (pp. 523, 524)
1. Youth antisocial behavior is more likely in poverty-stricken neighborhoods with a wide range of stressors, including poor-quality schools and high adult criminality.
2. Such community conditions heighten in young people a hostile view of people and relationships, a preference for immediate rewards, and a cynical attitude toward social conventions and moral norms.
3. Schools in these locales typically fail to meet students' developmental needs.
4. Ethnic and political prejudices further magnify the risk of angry, combative responses.
5. Children living amid the danger, chaos, and deprivation of inner-city ghettos and war-torn areas of the world are at risk for severe emotional stress, deficits in moral reasoning, and behavior problems.
    a. With the September 11, 2001, terrorist attacks, some U.S. children experienced extreme wartime violence firsthand, watching through classroom windows as the towers crumbled.
    b. During the following months, the distress reactions that were triggered declined, though more slowly for children with conflict-ridden parent–child relationships or preexisting adjustment problems.

I. Helping Children and Parents Control Aggression (pp. 523–525)
1. Treatment for aggressive children must break the cycle of hostilities between family members and promote effective ways of relating to others.
2. Interventions with preschool and school-age children have been most successful.
3. Parent Training
    a. Parent training programs based on social learning theory have been devised to improve the parenting of preschool and school-age children with conduct problems.

b. In one highly effective approach, *Incredible Years,* parents complete 18 weekly group sessions run by professionals who teach parenting techniques for promoting children's academic, emotional, and social skills and for managing disruptive behaviors.
c. The program also offers a complementary six-day training program for teachers, directed at improving classroom management strategies.
4. Social-Cognitive Interventions
   a. The social-cognitive deficits and distortions of aggressive children prevent them from empathizing with another person's pain and suffering.
   b. In such children, these responses may have to be directly taught.
      (1) School-based social-cognitive treatments focus on teaching children and adolescents to attend to relevant, nonhostile social cues and to generate effective social problem-solving strategies.
      (2) These interventions increase skill in solving social problems, decrease endorsement of beliefs supporting aggression, reduce hostile behaviors, and improve relationships with peers.
   c. Lacking resources to support such programs, many U.S. schools have implemented *zero tolerance policies,* which severely punish all disruptive and threatening behavior, major and minor, usually with suspension or expulsion.
      (1) Often these policies are applied inconsistently: Low-SES minority students are two to three times as likely to be punished.
      (2) Some studies find that by excluding students from school, zero tolerance heightens high school dropout and antisocial behavior.
5. Comprehensive Approaches
   a. Some researchers believe that effective treatment for serious, violent juvenile offenders must encompass parent training, social understanding, relating to others, and self-control.
   b. A program called EQUIP uses positive peer culture—an adult-guided but adolescent-conducted small group approach aimed at creating a prosocial climate.
      (1) Delinquents who participated in EQUIP displayed improved social skills and conduct during the following year compared with no-intervention controls.
      (2) The more advanced moral reasoning that emerged during group meetings seemed to have a long-term impact on antisocial youths' ability to inhibit lawbreaking behavior.
   c. Another program, *multisystemic therapy,* attempts to address the problems that occur when young people remain embedded in hostile home lives, poor-quality schools, antisocial peer groups, and violent neighborhoods.
      (1) In this program, counselors trained parents in communication and discipline skills; integrated violent youths into positive school, work, and leisure activities; and disengaged them from violent peers.
      (2) Compared with individual therapy, this intervention led to improved parent–child relations and school performance and a dramatic drop in number of arrests that persisted for two decades after treatment.
      (3) Multisystemic therapy also helped limit family instability in adulthood.

LECTURE ENHANCEMENTS

LECTURE ENHANCEMENT 12.1
Parental Discipline and Morality in Adolescents (p. 489)

Time: 5–10 minutes

Objective: To extend existing research on the relationship between parental discipline and morality in adolescents.

To extend existing research on the relationship between parental discipline and morality in adolescents, Patrick and Gibbs (2011) recruited 93 fifth, eighth, and tenth graders and their mothers. The researchers collected the following information:
   (1) Participants completed the Perceived Parental Discipline Questionnaire (PPD), which includes six conflict scenarios in which the child commits a transgression toward another person. Participants are then asked how their mother is likely to respond. For example, "You get angry at a friend and do some damage to the friend's things. Your mother is likely to respond by:"

- Power assertion: "Makes you go to your room." "Spanks you."
- Love withdrawal: "Tells you that you should be ashamed of yourself."
- Induction: "Asks how you would feel; suggests you put yourself in the other child's place."

Following each scenario, participants were also asked: On a scale of 1 to 5 (1 = very unfair; 5 = very fair), "How fair or appropriate would the thing she does most be in this situation?" "How do you feel when she does that?"

(2) Participants completed the Moral Self-Relevance Measure (MSR), which presents 16 questions that assess the importance of moral and non-moral qualities. For example:
- Moral: On a scale of 1 to 5 (1 = not important to me; 5 = extremely important to me), "How important is it to you that you are fair or just?"
- Non-moral: On a scale of 1 to 5 (1 = not important to me; 5 = extremely important to me), "How important is it to you that you are creative or imaginative?"

Findings indicated that participants viewed induction, particularly when combined with expressions of disappointment, as more appropriate or fair than power assertion or love withdrawal. The authors note that parental expression of disappointment may play a unique role in the development of a moral identity because it communicates to the child that he or she is capable of a higher standard of conduct. When looking at the relationship between discipline and moral development, adolescents exposed to induction were more likely than those exposed to love withdrawal or power assertion to endorse moral qualities, such as the importance of being fair and just, than non-moral qualities. Taken together, these findings suggest that when combined with disappointed expectations, induction continues to play an important role in adolescents' moral development.

Patrick, R. B., & Gibbs, J. C. (2011). Inductive discipline, parental expression of disappointed expectations, and moral identity in adolescence. *Journal of Youth and Adolescence*.

LECTURE ENHANCEMENT 12.2
The Relationship Between Community Service, Extracurricular Participation, and Civic Knowledge in High School and Civic Engagement in Adulthood (p. 508)

Time: 10–15 minutes

Objective: To examine the long-term consequences of high school community service, extracurricular participation, and civic knowledge.

As noted in the text, when young people engage in community service that exposes them to people in need or to public issues, they are especially likely to express a commitment to future service and to working toward important societal goals. To examine the long-term consequences of high school community service, extracurricular participation, and civic knowledge, Hart and colleagues (2008) used data from the National Educational Longitudinal Study. A total of 12,144 individuals were included in the analyses; data collection occurred in twelfth grade and eight years after high school graduation. The researchers collected the following information:

(1) In twelfth grade, participants were asked about three types of civic engagement—community service, extracurricular participation, and civic knowledge and courses. Questions included: "During the past two years, have you performed any unpaid volunteer or community service work? If so, was the service strictly voluntary?" "Was the service required for class or some other reason?" "How often did you perform community service: never/rarely, less than once a week, one to two times a week, or almost every day?" "During the past two years, have you participated in any extracurricular activities (for example, school government, sports, yearbook/newspaper, cheerleading, music, academic club)?" Civic knowledge was assessed using a standardized test, which focused on citizenship, American history, and geography. The researchers also had access to participants' completion of social science courses.

(2) In twelfth grade, civic attitude was assessed using the following question: On a scale of 1 to 3 (1 = not important; 3 = very important), "How important is it in your life to help others in your community?"

(3) When participants were approximately 26 years old, they were asked about voting and volunteering activities. For example: "In the past two years, have you voted in any local, state, or national election?" "Did you volunteer in a civic or community service organization in the past 12 months?"

Results indicated that community service participation—both voluntary and required for school—and extracurricular participation were strong predictors of adult voting and volunteering activities. In addition, adolescents who were involved in community service were more likely to view helping others as "very important" than adolescents who did not participate in community service. Civic knowledge in twelfth grade was not related to volunteerism but did predict adult voting practices.

However, this relationship was not strong. Thus, it seems that community service in high school, even when not on a voluntary basis, and extracurricular involvement are especially likely to predict civic engagement in adulthood. Furthermore, these activities seem to foster higher rates of civic engagement than coursework or knowledge of citizenship and American history.

Ask students to reflect on their own civic engagement. For example, are they registered to vote or do they plan to register to vote? Do they perform community service? What motivates them to do so? Do they do it voluntarily or is their service required for course credit? What early experiences, particularly those in high school, have contributed to their civic engagement?

Hart, D., Donnelly, T. M., Youniss, J., & Atkins, R. (2008). High school community service as a predictor of adult voting and volunteering. *American Educational Research Journal, 44,* 197–219.

LECTURE ENHANCEMENT 12.3
Adolescents' Perceptions of Rights Concerning Health (pp. 511–512)

Time: 5–10 minutes

Objective: To examine developmental changes in adolescents' perceptions of one's right to engage in risky behaviors.

To examine developmental changes in adolescents' perceptions of one's right to engage in risky behaviors, Flanagan, Stout, and Gallay (2008) recruited 1,536 adolescents and followed them for three years. Participants were divided into three age groups: early adolescents (12–13 years), middle adolescents (14–15 years), and late adolescents (16 years and older). During the second semester of each school year, the researchers collected the following information:

(1) Participants completed a survey about rights concerning health. The survey included two scales:
- Health as an Individual Right: "It's my body and I can do what I want with it." "If I want to smoke or drink, it's my choice."
- Public Health Beliefs: "If something is bad for your health, the government should tell you to avoid it." "Smokers need to be responsible and not smoke when little kids are around."

(2) Participants were presented with four hypothetical vignettes in which a friend was smoking cigarettes, drinking alcohol, using drugs, or planning to go to a party where alcohol would be served. Participants were then asked to rate how likely they were to intervene or ignore their friend's behavior.

Results indicated that between early and late adolescence, there was a steady increase in defense of health as an individual right. However, older adolescents were also more likely than younger adolescents to endorse the government's right to intervene in individual choices in behavior. The authors suggest that by late adolescence, young people develop a sophisticated understanding of health in which an individual's right to experiment with risky behaviors must be weighed against public welfare. Smoking cigarettes, for instance, does not just affect the smoker. It can also harm those who are exposed to the smoke.

For all age groups, endorsement of public health predicted one's belief that he or she had a right to intervene in a friend's risky behavior. In contrast, adolescents who emphasized individual rights over public health were less likely to intervene, saying that it was none of their business. Compared to boys, girls were more likely to endorse public health over individual rights and, consequently, were more likely to indicate that they would intervene in a friend's risky behavior.

Taken together, these findings show that perceptions of rights concerning health change over the adolescent years. Although with age, adolescents are more likely to defend health as an individual right, older adolescents also understand the government's right to constrain individual choices. Adolescents who believe that public health is more important than individual rights are more likely to intervene with a friend who smokes, drinks, or uses drugs.

How do findings on understanding of health as an individual right illustrate adolescents' advancing capacity to reason about competing moral and personal issues?

Flanagan, C. A., Stout, M., & Gallay, L. S. (2008). It's my body and none of your business: Developmental changes in adolescents' perceptions of rights concerning health. *Journal of Social Issues, 64,* 815–834.

LECTURE ENHANCEMENT 12.4
School-Age Children's Moral Reasoning About Physical and Relational Aggression (pp. 517–518)

Time: 10–15 minutes

Objective: To examine school-age children's moral reasoning about physical and relational aggression.

To examine children's moral reasoning about physical and relational aggression, Murray-Close, Crick, and Galotti (2008) recruited 639 fourth and fifth graders and collected the following information:

(1) Participants were administered the Moral Reasoning About Aggression (MRA) measure, which includes three physical aggression scenarios (for example, hitting a peer) and three relational aggression scenarios (for example, excluding a friend from your group because you are mad at him/her). For each scenario, participants were asked to provide three moral judgments of it:
- On a scale of 1 to 5 (1 = not wrong at all; 5 = extremely wrong), "How wrong is the behavior?"
- On a scale of 1 to 5 (1 = never; 5 = always), "How often would the behavior hurt the victim?"
- To identify the domain used to judge each act of aggression (moral, social-conventional, personal, or prudential—personal actions that are harmful to the self), participants were asked how they would view the behavior if there were no rule against it. For example: "If there were no rule against hitting others, it would be (a) OK because there is no rule against it (social-conventional); (b) OK, regardless of whether there is a rule, because the decision to hit another person is your own choice (personal); (c) wrong because the kid might hit you back and hurt you (prudential); or (d) wrong because it would hurt the kid if you hit him (moral)."

(2) Teachers rated children's physical and relational aggression in the classroom, as well their prosocial behaviors.

(3) A trained research assistant provided each child with a class roster and read aloud descriptions of physically aggressive and relationally aggressive behaviors. Children were then asked to select three male or female classmates who fit each description.

Results indicated that the majority of children regarded acts of physical and relational aggression from the perspective of the moral domain. That is, when considering the consequences of aggressive behavior, children tended to judge the behavior in terms of fairness and personal welfare. Participants also regarded physically aggressive behavior as more wrong and harmful than relationally aggressive behavior. According to Murray-Close, Crick, and Galotti, this finding is important from a developmental standpoint because it suggests that school-age children may not yet appreciate the extent of harm resulting from relational aggression. Results also revealed gender differences in moral judgments. Compared to boys, girls were more likely to judge aggressive acts as wrong, and they rated relationally aggressive acts as more harmful than did boys. Both boys and girls rated acts of physical aggression similarly.

Finally, peer and teacher ratings of aggression were related to children's performance on the MRA. Specifically, children's judgments of aggressive behavior were strongly related to their actual behavior, as reported by peers and teachers. Interestingly, aggressive children were more likely than their nonaggressive agemates to identify the harm associated with physical and relational aggression. Thus, these children are aware of the harm their behavior causes others but view it as an effective strategy for attaining their goals.

Murray-Close, D., Crick, N. R., & Galotti, K. M. (2008). Children's moral reasoning regarding physical and relational aggression. *Social Development, 15,* 345–372.

LEARNING ACTIVITIES

LEARNING ACTIVITY 12.1
True or False: Morality as the Adoption of Societal Norms (pp. 488–495)

Present the following activity as an in-class assignment or quiz.

Directions: Read each of the following statements and determine whether it is *True* (T) or *False* (F).

Statements:
_____ 1. According to Freud, morality emerges between ages 3 and 6.
_____ 2. Children who consistently experience induction tend to report overwhelming guilt.
_____ 3. Research consistently shows that operant conditioning is enough for children to acquire moral responses.
_____ 4. With fearless, impulsive children, gentle discipline is especially effective.
_____ 5. Frequent punishment promotes lasting changes in children's behavior.
_____ 6. Providing reasons for mild punishment (such as time out) leads to a far greater reduction in misbehavior than using punishment alone.
_____ 7. Parent–child similarities suggest that heredity contributes to the link between punitive discipline and children's adjustment difficulties.
_____ 8. Use of physical punishment is highest among low-SES ethnic minority parents.
_____ 9. Theories that regard morality as entirely a matter of internalizing norms are supported by many modern researchers because they are consistent with important ethical principles and social goals.
_____ 10. Cognitive-developmental theorists believe that children develop morally through construction, or actively attending to and interrelating multiple perspectives on situations in which conflicts arise and thereby deriving new moral understandings.

Answers:

1. T   6. T
2. F   7. T
3. F   8. T
4. F   9. F
5. F   10. T

LEARNING ACTIVITY 12.2
Supporting Young Children's Moral Development (pp. 488–495)

Ask students to pretend they must speak to a group of parents about supporting young children's moral development. Using research in the text as a guide, have students list information that they would include in the presentation. For example, what child-rearing practices and discipline strategies are likely to facilitate moral behavior? What discipline strategies should parents avoid, and why? How should parents match the strategies they use to consider children's temperaments? What are some alternatives to harsh punishment?

LEARNING ACTIVITY 12.3
Assessing Moral Reasoning (pp. 500–502)

Have students visit the website: *www.haverford.edu/psych/ddavis/p109g/kohlberg.dilemmas.html,* which presents four moral dilemmas and a series of questions. Students should select one dilemma, answer the questions, and evaluate their level of moral reasoning on the basis of research in the text. Next, have students select a moral dilemma and ask a friend, roommate, or family member to read it and respond to the questions. Students should then classify that individual's level of moral reasoning. Finally, ask students to reflect on the activity. Do they think these moral dilemmas accurately assess moral reasoning? Why or why not?

LEARNING ACTIVITY 12.4
Analyzing Letters to the Editor in Your Local Newspaper for Maturity of Moral Reasoning (pp. 504–506)

Letters to the editor in newspapers often present reasoning on moral issues. For example, the U.S. war in Iraq is a "hot" topic for debate and is sometimes objected to on moral grounds. Abortion, political corruption, and the death penalty are other topics that often appear in the newspaper. Have students select one or two letters, identify the moral issues raised, and attempt to classify the maturity of moral reasoning expressed in each according to Kohlberg's stages. Once students have completed the activity, discuss their findings. What level of moral reasoning is reflected most often in the letters?

LEARNING ACTIVITY 12.5
Observing Children's Conversations for Instances of Moral Understanding (pp. 510–512)

Preschoolers' first concepts of morality emerge through interactions with parents and peers. As early as age 2, children react to situations in which deviations from the way people should behave occur. For example, they point to destroyed property, such as spots on furniture or broken toys, with an expression of discomfort, often exclaiming, "Uh-oh!" In addition, they typically react with alarm to behaviors that are aggressive or that might otherwise harm someone. Have students visit a local child-care center or preschool and watch for instances in which children commit acts to which peers might object (for example, grabbing or breaking a toy, pushing another child to get one's way). Students should note statements that deal with morality. For instance, what kinds of behavior offend or upset children? How do children react when something "bad" occurs? How do children interact with peers who frequently transgress? In pretend play, how do children communicate their understanding of "right" and "wrong"?

LEARNING ACTIVITY 12.6
Children's Reactions to Violations of Moral Imperatives and Social Conventions (pp. 510–512)

This activity can be completed with Learning Activity 12.5. To illustrate children's early grasp of the distinction between moral imperatives and social conventions, ask students to spend a morning or afternoon observing in a preschool or child-care center, watching for instances in which moral imperatives and social conventions are violated. Have students record a description of each incident, along with how children and adults reacted. They should find that when a moral offense occurs (such as taking someone else's belongings), children react emotionally, describe their own injury or loss, tell another child to stop, or retaliate. An adult who intervenes is likely to call attention to the rights and feelings of the victim. In contrast, children often do not respond to violations of social convention. And adults tend to demand obedience without explanation, as when they state, "Say the magic word" or "Don't eat with your fingers."

LEARNING ACTIVITY 12.7
Observing Toddlers for Compliance and Self-Control (pp. 514–515)

Invite two or three toddlers and parents to your classroom for a demonstration of compliance and self-control. Prior to the demonstration, gather several age-appropriate toys and several boxes of raisins. If you do not have access to these materials, ask parents to bring toys and/or raisins from home.

Present the following activities: Ask the child (or have the parent ask the child) not to touch an interesting toy within arm's reach. Alternatively, hide some raisins under cups, and instruct the child to wait until you (or the parent) say it is all right to pick up a cup and eat a raisin. Have students note how easily each child is able to resist temptation. Then give the children several directions (for example, to bring you an object or to clean up some toys). Did older children exhibit more compliance and self-control? Did they also try to exert more independence and not comply with directives? How did parents respond to their child's behavior?

LEARNING ACTIVITY 12.8
Matching: The Other Side of Self-Control: Development of Aggression (pp. 517–518)

To help students understand various types of aggression, present the following activity as an in-class assignment or quiz.

Directions: Match each of the following terms with its correct description.

Terms:
_____ 1. Proactive aggression
_____ 2. Reactive aggression
_____ 3. Physical aggression
_____ 4. Verbal aggression
_____ 5. Relational aggression

Descriptions:

A. Damages another's peer relationships through social exclusion, malicious gossip, or friendship manipulation.
B. Harms others through physical injury—pushing, hitting, kicking, punching others, or destroying another's property.
C. An angry, defensive response to a provocation or a blocked goal and is meant to hurt another person.
D. Harms others through threats of physical aggression, name calling, or hostile teasing.
E. When children act out to fulfill a need or desire—obtain an object, privilege, space, or social reward, such as adult attention or peer admiration—and unemotionally attack a person to achieve their goals.

Answers:

1. E   4. D
2. C   5. A
3. B

LEARNING ACTIVITY 12.9
Applying Ecological Systems Theory to the Development of Aggressive Behavior (pp. 516–525)

In small groups, have students list factors associated with the development of aggression. Next, have them review ecological systems theory (Chapter 1, pp. 26–29). For each factor listed, students should indicate in which level of the environment it belongs. Encourage students to include examples of bidirectional influences and the role of third parties. Why must interventions for aggressive children target multiple levels of the environment?

ASK YOURSELF . . .

REVIEW: Describe evidence indicating that many morally relevant behaviors have roots in our evolutionary history. (pp. 486–487)

In the 1970s, biological theories of human social behavior suggested that many morally relevant behaviors and emotions have roots in our evolutionary history. This view was supported by the work of ethologists, who observed animals aiding other members of their species, often at great personal risk. For example, ants, bees, and termites show extremes of self-sacrifice. Among primates, chimpanzees (who are genetically closest to humans) conform to moral-like rules, which group members enforce in one another. Chimps also reciprocate favors, generously grooming and sharing food with those who have done the same for them, and engage in kind and comforting acts. On the basis of this evidence, researchers reasoned that evolution must have made similar biologically based provisions for moral acts in human beings.

In other species, most empathetic or self-sacrificing acts occur within family groups with common reproductive interests. Evolutionary theorists speculate that humans' unique capacity to act prosocially toward genetic strangers originated several million years ago in small hunting-and-gathering bands, including both kin and nonkin. To limit selfishness and maintain group functioning, humans developed informal systems of social exchange, acting benevolently toward others with the expectation that others might reciprocate in the future. Willingness of many members of a group to aid others and engage in self-sacrifice ensures that the majority of the group will survive and reproduce; therefore, traits that foster altruism undergo natural selection, becoming increasingly prominent in succeeding generations.

Chapter 12 Moral Development

CONNECT: Summarize the main features of the psychoanalytic and social learning perspectives on moral development. What shortcomings do these two views share? (pp. 488–491, 494–495)

Both psychoanalytic and social learning theory regard moral development as a matter of *internalization:* adopting societal standards for right action as one's own. According to Freud, morality emerges between ages 3 and 6, the period of the well-known Oedipus and Electra conflicts. Young children desire to possess the parent of the other sex but abandon this wish because they fear punishment and loss of parental love. To maintain their parents' affection, children form a *superego,* or conscience, by *identifying* with the same-sex parent, whose moral standards they adopt. Finally, Freud believed that children redirect the hostility previously aimed at the same-sex parent toward themselves, which evokes feelings of guilt whenever they disobey the superego. In Freud's view, moral development is largely complete by age 5 or 6.

According to the social learning perspective, morality is acquired just like any other set of responses: through reinforcement and modeling. Many studies show that having helpful or generous models increases young children's prosocial responses. Children are most willing to imitate models who are warm and responsive, exhibit competence and power, and display consistency between assertions and behavior. By the end of early childhood, children who have had consistent exposure to caring adults tend to behave prosocially even when a model is not present. They have internalized prosocial rules from repeated observations and encouragement by others.

Today, most researchers disagree with Freud's view of conscience development. In contrast to Freudian predictions, fear of punishment and loss of parental love do not motivate conscience formation. Rather, a combination of parental warmth and *inductive discipline*—in which an adult helps the child notice others' feelings by pointing out the effects of the child's misbehavior on others—is far more effective. And although Freud was correct that guilt is an important motivator of moral action, it is not the only force that compels us to act morally, nor is moral development complete by the end of early childhood. Rather, it is a gradual process, extending from the preschool years into adulthood.

Both psychoanalytic theory and social learning theory view moral development as a process of internalizing societal norms. Theories that take this view have been criticized because prevailing standards may be at odds with important ethical principles and social goals. Under these conditions, deliberate violation of norms is not immoral but justifiable and courageous. With respect to children, parental concern about internalization of societal norms is often accompanied by other goals. For example, parents may accept noncompliance at times if the child provides a reasonable justification. Cognitive-developmental theorists believe that individuals develop morally through *construction*—actively attending to and interrelating multiple perspectives on situations in which social conflicts arise and thereby attaining new moral understandings.

APPLY: Alice and Wayne want their two young children to develop a strong, internalized conscience and to become generous, caring individuals. List some parenting practices that would foster these goals, and explain why each is effective. (pp. 491, 494)

Many studies show that having helpful or generous models increases young children's prosocial responses. The following characteristics of models affect children's willingness to imitate:

- *Warmth and responsiveness:* Preschoolers are more likely to copy the prosocial actions of an adult who is warm and responsive than those of a cold, distant adult. Warmth seems to make children more attentive and responsive to the model and is itself an example of a prosocial response.
- *Competence and power:* Children admire and therefore tend to imitate competent, powerful models—especially older peers and adults.
- *Consistency between assertions and behavior:* When models say one thing and do another—for example, say that "it's important to help others" but rarely engage in helpful acts—children choose the most lenient standard of behavior that adults demonstrate.

Although its usefulness is limited, punishment can play a valuable role in moral development. The most effective forms of discipline encourage good conduct by building a mutually respectful bond with children, letting them know ahead of time how to act, and praising mature behavior. When parents do use punishment, they can increase its effectiveness in three ways:

(1) *Consistency:* Permitting children to act inappropriately on some occasions but scolding them on others confuses them, and the unacceptable act persists.
(2) *A warm parent–child relationship:* Children of involved, caring parents find the interruption in parental affection that accompanies punishment especially unpleasant. They want to regain parental warmth and approval as quickly as possible.
(3) *Explanations:* Providing reasons for mild punishment helps children relate the misdeed to expectations for future behavior. This approach leads to a far greater reduction in misbehavior than using punishment alone.

REFLECT: Did you display a strong, internalized conscience as a child? How do you think temperament, parenting practices, family living conditions, and cultural background affected your childhood moral maturity? (pp. 488–495)

This is an open-ended question with no right or wrong answer.

REVIEW: How do recursive thought and understanding of ideal reciprocity contribute to moral development? Why are Kohlberg's Stages 3 and 4 morally mature constructions? (pp. 497, 501–502, 509)

As school-age children gain the capacity for recursive thought, they understand that conflicts often arise because of multiple yet legitimate interpretations of the same reality. Through peer disagreements, in particular, children come to realize that people's perspectives on moral action can differ and that intentions, not concrete consequences, should serve as the basis for judging behavior. Through interacting as equals with peers, children learn to settle conflicts in mutually beneficial ways, relying on reciprocity. Older children and adolescents move beyond a crude, tit-for-tat understanding of reciprocity to a grasp of the importance of mutuality of expectations, or *ideal reciprocity*—the idea expressed in the Golden Rule: "Do unto others as you would have them do unto you." This concept helps young people realize that rules can be reinterpreted and revised to take individual motives and circumstances into account.

In Kohlberg's theory, individuals in Stages 3 and 4, the *conventional level* of morality, regard conformity to social rules as an important way of actively maintaining the current social system, thereby ensuring positive human relationships and societal order. Critics dispute Kohlberg's belief that moral maturity is not achieved until the postconventional level, Stages 5 and 6, when individuals define morality in terms of abstract principles and values that apply to all humanity, regardless of situation or society. For example, John Gibbs argues that "postconventional morality" should not be viewed as the standard of maturity against which other levels are judged. Rather, Gibbs finds maturity in a revised understanding of Stages 3 and 4 that emphasizes ideal reciprocity. He asserts that these stages are not "conventional," or based on social conformity, as Kohlberg assumed. Instead, they require profound moral constructions—an understanding of ideal reciprocity as the basis for relationships between people (Stage 3) and for widely accepted moral standards, set forth in rules and laws (Stage 4).

CONNECT: Do adolescents' efforts to resolve conflicts between personal choice and moral imperatives reflect their increasingly profound grasp of justice? Explain, citing examples. (pp. 512–513)

In diverse Western and non-Western cultures, adolescents' quest for identity and increasing independence leads to intensified concern with matters of personal choice during the teenage years. Young school-age children regard freedom of speech and religion as individual rights, even when laws exist that deny those rights, and view laws that discriminate against individuals as wrong and worthy of violating. By the end of middle childhood, children justify these views on the basis of democratic ideals, such as the importance of individual rights for maintaining a fair society.

As adolescents integrate personal rights with ideal reciprocity, they demand that the protections they want for themselves extend to others. For example, with age, teenagers are more likely to defend the government's right to limit individual freedom to engage in risky health behaviors, such as smoking and drinking, in the interest of the larger public good. Certain behaviors are classified differently in different cultures—viewed as moral imperatives by one culture but only as social conventions in another. But when children are asked about acts that obviously lead to harm or violate rights—for example, breaking promises, destroying another's property, or kicking harmless animals—cross-cultural similarity prevails. This is evidence that justice considerations are a universal feature of moral thought.

APPLY: Tam grew up in a small village culture, Lydia in a large industrial city. At age 15, Tam reasons at Kohlberg's Stage 3, Lydia at Stage 4. What factors probably account for the difference? (pp. 505–506)

Individuals in industrialized nations move through Kohlberg's stages more rapidly and advance to a higher level than do individuals in village societies, who rarely move beyond Stage 3. In village societies, moral cooperation is based on direct relations between people and does not allow for the development of advanced moral understanding, which depends on appreciating the role of larger social structures, such as laws and government institutions, in resolving moral conflict. Also, responses to moral dilemmas in collectivist cultures, including village societies, are often more other-directed than in Western Europe and North America.

Growing up in a small village culture, Tam would not have the opportunity to develop moral reasoning based on maintaining the larger social order. His moral reasoning is also likely to be influenced by a strong sense of the individual as vitally connected to the social group. In contrast, Lydia, growing up in a large industrial city, would have opportunities to observe larger social structures and to appreciate the importance of maintaining these institutions, and, depending on the specific culture in which she was raised, she might also place a higher value on individual rights and an appeal to an inner, private conscience—characteristics of Kohlberg's highest levels that may, in fact, represent a culturally specific way of thinking.

Chapter 12 Moral Development

REFLECT: Do you favor a cognitive-developmental or a pragmatic approach to morality, or both? What research evidence and personal experiences influenced your viewpoint? (pp. 496–506, 509–510)

This is an open-ended question with no right or wrong answer.

REVIEW: Cite factors that contribute to an improved ability to delay gratification from early to middle childhood. (pp. 515–516)

Cognitive development—in particular, gains in attention and mental representation—enables children to use a variety of effective self-instructional strategies that contribute to their resistance to temptation. In everyday situations, preschoolers find it difficult to keep their minds off tempting activities and objects for long. When their thoughts turn to a prohibited goal, the way they mentally represent it has much to do with their success at self-control. Teaching preschoolers to transform the stimulus in ways that de-emphasize its arousing qualities helps children shift attention and inhibit emotional reactivity, promoting delay of gratification.

During the school years, children become better at devising their own strategies for resisting temptation. By this time, self-control has become a flexible capacity for *moral self-regulation*—the ability to monitor one's own conduct, constantly adjusting it as circumstances present opportunities to violate inner standards.

When asked about situational conditions and self-instructions likely to help delay gratification, school-age children suggested a broader array of arousal-reducing strategies with age. But not until the late elementary school years did they mention techniques involving transformations of rewards or their own arousal states. Once this transforming ideation emerges, it greatly facilitates moral self-regulation.

CONNECT: Reread the section on adolescent parenthood in Chapter 5 (pages 217–219) and the section on adolescent suicide in Chapter 11 (pages 472–473). What factors do these problems have in common with chronic antisocial behavior? (pp. 520–521)

Adolescent parenthood is linked to a set of related, unfavorable family conditions and personal characteristics that negatively influence development over an extended time. Suicidal young people often have a family history of emotional problems and also are more likely to have experienced multiple stressful life events. In similar fashion, chronic antisocial behavior that emerges in childhood and endures is associated with certain characteristics of the child, such as irritability, fearlessness, impulsiveness, and overactivity, and also with a strife-ridden family life, poor parenting practices, aggressive peers, and exposure to televised violence—all strong predictors of both antisocial activity and reduced sensitivity to others' suffering. As with adolescent parenthood and suicide, family, community, and cultural influences can either heighten or reduce children's risk of sustaining a hostile interpersonal style that puts them at risk for chronic antisocial behavior.

APPLY: Zeke had been well behaved in elementary school, but around age 13 he started spending time with the "wrong crowd." At 16, he was arrested for property damage. Is Zeke likely to become a long-term offender? Why or why not? (pp. 520–521)

Zeke is not likely to become a long-term offender. Adolescent delinquency follows two paths of development—one with an onset of conduct problems in childhood and the second with an onset in adolescence. The early-onset type is far more likely to lead to a life-course pattern of aggression and criminality. For youths like Zeke who first display antisocial behavior around the time of puberty, conduct problems typically arise from typical adolescent novelty seeking and receptiveness to peer influence. Another factor may be a temporary decline in quality of parenting, perhaps related to the challenges of disciplining an unruly teenager. But in contrast to the early-onset type, late-onset adolescent delinquency does not arise from an inherited predisposition to aggressiveness that combines with inept parenting and other environmental factors to contribute to chronic antisocial involvements.

A few late-onset youths do continue to engage in antisocial acts, generally because the seriousness of their adolescent offenses has trapped them in situations that close off opportunities for responsible behavior. But Zeke's arrest for property damage does not fit this pattern of serious criminal involvement.

REFLECT: Describe a recent instance in which your cool processing system dominated your hot-system reactivity, enabling you to resist temptation. What did your cool processing system do to gain control? (p. 516)

This is an open-ended question with no right or wrong answer.

SUGGESTED READINGS

Arsenio, W. F., & Lemerise, E. A. (2010). *Emotions, aggression, and morality in children: Bridging development and psychopathology*. Washington, DC: American Psychological Association. Presents a diverse range of topics on emotional development, including biological and environmental influences, the importance of empathy, early parent–child and peer relations, the development of morality and aggression, the long-term consequences of childhood aggression, and research-based interventions for aggressive children.

Killen, M., & Rutland, A. (2011). *Children and social exclusion: Morality, prejudice, and group identity*. New York: Wiley-Blackwell. A compelling look at morality and children's experiences with prejudice, this book presents child and adolescent interviews, results from observational studies, and research on the effects of prejudice and group bias on children's development and well-being.

Nucci, L. (2008). *Nice is not enough: Facilitating moral development*. Upper Saddle River, NJ: Prentice Hall. Written by a leading expert in moral development, this book provides an extensive overview of developmental changes in moral understanding and explains how moral education can be incorporated into day-to-day classroom activities. Includes research-based strategies and sample lesson plans.

MEDIA MATERIALS

For details on individual video segments that accompany the DVD for *Child Development,* Ninth Edition, please see the DVD Guide for *Explorations in Child Development*. The DVD and DVD Guide are available through your Pearson sales representative.

Additional DVDs that may be useful in your class are listed below. These are not available through your Pearson sales representative, but you can order them directly from the distributors. (See contact information at the end of this manual.)

A Child's Mind: How Kids Learn Right & Wrong (2011, Magna Systems/Learning Seed, 34 min.). This program explores the effects of moral development on children's behavior, presents various theories of morality, and introduces the concept of the theory of mind. The program includes children's reactions to situations that challenge their morals, as well as interviews with experts who help explain how and why children develop as they do and discuss the importance of fostering moral development. An educator's guide is available.

Boys Will Be Boys, But What About Girls? Childhood Aggression and Gender (2008, Insight Media, 50 min.). This program explores relational aggression and examines its prevalence among girls and young women. Exploring three forms of relational aggression, it combines entertaining vintage footage from the television show *Candid Camera* with research findings.

Bully Girls (2006, Films Media Group/Meridian Production, 20 min.). Although bullying has traditionally referred to physical intimidation and violence—and in the past was considered a problem only among boys—experts are finding, as this program explains, that girls can perpetuate bullying as well. This program focuses on the increasing awareness of bullying among girls and on how, when, and why it occurs. An instructor's guide is available.

Encouraging Moral Development in Children (2006, Films Media Group, 14 min.). This program examines moral development in children and adolescents. Scenes from a busy preschool illustrate how toddlers absorb the concepts of right and wrong, personal responsibility, and compassion. Also featured is a roundtable session in which teens frankly discuss moral dilemmas, using their personal experiences as examples. Teaching materials are included.

Family Violence (2007, Insight Media, 30 min.). This program examines violent behavior within a family, including prevention and intervention programs that focus on combating the toxic effects of family violence.

Moral Ethics: Uncovering the Secrets of Childhood (2009, Insight Media, 27 min.). Using research on children's actions, this program explores the factors that shape children's moral behavior.

Morality: A Historical Perspective (2006, Insight Media, 127 min.). Questioning the concepts of morality, immorality, and the exclusivity of moral dilemmas to the human race, this program weighs goodness against the balance of human nature. It considers the contributions of religion, philosophy, and neuroscience to moral thought.

Morality: Judgments and Actions (2002, Davidson Films, 30 min.). Combining archival materials, a replication of a recent study with young children, and frank interviews with contemporary college students, this program summarizes much of recent research about moral development. It covers how children acquire morality and the distinctions that they are able to make early on about different types of rules that apply to everyday settings. It provides examples from a range of cultures. A learning guide is available.

Right and Wrong: Moral Development in Children (2006, Films Media Group/ BBC–Open University coproduction, 60 min.). This production, part of the series *Child of Our Time: A Year-by-Year Study of Childhood Development*, explores influences on moral development, including where children acquire their values, the age at which children begin to work out what is right and wrong, and whether young children can distinguish between actions that are morally deviant and those that simply violate a social convention. Viewers will watch as a group of 25 6-year-olds are presented with several moral dilemmas that assess their willingness to lie, cheat, and even destroy a photograph they are told is sentimentally valuable.

The Pandemic of Family Violence (2006, Insight Media, 48 min.). This program proposes that families are the basic units of socialization, and violence within the family both mirrors and determines violence within a society and between societies. Family violence is explored as a universal human rights issue.

CHAPTER 13
DEVELOPMENT OF SEX DIFFERENCES AND GENDER ROLES

CHAPTER-AT-A-GLANCE

Chapter Outline	Instruction Ideas	Supplements
Gender Stereotypes and Gender Roles pp. 530–535 Gender Stereotyping in Early Childhood • Gender Stereotyping in Middle Childhood and Adolescence • Individual and Group Differences in Gender Stereotyping • Gender Stereotyping and Gender-Role Adoption	Learning Objectives 13.1–13.3 Lecture Enhancements 13.1–13.2 Learning Activities 13.1–13.3 Ask Yourself p. 535	Test Bank Items 1–25, 125–126 Please contact your Pearson publisher's representative for a wide range of video offerings available to adopters.
Influences on Gender Stereotyping and Gender-Role Adoption pp. 535–547 Biological Influences • Environmental Influences	Learning Objectives 13.4–13.5 Ask Yourself p. 547	Test Bank Items 26–75, 127
Gender Identity pp. 547–553 Emergence of Gender Identity • Gender Identity in Middle Childhood • Gender Identity in Adolescence • Gender Schema Theory	Learning Objectives 13.6–13.8 Lecture Enhancement 13.3 Learning Activities 13.4–13.5 Ask Yourself p. 552	Test Bank Items 76–98, 128
To What Extent Do Boys and Girls *Really* Differ in Gender-Stereotyped Attributes? pp. 553–562 Mental Abilities • Personality Traits	Learning Objective 13.9 Learning Activity 13.6	Test Bank Items 99–120, 129
Developing Non-Gender-Stereotyped Children pp. 562–564	Learning Objective 13.10 Lecture Enhancement 13.4 Learning Activity 13.7 Ask Yourself p. 564	Test Bank Items 121–124, 130

BRIEF CHAPTER SUMMARY

At an early age, children adopt many gender-linked standards of their culture. The study of gender typing has responded to societal change, and the adoption of gender-typed beliefs and behaviors is no longer regarded as essential for healthy adjustment. Gender schema theory, an information-processing view of how children acquire gender-typed knowledge, combines social learning and cognitive-developmental approaches. Gender stereotypes and gender roles are the public face of gender; gender identity—perception of the self as relatively masculine or feminine in characteristics—is its private face.

Despite changes over the past four decades, strong beliefs persist about sex differences in personality. Instrumental traits are widely regarded as masculine and expressive traits as feminine. Gender stereotypes for physical characteristics, occupations, and activities or behaviors generally cast men in a more positive light than women.

Gender stereotyping begins in early childhood as children label their own and others' sex. Gender-stereotyped beliefs strengthen during early childhood and are well-established by age 5. As school-age children develop the capacity to integrate conflicting social cues, they display greater gender-stereotype flexibility, but children continue to disapprove of violations of gender-role expectations, especially by males.

Both individual and group differences in gender stereotyping exist. Boys hold more rigid views than girls, Caucasian-American children more than African-American children. Higher-SES adolescents and adults tend to hold more flexible views than their lower-SES counterparts.

Over the preschool years, gender-typed preferences and behaviors increase sharply, especially in boys. By middle childhood, knowledge of gender stereotypes is so universal that it cannot predict variations in children's behavior. But stereotype flexibility is a good predictor of gender-role adoption in middle childhood, suggesting that gender stereotypes affect behavior only when children incorporate those beliefs into their own gender identities.

Debate continues over biological and societal influences on gender differences. The role of biology is supported by cross-cultural similarities in gender stereotypes and by the influence of hormones on gender-role behavior. Sex hormones affect brain development and neural activity in many animal species, as well as in humans, affecting play styles and influencing preference for same-sex peers. But a wealth of evidence reveals that environmental forces powerfully support gender-role development.

Gender identity—a person's self-perception as masculine or feminine—is a good predictor of psychological adjustment. A substantial minority of people have a gender identity called androgyny, scoring high on both masculine and feminine characteristics. "Masculine" and androgynous children and adults have higher self-esteem than "feminine" individuals, and are more adaptable.

Preschool children develop gender constancy, an understanding that their gender is permanent and biologically based, but "gender-appropriate" behavior begins so early that it cannot simply be the result of gender constancy, but must reflect modeling and reinforcement.

School-age boys strengthen their identification with the masculine role, while girls become more androgynous. Adolescence is often accompanied by gender intensification, in which gender stereotyping of attitudes and behavior increases, though the evidence is mixed. Gender intensification typically declines by late adolescence.

Boys and girls do not differ in general intelligence but do vary in specific mental abilities, with girls ahead of boys in early language progress and boys ahead of girls in mathematical abilities by late childhood and early adolescence. Sex differences in personality are also in line with gender stereotypes, reflecting both biological and environmental factors. In industrialized nations, depression is more prevalent in adolescent girls than in boys, apparently as a result of a combination of stressful life events and gender-typed coping styles. By the second year, boys are more physically aggressive than girls, but sex differences in verbal and relational aggression are minimal. Again, both biological and environmental influences play a role.

To promote children's development beyond the constraints of traditional gender roles, adults can counteract children's readiness to absorb gender-linked associations by eliminating traditional gender roles from their own behavior. Once children notice gender stereotypes, adults can point out exceptions.

LEARNING OBJECTIVES

After reading this chapter, you should be able to answer the following:

13.1 Explain how the study of gender typing has responded to societal change. (p. 530)

13.2 Describe the development of gender stereotyping from early childhood into adolescence. (pp. 530–533)

13.3 Cite individual and group differences in gender stereotyping, and discuss the relationship between gender stereotyping and gender-role adoption. (pp. 533–534)

13.4 Discuss biological differences on gender stereotyping and gender-role adoption. (pp. 535–538)

13.5 Discuss environmental influences on gender stereotyping and gender-role adoption. (pp. 538–547)

13.6 Discuss androgyny as well as social learning and cognitive-developmental views of the development of gender identity in early childhood. (pp. 547–549)

13.7 What changes in gender identity occur in middle childhood and adolescence? (pp. 549–551)

13.8 Explain gender schema theory. (pp. 551–553)

13.9 Describe sex differences in mental abilities and personality traits, noting factors that contribute to those differences. (pp. 553–562)

13.10 Cite ways to reduce gender stereotyping in children. (pp. 562–563)

Chapter 13 Development of Sex Differences and Gender Roles

LECTURE OUTLINE

I. INTRODUCTION (pp. 529–530)
   A. At an early age, children adopt many gender-linked standards of their culture, and both boys and girls interact more with agemates of their own sex.
   B. Researchers who study gender typing investigate questions such as:
      1. Why do young children's play and social preferences become so strongly gender-typed, and how do these attitudes and behaviors change with age?
      2. Do societal expectations affect children's view of themselves as masculine or feminine beings, thereby limiting their potential?
      3. In what ways do heredity and environment contribute to the differences between the sexes?
   C. Perhaps more than any other area of child development, the study of gender typing has responded to societal change.
      1. Until the early 1970s, psychologists regarded the adoption of gender-typed beliefs and behaviors as essential for healthy adjustment.
      2. Today, many people recognize that some gender-typed characteristics, such as extreme aggressiveness and competitiveness in males and passivity and conformity in females, are serious threats to mental health.
   D. Major current approaches to the study of gender typing are social learning theory and cognitive-developmental theory, neither of which is sufficient by itself. An information-processing view, *gender schema theory,* combines elements of both theories.
   E. The following special terms have emerged in discussions of gender:
      1. **Gender stereotypes** are widely held beliefs about characteristics deemed appropriate for males and females.
      2. **Gender roles** are the reflection of these stereotypes in everyday behavior.
      3. **Gender identity** is the private face of gender—the perception of the self as relatively masculine or feminine in characteristics.
      4. **Gender typing** refers broadly to any association of objects, activities, roles, or traits with biological sex in ways that conform to cultural stereotypes of gender.

II. GENDER STEREOTYPES AND GENDER ROLES (pp. 530–535)
   A. Gender stereotypes have appeared in religious, philosophical, and literary works for centuries and persist despite growing awareness over the past four decades of the wide range of roles possible for each gender.
      1. **Instrumental traits,** reflecting competence, rationality, and assertiveness, are regarded as masculine.
      2. **Expressive traits,** emphasizing warmth, caring, and sensitivity, are viewed as feminine.
      3. Cross-cultural research reveals that the instrumental–expressive dichotomy is a widely held stereotype around the world.
      4. Other gender stereotypes involve physical characteristics, occupations, and activities or behaviors.
   B. The variety and broad acceptance of gender stereotypes suggest that they are deeply ingrained patterns of thinking. They cast men in a generally positive light and women in a generally negative light.
   C. Adults apply gender stereotypes to children with a special intensity.
   D. Gender Stereotyping in Early Childhood (pp. 531–532)
      1. Between 18 months and 3 years, children label their own and others' sex, using such words as *boy, girl, lady,* and *man.*
      2. Before age 2, children have begun to acquire commonly held, subtle associations with gender—men as rough and sharp, women as soft and round.
      3. Many children apply gender-stereotyped beliefs as blanket rules rather than as flexible guidelines.
      4. Most preschoolers do not yet realize that characteristics *associated with* being male or female do not *determine* a person's sex.
   E. Gender Stereotyping in Middle Childhood and Adolescence (pp. 532–533)
      1. Gender stereotyping of activities and occupations is well-established by age 5.
      2. During middle childhood and adolescence, knowledge of stereotypes increases in the areas of personality traits and achievement.
      3. Older children realize that gender-stereotypic attributes are not defining features of gender.
      4. Personality Traits
         a. Research in many countries reveals that stereotyping of personality traits increases steadily in middle childhood, becoming adultlike around age 11.

b. A large Canadian study found that the stereotypes acquired first reflected *in-group favoritism*.
c. Once trait stereotyping is well under way, children characterize the in-group and the out-group as having both positive and negative qualities.
d. Though both boys and girls view each gender as having more positive than negative traits, this effect is stronger for the in-group—evidence that in-group favoritism persists.
e. And girls express greater in-group favoritism and out-group negativity than boys.
5. Achievement Areas
a. Elementary school children often regard reading, spelling, art, and music as more for girls and mathematics, athletics, and mechanical skills as more for boys.
b. In both Asian and Western nations, boys tend to feel more competent than girls at math, science, and athletics, whereas girls feel more competent than boys at language arts.
c. Some gender-stereotyped beliefs among children may be changing. In several recent investigations, a majority of elementary and secondary school students disagreed with the idea that math is a "masculine" subject.
6. Toward Greater Flexibility
a. School-age children are knowledgeable about many gender stereotypes but also develop a more open-minded view of what males and females *can do*.
b. Researchers measure **gender-stereotype flexibility,** or overlap in the characteristics that children attribute to males and females.
c. Gender stereotypes become more flexible as children develop the cognitive capacity to integrate conflicting social cues.
d. By the end of the school years, most children no longer view gender-typed behavior (especially that of girls) as inborn and fixed.
e. But acknowledging that boys and girls *can* cross gender lines does not mean that children always *approve* of doing so.
f. Children displaying certain "cross-gender" behavior are likely to experience severe peer disapproval.
F. Individual and Group Differences in Gender Stereotyping (pp. 533–534)
1. By middle childhood, most children have extensive knowledge of gender stereotypes, but they vary widely in the makeup of their understanding.
2. The strongest group difference in gender stereotyping is sex-related: Boys hold more rigid gender-stereotyped views than girls throughout childhood and adolescence.
3. Evidence suggests that African-American children hold less stereotyped views of activities and achievement areas than do Caucasian-American children.
4. In adolescence and adulthood, higher-SES individuals tend to hold more flexible gender-stereotype views than their lower-SES counterparts.
G. Gender Stereotyping and Gender-Role Adoption (p. 534)
1. Over the preschool years, the same period in which children rapidly acquire stereotypes, gender-typed preferences and behaviors increase sharply, especially in boys.
2. But these parallel patterns do not tell us whether gender stereotyping shapes children's behavior.
3. By middle childhood, knowledge of gender stereotypes is so universal that it cannot predict variations in individual children's behavior.
4. Stereotype flexibility is a better predictor than stereotype knowledge of children's gender-role adoption in middle childhood, suggesting that gender stereotypes affect behavior only when children incorporate those beliefs into their own gender identities.

III. INFLUENCES ON GENDER STEREOTYPING AND GENDER-ROLE ADOPTION (pp. 535–547)
A. Biological Influences (pp. 535–538)
1. From an evolutionary perspective, males are genetically primed for dominance and females for intimacy, responsiveness, and cooperativeness.
2. Two sources of evidence have been used to support the role of biology:
a. Cross-cultural similarities exist in gender stereotypes.
b. Hormones influence gender-role behavior.

3. How Much Cross-Cultural Similarity Exists in Gender Typing?
   a. Cross-cultural findings reveal that most societies promote instrumental traits in males and expressive traits in females, although the magnitude of this difference varies widely.
   b. Although experience can profoundly influence gender typing, reversals of traditional gender roles are rare.
4. Sex Hormones and Gender Typing
   a. Sex hormones affect brain development and neural activity in many species and in humans.
   b. Play Styles and Preference for Same-Sex Peers
      (1) Studies show that androgens promote male-typical sexual behavior and aggression and suppress maternal caregiving in a wide variety of species.
      (2) At least some hormonal effects appear to extend to humans, as seen in children's preference for playmates of their own sex, which increases throughout the school years.
      (3) Hormones affect play styles, and as children interact with peers, they choose playmates whose interests and behaviors are compatible with their own.
      (4) Social pressures for "gender-appropriate" play and cognitive factors contribute to gender segregation, but sex hormones are also involved.
   c. Exceptional Sexual Development
      (1) Studies of girls with *congenital adrenal hyperplasia (CAH)*—a genetic disorder in which the adrenal system produces high levels of androgens from the prenatal period onward—support the view that prenatal androgen exposure influences certain aspects of "masculine" gender-role behavior.
      (2) In one study of children with *androgen insensitivity syndrome,* in which the testes produce normal levels of androgens but androgen receptors in body cells are impaired, the degree of reduction in prenatal androgen exposure predicted feminine gender-typed behavior, although child rearing also played a role.
      (3) Research on individuals reared as members of the other sex because they had ambiguous genitals indicates that most accepted their assigned sexual identity, though a substantial minority of CAH girls with masculinized genitals expressed considerable discomfort with being reared female.

B. Environmental Influences (pp. 538–547)
   1. Environmental forces provide powerful support for gender-role development.
   2. Perceptions and Expectations of Adults
      a. During childhood and adolescence, parents hold different perceptions and expectations of their sons and daughters.
      b. Parents of preschoolers respond more negatively to the idea of boys than girls crossing gender lines.
   3. Treatment by Parents
      a. Although differences in the way parents socialize boys and girls are small, consistent effects emerge when the evidence is examined closely.
      b. Infancy and Early Childhood
         (1) As early as the first few months of life, parents create different environments for boys and girls.
         (2) Parents also actively reinforce independence in boys and closeness and dependency in girls.
         (3) Parents unconsciously use language that highlights gender distinctions and informs children about traditional gender roles.
      c. Middle Childhood and Adolescence
         (1) During the school years, parents continue to demand greater independence from sons than from daughters.
         (2) Parents also hold gender-differentiated perceptions of and expectations for children's competencies in various school subjects. For example, mothers rate girls as better at English than boys who earn similar English grades.
         (3) Parents' differential treatment of boys and girls extends to the freedom granted children in their everyday lives, with parents granting more freedom and autonomy to boys.
      d. Mothers versus Fathers
         (1) In most aspects of differential treatment of boys and girls, fathers discriminate the most.
         (2) Parents seem especially committed to ensuring the gender typing of children of their own sex.
   4. Treatment by Teachers
      a. In some ways, preschool and elementary school teachers reinforce both boys and girls for "feminine" rather than "masculine" behaviors, valuing obedience over assertiveness.

b. Teachers also act in ways that maintain and even extend gender roles taught at home—for example, preschool teachers give girls more encouragement to participate in adult-structured activities, where compliance and bids for help occur more often than assertiveness.
c. Teachers often emphasize gender distinctions, using labeling that promotes gender stereotyping, in-group favoritism, and out-group prejudice in children.
d. As early as kindergarten, teachers give more overall attention (both positive and negative) to boys than to girls.
5. Observational Learning
a. Children's environments contain many gender-typed models, such as women as nurses.
b. Media portrayals are also gender typed.
c. Children who are exposed to nonstereotyped models are less traditional in their beliefs and behaviors.
6. Peers
a. The peer context is an especially potent source of gender-role learning.
b. Gender-Role Learning in Gender-Segregated Peer Groups
(1) By age 3, same-sex peers positively reinforce one another for gender-typed play and criticize one another for "cross-gender" activities.
(2) Children develop different styles of social influence in gender-segregated peer groups.
(3) Children form beliefs about the "correctness" of gender-segregated play that strengthen gender segregation and stereotyped activities.
(4) Some educators believe that forming mixed-sex activity groups in classrooms and recreation settings is vital for reducing gender stereotyping and broadening developmental possibilities for both sexes.
c. A short-term active intervention with elementary school children was successful at getting the children to counter peers' sexist statements.
d. Cultural Variations
(1) Cultures and subcultures differ in the extent of gender-typed communication within those groups.
(2) For example, African-American and Hispanic-American lower-SES girls are generally more assertive and independent in their interactions with one another and with boys than are Caucasian-American girls.
7. Siblings
a. Sibling effects on gender typing are more complex than peer influences because they depend on birth order and family size.
b. Younger siblings have little impact on older siblings' gender typing, but older siblings serve as powerful models for young siblings.
c. Studies have found that children with same-sex siblings are more gender-typed than those with no siblings, who, in turn, are more gender-typed than those with other-sex older siblings. Yet other research contradicts these findings.
d. When children are all of the same sex, parents sometimes relax pressures toward gender typing—for example, assigning "cross-gender" chores.

IV. GENDER IDENTITY (pp. 547–553)
A. *Gender identity* is a person's perception of the self as relatively masculine or feminine in characteristics.
1. Researchers can measure gender identity starting in middle childhood.
2. Although most people view themselves in gender-typed terms, a substantial minority, especially females, have a gender identity called **androgyny,** scoring high on *both* masculine and feminine characteristics.
3. Gender identity is a good predictor of psychological adjustment: "Masculine" and androgynous children and adults have higher self-esteem than "feminine" individuals, and are more adaptable.
B. Emergence of Gender Identity (pp. 548–549)
1. According to *social learning theory,* preschoolers first acquire gender-typed responses through modeling and reinforcement; only later do they organize these behaviors into gender-linked ideas about themselves.
2. *Cognitive-developmental theory* maintains that self-perceptions come before behavior and that over the preschool years, children develop **gender constancy**—a full understanding of the biologically based permanence of their gender, which combines *gender labeling, gender stability,* and *gender consistency*—and use this knowledge to guide their behavior.
3. Development of Gender Constancy
a. Kohlberg proposed that before age 6 or 7, children cannot maintain the constancy of their gender; but, rather, attain this understanding gradually, by moving through the following stages:

(1) **Gender labeling.** By the early preschool years, children can label their own sex and that of others correctly, but they do not understand that one's sex is permanent.
(2) **Gender stability.** Slightly older preschoolers have a partial understanding of the permanence of sex.
(3) **Gender consistency.** During the late preschool and early school years, children understand that sex is biologically based and remains the same even if a person dresses in "cross-gender" clothes or engages in nontraditional activities.
    b. Many studies confirm that the development of gender constancy follows this sequence and that mastery of gender constancy is associated with attainment of conservation.
    c. Gender constancy is also strongly related to the ability to pass verbal appearance–reality tasks.
  4. How Well Does Gender Constancy Predict Gender-Role Adoption?
    a. Only weak evidence exists for the cognitive-developmental theory that gender constancy is responsible for children's gender-typed behavior: "Gender-appropriate" behavior appears so early in the preschool years that modeling and reinforcement must contribute to its initial appearance, as social learning theory suggests.
    b. The cognitive changes that lead up to gender constancy do seem to facilitate gender typing.
    c. These findings suggest that once children form basic gender categories, they use them to acquire gender-relevant information about themselves and their social world.
    d. Gender-role adoption is more affected powerfully by children's beliefs about how close the connection must be between their own gender and their behavior than by their attainment of gender constancy.
C. Gender Identity in Middle Childhood (pp. 549–550)
  1. During middle childhood, boys' identification with the "masculine" role strengthens, while girls' identification with "feminine" characteristics declines.
  2. Girls are more androgynous than boys in both self-descriptions and choices of activities.
  3. The gender identity of school-age children expands to include several self-evaluations, which greatly affect their adjustment:
    a. *Gender typicality* is the degree to which the child feels similar to others of the same gender.
    b. *Gender contentedness* is the degree to which the child feels comfortable with his or her gender assignment.
    c. *Felt pressure to conform to gender roles* is the degree to which the child feels that parents and peers disapprove of his or her gender-related traits.
  4. *Gender-typical* and *gender-contented* children have been found to gain in self-esteem in middle childhood, in contrast to *gender-atypical* and *gender-discontented* children, who declined in self-worth.
  5. Gender-atypical children who experienced *intense pressure to conform to gender roles* experienced serious difficulties.
D. Gender Identity in Adolescence (pp. 550–551)
  1. Adolescence is typically accompanied by **gender intensification**—increased gender stereotyping of attitudes and behavior, and movement toward a more traditional gender identity.
  2. Gender intensification, when evident, seems stronger for adolescent girls.
  3. Biological, social, and cognitive factors account for gender intensification:
    a. Puberty magnifies sex differences in appearance, causing adolescents to spend more time thinking about themselves in gender-linked ways.
    b. When adolescents start to date, they often become more gender-typed as a way of increasing their attractiveness.
  4. Gender intensification typically declines by late adolescence, but not all affected young people move beyond it to the same degree.
  5. Teenagers who are encouraged to explore non-gender-typed options and to question the value of gender stereotypes are more likely to build an androgynous identity.
E. Gender Schema Theory (pp. 551–553)
  1. **Gender schema theory** is an information-processing approach that explains how environmental pressures and children's cognitions work together to shape gender typing.
  2. It integrates the various elements of gender typing—gender stereotyping, gender identity, and gender-role adoption—into a unified picture of how masculine and feminine orientations emerge and are often strongly maintained.
  3. Young children pick up gender-stereotyped preferences and behaviors from others and also organize their experiences into *gender schemas*—masculine and feminine categories that they use to interpret their world.

4. Individual differences exist in the extent to which children endorse gender-typed views.
    a. A *gender-schematic child* has a *gender-salience filter* that immediately makes gender highly relevant when he or she confronts new situations.
    b. A *gender-aschematic child* seldom views the world in gender-linked terms.

V. TO WHAT EXTENT DO BOYS AND GIRLS *REALLY* DIFFER IN GENDER-STEREOTYPED ATTRIBUTES? (pp. 553–562)
  A. Research on stable differences between males and females:
    1. Researchers have looked for stable differences between males and females and then for the biological and environmental roots of each variation.
    2. Researchers often use *meta-analysis*—reanalyzing the data of many investigations together—to avoid basing conclusions on single studies and small, potentially biased samples.
        a. Sex differences typically account for no more than 5 to 10 percent of individual differences in mental abilities and personality traits.
        b. Although a few considerable sex differences exist, males and females are more alike than different in developmental potential.
  B. Mental Abilities (pp. 554–558)
    1. Boys and girls do not differ in general intelligence, but they do vary in specific mental abilities.
    2. Many researchers believe that heredity is involved in the disparities, although experience plays a considerable role.
    3. Verbal Abilities
        a. Early in development, girls are ahead of boys in language progress, and throughout the school years, girls attain higher scores in reading achievement.
        b. Girls' advantage in reading and writing achievement increases in adolescence, with boys doing especially poorly in writing.
        c. These differences in literacy skills are believed to be major contributors to a widening gender gap in college enrollments, with males accounting for 43 percent of U.S. undergraduates.
        d. fMRI research suggests that girls are more efficient language processors than boys, but girls also receive more verbal stimulation from the preschool years through adolescence.
        e. Also, children view language arts as a "feminine" subject.
    4. Mathematical Abilities
        a. Some studies of mathematical abilities in early childhood find no disparities, whereas others show slight differences depending on the math skill assessed.
        b. Girls tend to be advantaged in counting, arithmetic computation, and mastery of basic concepts.
        c. But by late childhood and early adolescence, when math concepts and problems become more abstract and spatial, boys outperform girls, with the difference especially evident on tests requiring complex reasoning and geometry—a male advantage evident in most countries where both sexes have equal access to secondary education.
        d. The gender gap is small and has diminished over the past 30 years, but it is greater among the most capable students, although even this disparity has been shrinking.
        e. Accumulating evidence indicates that boys' advantage originates in boys' more rapid numerical memory and their superior spatial reasoning.
        f. Social pressures are also influential, as children often view math as a "masculine" subject, and parents typically think boys are better at it.
        g. This attitude encourages girls to blame their math errors on lack of ability, which undermines their performance on math achievement tests.
        h. In cultures that value gender equality, sex differences in secondary school students' math achievement are much smaller and, in one nation (Iceland), reversed.
  C. Personality Traits (pp. 558–562)
    1. Emotional Sensitivity
        a. Starting early in life, females are more emotionally sensitive than males.
            (1) Girls are slightly better than boys at inferring others' emotional states, especially at understanding self-conscious emotions.

(2) Girls express their feelings, except for anger, more freely and intensely in everyday interaction, and they are better than boys at identifying their feelings.
    b. Differences in emotional sensitivity are less consistently observed for empathy, sympathy, and prosocial behavior.
    c. Both biological and environmental explanations for sex differences in emotional sensitivity exist, but cultural expectations that girls be warm and expressive and boys be distant and self-controlled seem largely responsible for the gender gap in emotional sensitivity.
 2. Depression
    a. Depression is the most common psychological problem of adolescence.
    b. Depression increases sharply from ages 12 to 16 in industrialized nations, much more commonly in girls than in boys.
    c. Teenage girls are twice as likely as boys to report persistent depressed mood.
    d. The precise combination of biological and environmental factors leading to depression varies from one individual to the next.
       (1) Kinship studies reveal that heredity plays an important role.
       (2) Experience can also activate depression, promoting biological changes.
       (3) Parents of depressed children and adolescents show a high incidence of depression and other psychological disorders.
    e. Girls in industrialized nations appear to be more prone to depression as a result of a combination of stressful life events and gender-typed coping styles.
    f. Many adults misinterpret adolescents' depression, seeing it as just a passing phase. As a result, the overwhelming majority of depressed teenagers do not receive treatment.
 3. Aggression
    a. Sex differences in aggression have attracted more research attention than other sex differences.
       (1) By the second year, boys are more *physically aggressive* than girls, but sex differences in *verbal aggression* and *relational aggression* are minimal.
       (2) Girls often *appear* much more relationally aggressive than boys because many girls use relational tactics nearly exclusively, whereas boys draw on diverse means of inflicting harm.
       (3) Girls find relational aggression especially hurtful because of the high value they place on close relationships.
    b. Biological Influences
       (1) Most researchers believe that biology is involved in males' greater physical aggression because it is evident early in life, generalizes across cultures, and is found in many animal species.
       (2) Androgen hormones are believed to play a role in aggression, but children with CAH, who were exposed prenatally to abnormally high androgen levels, are not consistently more aggressive.
       (3) Sex hormones may influence brain functioning in ways that affect emotional reactions.
       (4) Environmental conditions have much to do with whether or not hormonally induced emotions and behaviors are channeled into aggressive acts.
    c. Environmental Influences
       (1) Coercive child-rearing practices promote aggressive behavior.
       (2) Boys are more likely than girls to be affected because parents more often use physical punishment with boys, which encourages them to adopt the same tactics.
       (3) Parents and teachers respond differently to boys' and girls' physical aggression, often positively reinforcing or ignoring physical aggression in boys while responding negatively to girls' assertive and aggressive acts.
       (4) Overall, biological predispositions and social encouragement jointly contribute to sex differences in aggression.

VI. DEVELOPING NON-GENDER-STEREOTYPED CHILDREN (pp. 562–564)
   A. Importance of reducing gender stereotyping:
      1. Persistent gender stereotypes can seriously limit children's developmental possibilities.
      2. Although biology clearly affects children's gender typing, a long human childhood ensures that experiences can greatly influence biologically based sex differences.

B. Strategies for reducing gender stereotyping and gender-role conformity:
1. Children need early experiences that counteract their readiness to absorb gender-linked associations in the larger culture.
2. Parents can eliminate traditional gender roles from their own behavior and from the alternatives they provide for children.
3. Once children begin to notice gender stereotypes, parents and teachers can point out exceptions.
4. Children who hold flexible beliefs about what boys and girls can do are more likely to notice instances of gender discrimination.

LECTURE ENHANCEMENTS

LECTURE ENHANCEMENT 13.1
The Acquisition of Gender Labels and Its Consequences for Development in Young Children (pp. 530–532)

Time: 5–10 minutes

Objective: To determine when children first acquire gender labels and consequences for gender-typed play.

To determine when children first acquire gender labels and consequences for gender-typed play, Zosuls and colleagues (2009) recruited 82 9-month-olds and followed them to age 21 months. Mothers were provided with diaries designed to document language development over the course of the study. During biweekly phone interviews with a member of the research team, mothers reported on their child's language production. The researchers were especially interested in the flexible production of gender labels (e.g., *girl, boy, man, woman*) and in gender self-labeling (calling oneself a *girl* or a *boy*). When participants were 17 and 21 months old, the researchers conducted home visits to videotape independent and mother–child play. Participants were provided with a variety of gender-stereotyped and gender-neutral toys—for example, a truck (masculine stereotyped); blocks (moderately masculine stereotyped); a baby doll (feminine stereotyped); a brush and comb set (moderately feminine stereotyped); and a sponge, nesting cups, a telephone, and people that fit in the truck (gender neutral). The amount of time the children spent in direct contact with each toy was recorded.

Findings indicated that, on average, children produced at least one gender label by 19 months of age, with the majority of 21-month-olds producing multiple labels. Both boys and girls engaged in gender-typed play at 17 and 21 months, with gender-typed play preferences increasing between these ages. Gender-typed play preferences were especially evident with the truck and the doll, which were the most gender-salient toys. Finally, results showed that gender labeling positively predicted increases in gender-typed play between 17 and 21 months.

Taken together, these findings suggest that gender labels appear in most toddlers' vocabularies by 19 months of age. Moreover, knowledge of gender categories likely contributes to early gender-typed play preferences.

Ask students to discuss how parents can reduce gender stereotyping in young children.

Zosuls, K. M., Ruble, D. N., Tamis-LeMonda, C. S., Shrout, P. E., & Bornstein, M. H. (2009). The acquisition of gender labels in infancy: Implications for gender-typed play. *Developmental Psychology, 45*, 688–701.

LECTURE ENHANCEMENT 13.2
Children's Flexibility in Reasoning About Gender (pp. 533–534)

Time: 10–15 minutes

Objective: To examine children's flexibility in reasoning about gender.

To assess children's flexibility in reasoning about gender, Conry-Murray and Turiel (2012) recruited 72 4-, 6-, and 8-year-olds (37 girls, 35 boys). Participants were presented with six hypothetical stories in which parents had to choose either their son or daughter for an activity. The stories involved attending a class, getting a toy, and getting a Halloween costume. Each story consisted of two situations reflecting male or female norms:
- Attending a class: Sending a child to a computer class (male norm) or a baby-sitting class (female norm)
- Getting a toy: Giving a child a toy truck (male norm) or a doll (female norm)
- Getting a Halloween costume: Giving a child a soldier costume (male norm) or a doll costume (female norm)

After each story, participants were given the following assessments:
1. *Judgments of parents' choice.* Children were asked if they thought the parents should choose the son or daughter. For example, "Who should the parents give the doll to, the daughter Elizabeth or the son Noah?" "Why should the parents choose him/her?"
2. *Knowledge of gender norms.* Children were asked which sex engages in the activity more. For example, "Do boys or girls usually play on computers more?"
3. *Generalizability.* Children were asked if it is acceptable for the gender norms to be reversed in another country. For example, "In another country, boys are usually baby-sitters more than girls. Is that OK or not OK?"
4. *Judgments or normative preferences.* Children were asked whether they perceived the gender norm as alterable. For example, "If the boy Mikey loves baby-sitting even more than the girl Emma, then who should go to the baby-sitting class?" "Why should the parents choose Mikey [or Emma]?"
5. *Rule legitimacy.* Children were asked about rules enforcing gender norms at school. For example, "The parents decided they wanted Mikey to go to the baby-sitting class, but there is a rule at school that only girls can go to the baby-sitting class. Is that rule OK or not OK?" "Why is it OK or not OK?"
6. *Rule legitimacy in another country.* Children were asked if it is acceptable for another country to have rules enforcing gender norms. For example, "In another country, they have the same rule that only girls can be baby-sitters. Is that rule OK or not OK in the other country?"

Overall, both younger and older children accepted that gender norms exist and should be followed, but believed that a reversal of gender norms in another culture was acceptable. The majority also indicated that parents should choose activities for their children based on these norms. However, most reported that personal preferences should take precedence over the application of gender norms. For example, when presented with the question: "If the boy Mikey loves baby-sitting even more than the girl Emma, then who should go to the baby-sitting class?" the majority of children indicated that Mikey should be able to attend the class. Older children were more likely than younger children to reject the imposition of rules on gender norms at school and judged such impositions as unfair. This finding is consistent with previous research showing that school-age children tend to judge exclusion based on gender or race as unfair. According to Conry-Murray and Turiel, this study suggests that even young children do not always perceive gender norms to be consistently fixed or morally obligatory.

Conry-Murray, C., & Turiel, E. (2012). Jimmy's baby doll and Jenny's truck: Young children's reasoning about gender norms. *Child Development, 83,* 146–158.

LECTURE ENHANCEMENT 13.3
More on the Consequences of Gender Typing for Psychological Adjustment (pp. 547–548, 550–551)

Time: 10–15 minutes

Objective: To extend existing research on the consequences of gender typing for psychological adjustment.

To extend existing research on the consequences of gender typing for psychological adjustment, DiDonato and Berenbaum (2011) recruited 401 undergraduate students (79 men, 322 women) and collected the following information:
1. Participants completed The Sex-Role Identity Scale (SRIS), which provides a global measure of masculinity and femininity and gender typicality (the extent to which an individual feels like a typical member of his/her own sex).
2. Participants were presented with a list of 60 gender-typed interests and, using a scale of 1 to 5 (1 = very much; 5 = not at all), were asked to indicate how much they enjoyed each activity.
3. Participants completed the Personal Attributes Questionnaire (PAQ), which measures instrumental traits (traditionally masculine characteristics, such as aggressive, competitive, and self-confident) and expressive traits (traditionally feminine characteristics, such as emotional, talkative, and nurturing).
4. Participants completed the Ambivalent Sexism Inventory (ASI). Ambivalent sexism consists of two components: hostile and benevolent sexism. Hostile sexism refers to the domination and degradation of women, whereas benevolent sexism encompasses subjectively positive attitudes of protection, idealization, and affection toward women. For example: "Women are inferior to men and need to be controlled." (hostile); "Women should forgo a career because they excel at child care." (benevolent) Participants also completed a scale focusing on whether they endorsed traditional or egalitarian attitudes toward women's roles and behaviors.

(5) To assess overall emotional adjustment, participants completed a personality questionnaire and self-esteem measure. The researchers were interested in participants' positive and negative emotionality. For instance, positive emotionality consists of positive well-being, achievement, and social closeness, whereas negative emotionality consists of high stress reactivity, aggression, and alienation. Research shows that individuals who rate high in negative emotionality often experience mental health problems like anxiety and depression. In contrast, those who rate high in positive emotionality tend to experience favorable mental health and are more resilient to stressful situations.

Findings indicated that favorable adjustment was linked to gender typicality, instrumentality, and flexible gender attitudes. That is, identifying with and feeling similar to others of one's sex, having more typically "masculine" than "feminine" traits, and endorsing egalitarian attitudes toward women's roles and behaviors predicted positive emotionality and more favorable mental health in both men and women. Individuals who scored low in gender typicality and who held sexist attitudes (particularly hostile attitudes) toward women rated high in negative emotionality and low in self-esteem. Gender-typed activity interests were unrelated to overall adjustment in male or female participants. That is, simply having interests in traditionally masculine or feminine activities was unrelated to self-esteem or emotionality.

Ask students to review Table 13.1 and note the characteristics with which they identify. Do students identify more with masculine traits, feminine traits, or a combination of both? How might their gender identity contribute to their emotional well-being?

DiDonato, M. D., & Berenbaum, S. A. (2011). The benefits and drawbacks of gender typing: How different dimensions are related to psychological adjustment. *Archives of Sexual Behavior, 40,* 457–463.

LECTURE ENHANCEMENT 13.4
Does Learning About Gender Discrimination Contribute to Adolescents' Occupational Judgments and Aspirations? (pp. 562–563)

Time: 10–15 minutes

Objective: To examine the consequences of learning about gender discrimination on adolescents' occupational judgments and aspirations.

To examine the consequences of learning about gender discrimination on adolescents' occupational judgments and aspirations, Pahlke, Bigler, and Green (2010) recruited 167 students between the ages of 10 and 14 years. Participants were randomly assigned to one of two treatment groups: the discrimination condition and the standard condition. In the discrimination condition, students were presented with biographical lessons on eight famous Americans (four men and four women). The lessons focused on an accomplished male and female doctor, writer, Supreme Court justice, and astronaut. Each female's biography included information about training and employment difficulties she experienced as a result of gender discrimination. Students in the standard condition were presented with the same biographies as those in the discrimination condition; however, statements about gender discrimination were removed from the lessons. Classroom teachers administered the following pre- and posttest measures:

- *Pretest measures:* Prior to beginning any lessons, classroom teachers administered two pretests: the Children's Occupations, Activities, and Traits—Attitude Measure (COAT—AM) and the Children's Occupations, Activities, and Traits—Personality Measure (COAT—PM). For the COAT—AM, participants were presented with a series of masculine (architect, plumber), feminine (house cleaner, librarian), and gender-neutral (artist, comedian) occupations. For each occupation, participants were asked to rate whether only men, only women, or both men and women should perform them. For the COAT—PM, participants were asked how interested they were in pursuing various masculine (e.g., scientist, construction worker), feminine (e.g., child-care teacher, nurse), and gender-neutral occupations (e.g., accountant, real estate agent). Participants were also asked how interested they were in the occupations presented in the biographical lessons.

- *Posttest measures:* In addition to readministering the COAT—AM and COAT—PM, teachers presented a series of questions focusing on participants' cognitive and emotional responses toward the lesson. For the cognitive component, participants were asked if they were satisfied with the lessons and whether or not they felt the lessons were accurate. For the emotional component, participants were asked if the lessons influenced their awareness of gender bias, interest in gender rights, and perceptions of affirmative action. To assess perceptions of gender discrimination, participants were asked: On a scale of 1 to 5 (1 = never, 5 = very often), "How often do you think gender discrimination happens today?" To determine if the lessons influenced participants' willingness to work in other-sex occupations, participants were presented with a series of jobs and asked to indicate how willing they were to work at each. Finally, at the end of the study, participants were presented with four additional biographies focusing on accomplished women. After the presentation, participants were asked to rate how likely it was that gender discrimination played a role in shaping the women's occupational outcomes.

Findings indicated that compared to participants in the standard condition, those in the discrimination condition reported higher levels of awareness of gender bias. One unexpected finding was that girls—but not boys—in the discrimination condition were more likely than participants in the standard condition to report an interest in gender-rights activism. According to Pahlke, Bigler, and Green, boys may view gender discrimination as working in their favor and, as a result, are unlikely to work toward eliminating it. It is also possible that boys do not perceive gender discrimination in the workplace as relevant to their own lives. Overall, girls in both conditions responded more positively to the lessons and viewed them as more accurate than boys. Although the lessons focused on both successful men and women, adolescent girls may have limited exposure to successful female role models in traditionally masculine occupations. Thus, the lessons may have been more interesting to girls than boys. Participants in both conditions reported that gender discrimination sometimes occurs in the workplace. Finally, compared to pretest scores on the COAT—AM and COAT—PM, posttest scores for students in both conditions indicated more egalitarian attitudes toward gender-stereotyped occupations. It is possible that simply hearing about successful women in traditionally masculine occupations modified the perceptions of students, regardless of whether or not the lessons included themes of gender discrimination.

Pahlke, E., Bigler, R. S., & Green, V. A. (2010). Effects of learning about historical gender discrimination on early adolescents' occupational judgments and aspirations. *The Journal of Early Adolescence, 30,* 854–894.

LEARNING ACTIVITIES

LEARNING ACTIVITY 13.1
Interviewing College Students About Masculine and Feminine Personality Traits (pp. 530–531)

Have students interview four college-age friends or acquaintances (two males and two females) about masculine and feminine personality traits. Students can use the following questions to guide their interviews: Tell me three or four personality traits common among women. Tell me three or four personality traits common among men. What are some physical characteristics and occupations associated with women? How about those associated with men? What are some activities or behaviors in which women excel? How about men? After completing their interviews, students should compare their findings with research presented in the text. For example, did the interviewees associate instrumental traits with men and expressive traits with women? Did their answers reveal gender stereotyping of physical characteristics, occupations, and activities/behaviors in which men and women excel? Were students surprised by any of the answers? Explain.

LEARNING ACTIVITY 13.2
Matching: Gender Stereotypes and Gender Roles (pp. 530–534)

Present the following exercise to students as an in-class assignment or quiz.

Directions: Match each of the following terms with its correct description.

Terms:
_____ 1. Gender stereotypes
_____ 2. Gender roles
_____ 3. Gender identity
_____ 4. Gender typing
_____ 5. Instrumental traits
_____ 6. Expressive traits
_____ 7. Gender-stereotype flexibility

Descriptions:

A. Traits reflecting competence, rationality, and assertiveness.
B. Overlap in the characteristics of males and females.
C. Widely held beliefs about characteristics deemed appropriate for males and females.
D. Refers broadly to any association of objects, activities, roles, or traits with biological sex in ways that conform to cultural stereotypes of gender.
E. The reflection of gender stereotypes in everyday behavior.
F. Traits emphasizing warmth, caring, and sensitivity.
G. The private face of gender—perception of the self as relatively masculine or feminine in characteristics.

Answers:

1. C   5. A
2. E   6. F
3. G   7. B
4. D

LEARNING ACTIVITY 13.3
Evaluating Commercial Toys for Aggressive and Gender-Stereotyped Themes (pp. 531–532)

Ask students to visit a local toy or department store and evaluate toys that might encourage violence and gender stereotyping. For example, to what extent do "masculine" toys emphasize violence and high activity and "feminine" toys emphasize quiet, home-based, and prosocial pursuits? Are "masculine" toys separated from "feminine" toys? Are gender-stereotyped toys heavily promoted at the front of the store or at the ends of aisles?

LEARNING ACTIVITY 13.4
Evaluating Gender Stereotyping in Children's Cartoons and Storybooks (pp. 548–549)

Have students watch several children's cartoons and/or obtain two or three children's picture and beginning-reader books. Using examples from the cartoons and books, ask students to describe how males and females are represented. Are characters portrayed in gender-stereotyped roles? Are males and females equally represented in exciting plot activities? Are the behaviors, attitudes, and characteristics of male and female characters strongly gender stereotyped? Are newer cartoons and books less gender stereotyped than those from a decade or more ago? Explain.

LEARNING ACTIVITY 13.5
Interviewing Young Children for Their Understanding of Gender Constancy (pp. 548–549)

Students can conduct informal interviews with children between the ages of 3 and 6 to assess their progress through the three stages of gender constancy. Materials needed for this activity are a boy and a girl paper doll, along with interchangeable paper clothing. To assess gender labeling, children can be asked to identify their own sex and that of each paper doll when it is dressed in a gender-appropriate fashion. For gender stability, children can be given the gender-appropriate version of the following question: "When you [a girl] grow up, could you ever be a daddy [or a man]?" Finally, gender consistency can be assessed by asking, "Could you be a [opposite sex of child] if you wanted to?" "If you wore [opposite-gender] clothes, what would you really be—a boy or a girl?" In addition, the boy paper doll can be dressed in female clothing and the girl in male clothing while the child watches. Then the child can be asked if each doll's sex is still the same (for example, "Is the boy doll still a boy now, or is he a girl? How come?").

LEARNING ACTIVITY 13.6
True or False: To What Extent Do Boys and Girls Really Differ in Gender-Stereotyped Attributes? (pp. 553–562)

Present the following activity as an in-class assignment or quiz.

Directions: Read each of the following statements and determine if it is *True* (T) or *False* (F).

Statements:

_____ 1. Sex differences in mental abilities and personality traits usually account for 25 to 35 percent of individual differences.
_____ 2. The gender gap in reading and writing achievement increases over adolescence, with boys doing especially poorly in writing.
_____ 3. In early adolescence, sex differences in mathematical abilities are especially evident on tests of complex reasoning and geometry.
_____ 4. Today, North American boys and girls reach advanced levels of high school math and science study in equal proportions.
_____ 5. Boys spend far more time playing video games than girls, which may contribute to boys' enhanced spatial scores.
_____ 6. Cultural expectations that girls be warm and expressive and boys be distant and self-controlled seem largely responsible for the gender gap in emotional sensitivity.
_____ 7. Adolescent boys and girls report similar levels of depressive symptoms.
_____ 8. Although children of both sexes report that relational aggression is very hurtful, girls find it especially so.
_____ 9. Children with CAH, who were exposed prenatally to abnormally high androgen levels, are consistently more aggressive than children without CAH.
_____ 10. Parents more often use physical punishment with girls, which encourages them to engage in aggressive behavior.

Answers:

1. F   6. T
2. T   7. F
3. T   8. T
4. T   9. F
5. T   10. F

LEARNING ACTIVITY 13.7
Reducing Gender Stereotyping in Children and Adolescents (pp. 562–563)

In small groups, have students create a list of recommendations for parents and teachers who want to reduce gender stereotyping in children and adolescents. For example, what can parents and teachers do to encourage children and teenagers to pursue activities that are traditionally associated with one gender? What are the potential short-term and long-term benefits of reducing children's gender stereotyping? Explain.

ASK YOURSELF . . .

REVIEW: Explain how young children's cognitive limitations combine with the social environment to contribute to rigid gender stereotyping in early childhood. (pp. 531–532)

During early childhood, gender-stereotyped beliefs strengthen—so much so that many children apply them as blanket rules rather than flexible guidelines. When children were asked whether gender stereotypes could be violated, half or more of 3- and 4-year-olds answered "no" to clothing, hairstyle, and play with certain toys. And most 3- to 6-year-olds do not want to be friends with a child who violates a gender stereotype—for example, a boy who wears nail polish or a girl who plays with trucks—or to attend a school where such violations are allowed.

When researchers labeled a target child as a boy or a girl and then provided either gender-typical or gender-atypical information about the child's characteristics, preschoolers usually based their judgments about the child only on the gender label, ignoring any specific information to the contrary. When 4-year-olds see a picture of a Scottish bagpiper wearing a kilt, they are likely to insist, "Men don't wear skirts!" During free play, preschoolers exclaim that girls can't be police officers and boys can't take care of babies. These one-sided judgments are a joint product of gender stereotyping in the environment and young children's cognitive limitations—in particular, their difficulty coordinating conflicting sources of information. Most preschoolers do not yet realize that characteristics *associated with* being male or female—activities, toys, occupations, hairstyle, and clothing—do not *determine* a person's sex. They have trouble understanding that males and females can differ in terms of their bodies while being similar in many other ways.

REVIEW: What factors allow for flexibility in gender stereotyping in middle childhood and adolescence? How is gender-stereotype flexibility related to gender-typed preferences and behavior? (pp. 533–534)

Gender-stereotype flexibility rises as children develop the cognitive capacity to integrate conflicting social cues. As they realize that a person's sex is not a certain predictor of his or her personality traits, activities, and behavior, they no longer view gender-typed behavior (especially that of girls) as inborn and fixed. Rather, they see it as socially influenced—affected by home rearing environments.

Stereotype flexibility is a better predictor than stereotype knowledge of children's gender-role adoption in middle childhood. Children who believe that many stereotyped characteristics are appropriate for both sexes (for example, that it is OK for girls to play with trucks) are more likely to cross gender lines in choosing activities, playmates, and occupational roles. This suggests that gender stereotypes affect behavior only when children incorporate those beliefs into their own gender identities—self-perceptions of what they can and should do at play, in school, and as future participants in society.

CONNECT: Describe parallels between the development of gender and ethnic attitudes (see Chapter 11, pages 477–478). (pp. 532–533)

Younger children's gender stereotyping begins by reflecting *in-group favoritism*—greater awareness of stereotypes that portray their own gender in a positive light. Once trait stereotyping is well under way, children characterize the in-group and the out-group as having both positive and negative qualities. Although both boys and girls view each gender as having more positive than negative traits, this effect is stronger for the in-group—evidence that in-group favoritism persists. And girls express greater in-group favoritism and out-group negativity than boys. But during the school years, stereotypes about which academic subjects and skill areas are "masculine" (mathematics, athletics, and mechanical skills) and which are "feminine" (reading, spelling, art, and music) influence children's preference for and sense of competence at certain subjects. Even when children of equal skill level are compared, boys tend to feel more competent than girls at math, science, and athletics, whereas girls feel more competent than boys at language arts.

Some gender-stereotyped beliefs about achievement may be changing. In recent investigations in Canada, France, and the United States, a majority of elementary and secondary school students disagreed with the idea that math is a "masculine" subject, but the overwhelming majority of these young people continued to view language arts as largely "feminine" and to believe that girls do better in language arts than in math. Even as school-age children become knowledgeable about a wide variety of gender stereotypes, they also develop a more open-minded view of what males and females *can do*—a trend that continues into adolescence.

Children's understanding of ethnicity follows a similar pattern. Most 3- and 4-year-olds have formed basic concepts of race and ethnicity and can label pictures, dolls, and people as "black" or "white." By the early school years, children absorb prevailing societal attitudes, associating power and privilege with white people and poverty and inferior status with people of color. By age 5 to 6, white children generally evaluate their own racial group favorably and other racial groups less favorably or negatively, and this *in-group favoritism* strengthens until age 7 to 8. Young ethnic minority children often display a reverse pattern: *out-group favoritism,* or greater liking for the privileged ethnic majority. *Out-group prejudice* appears among white children during the early school years but gradually declines as children become capable of classifying the social world in multiple ways. After age 7 to 8, both majority and minority children express in-group favoritism, and white children's prejudice against out-group members often weakens.

APPLY: After 9-year-old Dennis enrolled in an after-school cooking class, his friends Tom and Bill began teasing him relentlessly. Cite evidence that explains this negative reaction to Dennis's "cross-gender" behavior. (p. 533)

Acknowledging that boys and girls *can* cross gender lines does not mean that children always *approve* of doing so. In one longitudinal study, between ages 7 and 13, children of both genders became more open-minded about girls being offered the same opportunities as boys, but the change was less pronounced for boys. And many school-age children take a harsh view of certain violations of gender stereotypes, especially when boys engage in "cross-gender" acts, which children regard as nearly as bad as moral transgressions. When Tom and Bill tease Dennis about his voluntary participation in a cooking class, they are reflecting these typical negative evaluations of a male who engages in a behavior strongly associated with girls.

REVIEW: Summarize parent, peer, and sibling influences on gender-role adoption. Why are sibling influences more complex than parent and peer influences? (pp. 539–542, 544, 546–547)

Early in development, parents provide many experiences—through play materials and social interaction—that promote assertiveness, exploration, engagement with the physical world, and emotional restraint in boys and imitation, reliance on others, and emotional sensitivity in girls. These experiences, in turn, give young children a rich array of cues for constructing a view of the world that emphasizes stereotypical gender distinctions.

In middle childhood, parents usually behave in a more mastery-oriented fashion with sons than with daughters and, consistent with their interaction patterns, hold gender-differentiated perceptions of and expectations for children's competencies in various school subjects. Parents' differential treatment extends to the freedom granted to children in their everyday lives. Parents tend to use more directive speech with girls than with boys, and mothers of sons more often pair control with autonomy granting when insisting that children meet their daily responsibilities. Parents typically give boys more freedom to range farther from home without supervision and assign them chores that take them into the surrounding world, such as yard work and errands. Parents, especially fathers, seem especially committed to ensuring the gender typing of children of their own sex. In addition to spending more time with children of their own sex, they are also more vigilant about monitoring the activities of same-sex children while the children are away from home.

Because most children associate almost exclusively with peers of their own sex, the peer context is an especially potent source of gender-role learning. By age 3, same-sex peers positively reinforce one another for gender-typed play by praising, imitating, or joining in. In contrast, when preschoolers engage in "cross-gender" activities, peers criticize them; pressure them to change their behavior; and, in extreme cases, harass and physically attack them. Boys are especially intolerant of "cross-gender" play in other boys. Over time, children come to believe in the "correctness" of gender-segregated play, which further strengthens gender segregation and stereotyped activities.

Growing up with siblings of the same or the other sex also affects gender typing. But sibling effects are more complex than peer influences because they depend on birth order and family size. Whereas younger siblings have little impact on older siblings' gender typing, older siblings serve as powerful models for younger siblings. Studies that report a *modeling and reinforcement effect* (an increase in gender typing among same-sex siblings) focus on children from two-child families. In contrast, studies reporting a *differentiation effect* often include children from larger families, where siblings are more likely to strive to be different from one another. In particular, families in which all children are of the same sex may provide special opportunities to step out of traditional gender roles. For example, children in these families are more likely to be assigned "cross-gender" chores or to be given gender-atypical toys.

CONNECT: Using research in this chapter and in Chapter 11 (see page 467), explain why girls are more susceptible than boys to learned helplessness in achievement situations. (pp. 539–541, 542–543)

Parents' gender-differentiated perceptions of and expectations for children's competencies in various school subjects tend to reinforce learned helplessness in girls. In longitudinal research, mothers rated first-grade sons as more competent than daughters at math, regardless of their child's actual performance. Mothers' gender-typed judgments, in turn, influenced children's self-perceptions of math ability, the effort they devoted to math, and later math achievement. When participants were followed up two years after high school graduation and again at age 24 to 25, mothers' early perceptions no longer predicted sons' outcomes but continued to predict daughters' self-perceptions and also their career choices. Young women whose mothers had regarded them as highly capable at math were far more likely to choose a physical science career. Yet mothers rarely made such optimistic judgments about girls.

Teachers, too, may reinforce learned helplessness in girls. Like parents, preschool teachers give girls more encouragement to participate in adult-structured activities, where compliance and bids for help occur more often than in the unstructured pursuits favored by boys. Teachers often emphasize gender distinctions in the ways they label behavior, and they more often interrupt girls than boys during conversation, thereby promoting boys' social dominance and girls' passivity. Finally, teachers tend to praise boys for their academic knowledge and girls for their obedience.

APPLY: List findings indicating that language and communication—between parents and children, between teachers and children, and between peers—powerfully affect children's gender stereotyping and gender-role behavior. What recommendations would you make to counteract these influences? (pp. 539–544, 545)

Language is a powerful *indirect* means for teaching children about gender stereotypes and gender roles. Even parents who believe strongly in gender equality unconsciously use language that highlights gender distinctions and informs children about traditional gender roles, and gender-typed play contexts amplify these communication differences. For example, when playing housekeeping, mothers engage in high rates of supportive, emotional talk with girls. In a detailed analysis of conversations about picture books between mothers and children, even when mothers' directly expressed attitudes about gender stereotypes were neutral, they frequently affirmed stereotypes voiced by their children—for example, the idea that "only boys" can be sailors. And mothers in this study often called attention to gender even when it was not necessary—asking, for example, "Is that a he or a she?"—and expressed *generic utterances* broadly referring to many, or most, males or females.

In middle childhood, parents use more directive speech (imperatives and specific suggestions) with girls than with boys. And mothers of sons more often pair control with autonomy granting. Whereas they usually ask boys to make decisions, parents tend to decide for girls. Teachers, too, often emphasize gender distinctions, as when they say, "Boys, I wish you'd quiet down like the girls!"—labeling that promotes gender stereotyping, in-group favoritism, and out-group prejudice in children. At older ages, teachers praise boys for their academic knowledge and girls for their obedience, and they more frequently use disapproval and controlling discipline with boys in an expectation that boys will misbehave more often than girls.

By age 3, same-sex peers positively reinforce one another for "gender-appropriate" play by praising, imitating, or joining in. In contrast, when preschoolers engage in "cross-gender" activities—for example, when boys play with dolls or girls with cars and trucks—peers criticize them.

Parents and other adults can combat children's gender stereotyping by refraining from labeling gender when it is unnecessary to do so, from using generic expressions about gender, and from affirming children's stereotypical claims. Furthermore, children who are exposed to nonstereotyped models at home are less traditional in their beliefs and behaviors. Children who frequently see their parents cross traditional gender lines less often endorse gender stereotypes.

Some educators believe that forming mixed-sex activity groups in classroom and recreational settings is a vital means of reducing gender stereotyping and broadening developmental possibilities for both sexes. To be successful, however, interventions may have to modify the styles of social influence typically learned in same-sex peer relations. In one successful intervention, an elementary school with an explicit curricular goal of creating a gender-equitable climate found that children benefited from direct instruction in ways of combating peers' sexist remarks. Children in an active intervention condition were explicitly taught rhyming retorts to sexist remarks—for example, "You can't say that boys [girls] can't play." The use of these techniques spread to children who were not part of the active intervention group, suggesting that active training in combating sexism can contribute to a school climate that respects and protects individual differences in children's gender typing.

REFLECT: In early and middle childhood, did you play mostly with peers of your own sex? What gender-linked attitudes and behaviors were emphasized in your peer associations? How did you view members of the other sex? (pp. 544, 546)

This is an open-ended question with no right or wrong answer.

REVIEW: Describe the general path of gender identity development, from early childhood through adolescence, noting differences between boys and girls. (pp. 548–551)

According to *social learning theory,* behavior comes before self-perceptions. Preschoolers first acquire gender-typed responses through modeling and reinforcement and only later organize these behaviors into gender-linked ideas about themselves. In contrast, *cognitive-developmental theory* maintains that self-perceptions come before behavior. Over the preschool years, children acquire a cognitive appreciation of the permanence of their sex. They develop *gender constancy*—a full understanding that their gender is biologically based and permanent.

Kohlberg proposed that before age 6 or 7, children cannot maintain the constancy of their gender, just as they cannot pass Piagetian conservation problems. They attain this understanding only gradually, by moving through three stages of development: *gender labeling, gender stability,* and *gender consistency.* During middle childhood, boys' and girls' gender identities follow different paths. Self-rating on personality traits reveals that from third to sixth grade, boys strengthen their identification with the "masculine" role, while girls' identification with "feminine" characteristics declines. While still leaning toward the "feminine" side, girls are more androgynous than boys—more likely than boys to describe themselves as having "other-gender" characteristics. This difference is also evident in children's activities. Whereas boys usually stick to "masculine" pursuits, girls experiment with a wider range of options. Besides cooking, sewing, and baby-sitting, they join organized sports teams and work on science projects. And girls are more likely than boys to consider future work roles stereotyped for the other gender, such as firefighter or astronomer.

The arrival of adolescence is typically accompanied by *gender intensification*—increased gender stereotyping of attitudes and behavior and movement toward a more traditional gender identity. Biological, social, and cognitive factors are involved. As puberty magnifies sex differences in appearance, adolescents may spend more time thinking about themselves in gender-linked ways. Pubertal changes may also prompt gender-typed pressures from others. By late adolescence, gender intensification typically declines, especially in teenagers who are encouraged to explore non-gender-typed options and to question the value of gender stereotypes for themselves and their society.

CONNECT: How might factors that affect identity development in general (see pages 472–474 in Chapter 11) influence gender identity in adolescence? Which influences would likely protect against gender intensification? (p. 551)

Gender intensification typically declines by late adolescence, but not all affected young people move beyond it to the same degree. Teenagers who are encouraged to explore non-gender-typed options and to question the value of gender stereotypes for themselves and their society are more likely to build an androgynous identity. Thus, the social environment is a major force in promoting gender-role flexibility in adolescence, just as it was at earlier ages.

The influences that protect against gender intensification are similar to those that support adolescent identity development in general. For example, teenagers whose families serve as a "secure base" from which they can confidently move out into the wider world tend to be in a state of moratorium or identity achievement. In contrast, those who may be close to their parents but do not feel free to explore various options tend to be in a foreclosed identity status, unable to move beyond parental expectations, which may reflect gender stereotypes.

Teenagers' close friends, like parents, can act as a secure base for the exploration that promotes identity development. And interaction with diverse peers encourages adolescents to explore values and role possibilities. In school, classrooms that promote high-level thinking, teachers and counselors who encourage academic self-development, meaningful extracurricular and community activities, and vocational training that immerses adolescents in the real world of adult work all promote identity development, including exploration of non-gender-stereotyped life possibilities.

APPLY: While looking at a book, 4-year-old Roger saw a picture of a boy cooking at a stove. Later, he recalled the person in the picture as a girl. Using gender schema theory, explain Roger's memory error. (pp. 551–552)

Gender schema theory is an information-processing approach that integrates the various elements of gender typing—gender stereotyping, gender identity, and gender-role adoption—into a unified picture of how masculine and feminine orientations emerge and are often strongly maintained. At an early age, children pick up gender-stereotyped preferences and behaviors from others. At the same time, they organize their experiences into *gender schemas,* or masculine and feminine categories, that they use to interpret their world. Gender-schematic thinking is so powerful that when children see others behaving in "gender-inconsistent" ways, they often cannot remember the behavior or distort their memory to make it "gender consistent." In Roger's gender schemas, cooking is "a girl's job," so when he sees a picture of a boy cooking at a stove, he later recalls the person in the picture as a girl.

REFLECT: In early adolescence, did you and your friends display gender intensification? Describe examples. When did this concern with gender appropriateness decline? (pp. 550–551)

This is an open-ended question with no right or wrong answer.

REVIEW: Cite evidence that both biological and environmental factors contribute to girls' advantage in verbal abilities and to boys' advantage in mathematical reasoning. (pp. 554–558)

Early in development, girls are slightly ahead of boys in language progress. Girls have a biological advantage in earlier development of the left hemisphere of the cerebral cortex, where language is usually localized. But environmental factors also play a role. Girls receive more verbal stimulation from the preschool years through adolescence. Further, children view language arts as a "feminine" subject. And as a result of the high-stakes testing movement, students today spend much time at their desks being taught in a regimented way—an approach that is at odds with boys' higher activity level, assertiveness, and incidence of learning problems. Finally, high rates of divorce and out-of-wedlock births mean that more children today grow up without the continuous presence of a father who models and encourages good work habits and skill at reading and writing.

In mathematics, girls tend to be advantaged in counting, arithmetic computation, and mastery of basic concepts, perhaps because of their better verbal skills and more methodical approach to problem solving. But by late childhood and early adolescence, when math concepts and problems become more abstract and spatial, boys outperform girls in math, especially on tests requiring complex reasoning and geometry, and in science. This male advantage is evident in most countries where both sexes have equal access to secondary education. Although the gap is small and has diminished over the past generation, it is greater among the most capable students.

Some researchers believe that heredity contributes substantially to the gender gap in math, especially to the tendency for more boys to be extremely talented. Accumulating evidence indicates that boys' superior reasoning ability originates in two skill areas: (1) their more rapid numerical memory, which permits them to devote more energy to complex mental operations, and (2) their superior spatial reasoning, which enhances their mathematical problem solving. But social pressures are also influential. Many children view math as a "masculine" subject, and parents typically think boys are better at it—an attitude that encourages girls to view themselves as having to work harder at math to do well, to blame their errors on lack of ability, and to regard math as less useful for their future lives. These beliefs reduce girls' self-efficacy at doing math, undermining their performance on math achievement tests and their willingness to consider math- or science-related careers in college. Stereotype threat—the fear of being judged on the basis of a negative stereotype—also causes girls to do worse than their abilities allow on difficult math problems. As a result of all these influences, even highly talented girls are less likely to develop effective math reasoning skills.

REVIEW: Explain possible *indirect* links between androgen hormones and boys' greater physical aggression, noting the influence of both family and peer-group experiences. (pp. 561–562)

Androgen hormones, which are related to aggression in animals, are also believed to play a role in humans. However, children exposed prenatally to abnormally high androgen levels are not consistently more aggressive, suggesting that the impact of male sex hormones on aggression may be indirect. That is, androgens may promote certain behaviors that, in some circumstances, increase the likelihood of aggressive outcomes.

One possibility is that prenatal androgens promote physical activity and competitiveness—behaviors likely to change into aggression in certain situations. For example, one study found that whereas group size had no impact on girls' competitive behavior, boys displayed nearly twice as much competitive behavior in larger groups. Compared with girls, boys spend more time playing in large groups—an attraction, according to evolutionary theorists, adapted to preparing them for the competitive adult life of their male ancestors. Large groups, in turn, serve as contexts in which competition may promote aggression.

Another hypothesis is that sex hormones influence brain functioning in ways that affect emotional reactions. In this view, hormone levels induce more frequent displays of excitement, anger, or anxiety, which make aggression more likely under certain conditions. Consistent with this prediction, adolescent boys with high androgen levels are more dominant and, therefore, more likely to respond with aggression when provoked by peers.

Environmental factors also play a role. Coercive child-rearing practices promote aggressive behavior. Boys are more likely than girls to be affected because parents more often use physical punishment with boys, which encourages them to adopt the same tactics in their own relationships. The stereotypical view that "boys will be boys" may lead many adults to overlook or tolerate boys' hostility unless it is extreme, so that boys receive tacit approval for physical aggression, whereas girls suppress it. It is not surprising, then, that school-age boys expect less parental disapproval and report feeling less guilty for aggression than girls.

Gender-segregated peer groups extend adults' lessons about expressing aggression. In one study, emotionally reactive preschool and kindergarten boys who mostly played with other boys showed an increase in teacher-reported problem behaviors, such as fighting and defiance to adults, over the school year. Among emotionally reactive girls who often played with other girls, the opposite effect was seen: Problem behaviors decreased over the course of the year.

CONNECT: Using Bronfenbrenner's ecological systems theory (see Chapter 1, page 26), describe steps that can be taken at each level of the environment to reduce gender stereotyping in children. (pp. 562–563)

Although biology clearly affects children's gender typing, substantial revisions in gender roles and relationships between males and females—along with wide individual, family, and cultural variations—reveal that most aspects of gender typing are not built into human nature but, rather, can be greatly influenced by children's experiences. At the most basic levels of the environment, the microsystem and the mesosystem, parents and teachers should make a special effort to delay young children's learning of gender-stereotyped messages. Adults can begin by eliminating traditional gender roles from their own behavior and from the alternatives they provide for children. For example, mothers and fathers can take turns making dinner, bathing children, and driving the family car and can provide sons and daughters with both trucks and dolls, both pink and blue clothing. Teachers can make sure all children spend some time each day in both adult-structured and unstructured activities. Adults can avoid using language that conveys gender stereotypes and can shield children from media presentations that do the same.

Once children notice the wide array of gender stereotypes that exist at the levels of the exosystem and macrosystem, in the larger society and culture, parents and teachers can point out exceptions. For example, they can arrange for children to see men and women pursuing nontraditional careers and can explain that interests and skills, not sex, should determine a person's occupation. With older children, adults can discuss the historical roots and current consequences of gender inequalities—why, for example, there has not yet been a female U.S. president, why fathers rarely stay home with young children, and why stereotyped views of men and women are hard to change. As these efforts help children build concepts of themselves and their social world that are not limited by a masculine–feminine dichotomy, they contribute to the transformation of societal values, bringing us closer to a time when people will be released from the constraints of traditional gender roles.

APPLY: Thirteen-year-old Donna, who has a "feminine" gender identity, reached puberty early, is dissatisfied with her physical appearance, and often ruminates about how well her peers like her. Explain why Donna is at risk for depression. (p. 560)

Research suggests that stressful life events and gender-typed coping styles are responsible for girls' higher rates of depression in industrialized nations. Early-maturing girls are especially prone to depression, particularly when they also face other stressful life events. And the gender intensification may strengthen girls' passivity, dependency, and tendency to ruminate on (repetitively mull over) their anxieties and problems—maladaptive approaches to the tasks expected of teenagers in complex cultures. Consistent with this explanation, teenagers who identify strongly with "feminine" traits, as Donna does, ruminate more and tend to be more depressed, regardless of their sex. Girls who repeatedly feel overwhelmed develop an overly reactive physiological stress response and cope more poorly with challenges in the future. In this way, stressful experiences and stress reactivity feed on one another, sustaining depression.

SUGGESTED READINGS

Brettell, C. B., & Sargent, C. F. (2009). *Gender in cross-cultural perspective*. Upper Saddle River, NJ: Prentice Hall. A comprehensive approach to understanding gender development, this book examines cultural influences on gender roles and ideology throughout the world, including the evolution of sex differences, rites of passage for boys and girls, gender and violence, and historical depictions of men and women.

Eliot, L. (2010). *Pink brain, blue brain: How small differences grow into troublesome gaps*. Boston, MA: Houghton Mifflin. Drawing on the field of neuroplasticity, this book examines biological and environmental contributions to the development of sex differences. The author presents research on how parents, peers, educators, and the media can exacerbate small, genetically based sex differences. Also discussed are strategies for combating harmful gender stereotypes.

Meyer, E. J. (2010). *Gender and sexual diversity in schools*. New York: Springer-Verlag. Presents current research on gender and sexual diversity in public schools. Topics include: creating equitable learning environments, working with same-sex parents, integrating gender and sexual diversity into the curriculum, preventing sexual harassment and bullying, creating gay–straight alliances, and strategies for supporting transgendered students.

MEDIA MATERIALS

For details on individual video segments that accompany the DVD for *Child Development,* Ninth Edition, please see the DVD Guide for *Explorations in Child Development*. The DVD and DVD Guide are available through your Pearson sales representative.

Additional DVDs that may be useful in your class are listed below. These are not available through your Pearson sales representative, but you can order them directly from the distributors. (See contact information at the end of this manual.)

Becoming Me: The Gender Within (2009, Insight Media, 40 min.). Questioning what determines a person's gender, this program features five transgendered individuals between the ages of 20 and 50 who discuss their personal stories, including the experience of gender confusion. It also explores sexual reassignment surgery.

Boy to Girl to Man: Disproving the Theory of Gender Neutrality (2004, Films Media Group, 50 min.). Originally a BBCW broadcast titled *Dr. Money and the Boy with No Penis,* this film tells the story of David Reimer, who lost his penis as a result of a botched circumcision. On the advice of Dr. John Money, a pioneering gender-reassignment specialist, David was renamed Brenda and raised as a girl. Using interview footage of David, conversations with his family, and transcripts of meetings between Dr. Money and his tormented patient, this program recounts the medical and psychological ordeals that Reimer underwent, both as Brenda and then as David again, before his suicide in 2004.

Clinical Depression in Children (2004, Aquarius Health Care Media, 19 min.). Although more than three million teenagers in the United States suffer from depression, the illness is often not recognized. This program discusses the warning signs of adolescent depression and profiles two young women who have struggled with it. The program offers expert commentary on treatment.

Cry for Help (2009, Films Media Group, 60 min.). This program features adolescents and young adults who are confronting depression, anxiety, and mental illness; parents who are unaware of what may be troubling their own children; and those on the front lines of prevention and care. Distributed by PBS.

Divide of the Sexes: Gender Roles in Childhood (2008, Films Media Group/BBC–Open University coproduction, 60 min.). This program features a group of 25 8-year-olds who demonstrate various aspects of gender typing. It examines the questions of whether our celebrity culture influences the self-esteem of young girls and whether children are growing up too quickly in an atmosphere dominated by sex and consumerism. Among the children depicted in this film are Nathan, whose parents have taken steps to ensure that he grows up without stereotypes; Helena, who has embraced her femininity; and Tyrese, who displays male aggression.

From Depression to Discovery: A Teenager's Guidebook (2005, Films Media Group/Cambridge Educational Production, 25 min.). Using expert commentary and interviews with teenagers diagnosed with depression, this program exposes common myths and misconceptions about clinical depression, such as the idea that it does not affect young people. It also presents symptoms of depression and current treatment options. A teacher's guide is included.

Gender (2002, Insight Media, 30 min.). In this program, sociologists explain how social expectations influence gender typing. This program describes the difference between "sex" and "gender," defines gender as a cultural phenomenon, and examines gender inequality and gender stratification.

How Boys and Girls Differ: The First Six Years (2002, Learning Seed, 20 min.). This program explores the developmental differences between boys and girls as an essential element of understanding child development. For example, girls have more acute hearing than boys and begin talking a little earlier, while boys show superior spatial intelligence even in the first year of life. The program examines what these and other sex differences mean for parents and caregivers and whether and how they contribute to gender stereotypes.

Me, My Sex, and I: Disorders of Sexual Development (2011, Films Media Group/BBC, 50 min.). Questioning the deeply ingrained assumption that every person can be designated either male or female, this program features people born with ambiguous genitalia or what has often been called "intersex" anatomy. This condition has long been shrouded in shame and secrecy, even though disorders of sexual development (DSDs) are estimated to appear in almost one in 50 births. The program explores the insights of people living with DSDs and of the parents of children born with DSDs.

Middle Sexes: Redefining He and She (2005, Insight Media, 75 min.). Featuring a case study of an 8-year-old boy who is widely considered to be a female trapped in a male body, this program explores the lives of those who do not conform to rigid gender concepts.

Sexual Minority Adolescents (2005, Insight Media, 50 min.). Featuring gay and lesbian youths and the commentary of experts, this program considers the experiences of gay, lesbian, and bisexual (GLB) adolescents, including the challenges associated with establishing a healthy GLB identity.

Sexual Stereotypes in the Media (2008, Films Media Group, 38 min.) Using clips of television programs and television and print advertisements, this program explores some of the many commercial, cultural, psychological, and sociological forces that have shaped sexual stereotypes in the media.

The Problem with Boys: Falling Behind in School and Life (2004, Films Media Groups, 41 min.). According to current education statistics, boys now perform poorly compared with girls—and with boys of previous generations. This program presents insights from experts in child development on the causes of this trend. Teacher training, curriculum design, literacy instruction, role models, pop culture, and male behavioral tendencies are addressed.

The Role of Gender (2007, Insight Media, 30 min.). This program examines the ways humans learn about gender from an early age. It also considers how gender roles, expectations, and assumptions are changing.

Understanding the Differences Between Men and Women (2005, Insight Media, 30 min.). This program discusses the biological, anthropological, and environmental and social forces that account for the differences between men and women and that contribute to the development of gender identity in the United States.

CHAPTER 14
THE FAMILY

CHAPTER-AT-A-GLANCE

Chapter Outline	Instruction Ideas	Supplements
Origins and Functions of the Family p. 568	Learning Objective 14.1 Learning Activity 14.9	Test Bank Items 1–6, 126 Please contact your Pearson publisher's representative for a wide range of video offerings available to adopters.
The Family as a Social System pp. 569–573 Direct Influences • Indirect Influences • Adapting to Change • The Family System in Context	Learning Objective 14.2 Lecture Enhancement 14.1 Learning Activities 14.1, 14.9 Ask Yourself p. 573	Test Bank Items 7–20
Socialization Within the Family pp. 573–584 Styles of Child Rearing • What Makes the Authoritative Style Effective? • Adapting Child Rearing to Children's Development • Socioeconomic and Ethnic Variations in Child Rearing	Learning Objectives 14.3–14.4 Lecture Enhancement 14.2 Learning Activities 14.2–14.3, 14.9 Ask Yourself p. 584	Test Bank Items 21–66, 127–128
Family Lifestyles and Transitions pp. 584–599 From Large to Small Families • One-Child Families • Adoptive Families • Gay and Lesbian Families • Never-Married Single-Parent Families • Divorce • Blended Families • Maternal Employment and Dual-Earner Families • Child Care • Self-Care	Learning Objectives 14.5–14.9 Lecture Enhancements 14.3–14.4 Learning Activities 14.4–14.7, 14.9 Ask Yourself p. 599	Test Bank Items 67–112, 129–131
Vulnerable Families: Child Maltreatment pp. 599–604 Incidence and Definitions • Origins of Child Maltreatment • Consequences of Child Maltreatment • Preventing Child Maltreatment	Learning Objective 14.10 Learning Activities 14.8–14.9 Ask Yourself p. 604	Test Bank Items 113–125, 132

BRIEF CHAPTER SUMMARY

The family is the child's first, and longest-lasting, context for development. Families are pervasive in human societies, going back to our hunting-and-gathering ancestors, and parenting is universally important in children's lives. The family unit historically performed a number of vital functions for society: reproduction, providing economic services, maintaining social order, socializing the young, and providing emotional support. As societies became more complex, other institutions developed to help with some of these roles, but reproduction, socialization, and emotional support remain the province of the family.

Today, the family is seen as a social system—a dynamic, ever-changing network of interdependent relationships that exerts both direct and indirect influences on children. The family is also affected by surrounding social contexts—both formal organizations, such as the school or workplace, and informal social networks of relatives, friends, and neighbors.

Child-rearing styles are combinations of parenting behaviors occurring over a wide range of situations, creating an enduring child-rearing climate. The most successful approach, the authoritative style, involves high acceptance and involvement, adaptive control techniques, and appropriate autonomy granting. The authoritarian style is high in coercive behavioral and psychological control and low in autonomy granting. Parents with a permissive style are warm and accepting but do not provide appropriate behavioral control. Finally, uninvolved parents show low acceptance and involvement along with little control. Children's characteristics contribute to the ease with which parents can apply the authoritative style, but effective parenting also can modify difficult children's maladaptive styles.

In middle childhood, parents engage in coregulation, exercising general oversight while giving children increasing responsibility for moment-by-moment decision making. In adolescence, the salient task of striving for autonomy is facilitated by warm, supportive parent–adolescent ties. Stressors accompanying poverty weaken the family system, with devastating effects on children's development. Affluent parents, as well, often fail to engage in family interaction and parenting that promote healthy development.

Although authoritative parenting is broadly advantageous, ethnic minority parents often have distinct child-rearing beliefs and practices reflecting cultural values and family context—for example, the effective use of more controlling strategies by some low-SES African-American parents, or the insistence on respect for parental authority in Hispanic, Asian Pacific Island, and Caribbean families of African and East Indian origin. In many ethnic minority groups, extended-family households are a vital feature of family life.

Families in industrialized nations have become more diverse, with fewer births per family unit, more adults wanting to adopt children, more openly gay and lesbian parents, and more never-married parents. High rates of divorce, remarriage, and maternal employment have also reshaped the family system. Although sibling relationships bring many benefits, only children are not spoiled and, in some respects, may be advantaged. Adopted children, particularly those adopted past infancy, have more learning and emotional difficulties than other children, and by adolescence, their lives are often complicated by unresolved curiosity about their roots. By adulthood, however, most adoptees are well-adjusted. Research on gay and lesbian families indicates that their children do not differ from children of heterosexuals in adjustment or gender-role behavior.

In the United States, the largest group of never-married parents is African-American young women, who are likely to tap their extended families for help in child rearing. Divorce rates in industrialized countries, after rising dramatically, stabilized in most countries. Of the 45 percent of American marriages that end in divorce, half involve children. The effects of divorce on children vary according to the child's age and sex, but the overriding factor in positive adjustment following divorce is effective parenting. Many divorced parents remarry, and their children then experience life in a blended family; some of these remarried parents will also divorce.

More than three-fourths of U.S. mothers of school-age children are employed. Children whose mothers enjoy their work and remain committed to parenting show favorable adjustment. Part-time employment, flexible work schedules, and job sharing are associated with positive child adjustment, but when employment is stressful because of time demands or other reasons, children are at risk for ineffective parenting.

High-quality child care is important for working parents, and early intervention can enhance development in economically disadvantaged children. Because the United States does not have national child-care policies, it lags behind other industrialized nations in the supply, affordability, and quality of child care. Self-care children who regularly look after themselves after school do well if they have a history of authoritative child rearing, parental monitoring, and regular after-school chores. Good "after-care" programs also aid school performance and emotional and social adjustment, with low-SES children showing special benefits.

Child maltreatment, including physical abuse, sexual abuse, neglect, and emotional abuse, has always existed but is especially common in large industrialized nations. Children who are challenging to raise are more likely to be abused, and once abuse begins, it can become part of a self-sustaining cycle. Most abusive and neglectful parents are socially isolated, and some are influenced by societal mores that condone the use of violence to solve problems.

Chapter 14 The Family

Maltreated children are impaired in development of attachment, emotional self-regulation, empathy and sympathy, self-concept, social skills, and academic motivation. They are also more likely to suffer central nervous system damage. Successful prevention of child maltreatment requires efforts at the family, community, and societal levels.

LEARNING OBJECTIVES

After reading this chapter, you should be able to answer the following:

14.1 Discuss evolutionary origins of the family, and cite functions contemporary families perform for society. (p. 568)

14.2 Describe the social systems perspective on family functioning. (pp. 569–572)

14.3 Discuss child-rearing styles, and explain how effective parents adapt child rearing to children's growing competence. (pp. 573–580)

14.4 Describe socioeconomic and ethnic variations in child rearing, including the impact of affluence and poverty. (pp. 580–584)

14.5 Describe the influence of family size on child rearing, and explain how sibling relationships affect development. (pp. 584–588)

14.6 How do children fare in adoptive, gay and lesbian, and never-married single-parent families? (pp. 588–590)

14.7 What factors influence children's adjustment to divorce and blended-family arrangements? (pp. 590–595)

14.8 How do maternal employment and life in dual-earner families affect children's development? (pp. 595–596)

14.9 Discuss the influence of child-care quality on preschoolers' development and the impact of self-care on school-age children's adjustment. (pp. 596–599)

14.10 Discuss the origins of child maltreatment, its consequences for development, and prevention strategies. (pp. 599–604)

LECTURE OUTLINE

I. INTRODUCTION (p. 567)
   A. The family is the child's first, and longest-lasting, context for development, and parenting is universally important in children's lives.
   B. Although other contexts also mold children's development, none equals the family in influence.
   C. The family is a *social system* with many interacting influences on the child.

II. ORIGINS AND FUNCTIONS OF THE FAMILY (p. 568)
   A. The family in its most common form—an enduring commitment between a man and a woman who feed, shelter, and nurture their children until they reach maturity—arose tens of thousands of years ago among our hunting-and-gathering ancestors.
   B. Evolutionary origins of the family:
      1. The human family enhanced survival by ensuring a relatively even balance of male hunters and female gatherers within a social group, thereby providing protection against starvation at times when game was scarce.
      2. An extended relationship between a man and a woman increased male certainty that a newborn baby was *his* offspring, motivating him to care and provide for mother and child.
      3. Larger kin networks increased the chances of successful competition with other humans for resources.
   C. The family unit performed the following vital services for society:
      1. *Reproduction:* Replacing dying members.
      2. *Economic services:* Producing and distributing goods and services.
      3. *Social order:* Devising procedures for reducing conflict and maintaining order.
      4. *Socialization:* Training the young to become competent, participating members of society.
      5. *Emotional support:* Helping others surmount emotional crises and fostering in each person a sense of commitment and purpose.

D. Increasing role of other societal institutions:
   1. As societies became more complex, the demands placed on the family became too much for it to sustain alone.
   2. Consequently, other institutions developed to assist with certain functions, and families became linked to larger social structures, such as political, legal, and religious institutions and schools.
   3. Economic tasks have largely been taken over by institutions that make up the world of work.
E. Roles of the contemporary family:
   1. The family still assumes primary responsibility for the functions especially concerned with children: reproduction, socialization, and emotional support.
   2. Researchers investigating how families fulfill these functions take a **social systems perspective,** viewing the family as a complex set of interacting relationships influenced by the larger social context.

III. THE FAMILY AS A SOCIAL SYSTEM (pp. 569–573)
   A. The social systems perspective on family functioning:
      1. This perspective grew out of researchers' efforts to explain the complex patterns of interaction among family members.
      2. It has much in common with Bronfenbrenner's *ecological systems theory*.
      3. In this view, the *family system* is a network of interdependent relationships, within which family members mutually affect one another by means of *bidirectional influences*.
   B. Direct Influences (p. 569)
      1. When parents are firm but warm in dealing with their children, children tend to comply with their requests, which, in turn, leads parents to be warm and gentle in the future.
      2. Parents who discipline with harshness and impatience tend to have children who resist and rebel, which, in turn, may increase parental use of punishment, leading to more unruliness.
   C. Indirect Influences (pp. 569–571)
      1. Interaction between any two family members is affected by others present in the setting—what Bronfenbrenner called the effect of *third parties*.
      2. Third-party effects, from the parents' marital relationship to relationships with grandparents and others, can either support or undermine development.
         a. When the marital relationship is warm, mothers and fathers are more likely to engage in effective **coparenting,** mutually supporting each other's parenting behaviors.
         b. Children who are chronically exposed to angry, unresolved parental conflict have myriad problems related to disrupted emotional security and emotional self-regulation.
         c. When parental arguments strain children's adjustment, other family members, such as grandparents, may help restore effective interaction.
   D. Adapting to Change (p. 571)
      1. In Bronfenbrenner's theory, the family functions as a *chronosystem* in which the interplay of forces is ever-changing, as each member adapts to the development of other members.
      2. As children acquire new skills, parents adjust the way they treat them.
      3. Parents' development affects children as well, especially in adolescence, when parent and teenager must accommodate changes in each other.
   E. The Family System in Context (pp. 571–572)
      1. From a social systems perspective, surrounding social contexts—the *mesosystem* and *exosystem* of Bronfenbrenner's model—influence family relationships.
      2. These include both *formal organizations,* such as school, and *informal social networks* of relatives, friends, and neighbors.
         a. In unstable inner-city neighborhoods with poor community services, family violence, child abuse and neglect, youth antisocial activity, and adult criminality are especially high.
         b. In contrast, strong family ties to the surrounding context reduce youth adjustment problems.
      3. Links between family and community provide *social support,* with the following benefits:
         a. *Parental self-worth* is enhanced when a neighbor or relative tries to relieve a parent's concern, which leads to more sensitive and involved interaction between parent and children.
         b. The community facilitates *parental access to valuable information and services*.
         c. Friends and other community members can provide *child-rearing controls and role models*.

Chapter 14 The Family

   d. Through *direct assistance with child rearing,* family–neighborhood ties can reduce the impact of ineffective parenting.
   e. The Better Beginnings, Better Futures Project of Ontario, Canada, which includes a component focused on improving the quality of the neighborhood as a place to live, has been shown to provide wide-ranging benefits to children in the neighborhoods studied.

IV. SOCIALIZATION WITHIN THE FAMILY (pp. 573–584)
   A. Styles of Child Rearing (pp. 573–575)
      1. **Child-rearing styles** are combinations of parenting behaviors that occur over a wide range of situations.
      2. Three features consistently differentiate an effective style from less effective ones:
         a. *Acceptance* of the child and *involvement* in the child's life
         b. *Behavioral control* of the child
         c. *Autonomy granting*
      3. Authoritative Child Rearing
         a. The **authoritative child-rearing style,** the most successful approach, involves high acceptance and involvement, adaptive control techniques, and appropriate autonomy granting.
            (1) Authoritative parents are warm and sensitive to their child's needs.
            (2) They establish an enjoyable, emotionally fulfilling parent–child relationship.
            (3) They exercise firm, reasonable control, insisting on appropriate maturity, giving reasons for their expectations, and using disciplinary encounters as "teaching moments."
            (4) They engage in gradual, appropriate *autonomy granting*.
         b. Authoritative parenting is linked to many aspects of competence in childhood and adolescence, including an upbeat mood, self-control, and academic achievement.
      4. Authoritarian Child Rearing
         a. The **authoritarian child-rearing style** is low in acceptance and involvement, high in coercive behavior control, and low in autonomy granting.
            (1) Authoritarian parents exert control by commanding and criticizing, make decisions for their child, expect unquestioning obedience, and hold excessively high expectations.
            (2) Children of authoritarian parents are anxious and unhappy, are low in self-esteem, tend to react with hostility when frustrated, and typically do poorly in school.
         b. In addition to unwarranted behavioral control, authoritarian parents also use **psychological control**—in which they attempt to take advantage of children's psychological needs by intruding on and manipulating their verbal expressions, individuality, and attachments to parents.
            (1) When dissatisfied, these parents withdraw love.
            (2) Children subjected to this parenting style exhibit adjustment problems involving both anxious, withdrawn and defiant, aggressive behaviors.
      5. Permissive Child Rearing
         a. The **permissive child-rearing style** is warm and accepting but uninvolved.
            (1) Permissive parents are either overindulgent or inattentive, engaging in little behavioral control.
            (2) Instead of gradually granting autonomy, they allow children to make many decisions for themselves at an age when they are not yet capable of doing so.
         b. Children of permissive parents are impulsive, disobedient, and rebellious; are overly dependent on adults; and show poorer school achievement.
      6. Uninvolved Child Rearing
         a. The **uninvolved child-rearing style** combines low acceptance and involvement with little behavior control and general indifference to issues of autonomy.
            (1) Uninvolved parents may be detached and depressed.
            (2) They may respond to the child's immediate demands while failing to engage in strategies to promote long-term goals.
         b. At its extreme, uninvolved parenting is a form of child maltreatment called *neglect,* which disrupts virtually all aspects of development.
   B. What Makes the Authoritative Style Effective? (pp. 575–577, 578)
      1. The relationship between the authoritative style and children's competence is open to interpretation.

a. Children's characteristics, such as a cooperative disposition, do contribute to the ease with which parents can use the authoritative style; negative children are more likely to evoke inconsistent, coercive discipline.
b. Longitudinal evidence indicates that authoritative child rearing promotes maturity and adjustment in children of diverse temperaments.
2. Over time, the relationship between parenting and children's attributes becomes increasingly bidirectional as each participant modifies the actions of the other and forms expectancies for the other's behavior.
3. Most children and adolescents regard the authoritative child-rearing style as a well-intentioned parental effort to increase their competence and, as a result, gradually respond with increased cooperation and maturity.
4. Authoritative child rearing seems to create a *positive emotional context* for parental influence:
   a. Warm, involved parents who are secure in the standards they hold for their children provide models of caring concern and of confident, self-controlled behavior.
   b. Children are far more likely to comply with and internalize behavioral control that appears fair and reasonable, not arbitrary.
   c. Authoritative parents make demands and engage in autonomy granting that fits with children's ability to take responsibility for their own behavior.
5. A few theorists claim that parents' genetically influenced child rearing merely enhances children's built-in propensities, but this view—that parenting has little impact on children's development—has been rebutted by a host of research findings.

C. Adapting Child Rearing to Children's Development (pp. 577–580)
1. Authoritative parents continually adapt to children's increasing competence.
2. A gradual increase in autonomy granting promotes favorable development.
3. Parenting in Middle Childhood: Coregulation
   a. For those who have established an authoritative style in the early years, child rearing now becomes easier.
      (1) Reasoning is more effective with school-age children.
      (2) Parents can gradually shift responsibility for daily activities from adult to child by engaging in **coregulation,** exercising general oversight while letting children take charge of moment-by-moment decision making.
   b. School-age children often turn to parents for affection, advice, and assistance.
4. Parenting in Adolescence: Fostering Autonomy
   a. During adolescence, striving for **autonomy**—a sense of oneself as a separate, self-governing individual—becomes a salient task.
   b. Autonomy includes both an *emotional component*—relying more on oneself—and a *behavioral component*—making decisions independently.
   c. Changes within the adolescent support autonomy.
      (1) Puberty triggers psychological distancing from parents, and parents grant young people more opportunities to regulate their own activities.
      (2) Gradually, adolescents solve problems and make decisions more effectively.
      (3) Adolescents *deidealize* their parents, making them less willing to bend to parental authority than earlier.
   d. Effective parenting of adolescents strikes a balance between *connection* and *separation*.
      (1) Warm, supportive parent–adolescent ties foster adolescent autonomy, but parents who are coercive or psychologically controlling interfere with its development.
      (2) Consistent parental monitoring of adolescents' daily activities, through a relationship in which the teenager willingly discloses information, predicts favorable outcomes.
      (3) Teenagers with immigrant parents from cultures that place a high value on family closeness and obedience to authority may develop *acculturative stress,* which is associated with a rise in depressive symptoms and deviant behavior.
   e. Throughout adolescence, the quality of the parent–child relationship is the single most consistent predictor of mental health.
      (1) In well-functioning families, young people remain attached to parents and seek their advice, but in a context of greater freedom.
      (2) Mild conflict facilitates adolescent identity and autonomy by helping family members learn to express and tolerate disagreement.
   f. By middle to late adolescence, harmonious parent–child interaction is on the rise.

D. Socioeconomic and Ethnic Variations in Child Rearing (pp. 580–584)
   1. Although the authoritative style predicts favorable development in children and adolescents varying widely in SES and culture, SES and ethnic differences do exist.
   2. Socioeconomic Status
      a. Circumstances affecting family functioning vary with changes in each component of SES (education, occupational prestige and skill, and income).
      b. Education and earnings are powerfully influential, with occupation playing a lesser role.
      c. SES is linked to timing of parenthood, to family size, and also to child-rearing values.
      d. SES differences are reflected in family interaction.
         (1) Higher-SES parents talk to, read to, and otherwise stimulate their young children more.
         (2) With older children and adolescents, higher-SES parents set higher academic developmental goals and allow their children to make more decisions.
         (3) Commands, criticism, and physical punishment occur more often in low-SES households.
      e. Education contributes substantially to SES-related variations in child rearing:
         (1) Through more extensive schooling, higher-SES parents have learned to think about abstract, subjective ideas and, thus, to invest in their children's cognitive and social development.
         (2) Greater economic security permits higher-SES parents to devote more time and resources to nurturing their children's psychological characteristics.
         (3) High levels of stress sparked by economic insecurity contribute to low-SES parents' reduced provision of stimulating interaction and activities as well as greater use of coercive discipline.
      f. SES also influences parents' sense of control over their own lives, which affects parenting style.
   3. Poverty
      a. When families slip into poverty, effective parenting and children's development are profoundly threatened.
      b. The constant stressors that accompany poverty gradually weaken the family system, as daily crises lead to parental depression and irritability, with negative effects on children.
      c. Negative outcomes are especially severe in single-parent families, in families who live in poor housing and dangerous neighborhoods, and in homeless families.
      d. Reduced parental involvement and depleted home learning environments profoundly affect poor children's cognitive and emotional well-being.
   4. Affluence
      a. Affluent parents—those in prestigious occupations with very high incomes—too often fail to engage in family interaction and parenting that promote healthy development.
      b. Affluent youths who are troubled report less emotional closeness and supervision from parents.
   5. Ethnicity
      a. Although authoritative parenting is broadly advantageous, ethnic minority parents often have distinct child-rearing beliefs and practices that reflect cultural values and family context.
      b. Chinese parents describe their parenting as less warm and more controlling than Western parents.
      c. Hispanic, Asian Pacific Island families, and Caribbean families of African and East Indian origin pair insistence on respect for parental authority with high parental warmth, a combination that promotes competence and strong feelings of family loyalty.
      d. Low-SES African-American parents tend to expect immediate obedience.
         (1) For families living in depleted neighborhoods with few social supports, strict control may prevent antisocial involvements.
         (2) Firm control may also promote self-reliance, self-regulation, and watchfulness in risky surroundings.
         (3) Low-SES African-American parents who use more controlling strategies tend to have more cognitively and socially competent children.
      e. The **extended-family household,** in which one or more adult relatives live with the parent–child nuclear family unit, is a vital feature of family life in many ethnic minority groups that has enabled many families to rear children successfully, despite poverty and prejudice.

V. FAMILY LIFESTYLES AND TRANSITIONS (pp. 584–599)
   A. Families in industrialized nations have become more diverse, but from a social systems perspective, regardless of family form, children's well-being depends on the quality of family interaction.

B. From Large to Small Families (pp. 584–587)
   1. The average number of children per American woman has declined dramatically since 1960.
      a. Smaller family size is more compatible with a woman dividing her energies between family and work.
      b. This change also reflects many couples' decision to postpone parenthood until they are well-established professionally and secure economically.
      c. The expense of raising children also contributes to a smaller family size.
   2. Family Size and Child Development
      a. Prevailing attitudes suggest that large families produce less intelligent children, because of the availability of more parental attention and material resources per child.
      b. In longitudinal research, children's IQs did not decline with later birth order, contradicting the assumption that large families produce less intelligent children.
      c. However, the larger the family, the lower the IQ of all siblings, perhaps as a result of the strong trend for mothers lower in intelligence to give birth to more children.
      d. Among children of bright, economically advantaged mothers, the family size–IQ correlation disappeared.
   3. Growing Up with Siblings
      a. Eighty percent of North American and European children grow up with at least one sibling.
      b. Siblings have both direct and indirect influences on many aspects of development.
      c. Emergence of Sibling Relationships
         (1) The arrival of a baby brother or sister is a difficult experience for most preschoolers, yet a rich emotional relationship soon develops between siblings.
         (2) Older children show affection and sympathetic concern for younger siblings; babies are comforted by the presence of older siblings; and children treat older siblings as attachment figures.
         (3) Sibling interactions become unique contexts in which social competence expands, especially as younger siblings take a more active role in play.
         (4) Positive sibling ties predict favorable adjustment, even among hostile children at risk for social difficulties.
         (5) Individual differences in sibling relationships are affected by a number of factors, including children's temperament and maternal warmth toward both children.
      d. Sibling Relationships in Middle Childhood
         (1) Sibling rivalry tends to increase in middle childhood as children participate in a wider range of activities, leading parents to make more comparisons between them.
         (2) Despite conflicts, siblings continue to rely on one another for companionship and support.
         (3) But destructive sibling conflict in middle childhood is associated with detrimental outcomes, including conflict-ridden peer relationships.
         (4) Providing parents with training in mediation increases siblings' awareness of one another's perspectives and reduces animosity.
      e. Sibling Relationships in Adolescence
         (1) As younger siblings become more self-sufficient, they accept less direction from their older brothers and sisters, and sibling influence declines.
         (2) As teenagers become more involved in friendships and romantic relationships, they invest less time and energy in their siblings.
         (3) Overall, siblings who established a positive bond in childhood continue to display greater affection and caring, which contribute to more favorable adolescent adjustment.
         (4) Culture also influences the quality of sibling relationships.
         (5) Warm adolescent sibling relationships contribute to more gratifying friendships.
C. One-Child Families (pp. 587–588)
   1. Sibling relationships are not essential for healthy development.
   2. Only children are not spoiled, as is widely believed, but are even advantaged in some respects.
      a. Compared to children with siblings, only children are higher in self-esteem and achievement motivation and attain higher levels of education.
      b. Only children do tend to be less well-accepted in the peer group, perhaps because they have not had opportunities to learn effective conflict-resolution strategies through sibling interactions.
      c. In China, where a one-child family policy has been enforced in urban areas for more than three decades, only children are advanced in cognitive development and academic achievement.

Chapter 14 The Family

- (1) China's birth rate is now lower than that of many developed nations, and its elderly population is rapidly increasing while its working-age population has leveled off—an imbalance that threatens the country's economic progress.
- (2) Because sons are more highly valued than daughters, the policy has resulted in an epidemic of abortions of female fetuses and abandonment of girl babies, yielding a vastly skewed population sex ratio.

D. Adoptive Families (pp. 588–589)
 1. Adults who are infertile, who are likely to pass along a genetic disorder, or who are older and single but want a family are turning to adoption in increasing numbers.
 2. Because the availability of healthy babies has declined, more people in North America and Western Europe are adopting from other countries or accepting children who are past infancy or who have known developmental problems.
 3. Adopted children and adolescents tend to have more learning and emotional difficulties than other children, a difference that increases with the child's age at the time of adoption.
    a. The biological mother may have experienced prenatal stress, poor diet, or inadequate medical care.
    b. Children adopted after infancy are more likely than their nonadopted peers to have a preadoptive history of lack of parental affection, neglect, or deprived institutional rearing.
    c. Adoptive parents and children, who are genetically unrelated, are less alike in intelligence and personality than are biological relatives.
 4. Most adopted children fare well, and those with preexisting problems usually make rapid progress.
 5. By adolescence, adoptees' lives are often complicated by unresolved curiosity about their roots; nevertheless, most adoptees appear optimistic and well-adjusted as adults.
 6. When parents have been warm, open, and supportive in their communication about adoption, their children typically forge a positive sense of self.

E. Gay and Lesbian Families (pp. 589–590)
 1. About 20 to 35 percent of lesbian couples and 5 to 15 percent of gay couples are parents, most through previous heterosexual marriages, some through adoption, and a growing number through reproductive technologies.
 2. Although a few U.S. states ban gay and lesbian adoptions, other U.S. states hold that sexual orientation by itself is irrelevant to custody of children.
 3. Findings indicate that gay and lesbian parents are as committed to and effective at child rearing as are heterosexual parents.
 4. Children of homosexuals have not been found to differ from the children of heterosexuals in mental health, peer relations, or gender-role behavior.
 5. Children of gay and lesbian parents can be distinguished from other children mainly by issues related to living in a nonsupportive society.

F. Never-Married Single-Parent Families (p. 590)
 1. About 40 percent of U.S. births are to single mothers, more than double the percentage in 1980.
 2. While teenage parenthood has declined, unwed motherhood among women in their twenties and older has risen, especially among those in their thirties and forties in high-status occupations.
 3. In the United States, African-American young women make up the largest group of never-married parents.
    a. About 64 percent of births to black mothers in their twenties are to women without a partner, compared with 28 percent of births to white women.
    b. Job loss, persistent unemployment, and consequent inability of many black men to support a family contribute to the number of African-American never-married, single-mother families.
 4. Never-married African-American mothers tap the extended family for help in child rearing.
    a. About one-third get married, though not necessarily to the child's biological father, within nine years after birth of their first child.
    b. These families function much like other first-marriage parents and do not report the child-rearing difficulties usually associated with remarriage.
 5. For low-SES women, never-married parenthood generally increases financial hardship, and many children in single-mother homes display adjustment problems associated with economic adversity.
 6. Children of never-married mothers who lack a father's warmth and involvement show less favorable cognitive development than children in low-SES, first-marriage families.
 7. Over time, most unwed fathers spend less and less time with their children.

8. Strengthening social support, education, and employment opportunities for low-income parents would greatly enhance the well-being of unmarried mothers and their children.

G. Divorce (pp. 590–594)
1. Divorce rates in industrialized countries rose dramatically between 1960 and 1985, then stabilized in most countries; the United States has the highest divorce rate in the world.
2. Of the 45 percent of American marriages that end in divorce, half involve children.
    a. One-fourth of U.S. children live in single-parent households.
    b. Most live with their mothers, but the percentage in father-headed households has increased steadily, to about 12 percent.
3. Divorce is not a single event in the lives of parents and children but, rather, a transition leading to a variety of new living arrangements, accompanied by changes in housing, income, and family roles and responsibilities.
4. Many studies have reported that marital breakup is stressful for children, but great individual differences exist, depending on factors such as the custodial parent's psychological health.
5. Immediate Consequences
    a. Family conflict often rises around the time of divorce as parents try to settle disputes over children and possessions.
    b. Mother-headed households typically experience a sharp drop in income.
    c. The transition from marriage to divorce often leads to high maternal stress, depression, and anxiety, and to a disorganized family situation.
    d. Contact with noncustodial fathers decreases over time.
    e. About 20 to 25 percent of children in divorced families display severe problems, compared with about 10 percent in nondivorced families.
    f. Children's Age
        (1) Preschool and early school-age children often blame themselves for a marital breakup and fear that both parents may abandon them.
        (2) Many school-age and adolescent youngsters also react strongly.
        (3) Some children display more mature behavior, willingly taking on household tasks and care of younger siblings; but if demands are too great, these children may eventually become resentful.
    g. Children's Temperament and Sex
        (1) The problems of temperamentally difficult children are magnified by exposure to stressful life events and inadequate parenting.
        (2) Easy children also cope better with adversity.
        (3) Girls sometimes respond to divorce with internalizing reactions, such as crying, self-criticism, and withdrawal.
        (4) Children of both sexes frequently show demanding, attention-getting behavior.
        (5) These declines in psychological well-being contribute to the poorer academic achievement of children of divorce.
        (6) Research reveals that sons of divorcing couples, long before the breakup, display higher rates of impulsivity, defiance, and aggression that may have been caused by their parents' marital problems while also contributing to them.
6. Long-Term Consequences
    a. Most children show improved adjustment by two years after divorce.
    b. Overall, children and adolescents of divorced parents score slightly lower than children of continuously married parents in academic achievement, self-esteem, and social competence.
    c. Divorce is linked to children's problems with sexuality and development of intimate ties.
    d. The overriding factor in positive adjustment after divorce is effective parenting.
    e. When the custodial parent is the mother, a good father–child relationship is also important, leading to lower levels of defiance and aggression and, for girls, protection against early sexual activity and unhappy romantic involvements.
    f. Several studies report better outcomes for sons when the father is the custodial parent.
    g. Remaining in an intact but high-conflict family is worse for children than making the transition to a low-conflict single-parent household.
    h. Parents who can set aside their disagreements and support each other in their child-rearing roles increase the chances that their children will grow up competent, stable, and happy.

Chapter 14 The Family

7. Divorce Mediation, Joint Custody, and Child Support
   a. *Divorce mediation* is a series of meetings between divorcing couples and a trained professional aimed at reducing family conflict, including legal battles over child custody.
   b. To further encourage parents to resolve their disputes, parent education programs are becoming common. Because of the demonstrated impact of such programs on parental cooperation, courts in many U.S. states may require parents to attend a program.
   c. *Joint custody,* an increasingly common option, grants divorced parents equal say in important decisions about their children's upbringing. The children in such families tend to be better-adjusted than their counterparts in sole maternal-custody homes.
   d. Many single-parent families depend on child support from the absent parent.
      (1) All U.S. states have procedures for withholding wages from parents who fail to make these payments.
      (2) Noncustodial fathers who have generous visitation schedules are more likely to pay child support regularly.

H. Blended Families (pp. 594–595)
   1. About 60 percent of divorced parents remarry within a few years, and others *cohabit,* or share a sexual relationship and a residence with a partner outside of marriage.
   2. Parent, stepparent, and children form a new family structure called the **blended, or reconstituted, family.**
      a. For some children, this expanded family network is positive, but most children in blended families have more problems than children in stable, first-marriage families.
      b. Switching to stepparents' new rules and expectations can be stressful, and children may regard steprelatives as intruders.
   3. Mother–Stepfather Families
      a. The mother–stepfather family is the most common form of blended family.
      b. Boys tend to adjust quickly, especially if a stepfather is warm, does not exert authority too quickly, and offers relief from coercive mother–son interaction.
      c. Stepfathers who marry rather than cohabit are more involved in parenting, but girls often have difficulty with their custodial mother's remarriage.
      d. Older school-age children and adolescents of both sexes display more acting-out behavior than their peers not in stepfamilies.
   4. Father–Stepmother Families
      a. Noncustodial fathers who remarry often have reduced contact with their biological children, but when fathers have custody, children typically react negatively to their remarriage.
         (1) Children living with fathers may start out with more problems.
         (2) The father may have custody because of a very close relationship with the child, which his remarriage disrupts.
      b. Girls, especially, have a hard time getting along with stepmothers.
   5. Support for Blended Families
      a. Parenting education and couples counseling can help parents and children adapt to the complexities of blended families.
      b. Effective approaches encourage stepparents to move into their new roles gradually.
      c. The divorce rate for second marriages is even higher than that for first marriages; the more marital transitions children experience, the greater their difficulties.

I. Maternal Employment and Dual-Earner Families (pp. 595–596)
   1. More than three-fourths of U.S. mothers of school-age children are employed.
   2. The impact of maternal employment on early development depends on the quality of child care, the continuing parent–child relationship, fathers' participation in caregiving, and the mother's work satisfaction.
   3. Maternal Employment and Child Development
      a. When mothers enjoy their work and remain committed to parenting, children show favorable adjustment.
         (1) Girls, especially, profit from the image of female competence.
         (2) Employed mothers who value their parenting role are more likely to use authoritative child rearing and coregulation.
         (3) Maternal employment often leads fathers to take on greater child-care responsibility.
      b. When employment places heavy demands on a mother's or a father's schedule or is stressful for other reasons, children are at risk for ineffective parenting.

c. Part-time employment and flexible work schedules are associated with parents' enhanced satisfaction with family life and good adjustment in children and adolescents.
4. Support for Employed Parents and Their Families
   a. In dual-earner families, the father's willingness to share child-care responsibilities is a crucial factor.
   b. Compared to three decades ago, today's U.S. fathers are far more involved in child care, but their increased participation has resulted in a growing number of fathers who also report work–family life conflict.
   c. Employed parents need assistance from work settings and communities in their child-rearing roles, including opportunities for part-time employment, flexible schedules, and job sharing.

J. Child Care (pp. 596–597, 598)
   1. Over the past several decades, the number of young children in child care in the United States has steadily increased to more than 60 percent.
   2. Over half of 3- to 6-year-olds not yet in kindergarten are cared for in child-care centers, with the remainder in family child-care homes or looked after informally by a relative or their fathers.
   3. Nearly one-fourth of preschoolers, most from low-income families, experience several types of care at once, usually involving multiple caregivers and longer hours in child care.
   4. With age, children typically shift from home-based to center care.
   5. Early intervention can enhance the development of economically disadvantaged children; however, much U.S. child care is of poor quality.
      a. Externalizing difficulties are especially likely to endure through middle childhood and into adolescence after extensive exposure to mediocre care.
      b. Good child care enhances development, especially for low-SES children—effects that persist into elementary school and, for academic achievement, into adolescence.
   6. The ingredients of high-quality child care for preschoolers include small group size and caregiver–child ratio, and caregivers who have college-level specialized preparation.
   7. Much U.S. child care is both expensive and substandard.
   8. Because the United States does not have national child-care policies, it lags behind other industrialized nations in supply, quality, and affordability of child care.

K. Self-Care (pp. 597–599)
   1. **Self-care children** are those who regularly look after themselves for some period of time during after-school hours.
   2. An estimated 5 million 5- to 14-year-olds in the United States are self-care children.
   3. Self-care rises dramatically with age. It also increases with SES.
   4. Some studies report negative effects of self-care on children, while others show no such effects—apparent contradictions that seem to be explained by children's maturity and the way they spend their time.
   5. Throughout middle childhood and early adolescence, attending after-school programs with well-trained staff and skill-building activities is linked to good school performance and emotional and social adjustment.
   6. Low-SES children who participate in "after-care" programs offering academic assistance and enrichment activities show special benefits, but good after-care is in especially short supply in low-income neighborhoods.

VI. VULNERABLE FAMILIES: CHILD MALTREATMENT (pp. 599–604)
   A. Incidence and Definitions (pp. 599–600)
      1. Child maltreatment has only recently been widely acknowledged and investigated by researchers.
      2. Child maltreatment takes several forms:
         a. *Physical abuse* includes assaults, such as kicking or punching, that inflict physical injury.
         b. *Sexual abuse* includes fondling, intercourse, exhibitionism, and other forms of sexual exploitation.
         c. *Neglect* is failure to meet a child's basic needs for food, clothing, medical attention, education, or supervision.
         d. *Emotional abuse* includes acts, such as intimidation and humiliation, that could cause serious mental or behavioral disorders.
      3. Parents commit more than 80 percent of abusive incidents, other relatives about 5 percent; the remainder are perpetrated by parents' unmarried partners, school officials, camp counselors, and other adults.
   B. Origins of Child Maltreatment (pp. 600–602)
      1. Although child abuse is more common among disturbed parents, there is no single "abusive personality type"; parents who were abused as children do not necessarily become abusers.

2. Research viewing family functioning from a social systems perspective found that many interacting variables, at the family, community, and cultural levels, contribute to maltreatment.
3. The Family
   a. Within the family, children whose characteristics make them more challenging to rear—for example, children who are temperamentally difficult—are more likely to become targets of abuse; but child factors only slightly increase the risk of abuse.
   b. Maltreating parents are less skillful than other parents in handling discipline; they also suffer from biased thinking about their child, evaluating transgressions as worse than they are.
   c. Once abuse begins, it becomes part of a self-sustaining negative relationship.
   d. Most parents have enough self-control not to respond to their children's misbehavior or developmental problems with abuse; other factors combine with these conditions to prompt an extreme response.
      (1) Unmanageable parental stress is strongly associated with maltreatment.
      (2) Conditions such as low income, marital conflict, and domestic violence increase the chances that parents will vent their frustrations by lashing out at their children.
4. The Community
   a. The majority of abusive and neglectful parents are isolated from both formal and informal social supports.
      (1) Because of their life histories, many have learned to mistrust and avoid others.
      (2) Maltreating parents are more likely to live in unstable, run-down neighborhoods that provide few links between family and community.
   b. These parents have no one to turn to for help in stressful times.
5. The Larger Culture
   a. Societies that view violence as an appropriate way to solve problems set the stage for child abuse.
   b. In the United States, widespread support exists for use of physical force with children.
   c. All industrialized nations except the United States and France prohibit corporal punishment in school.
C. Consequences of Child Maltreatment (p. 602)
   1. The family circumstances of maltreated children impair the development of attachment, emotional self-regulation, empathy and sympathy, self-concept, social skills, and academic motivation.
   2. These youngsters show serious adjustment problems, including school failure, severe depression, aggressive behavior, peer difficulties, substance abuse, and violent crime.
   3. Hostile cycles of parent–child interaction are especially severe for abused children. Also, partner abuse is strongly associated with child abuse in families, creating a home life that overflows with adult conduct that leads to profound distress.
   4. Demeaning parental messages to children result in low self-esteem, high anxiety, and depression.
   5. At school, maltreated children present serious discipline problems.
   6. Repeated abuse is associated with central nervous system damage, increasing the chances that abused children's cognitive and emotional problems will endure.
D. Preventing Child Maltreatment (pp. 603–604)
   1. Efforts to prevent child maltreatment must be directed at the levels of family, community, and society as a whole, within which it is embedded.
   2. Suggested approaches include teaching high-risk parents effective child-rearing strategies and developing broad social programs aimed at improving economic conditions and community services for at-risk families.
      a. Providing social supports to families is effective in easing parental stress.
      b. A trusting relationship with another person is the most important factor in preventing mothers with childhood histories of abuse from repeating the cycle with their children. Parents Anonymous helps child-abusing parents learn constructive parenting practices, largely through social supports.
      c. Healthy Families America identifies families at risk for maltreatment during pregnancy or at birth and provides three years of home visitation, in which a trained worker helps parents manage crises, encourages effective child rearing, and puts parents in touch with community services.
      d. Another home-visiting program shown to reduce child abuse and neglect is the Nurse–Family Partnership.
   3. Many experts believe that child maltreatment cannot be eliminated as long as violence is widespread and harsh physical punishment is considered acceptable.
   4. Child maltreatment remains a crime that is difficult to prove, because the only witnesses are usually the child victims or other loyal family members.

5. Even when the evidence is strong, judges are reluctant to remove children permanently from the family.
6. When parents are unlikely to change their behavior, the drastic step of separating parent from child and legally terminating parental rights is the only justifiable course of action.

LECTURE ENHANCEMENTS

LECTURE ENHANCEMENT 14.1
Marital Satisfaction and Father Involvement During the Transition to Parenthood (p. 570)

Time: 10–15 minutes

Objective: To extend existing research on marital satisfaction and father involvement during the transition to parenthood.

To examine the relationship between marital satisfaction and father involvement during the transition to parenthood, Lee and Doherty (2009) recruited 141 couples during the second trimester of pregnancy and followed them through 12 months postpartum. Participants were randomly assigned to one of two groups—an eight-session educational intervention focusing on parental attitudes and skills or an assessment-only control group. The researchers collected the following information:

(1) During the second trimester of pregnancy, at 6 months postpartum, and at 12 months postpartum, fathers completed the Dyadic Adjustment Scale (DAS), which assesses couples' marital satisfaction.
(2) To measure father involvement at 6 and 12 months postpartum, fathers completed diaries of (a) quantity (time spent with the child) and (b) quality (skills in interacting with the child). The diaries were divided into 15-minute blocks of time for a 24-hour period. Over the course of three days, which included both workdays and at-home days, fathers reported on the baby's activities, their own activities, and their partner's activities. The researchers were interested in the following types of father–child interaction:
    - Engaged interaction time—the amount of time in which the father is actively interacting and/or in direct contact with the child, including face-to-face interactions.
    - Parallel interaction time—the amount of time in which the father and infant are involved in activities together, but the father is not giving full attention to the infant; and the amount of time in which the father and infant are engaged in unrelated activities in close proximity, and interaction can be assumed.
    - Accessibility time—the amount of time in which the father is physically available but not interacting with the infant.
(3) To measure quality of father involvement at 6 and 12 months postpartum, infant–father interactions were recorded in the home during a 5-minute play exercise. Trained researchers then coded the interactions according to six indicators—warmth and emotional support, intrusiveness in the child's activity, engagement with the child, positive affect, negative affect, and father–child dyadic synchrony.
(4) To assess attitudes toward father involvement, participants completed the Father Attitude Scale (FAS). Using a five-point Likert scale (1 = disagree a lot; 5 = agree a lot), fathers responded to statements like: "It is essential for the child's well-being that fathers spend time interacting and playing with their children." "A father should be as heavily involved in the care of his child as the mother."

Results indicated that marital satisfaction before childbirth was strongly related to father involvement at 6 and 12 months postpartum. That is, fathers who reported higher levels of marital satisfaction during the second trimester of pregnancy spent more time with their babies, particularly in face-to-face (engaged) interaction, than fathers who reported low levels of marital satisfaction. During playtime, maritally satisfied fathers also demonstrated more warmth and emotional support, higher levels of father–child dyadic synchrony, and less intrusiveness with their babies. Fathers who experienced a decline in marital satisfaction from the second trimester of pregnancy to 6 and 12 months postpartum tended to spend less time with their babies over the course of the study. Finally, positive attitudes toward father involvement predicted both quality and quantity of time fathers spent with their babies.

Using findings from this study and research presented in the text, ask students to explain how marital quality and father involvement contribute to child development and well-being. How might bidirectional influences between fathers and babies contribute to developmental outcomes? How about bidirectional influences between mothers and fathers?

Lee, C-Y. S., & Doherty, W. J. (2009). Marital satisfaction and father involvement during the transition to parenthood. *Fathering, 5,* 75–96.

LECTURE ENHANCEMENT 14.2
Intergenerational Cultural Dissonance in Parent–Adolescent Relationships (pp. 580–581, 582–584)

Time: 10–15 minutes

Objective: To examine intergenerational cultural dissonance in parent–adolescent relationships using a sample of Chinese-American and European-American adolescents.

Research indicates that differential acculturation between adolescents and immigrant parents can lead to intergenerational cultural dissonance in which adolescents endorse mainstream norms to a greater extent than their parents. This generational cultural gap often carries over to the parent–child relationship. To extend existing research on intergenerational cultural dissonance in parent–adolescent relationships, Wu and Chao (2011) recruited 634 U.S. high school students—249 Chinese-American adolescents (95 first-generation and 154 second-generation) and 385 European-American adolescents. The researchers collected the following information:

(1) To assess adolescents' perceptions of parental warmth, participants completed the Acceptance–Rejection subscale of the Children's Report on Parent Behavior Inventory (CRPBI). The subscale measures the degree to which adolescents perceive their parents as warm and responsive, as well as their ideals for parental warmth.

(2) To assess adolescents' perceptions of open parent–child communication, participants completed the Open Family Communication subscale. Sample questions include: On a scale of 1 to 5 (1 = strongly disagree; 5 = strongly agree), "My parent is always a good listener." "It's very easy for me to express all my true feelings to my parent."

(3) To assess adolescents' perceptions of parental devotion, sacrifice, thoughtfulness, and anticipation of the child's needs, participants completed the Chinese Parent–Adolescent Relationships Scale. For example: On a scale of 1 to 5 (1 = never; 5 = always), "How often does your parent sacrifice spare time for you?"

(4) To assess adolescents' internalizing and externalizing problems, participants completed the Child Behavior Checklist (CBCL). The internalizing subscale focuses on social withdrawal, anxiety and depression, and somatic complaints (e.g., headaches, stomachaches, dizziness). The externalizing subscale focuses on rule breaking (e.g., alcohol or drug use) and aggressive behavior.

Findings revealed that second-generation Chinese-American adolescents reported the lowest levels of perceived parental warmth and open communication. Compared to European-American adolescents, first-generation Chinese-American adolescents reported lower levels of parental warmth but not open communication. It is important to note that the cultural dissonance reported by Chinese-American adolescents reflected their perceptions of, rather than their ideals for, their relationships with parents. In fact, Chinese-American participants reported ideals for parental warmth and communication similar to those of European-American participants.

Another important finding was that discrepancies in parental warmth (desiring more or less parental warmth than the adolescent receives) predicted higher rates of internalizing problems for Chinese-American participants than for their European-American counterparts. Specifically, Chinese-American participants who desired more warmth from their parents reported higher rates of internalizing problems, such as anxiety, depression, and somatic complaints. Interestingly, European-American adolescents experienced lower rates of externalizing problems when their parents were perceived as warmer than desired. According to Wu and Chao, among European-Americans, parents who are perceived as warmer than desired may engage in more control or enforce more standards for behavior, which results in reduced rates of externalizing problems. Discrepancies in the desire for parent–adolescent open communication did not predict behavioral problems in any of the groups. It is possible that adolescents view communication difficulties with parents as somewhat normative and, therefore, not a sign of serious relationship problems. Finally, for Chinese-American adolescents, perceptions of high parental devotion, sacrifice, and thoughtfulness served a protective function against behavioral problems, even when parental warmth was lower than desired.

Wu, C., & Chao, R. K. (2011). Intergenerational cultural dissonance in parent–adolescent relationships among Chinese and European Americans. *Developmental Psychology, 47,* 493–508.

LECTURE ENHANCEMENT 14.3
Elder Sibling Closeness and Younger Sibling Substance Use (pp. 585–587)

Time: 5–10 minutes

Objective: To determine if elder sibling closeness protects younger siblings from substance use.

To determine if elder sibling closeness protects younger siblings from substance use, Samek and Rueter (2011) recruited 613 adolescent sibling pairs (206 biological sibling pairs, 407 adopted sibling pairs). The mean age for older siblings at the beginning of the study was 16.1 years; the mean age for younger siblings was 13.8 years. Data collection occurred in two waves—at the beginning of the study and again 3.5 years later. During both waves, the researchers collected the following information:

(1) To assess sibling emotional and behavioral closeness, participants completed the Sibling Relationship Questionnaire (SRQ). For example: On a scale of 1 to 5 (1 = Hardly at all; 5 = Extremely much), "How much is there a strong feeling of love between you and this sibling?" "How much do you and this sibling go places and do things together?"

(2) Participants completed the Computerized Substance Use Assessment (CSA), which measures tobacco, alcohol, and marijuana use. Participants indicated whether or not they had used any of the three substances, as well as the frequency of use over the past 12 months.

Findings indicated a significant relationship between elder sibling substance use and younger sibling substance use, regardless of gender and genetic relationship. In both natural and adoptive families where older siblings used tobacco, alcohol, or marijuana, younger siblings were also likely to use these substances, even if the sibling differed in gender. In contrast, in families where older siblings did not use tobacco, alcohol, or marijuana, younger siblings were also unlikely to use them. In addition, siblings who felt behaviorally and emotionally close to one another were less likely to engage in substance use. The authors note that most research on adolescent substance use focuses on the influence of peers. However, as this study illustrates, older siblings can serve as important role models to younger siblings. Within the family system, sibling emotional closeness may help prevent younger sibling substance use.

In addition to helping prevent substance use, what are some additional benefits of warm sibling ties during childhood and adolescence? How can parents nurture sibling relationships?

Samek, D. R., & Rueter, M. A. (2011). Considerations of elder sibling closeness in predicting younger sibling substance use: Social learning versus social bonding explanations. *Journal of Family Psychology, 25,* 931–941.

LECTURE ENHANCEMENT 14.4
Long-Term Consequences of Nonmaternal Child Care in Infancy and Early Childhood (pp. 595–597)

Time: 10–15 minutes

Objective: To examine the long-term consequences of nonmaternal child care in infancy and early childhood.

To examine the long-term consequences of early nonmaternal child care, Vandell and colleagues (2010) recruited 1,364 children and their mothers and followed them from birth to age 15. The researchers focused on three aspects of child care from birth through 4½ years: type of care, quantity of care, and quality of care. Every three to four months, researchers interviewed mothers about child-care arrangements since the previous interview, including location (child-care home, center-based care, father care, or grandparent care) and number of hours per week. The researchers were primarily interested in hours spent in nonrelative care. When children were ages 6, 15, 24, 36, and 54 months, researchers visited participants' current child-care settings and completed the Observational Record of the Caregiving Environment (ORCE). The ORCE focuses on caregiver intrusiveness and stimulation of development, caregiver availability, positive regard for the child, and child unoccupied/watching behavior. The researchers also collected information on cognitive and academic functioning when children were in first, third, and fifth grades. At age 15, participants completed a standardized intelligence test and provided self-reports of risk-taking behaviors, impulsivity, and externalizing problems. For example, participants were asked about alcohol and drug use, theft, property damage, ability to control behavior, and aggression.

In addition to child measures, the researchers gathered information on maternal and family characteristics. When children were ages 6, 15, 24, 36, and 54 months, mothers provided information on demographic variables, including maternal education, family ethnicity, family income, and presence of a father or partner in the home. Home visits were also completed at the above time periods, with researchers conducting observations of maternal sensitivity toward the child and environmental quality. During the home visits, mothers were administered a standardized depression inventory. Finally, when participants were age 15, parenting quality was assessed using a videotaped discussion of mothers describing areas of disagreement—such as chores, homework, and money—between themselves and their teenagers. The researchers coded tapes according to supportive presence, respect for autonomy, and hostility.

Results indicated that both quality and quantity of early child care predicted academic and behavioral outcomes at age 15. Compared to participants enrolled in lower-quality child-care settings, those in high-quality settings scored higher on cognitive and achievement measures gathered in first, third, and fifth grades and on the intelligence test administered at age 15. In addition, findings indicated that the more hours children spent in nonmaternal care between birth and age 4½, the higher they scored on measures of risk taking, impulsivity, and externalizing problems in adolescence. This relationship was especially strong for children enrolled in lower-quality child-care settings, regardless of maternal education, family ethnicity, family income, or presence of a partner in the home.

Taken together, these findings support previous research on the importance of high-quality child-care experiences for young children. The cognitive and achievement benefits of attending high-quality child care in infancy and early childhood are enduring, with effects still evident 10 years after school entry. Findings also suggest that young children who spend long hours in low-quality nonmaternal child care are at risk for serious behavior problems in adolescence.

Vandell, D. L., Burchinal, M., Vandergrift, N., Belsky, J., & Steinberg, L. (2010). Do effects of early child care extend to age 15 years? Results from the NICHD Study of Early Child Care and Youth Development. *Child Development, 81,* 737–756.

LEARNING ACTIVITIES

LEARNING ACTIVITY 14.1
Creating a Pamphlet About the Transition to Parenthood (p. 570)

Present the following scenario to students:

> A local social service agency has asked you to create a pamphlet for expectant mothers and fathers about the transition to parenthood. Using research in the text as a guide, list information that you would include in your pamphlet. For example, what changes can parents anticipate after the baby arrives? Does the arrival of a new baby cause significant marital strain? How can parents support one another during and after the transition to parenthood? How might additional births affect the family system?

LEARNING ACTIVITY 14.2
Observing Styles of Child Rearing (pp. 573–575)

Have students review the four styles of child rearing on pages 573–575. Next, suggest that they observe and record conflicts between parents and children in a variety of public settings (for example, shopping malls, grocery stores, and toy stores). Checkout counters, where candy and other items designed to appeal to children are displayed, are especially good locations for observing such interactions. Students should describe and classify parents' handling of conflicts according to the child-rearing styles, providing a rationale for each classification. Remind students to check with store personnel before they situate themselves for an extended period for observation.

LEARNING ACTIVITY 14.3
Identifying Styles of Child Rearing (pp. 573–575)

To help students better understand and discern between the four types of child rearing, have them complete the following exercise as an in-class activity or quiz.

Directions: Read each of the statements, and determine whether each pertains to an authoritative (AE), authoritarian (AN), permissive (P), or uninvolved (U) style of child rearing.

Statements:

_____ 1. Parents who use this child-rearing style are low in acceptance and involvement, high in coercive control, and low in autonomy granting.
_____ 2. This child-rearing style combines low acceptance and involvement with little control and general indifference to autonomy granting.
_____ 3. At its extreme, this type of parenting is a form of child maltreatment called neglect.
_____ 4. This child-rearing style is warm and accepting, but parents are either overindulging or inattentive.
_____ 5. The most successful approach to child rearing, this style involves high acceptance and involvement, adaptive control techniques, and appropriate autonomy granting.
_____ 6. Children who experience this type of child rearing are anxious, unhappy, low in self-esteem and self-reliance, and tend to react with hostility when frustrated.
_____ 7. Children of these parents are impulsive, disobedient, and rebellious.
_____ 8. Research shows that this child-rearing style promotes maturity in children of diverse temperaments.
_____ 9. Although some parents believe in this approach, many others simply lack the confidence in their ability to influence their child's behavior.
_____ 10. These parents engage in both unwarranted direct control and psychological control, in which they intrude on and manipulate children's verbal expression, individuality, and attachments to parents.

Answers:

1. AN   6. AN
2. P   7. P
3. U   8. AE
4. P   9. P
5. AE   10. AN

LEARNING ACTIVITY 14.4
True or False: Family Lifestyles and Transitions (pp. 584–599)

Present the following exercise as a quiz or in-class assignment.

Directions: Read each of the following statements and indicate whether it is *True* (T) or *False* (F).

Statements:

_____ 1. Sibling rivalry tends to decrease in middle childhood.
_____ 2. Research confirms that only children tend to be spoiled and selfish.
_____ 3. Despite concerns about their origins, most adoptees appear optimistic and well-adjusted as adults.
_____ 4. Children of homosexual parents tend to be confused about their sexual orientation and experience significant adjustment problems.
_____ 5. In the United States, the largest group of never-married parents is African-American young women.
_____ 6. About 40 percent of children in divorced families display severe adjustment problems.
_____ 7. Compared to girls, boys of divorcing parents tend to receive less emotional support from mothers, teachers, and peers.
_____ 8. Older school-age children and adolescents of both sexes display more irresponsible, acting-out, and antisocial behavior than their peers not in stepfamilies.
_____ 9. Overall, children of employed mothers exhibit more behavioral and emotional problems than their peers.
_____ 10. High-quality child care enhances cognitive, language, and social development, especially for low-SES children.

Answers:

1.	F	6.	F
2.	F	7.	T
3.	T	8.	T
4.	F	9.	F
5.	T	10.	T

LEARNING ACTIVITY 14.5
Applying Ecological Systems Theory to Divorce (pp. 590–594)

In small groups, have students list factors that contribute to divorce, including the consequences of divorce for children and adolescents. Next, direct students to the discussion of ecological systems theory (Chapter 1, pages 26–29). For each factor listed, have students determine in which level of the environment it belongs. How does each level of the environment contribute to children's outcomes following divorce? How do community-based services help both children and their families adjust to divorce?

LEARNING ACTIVITY 14.6
Conducting a Mock Seminar for Stepparents and Their Spouses (pp. 594–595)

Ask students to pretend they must speak at a seminar for new stepparents and their partners. Using research in the text as a guide, what information would students include in the seminar? For example, what topics should be addressed? How might blended families work together to make a smooth transition? What conflicts between stepparents and parents, and between stepparents and children, might arise, and how should they be dealt with? How can stepparents develop a warm bond with their stepchildren? Where can family members go to get help if problems persist?

LEARNING ACTIVITY 14.7
Families and Work Institute (pp. 595–596)

The Families and Work Institute is a nonprofit organization developed in 1989 to research the relationship between work and family. Visit the website, *www.familiesandwork.org*. Under Research and Publications, select one of the research reports available for download. Why was this study conducted? Using information presented in the text, how might the results of this study benefit working mothers or dual-earner families? Can you think of ways in which the results can be used to support public policy for equal pay and equal employment opportunities for women?

LEARNING ACTIVITY 14.8
Finding Out About Supports for Sexually Abused Children in Your Community (pp. 601, 603–604)

Once child sexual abuse has been reported, legal proceedings can begin for the perpetrator, but what happens to the child? If students suddenly discovered that the child of a good friend had been the victim of sexual abuse, what information or suggestions could they make regarding supports for the child? To find out, have students contact the children's protective services department in their area and request information about support services for sexually abused children. For instance, are children always removed from the home environment? If so, where are they placed? What support groups or counseling facilities are available for sexual abuse victims? Do supports focus on families as a whole or just children?

LEARNING ACTIVITY 14.9
Examining Popular Books on Parenting

Ask students to visit a local library or bookstore and examine two popular books on parenting. As they review the books, students should briefly summarize the topics presented (for example, balancing work and family, changes in the family system after the arrival of a new baby, parent education, single parenthood, divorce, parenting teenagers). Is the advice presented in the books supported by research in the text? Why or why not?

ASK YOURSELF . . .

REVIEW: Links between family and community are essential for children's well-being. Provide examples and research findings that support this idea. (pp. 571–572)

In unstable inner-city neighborhoods with dilapidated housing; schools, parks, and playgrounds in disarray; and lack of community centers, these disruptions in community life introduce stressors that undermine parental warmth, involvement, and monitoring, while increasing parental harshness and inconsistency. In such neighborhoods, family violence, child abuse and neglect, children's problem behavior, youth antisocial activity, and adult criminality are especially high. In contrast, strong family ties to the surrounding social context—as indicated by contact with friends and relatives, organized youth activities, and regular church, synagogue, or mosque attendance—reduce family stress and youth adjustment problems. Links between family and community provide social support, which leads to many benefits, including a rise in parental self-worth, parental access to valuable information and services, child-rearing controls and role models, and direct assistance with child rearing.

As one example, the Better Beginnings, Better Futures Project of Ontario, Canada, based in a local elementary school in a poverty-stricken community, provided 4- to 8-year-olds with in-class, before- and after-school, and summer enrichment activities. Workers also visited each child's parents regularly, informed them about community resources, and encouraged their involvement in their child's school and in neighborhood life. Another program component focused on improving the quality of the neighborhood by organizing leadership training and adult education programs, neighborhood safety initiatives, and special events and celebrations. Evaluations as children reached grades 3, 6, and 9 revealed wide-ranging benefits compared with children and families living in other poverty-stricken neighborhoods without this set of programs. Benefits included parents' sense of improved marital satisfaction, family functioning, effective child rearing, and community involvement, and gains in children's academic achievement and social adjustment, including positive relationships with peers and adults, prosocial behavior, self-regulation, and a reduction in emotional and behavior problems.

CONNECT: How does the goodness-of-fit model, discussed in Chapter 10 (see page 426), illustrate central features of the social systems perspective on family functioning? (p. 569)

The goodness-of-fit model describes how temperament and environment can work together to produce favorable outcomes. An effective match, or "good fit," between child-rearing practices and a child's temperament promotes favorable development and psychological adjustment. But when a "poor fit" exists, the outcome is likely to be distorted development and maladjustment.

Similarly, the social systems perspective on family functioning maintains that bidirectional influences exist whereby family members mutually influence one another. Further, both goodness-of-fit and family systems theory state that parents do not mechanically shape their children. Rather, psychological adjustment and well-being are joint products of the child's characteristics and the family environment.

APPLY: At the mall, you see a father getting angry with his young son. Using the social systems perspective, list as many factors as you can that might account for the father's behavior. (pp. 569, 571–572)

The social systems perspective emphasizes the existence of *bidirectional influences,* whereby family members mutually influence one another. Parents who discipline with harshness and impatience tend to have children who refuse and rebel. Because the child's behavior is stressful for parents, they may increase their use of punishment, leading to more unruliness by the child. In this way, parent and child mutually contribute to sustaining each other's behavior.

According to the social systems perspective, interaction between any two family members is also affected by *third parties*—others present in the setting. For example, parents whose marriage is tense and hostile often interfere with each other's child-rearing efforts, are less responsive to their children's needs, and are more likely to criticize, express anger, and punish, as this father is doing.

The social systems perspective also views the family as affected by surrounding social contexts. If this father and son live in a run-down, impoverished neighborhood characterized by dilapidated housing, a high crime rate, and a lack of community centers, these factors in the social context, along with a lack of strong ties to the community, may have introduced stressors into this family's life that undermine the father's warmth and involvement and increase his tendency to resort to harsh punishment.

REFLECT: Did any third parties—grandparents, aunts or uncles, or others—influence your relationship with your parents when you were a child? Describe how they affected interactions within your family. (p. 571)

This is an open-ended question with no right or wrong answer.

REVIEW: Explain why authoritative parenting is linked to favorable academic and social outcomes among children and adolescents. Is the concept of authoritative parenting useful for understanding effective parenting across cultures? Explain. (pp. 573–574, 576, 582–583)

The authoritative child-rearing style involves high acceptance and involvement, adaptive control techniques, and appropriate autonomy granting. Authoritative parents are warm, attentive, and sensitive to their child's needs. They establish an enjoyable, emotionally fulfilling parent–child relationship that draws the child into close connection. At the same time, authoritative parents exercise firm, reasonable behavioral control: They insist on appropriate maturity, give reasons for their expectations, use disciplinary encounters as "teaching moments" to promote the child's self-regulation, and monitor their child's whereabouts and activities. Furthermore, authoritative parents engage in gradual, appropriate *autonomy granting*, allowing the child to make decisions in areas where he is ready to make choices. They also encourage the child to express her thoughts, feelings, and desires, and they engage in joint decision making to resolve disagreements when possible, increasing the likelihood that the child will listen to their perspective in situations where compliance is vital.

Throughout childhood and adolescence, authoritative parenting is linked to many aspects of competence—an upbeat mood, self-control, task persistence, academic achievement, cooperativeness, high self-esteem, responsiveness to parents' views, and social and moral maturity. Over time, the relationship between parenting and children's attributes becomes increasingly bidirectional, so that parental monitoring promotes responsible youth behavior, which in turn leads to gains in parental knowledge. Parents who exert appropriate oversight are likely to parent effectively in other ways as well, giving adolescents both less opportunity and less reason to engage in delinquency. In sum, authoritative child rearing seems to create a positive emotional context for parental influence.

Although authoritative parenting is broadly advantageous, ethnic minority parents often have distinct child-rearing beliefs and practices that reflect cultural values and family context:

(1) Compared with Western parents, Chinese parents describe their parenting as less warm and more controlling, and they are more likely than American parents to shame a misbehaving child, withdraw love, and use physical punishment. When these practices become excessive, resulting in an authoritarian style high in psychological or coercive control, Chinese children display the same negative outcomes seen in Western children: poor academic achievement, anxiety, depression, and aggressive behavior.

(2) In Hispanic families, Asian Pacific Island families, and Caribbean families of African and East Indian origin, firm insistence on respect for parental authority is combined with high parental warmth—a combination that promotes competence and strong feelings of family loyalty.

(3) Although wide variation exists, low-SES African-American parents tend to expect immediate obedience. For families living in depleted, crime-ridden neighborhoods, with few social supports, this strict parental control may have a positive effect, preventing antisocial involvements. Children of low-SES African-American parents who use more controlling strategies tend to be more cognitively and socially competent, and most of these parents combine strict, "no-nonsense" discipline with warmth and reasoning—authoritative practices that predict favorable adjustment, regardless of ethnicity.

CONNECT: How do factors that promote autonomy in adolescence also foster identity development? (To review the influence of parenting on identity, see page 473 in Chapter 11.) (pp. 578–580)

The development of autonomy is closely related to adolescents' quest for identity. Young people who successfully construct personally meaningful values and life goals are autonomous. They have given up childish dependence on parents for a more mature, responsible relationship.

A variety of changes within the adolescent support autonomy. For example, puberty triggers psychological distancing from parents. In addition, as young people look more mature, parents give them more freedom to think and decide for themselves, more opportunities to regulate their own activities, and more responsibility. Cognitive development also paves the way for autonomy as well as for identity development. Gradually, teenagers solve problems and make decisions more effectively. And an improved ability to reason about social relationships leads adolescents to *deidealize* their parents, viewing them as "just people," so that they no longer bend as easily to parental authority as they did when younger.

Warm, supportive parent–child ties that permit young people to explore ideas and social roles foster both autonomy and identity development. Effective parenting of adolescents strikes a balance between *connection* and *separation,* so that parental control gradually relaxes without breaking the parent–child bond. This means establishing guidelines that are flexible and open to discussion. The mild parent–child conflict that typically occurs facilitates adolescent identity and autonomy by helping family members learn to express and tolerate disagreement.

APPLY: Prepare a short talk for a parent–teacher organization, maintaining that parents matter greatly in children's lives. Support each of your points with research evidence. (p. 578)

Parents—though not the sole influence—exert a profound influence on children's development. Well-designed research reveals that the relation between parenting and children's development is sometimes substantial. For example, when parents engage in joint problem solving with their adolescent youngsters; establish firm, consistent control; and monitor the adolescent's whereabouts, research shows strong negative relationships with antisocial behavior.

When weak associations between parenting and children's development are found, they are not necessarily due to the feeble impact of parenting. Rather, some child-rearing practices affect different children in different ways. And although parents respond differently to children with different temperaments, this relationship is not just a reactive one: Parents can modify the maladaptive styles of impulsive, difficult, and shy children.

Powerful evidence that parents matter comes from experiments with parenting interventions, which show that when child rearing improves, children's development changes accordingly. Parents also influence children's peer relations. Beginning in the preschool years, parents propel children toward certain peers by managing their social activities. Further, authoritative child rearing affects the values and inclinations adolescents bring to the peer situation and, therefore, their choice of friends and their peer interactions and activities.

Finally, some parenting influences are difficult to measure. Many people report memorable moments with parents that made a lasting impression. In contrast, a parent's broken promise or discovered deception can destroy parent–child trust and change the impact of future parenting. Overall, parenting effects combine in complex ways with many other factors, including heredity and peers. As one example of the way nature and nurture are interwoven throughout development, the contribution of each factor cannot be partitioned neatly from the others.

REFLECT: How would you classify your parents' child-rearing styles? What factors might have influenced their approach to child rearing? (pp. 573–575)

This is an open-ended question with no right or wrong answer.

REVIEW: Describe and explain changes in sibling relationships from early childhood to adolescence. What can parents do to promote positive sibling ties? (pp. 585–587)

Siblings influence development both directly, through relationships with one another, and indirectly, through the impact of an additional child on parents' behavior. For most preschoolers, the arrival of a baby brother or sister is a difficult experience. Realizing that they must now share their parents' attention and affection, they often become demanding, clingy, and deliberately naughty for a time. Attachment security also declines, especially for children over age 2 and for those with mothers under stress. Yet resentment is only one feature of a rich emotional relationship that soon develops between siblings. Older children also show affection and sympathetic concern—kissing and patting the baby and calling their mother to come when the infant cries. By the end of the first year, babies typically spend much time with older siblings and are comforted by their presence during short parental absences. Throughout childhood, children turn to older siblings for comfort in stressful situations when parents are unavailable.

Because of their frequency and emotional intensity, sibling interactions become unique contexts in which social competence expands. Between their second and fourth birthdays, younger siblings take a more active role in play. Siblings who are close in age often engage in joint pretend, talk about feelings, tease, deceive, and assert their own wants and needs when conflict arises. The skills children acquire during sibling interaction contribute to understanding of emotions and other mental states, perspective taking, moral maturity, and competence in relating to other children.

In middle childhood, sibling rivalry tends to increase. As children participate in a wider range of activities, parents often compare siblings' traits and accomplishments. For same-sex siblings who are close in age, parental comparisons are more frequent, resulting in more quarreling and antagonism. Nevertheless, most school-age siblings continue to rely on each other for companionship and assistance.

Like parent–child relationships, sibling interactions adapt to development at adolescence. As younger siblings become more self-sufficient, they accept less direction from their older brothers and sisters, and sibling influence declines. And as adolescents become more involved in friendships and romantic relationships, they invest less time and energy in their siblings, who are part of the family from which they are trying to establish autonomy. As a result, sibling relationships often become less intense, in both positive and negative feelings.

Parenting is influential in sibling relationships. For example, maternal warmth toward both children is related to positive sibling interaction among young siblings and to preschoolers' support of a distressed younger sibling. And mothers who frequently play with their children and head off potential conflicts by explaining the toddler's wants and needs to the preschool sibling foster sibling cooperation. In contrast, maternal harshness and lack of involvement result in increasingly antagonistic sibling relationships. During middle childhood, when parents tend to compare siblings' traits and accomplishments, the child who gets less parental affection, more disapproval, or fewer material resources is likely to be resentful and show poorer adjustment over time. Finally, sibling interaction in adolescence continues to be affected by relationships with parents. Teenagers whose parents are warm and supportive have more positive sibling ties. And mild sibling differences in perceived parental affection no longer trigger jealousy but, instead, predict increasing sibling warmth.

CONNECT: Review research on resilience in Chapter 1 (see pages 10–11). Are factors that foster resilience similar to those that promote favorable adjustment to parental divorce and blended families? Explain. (pp. 591–593, 594–595)

A number of factors that foster resilience are similar to those that promote favorable adjustment to divorce and remarriage. Children who have an easy temperament tend to have an optimistic outlook on life and a special capacity to adapt to change. They are less often targets of parental anger and are also better at coping with adversity. Resilient children are also more likely to display more mature behavior after divorce, taking on family and household tasks, care of younger siblings, and emotional support of a depressed, anxious parent.

Effective parenting is the overriding factor in children's positive adjustment following divorce, and children who have the qualities that foster resilience are more likely to have a warm relationship with the custodial parent that makes such parenting more likely. They are also likely to be more open to gradually forming a warm relationship with a stepparent and stepsiblings. Finally, the availability of caring extended-family members, teachers, siblings, and friends—another factor known to promote resilience in children—also reduces the likelihood that divorce will result in long-term difficulties.

APPLY: Steve and Marissa are in the midst of an acrimonious divorce. Their 9-year-old son, Dennis, has become hostile and defiant. How can Steve and Marissa help Dennis adjust? (p. 594)

Steve and Marissa can take a number of concrete steps to help Dennis adjust to their divorce:
(1) They should shield Dennis from parental conflict. If one parent expresses hostility, the other should avoid responding in kind.
(2) They should provide Dennis with as much continuity, familiarity, and predictability as possible. Children adjust better when their lives have some stability—for example, the same school, bedroom, babysitter, playmates, and daily schedule.
(3) They should explain the divorce to Dennis, providing a reason that he can understand, assuring him that he is not to blame, and telling him what to expect.
(4) They should emphasize the permanence of the divorce, so that Dennis does not fantasize about his parents getting back together.
(5) They should acknowledge and respond sympathetically to Dennis's feelings, offering a supportive, understanding response when he expresses sadness, fear, and anger.
(6) They should engage in authoritative parenting, providing affection and acceptance, reasonable demands for mature behavior, and consistent, rational discipline.
(7) Finally, they should promote Dennis's continuing relationship with both parents, enlisting the help of extended-family members in not taking sides.

REFLECT: What after-school child-care arrangements did you experience in elementary school? How do you think they influenced your development? (pp. 596–597)

This is an open-ended question with no right or wrong answer.

REVIEW: Explain how personal and situational factors that contribute to child maltreatment illustrate the social systems perspective on family functioning. (pp. 599–600, 602)

Researchers have discovered that many interacting variables—at the family, community, and cultural levels—contribute to child abuse and neglect. Within the family, children whose characteristics make them more challenging to rear are more likely to become targets of abuse. These include premature or very sick babies and children who are temperamentally difficult, are inattentive or overactive, or have other developmental problems. But whether such children are maltreated largely depends on parents' characteristics. Maltreating parents are less skillful than other parents in handling discipline confrontations and getting children to cooperate in working toward common goals. They often evaluate children's transgressions as worse than they are and feel powerless in parenting. Once abuse begins, it quickly becomes part of a self-sustaining relationship. The small irritations to which abusive parents react soon become bigger ones, and parental harshness increases. By the preschool years, abusive and neglectful parents seldom interact with their children, and when they do, the communication is almost always negative.

Most parents have enough self-control not to respond with abuse to their children's misbehavior or developmental problems. Other factors combine with these conditions to prompt an extreme response. Unmanageable parental stress is strongly associated with maltreatment. Abusive parents react to stressful situations with high emotional arousal. And such stressors as low income, low education, unemployment, alcohol and drug use, marital conflict, domestic violence, overcrowded living conditions, frequent moves, and extreme household disorganization are common in abusive homes. These conditions increase the chances that parents will be too overwhelmed to meet basic child-rearing responsibilities or will vent their frustrations by lashing out at their children.

CONNECT: After reviewing factors linked to adolescent parenthood (Chapter 5, pages 218–219), explain why it places children at risk for abuse and neglect. (pp. 600, 602)

Teenagers who become parents often face stressful life circumstances that are compounded after the baby is born. They are far more likely to be poor than their agemates who postpone childbearing. Their backgrounds often include low parental warmth and involvement, domestic violence and child abuse, repeated parental divorce and remarriage, adult models of unmarried parenthood, and residence in neighborhoods where other adolescents also display these risks. Girls at risk for early pregnancy do poorly in school, engage in alcohol and drug use, have a childhood history of aggressive and antisocial behavior, associate with deviant peers, and experience high rates of depression. All of these factors place the children of adolescent parents at risk for abuse and neglect.

Additional factors put these children at risk: Compared with adult mothers, adolescent mothers know less about child development, have unrealistically high expectations of their infants, perceive their babies as more difficult, and interact less effectively with them. These personal and situational factors increase the chances that adolescent parents will be too overwhelmed to meet basic child-rearing responsibilities or will vent their frustrations by lashing out at their children. In addition, isolation from formal and informal supports, which puts children at risk for abuse and neglect, is common among adolescent parents.

APPLY: Claire told her 6-year-old daughter to be careful never to talk to or take candy from strangers. Why is Claire's directive not adequate to protect her daughter from sexual abuse? (p. 601)

Claire's directive is not adequate to protect her daughter from sexual abuse because abusers are usually not strangers. Typically, the abuser is either a parent or someone the parent knows well—a father, stepfather, or live-in boyfriend or, somewhat less often, an uncle or older brother. And even in cases that involve a nonrelative, the abuser is usually someone the child has come to know and trust.

REFLECT: Describe a challenging time for your family during your childhood. What aspects of the experience increased stress? What factors helped you and your parents cope with adversity?

This is an open-ended question with no right or wrong answer.

SUGGESTED READINGS

Crosson-Tower, C. (2010). *Understanding child abuse and neglect.* Upper Saddle River, NJ: Prentice Hall. A comprehensive look at child maltreatment, this book examines the history of child abuse and neglect, presents case studies, and addresses treatment options for abused children and their caretakers.

Fox, B. (2009). *When couples become parents: The creation of gender in the transition to parenthood.* Toronto: University of Toronto Press. Examines the many surprises and challenges of negotiating the transition to parenthood, with an emphasis on how gender roles often change during the first year. Other topics include the importance of family support, combining work and family, and strategies new parents can use to cope with the challenges of parenthood.

Pedro-Carroll, J. (2010). *Putting children first: Proven parenting strategies for helping children thrive through divorce.* New York: Avery/Penguin. Using up-to-date research findings, this book examines the short- and long-term consequences of parental divorce on children's development. Topics include preparing children for the separation, dealing with parent–child conflict, supporting children's resilience, and navigating new relationships and remarriage.

MEDIA MATERIALS

For details on individual video segments that accompany the DVD for *Child Development,* Ninth Edition, please see the DVD Guide for *Explorations in Child Development*. The DVD and DVD Guide are available through your Pearson sales representative.

Additional DVDs that may be useful in your class are listed below. These are not available through your Pearson sales representative, but you can order them directly from the distributors. (See contact information at the end of this manual.)

A Home for Maisie (2011, Films Media Group/BBC, 58 min.). This program is about 7-year-old Maisie, a child in foster care who had suffered abuse and neglect almost all her life. Although she desperately wanted to be adopted, her early experiences left her with a vast store of anger, confusion, and distrust, and several families who planned to adopt her returned her to the foster care system. The program follows Maisie and the couple who will ultimately adopt her and who helped Maisie overcome her traumatic past to some degree, with the assistance of an agency that specializes in counseling the most damaged children.

Breaking the Cycle of Abuse (2009, Films Media Group, 39 min.). This edition of *Primetime* spotlights three primary caregivers of one or more young children—a 63-year-old grandmother, a 36-year-old mother, and a 29-year-old father—who are hoping to break the cycle of child abuse by taking part in a mentoring program for at-risk caregivers. The caregivers in this program are filmed both at their worst and at their best as they begin to apply the new behavior-modification techniques to the children's actions as well as their own. Commentary is provided by Alan Kazdin, director of the Yale University Parenting Center and Child Conduct Clinic and author of *The Kazdin Method for Parenting the Defiant Child*.

Families Talk About…Fathers Matter (2004, Insight Media, 19 min.). In this program, urban fathers reflect on what it means to be a father in married, single, and divorced households.

Families Talk About…Single Parenting (2004, Insight Media, 21 min.). This program features interviews with urban parents who have sole custody of their children. They discuss the unique pressures their families face and explain how they have learned to overcome obstacles.

Families Today and Tomorrow (2007, Insight Media, 30 min.). This program examines contemporary families, including single-parent families, stepfamilies, and multigenerational families. It also looks at increasing racial and ethnic diversity resulting from rising immigration rates and emphasizes the vital role of the family in the United States.

Family Matters: Family Types (2005, Insight Media, 30 min.). This program considers the diversity of family forms, including cultural shifts in the ways people think about families.

Fitting in: Socialization (2005, Insight Media, 30 min.). This program explains how culture begins with the family and then extends to such agents of socialization as school, peer group, and mass media.

Flesh and Blood: Sibling Rivalry (2006, Films Media Group, 60 min.). Part of the series *Child of Our Time 2006,* this BBC/Open University coproduction features a group of 25 6-year-olds as they demonstrate the significance of sibling rivalry and bonding. The program also examines recent theories suggesting that relationships among siblings in a nuclear family—rather than those between parent and offspring—are the most meaningful to an individual's growth.

Recognizing Child Abuse (2007, Films Media Group/Meridian Productions, 25 min.). Noting that child abuse often goes unnoticed, this program spells out the four *R*s of child abuse: the harsh reality of its presence in our society, the results it leads to, the many ways to recognize it, and the proper channels for reporting it. Each of these aspects is explained through dramatizations and interviews with education and child welfare experts. A presenter's guide is available online.

The History of Parenting Practices (2006, Insight Media, 20 min.). This program explores seminal events in the history of parenting techniques and considers the ways in which government policies have affected parenting practices over the past century. It also examines influential child development theories that have shaped the ways in which parents raise their children.

The Power of Family: Types of Families and Family Development (2008, Films Media Group, 23 min.). This program examines different types of families—such as traditional, single-parent, and extended—and the roles the families play in the physical, emotional, intellectual, social, and moral development of their members. Topics also include stresses on the family structure and the "changing seasons" of the family cycle. Educational resources are available online.

The Roots of Violence, Addiction, and Neglect (2006, Magna Systems/Linkletter Media, 33 min.). Hosted by Art Linkletter and featuring family specialist John Bradshaw, this program explores the lives of children brought up in families where violence, addiction, and neglect were present. It highlights the impact parents have on their children and the difficulty of the healing process.

Why Can't a Woman Succeed Like a Man? (2009, Insight Media, 60 min.). This program questions whether women can, should, or even want to "have it all" by pursuing a career and raising a family. It examines gender inequality and looks at such issues as the societal assumption that women should be more responsible for child rearing than men.

CHAPTER 15
PEERS, MEDIA, AND SCHOOLING

CHAPTER-AT-A-GLANCE

Chapter Outline	Instruction Ideas	Supplements
Peer Relations pp. 607–628 Development of Peer Sociability • Influences on Peer Sociability • Friendship • Peer Acceptance • Peer Groups • Dating • Peer Pressure and Conformity	Learning Objectives 15.1–15.5 Lecture Enhancement 15.1 Learning Activities 15.1–15.5 Ask Yourself pp. 613, 618, 622, 628	Test Bank Items 1–64, 126–128 Please contact your Pearson publisher's representative for a wide range of video offerings available to adopters.
Media pp. 629–637 Television • Computers, Cell Phones, and the Internet • Regulating Media Use	Learning Objectives 15.6–15.7 Lecture Enhancement 15.2 Learning Activities 15.6–15.7 Ask Yourself p. 637	Test Bank Items 65–84, 129
Schooling pp. 637–650 Class and Student Body Size • Educational Philosophies • School Transitions • Teacher–Student Interaction • Grouping Practices • Teaching Students with Special Needs • Parent–School Partnerships • How Well-Educated Are American Young People?	Learning Objectives 15.8–15.12 Lecture Enhancements 15.3–15.4 Learning Activities 15.8–15.9 Ask Yourself p. 650	Test Bank Items 85–125, 130–131

BRIEF CHAPTER SUMMARY

Beyond the family, the forces that most strongly influence children and adolescents are peers, media, and school. Peer bonds are vital for social competence, and parent and peer relations complement one another. During the preschool years, as children become increasingly self-aware and better at communicating and understanding others' thoughts and feelings, their skill at interacting with peers improves rapidly. Sharing, helping, and other prosocial acts increase in middle childhood, as does rough-and-tumble play, which may help children establish a dominance hierarchy that serves the adaptive function of limiting aggression.

Parents exert both direct and indirect influence on peer sociability; situational factors, such as age mix, and cultural values also play a role. Authoritative parenting provides a firm foundation for competence in relating to agemates. Peer contact rises in adolescence in all societies, but especially in industrialized nations, in which young people spend most of each weekday with agemates in school.

In early childhood, friendships are based on shared pleasurable activity; as children grow older, friendship becomes more abstract, and trust becomes its defining feature. Teenagers emphasize intimacy, mutual understanding, and loyalty as the qualities they seek in a friend. Friendships are remarkably stable at all ages. Friends behave more prosocially with one another but also disagree and compete more. From middle childhood on, friends resemble one another in personality and prosocial behavior. Sex differences in friendships emerge in middle childhood: Emotional closeness is more common between girls than between boys.

Peer acceptance, or likability, contributes uniquely to children's adjustment. Researchers have identified four categories of peer acceptance: popular, rejected, controversial, and neglected. Controversial children display a blend of positive and negative social behaviors. Neglected children, surprisingly, are usually well-adjusted. Rejected children may benefit from interventions. Peer groups are collectives of children that generate unique values and standards for behavior and a social structure of leaders and followers. In early adolescence, peer groups evolve into same-sex cliques, several of which may combine to form a crowd. Eventually, mixed-sex cliques form, and by late adolescence, crowds decline in importance.

The beginning of dating is regulated by cultural expectation, and the achievement of intimacy in adolescent dating relationships lags behind that of friendships. Warm, caring romantic ties in adolescence have a positive relationship to gratifying, committed relationships in emerging adulthood. Conformity to peer pressure is greater in adolescence than earlier or later, but authoritative child rearing is related to resistance to peer pressure.

Television remains the dominant form of youth media, but computers now exist in most American homes and in virtually all school classrooms. The cell phone has become the favored channel of communication between teenagers and their friends, and young people also use it for diverse entertainment purposes. Extensive TV watching is associated with family, peer, and health difficulties. Televised violence promotes hostile thoughts and emotions, aggression, and a violent worldview. TV also conveys ethnic and gender stereotypes. Educational television can promote children's cognitive and academic skills, emotional and social understanding, and prosocial behavior. But heavy viewing of entertainment TV detracts from reading time, school success, and social experiences.

Computers can offer rich educational benefits for children and adolescents, but the growing use of computers has raised concerns about a "digital divide" between gender and SES groups in computer skills. Recent survey evidence reveals that U.S. children and adolescents, on average, use the computer a half-hour a day for schoolwork and 1½ hours for pleasure. Teenagers' online communication with preexisting friends, through such means as texting and instant messaging, promotes friendship closeness.

In the United States, the pendulum has swung back and forth between two philosophical approaches to education: the traditional classroom, in which the teacher is the sole authority, and the constructivist classroom, which encourages students to construct their own knowledge. Today, many preschool and kindergarten teachers feel increased pressure to stress teacher-directed academic training, despite grave concerns about its appropriateness.

Homogeneous grouping in elementary school is linked to poorer-quality instruction and declines in self-esteem and achievement for children in low-ability groups, and in the United States, high school tracking extends earlier educational inequalities. Low-SES students are at risk for unfair placement in noncollege tracks. U.S. legislation mandates that schools place children who require special supports for learning in the "least restrictive" environments that meet their educational needs. The effectiveness of inclusive classrooms depends on the severity of the child's disability and on the availability of additional support.

In international comparisons of academic achievement, U.S. students typically perform at or below the averages, and compared with top-achieving nations, the United States is far less equitable in the quality of education it provides to its low-income and ethnic minority students. Research on learning environments in Asian nations highlights social forces that foster strong student learning, including the cultural valuing of effort.

Unlike some European nations, the United States has no widespread vocational training system to help non-college-bound adolescents prepare for skilled business and industrial occupations and manual trade.

LEARNING OBJECTIVES

After reading this chapter, you should be able to answer the following:

15.1 Trace the development of peer sociability from infancy into adolescence, and discuss various influences on peer sociability. (pp. 608–613)

15.2 Describe developing concepts and characteristics of friendships in childhood and adolescence, as well as implications of friendship for psychological adjustment. (pp. 613–618)

15.3 Describe categories of peer acceptance, the relationship of social behavior to likability, and ways to help rejected children. (pp. 618–622)

15.4 Discuss peer group formation and dating relationships, including their consequences for development. (pp. 622–625)

15.5 What factors influence conformity to peer pressure in adolescence? (pp. 625–628)

15.6 Discuss the influence of television on children's development. (pp. 629–632)

15.7 Discuss computer, cell phone, and Internet use by children and adolescents, noting benefits and concerns. (pp. 632–636)

15.8 How do class and student body size and educational philosophies affect academic and social development? (pp. 637–640)

15.9 Cite factors that influence adjustment following school transitions in early childhood and in adolescence. (pp. 640–642)

15.10 Discuss the role of teacher–student interaction and grouping practices in academic achievement. (pp. 643–645)

15.11 Under what conditions is placement of students with special needs in regular classrooms successful, and how can schools increase parent involvement in education? (pp. 646–647)

15.12 How well are American young people achieving compared with their counterparts in other industrialized nations, and what problems do non-college-bound youths face in preparing for a vocation? (pp. 647–650)

LECTURE OUTLINE

I. PEER RELATIONS (pp. 607–628)
   A. Parent and peer relations complement one another.
      1. A secure attachment bond and authoritative parenting grant children the confidence and social skills they need to enter the world of peers and form gratifying peer relationships.
      2. Peer interaction, in turn, enables children to expand their social-cognitive knowledge and social skills, which are vital sources of support in threatening situations.
   B. Development of Peer Sociability (pp. 608–611)
      1. In cultures where agemates have regular contact during the first year of life, peer sociability begins early, gradually evolving into the complex, well-coordinated exchanges of childhood and adolescence.
      2. Infant and Toddler Beginnings
         a. In pairs of infants brought together in a laboratory, looking accompanied by touching is present at 3 to 4 months, peer-directed smiles and babbles by 6 months.
         b. Though limited, peer sociability is present in the first two years and is promoted by the early caregiver–child bond.
         c. Toddlers who have a warm parental relationship or who attend high-quality child care display more positive peer exchanges and show more socially competent behavior as preschoolers.
      3. The Preschool Years
         a. As children become increasingly self-aware and better at communicating and understanding others' thoughts and feelings, their skill at interacting with peers improves rapidly.
         b. Mildred Parten proposed that social development proceeds in a three-step sequence:
            (1) **Nonsocial activity** is unoccupied, onlooker behavior and solitary play.
            (2) In **parallel play,** a child plays near other children with similar materials but does not try to influence their behavior.
            (3) Two forms of true social interaction are **associative play,** in which children engage in separate activities but exchange toys and comment on one another's behavior, and **cooperative play,** a more advanced type of interaction in which children orient toward a common goal, such as acting out a make-believe theme.
         c. Although these play forms emerge in the order suggested by Parten, all coexist during the preschool years.
         d. It is the *type,* rather than the amount, of solitary and parallel play that changes during early childhood, with older children engaging in play that demonstrates greater *cognitive maturity* than younger children's play.
         e. Only certain types of nonsocial activity—such as aimless wandering and hovering near peers—are cause for concern.
         f. Some preschoolers with low rates of peer interaction are neither socially anxious nor impulsive but simply like to play by themselves.
         g. *Sociodramatic play,* which becomes especially common during the preschool years, is an advanced form of cooperative play that supports cognitive, emotional, and social development.
         h. With age, preschoolers' disagreements center less on toys and other resources and more on differences of opinion.
      4. Middle Childhood and Adolescence
         a. Formal schooling exposes children to agemates who vary in many ways, contributing to their awareness of a multiplicity of viewpoints.
         b. Peer communication profits from improved perspective taking.
         c. School-age children apply their emotional and social knowledge to peer interaction.
         d. Sharing, helping, and other prosocial acts increase in middle childhood.
         e. Another form of peer interaction that emerges in the preschool years and peaks in middle childhood is the friendly chasing and play-fighting called **rough-and-tumble play.**

(1) This type of play is similar to the social behavior of young mammals.
(2) It is more common among boys.
(3) In our evolutionary past, rough-and-tumble play may have been important for developing fighting skill and establishing a **dominance hierarchy**—a stable ordering of group members that predicts who will win when conflict arises.
(4) A consistent lineup of winners and losers develops and becomes increasingly stable in middle childhood and adolescence, especially among boys.
(5) As adolescents reach physical maturity, individual differences in strength become apparent, and rough-and-tumble play declines.
    f. Over middle childhood, children interact increasingly often with peers; by mid-adolescence, more time is spent with peers than with any other social partners.
C. Influences on Peer Sociability (pp. 611–613)
1. Children first acquire skills for interacting with peers within the family.
2. Direct Parental Influences
    a. Preschoolers whose parents frequently arrange informal peer contact tend to have larger peer networks and to be more socially skilled.
    b. Parents' skillful suggestions for managing conflict, discouraging teasing, and entering a play group are associated with preschoolers' social competence and peer acceptance.
    c. In middle childhood and adolescence, heavy provision of parental guidance is usually aimed at children with peer-relationship problems.
    d. Parental monitoring of children's activities protects school-age children and adolescents from antisocial involvements.
3. Indirect Parental Influences
    a. Child-rearing variables, such as inductive discipline and authoritative parenting, influence peer relations indirectly by offering a firm foundation for competence in relating to agemates.
    b. Coercive behavioral control, including harsh physical punishment, and psychological control engender poor social skills and aggressive behavior.
    c. Secure attachments to parents are linked to more harmonious peer interactions, larger peer networks, and more supportive friendships throughout childhood and adolescence.
    d. Parent–child play seems to be a particularly effective context for promoting peer-interaction skills.
    e. The quality of parents' own social networks is associated with children's social competence.
4. Age Mix of Children
    a. In age-graded settings, children typically interact with others close in age, but in cultures where children are not segregated by age for schooling and recreation, cross-age interaction is common.
    b. The theories of Piaget and Vygotsky suggest different benefits from same- versus mixed-age interaction.
(1) Piaget emphasized experiences with children equal in status who challenge one another's viewpoints, thereby promoting cognitive, social, and moral development.
(2) Vygotsky believed that children profit from interacting with older, more capable peers, who model and encourage more advanced skills.
    c. Among preschoolers, the play of younger children is more cognitively and socially mature in mixed-age than in single-age classrooms.
    d. However, the oldest school-age children in mixed-age settings prefer same-age companions.
    e. Children benefit from both same-age and mixed-age relationships.
5. Cultural Values
    a. Peer sociability in collectivist societies, which stress group harmony, differs from that in Western individualistic cultures.
(1) Children in India typically play in large groups that require high levels of cooperation.
(2) Chinese preschoolers are more willing than their American counterparts to include a quiet, reserved child in play.
    b. Cultural beliefs about the importance of play affect early peer associations.
(1) Caregivers who view play as mere entertainment are less likely to encourage pretend than those who value its cognitive and social benefits.

(2) Preschool-age children of Korean-American parents, who emphasize task persistence as crucial for learning, spend less time than Caucasian-American children at joint make-believe and more time unoccupied and in parallel play.
- c. Western-style sociodramatic play may be particularly important for social development in societies where children's and adults' worlds are distinct.
- d. Peer contact rises in adolescence in all societies but particularly in industrialized nations, in which young people spend most of each weekday with agemates in school.

D. Friendship (pp. 613–618)
1. **Friendships** are close relationships involving companionship in which each partner wants to be with the other.
2. Thinking About Friendship
    a. To an adult, friendship is a consensual relationship involving companionship, sharing, and understanding of thoughts and feelings.
    b. For children, friendship begins more concretely, as pleasurable activity.
    c. Children's changing ideas about friendship follow a three-stage sequence:
        (1) Preschool children (ages 4 to 7) view a friend as a handy playmate but do not perceive friendship as having a long-term, enduring quality.
        (2) School-age children (ages 8 to 10) have a more complex, psychologically based view of friendship as characterized by mutual *trust* and assistance.
        (3) For teenagers (ages 11 to 15), friendship is about *intimacy, mutual understanding,* and *loyalty*.
3. Characteristics of Friendships
    a. Friendship Selectivity and Stability
        (1) Whereas preschoolers say they have lots of friends, school-age children grow more selective. In adolescence, the number of best friends declines.
        (2) Friendships are remarkably stable at all ages, but for younger children, stability is largely a function of the constancy of social environments, such as school and neighborhood.
        (3) Context continues to be influential at older ages, with friendships spanning several situations—such as school or religious institution—more likely to persist.
        (4) At the same time, stability increases with age as friendships become psychologically based.
    b. Interaction Between Friends
        (1) Preschoolers give twice as much reinforcement to children they identify as friends.
        (2) Spontaneity, intimacy, and sensitivity characterize rewarding friendships very early.
        (3) A more mature understanding of friendship seems to spark greater prosocial behavior between friends.
        (4) Cooperation, generosity, mutual affirmation, and self-disclosure continue to rise into adolescence.
        (5) Friends also disagree and compete with one another more than do nonfriends.
        (6) Friendship provides an important context in which children learn to tolerate criticism and resolve disputes.
    c. Resemblance Between Friends
        (1) In childhood and adolescence, the attributes on which friends are most alike are age, sex, ethnicity, and SES; but from middle childhood on, they also resemble one another in personality, academic achievement, and prosocial behavior.
        (2) In adolescence, friends tend to be similar in identity status, educational aspirations, and willingness to engage in lawbreaking acts.
        (3) In-group favoritism and out-group prejudice may influence the choice of friends.
        (4) As young people enter a wider range of school and community settings, they choose some friends who differ from themselves.
        (5) As they forge a personal identity, adolescents may seek friends with differing attitudes and values as a way of exploring new perspectives.
        (6) Children and adolescents are more likely to form friendships with agemates of other ethnicities when they attend ethnically diverse schools and live in integrated neighborhoods.
4. Sex Differences in Friendships
    a. In middle childhood, children report a consistent sex difference in friendships:
        (1) Emotional closeness is more common between girls than between boys; girls frequently get together to "just talk," and their exchanges contain more self-disclosure.

(2) Boys more often gather for an activity, such as sports, and tend to have discussions that focus on recognition and mastery issues.
- b. Androgynous boys are as likely as girls to form intimate same-sex ties, whereas highly "masculine" boys are less likely to do so.
- c. When friends focus on their deeper thoughts and feelings, they tend to *coruminate* about problems and negative emotions; this can trigger anxiety and depression.
- d. In early adolescence, young people who are either very popular or very unpopular are more likely to have other-sex friends.
- e. Girls have more other-sex friends than boys, a difference that widens with age as teenage girls form friendships with boys who are somewhat older.

5. Friendship and Adjustment
   - a. Warm childhood and adolescent friendships that are high in trust, intimate sharing, and support contribute to many aspects of psychological health and competence into early adulthood.
     (1) Close friendships provide opportunities to explore the self and develop a deep understanding of another.
     (2) Close friendships provide a foundation for future intimate relationships.
     (3) Close friendships help young people deal with the stresses of everyday life.
   - b. Some friendships interfere with well-being.
     (1) Beginning in the preschool years, conflict-ridden interactions between aggressive friends are associated with poor adjustment.
     (2) Children with aggressive friends increase in antisocial behavior over time.
   - c. Children who have no friends usually have undesirable personalities; without supportive friendships, their maladaptive behaviors tend to persist.

E. Peer Acceptance (pp. 618–622)
  1. **Peer acceptance** refers to likability: the extent to which a child is viewed by a group of agemates, such as classmates, as a worthy social partner.
     - a. Unlike friendship, peer acceptance is not a mutual relationship but a one-sided perspective, involving the group's view of an individual.
     - b. Better-accepted children tend to have more friends and more positive relationships with them.
  2. To assess peer acceptance, researchers use self-reports that measure *social preferences* or assess *social prominence*.
  3. Children's self-reports yield four general categories of peer acceptance.
     - a. **Popular children** get many positive votes.
     - b. **Rejected children** are disliked.
     - c. **Controversial children** receive many votes, both positive and negative.
     - d. **Neglected children** are seldom mentioned, either positively or negatively.
  4. About two-thirds of students in a typical elementary school classroom fit one of these categories; the remaining one-third are *average* in peer acceptance.
  5. Peer acceptance is a powerful predictor of current and later psychological adjustment.
     - a. Rejected children are anxious, unhappy, disruptive, and poorly achieving.
     - b. Peer rejection in middle childhood is also strongly associated with poor school performance, dropping out, antisocial behavior, and delinquency in adolescence.
  6. Children's characteristics combined with parenting practices may largely explain the link between peer acceptance and psychological adjustment.
     - a. School-age children with peer relationship problems are more likely to have experienced family stress and insensitive child rearing.
     - b. Rejected children evoke reactions from peers that contribute to their unfavorable development.
  7. Determinants of Peer Acceptance
     - a. Popular Children
       (1) Most popular children are **popular-prosocial children,** who combine academic and social competence.
       (2) **Popular-antisocial children** includes "tough" boys—athletically skilled but poor students who cause trouble and defy adult authority—and relationally aggressive boys and girls who enhance their own status by ignoring, excluding, and spreading rumors about other children.

b. Rejected Children
   (1) **Rejected-aggressive children** show high rates of conflict, physical and relational aggression, and hyperactive, inattentive, and impulsive behavior.
   (2) **Rejected-withdrawn children** are passive and socially awkward—timid children who are overwhelmed by social anxiety.
   (3) As early as kindergarten, peers exclude rejected children.
   (4) Some rejected children have no friends—a circumstance linked to low self-esteem, mistrust of peers, and severe adjustment difficulties.
   (5) Both rejected-aggressive and rejected-withdrawn children are at risk for peer harassment, but rejected-withdrawn children are especially likely to be victimized by their peers.
c. Controversial and Neglected Children
   (1) Controversial children are hostile and disruptive but also engage in positive, prosocial acts.
   (2) Controversial children have as many friends as popular children and are happy with their peer relationships.
   (3) They often bully agemates to get their way and engage in relational aggression.
   (4) Neglected children, once thought to be in need of treatment, are usually well-adjusted and do not report feeling unhappy about their social life.
   (5) Neglected status, like controversial status, is often temporary.
8. Helping Rejected Children
   a. Interventions to improve the peer relations and psychological adjustment of rejected children usually involve coaching, modeling, and reinforcing positive social skills.
   b. Another approach focuses on training in perspective taking and social problem solving.
   c. For rejected children whose behaviors originate in a poor fit between the child's temperament and parenting practices, effective interventions may need to focus on improving parent–child interactions.
F. Peer Groups (pp. 622–624)
1. By the end of middle childhood, children form **peer groups,** collectives that generate unique values and standards for behavior and a social structure of leaders and followers.
2. First Peer Groups
   a. Peer groups organize on the basis of proximity and similarity in sex, ethnicity, academic achievement, popularity, and aggression.
   b. The practices of these informal groups lead to a "peer culture" that typically includes a specialized vocabulary, dress code, and place to "hang out."
   c. Most school-age children judge a group's decision to exclude a peer to be wrong.
      (1) Nevertheless, children do exclude peers, often with relationally aggressive tactics.
      (2) Peer groups frequently oust no-longer-"respected" children.
   d. School-age children's desire for group belonging also can be satisfied through formal group ties such as scouting and religious youth groups.
3. Cliques and Crowds
   a. The peer groups of early adolescence are organized around **cliques,** groups of about five to eight members who are friends and, therefore, usually resemble one another in family background, attitudes, values, and interests.
   b. Among Western adolescents attending high schools with complex social structures, often several cliques with similar values form a larger, more loosely organized group called a **crowd.**
   c. When adolescents join a clique or crowd, it can modify their beliefs and behaviors, but family experiences affect the extent to which adolescents become like group members over time.
   d. As interest in dating increases, mixed-sex cliques form, providing boys and girls a chance to interact with the other sex without having to be intimate.
   e. By late adolescence, the mixed-sex clique disappears and crowds also decline in importance.
G. Dating (pp. 624–625)
1. The hormonal changes of puberty increase sexual interest, but cultural expectations determine when and how dating begins.
   a. Asian youths start dating later and have fewer dating partners than young people in Western societies, which tolerate and even encourage early romantic involvements from middle school on.
   b. Early adolescents tend to mention recreation and achieving peer status as reasons for dating.

c. By late adolescence, young people seek dating partners who offer companionship, affection, and social support.
2. The achievement of intimacy in adolescent dating relationships lags behind that between friends.
3. Positive relationships with parents and friends contribute to the development of warm romantic ties.
4. Perhaps because early adolescent dating relationships are stereotyped, early, frequent dating is related to drug use and poor academic achievement.
5. These factors, along with a history of uninvolved parenting and aggression in family and peer relationships, increase the likelihood of dating violence.
6. Gay and lesbian youths face special challenges in initiating and maintaining visible romances.
   a. Their first dating relationships seem to be short-lived and to involve little emotional commitment because they fear peer harassment and rejection.
   b. Many have difficulty finding a same-sex partner because their gay and lesbian peers have not yet come out.
7. Warm, caring romantic ties in adolescence are positively related to gratifying, committed relationships in early adulthood.

H. Peer Pressure and Conformity (pp. 625–628)
1. Conformity to peer pressure is greater during adolescence than in childhood or early adulthood.
2. Peer conformity is a complex process that varies with the adolescent's age, current situation, need for social approval, and culture.
3. Adolescents feel greatest pressure to conform to obvious aspects of the peer culture—dress, grooming, and participation in social activities.
4. Peer pressure to engage in proadult behavior, such as cooperating with parents and getting good grades, is also strong.
5. Resistance to peer pressure strengthens with age, though wide individual differences exist and personal characteristics make a difference.
6. Authoritative child rearing is also influential.
   a. Teenagers whose parents are supportive and exert appropriate oversight respect their parents, and their attitude lessens unfavorable peer pressure.
   b. Adolescents whose parents exert either too much or too little control tend to be highly peer-oriented. Youths who bend easily to peer influence display wide-ranging problems.

II. MEDIA (pp. 629–637)
   A. Although television remains the dominant form of youth media, computers now exist in most American homes and in virtually all school classrooms.
   B. The cell phone has become the favored channel of communication between teenagers and their friends, and young people also use it for diverse entertainment purposes.
   C. U.S. 8- to 18-year-olds devote an average of 7½ hours a day to entertainment media of all kinds.
   D. Television (pp. 629–632)
      1. Exposure to television is almost universal in the industrialized world.
      2. Widespread concern about television's negative impact on children and youths is warranted, but if TV programming were improved, television could be a powerful means of strengthening cognitive, emotional, and social development.
      3. How Much Television Do Children View?
         a. Each week, U.S. preschoolers spend about 10 to 18 hours, school-age children about 24 hours, and adolescents about 32 hours watching TV.
         b. Children vary in their attraction to television.
            (1) From early childhood on, boys watch slightly more TV than girls.
            (2) Low-SES, African-American, and Hispanic children are more frequent viewers.
            (3) Extensive TV viewing is associated with family and peer difficulties.
      4. Television and Social Learning
         a. Since the 1950s, researchers and public citizens have been concerned about television's influence on the attitudes and behaviors of young viewers.
         b. Aggression
            (1) In the United States, 57 percent of TV programs between 6 a.m. and 11 p.m. contain violent scenes, and violent content is 9 percent above average in children's programming.

(2) Reviewers of thousands of studies have concluded that television violence increases the likelihood of hostile thoughts and emotions and of verbally, physically, and relationally aggressive behavior.
(3) Longitudinal studies show that time spent watching TV in childhood and early adolescence predicted aggressive behavior in late adolescence and early adulthood.
(4) TV violence "hardens" children to aggression, making them more willing to tolerate it in others.
  c. Ethnic and Gender Stereotypes
    (1) Although educational programming for children is sensitive to issues of equity and diversity, commercial entertainment TV conveys ethnic and gender stereotypes.
    (2) African Americans, Hispanics, and other ethnic minorities are underrepresented, and women appear less often than men.
    (3) Minorities are more likely than whites to be depicted in secondary or lower-status roles.
    (4) Female characters tend to be portrayed as young, attractive, emotional, and victimized, and are often sexualized, shown in scanty clothing.
    (5) TV viewing is linked to gender-stereotyped attitudes and behaviors in children and adolescents.
  d. Consumerism
    (1) The marketing industry aimed at selling products to youths has exploded, exposing U.S. children and adolescents to tens of thousands of TV commercials each year.
    (2) Because many children's shows contain characters and props that are themselves products, the boundary between programs and commercials is blurred.
    (3) Preschoolers and young elementary school children seldom grasp the selling purpose of TV ads.
    (4) Research suggests that the heavy bombardment of children with advertising contributes to a variety of child and youth problems, including family stress and overweight and obesity.
    (5) The more adolescents are exposed to cigarette and alcohol ads, the more likely they are to smoke and drink.
  e. Prosocial Behavior
    (1) Television that includes acts of cooperating and comforting can increase children's prosocial behavior.
    (2) Much TV mixes prosocial and antisocial messages, yet prosocial programs promote children's kind acts only when they are free of violent content.
 5. Television, Academic Learning, and Imagination
  a. Since the early days of television, educators have been interested in its potential for strengthening academic and social skills, especially among low-SES children.
    (1) *Sesame Street,* especially, was created to foster children's learning.
    (2) *Sesame Street* is broadcast in 140 countries, making it the most widely viewed children's program in the world.
  b. Time devoted to watching children's educational programs is associated with gains in early literacy and math skills and to academic progress in elementary school.
  c. Watching slow-paced children's programs with easy-to-follow narratives leads to more elaborate make-believe play than viewing programs that simply provide information.
  d. Watching entertainment TV—especially heavy viewing—detracts from children's and adolescents' reading time, school success, and social experiences.
E. Computers, Cell Phones, and the Internet (pp. 632–635)
 1. Unlike TV, computers and cell phones offer *interactive* media forms, through a wide range of learning, entertainment, and communication tools.
 2. More than 90 percent of U.S. children and adolescents live in homes with one or more computers, 80 percent of which have an Internet connection.
 3. Virtually all U.S. public schools have integrated computers into their instructional programs.
 4 Recent survey evidence reveals that U.S. children and adolescents, on average, use the computer a half-hour a day for schoolwork and 1½ hours for pleasure.
 5. Computers and Academic Learning
  a. Computers can have rich educational benefits; in classrooms, children more often collaborate in computer activities than in other pursuits.
  b. When children use a computer for word processing, their written products tend to be longer and of higher quality.

c. Older children often use the computer for schoolwork, mostly to search the Web for information and to prepare written assignments—activities linked to improved academic achievement.
d. The learning advantages of computers raise concerns about a "digital divide" between SES and gender groups.
    (1) Poverty-stricken children are least likely to have home computers and Internet access.
    (2) By the end of elementary school, boys spend more time with computers than girls. In one large survey, many more boys than girls rated their computer skills as "excellent."
6. Video Games
    a. On average, U.S. school-age and adolescent boys spend nearly one-third of their computer time playing games—three times as much as girls.
    b. Speed-and-action video games foster selective attention and spatial skills in boys and girls alike. Extensive game playing, however, is negatively related to school performance.
    c. Playing violent computer games increases hostility and aggression, and video games also are full of ethnic and gender stereotypes.
7. Cell Phones, the Internet, and Communication
    a. Cell-phone texting has become the preferred means of electronic interaction between teenage friends, with cell calling second, followed by social networking sites.
    b. These forms of online interaction seem to support friendship closeness.
    c. Although mostly communicating with friends they know, adolescents are also drawn to meeting new people over the Internet.
    d. Through online ties, young people explore central adolescent issues.
    e. But online communication also poses dangers. For example, adolescents who lack protective networks may be overly trusting and may also find deceptions and harassment in Internet relationships particularly painful.
F. Regulating Media Use (pp. 635–636)
    1. In the United States, the First Amendment right to free speech has hampered efforts to regulate TV broadcasting.
        a. Instead, all programs must be rated for violent and sexual content, and all new TV sets are required to contain the V-chip, which allows parents to block undesired material.
        b. Parents bear most responsibility for regulating their children's exposure to inappropriate media content.
        c. Yet surveys indicate that the parents of 20 to 30 percent of U.S. preschoolers and about half of school-age children and early adolescents do not limit TV or computer use at home.
    2. The overwhelming majority of U.S. parents provide their child with a cell phone.
        a. Less than half of the parents limit the number of minutes their child may use the phone, and less than one-third restrict the number of text messages their child may send or receive.
        b. Yet when parents limit texting, adolescents less often report regretting a text message they sent.

III. SCHOOLING (pp. 637–650)
A. Research looking at schools as complex social systems provides important insights into how they powerfully affect development.
B. Class and Student Body Size (pp. 637–638)
    1. Being in small classes from kindergarten through third grade predicts higher academic achievement in later grades.
    2. Small class size is beneficial for several reasons.
        a. Teachers spend less time disciplining and more time teaching.
        b. Children who learn in smaller groups show better concentration and higher-quality class participation.
    3. In secondary school, the size of the student body profoundly affects school life: Members of smaller schools report more social support and caring as well as greater school engagement.
        a. Small secondary schools give students opportunities to enter a greater number and variety of activities and to hold more positions of leadership.
        b. Extracurricular participation focusing on the arts, community service, and vocational development promotes diverse aspects of adjustment.
        c. In small schools, potential dropouts are far more likely to join in activities.

C. Educational Philosophies (pp. 638–640)
   1. Traditional versus Constructivist Classrooms
      a. In the **traditional classroom,** the teacher is the sole authority for knowledge, rules, and decision making and does most of the talking.
         (1) Students are relatively passive—listening, responding when called on, and completing teacher-assigned tasks.
         (2) Student progress is evaluated by how well they keep pace with a uniform set of standards for their grade.
      b. In the **constructivist classroom,** students are encouraged to construct their own knowledge.
         (1) Many constructivist approaches are grounded in Piaget's view of children as active agents who reflect on and coordinate their own thoughts, rather than absorbing those of others.
         (2) Constructivist classrooms feature richly equipped learning centers, small groups and individuals solving self-chosen problems, and a teacher who guides and supports in response to children's needs.
         (3) Students are evaluated by considering their progress in relation to their own prior development.
      c. In the United States, constructivist classrooms gained in popularity in the 1960s and early 1970s, but then a "back to basics" movement arose, and classrooms returned to traditional instruction.
      d. This style, still prevalent today, has become increasingly pronounced as a result of the U.S. No Child Left Behind Act.
      e. Constructivist settings are associated with many other benefits, such as gains in critical thinking and more positive attitudes toward school.
      f. Yet despite grave concerns about its appropriateness, even preschool and kindergarten teachers have felt increased pressure to stress teacher-directed, academic training.
   2. New Philosophical Directions
      a. **Social-constructivist classrooms** represent new approaches to education grounded in Vygotsky's sociocultural theory.
      b. In these classrooms, children participate in a wide range of challenging activities with teachers and peers, with whom they jointly construct understandings.
      c. As children *appropriate* the knowledge and strategies generated from working together, they become competent, contributing members of their classroom community.
      d. Vygotsky's emphasis on the social origins of complex mental activities has inspired the following educational themes:
         (1) Teachers and children function as partners in learning.
         (2) Children gain experience with many types of symbolic communication in meaningful activities.
         (3) Teaching is adapted to each child's zone of proximal development.
      e. Another Vygotsky-based innovation makes collaboration a schoolwide value, transforming classrooms into **communities of learners.**
         (1) Teachers guide the overall process of learning, but no other distinction is made between adult and child contributors. All participate in joint endeavors.
         (2) Classroom activities often consist of long-term projects that address complex real-world problems.
D. School Transitions (pp. 640–642)
   1. The timing of transitions from one school level to the next affects students' achievement and adjustment.
   2. Early Adjustment to School
      a. In longitudinal research extending over the school year, the ease with which kindergartners made new friends and related to their teachers predicted cooperative participation in classroom activities and self-directed completion of learning tasks.
      b. Those with weak emotional self-regulation skills and argumentative, aggressive, or peer-avoidant styles established poor-quality relationships and made few friends.
      c. Some experts propose that readiness for kindergarten be assessed in terms of both academic skills and social skills.
   3. School Transitions in Adolescence
      a. In early adolescence, students typically move from an intimate elementary school classroom to a much larger secondary school where they must shift between classes.
      b. With each school change—from elementary to middle and then to high school—adolescents' grades decline partly due to tighter academic standards.
      c. The transition to secondary school often brings less personal attention.

d. Students rate their middle school learning experiences less favorably than their elementary school experiences, and many young people feel less academically competent and experience a drop in motivation.
e. Adolescents facing added strains at each transition, such as family disruption and low levels of parental involvement, are at greatest risk for self-esteem and academic difficulties.
f. The high school transition is particularly challenging for African-American and Hispanic students who move to a new school with substantially fewer same-ethnicity peers.
4. Helping Adolescents Adjust to School Transitions
a. School transitions often lead to environmental changes that fit poorly with adolescents' developmental needs.
(1) They disrupt close relationships with teachers at a time when adolescents need adult support.
(2) They reduce decision making and choice as the desire for autonomy is increasing.
b. Parental involvement, monitoring, autonomy granting, and emphasis on mastery rather than merely good grades are associated with better adjustment.
c. A "critical mass" of same-ethnicity peers helps teenagers feel socially accepted and reduces fear of out-group hostility.
d. Teenagers' perceptions of the sensitivity and flexibility of their school learning environments contribute substantially to successful school transitions.
E. Teacher–Student Interaction (p. 643)
1. Elementary and secondary school students describe good teachers as caring, helpful, and stimulating—behaviors associated with gains in students' motivation, achievement, and favorable peer relations.
2. But too many U.S. teachers emphasize repetitive drill over higher-level thinking.
3. Well-behaved, high-achieving students typically get more encouragement and praise, whereas unruly students have more conflicts with teachers and receive more criticism from them.
4. Overall, higher-SES students—who tend to be higher achieving and to have fewer learning and behavior problems—have more sensitive and supportive relationships with teachers.
5. Teachers' attitudes toward students can lead to **educational self-fulfilling prophecies,** whereby children may adopt teachers' positive or negative views and start to live up to them.
6. Teacher expectations have a greater impact on low achievers than high achievers.
F. Grouping Practices (pp. 643–645)
1. Grouping in Elementary School
a. *Homogeneous* groups or classes can be a potent source of self-fulfilling prophecies.
(1) Low-group students—who as early as first grade are disproportionately low-SES, minority, and male—get more drill on basic facts and skills, engage in less discussion, and progress at a slower pace.
(2) Gradually, they decline in academic self-esteem and motivation and fall further behind in achievement.
b. Magnet schools foster heterogeneous learning contexts; another way schools can increase the *heterogeneity* of student groups is to combine two or three adjacent grades.
c. In *multigrade classrooms,* academic achievement, self-esteem, and attitudes toward school are usually more favorable than in the single-grade arrangement.
2. Grouping in High School
a. By high school, some homogeneous grouping is unavoidable because certain aspects of education must dovetail with the young person's educational and vocational plans.
b. In the United States, high school students are counseled into college preparatory, vocational, or general education tracks, a system that perpetuates educational inequalities of earlier years.
c. Longitudinal research following U.S. students from eighth to twelfth grade reveals that assignment to a college track accelerates academic progress, whereas assignment to a vocational or general education track decelerates it.
d. Breaking out of a low academic track is difficult. Track or course enrollment is generally based on past performance, which is limited by placement history.
e. High school students are separated into academic and vocational tracks in virtually all industrialized nations.
f. By adolescence, SES differences in quality of education and academic achievement are greater in the United States than in most other industrialized countries.
G. Teaching Students with Special Needs (p. 646)
1. Children with Learning Difficulties
a. U.S. legislation mandates that schools place children who require special supports for learning in the "least restrictive" environments that meet their educational needs.

- b. In **inclusive classrooms,** students with learning difficulties learn alongside typical students in the regular educational setting for part or all of the school day.
- c. An increasing number of students experience *full inclusion*—full-time placement in regular classrooms.
- d. Some students in inclusive classrooms have *mild mental retardation*.
- e. The largest number—5 to 10 percent of school-age children—have **learning disabilities,** great difficulty with one or more aspects of learning, usually reading.

2. How Effective Are Inclusive Classrooms?
   - a. Some included students benefit academically, but many do not.
   - b. Achievement gains depend on both the severity of the disability and the support services available.
   - c. Children with disabilities are often rejected by regular-classroom peers, and those with mental retardation are overwhelmed by the social skills of their classmates; they cannot interact adeptly in a conversation or game.
   - d. Many children do best when they receive instruction in a resource room for part of the day and in the regular classroom for the remainder.
   - e. Special steps must be taken to promote positive peer relations in inclusive classrooms.

H. Parent–School Partnerships (p. 647)
   1. For all students, parent involvement in education, such as keeping tabs on the child's progress, promotes academic motivation and achievement.
   2. In low-income, high-risk neighborhoods, families face daily stresses that reduce their energy for school involvement, but stronger home–school links can relieve some of this stress.
   3. Schools can build parent–school partnerships by strengthening personal relationships between teachers and parents and showing parents how to support their child's education at home.

I. How Well-Educated Are American Young People? (pp. 647–650)
   1. Societal values, school resources, quality of teaching, and parental encouragement all affect children's learning.
   2. Cross-National Research on Academic Achievement
      - a. In international studies of reading, mathematics, and science achievement, young people in China, Korea, and Japan are consistently top performers.
      - b. Among Western nations, Australia, Canada, Finland, the Netherlands, and Switzerland are also in the top tier, but U.S. students typically perform at or below the international averages.
      - c. According to international comparisons, instruction in the United States is less challenging, more focused on absorbing facts, and less focused on high-level reasoning and critical thinking than in other countries.
      - d. Compared with top-achieving nations, the United States is far less equitable in the quality of education it provides to its low-income and ethnic minority students.
      - e. Finnish education is grounded in equal opportunity for all—a policy that has nearly eliminated SES variations in achievement.
      - f. Research on learning environments in Asian nations, such as Japan, Korea, and Taiwan, highlights social forces that foster strong student learning, including the cultural valuing of effort.
   3. Vocational Preparation of Non-College-Bound Adolescents
      - a. The one-third of U.S. young people who graduate from high school without plans to go to college are more likely to find employment than those who drop out.
      - b. However, changes in the labor market over the past several decades have drastically reduced viable work opportunities for high school graduates.
      - c. About 20 percent of recent U.S. high school graduates who do not continue their education are unemployed.
      - d. In high school, about one-fourth of U.S. adolescents are employed, typically at low-level jobs. A heavy commitment to such jobs is harmful.
      - e. In contrast, participation in work–study programs or other jobs that provide academic and vocational learning opportunities is related to positive school and work attitudes, achievement, and reduced delinquency.
      - f. Yet high-quality vocational preparation for non-college-bound U.S. adolescents is scarce.
      - g. Unlike some European nations—such as Germany, which has a successful system—the United States has no widespread training systems to prepare youths for skilled business and industrial occupations and manual trades.

LECTURE ENHANCEMENTS

LECTURE ENHANCEMENT 15.1
Does Interparental Conflict Contribute to Quality of Early Peer Relations? (pp. 611–612)

Time: 10–15 minutes

Objective: To examine the relationship between interparental conflict and quality of early peer relations.

To determine whether interparental conflict contributes to early peer relationships, David and Murphy (2008) recruited 62 preschoolers from middle-class, two-parent households. The researchers collected the following information:

(1) Research assistants conducted structured observations of participants during classroom free play and playground time. Each child was observed daily over the course of several weeks. The research assistants used a 5-point scale to code the amount of peer interaction (1 = no peer interactions; 5 = active physical/verbal exchange) for virtually all of the observation. They also coded problematic peer relations, including hostility toward others, frequency of negative affect (e.g., facial and verbal cues and body postures), and provoking events, such as arguing, hitting, or giving dirty looks.

(2) Teachers completed a measure of social competence that assesses children's popularity with peers and overall social skills. Each item on the scale contains two opposing statements. For example, "This child finds it hard to make friends," or "For this child, it's pretty easy to make friends."

(3) To measure interparental conflict (IPC), mothers completed the Conflict and Problem-Solving Scales (CPS) based on their relationship with their current husband. The CPS assesses the frequency of minor ("spats") and major ("big fights") conflicts over the past year. For example: On a scale of 1 to 6 (1 = once a year or less; 6 = just about every day), "My partner and I have big fights." Mothers were also asked about how often they yell, make accusations, and insult their spouse during arguments.

(4) Teachers filled out a temperament scale that measured 15 dimensions of temperament. For the purposes of this study, the researchers were primarily interested in two aspects of temperament—effortful control and positive emotionality.

Results indicated that IPC by itself did not necessarily predict problematic peer relations. However, effortful control moderated the relationship between IPC and peer difficulties. Specifically, children who were exposed to high levels of IPC and who scored low on effortful control had low rates of peer interaction and when they did interact with peers, were often hostile, demonstrated negative affect, and engaged in low rates of positive emotionality. In contrast, children who were exposed to high levels of IPC but also scored high in effortful control tended to have high rates of peer interaction and their interactions were generally positive. According to David and Murphy, one explanation for the moderating role of effortful control is that children low in emotional regulation are easily aroused during stressful situations, such as interparental or peer conflict. Over time, these children tend to have difficulty interpreting and responding appropriately to social situations, often acting out when overwhelmed.

In addition to effortful control, gender moderated the relationship between IPC and peer difficulties. High IPC predicted low rates of peer interaction for girls but predicted high rates of peer interaction for boys. This suggests that when exposed to IPC, girls are more likely to withdraw from social situations, whereas boys are likely to seek out peers. Socialization differences between boys and girls—boys' tendency toward agency and self-interest and girls' tendency toward interpersonal connectedness—may explain this gender difference. During stressful situations, girls may be more likely to withdraw as a way of avoiding negative peer interactions. In contrast, boys spend more time in large peer groups than girls, and boys from high conflict homes may be especially likely to seek out peers as a source of comfort. However, more research is needed to verify these interpretations.

Have students return to Chapter 1 and review the concept of resilience (page 10). What factors within the child and his or her environment might help buffer against the effects of high interparental conflict? How might teachers and other adults in the child's life help foster resilience?

David, K. M., & Murphy, B. C. (2008). Interparental conflict and preschoolers' peer relations: The moderating roles of temperament and gender. *Social Development, 16,* 1–23.

LECTURE ENHANCEMENT 15.2
The Effects of Electronic Media on Children's Achievement and Behavior (pp. 629–636)

Time: 10–15 minutes

Objective: To extend existing research on the effects of electronic media on children's academic achievement and behavior.

To extend existing research on the effects of electronic media on children's academic achievement and behavior, Hofferth (2010) used existing data on 1,226 6- to 12-year-olds who were participating in the Panel Study of Income Dynamics. Time 1 data was collected when participants were between the ages of 6 and 12 years. Time 2 data was collected when participants were between the ages of 12 and 18 years.

- At Time 1 and Time 2, participants or their parents were asked to complete a time diary, which focused on children's activities over a 24-hour period. The researchers were interested in the amount of time children spent sleeping, watching TV, using a computer, studying, reading, playing video games, playing outdoors, participating in sports, and non-video game/non-computer playing. Time spent at school was used to adjust for non-school leisure time.
- At Time 1 and Time 2, parents completed the Behavior Problems Index, which measures internalizing (fearful, anxious, sad, withdrawn) and externalizing (impulsive, aggressive, moody, disobedient) disorders.
- At Time 1 and Time 2, participants were administered three achievement subtests—letter–word identification (measures the ability to identify and respond to letters and words), passage comprehension (measures reading comprehension), and applied problems (measures the ability to analyze and solve numerical problems).

Results indicated that participants spent the majority of their free time watching TV, which increased from 13 hours per week at Time 1 to 14 hours per week at Time 2. When using the computer, the majority of children's time was spent playing games, followed by communications (such as e-mail and instant messaging). Although boys and girls spent similar amounts of time on the computer, boys devoted most of their time to game playing, whereas girls spent the majority of their time in communications. Between Time 1 and Time 2, non-video game/non-computer time decreased, while time spent on computers or playing video games increased by 12 percent. Participants devoted the least amount of their computer time to studying or homework.

Results also indicated that low to moderate computer use at Time 1 was positively related to reading and applied problem solving at Time 2, particularly for girls. According to Hofferth, girls are more likely to use the computer for educational games, whereas boys more often spend their computer time playing strategy or adventure games. Low to moderate video game playing also predicted higher scores on applied problem solving. When looking at the relationship between media use and behavior problems, increased computer use in girls predicted lower rates of internalizing problems, whereas increased video game play predicted higher rates of externalizing problems. This finding makes sense when considering how boys and girls spend their media time. Girls are more likely to spend their time engaged in social networking, which can be a protective factor against anxiety and depression. In contrast, boys are more likely to spend their time playing violent video games, which can lead to aggression, moodiness, and disobedience. As noted in the text, low to moderate rates of media consumption can lead to positive academic and behavioral outcomes, whereas high rates of media consumption can be detrimental to children's learning and emotional well-being.

What are some strategies that adults can use to protect children from the undesirable effects of TV and computer use?

Hofferth, S. L. (2010). Home media and children's achievement and behavior. *Child Development, 81,* 1598–1619.

LECTURE ENHANCEMENT 15.3
Effortful Control, Quality of Social Relationships, Classroom Participation, and Academic Competence in School-Age Children (pp. 637–647)

Time: 10–15 minutes

Objective: To examine the relationship between effortful control, quality of social relationships, classroom participation, and academic competence in school-age children.

To extend existing research on factors that contribute to academic competence in school-age children, Valiente, Lemery-Chalfant, and Reiser (2008) recruited 264 7- to 12-year-olds and collected the following information:

(1) Parents and children completed a measure of effortful control that focused on attention shifting, activation control, and inhibitory control. Sample questions included:

- Attention shifting: "I am [Your child is] good at keeping track of several different things that are happening around me [him/her]."
- Activation control: "If I have [your child has] a hard assignment to do, I get [he/she gets] started right away."
- Inhibitory control: "When someone tells me [your child] to stop doing something, it is easy for me [him/her] to stop."

(2) Teachers and children completed the Student–Teacher Relationship Scale, which assesses closeness and conflict between teachers and students.

(3) Parents and teachers completed the Perceived Competence Scale for Children, which measures socially appropriate behavior (e.g., "This child is usually well-behaved.") and popularity (e.g., "This child has a lot of friends.").

(4) Teachers completed the Teacher Rating Scale of School Adjustment, which focuses on children's classroom participation. For example: On a scale of 0 to 2 (0 = doesn't apply; 2 = certainly applies), "This child follows instructions." "This child challenges him/herself to do well in school."

(5) To assess academic competence, the researchers collected school records at the end of the school year, including tardies, absences, and fall and spring grade point averages (GPAs).

Findings indicated that effortful control was positively related to students' grades and negatively related to student absences. Children who scored high in effortful control also had more positive relationships with teachers, were rated higher in social competence, and participated more in classroom activities than children who scored low in effortful control. Based on the data analyses, it seems that quality of teacher–child relationships, social competence, and classroom participation may mediate the relationship between effortful control and GPA. According to Valiente, Lemery-Chalfant, and Reiser, one reason children high in effortful control perform well in school is because they have favorable social relationships, both with teachers and peers. These children are also more likely to enjoy school and participate actively in class, which contributes to higher achievement and fewer absences.

Valiente, C., Lemery-Chalfant, K., & Reiser, M. (2008). Prediction of children's academic competence from their effortful control, relationships, and classroom participation. *Journal of Educational Psychology, 100*, 67–77.

LECTURE ENHANCEMENT 15.4
School Recess and Classroom Behavior (p. 639)

Time: 5–10 minutes

Objective: To examine the relationship between school recess and classroom behavior in school-age children.

As noted in the text, although recess has diminished or disappeared in many U.S. elementary schools, children with access to recess periods are more attentive and enjoy school more than agemates who do not have daily recess. To determine how many U.S. school-age children actually have access to recess and to compare the classroom behavior of those with and without daily recess, Barros, Silver, and Stein (2009) used existing data on 11,624 third graders who were participating in the Early Childhood Longitudinal Study (ECLS). The ECLS focuses on the educational experiences of children from kindergarten through middle school. The researchers collected the following information:

(1) Teachers completed a questionnaire about the number of days per week and times per day students had recess and the duration of each recess period.

(2) Using a 5-point scale, teachers rated children's classroom behavior (1 = misbehaves very frequently and is almost always difficult to handle; 5 = behaves exceptionally well).

(3) Demographic information, school characteristics (e.g., private vs. public, school size, location), and classroom characteristics (e.g., number of students, proportion of students eligible for free lunch) were available from the ECLS.

Results indicated that 30 percent of the participants had no access to recess. Children without scheduled recess were more likely to be African American or Hispanic, to live in a medium- or large-sized city, to come from low-SES backgrounds, and to attend public rather than private schools. Barros, Silver, and Stein point out that children from disadvantaged backgrounds may benefit especially from recess. These children often live in unsafe neighborhoods, and recess may be one of the few opportunities they have to acquire social skills from playing with other children. Teacher ratings of classroom behavior showed that even 15 minutes of daily recess contributed to better classroom behavior. That is, compared to children who received no recess, those who had at least a 15-minute break during the day were more attentive and less disruptive in the classroom. Thus, these results provide additional evidence that recess has important consequences for classroom learning and behavior.

According to the text, how does recess contribute to physical, academic, and social skills in school-age children? What factors have led to the decline in recess in U.S. schools?

Barros, R. M., Silver, E. J., & Stein, R. E. (2009). School recess and group classroom behavior. *Pediatrics, 123,* 431–436.

LEARNING ACTIVITIES

LEARNING ACTIVITY 15.1
Development of Peer Sociability: Fostering Preschoolers' Peer Relations (pp. 611–613)

Have students form small groups and respond to the following scenario:

> Clint and Adrianne are the parents of 3-year-old Morgan. They currently live in the country, where Morgan rarely has opportunities to interact with other children. Clint and Adrianne are not sure if they should arrange a play group for Morgan or if they should simply wait until Morgan is old enough for kindergarten. On the basis of research presented in the text, how would you respond to Clint and Adrianne's concern? What are the benefits of peer relations during the preschool years?

LEARNING ACTIVITY 15.2
Interviewing a School-Age Child or an Adolescent About Friendship (pp. 613–618)

Ask students to interview a school-age child or an adolescent about his or her concept of friendship, using the following questions: "Who is your best friend?" "Why is [child's name] your best friend?" "How long have you and [child's name] been friends?" "Is there a reason you like [child's name] more than anyone else?" Students should record the child's/adolescent's answers and compare them to research in the text. For example, did the individual mention personal qualities and trust? Does the child's/adolescent's best friend share similar interests? Explain. Spend some class time discussing students' findings. Did children and adolescents emphasize different qualities?

LEARNING ACTIVITY 15.3
Matching: Peer Acceptance and Peer Groups (pp. 618–625)

Present the following activity as a quiz or an in-class assignment.

Directions: Match each of the following terms with its description.

Terms:
_____ 1. Peer acceptance
_____ 2. Popular-prosocial children
_____ 3. Popular-antisocial children
_____ 4. Rejected-aggressive children
_____ 5. Rejected-withdrawn children
_____ 6. Peer victimization
_____ 7. Peer groups
_____ 8. Cliques
_____ 9. Crowd

Descriptions:

A. A subtype of popular children, which emerges in late childhood and early adolescence, and consists of aggressive youngsters.
B. Collectives that generate unique values and standards for behavior and a social structure of leaders and followers.
C. Children who show severe conduct problems—high rates of conflict, physical and relational aggression, and hyperactive, inattentive, and impulsive behavior.
D. Often several cliques with similar values form a larger, more loosely organized group.
E. Refers to likability—the extent to which a child is viewed by agemates, such as classmates, as a worthy social partner.
F. Groups of five to eight members who are friends and, therefore, tend to resemble one another in family background, attitudes, values, and interests.
G. The majority of popular children combine academic and social competence.
H. A subgroup of rejected children who are passive and socially awkward.
I. A particularly destructive form of interaction in which certain children become targets of physical attacks or other forms of abuse.

Answers:

1. E
2. G
3. A
4. C
5. H
6. I
7. B
8. F
9. D

LEARNING ACTIVITY 15.4
Observing Adolescent Peer Groups (pp. 622–625)

Suggest that students visit a typical teenage gathering place, such as a mall, arcade, fast-food restaurant, or movie theater, and answer the following questions: Are peer groups large or small? Same-sex or mixed? Are there differences in the ways boys and girls interact? How close do same-sex groups stand? How about mixed-sex groups? Is there anything noteworthy about group members' dress? What age differences are apparent? Once students have completed this activity, ask them to share some of their observations in class.

LEARNING ACTIVITY 15.5
Interviewing College-Age Students About Experiences with Peer Pressure (pp. 625–627)

Have students interview two or three college-age friends about past experiences with peer pressure. Students can use the following questions for their interviews:

(1) Did you encounter peer pressure in adolescence? If so, briefly describe what kinds of peer pressure you experienced.
(2) As a teenager, did your friends ever encourage you to engage in antisocial acts? If so, how did you handle the pressure?
(3) Did you ever give in to peer pressure? If so, why? What, if any, consequences did you experience as a result? For instance, how did your parents and friends react?
(4) Did you ever experience peer pressure that went against your personal beliefs or family values? If so, how did you handle it?

After students complete their interviews, ask them to compare answers with research presented in the text. For example, did respondents primarily encounter peer pressure in early adolescence? Did friends discourage antisocial behavior? Did respondents resist peer pressures that went against their personal beliefs and family values?

Chapter 15 Peers, Media, and Schooling

LEARNING ACTIVITY 15.6
Young Children's Exposure to Electronic Media (pp. 629–636)

Engage students in a debate about young children's exposure to electronic media. For instance, what are the pros and cons of exposure to television, computers, and video games? In students' opinion, should young children have access to electronic media? Why or why not? For students who support the use of electronic media with young children, how much exposure is too much?

LEARNING ACTIVITY 15.7
Internet Friendships (pp. 634–635)

Have students interview two or three college-age friends about using the Internet to meet new people. The following questions may be helpful:
    (1) How do you feel about meeting new people on the Internet?
    (2) Have you ever met a friend or romantic partner on the Internet? If so, are you still in contact with that person? Was the individual honest and straightforward about him- or herself? Explain.
    (3) If you have met someone on the Internet, did you feel safe and supported by this person? Why or why not?
    (4) If you have not used the Internet to meet new people, will you do so in the future? Why or why not?
    (5) If you have used the Internet to meet new people, will you continue to do so in the future? Why or why not?
    (6) What are the benefits of meeting new people on the Internet? What are some potential risks?

After completing this activity, ask students to bring the interviews to class for discussion. For example, did the majority of respondents indicate that they had met new people on the Internet? Did they experience any problems with their online friend or romantic partner? For respondents who have never used the Internet to meet new people, what reasons did they give for this decision? Did the respondents seem to understand the potential dangers of meeting people online? Were students surprised by any of the findings?

LEARNING ACTIVITY 15.8
Observing in a Junior High or High School Classroom (pp. 637–645)

If possible, arrange for small groups of students to observe for a 1- to 2-hour period in a junior high or high school classroom. Students should indicate whether or not the following characteristics, which support academic and social learning, were present:
    (1) Small class size
    (2) Educational philosophy
    (3) Challenging learning activities
    (4) Learning activities that involve communication and collaboration
    (5) Teachers who promote high-level thinking
    (6) Teachers who are responsive and encouraging

Using examples from their observation and research in the text, how would students rate the quality of the classroom environment? How did their observations compare to their own schooling experiences?

LEARNING ACTIVITY 15.9
Helping Students Adjust to School Transitions (pp. 640–642)

Present the following scenario to students:

> You have been invited to speak at a local school district about school transitions. Educators from elementary schools, middle schools, and high schools will be present for your discussion. What information will you include in your presentation? What should educators know about the effects of school transitions? How can schools help students adjust to school transitions? What educational practices or school characteristics tend to undermine student adjustment following a transition?

ASK YOURSELF . . .

REVIEW: Among children who spend much time playing alone, what factors distinguish those who are likely to have adjustment difficulties from those who are well-adjusted and socially skilled? (p. 609)

Only certain types of nonsocial activity—aimless wandering, hovering near peers, and functional play involving immature, repetitive motor action—are linked to adjustment difficulties. Preschoolers who behave reticently, by watching peers without playing, are usually temperamentally inhibited—high in social fearfulness. And those who engage in solitary, repetitive behavior (banging blocks, making a doll jump up and down) tend to be immature, impulsive youngsters who find it difficult to regulate anger or aggression. Both reticent and impulsive children, especially boys, experience peer ostracism.

But other preschoolers with low rates of peer interaction are not socially anxious or impulsive. They simply prefer to play alone, and their solitary activities are positive and constructive. Teachers encourage such play by setting out art materials, books, puzzles, and building toys. Children who spend much time at these activities are usually well-adjusted youngsters who, when they do play with peers, show socially skilled behavior.

CONNECT: What aspects of parent–child interaction probably account for the relationship between attachment security and children's peer sociability? (*Hint:* See Chapter 10, pages 434 and 437). (pp. 608, 611–612)

Though limited, peer sociability is already present in the first two years and is promoted by the early caregiver–child bond. From interacting with sensitive adults, babies learn how to send and interpret emotional signals in their first peer associations. Consistent with this idea, toddlers who have a warm parental relationship engage in more positive and extended peer exchanges. These children, in turn, show more socially competent behavior as preschoolers.

Secure attachments to parents are linked to more responsive, harmonious peer interactions, larger peer networks, and warmer, more supportive friendships throughout childhood and adolescence. The sensitive, emotionally expressive parental communication that contributes to attachment security may be responsible. In one study, researchers observed parent–child conversations and rated them for the strength of the mother–child bond, as indicated by exchanges of positive emotion and parental sensitivity to the child's statements and feelings. Kindergartners who were more emotionally "connected" to their mothers displayed more empathy and prosocial behavior toward their classmates. This empathic orientation, in turn, was linked to more positive peer ties.

Parent–child play seems particularly effective for promoting peer interaction skills. During play, parents interact with their child on a "level playing field," as peers do. Highly involved, emotionally positive, and cooperative play between parents and preschoolers is associated with more positive peer relations.

APPLY: Three-year-old Ben lives in the country, with no other preschoolers nearby. His parents wonder whether it is worth driving Ben into town once a week to participate in a peer play group. What advice would you give Ben's parents, and why? (pp. 611–612)

Preschoolers whose parents frequently arrange informal peer play activities tend to have larger peer networks and to be more socially skilled. In providing play opportunities, parents show children how to initiate peer contacts and encourage them to be good "hosts" who consider their playmates' needs. Peer play activities also give parents an opportunity to influence children's peer interaction skills by offering guidance on how to act toward others. Children's skill at managing conflict, discouraging teasing, and entering a play group is associated with social competence and peer acceptance. Because Ben lives in an area where he has no social contact with peers, his parents should enroll him in the peer play group to increase his social competence.

REFLECT: What did your parents do, directly and indirectly, that might have influenced your peer relationships in childhood and adolescence? (pp. 611–612)

This is an open-ended question with no right or wrong answer.

REVIEW: Describe unique qualities of interaction between close friends, and explain how they contribute to development. (p. 615)

At all ages, friends have special ways of interacting. Preschoolers, for example, offer twice as much reinforcement—greetings, praise, and compliance—to children they identify as friends, and they also receive more from them. In middle childhood, a more mature understanding of friendship seems to spark greater prosocial behavior between friends. When working on a task together, school-age friends help, share, refer to each other's comments, and spend more time focused than preschool friends do. Cooperation, generosity, mutual affirmation, and self-disclosure continue to rise into adolescence—trends

Chapter 15 Peers, Media, and Schooling

that may reflect greater effort and skill at preserving the relationship and increased sensitivity to a friend's needs. Adolescents are also less possessive of friends than they were in childhood, recognizing that their friends need a degree of autonomy, just as they themselves do.

Friends not only behave more prosocially but also disagree and compete with each other more than nonfriends. Because children regard friendship as based on equality, they seem especially concerned about losing a contest to a friend. Also, when children hold differing opinions, friends are more likely to voice them. At the same time, school-age and adolescent friends use negotiation to resolve conflicts more often than nonfriends do. Friends seem to realize that close relationships can survive disagreements if both parties are secure in their liking for one another. Clearly, friendship provides an important context in which children learn to tolerate criticism and resolve disputes.

REVIEW: Why are aggressive children's friendships likely to magnify their antisocial behavior? (p. 616)

When aggressive children make friends, the relationship is often riddled with hostile interaction and is at risk for breakup, especially when just one member of the pair is aggressive. Aggressive girls' friendships are high in self-disclosure but full of relational hostility, including jealousy, conflict, and betrayal. Friendships between aggressive boys involve frequent expressions of anger, coercive statements, physical attacks, and enticements to rule-breaking behavior, as well as relational aggression. These findings indicate that the social problems of aggressive children operate within their closest peer ties.

CONNECT: Cite similarities in the development of self-concept, described in Chapter 11 (pages 456, 458), and ideas about friendship. Explain how the discussion among Stu, Pete, Jessamyn, and Katy in the introduction to this chapter reflects friendship expectations that typically emerge at adolescence. (pp. 614–616)

As their self-concepts develop, school-age children begin to make frequent social comparisons—judgments of their own appearance, abilities, and behavior in relation to those of others. Also, children look to more people for information about themselves, and their self-descriptions include frequent references to social groups. In adolescence, self-concept becomes increasingly vested in feedback from close friends.

Similarly, during the school years, children's concepts of friendship become more complex and psychologically based. Friendship is no longer just a matter of having a handy playmate but, rather, is a mutually agreed-on relationship in which children like each other's personal qualities and respond to each other's needs and desires. In addition, children select friends who share similar personality traits and levels of peer popularity and academic achievement.

The friendships described in the introduction illustrate how adolescents choose their friends on the basis of similar interests and personality traits. As children mature, they begin looking past superficial traits, such as popularity, and seek friends who are similar to themselves, as indicated in Jessamyn's comment about losing interest in her friends from fifth grade who tried too hard to be popular. In addition, as revealed by Pete's comment that "a friend has to be somebody who makes you feel good about yourself," adolescents' concepts of friendship focus on psychological qualities—in particular, intimacy. Pete would not be likely to form a close friendship with someone who wasn't caring and responsive to his needs.

APPLY: Ralph, a high school junior of Irish Catholic background, befriended Jonathan, a Chinese-American of Buddhist faith. Both boys are from middle-SES homes and are good students. Why might Ralph seek out a friend both similar to and different from himself? (pp. 616–617)

The value adolescents attach to feeling "in sync" with their friends suggests that friends will become increasingly similar in attitudes and values with age. Actually, the attributes on which friends are most alike throughout childhood and adolescence are age, sex, ethnicity, and SES. But from middle childhood on, friends also resemble one another in personality, popularity, academic achievement, prosocial behavior, and judgments of other people. And in adolescence, friends tend to be alike in identity status, educational aspirations, political beliefs, and willingness to try drugs and engage in lawbreaking acts. Nevertheless, as teenagers enter a wider range of school and community settings, they also choose some friends who differ from themselves. The task of forging a personal identity at times leads adolescents to befriend peers with differing attitudes and values, as a means of exploring new perspectives within the security of compatible relationships. Furthermore, teenagers often judge commonality in certain attributes as more important than in others. In the case of Ralph and Jonathan, both boys share some similar attributes: They are from middle-SES homes and are good students. Commonality in these attributes may be particularly important to them, while their differences in ethnicity and religious faith allow them to explore new perspectives in these areas. Children and adolescents are more likely to form friendships with agemates of different ethnicities if, like Ralph and Jonathan, they attend the same, ethnically diverse school and live in an integrated neighborhood. Through such friendships, these young people come to view ethnically different peers as individuals rather than through the lens of stereotypes.

REVIEW: Why are rejected children at risk for maladjustment? What experiences with peers probably contribute to their serious, long-term adjustment problems? (pp. 619–620)

Rejected children, especially, are anxious, unhappy, disruptive, poorly achieving children with low self-esteem. Both teachers and parents view them as having a wide range of emotional and social problems. Peer rejection in middle childhood is also strongly associated with poor school performance, absenteeism, dropping out, substance abuse, depression, antisocial behavior, and delinquency in adolescence and with criminality in early adulthood.

Rejected-aggressive children are usually deficient perspective takers, misinterpreting the innocent behaviors of peers as hostile, blaming others for their social difficulties, and acting on their angry feelings. Unlike popular-aggressive children, who use aggression skillfully to attain status, rejected-aggressive children display blatantly hostile, acting-out behavior, which triggers scorn and avoidance in their peers. Rejected-withdrawn children, a smaller subgroup, are passive, socially awkward, and overwhelmed by social anxiety. They hold negative expectations for treatment by peers and fear being scorned and attacked. Like their aggressive counterparts, they typically feel like retaliating rather than compromising in peer conflicts, although they less often act on those feelings. Rejected children are excluded by peers as early as kindergarten. Rejection, in turn, further impairs their biased social information processing, heightening their hostility. Soon, rejected children's classroom participation declines, their feelings of loneliness and depression rise, their academic achievement falters, and they want to avoid school. Most have few friends, and some have none—a circumstance linked to low self-esteem, mistrust of peers, and severe adjustment difficulties.

CONNECT: Cite parenting influences on children's social skills, and explain why interventions that focus only on the rejected child are unlikely to produce lasting changes in peer acceptance (see page 619). What changes in parent–child relationships are probably necessary? (pp. 620, 622)

Parents influence children's social skills both directly, through attempts to influence children's peer relations, and indirectly, through their child-rearing practices and play behaviors. For instance, because young children are limited in their ability to find playmates, they depend on parents to help them establish rewarding peer associations. Preschoolers whose parents frequently arrange informal peer contact tend to have larger social networks and to be more socially skilled. Parents also influence children's social relations by offering guidance on how to act toward others. Furthermore, inductive discipline and authoritative parenting offer a firm foundation for competence in relating to agemates.

Because rejected children's socially incompetent behaviors often originate in a poor fit between the child's temperament and parenting practices, interventions that focus on the child alone may not be sufficient. If the quality of parent–child interaction does not change, rejected children may soon return to their old behavior patterns. Children with a difficult temperament benefit from warm, accepting parenting that makes firm but reasonable demands for behavior, and such children may benefit especially from authoritative child rearing that includes coaching, modeling, and reinforcing positive social skills.

APPLY: Each day on the school bus and during recess, Jodee—a quiet, sensitive fifth grader—was pushed, pelted with gravel, and showered with insults by her classmates. Following the advice of her well-meaning parents, she tried to ignore her tormentors. What factors made Jodee susceptible to peer victimization? How can it be prevented? (p. 621)

About 25 percent of children are repeatedly victimized, and these chronic victims tend to have certain characteristics in common. They are passive when active behavior is expected. On the playground, they hang around chatting or wander on their own. When bullied, they give in, cry, and assume defensive postures. Biologically based traits—an inhibited temperament and a frail physical appearance—contribute to victimization. In Jodee's case, her lack of response to her tormentors may lead her bullying peers to view her as "easy prey."

Interventions that change victimized children's negative opinions of themselves and that teach them to respond in nonreinforcing ways to their attackers are helpful. Another way to assist children like Jodee is to help them acquire the social skills needed to form and maintain a gratifying friendship. When children have a close friend whom they can turn to for help, bullying episodes end quickly. But although modifying victimized children's behavior can help, this does not mean that they are to blame for their abuse. The best way to reduce bullying is to change youth environments, promoting prosocial attitudes and behaviors, and enlisting young people's cooperation. Effective approaches include developing school and community codes against bullying, teaching peer bystanders to intervene, enlisting parents' assistance in changing bullies' behaviors, strengthening adult supervision of high-bullying areas in schools, and (if necessary) moving socially prominent bullies to another class or school.

REFLECT: Name several classmates from your high school days who were high in *social prominence*—admired by many peers. Describe these classmates' attributes. Were they also *socially preferred*—that is, peers whom you and your friends liked personally? Explain. (p. 618)

This is an open-ended question with no right or wrong answer.

REVIEW: Describe the distinct positive functions of friendships, cliques, and crowds. What factors lead some friendships and peer-group ties to be harmful? (pp. 622–624)

Whereas friendships contribute to the development of trust, sensitivity, and intimacy, peer groups provide practice in cooperation, leadership, followership, and loyalty to collective goals. *Cliques* are groups of about five to eight members who are friends and, therefore, usually resemble one another in family background, attitudes, values, and interests. For girls, the clique is a context for expressing emotional closeness and predicts academic and social competence. Among Western adolescents attending high schools with complex social structures, several cliques with similar values may form a larger, more loosely organized group called a *crowd*. Crowd membership is based on reputation and stereotype, granting the adolescent an identity within the larger social structure of the school. In mid-adolescence, mixed-sex cliques form, providing boys and girls with models for how to interact with the other sex and a chance to do so without having to be intimate. By late adolescence, both cliques and crowds decline in importance as adolescents settle on personal values and goals.

Peer group experiences give children opportunities to experiment with and learn about the functioning of social organizations. However, peer groups—at the instigation of their leaders, who can be skillfully aggressive—frequently oust no-longer-"respected" children. Some of these cast-outs, whose own previous hostility toward outsiders reduces their chances of being included elsewhere, turn to other low-status peers with poor social skills. Socially anxious children, when ousted, often become increasingly peer-avoidant and thus more isolated. In either case, opportunities to learn socially competent behavior diminish.

CONNECT: How might gender intensification, discussed on page 550 in Chapter 13, contribute to the shallow quality of early adolescent dating relationships? (pp. 624–625)

Gender intensification in early adolescence involves increased conformity to gender stereotypes in attitudes and behavior and movement toward a more traditional gender identity. When young people start to date, they typically mention recreation and achieving peer status as reasons for dating and often become more gender-typed as a way of increasing their attractiveness. Relationships based on these criteria tend to be shallow and stereotyped. In later adolescence, gender intensification declines as young people become ready for greater psychological intimacy based on self-understanding. As a result, older teens are more likely than early adolescents to seek out dating partners who offer companionship, affection, and social support.

APPLY: Thirteen-year-old Mattie's parents are warm, firm in their expectations, and consistent in monitoring her activities. Is Mattie likely to succumb to unfavorable peer pressure? Explain. (pp. 625–627)

Because of greater concern with what their friends think of them, early adolescents like Mattie are more likely than either younger or older individuals to give in to peer pressure. However, Mattie's parents have an authoritative child-rearing style, characterized by warmth and consistency in monitoring her activities. Authoritative child rearing is related to resistance to peer pressure. Teenagers whose parents are supportive and exert appropriate oversight respect their parents and, therefore, usually follow their rules and consider their advice. Therefore, it is unlikely that Mattie will succumb to unfavorable peer pressure.

REFLECT: How did family experiences influence your crowd membership in high school? How did your crowd membership influence your behavior? (pp. 623–624)

This is an open-ended question with no right or wrong answer.

REVIEW: Describe research findings on the academic and social benefits of television and computer use. (pp. 632–635)

Time devoted to watching children's educational programs is associated with gains in early literacy and math skills and to academic progress in elementary school. Consistent with these findings, one study reported a link between preschool viewing of *Sesame Street* and other similar educational programs and getting higher grades, reading more books, and placing more value on achievement in high school. Watching children's programs with slow-paced action and easy-to-follow narratives, such as *Arthur, The Magic School Bus,* and *Wishbone,* leads to more elaborate make-believe play in early childhood and to greater recall of program content and gains in vocabulary and reading skills in the early elementary school grades than viewing programs that simply provide information.

Computers can also have rich educational benefits. In classrooms, small groups often gather around computers, and children more often collaborate in computer activities than in other pursuits. In childhood and adolescence, nongame computer use is associated with literacy progress. Using the computer for word processing enables children to write freely, experimenting with letters and words without having to struggle with handwriting. Because they can revise their text's meaning and style and also check their spelling, they worry less about making mistakes. As a result, their written products tend to be longer and of higher quality. And as children get older, they increasingly use the computer for schoolwork, mostly to search the Web for information needed for school projects and to prepare written assignments—activities linked to improved academic achievement.

In terms of social benefits, television that includes acts of cooperating, helping, and comforting can increase children's prosocial behavior. In one study, when second to sixth graders were asked to name their favorite educational TV shows and say what they learned from them, the children not only named many prosocial programs but also accurately described the lessons the programs conveyed.

Adolescents frequently use the Internet to communicate with friends. Girls' online interactions seem to support friendship closeness. In several studies, as amount of online messaging between preexisting friends increased, so did young people's perceptions of intimacy in the relationship and sense of well-being. Although mostly communicating with friends they know, adolescents are also drawn to meeting new people over the Internet. Nearly three-fourths of U.S. teenagers now use social networking sites such as MySpace and Facebook, along with blogs, message boards, and chat rooms. Through these online ties, young people explore central adolescent issues—sexuality, challenges in parent and peer relationships, and identity issues, including attitudes and values—in contexts that grant anonymity and, therefore, may feel less threatening than similar conversations in the real world. Online interactions with strangers also offer some teenagers vital sources of support. Socially anxious youths, for example, may engage in Internet communication to relieve loneliness while practicing and improving their social skills. And teenagers suffering from depression, eating disorders, and other problems can go to message boards where participants provide informal mutual assistance, including a sense of group belonging and acceptance.

APPLY: Thirteen-year-old Tommy spends hours each afternoon surfing the Web, instant messaging with online friends he has never met, and playing computer games. Explain why his parents should intervene. (pp. 634–636)

An increasing number of studies indicate that playing violent video games, like watching violent TV, increases hostility and aggression, especially in boys, who are more avid players than girls. Compared with infrequent users, "passionate" game players tend to be anxious, withdrawn young people who use games to escape from unpleasant family and school experiences. Excessive playing of fantasy games can blur the distinction between virtual and real life. Because Tommy is spending a great deal of time playing computer games, his parents should intervene to ensure that he does not become addicted to game playing, isolated from his peers, and alienated from school.

Instant messaging between friends who actually know one another seems to support friendship closeness. But adolescents also frequently use the Internet to meet new people, and these online ties can pose dangers. In a survey of a nationally representative sample of U.S. 10- to 17-year-old Internet users, 14 percent reported having formed online friendships or romances. Although some of these youths were well-adjusted, many reported high levels of conflict with parents, peer victimization, depression, and delinquency, and spent extensive time on the Internet. These findings suggest that troubled youths may turn to the Internet to relieve feelings of isolation and rejection—motivations that make them especially vulnerable to exploitation. Because Tommy is spending his time instant messaging with online friends he has never actually met, his parents should intervene in this activity as well.

CONNECT: Which subtypes of popular and rejected children, described on page 619, are most likely to be attracted to violent media? Explain. (pp. 630–631)

The largest subgroup of rejected children is rejected-aggressive children, who are more extremely antagonistic than popular-aggressive children and thus likely to show severe conduct problems. Aggressive children and adolescents have a greater appetite for TV and other media violence, and boys devote more time to violent media than girls, in part because of male-oriented themes of conquest and adventure and also because lead characters tend to be male. Even in nonaggressive children, violent TV sparks hostile thoughts and behavior, but its impact is more intense in aggressive children.

REFLECT: How much and what kinds of television viewing and computer use did you engage in as a child and adolescent? Did your parents have rules about TV and computer time, and did they enforce those rules? How do you think your home media environment influenced your development? (pp. 629–636)

This is an open-ended question with no right or wrong answer.

REVIEW: List educational practices that promote positive attitudes toward school, academic motivation, and achievement, and explain why each is effective. (pp. 637–644)

Small class size: With fewer children, teachers spend less time disciplining and more time teaching and giving individual attention. Children who learn in smaller groups show better concentration, higher-quality class participation, and more favorable attitudes toward school.

Small student body size: In high school, student body size is the relevant physical context. Members of smaller schools report more social support and caring as well as greater school engagement. In schools with no more than 500 to 700 students, young people have an opportunity to get involved in a greater number and variety of extracurricular activities and to hold more positions of responsibility and leadership. Adolescents with academic, emotional, and social problems are especially likely to benefit from extracurricular pursuits that require them to take on meaningful roles and responsibilities.

Educational philosophies: A *constructivist classroom,* in contrast to a traditional classroom, encourages students to construct their own knowledge. Many constructivist approaches are grounded in Piaget's theory, which views children as active agents who reflect on and coordinate their own thoughts, rather than absorbing those of others. A constructivist classroom provides richly equipped learning centers where small groups and individuals solve self-chosen problems, while the teacher offers guidance and support in response to children's needs. Constructivist settings are associated with gains in critical thinking, greater social and moral maturity, and more positive attitudes toward school.

School transitions: Positive school attitudes and better achievement can be promoted by counteracting the decline in personal attention and active classroom participation that accompanies the transition to secondary school. In the first year after a school transition, homerooms can be provided in which teachers offer academic and personal counseling and work closely with parents to promote favorable school adjustment. To increase social support, students can also be assigned to classes with several familiar peers or a constant group of new peers. In addition, taking steps to minimize competition and differential treatment by ability is helpful. In schools that intervene in these ways, adolescents are less likely to decline in school performance.

Teacher–student interaction: When elementary and secondary teachers are caring, helpful, and stimulating, students gain in motivation and achievement. Positive teacher expectations for students' achievement are associated with higher achievement, especially for low-achieving students.

Grouping practices: Heterogeneous student groups limit the effects of educational self-fulfilling prophecies. For example, in multigrade classrooms, academic achievement, self-esteem, and attitudes toward school are usually more favorable than in the single-grade arrangement, perhaps because multigrade classrooms often decrease competition and increase harmony. When teachers assist heterogeneous groups in peer tutoring and collaboration, such groups are desirable into middle or junior high school, effectively supporting the achievement of students who vary widely in academic progress.

CONNECT: What common factors contribute to the high academic achievement of students in Asian nations and to the academic success of immigrant youths, discussed on page 53 in Chapter 2? (pp. 647–648)

A number of common factors contribute to the high academic achievement of students in Asian nations and that of immigrant youths. These include cultural valuing of academic achievement, emphasis on effort, parent involvement in their children's education, provision of high-quality education for all students, and more time devoted to academic instruction.

APPLY: Ray is convinced that his 5-year-old son Trip would learn more in school if only Trip's kindergarten would provide more teacher-directed lessons and worksheets and reduce the time devoted to learning-center activities. Is Ray correct? Explain. (p. 639)

Many preschool and kindergarten teachers have felt increased pressure to stress teacher-directed, academic training in an effort to increase student achievement. In fact, these approaches undermine children's motivation and emotional well-being. Young children who spend much time passively sitting and doing worksheets, as opposed to being actively engaged in learning centers, display more stress behaviors (such as wiggling and rocking), have less confidence in their abilities, prefer less challenging tasks, and are less advanced in motor, academic, language, and social skills at the end of the school year. Follow-ups reveal lasting effects through elementary school in poorer study habits and achievement. These outcomes are strongest for low-SES children, with whom teachers more often use an academic approach—a disturbing trend in view of its negative impact on motivation and emotional well-being.

REFLECT: Describe your experiences in making the transition to middle or junior high school and then to high school. What made these transitions stressful? What helped you adjust? (pp. 641–642)

This is an open-ended question with no right or wrong answer.

SUGGESTED READINGS

Cartledge, G. Y., Gardner, R., & Ford, D. Y. (2008). *Teaching diverse learners*. Newark, NJ: Prentice Hall. A collection of chapters focusing on the educational needs of culturally and racially diverse learners, including children with special needs. Other topics include research on gifted and talented students, assessment and testing, and strategies for enhancing social and academic skills.

Jamieson, P. E. (2009). *The changing portrayal of adolescents in the media since 1950*. New York: Oxford University Press. Presents a compelling look at how adolescents have been portrayed in the media for the past 60 years, including how these portrayals contribute to adolescent behavior. The author contends that a drastic increase in media consumption—from television to music to the Internet—has contributed to current trends in gender and ethnic representation, sexuality, substance use, violence, and even suicidal behavior among teens.

Klein, J. (2012). *The bully society*. New York: New York University Press. Examines three decades of research on peer victimization in American society. The author argues that a diverse range of factors contribute to bullying among children, including a cultural emphasis on competiveness, gender expectations, academic difficulties, and mental health problems.

MEDIA MATERIALS

For details on individual video segments that accompany the DVD for *Child Development,* Ninth Edition, please see the DVD Guide for *Explorations in Child Development*. The DVD and DVD Guide are available through your Pearson sales representative.

Additional DVDs that may be useful in your class are listed below. These are not available through your Pearson sales representative, but you can order them directly from the distributors. (See contact information at the end of this manual.)

Beyond Good and Evil: Children, Media, and Violent Times (2003, Insight Media, 37 min.). This program explores the impact of political rhetoric on children. It considers how the good-versus-evil narratives that circulated in the media following September 11 were integrated into video games, cartoons, and movies.

Cyberbullying: Cruel Intentions (2006, Films Media Group, 40 min.). This *ABC News* program reports on how cell phones, digital cameras, and personal Web sites encourage and amplify the frequent cruelty of teen behavior. With the help of an experiment conducted by Brigham Young University child development researchers, the program analyzes the behavior of a group of teenage girls as they use online verbal innuendos and emotional attacks to vie for attention and create a social hierarchy. The program also looks at the difficulties parents face in monitoring what their children do on the Internet.

Ecstasy: Happiness in a Pill? A 48 Hours/MTV News *Report* (2005, Films Media Group, 44 min.). This edition of *48 Hours* takes a broad look at the drug ecstasy. Case studies involving a high school student, two college students, and a single mother of three serve as platforms for investigating ecstasy's role as a gateway drug, the spread of potentially lethal copycat drugs, and how the controversial group DanceSafe helps ecstasy abusers at raves distinguish between ecstasy and other drugs.

Educational Psychology in the Classroom (2010, Insight Media, 30 min.). This program explores instructional design, curriculum development, organizational learning, special education, and classroom management. It outlines the cognitive, academic, social, and moral goals of learning and presents behavioral, cognitive, functionalist, and constructivist theories of learning.

Girl Bullying: Girls Can't Be Bullies? (2005, Aquarius Health Care Media, 26 min.). This program addresses relational aggression, or "girl bullying," as it is commonly called. It features girls who were bullied as children, often by their own friends, as well as the mother of a bullied girl who struggles to help her child. Three experts in the field, as well as a teen mentor, discuss this problem.

Handling Peer Pressure (2011, Films Media Group/Cambridge Education Production, 30 min.). This program explores peer group influences: how they can cause young people to change their attitudes, values, or behaviors in order to conform, and what can be done to avoid their pitfalls. Topics include positive, negative, direct, and indirect peer pressure; cultural forces, especially media-driven ones; and media stereotypes about what it means to be attractive, smart, or successful. An instructor's guide is available online.

How Come You Walk Funny? (2004, Fanlight Productions, 47 min.). This video profiles a unique experiment in early childhood education. At Toronto's Bloorview MacMillan Children's Center, 21 4-to-6-year-olds, half of whom use walkers, crutches, or wheelchairs, take part in a "reverse integration" kindergarten classroom. Shown in this program are parents who have chosen to enroll their non-disabled kids in a school designed for children with physical disabilities. The school's goals are to promote inclusive behavior in non-disabled children and self-advocacy skills in those with disabilities.

Kids and Bullying (2010, Films Media Group, 29 min.). In this *ABC News* program, correspondent Chris Cuomo talks to families, children, educators, and lawmakers to find out why so many school children are victims of bullying. He listens to the bullied, confronts the instigators of bullying, and takes viewers inside the Alliance School—a no-hate, no-bullying zone in Milwaukee, Wisconsin, the only middle school of its kind in the United States.

Learning Curves: Education (2005, School Media Associates, 30 min.). This program examines the link between quality of education and socioeconomic status, race, and culture. Topics covered included different approaches families take to educating their children and the growth in home schooling as an alternative to conventional education.

Life at 5: Great Expectations (2010, Films Media Group, 52 min.). Proposing that a good start to school depends on the ability to communicate effectively, a talent for fitting in well with others, and an ambition to learn, this program tracks the challenges, setbacks, and successes in the lives of a half-dozen 5-year-olds as they prepare for the world of organized education. Part of the series *Life at 1, 3, and 5: A Longitudinal Study in Childhood Development*.

Sexual and Racial Stereotypes in the Media (2008, Films Media Group, 2-part series, 38 and 42 min.). This two-part series scrutinizes the media to both expose and understand common sources of bias. Expert commentary is provided by Carolyn Kitch, director of the Mass Media and Communication program at Temple University; Oscar Gandy, professor emeritus at the Annenberg School for Communication; and NPR's Bob Garfield, cohost of *On the Media*.

Spin the Bottle: Sex, Lies & Alcohol (2004, Media Education Foundation, 45 min.). This program examines the role of contemporary popular culture in glamorizing excessive drinking and high-risk behaviors. Award-winning media critics Jackson Katz and Jean Kilbourne contrast these distorted representations with the often disturbing and dangerous ways that alcohol consumption affects the lives of real young men and women. A study guide is available online.

Teen Romance: What's Risky, What's Not? (2009, Films Media Group/Cambridge Educational Production, 32 min.). This program explores love, sex, and friendship among teenagers. With candid discussions about jealousy, trust, peer pressure, and effective communication, it focuses on the mental and emotional aspects of teenage sex and romance, as well as strategies for coping with rejection and breakups. Also discussed are "cyber relationships," both friendly and romantic, and what is gained and what is lost when the computer mediates human connections.

The "In" Crowd and Social Cruelty (2002, Films Media Group, 41 min.). In this *ABC News* special, correspondent John Stossel visits middle and high schools to examine why kids dish out abuse, why they take it, and what parents and school administrators have done to address such behavior. This program features discussions with students as well as with psychologist Michael Thompson, author of *Best Friends, Worst Enemies,* about the factors that lead some people to be popular and others unpopular.

ADDITIONAL INSTRUCTIONAL IDEAS

For additional instructional ideas, visit MyDevelopmentLab, an interactive multimedia resource that is designed to reinforce text concepts through controlled assessments, extensive video footage, simulations, biographies of major theorists in the field, careers in child development, and other interactive activities that are unique to *Child Development*. Below are sample activities that can be used for classroom instruction or out-of-class assignments.

Sample Videos and Simulations Featured on MyDevelopmentLab

Chapter 1

MDL Video: Resilience: Mentoring At-Risk Children
MDL Simulate: Ecological Systems Theory

Chapter 2

MDL Simulate: Distinguishing Independent and Dependent Variables
MDL Simulate: Ethics in Psychological Research

Chapter 3

MDL Video: Parenting a Child with a Genetic Disorder
MDL Video: Childbirth
MDL Video: Preterm Birth
MDL Simulate: Alien Gene Lab

Chapter 4

MDL Video: Newborn States
MDL Video: Motor Development in Infancy
MDL Simulate: Newborn Reflexes
MDL Simulate: Experiencing the Visual Cliff

Chapter 5

MDL Video: Motor Development and Play: The Children's Circus
MDL Video: Childhood Obesity
MDL Video: Adolescent Parenthood
MDL Simulate: Brain Development
MDL Simulate: Early versus Late Pubertal Timing

Chapter 6

MDL Video: Make-Believe Play: Sophie, Age 2½ and Alison, 4 Years
MDL Video: Understanding of Death
MDL Video: Cooperative Learning
MDL Simulate: Piaget and Vygotsky

Chapter 7

MDL Video: ADHD
MDL Video: Mathematics: A Second-Grade Math Lesson
MDL Simulate: Working Memory

Chapter 8

MDL Video: Home Environment and Mental Development
MDL Video: Jumpstart: Promoting Early Literacy and School Readiness
MDL Simulate: Gardner's Theory of Multiple Intelligences

Chapter 9

MDL Video: Supporting Early Language Learning: Storybook Reading
MDL Video: Acquiring Conversational Skills

Chapter 10

MDL Video: Early Emotional Development
MDL Video: Multiple Attachments: Fathers
MDL Simulate: Recognizing Facial Expressions of Emotion
MDL Simulate: The Strange Situation

Chapter 11

MDL Video: Understanding of False Belief
MDL Video: Autism
MDL Video: Self-Concept

Chapter 12

MDL Video: Early Morally Relevant Self-Control
MDL Video: Delinquency
MDL Simulate: Development of Moral Reasoning

Chapter 13

MDL Video: Gender Typing
MDL Video: Gender Constancy

Chapter 14

MDL Video: Transition to Parenthood
MDL Video: Quality Child Care
MDL Video: Child Abuse
MDL Simulate: Child-Rearing Styles

Chapter 15

MDL Video: Peer Acceptance
MDL Video: Friendship in Adolescence
MDL Video: Adolescent Dating
MDL Simulate: Peer Acceptance
MDL Simulate: Name That Educational Philosophy

MEDIA DISTRIBUTION INFORMATION

ACT Media Productions Inc.
1365 North Winchester Street
Olathe, KS 66061-5880
Phone: 1-800-745-5480

Annenberg Media
P.O. Box 55742
Indianapolis, IN 46205-0742
Phone: 1-800-LEARNER (1-800-532-7637)
Fax: 1-317-579-0402
E-mail: order@learner.org
www.learner.org

Aquarius Health Care Media
30 Forest Road
P.O. Box 249
Millis, MA 02054
Phone: 1-508-376-1244
Fax: 1-508-376-1245
www.aquariusproductions.com

Cambridge Documentary Films, Inc.
P.O. Box 390385
Cambridge, MA 02139-0004
Phone: 1-617-484-3993
Fax: 1-617-484-0754
E-mail: mail@cambridgedocumentaryfilms.org
www.cambridgedocumentaryfilms.org

Child Development Media, Inc.
5632 Van Nuys Blvd., Suite 286
Van Nuys, CA 91401
Phone: 1-800-405-8942
Fax: 1-818-989-7826
E-mail: info@childdevelopmentmedia.com
www.childdevelopmentmedia.com

Davidson Films, Inc.
735 Tank Farm Road, Suite 210
San Luis Obispo, CA 93401
Phone: 1-888-437-4200
Fax: 1-805-594-0532
E-mail: dfi@davidsonfilms.com
www.davidsonfilms.com

Discovery Channel
Discovery Store
Phone: 1-800-889-9950
http://store.discovery.com

Fanlight Productions
c/o Icarus Films
32 Court Street, 21st Floor
Brooklyn, NY 11201
Phone: 1-800-876-1710
Fax: 1-718-488-8642
E-mail: info@fanlight.com
www.fanlight.com

Films for the Humanities & Sciences
132 West 31st Street
17th Floor
New York, NY 10001
Phone: 1-800-322-8755
Fax: 1-800-329-6687
E-mail: custserv@films.com
http://ffh.films.com

Films Media Group
132 West 31st Street
17th Floor
New York, NY 10001
Phone: 1-800-322-8755
Fax: 1-800-329-6687
E-mail: custserv@films.com
http://ffh.films.com

Insight Media, Inc.
2162 Broadway
New York, NY 10024-0621
Phone: 1-800-233-9910
Fax: 1-212-799-5309
E-mail: custserv@insight-media.com
www.insight-media.com

Learning Seed
641 West Lake Street, Suite 301
Chicago, IL 60661
Phone: 1-800-634-4941
Fax: 1-800-998-0854
E-mail: info@learningseed.com
www.learningseed.com

Magna Systems, Inc.
641 West Lake Street, Suite 301
Chicago, IL 60661
Phone: 1-800-203-7060
Fax: 1-800-327-1443
E-mail: info@magnasystems.com
www.magnasystems.com

Media Education Foundation
60 Masonic St.
Northampton, MA 01060
Phone: 1-800-897-0089
Fax: 1-800-659-6882
E-mail: info@mediaed.org
www.mediaed.org

National Geographic Channel
National Geographic Catalog/Online
777 South State Road 7
Margate, FL 33068
Phone: 1-888-225-5647
http://shop.nationalgeographic.com

PBS Home Video
Phone: 1-800-531-4727
www.shoppbs.org/home

PHD Lowe Productions
#188-P.O. Box 8000
Abbotsford, BC V2S 6H1
Canada
Phone: 1-604-854-8130
E-mail: phd-lowe@shaw.ca
www.vygotskydocumentary.com

School Media Associates
5815 Live Oak Parkway, Suite 2-B
Norcross, GA 30093-1700
Phone: 1-800-451-5226
Fax: 1-770-441-8529
E-mail: info@smavideo.net
www.smavideo.com